LINGUISTIC TURNS, 1890–1950

Linguistic Turns, 1890–1950

Writing on Language as Social Theory

KEN HIRSCHKOP

OXFORD
UNIVERSITY PRESS

OXFORD
UNIVERSITY PRESS

Great Clarendon Street, Oxford, OX2 6DP,
United Kingdom

Oxford University Press is a department of the University of Oxford.
It furthers the University's objective of excellence in research, scholarship,
and education by publishing worldwide. Oxford is a registered trade mark of
Oxford University Press in the UK and in certain other countries

© Ken Hirschkop 2019

The moral rights of the author have been asserted

First Edition published in 2019

Impression: 1

All rights reserved. No part of this publication may be reproduced, stored in
a retrieval system, or transmitted, in any form or by any means, without the
prior permission in writing of Oxford University Press, or as expressly permitted
by law, by licence or under terms agreed with the appropriate reprographics
rights organization. Enquiries concerning reproduction outside the scope of the
above should be sent to the Rights Department, Oxford University Press, at the
address above

You must not circulate this work in any other form
and you must impose this same condition on any acquirer

Published in the United States of America by Oxford University Press
198 Madison Avenue, New York, NY 10016, United States of America

British Library Cataloguing in Publication Data

Data available

Library of Congress Control Number: 2018958832

ISBN 978-0-19-874577-8

Printed and bound in Great Britain by
Clays Ltd, Elcograf S.p.A.

Links to third party websites are provided by Oxford in good faith and
for information only. Oxford disclaims any responsibility for the materials
contained in any third party website referenced in this work.

To my father, Ray Hirschkop

Preface and Acknowledgements

This book was inspired by something I was researching, something I was teaching, and something that annoyed me. The research was on M. M. Bakhtin: in the course of looking at his intellectual trajectory, I could see there was a distinct moment in the late 1920s when he turned what had been an ethical philosophy into a theory of discourse and novelistic style. In a brief period of time, the architectonics of moral experience became the dynamics of prose style, the dangers of Kantian theory became poetic monologism, and the moral force of his earlier philosophy became a property of certain kinds of language. I had heard of 'linguistic turns': now I was seeing one in person. Everyone who reads Bakhtin thinks the force invested in what he called 'novelistic discourse' is extravagant; I realized that, to some extent, that force had been transplanted.

At about the same time, my teaching responsibilities included introducing students to the works of Saussure. Like any responsible teacher, I thought about how to make this as interesting as possible for the students (and, I suppose, for myself as well). This quest led me to look into the history of Saussure's work in general linguistics and the process whereby what had been a few lecture courses became a central work in the human sciences. Saussure thought of language as a social institution; I therefore should not have been surprised to learn that some of his ideas about language were not, strictly speaking, linguistic in origin, but had been borrowed from other spheres of social theory: from sociology, crowd theory, social contract theory, and neoclassical economics. When Saussure revolutionized the study of language, he was writing about language, but never just language, in the sense that one can never write about the structure of any social institution in complete isolation.

What annoyed me was quite straightforward. The advent of structuralism and post-structuralism in the humanities had led to a great deal of confident, excited talk (in which I was a very willing participant). Much of that talk was about how language mediated between ourselves and the world around us, how it structured that world for us by means of its 'differences', how it could disguise or hide the very process of structuring, and how its inner slipperiness meant we could no longer be certain of very much. Over time these claims became more elaborate—people working in literature, political theory, history and cultural studies would adopt an account of language and then use it to make substantial historical claims or political claims in their discipline, as if theories of language (Saussure, Wittgenstein, speech act theory, Foucault) had political or social affiliations. We probably don't need much in the way of examples here. Lyotard's argument against grand narratives in *The Postmodern Condition* appealed to and relied on Wittgenstein's philosophy.[1]

---

[1] '[T]he observable social bond is composed of language "moves"', Jean-François Lyotard, *The Postmodern Condition: A Report on Knowledge*, trans. Geoff Bennington and Brian Massumi (Manchester: Manchester University Press, 1984), 11.

Judith Butler thought the idea of the performative, drawn initially from speech act theory, together with Foucault's concept of discourse, demonstrated the fragile nature of identity in general and gender identity in particular, with serious consequences for feminist and queer politics.[2] Ernesto Laclau and Chantal Mouffe argued that post-structuralist theories of signification—artfully combined with a certain reading of Gramsci—demolished Marxist claims for the primacy of proletarian struggle in political revolutions.[3] Gareth Stedman Jones claimed if you took the linguistic turn seriously enough, you arrived at a different interpretation of eighteenth-century political radicalism.[4] In some cases, writers told us both that it was impossible to grasp the world yet possible to grasp—to understand—how and why language made it impossible to grasp the world. Given what I'd figured out concerning Bakhtin and Saussure, I was coming to realize that people were able to draw political tendencies and conclusions out of accounts of language because the accounts already had political and social ideas embedded in them. You couldn't talk about language without talking about a great deal else.

There was a moment when I thought I would do something quite polemical in relation to what annoyed me, but that moment passed, happily, and I knew that I needed to look not at the theories of language that were circulating around me, but at the theories that had got the ball rolling at the beginning of the twentieth century. The more I looked into the matter, the more interesting and urgent it became. For the early twentieth century was also the moment in Europe when societies had to figure out what to do about the democratization of their political and social worlds and how to square this democratization with the ever more popular idea of the political nation-state. Language itself was involved in that crucial political struggle, but it also had become a way to think about that struggle, to think about what a nation was, what consent was, how we made collective decisions, or didn't, and what the basis of a democratic social order might be. The extravagance of the investment Bakhtin had made in language and the extravagance of the investment structuralists and post-structuralists were making in language suddenly had a potential source—and I had a potential thesis.

Elaborating that thesis and finding evidence to support it turned out to be a rather lengthy endeavour. I already had Bakhtin and Saussure to hand, and any study of linguistic turns had to reckon with analytic philosophy, which had given us the phrase 'linguistic turn' in the first place. I didn't have to look hard for more linguistic turns; in fact, I hardly had to look at all. Several figures I'd been interested in all along—Walter Benjamin, the Russian linguist G. O. Vinokur, Gramsci—were implicated in the phenomenon I'd just framed for myself and many others were a single degree of separation from the writers I'd assembled (Cassirer, Russian

---

[2] Thus: 'This theoretical inquiry has attempted to locate the political in the very signifying practices that establish, regulate and deregulate identity.' Signifying practice, in its turn, was a theory of language drawn from the world of post-structuralism, mostly Foucault. Judith Butler, *Gender Trouble* (New York: Routledge, 1990), 147.

[3] Ernesto Laclau and Chantal Mouffe, *Hegemony and Socialist Strategy* (London: Verso, 1985).

[4] Gareth Stedman Jones, 'The Determinist Fix: Some Obstacles to the Further Development of the Linguistic Approach to History in the 1990s', *History Workshop Journal* 42 (1996): 19–35.

Futurism and Formalism, Ogden and Richards, Sorel). I could have gone on adding names to the list indefinitely.

To many friends and loved ones, this appeared to be my plan. I have to thank them in the first place for persuading me that it was not a good plan. Several of them helped bring the project to a conclusion by agreeing to read the manuscript in part or as a whole. Individual chapters (or early papers that eventually became chapters) were read by Craig Brandist, Mika Lähteenmaki, Galin Tihanov, Terry Eagleton, Patricia Marino, Harsha Ram, Tony Crowley, Richard Hogg, Bruce Robbins, Rebecca Tierney-Hynes, Paul Hamilton, and Jonathan Doering. Each provided me with detailed criticism and useful suggestions about where to look next and often they pushed me to think harder about matters I'd tried to finesse. Nigel Vincent read Part I in its entirety and gave me the benefit of his wide-ranging erudition, but he also alerted me to linguistic traditions I'd been unaware of, saved me from some foolish generalizations, and prompted me to calibrate my rhetoric to the matter at hand. Sascha Bru read the manuscript in its entirety and knew right off the bat what I was trying to do: his generous advice helped broaden the horizons of the work, sharpened its argument, and helped me be bolder when being bold was called for. John E. Joseph, my wonderful reader for OUP, responded to the project with notes and advice that were erudite, insightful, sympathetic, and witty: his careful and demanding engagement with the text made the process of revising it rewarding and even enjoyable. Scott McCracken read through the manuscript several times, often at disturbingly short notice: his pointed and shrewd criticisms, combined with his unwavering belief in the project as a whole, shaped the work profoundly and have put me eternally in his debt. It would have been a different, much poorer book without him.

Papers based on the research have been delivered at Manchester Metropolitan University, the University of Salford, Lancaster University, Stirling University, the University of Sussex, New York University, Yale University, Queen's University (Ontario), the Katholieke Universiteit Leuven, the Toronto Semiotic Circle, and at many conferences. In every case, colleagues listened carefully and made excellent and thoughtful suggestions about what to do next, not all of which, regrettably, I could follow up. As will become abundantly clear in the following pages, I cannot claim to be expert in any of the fields I've covered, save the work of Bakhtin. Given the range of what is attempted here and, frankly, the difficulty of the project, I have depended, even more than usually, on input and criticism from a wide range of colleagues in humanistic scholarship. As ever, my name is on the cover, but the project is collective. Nevertheless, where there are errors and hasty, ill-advised conclusions, the blame lies with me.

Of course, one needs collegiality of the day-to-day kind, and for this I want to thank my colleagues at the Universities of Manchester and Waterloo, who offered warm support and a stimulating environment—I've greatly enjoyed working with them and I want to offer particular thanks for the intellectual companionship of David Alderson, Richard Kirkland, Howard Booth, Tony Crowley, Kevin McGuirk, Randy Harris, Michael McDonald, Win Siemerling, and Rebecca Tierney-Hynes. I want also to offer thanks to the many librarians who have helped me directly and indirectly in my work, including those at: the British Library; the libraries at the Universities of Manchester, Waterloo, and Toronto; McMaster University Library; Houghton and Widener Libraries at Harvard; Helsinki University Library; Sterling Library at Yale; and the Russian State Library in Moscow. Without their intelligence and dedication, the scholarship necessary for a project like this would be impossible. One needs space to work and think, of course—those libraries and my home provided much of the space, but many of the ideas in this book depended on time in the Jet Fuel coffee shop in Toronto (thanks to the staff there) and long walks with the dog in nearby Riverdale Park (thanks to the City of Toronto).

At an early stage of the research, the Leverhulme Trust granted me a research fellowship that allowed me to focus on this research for a full academic year: I'm grateful to them for this invaluable aid and for their continued support for scholarship in the humanities.

Authors provide text; publishers create books. This one was created by the excellent work of my editors at Oxford University Press, Jacqueline Norton and Aimee Wright, my production managers Alamelu Vengatesan and Seemadevi Sekar, and my patient copyeditor Joanna North. My deepest thanks to them and the other people who made this book.

I have enjoyed working on the book: quite a lot, to be honest. Those around me, I have reason to believe, have enjoyed it a good deal less. I thank my partner Joanne Hurley for supporting what seemed to be a crazy, endless project and for giving me a reason to look forward to every day. My children Jacob and Roisin urged me to finish, occasionally evinced interest in the work, and made the last several years a boundless, undeserved pleasure. I am fortunate to have the support and love of my sister and her partner, as well as the joy of knowing my brother and his. The efforts of my family have been complemented by the kindness and patience of many friends, who kept my spirits up and my confidence high. I can't name them all, but you know who you are, though you don't know just how much you've done for me over the many years.

Parts of Chapter 5 were previously published in the journal *Modernist Cultures*, as 'Language in 1910 (and after): Saussure, Benjamin and Paris'; they are reproduced with permission of Edinburgh University Press though PLS Clear. I want to thank the editors, Andrzej Gasiorek and Deborah Longworth, for kindly giving the material its first airing.

Contents

Note on Translations and References   xiii

1. Introduction: Linguistic Turns as Social Theory   1

PART I. ORDER

2. 'Grammar, for example, can only be studied in the crowd': Reason, Analogy, and the Nature of Social Consent   29
   (Ferdinand de Saussure)
3. The Ship of Logic on the High Seas of Discourse   53
   (Gottlob Frege, Bertrand Russell, Ludwig Wittgenstein, a little Gilbert Ryle)
4. Saussure and the Soviets   105
   (S. I. Kartsevskii, G. O. Vinokur, L. Iakubinskii)
5. On the Diversity—and Productivity—of Language   128
   (M. M. Bakhtin, Walter Benjamin, Saussure)

PART II. MYTH

6. Do They Believe in Magic? The Word as Myth, Name, and Art   159
   (C. K. Ogden and I. A. Richards, Frege, George Orwell, Bakhtin, Saussure)
7. Myth You Can Believe In   184
   (Ernst Cassirer, Viktor Shklovskii, Velimir Khlebnikov, Roman Jakobson, Benjamin)

   Excursus: Reversing Out—Sorel's Heroic Myth, Gramsci's Slow Magic   237
8. High Anxiety, Becalmed Language: Ordinary Language Philosophy   247
   (Wittgenstein, J. L. Austin)

   Conclusion: Motorways and Cul-de-Sacs—What the Linguistic Turns Turned To   271

Bibliography   285
Index   315

Note on Translations and References

I have used existing English translations for all texts in French, German, and Italian, except where none are available. If the translation has been amended in any way, this is indicated in the notes. Saussure's *Course in General Linguistics* has two existing translations, an early one by Wade Baskin and a later one by Roy Harris. I have used Harris's in almost all cases, but where Baskin's is preferred I mention this in the accompanying note.

Translations from Russian are my own, though I have naturally benefited from the existing ones. The complicated case is, of course, Bakhtin's. Almost every existing English translation has relied on a Russian text that we now know was severely edited or censored, owing to a number of circumstances. I've therefore translated from the recent scholarly edition of Bakhtin's works, the *Sobranie sochinenii* [*Collected Works*], published between 1996 and 2012 in Moscow under the editorship of S. G. Bocharov, except where the text in question was a book published during Bakhtin's lifetime, i.e., the books on Dostoevsky and Rabelais. For all Bakhtin translations the first page reference will be to the Russian text I've used, the second to an available English translation, details of which I provide in the notes.

1

Introduction
Linguistic Turns as Social Theory

We talk and write incessantly, and some of our talking and writing is devoted to the language we use when doing it. But there are times when talk about language expands and acquires a new urgency, leading to dramatic changes in the way we think about it. The moment when rhetoric flowered in ancient Athens and Syracuse was one such episode; the explosion of interest in the origin of language in eighteenth- and nineteenth-century Europe was another. Such sudden intensifications of concern are provoked in part by changes in the condition and form of language itself, but they reach fever pitch because in these moments language is invested with larger worries: worries about new forms of communication, about the relationship of discourse to politics, and about the existence and nature of the social order itself. To adapt a comment of Antonio Gramsci's, every time the question of language surfaces, 'it means that a series of other problems are coming to the fore'.[1]

This book is devoted to a recent moment of this kind. In the last decades of the nineteenth century and the first half of the twentieth, a striking number of intellectuals in Europe were gripped by the sense that confusions about language were everywhere and everywhere responsible for both local intellectual disorders and larger social ones. They believed that language itself was fundamentally misunderstood and that its significance for the society around them had been fundamentally misunderstood as well. They responded by executing a series of 'linguistic turns', in which they both reorganized their intellectual fields around language and argued for a new understanding of language itself. The results—in philosophy, in linguistics, in literary criticism, in anthropology, in political theory—were dramatic and long-lasting. But scholars have tended to examine these turns in isolation, as episodes in the development of individual figures and disciplines. In this book we look at these turns in concert, as a whole, as a comprehensive reconceptualization and revaluation of language in the modernist moment.

Scholars have not examined the turns in concert because they have not thought about 1890 to 1950 as a historical moment of linguistic *turns*. They have typically understood it as the moment of '*the* linguistic turn', in the singular, executed uniquely in philosophy. Even the philosophers whom we now credit with this

---

[1] Gramsci, in the original, refers specifically to the problem of an Italian 'national language'; Antonio Gramsci, *Selections from Cultural Writings*, trans. William Boelhower (London: Lawrence & Wishart, 1985), Prison Notebook 29, §3 (183).

turn—some combination of Gottlob Frege, Bertrand Russell, Ludwig Wittgenstein, and J. L. Austin—did not know that was what they were doing at the time, though they felt they were doing something revolutionary. It was only in 1952, when the dust was beginning to clear, that Gustav Bergmann observed that '[o]f late philosophy has taken a linguistic turn'.[2] Bergmann thought the advance guard of what was then called 'linguistic philosophy' had transformed the discipline by means of (as Bergmann later put it) a 'fundamental gambit as to method': the conviction that philosophers should 'talk about the world by means of talking about a suitable language'.[3] From the final decades of the nineteenth century through the early decades of the twentieth, philosophers in England and Austria had recast familiar philosophical issues as problems with language: in order to understand what an object was, what it meant to be responsible, or what it meant to know something, one had to understand the word 'object', the word 'responsibility', and the verb 'to know'—understand either by logical analysis or by an assessment of how it is used. The change prompted the rise of a 'linguistic philosophy' that thought of itself as revolutionizing the discipline; for several decades it looked like the move that would finally set philosophical discussion on the right path.

But at the same time that Frege, Russell, and Wittgenstein wondered about the nature of logical symbols, the literary critic Viktor Shklovskii cried for the 'resurrection of the word', the native metaphoric energy of which was being slowly dissipated by habit. Seeing words, hearing words, apprehending them in their original density would make not only for better art, he claimed, but better everything else as well: the resurrection of the word would also be 'the resurrection of things'.[4] Shklovskii's plea for the powers of the word would find itself complemented by developments in the study of language proper, in which Saussure argued that linguists had not been looking at language at all, but at a confused and disordered set of facts. Saussure would redirect the attention of linguists (and, when his text reached Russia, literary critics) to a new object, 'language in general', which would have a systematic form and shape no one had acknowledged before. When Wittgenstein's *Tractatus*—the book destined to become the old testament of analytic philosophy—was published, C. K. Ogden (who would translate the *Tractatus* into English) and I. A. Richards began work on a critique of the 'word magic' that was making normally sane and rational Europeans do crazy things. As they were preparing a study of 'symbolism' that would destroy the magical force of language, Ernst Cassirer, the accomplished neo-Kantian philosopher of science, was concluding that a systematic philosophy of the modern age should take the shape of a 'philosophy of symbolic form' that would explain the power of magic as well as the force of language. As its second volume came out, Antonio Gramsci, the Secretary of the Italian Communist Party and former advanced student in historical linguistics, was imprisoned by Mussolini; in the

---

[2] Gustav Bergmann, 'Two Types of Linguistic Philosophy', *Review of Metaphysics* 5.3 (1952): 417.
[3] Gustav Bergmann, 'Strawson's Ontology', *Journal of Philosophy* 57.19 (1960): 607.
[4] Viktor Shklovskii, *Voskreshenie slova* (St Petersburg: Z. Sokolinskago, 1914), 1. Translation: 'The Resurrection of the Word (1914)', in Stephen Bann and John E. Bowlt (eds.), *Russian Formalism* (Edinburgh: Scottish Academic Press, 1973), 41.

eleven remaining years of his short life, he would demonstrate that linguistics offered a model for the working of political leadership and ideological change. Left-wing politics would also find inspiration in a philosophy of language in the work of Walter Benjamin, although Benjamin's conception of language and his conception of political commitment were as different from Gramsci's as could be. There is perhaps no more confused assimilation of philosophy of language to politics than that propounded by Bakhtin, who spent a decade on a mammoth project of ethical philosophy, which he then, in the space of a couple of years, rewrote as a theory of 'novelistic discourse' in the late 1920s.

It's a remarkable constellation of thinkers, all of whom decide within a relatively brief span that they need the study of language to solve problems that are disciplinary and theoretical, but not only disciplinary and theoretical. Since Benjamin himself made the concept of a 'constellation' theoretically respectable, though, we have tended to forget that constellations were originally instances of reading too much into coincidental facts, of projecting human conceptions onto the indifferent and random appearance of the stars. Is the simultaneous appearance of so many linguistic turns also a coincidence? It could be: but the wager of this book is that it is not. And if the argument works, then we need to look at these turns, up till now seen and interpreted in isolation, in a very different light. From within each discipline or sphere, a linguistic turn appears to be the fruit of sustained reflection on a set of issues unique to that discipline, be it logic, linguistics, or literary criticism; it's a moment of intellectual insight and progress, even revolutionary progress. If we see the same turn, however, as one element of a constellation, it appears in a different guise. Maybe one field turns to language to solve problems peculiar to its discipline. When several do, when attention to 'language' is simultaneously the key to advance in philosophy, to the revitalization of literature and literary criticism, to neo-Kantian philosophy of culture, to the reform of English political thinking, to the renewal of European communism and syndicalism, something else is going on.

In the period from 1890 to 1950 'language' didn't just attract the attention of a couple of stray but innovative thinkers—it seized the imagination of intellectuals throughout Europe. A couple of the resulting romances—the turn in analytic philosophy, the rise of linguistic structuralism—are well known because they left a great many progeny, but others—short-lived, childless affairs—have been neglected. That not every turn was equally successful lends weight to the suspicion that intellectual issues were not the only thing urging a greater role for language. That even the successful, 'productive' turns had an endpoint is perhaps even more telling. At its inception the linguistic turn in analytic philosophy was regarded as an irrevocable step forward, but we see now it was an historical moment. When Russian Formalists turned literary criticism into the theory of poetic language, they thought they had put criticism on a respectable, scientific path, and for a while it seemed they were right. As late as 1982 a confident Paul de Man would equate literary theory itself with 'the introduction of linguistic terminology in the metalanguage about literature'; but then Theory itself would stall, and the linguistic turn in literary criticism would give way to a cultural turn, to political criticism, to psychoanalysis and the love of literature.[5] The linguistic turns we will explore look like on-ramps to scientific progress, but the path they take turns out to be circuitous: not a useless detour but a route which is nevertheless eventually abandoned.

Many linguistic turns, but not, as it happens, many turns to a single object. For one of the most curious features of this constellation is that, although each writer claims to have grasped the necessity of confronting language, the word, the symbol, in all its intractability and complexity, each writer has a quite different idea of what language *is*. Language will be a system to some, a form of behaviour to others, a sphere of symbols conveying logical ideas (imperfectly) to another group, a set of tools, pictures, or games to Wittgenstein, depending on when you asked. Even Bergmann, when he first named 'the linguistic turn', had to admit that '[f]rom this common origin two distinct types of linguistic philosophy have developed' that, though courteous to each other, lacked 'mutual appreciation'.[6] There is, in short, firm agreement on the need to get to grips with language and to acknowledge that it is not a mere medium of communication, and equally firm disagreement on what sort of thing language might be instead.

This odd difference of perspective, however, makes more sense if we think of 'language' not as an object to which one turned, but as a *problem* that compelled or demanded attention. In the early twentieth century language became a problem, not only in the intellectual sense of being hard to comprehend, but also in the sense that it was causing problems, serious problems of a social, cultural, political, and philosophical kind. What the linguistic turns of the time share is not a definition of language, but anxieties and hopes that coalesce around it, that seem to stick to it and express themselves through it. In the period of European modernism language became invested with new possibilities—with an extraordinary *force*, for good or ill. A force that demanded some kind of assessment and reckoning, an engagement with a 'language' that had somehow lost its way.

The predicament is neatly captured in the title of Walter Benjamin's notorious 1916 essay, 'On Language as Such and Human Language'. It's as if the language that confronts the intellectuals of the time is internally ruptured, turned against itself, imbalanced or out of whack. Benjamin would contrast the immediate power of what he called pure language with the human language that had fallen 'into the abyss of the mediateness of all communication, of the word as means, of the empty word, into the abyss of prattle'.[7] The complaint that language had been drained of its native force would be echoed by Shklovskii, who regarded the language we actually spoke as a thin, insipid medium, robbed of its 'poetic' magic. Writers like Wittgenstein or J. L. Austin would point their fingers in a different direction (at other philosophers for the most part) and talk about the ways in

---

[5] Paul de Man, 'The Resistance to Theory', in *The Resistance to Theory* (Minneapolis: University of Minnesota Press, 1986), 8.

[6] Bergmann, 'Two Types of Linguistic Philosophy', 417.

[7] Walter Benjamin, 'On Language as Such and on the Language of Man', in *Selected Writings: Volume 1, 1913–1926*, trans. Edmund Jephcott et al. (Cambridge, MA: Harvard University Press, 1996), 72. I have altered the translation of the title, as 'Human Language' seems to me preferable to the antiquated phrase 'Language of Man'.

which our language was led astray, although they would only hint at the larger ramifications. Whereas for someone like Heidegger no ramification could ever be large enough: he therefore spoke urgently and melodramatically of the need 'to regain the unimpaired strength of language and words', because 'the misuse of language in idle talk, in slogans and phrases, destroys our authentic relation to things'.[8] Idle talk, slogans, and phrases were commonly mentioned dangers, pressing practical issues that demanded a response. But what is distinctive and striking is that in nearly every instance the language to which writers turn lacks coherence or ontological consistency, as if language, however conceived, possessed both an inner elegance and a set of bad habits from which it had to be forcibly weaned. Language had acquired a certain density, but it was not inert or thing-like: on the contrary, it appeared as something with inner tendencies and pressures, which could push it in one direction or another. Its analysis, therefore, was never merely contemplative: it was always the struggle for a certain kind of language and a certain form of lucidity, a struggle which would unlock a force, coherence, and lucidity lying within language itself.

The forcefulness of language was not entirely its own: some of it was, so to speak, borrowed. Look, for example, at the justification for philosophy's linguistic turn made by one of the field's most prominent figures, the American philosopher W. V. O. Quine, who suggested in his book *Word and Object* that '[w]ords, or their inscriptions, unlike points, miles, classes, and the rest, are tangible objects of the size so popular in the marketplace, where men of unlike conceptual schemes communicate at their best.'[9] Philosophy had been marred by constant skirmishing and fruitless battles between competing *Weltanschauungen* (world-views); focusing on words would make philosophical discussion civil and progress possible. But the language in which Quine talks about language is telling: the civilizing force language exerts is that of the marketplace, and markets, according to Quine, are spheres of peaceable human interaction, where the logic of commerce renders ideological difference moot. What looks like a turn to mere words, to the stuff of language, is in fact an appeal to language-as-a-market, an appeal to language *because* it's a market and an appeal to markets as a way to keep the peace. That appeal had some history behind it. As the political philosopher Pierre Rosanvallon has pointed out, in the nineteenth century the market emerges as the model for 'a self-regulating civil society', in which the impersonality of transactions replaces all political authority, political struggle, and political will.[10] One could therefore appeal to the market as an alternative sphere of public authority, an alternative to the strife and drama of politics. Quine's opening line in *Word and Object* had been 'Language is a social art.'[11] But to describe the manner and mode of language's social being, to describe what kind of society language might be—and what pressures that society would

---

[8] Martin Heidegger, *An Introduction to Metaphysics*, trans. Ralph Manheim (New Haven and London: Yale University Press, 1959), 13–14.
[9] W. V. O. Quine, *Word and Object* (Cambridge, MA: MIT Press, 1960), 272.
[10] Pierre Rosanvallon, 'The Market, Liberalism, and Anti-Liberalism', in *Democracy Past and Future* (New York: Columbia University Press, 2006), 53.
[11] Quine, *Word and Object*, ix.

bring to bear on the discussions of philosophers—he had had to go beyond language, calling on the resources of social theory.

Not everyone was as forthright as Quine. Some writers turning to language—Wittgenstein, Cassirer, Shklovskii, for example—invoked concepts of social theory rarely and obliquely; others—say, Ogden and Richards—thought a linguistic turn would have a direct payoff politically and socially. Where intellectuals didn't borrow concepts or theory, however, they borrowed force and tension, a force and tension that language could embody, host, or refract, depending on how one imagined the 'social art' of language related to the larger social world surrounding it. Which is to say that while it is no doubt true that the 'language' writers turned to had problems, was in some sense distorted or awry, these problems were not just its own problems. The disagreements that Europe's linguistic turns were supposed to resolve were inevitably couched in terms of an intellectual discipline, but the continent on which they took place was racked by a kind and level of disagreement that threatened its very existence. In the early twentieth century the ruptures, forces, and inconsistencies that defined language, that made it compelling and fascinating, stand metonymically for ruptures and inconsistencies that seem to plague the European body politic, ruptures expressed in certain specifically linguistic phenomena to be sure—in novelties like the radio broadcast, the mass newspaper, the talkie film, state propaganda—but in no way exhausted by them.

Metonymically: which is to say, part for whole, cause for effect, container for the contained, and so on. Metonymically: as when Ogden and Richards would point to the way word magic or myth was inflaming the newly enfranchised masses; or Shklovskii and Orwell to the way *cliché* and habit were wearing away our linguistic attentiveness; or Sorel to how parliamentary wrangling was weakening the resolve of the working class; or Saussure to how language itself was conservative and impossible to revolutionize. In each case, there is a genuine linguistic issue with powerful discursive forces in play, but also something more—the absorption of larger social and political problems into language, not because a society is 'like' a language (though we find that kind of metaphoric modelling, too) but because the sociopolitical ruptures and forces of the day work themselves out in part *through* language. Metonymically, finally, because this seems to me the right way to think about the relationship language has to the social world (and by extension, linguistic theory to social theory) in general. If I may lay a few of my theoretical cards on the table (not all: this is seven-card stud for theorists) I believe an adequate philosophy of language, one grounded in social theory, doesn't think of language as a reflection of the social world, a function of it, or something 'caused' by it, but as an institution which is always 'part' of it, but not always part of it in exactly the same way. Metonymy is the figure that fits that bill.

LANGUAGE AND THE CRISIS OF DEMOCRACY

What kinds of social ruptures? Studies of European modernism—its literature, music, visual art, emerging popular culture—invariably refer to one or more 'crises'

Introduction: Linguistic Turns as Social Theory

of the early twentieth century. The description is obviously justified: this is, after all, the time in which Europe tore itself apart in two massive wars, inflicted continuous suffering on the peoples who lived in its colonies, witnessed the emergence of political movements like feminism and civil rights, and discovered the mass media and the modern city. Even its rare moments of political 'normality' are haunted by Walter Benjamin's apt observation '[t]hat things "just keep on going" *is* the catastrophe'.[12] But a crisis is also a crossroads or turning point, a moment for decision, and the crisis relevant here is a particular decision that European societies continually made and then remade, obsessively, in the first half of the twentieth century. For they needed to make, but could not make, a decision about 'democracy'.

In *Dark Continent: Europe's Twentieth Century*, Mark Mazower notes that democracy was not, current triumphalism notwithstanding, 'rooted deeply in Europe's soil'.[13] It was, in fact, extraordinarily fragile in the period between 1918 and 1939, when its institution was at best halting and unconvincing, and when support for democracy and its principal mechanism, the parliament, often turned out to be less than half-hearted. The short-lived Weimar Republic, from the outset a kind of messy compromise with few real adherents, continually under threat from the socialist Left, the aristocratic 'Junker' Right, and the newly emerging fascist movement, was the poster-child for this kind of anaemic democracy.

Matters had initially looked more promising. When the Russian, Austro-Hungarian, and Ottoman Empires tumbled, opening the door to the establishment of new 'national' democracies, elaborate constitutions provided a framework for new nations. Constitution-making aimed, in Mazower's words, 'to "rationalize" power and sweep away the inconsistencies and irrational residues of the old feudal order'.[14] The paradigmatic form would be the democratic republic affirming the sovereignty of the people and vesting their power in a strong parliament: this kind of arrangement sprung up, with variations of emphasis, in postwar Germany, Poland, Czechoslovakia, Lithuania, Greece, Ireland, and Hungary, among other places. In those countries that already had parliamentary rule, the pressure for democracy took the form of extensions of the suffrage and the rise of independent working-class movements. In Britain the business begun in the Reform Acts of the nineteenth century continued into the twentieth century, as universal male suffrage was granted in 1918 and a powerful and militant feminist movement pushed for the rights that would be granted in 1928. By the beginning of the First World War, extensions to the franchise had doubled or even tripled the electorate in Belgium, Finland, and Norway, while universal manhood suffrage had been granted in Austria and Italy.[15] Such developments, as Eric Hobsbawm has noted,

---

[12] Walter Benjamin, 'N [Re the Theory of Knowledge, Theory of Progress]', trans. Leigh Hafrey and Richard Sieburth, in Gary Smith (ed.), *Benjamin: Philosophy, Aesthetics, History* (Chicago: University of Chicago Press, 1989), N9a, 1 (64).

[13] Mark Mazower, *Dark Continent: Europe's Twentieth Century* (London: Allen Lane, 1998), xi.

[14] Mazower, *Dark Continent*, 5.

[15] Figures from Eric Hobsbawm, *The Age of Empire: 1875–1914* (London: Weidenfeld & Nicolson, 1995), 85–6. For a vivid account of how Habsburg Empire voters embraced their recently granted

'were viewed without enthusiasm by the governments that introduced them', which sought various means of controlling the newly enfranchised 'people'.[16]

Democracy, or democratization, was not, however, only a matter of parliamentary democracy. It also meant the entrance of popular groups, working-class or agrarian, onto the political scene in other ways: through the creation of mass parties and unions, through strikes and demonstrations (often the catalyst of constitutional change), through new cultural institutions—newspapers, theatres, educational associations, and the like—that created the basis for a kind of 'mass' urban culture that did not yet need the assistance of media technologies. And, in this context, 'urban' is as important a qualifier as 'mass', for this was a culture centred in European cities that grew dramatically and that spawned the great working-class neighbourhoods that would become centres of political action and resistance in the twentieth century. The emerging twentieth-century democracy was not a democracy of peasants, who coexisted, in Marx's famous phrase, like potatoes in a sack, at once similar and separate, but a democratic movement that drew its strength from urban patterns of association.

'By the 1930s', however, 'parliaments seemed to be going the way of kings.'[17] It turned out that there were other ways to organize modern European societies than parliamentary democracy, and these forms could accommodate 'mass' society in a more authoritarian manner: some would even claim to be more democratic than the parliamentary regimes they displaced. Nations and their peoples remained, but liberal democracy 'might have to be sacrificed if the Nation was to survive'.[18] There was Communism in Russia and the other Soviet Socialist Republics, fascism in Germany and Italy, and a variety of right-wing authoritarian regimes in Hungary, Spain, Portugal, and elsewhere. The new fascist regimes differed from the classic monarchical-aristocratic regimes in their embrace of mass politics and populist ideologies. Those who railed against parliamentary rule and its messy procedures invoked not just the good of the Nation, but the principle of democracy itself in their arguments. Thus Georges Sorel would rail against parliamentary socialists for defanging popular struggles best expressed by violent acts, and Carl Schmitt would insist that 'the distinction between liberal parliamentary ideas and mass democratic ideas cannot remain unnoticed any longer'.[19]

Schmitt's example reminds us of something else: democracy itself had its ambiguities. Conceived of as the political expression of nation-building projects, as the means by which a people asserted its political right and power, it could easily take a decidedly illiberal or racist form. Schmitt argued that the principle of democracy entailed a unified 'people' or demos, not the wrangling of parliamentary parties, and that 'dictatorial and Caesaristic methods not only can produce the acclamation

---

rights, see the marvellous opening of Pieter M. Judson's *The Habsburg Empire: A New History* (Cambridge, MA: Harvard University Press, 2016), 1–4.

[16] Hobsbawm, *Age of Empire*, 86.   [17] Mazower, *Dark Continent*, 2.
[18] Mazower, *Dark Continent*, 25.
[19] Carl Schmitt, 'Preface to the Second Edition (1926): On the Contradiction between Parliamentarism and Democracy', in *The Crisis of Parliamentary Democracy*, trans. Ellen Kennedy (Cambridge, MA: MIT Press, 1988), 2.

of the people but can also be a direct expression of democratic substance and power'.[20] The problem was not merely one of Schmitt's fantasizing. As Mazower points out, 'the new democracies tended to be exclusionary and antagonistic in their ethnic relations': states built on the basis of nationality inevitably spawned national minorities which appeared *prima facie* to be threats to national unity.[21] The problem was not confined to the newer democracies, either: in the 1890s France had shown just how uncomfortable its elites were with the modern society on its horizon when it tore itself to pieces in the Dreyfus affair. That democracy didn't imply any kind of liberal respect for different nationalities, or any kind of 'multicultural' thinking about citizenship or nationhood was made clear in the treatment accorded to Jews in modern Europe. Mazower again:

> Because democracy was about the creation of *national* communities, it was generally anti-Semitic, or at least more ready to allow anti-Semitism to shape policy—through separate electoral colleges, for example, or entry quotas into the universities and civil-service posts—than old-fashioned royalists had been.[22]

How to handle this mass society, a society full of urbanized people, working and lower middle class, now educated and enfranchised, ready to participate, in one way or another, in the cultural and political life of the nation? Modern Europe could not make up its mind.

In this context, the question of democracy was more than a matter of deciding on appropriate government institutions or procedures. It was the question of social and political order itself, the urgent matter of figuring out how to maintain order and cohesion in societies that had been rendered dynamic and unruly by the political and economic transformations of the nineteenth century. Rosanvallon has described these changes as leading to 'the extension, and one might even say the unleashing, of the political', that is, a burdening of political life with new tasks it must assume when the old 'natural' order has been dissolved by capitalism and political revolution.[23] The entrance of 'the people' onto the political and social stage makes the social order itself amorphous, even unrepresentable:

> The people is like Janus: it has two faces. It is at once a danger and a possibility. It menaces the political order at the same time as it grounds it [...] Whence the central problem: it is at the very moment that the principle of popular sovereignty triumphs that its face, in a sense, becomes problematic.[24]

The result is an endless anxiety—one that haunts us still—about the constitution of the social order itself. For 'the people' both define the substance of the nation and yet appear to ruling classes as an unpredictable and destabilizing force within it.[25]

---

[20] Schmitt, 'Parliamentarism and Democracy', 17.   [21] Mazower, *Dark Continent*, 41.
[22] Mazower, *Dark Continent*, 59.
[23] Pierre Rosanvallon, 'Toward a Philosophical History of the Political', in *Democracy Past and Future*, 61.
[24] Pierre Rosanvallon, 'Revolutionary Democracy', in *Democracy Past and Future*, 84–5.
[25] On current anxieties about how democracy is rendering societies ungovernable, see Jacques Rancière, *Hatred of Democracy*, trans. Steve Corcoran (London: Verso, 2009).

If we go back to the beginning of this period, when anxieties about the social order and the role of the people within it were intensifying, we see that several intellectuals concerned with language make an interesting move. In the late nineteenth century, after the Paris Commune, a few linguists make the novel claim that language has always been 'of the people'. 'Universal suffrage has not always existed in politics; it has always existed in the domain of language', claimed the nineteenth-century French linguist, Arsène Darmesteter.[26] If it had, linguists were not always willing to recognize it. Carita Klippi has shown how Darmesteter, Michel Bréal, and Victor Henry gradually made popular usage the test of what belonged to 'the language', displacing an earlier belief in the priority of written sources and standard forms.[27] This 'linguistic communism', as Pierre Bourdieu dubbed it, was not without its ambiguities.[28] On the one hand, it broke with the prescriptivist idea—embodied in earlier dictionaries and guides to elocution—that popular usage tended to degrade or corrupt a language that had, at an earlier point in time, been purer or more logically structured. At the same time, it could be taken to imply that because language was the product of collective activity, everyone in that collective played an equal role in determining its shape and substance. It is, of course, the reflected image of the problem facing democratizing nations. The political community of the nation was expanding until it included most of its adult citizens; 'language' was expanding so that it represented the speech of more or less the same group. It was this isomorphism that made it possible for problems in the political and social field to be represented and worked through as problems in the linguistic field.

LANGUAGE AND THE PEOPLE IN THE NINETEENTH CENTURY

Of course, the identification of language with nation and people was nothing new: it had been established by an earlier generation of language-obsessed intellectuals, the comparative philologists of the nineteenth century. For 'language' lay at the centre of the nineteenth century's intellectual universe as well. The invention of comparative philology as a method and a discipline by Friedrich Schlegel, Franz Bopp, Rasmus Rask, and Jacob Grimm gave the study of language both an empirical and scientific character and a strikingly practical orientation. On the one hand, comparative philology produced a method: linguistic forms, at both the phonetic and the morphological level, would be explained as the result of systematic, often 'lawlike' historical change, change which could be charted by careful observation

---

[26] Arsène Darmesteter, *The Life of Words as the Symbols of Ideas* (London: Kegan Paul, Trench & Co., 1886), 109.
[27] Carita Klippi, 'Vox populi, Vox Dei: The "People" as an Agent of Linguistic Norm', *Language & Communication* 26 (2006): 356–68.
[28] Pierre Bourdieu, 'The Production and Reproduction of Legitimate Language', in *Language and Symbolic Power*, trans. Gino Raymond and Matthew Adamson (Cambridge, MA: Harvard University Press, 1991), 43.

and arguments that were open to empirical checking and refutation. The results of comparative philology would be elaborate, scientific accounts of the genealogy and development of the world's languages. On the other hand, although its source materials came from language that was variable and constantly changing, its conclusions centred on distinct 'languages', with a comprehensible internal structure. During the springtime of nations, this could not be an innocent gesture. Possession of a distinct language with a well-attested history appeared to be a *sine qua non* of any group aspiring to independent nationhood in nineteenth- and twentieth-century Europe. So while comparative philologists created the history of Europe's languages, those languages were codified and purified in grammatical studies and historical dictionaries, the Oxford English Dictionary, Littré and Grimm among them, and lovingly refined in novels, now thought of as elements of a 'national' literature.

That these two strands of the comparative philological project could not be disentangled, that the political dimension could not be fenced off from scientific aspirations is evident from one of the most detailed and thoughtful histories of the period, Anna Morpurgo Davies's *Nineteenth-Century Linguistics*. The story Morpurgo Davies wants to tell is of the emergence of a 'data-oriented linguistics', in which 'progress was seen as defined by the accumulation of concrete results and by the diminishing number of unsolved problems'.[29] But as Morpurgo Davies herself demonstrates, this project can never quite shake off something one would have hoped was alien to it: ideas of cultural nationalism, aspirations to tie one's own language to a distinguished ancestor, the desire to link the genealogy of languages to the movements of distinct 'peoples' across Europe and Asia. At the beginning, Friedrich Schlegel's 1808 book *On the Language and Wisdom of the Indians* will open with 'a purely linguistic demonstration of the genealogical links between Sanskrit and the other languages [ancient European ones, KH]', but these will be followed by Orientalist disquisitions on Indian philosophy and speculations on the migrations of peoples.[30] Schlegel will also initiate both a commitment to the typological classification of languages—in his case, an overarching distinction between organic and mechanical languages—and the evaluative conviction that one class of language is culturally or epistemologically superior to the others (a pattern that will work itself all the way down to Cassirer, as we shall see later). Franz Bopp, the first to hold an institutional chair in the subject of 'general linguistics' will, in the careful words of Morpurgo Davies, 'create a working style which survived when some of his assumptions and his conclusions had gone out of fashion or had been forgotten'.[31]

And then, of course, there is Jacob Grimm, author of the comprehensive *Deutsche Grammatik* of 1819–40, collector of folklore, co-discoverer (with the Dane, Rasmus Rask) of systematic phonetic change, and ardent German patriot. On the one hand, a man wholly devoted to the detailed empirical examination of all things

---

[29] Anna Morpurgo Davies, *History of Linguistics, Volume IV: Nineteenth-Century Linguistics* (London: Longman, 1998), 19.
[30] Morpurgo Davies, *Nineteenth-Century Linguistics*, 70.
[31] Morpurgo Davies, *Nineteenth-Century Linguistics*, 135.

German; on the other hand, a scholar who believed, as Morpurgo Davies notes, 'in a direct link not only between the history of words and the cultural and historical development of a nation but also between the development of the more structured parts of language and that of culture in the broadest possible sense'.[32] 'Our language', Grimm asserted, 'is also our history': this meant, in practice, that apparently technical features of the Germanic languages reflected the distinguishing characteristics of the Germanic peoples.[33] So, for example, the phenomenon of *Ablaut*—when variation in a root vowel corresponds to a grammatical distinction, such as English *swim/swam*—was not only described as 'a fundamental and exclusive characteristic that runs through all the German languages and distinguishes them from most others' but also as 'the form in which the spirit of the German language appears'.[34] Grimm's most famous technical discovery, known as Grimm's Law or the Grimm–Rask Law, was given a similar cultural spin. Grimm had discovered a series of systematic shifts in consonants between Greek and Gothic (a precursor of modern German), which was followed by a shift in the same consonants between Gothic and Old High German in the Middle Ages: among them would be the shift from Greek *p* to Gothic *f* and then High German *v* or the shift from Greek *t* to Gothic *th* and then Old High German *d*.[35] The latter shift would help create the split that defined German, but it did more than that, for it was 'connected with the violent progress and craving for freedom found in Germany at the beginning of the Middle Ages'.[36] In the meantime, Grimm's German compatriots will suggest new typologies of language, of which the best known may be Wilhelm von Humboldt's distinction between inflecting, agglutinative, and isolating languages (roughly speaking: languages that mark grammatical distinctions with a suffix that may modify the root, languages that mark each distinction with a separate, fully-formed morpheme, and languages that rely on word order and prepositions to do the job). Here, too, the structure of language is meant to reflect or embody the spirit of the nation that uses it. And while, according to Humboldt, '*nations*, as such, are truly and immediately creative' in the languages they make, each presumably in their own way, there are more and less impressive ways in which to be creative.[37] Agglutination, for example, works by a '*compounding* used

---

[32] Morpurgo Davies, *Nineteenth-Century Linguistics*, 139.

[33] Jakob Karl Ludwig Grimm, *On the Origin of Language* [1851], trans. Raymond A. Wiley (Leiden: Brill, 1984), 20.

[34] Jacob Grimm, *Deutsche Grammatik*, Vol. 1 (1819 edition), 546 and Vol. 2, 73, as quoted and translated in Kevta E. Benes, 'German Linguistic Nationhood, 1806–66: Philology, Cultural Translation, and Historical Identity in Preunification Germany' (PhD dissertation, University of Washington, 2001), 112, 113.

[35] In order to illustrate these shifts more easily we can substitute Latin for Greek and English for Gothic (because Latin and Greek shared much of the same sound system and English retained the Gothic consonants that changed in Old High German). Thus Latin *pater* becomes English *father* and German *Vater*, while Latin *tu* becomes English *thou* and German *du*.

[36] Jacob Grimm, *Geschichte der deutschen Sprache*, vol. 1 (1848), 416, as quoted and translated in Morpurgo Davies, *Nineteenth-Century Linguistics*, 139.

[37] Wilhelm von Humboldt, *On Language: The Diversity of Human Language-Structure and its Influence on the Mental Development of Mankind*, trans. Peter Heath (Cambridge: Cambridge University Press, 1988), 42.

as inflection, an inflecting, therefore, deliberate but not brought to perfection—a more or less mechanical adding, not a truly organic accretion'.[38]

What binds sonorous claims for national character to the minute, scientific business of detailed linguistic observation? The thread that stitches them together will be belief in the 'genius' or peculiar spirit of a language. As Christiane Schlaps has shown, the earlier idea that each language had a distinctive 'genius'—a pattern of grammatical forms, a characteristic lexicon—was repurposed in the nineteenth century as an explanation of each language's historical development: its 'genius' was now 'a personified driving force behind the teleological historical development of a language', dictating the direction a particular language's evolution would take.[39] Grimm could thus speak of how the 'eternally vigilant genius of language' causes it to 'choose' certain forms of expression over others and allows it to heal whatever wounds the accidents of history may visit upon it.[40] The phonetic changes charted by comparative philology took place behind the backs of the language's speakers, even though the language had no other existence except as the output of speakers. If these changes were not to be random, one needed some collective entity, something supra-individual, to ground them. The genius or spirit of a language—Grimm's term is *Sprachgeist*—provides a principle of development, a force within language that can easily be allied or even merged with a national spirit or character.

We ought to stop and take note, however, of the collective entity that *isn't* selected by the comparative philologists to guide language: the modern European state. We ought also to take note of the irony that the state is elided from the theory of language precisely at the time when it becomes rather important to actually existing languages in Europe. The dictionaries and the literary culture so central to the establishment of national languages were the work of civil society for the most part—cultural intellectuals working in universities or independent writers. But the state also had a significant role in the definition, spread, and maintenance of a national language, by virtue of the systems of state education minted in the late nineteenth century. Insofar as literacy was the first order of business in public education, states had to decide what sort of language had to be imparted to the young citizenry. Which is to say that the state had a directive role in language (as did the intellectuals of civil society), guiding its development and evolution consciously and thoughtfully.[41]

---

[38] Humboldt, *On Language*, 106. Grimm's position was more complicated. While he regrets the loss of inflections that produces the Romance and Germanic languages out of Latin and Gothic, he argues that inflected languages 'had to yield to the striving for a still greater freedom of thought' made possible by the use of prepositions and particles. Grimm, *On the Origin of Language*, 21.

[39] Christiane Schlaps, 'The "Genius of Language": Transformations of a Concept in the History of Linguistics', *Historiographia Linguistica* 31.2–3 (2004): 376.

[40] Jacob Grimm, 'Über das pedantische in der deutschen sprache', *Kleinere Schriften* I (1864), 340, quoted in Schlaps, 'The "Genius of Language"', 378.

[41] On the establishment and directing of 'standard English' see Tony Crowley's brilliant study, *Standard English and the Politics of Language*, 2nd edn. (Basingstoke: Palgrave Macmillan, 2003). On the role of literary French in the education system, see Etienne Balibar and Pierre Macherey, 'On Literature as an Ideological Form', in Robert Young (ed.), *Untying the Text* (London: Routledge & Kegan Paul, 1981), 79–99.

That kind of collective activity finds no echo in the work of comparative philologists in part, of course, because they are mesmerized by the seemingly organic cultures of the past (ancient Greece, Rome, Persia, India). The hegemony of ancient cultures, however, was slowly being eroded, as the atomized nature of modern Europe became clearer and sharper, throwing the lack of social order into relief. You can see this dawning recognition in the theoretical programme of the so-called Neogrammarians of the 1870s and 1880s. In what is usually regarded as their manifesto, the preface to the first volume of their *Morphological Investigations* (1878), Hermann Osthoff and Karl Brugmann argued that the laws and processes of linguistic development that governed the modern vernaculars were the very same as those that governed the classical tongues—Greek, Latin, Sanskrit, and the hypothetical Indo-European mother language. Rather than focus attention on the reconstruction of languages long gone, the comparative linguist should learn about language by examining its recent history in 'fields like Germanic, Romance and Slavic', where there was not only a continuous record of textual material but also a connection 'with genuine popular speech, with the common language of communication and colloquial speech'.[42] This was justified by a ringing endorsement of the linguistic present. Comparative linguistics had to be guided by two principles:

> first, that language is not a thing which leads a life of its own outside of and above human beings, but that it has its true existence only in the individual, and hence that all changes in the life of a language can only proceed from the individual speaker; and second, that the mental and physical activity of man must have been at all times essentially the same when he acquired a language inherited from his ancestors and reproduced and modified the speech forms which had been absorbed into his consciousness.[43]

Olga Amsterdamska has cleverly described the Neogrammarian move as a 'philosophical "equalization" of ancient and modern languages': the idealized notion of an original language organically rooted in a stable culture would no longer provide the model of a language.[44] In fact, the equalization decisively tilted the field in favour of the modern present, or, to be more precise, a particular conception of the modern present. To say that language had its true existence only in the individual and that change originated with the individual speaker was to dissolve any particular language into millions of distinct utterances, was to say that, in truth, languages themselves had no real boundaries and were miracles of collective coordination, guided who-knows-how by some mysterious mechanism. Hermann Paul, the acknowledged theoretician of the Neogrammarians, would accordingly define '[t]he true object of philological study' as 'the entire sum of the products of the linguistic

---

[42] Hermann Osthoff and Karl Brugmann, 'Preface', *Morphological Investigations in the Sphere of the Indo-European Languages* (Leipzig, 1878), in Winfred P. Lehmann (ed.), *A Reader in Nineteenth-Century Historical Indo-European Linguistics* (Bloomington: Indiana University Press, 1967), 200, 201.

[43] Osthoff and Brugmann, 'Preface', 204.

[44] Olga Amsterdamska, *Schools of Thought: The Development of Linguistics from Bopp to Saussure* (Dordrecht: D. Reidel, 1987), 139.

activity of the entire sum of individuals in their reciprocal relations'.[45] Having defined the object of his attention as something so mutable, amorphous, and complicated as to be virtually impossible to take in, he at once admitted that the best one could hope for would be 'to get a general idea of the play of the forces at work in this huge complex'.[46]

In the face of such atomism and the conviction, shared by Osthoff, Brugmann, and Paul, that a modern unhistorical psychology was the key to understanding the acts of individual speakers, the Neogrammarians retained a conservative conception of their discipline. When Brugmann composed one of the last great comparative compendia, his *Comparative Grammar of the Indo-Germanic Languages*, he introduced its discussion of eleven 'indo-germanic' tongues with the claim that: 'The science of the Indg. [Indo-germanic, KH] languages forms, like Indg. Mythology, a section of Indg. "*Philology*", i.e., of that science, which has to investigate the intellectual development of the Indg. peoples from the time before their separation up to the present day.'[47] *Like* mythology, because language and myth are but different media or expressions of the culture of a people, here thrust back in time so that the Indo-Germanic language family has an imaginary 'national' correlate. However willing he was to think of language as disordered and individualized, for Brugmann 'linguistics is not a separate discipline but a research area within the various philological fields', which will remain divided on national-cultural grounds.[48]

The contradiction did not go unremarked upon. Michel Bréal—prominent linguist, coiner of the term 'semantics', and notable Dreyfusard—appreciated the scientific achievement of comparative philology, but was scathing about the nationalism that deformed it. In comparative philology, as he put it '[t]he mystical theory and the naturalist theory [...] gradually amalgamated'.[49] It's thus no accident that Bréal's short article 'Is Linguistics a Natural Science?', published as an appendix to his *Essay on Semantics*, was in fact an abridged version of a piece with a significantly different title, 'Language and Nationality', for nationality was the secret 'intellectual' substrate of the nineteenth-century conviction in the lawlike nature of linguistic change.[50] To claim that a language was national was, Bréal realized, to make a claim not just about the *scale* of the collective that supported it, but about the unconscious *form* of that collective as well. The principle of nationality, he observed, was used by peoples 'to subordinate their destiny to that of ancestors long since dead, and to diminish any freedom and reason which the world has

---

[45] Hermann Paul, *Principles of the History of Language*, trans. from the 2nd edn. by H. A. Strong (London: Swan Sonnenschein, Lowrey & Co., 1888), 2.

[46] Paul, *Principles*, 3.

[47] Karl Brugmann, *Elements of the Comparative Grammar of the Indo-Germanic Languages, Vol. I: Introduction and Phonology*, trans. Joseph Wright, (London: Trübner & Co., 1888), 1. 'Indo-Germanic', coined in 1823, described the family of languages that we now know (thanks to a later coinage) as 'Indo-European'. See also Benes, 'German Linguistic Nationhood', 65.

[48] Amsterdamska, *Schools of Thought*, 136.

[49] Michel Bréal, 'Language and Nationality', in *The Beginnings of Semantics: Essays, lectures and reviews*, ed. and trans. George Wolf (London: Duckworth, 1991), 202.

[50] George Wolf, translator of 'Language and Nationality', points out that the abridged version was published as 'La linguistique est-elle une science naturelle?' in the 6th edn. of the *Essai de sémantique*; Bréal, 'Language and Nationality', 199n.

managed to gain'.[51] Unsurprisingly, belief in the national character of language exhibited 'a fundamental disdain for reason. A certain caste pride was mixed in: the notion of privileged races, including of course one's own, was not be shunned.'[52]

Bréal was ready to acknowledge that linguistic order had to be made, created by a collective of individuals, that there was no natural principle, national or racial, that could ground it. A people would therefore shape their language not by swimming with the tide of some spontaneously evolving spirit but by means of a collective 'intelligence, hidden and yet so alert, which takes advantage of the smallest accidents to furnish thought with new resources'.[53] The grammatical categories and lexical richness of language are, for Bréal, the fruit of human reason, which slowly but surely perfects its most precious instrument, discarding words and categories that are useless, while creating those it needs and desires out of the historical stuff it inherits. Perfection and improvement arise from a process of collective hit-and-miss, as the product of countless individual acts of speech, the happy result, as he put it, 'of thousands, of millions, of billions of furtive attempts', culminating in a linguistic instrument both reasonable and orderly.[54] In this respect Bréal figures as a crucial transitional or intermediary figure. He thought of languages as the expression of collective will, but a will that arises from countless and apparently random interactions, an intelligence that is no one's in particular.

'LANGUAGE IN GENERAL' IN THE TWENTIETH CENTURY

What, then, is the moment that separates the nineteenth century's prodigious investments in language—as a model of evolutionary historical change and a resource for nationalism—from the linguistic turns of the early twentieth century? We could describe it as the moment when one no longer takes the orderliness and homogeneity of language for granted, when the unleashing of the political enters the heart of language, turning its shape and cohesiveness into a problem that must be solved. It could be described in disciplinary terms, as the moment when the obsession with 'language' migrates from the cultural world of philology, folklore, and nationalism to the somewhat different spheres of psychology, philosophy, logic, and literary criticism. But we can also define this dramatic break concretely, metonymically if you will, as the moment when Bréal's young colleague, Ferdinand de Saussure, realizes with a sinking heart that he's going to have to put aside his work on Indo-European languages in order to examine something quite different

---

[51] Bréal, 'Language and Nationality', 215.

[52] Bréal, 'Language and Nationality', 202. For a strikingly vigorous and sympathetic account of Bréal's critique, see Hans Aarsleff, 'Bréal vs. Schleicher: Reorientation in Linguistics during the Latter Half of the Nineteenth Century', in *From Locke to Saussure: Essays on the Study of Language and Intellectual History* (Minneapolis: University of Minnesota Press, 1982), 293–334.

[53] Michel Bréal, *Semantics: Studies in the Science of Meaning*, trans. Mrs Henry Cust (New York: Dover, 1964), 86.

[54] Bréal, *Semantics*, 7.

Introduction: Linguistic Turns as Social Theory

and more worrying, 'language in general'. The realization comes in an oft-quoted letter Saussure writes to Antoine Meillet in 1894:

> Ultimately, the only aspect of a language that interests me is its picturesque or quasi-ethnographic side—what distinguishes it from others as the property of a particular people with certain origins. But I have lost the pleasure of unreservedly devoting myself to such study [...]
>
> The utter inadequacy of current terminology, the necessity of reforming it and, in order to do that, of demonstrating what sort of object language is, continually spoils my pleasure in philology, even though I have no dearer wish than not to have to concern myself with the nature of language in general.[55]

In the past lies the tradition of comparative philology in which Saussure had been trained and which he clearly enjoys—the ethnographic examination and appreciation of particular languages; pressing towards the future, the demand to confront 'language in general'. Just ploughing ahead in the existing manner is not an option, because Saussure knows it is 'necessary to show the linguist *what he is doing*' (and also knows it will be 'an enormous amount of work').[56] He will ruminate on 'language in general' in a series of notes in the 1890s and in some lectures at the University of Geneva, but come to no firm conclusions. He will be forced to confront it again when the death of a colleague at the University of Geneva compels him to deliver three series of lectures on 'general linguistics' between 1907 and 1911. In the last of these lecture courses, Saussure will begin by admitting, that language 'is manifested in an infinite diversity of languages' and '[o]ne must therefore begin with what is given: languages; then, draw out what is universal: the language [*la langue*]'.[57] But though Saussure makes it sound as if he'll assemble 'the language' from the features of particular languages, by mere abstraction, this will turn out to be impossible. For the linguist is immediately faced with the obstacle 'that there is no homogeneous entity which is the language, but only a conglomerate of composite items'.[58]

Hermann Paul and his colleagues had *seen* the problem—how does this activity called language hang together, what are the forces at work in it?—without quite admitting the seriousness of it. Saussure would start by admitting there was a problem and would never let anyone forget it. In the notes he made for a book on general linguistics in 1893–4, he confessed that 'language does not in any of its manifestations present a substance, but rather combined or isolated *actions* of

---

[55] Ferdinand de Saussure, Letter to Antoine Meillet, 4 January 1894, translated by Gregory Elliott in Françoise Gadet, *Saussure and Contemporary Culture* (London: Hutchinson Radius, 1989), 19.

[56] Saussure, Letter to Meillet, 4 January 1894, 19.

[57] Ferdinand de Saussure, Lecture of 4 November 1910, in Robert Godel, *Les sources manuscrites du Cours de Linguistique Générale de F. de Saussure* (Geneva: Libraire Droz, 1969), 77. The content of Saussure's three lecture courses in general linguistics is known from detailed notes taken by various students. For the two later courses (1908–9, 1910–11), there are two different sets of notes now available. While I quote here from Godel's reconstruction of the course, based on the notes taken by one G. Dégallier, hereafter I'll refer to a later, fuller reconstruction of the course based on notes by Emil Constantin (which were not available to Godel).

[58] Ferdinand de Saussure, *Saussure's Third Course of Lectures on General Linguistics (1910–1911)*, ed. Eisuke Komatsu, trans. Roy Harris (Oxford: Pergamon Press, 1993), Lecture of 4 November 1910, 6a.

physiological, physical, or mental forces'.[59] No substance, no readily available object: instead the place in which a series of different forces, not necessarily commensurable with one another, intersect. Therefore there would be no 'luminous synthesis of the language system, starting out from a given principle'; language 'can only be understood with the help of four or five principles, intertwining constantly'. Saussure knew he was navigating unknown and uncertain territory: in a book on 'language in general', 'each paragraph must be set like a solid object planted firmly in the marsh, marking the route both forward and backward'.[60]

To cut a path through the marsh, one would have to be brutal and decisive; to Saussure's enduring credit he was, despite some well-documented hesitations. Linguistics would have to reorientate itself around this new object, *la langue*—variously translated as 'the language', 'the language structure', and 'the language system'—which was by no means an abstraction from the composite, amorphous, endlessly changing universe of *langage*. It represented the system of language as it existed in the instant when one spoke or understood something spoken: more precisely, it was the system, the order or set of relationships that made it possible to say something or understand something in the first place. The order was, Saussure would have been the first to admit, something of a fiction: he could never say exactly where this system was to be found (in the mind of a single speaker, as the average of a community of speakers, in dictionaries and grammars?).[61] One could only find it by cutting away a great mass of linguistic underbrush, which would henceforth be declared either a matter of 'external' linguistics (political factors, cultural and ethnological matters, questions of migration and geography) or 'diachronic', i.e., relating to the constant mutations that change the system from one instant to the next. The new object would set linguistics on a new and productive path, from which it has, in many respects, not strayed since Saussure's time.[62]

It's a linguistic turn within linguistics: a linguistic turn, and not just a change of scientific paradigm (in Kuhn's sense), because it looks to 'language in general' for forces that will somehow order the composite, heterogeneous world of speech. For all the talk of objectivity and science, *la langue*, as we'll see in the following chapters, is not a state of language, but a way of directing and guiding the force of

---

[59] Ferdinand de Saussure, 'Notes for a Book on General Linguistics, I (1893–1894)', in *Writings in General Linguistics*, trans. Carol Sanders, Matthew Pires, and Peter Figueroa (Oxford: Oxford University Press, 2006), 136.

[60] Saussure, 'Discourse as a site of modifications—Organization of this book', in *Writings in General Linguistics*, 65.

[61] In the *Course in General Linguistics*, *la langue* is described as: 'a collection of necessary conventions' (9); 'some sort of average' (13); 'the sum of word-images stored in the minds of all individuals' (13); 'a storehouse filled by the members of a given community' (13); and what is represented in 'dictionaries and grammars' (15). These translations are taken from Ferdinand de Saussure, *Course in General Linguistics*, trans. Wade Baskin (London: Fontana, 1974). In presenting Saussure in English I will sometimes use Baskin's translation, sometimes the later one by Roy Harris (London: Duckworth, 1983), and sometimes an amended version made in consultation with Tullio de Mauro's critical edition (*Cours de linguistique générale*, ed. Tullio de Mauro (Paris: Payot, 1985).

[62] The extent of Saussure's influence in American linguistics is a matter of dispute. On the indigenous sources of American 'descriptivism', see Julia S. Falk, 'Saussure and American Linguistics', in Carol Sanders (ed.), *The Cambridge Companion to Saussure* (Cambridge: Cambridge University Press, 2004), 107–23.

language. Nor will Saussure pretend that this language system is disengaged from the social world in which it operates. Having cut his way through the marsh, he lights on a new aquatic metaphor, to which he'll recur throughout his writings on 'general linguistics':

> A sign system is destined for a community just as a ship is for the sea. Its only role is that of allowing comprehension between people in groups large or small, but not for the use of a sole individual. This is why, contrary to appearance, semiological phenomena, of whatever kind, are never devoid of the social, collective element. The community and its laws are among their *internal*, rather than *external* elements, as far as we are concerned.[63]

Of course, 'the community and its laws' are not a stable object: societies change under the pressure of innovation, political revolution, and counter-revolution, and at any one point the globe may play host to a quite diverse set of communities. That much would have been painfully obvious to any European intellectual of the time. But to allow this kind of historical contingency into *la langue* would have been tantamount to admitting that language was simply too mutable at its core to permit any kind of permanent definition. Saussure therefore has both disciplinary reasons and sociopolitical reasons for believing one must make stability and cohesion defining features of 'language in general'. In his texts the search for a stable object of linguistic inquiry becomes a way of thinking about what might stabilize 'the community and its laws'.

Saussure is exemplary, but not unique. 'Language in general', *die Sprache überhaupt*, слово как таковое, 'the symbol', 'language with a capital L': each linguistic turn will feature an appeal to a modernist, universal object, or rather, to a linguistic force or tension intrinsic to language as such, but not coterminous with actually existing language. Language itself will appear as fractured, divided against itself or unable to perform the tasks assigned to it. Its problems will be myriad: a tendency to dissolve into a mere aggregate of individual actions, the disjunction between rational and irrational aspects of its ordering, a tendency to tedious *cliché* and prefabricated speech, its liability to utterances full of 'word magic', at once forceful and unreasonable. The solutions will claim that the resources needed to tame or solve the problems posed by language will be drawn from language itself, which has to be prodded, shaped, exploited, rid of dangerous excrescences. For intellectuals throughout Europe, language will be both the problem and the solution.

It can be both because the problem and the solution concern far more than language: those who take the linguistic turn are doing social theory by other means. Sometimes quite self-consciously, as we shall see, and sometimes with utter conviction that words are all that matter to them. In each case we will see that an idea of 'language as such', of a language within language, is what mediates between the surface concerns of the argument and the problem of democracy and social order that endows it with its shape and urgency. Language will be a metonym for this problem, but not a simple one-to-one figure: its inconsistency, which gives rise to

---

[63] Saussure, 'Sign systems—Community', in *Writings in General Linguistics*, 203.

a 'language as such' within it, is a metonym for mass democracy, understood as a challenge to the prevailing order and a social and political problem to be solved.

THE SHAPE OF THE BOOK: THREE CLAIMS

The argument of this book can therefore be separated, with only a little violence, into three related claims. The first is simply that in the late nineteenth and early twentieth centuries there were multiple linguistic turns and that we need to think of them as a whole, as a constellation across Europe. I believe the very breadth of the book, the number and variety of writers discussed, provides compelling evidence for that claim. But though the spectacle is grand enough, it is by no means all-inclusive. One has to admit at the outset that it would be well beyond both my competence and my energy (and perhaps my lifespan) to examine European linguistic turns comprehensively. In what follows I discuss instances of them in Britain, Switzerland, Germany, Austria, France, Italy, and Russia (Soviet and pre-Soviet). That is, of course, a somewhat odd construction of Europe and one likely to annoy many of its current inhabitants. It excludes most of Eastern and Central Europe, all of Scandinavia, the Low Countries, and the Iberian Peninsula. It also ignores the fact that most of those nations were also the ruling centres of empires. The fact of extensive colonies—in which language was a pressing question and democracy non-existent—has a clear bearing on the investments these nations made in language and its political significance, but I lack the expertise to address it.

Even given these limitations, there are many omissions, which—if I can invoke the reader's trust—I regret greatly. Martin Buber wants to characterize Jewish religious life in terms of 'basic words'. Vienna, with its own pressing language question, is home to Karl Kraus on the one hand and the Vienna Circle on the other. There are Fritz Mauthner and Gustav Landauer, whose explicit melding of politics and language make them ideal candidates. There's the Prague Linguistic Circle and Havranek. There is Victoria Welby, a significant European figure, who deserves far more than the cursory treatment she gets here and whose serious inclusion would have broken up the all-male tedium of my cast. And there are two whose absence may strike a dagger in the heart of the whole project: Freud and Heidegger. What can I say? I started juggling, and at a certain point adding another ball seemed impossible.

The second claim is that language draws such a crowd because crowds have become a problem: in the linguistic turns of the early twentieth century, language is a metonym for problems of social order and social division, democracy and consent, nationality and difference. These problems circulate around the problem of mass democracy, which by the beginning of the twentieth century had become a political question throughout Europe. Mass democracy was not a mere quantitative extension of what came before: it entailed new constituencies, new forms of organization, new procedures, and new forces. In some linguistic turns, the metonymic relation between language and the problem of democracy is explicit: Ogden and Richards think we need a theory of symbolism to prevent the demagoguery that threatens mass democracy; Gramsci thinks a national-popular form of Italian is part of cultural hegemony. In other cases, say that of Shklovskii, language is appealed to as a force that might revivify social life, but the connection with political matters is oblique. In the linguistic turn taken by analytic philosophy, politics arises only as the seemingly random subject of example sentences.

The claim is not, of course, that literary critics, linguists, or philosophers were interested in words because of the democratic crisis challenging Europe: they had a natural interest in words and would have paid them careful attention in any case. The claim is that the kind of investment they place in language—it figures as a force and not just a neutral field—and the way in which they configure language (ruptured from within, in need of renewal or redemption) are the signs of the political and social crisis.

Hence the third claim: that the distinguishing feature of these linguistic turns is a commitment to some version of 'language as such', a force or structure within language that can provide the vitality, the order, the lucidity, or some combination of these, necessary to cure language of its present ills. Happily, many of the writers we examine explicitly invoke something along these lines, but where they don't I will show that the conception is there even if the name isn't.

The claims imply one another: the assertion that there are many linguistic turns depends in part upon the idea that we define them by their attention to 'language as such'; that the democratic crisis provokes the turns is the explanation for why there are so many of them in such different areas in a discrete period of time; the role and significance of 'language as such' depends upon the claim that it arises to help resolve a larger social crisis; and so on. They do not, however, demand each other: it's possible for the reader to be persuaded by one or two, but not all. If the reader comes away convinced that from now on we should think of the early twentieth century as the moment of linguistic turns (and therefore linguistic turns as a characteristic move within the historical event of modernism), the book will have at least opened up a new research area. If they also believe that a commitment to 'language as such' is what unites these turns, I'll consider the book a success. If people are persuaded that these turns are in part attempts to do social theory metonymically, that they are wrestling with the social and political problems posed by mass democracy in Europe, my happiness will be complete.

These claims unite the book and they constitute its basic case. But it is in the nature of the beast that they cannot be cashed out in a single historical narrative. The linguistic turns make up a constellation, not a story; they are a series of responses to a crisis, the significance of which becomes clearer when you see them together, but the responses are only occasionally related by influence or direct connection. We'll see that Ogden translated Wittgenstein, that Jakobson read and lectured on Saussure, and that Cassirer read practically everyone. But for the most part, writers who became heavily invested in the force of 'language as such' didn't know that other, contemporary writers had similar investments. As a result, though there's a story to tell here, it has to be told episodically and thematically.

Very roughly, the problems posed by mass democracy can be divided into problems of order on the one hand and problems of myth on the other; the book's two parts follow from that. In the episodes contained in Part I, 'Order', the focus is on how a society grounded in 'the people' can be both consensual and orderly. The unleashing of the political Rosanvallon describes means society now has to be *instituted*, and instituted democratically: there is no natural order of estates, no organic corporate hierarchy, on which one can found the structure of the polity. If we are already used to thinking of language as embodying 'the nation'—thanks in large part to the work of the nineteenth century—then the problem of social order can be framed as a question about the cohesiveness of language: how is a whole woven and maintained from 'the combined or isolated *actions* of physiological, physical, or mental forces', the incoherent, amorphous, and mutable stuff of speech? Such an order must command consent, although consent does not, as we shall see, mean reason and argument as well. (As Habermas pointed out many years ago, and I will remind the reader repeatedly in the pages to come, the enlargement of the public sphere in the nineteenth century went hand-in-hand with the blunting of its argumentative features.)[64]

The first chapter of Part I explores this question through a discussion of the role of analogy in Saussure's new linguistics. Analogy may seem like a minor linguistic byway; in fact, in it are condensed a series of critical questions about linguistic order. By the twentieth century, analogy was understood as the principle that underlay the systematicity and orderliness of language, but it was also understood to be a psychological process. Did it involve reasoning (which would mean that the consent grounding language was a reasoned consent)? This was the question Saussure wrestled with in his lectures on general linguistics. In this chapter we observe the wrestling and see how a conservative version of 'language as such'—language as such as embodying an unconscious consent—emerges victorious.

Analogy would also play a role in the linguistic turn urged on by Ludwig Wittgenstein. In Chapter 3 we look at the linguistic turn in analytic philosophy as it emerges from Gottlob Frege, gains momentum in Bertrand Russell, and finds elaboration in the early and middle work of Ludwig Wittgenstein. This linguistic turn in philosophy would ultimately produce a great many different kinds of philosophical practice, but its initial impulse is a sense that ordinary language—the language in which we hold conversations and compose non-philosophical prose—is logically deceptive or 'muddled'. The characteristic move of linguistic philosophy will therefore be the translation and rephrasing of statements—making these statements clearer *without changing their content*. Why actually existing language is muddled or how one goes about making it clearer will be a topic of continual dispute, leading to various, even irreconcilable versions of linguistic philosophy. But the basic goal and the procedure stay the same: to bring to the surface a lucidity that is lurking within language, needing only to be coaxed out. Of course, the lucidity will itself be a matter of words—no matter what a proposition is, it will require symbols for expression—and eventually many of the analytic philosophers will decide that we don't need different words, but a sharper

---

[64] Jürgen Habermas, *The Structural Transformation of the Public Sphere: An Inquiry into a Category of Bourgeois Society*, trans. Thomas Burger and Frederick Lawrence (Cambridge, MA: MIT Press, 1989), Parts V and VI.

understanding of the words we usually employ. But this conundrum—being caught within language, having only words and symbols at one's disposal, but feeling that the words and symbols are somehow a problem—will permanently afflict the discipline.

What is at stake in this drive towards clarification? First is intersubjectivity: the drive to clarity entails, at least at its beginning, a stripping away of every intersubjective, temporal element in discourse, every trace in it of a definite time and place, as if intersubjectivity itself were an obstacle to communication. To put it a different way: philosophy will, yet again, take up arms against everything *rhetorical* in language, those features of language that turn the naked assertion into a concrete effort to be persuasive (and therefore to persuade someone in particular, on a definite occasion). Second is the relationship of professional expertise to democracy, because a language clarified by professional philosophers is a substitute for the objectivity of the public sphere. The clarifying, logical analysis of statements by professional philosophers offers itself as a substitute source of objectivity, at a point in political history when many European nations are extending the franchise and fearing the consequences. Finally, there is belief in language itself. When Wittgenstein and his fellow philosophers surrender the project of logical analysis for a different kind of clarification, one which depends on the making and deciphering of analogies, they ground their practice on the assumption that language always 'works': that it is itself successful at representing and communicating and fails only when external circumstances disturb its inner workings.

Chapter 4 returns to Saussure and the contention that 'language in general' is a social institution, but a uniquely conservative one. To produce this version of 'language' he had to strike a precarious balance between grounding language in the agreement of those who used it (and nothing else) and ensuring that agreement was neither conscious nor liable to reasoned dispute. The ambiguities of his position come to the fore when his claim that language is a social institution is taken up enthusiastically by linguists working in the newly created Soviet Union. In Chapter 4 I focus on three particular linguists, all of whom consider whether, from the perspective of Saussure's work, a linguistic revolution is possible. One, S. I. Kartsevskii, does not want such a revolution and believes Saussure tells us why it is not possible. Another, G. O. Vinokur, both desires it and believes Saussure has provided tools for its realization. A third, Lev Iakubinskii, shares Vinokur's enthusiasm but sees Saussure's linguistics as an obstacle. The problem is not one of misinterpretation, for this varied reception reveals the striking inconsistency of Saussure's conception of the community and its laws.

The sense that language was constantly productive and mutable, that it was a source of constant innovation and change, coexisted uneasily with the stability promised by theories of linguistic consent. Comparative philology had sought to rationalize that productivity by subsuming it under natural laws. In Chapter 5 I borrow Walter Benjamin's description of the 'narcotic historicism' of nineteenth-century Paris (expressed in its arcades, panoramas, wax museums, and architecture) and apply it to comparative philology, suggesting that, in effect, it creates 'museums' of language. One can then follow this comparison through and view some forms of twentieth-century modernism as attempts to liberate the force bound up in historicist forms. In this context, one can interpret Saussure, Bakhtin, and Benjamin as each unleashing the productivity and creativity of language that had been explained (and confined) in the phonetic laws discovered in the previous century. Bakhtin does so by counterpoising heteroglossia with myth; Saussure does so by invoking a model of linguistic change modelled on urban life and the republican social contract; Benjamin does so in his theory of translation, which aims to recover a native linguistic energy from the diversity of actually existing languages. In their different ways, these paeans to linguistic productivity draw attention to another feature of mass democracy: its urban character.

In Part II, 'Myth', I focus on a notable tendency of 'language as such' that alarms most intellectuals, but excites a few: its penchant for 'word magic' and myth, words and phrases packed with an immediate force and power, a force that seems to inhere in the words themselves. In the case of myth and magic, the reference to the perilous state of Europe is not mediated or analogical but direct: mythic, magical discourse created confusion in the public, diverted the power of reason and created a dangerous, 'charismatic' kind of mass politics. Or else—as those excited by it claimed—mythic language was the only hope of reviving a politics that had been robbed of life by bureaucratic haggling and the manoeuvres of parliament, the force that might inspire the popular masses and lead them to active participation in the life of the nation.

Chapter 6 is devoted to those hostile to myth, who believe that myth must be defeated and who have a strategy for defeating it. The strategies are varied: Ogden and Richards turn to science, Frege to logic, Orwell to a particular kind of prose, Bakhtin to the novel, and Saussure to language itself. Antipathy to myth and word magic is sometimes framed in explicit political terms (in Ogden and Richards, Orwell, and Bakhtin) and sometimes not. My claim is that myth figures as a tendency of 'language as such' that must be vigilantly monitored and countered with alternative forms of discourse; lurking within the fear of myth is nervousness about demagoguery within popular democratic politics.

Chapter 7 is given over to the enthusiasts of myth, who argue that, on the contrary, it represents the lifeblood of language without which any polity is doomed. We begin with a discussion of Ernst Cassirer's theory of myth, before turning to the Russian Formalists and Futurists—ready to resurrect the word—and conclude with Walter Benjamin's insistence on the power and magic of pure language. For Walter Benjamin, for Viktor Shklovskii and many of his Futurist brethren, the 'word as such' has to be rescued from the deadening 'bourgeois' language of the present. Language is out of whack, but what has distorted it is precisely its misuse as a mere tool of communication (the aforementioned 'abyss of prattle'), against which one has to defend language as *naming*. The problem is not, according to these writers, that myth threatens the liberal polity, but that liberalism itself, embodied in the deadening language of public life, threatens democracy. Following this chapter is an excursus on two figures who present a kind of linguistic turn in reverse: Georges Sorel and Antonio Gramsci. For they are political thinkers who make linguistic ideas, ideas of myth in particular, central to their political strategies. Sorel will look to myth as an alternative form of organizing and motivating the political masses; Gramsci will look to Sorel as a source for ideas about popular mobilization, which he, however, will embody not in an instantaneous call to arms, but in the institutional struggle for hegemony.

Chapter 8 returns to 'linguistic philosophy', but now a different kind, represented by the middle and late work of Wittgenstein and the writing of J. L. Austin. In what came to be called, rightly or wrongly, ordinary language philosophy, myth emerged not from charismatic demagogues but from the fervid minds of scientistic intellectuals. Wittgenstein and Austin share the conviction that 'language as such' is the antidote to the metaphysical entanglements that arise when, in Wittgenstein's famous phrase, 'language *goes on holiday*'.[65] The claim, however, is that language as such is language unhindered, 'our common stock of words', as Austin put it, as used in the mundane practical matters of life.[66] But, as we will see, this ordinary version of 'language as such' is not simply present to the naked eye and ear, but is only available as the end result of strategies of philosophical clarification, which make language a manifestation of life. The chapter therefore focuses on Wittgenstein's idea of the perspicuous representation and Austin's techniques of drawing out distinctions. Unlike the other chapters in this book, this one pays attention to pleasure, in particular the pleasure Wittgenstein and Austin get from a clarifying look at ordinary life. That language always works turns out not to be a mere fact, but also a source of satisfaction for some philosophers. But as we'll see, in Wittgenstein's case the satisfaction one draws from seeing language at work is weakened by an undercurrent.

The Conclusion examines the situation after the Second World War. There we see how the social democratic settlement in Western Europe gives birth to the new linguistic turns known as structuralism. We explore this by looking at how Roland Barthes combines ideas from Saussure with a project for a radical analysis of French everyday life in the *Mythologies*.

Why does any of it matter? The pat answer is that it always matters whether or not we understand the history whose work we inherit. I don't subscribe to all of Benjamin's philosophy of history, but he's entirely right to claim that for the historian '*even the dead* will not be safe from the enemy if he is victorious'.[67] But there are specific reasons why this particular issue matters. It was, indirectly, a struggle over what a democratic society would look like: what would hold it together, how its collective agreements would be established and maintained, how it might be more than a set of empty procedures. It was, directly, a debate on what role language would play in the political crises and problems of the time: whether it was itself a unifying force, whether it existed 'consensually', what role its mythic forms should play in political life and what role everyday language—as opposed to technical jargons—should play. In essence, this was a

---

[65] Ludwig Wittgenstein, *Philosophical Investigations*, revised 4th edn., trans. G. E. M. Anscombe, P. M. S. Hacker, and Joachim Schulte (Oxford: Wiley-Blackwell, 2009), §38 (23e).
[66] J. L. Austin, 'A Plea for Excuses', in *Philosophical Papers*, 3rd edn. (Oxford: Oxford University Press, 1979), 182.
[67] Walter Benjamin, Thesis VI, 'On the Concept of History', in *Selected Writings: Volume 4, 1938–1940*, trans. Edmund Jephcott and others (Cambridge, MA: Harvard University Press, 2003), 391.

debate on what rhetoric should look like in modern democracies (if one wanted a longer book, one would add to it the revival of rhetoric in the early twentieth century in the works of Kenneth Burke and Chaim Perelman). Rhetoric, as the doctrine and practice of persuasive discourse in democratic society, had fallen into disuse in modern society, victim of Romanticism on one side and rival theories of language on the other. In a sense, the linguistic turns of the early twentieth century are, without quite knowing it, attempts to thrash out once more the questions that rhetoric was meant to confront.

But there is one more reason why this matters, and that is the subject of this book's Conclusion. The linguistic turns of 1890 to 1950 may have faded, but they left an inheritance that was exploited with some gusto by the following generations. The structuralist and post-structuralist enthusiasms of the later twentieth century depended on ideas about language put forward in the earlier part of the century, ideas people were quick to draw political conclusions from. My argument, to put it in the briefest possible way, is that the politics people were able to extract from theories of discourse at the end of the twentieth century were the politics that had been put into them at the beginning. That is one more reason why unearthing this past makes a difference.

PART I
ORDER

2

'Grammar, for example, can only be studied in the crowd'
Reason, Analogy, and the Nature of Social Consent

(Ferdinand de Saussure)

The moments when the writers we examine seem most indecisive, confused, or tortured are often the moments when they say the most about the issues in play. For Saussure that moment is his confrontation with what is known as 'analogy'. In linguistics, analogy is a mechanism that produces new forms in a language, and that, by producing these forms, reinforces certain existing patterns of word-derivation and grammatical inflection. The plural *cows* was created in sixteenth- and seventeenth-century English as an alternative to the existing plural for *cow*, the now antiquated *kine*. It was created by analogy with already existing forms, such as the pair *pig* : *pigs*. When *cows* became the preferred plural for the bovine beast, it meant both that a new word had established itself in English usage and that a particular grammatical pattern of making plurals (adding *-s*) had been reinforced in English.

For those familiar with Saussure and his most famous work, the *Course in General Linguistics* [*Cours de linguistique générale*], it probably sounds like an odd place to start. The *Cours* had been edited by Saussure's colleagues Charles Bally and Albert Sechehaye after his death in 1913. According to Robert Godel, Bally and Sechehaye made the skeleton of this work from notes that students had taken of Saussure's three series of lectures on general linguistics in 1907, 1908–9 and 1910–11, adding to it material drawn from a variety of Saussure's own notes dating as far back as 1891.[1] The two editors used the final lecture series as the organizational template for the work, arranging the material, roughly speaking, in the order it had been presented there. When topics had been covered in greater depth in an earlier series, Bally and Sechehaye used the older material to fill in the gaps. In the published edition of the *Cours*, the topic of analogy occupies two short chapters in the part dedicated to 'Diachronic Linguistics'. The *Cours* is famous for having established the scientific priority of the 'synchronic' point of view, which included the

---

[1] Robert Godel, *Les sources manuscrites*, in particular chapter 3, 'Le travail des éditeurs'. It is worth noting that Bally and Sechehaye did not have at their disposal all the lecture notes that have since come to light. In particular, they didn't have Emil Constantin's very full notes to the third course of lectures, which were only discovered in 1958 and were published in full in 1993.

idea that every language was a system of signs, in which each meaningful unit gained its identity—as a recognizable sound pattern attached to a determinate meaning—from its relations to the other signs in the system. In a text best known for establishing the arbitrary and conventional nature of signs, the material collected under the rubric of 'diachronic linguistics', discussions of phonetic and analogical change, is bound to seem like something left over from the linguistic past.

It was, however, not always so. In the first course of lectures on general linguistics delivered by Saussure in Geneva in January–July 1907, the topic of analogical change dominated. In fact, it's fair to say that in this course the topic of general linguistics was effectively the study of diachronic linguistics: in the published notes, 27 pages of material on linguistics in general are followed by 27 pages on 'Phonetic evolutions', 49 pages on 'Analogical changes', and 20 pages on the internal and external history of the Indo-European languages (although some additional lecture material on the history of the Indo-European languages was left out of the published version of the lectures).[2] It's tempting to ascribe this emphasis to the immediate situation in which the course was delivered. In his recent biography of Saussure, John Joseph has pointed out that Saussure was assigned the teaching of this course at the last minute. Up till 1907 general linguistics at Geneva had been taught by the chair in this topic, Joseph Wertheimer, whose sudden retirement due to ill health looks to have thrown the Faculty of Arts into one of those crises of teaching provision familiar to anyone working in a university. Rather than appoint a new chair, the university decided to assign responsibility for general linguistics to Saussure, who up to then had been teaching Indo-European languages and linguistics (this kind of solution will also be familiar to anyone working in a university).[3] The course began midway through the first semester and there's good reason to think Saussure didn't have time to think through how to present it. Maybe he just tried to generalize from the kind of historical linguistics he was already teaching?

But the role played by analogy in Saussure's theory of language belies this explanation. As that which enforces and maintains regularity in a language, analogy is cast as the underlying principle of the language system itself, to the point where Saussure introduces what will be one of his most critical innovations—the distinction between *langue* and *parole* which opens the published *Cours*—as a consequence of his theory of analogy. For all its initial prominence, 'analogy' will virtually disappear as a topic in the next two series (the material on analogy in the published *Cours* is drawn largely from the 1907 lectures). Was this because Saussure did not know what to do with it, or because he was unhappy with his formulations? Before broaching the critical questions, it is probably necessary to back up a bit and make clear why analogy would have been so important in the first place.

---

[2] Ferdinand de Saussure, *Saussure's First Course of Lectures on General Linguistics (1907)*, ed. Eisuke Komatsu, trans. George Wolf (Oxford: Pergamon Press, 1996). On Riedlinger's notes on lectures on Indo-European languages, excluded from the published version, see John E. Joseph, *Saussure* (Oxford: Oxford University Press, 2012), 514.

[3] Joseph, *Saussure*, 489–91.

ANALOGY: A STICKING POINT IN THE HISTORY OF LINGUISTICS

In nineteenth-century comparative philology, analogy had come to be seen as a problem. After some initial toing and froing over method, the comparativists decided that the most reliable evidence for tracing the evolution of languages was systematic sound change, as exemplified in regularities like the Grimm-Rask Law. Sound change was deemed to be lawlike in the sense that, if you specified the conditions in sufficient detail, a shift from one consonant to another or one vowel to another took place throughout the language in question. Thus the *-s-* sound in the Indo-European mother language was replaced by the *-r-* sound in Latin whenever the *-s-* was 'intervocalic', that is, surrounded by two vowels; this produced *gene-r-is* in Latin, which one could contrast with the Greek *gene-s-is*, in which the original Indo-European *-s-* had not been subject to change.[4] For the early comparative philologists, sound change was disruptive and even degenerative: Grimm would claim that as a result of consonant changes in the Germanic languages '[a] mass of roots are obscured', i.e., that sound changes disturbed the correspondence of sound and meaning that characterized earlier, purer forms of language like Latin.[5] Saussure did not think sound change was disruptive, but he nevertheless provided a classic example of this obscuring in his lectures: by virtue of sound changes the Latin pair *decem/undecim* (10/11, or, to be precise, 10/10 +1) became in French *dix/onze*, in which there appears to be no logical relation between the two terms.[6] But however much it may have upset the order of Latin, Greek, or Sanskrit, sound change was systematic, and it made possible the establishment of clear lines of descent from one state of a language, or one language, to another.

Except where analogy intervened. At times, linguistic forms changed not on account of sound changes that were regular and lawlike because they were 'unconscious' (on which more, later), but because speakers invented new forms on the basis of analogies with existing ones. When, in Latin, intervocalic *-s-* became intervocalic *-r-*, the accusative singular of Latin *honos* (honour), *honosem*, became *honorem*, while the *-s* in the nominative singular form *honos*, being final, did not change. However, speakers of Latin compared the new form *honorem* with other instances of the accusative singular like *oratorem*, for which the nominative singular was *orator*, and they invented a new nominative singular for Latin 'honour', by means of the analogy *oratorem : orator = honorem : honor*.[7] The rest, as they say, is history.

Initially, the history produced by this kind of 'false' analogizing was considered bad history.[8] First, because it muddied the waters of sound change. Someone looking

---

[4] See Saussure, *Course in General Linguistics* (1983), 145.
[5] Grimm, *On the Origin of Language*, 21.   [6] Saussure, *First Course*, 48a.
[7] Saussure, *Course in General Linguistics* (1983), 160–4.
[8] The categorization of analogy as 'false analogy' was first made by the philologist August Friedrich Pott. See Gerda Hassler, '"Analogy": The History of a Concept and a Term from the 17th to the 19th Century', in Douglas A. Kibbee (ed.), *History of Linguistics 2005: Selected Papers from ICHOLS X* (Amsterdam: John Benjamins, 2007), 164.

at the pair *honor : honorem* and its predecessor, *honos : honosem*, would be at a loss to come up with a principle to explain the change, because not all instances of Latin final *-s* had undergone sound change. Secondly, analogy was frequently based on, and propounded, a 'mistaken' view of the grammatical structure of a language, insofar as it segmented the word in the wrong place. When English speakers use analogy to create words like *beautician* or *mortician* on the model of *electrician* and *logician*, they mistake *-ician* for a suffix. In fact, *-ician* arises because the derivational suffix *-ian*, when attached to words like *electric* or *logic*, softens the final consonant of the root: segmenting the word at *-ician* implies that the original roots are *electr* and *log*, which is obviously false. Analogical change therefore, as Saussure remarked in an early formulation, 'has the characteristic of being a historical error, of an offense against the language'.[9] It produced forms that unsettled the order of the language seen from an etymological point of view and it created new and bizarre forms, whose past became indecipherable.

These problems were, in fact, the consequences of a deeper one: analogical change was understood as the result of a conscious intervention in the language, a change that required the intelligent comparison of existing forms and the creation of a new form on that basis. 'Conscious' interventions in the path of linguistic evolution were disturbing, not only because they were often mistaken from an etymological point of view, but also because they were necessarily unpredictable and irregular. The kind of history that resulted was 'human', a subjective and capricious intrusion into what should have been a lawlike 'natural-historical' process. The irony here is that when analogy was first established as a characteristic of languages, as the process that made for grammatical consistency and thus grammatical 'rules', it was opposed to human caprice and was the very foundation of the orderliness and regularity of language. In the text containing the classic defence of analogy, Book X of Varro's *De lingua latina* [*On the Latin Language*], the author distinguished between regular, systematic patterns of inflection that exhibited analogy and the 'imposition' of names by human invention. '[M]orphological variation of this kind', he remarks, 'in the popular usage of words is weakly motivated, because it has its source in the arbitrary determination of the speech community: therefore in this process in speaking there is more anomaly than analogy.'[10] 'Will' was manifest in the anomalous creation of names, whereas the analogies manifest in systems of word declension and conjugation were 'natural': 'for each of us imposes a name as he wishes but declines it as nature desires'.[11]

Varro dotted his text with references to analogies in the natural world, to underscore the accord between a language governed by analogy and the natural order of things. In her short history of the concept's interesting evolution, Gerda Hassler notes that from the Renaissance through the eighteenth century analogy was regarded as the principle behind existing language and the guarantee of its reasonableness.

---

[9] Saussure, *First Course*, 57a.

[10] Varro, *De lingua latina X*, trans. and ed. Daniel J. Taylor (Amsterdam: John Benjamins, 1996), chapter 16 (65).

[11] Varro, *De lingua latina X*, chapter 53 (81).

In an article by Nicolas Beauzée in the *Encyclopédie méthodique* of 1782 analogy would be celebrated as that which, in Hassler's paraphrase, 'fell from heaven during mankind's creation in order to determine the form of language'.[12]

Perhaps after the French Revolution some intellectuals felt less confident about unleashing the power of reason. Or perhaps analogy fell victim to the new conviction that the study of language was the study of the history of language, the study of language change first and foremost, and the study of language structure as a means of ascertaining language change. In the organicist, nationalist, and occasionally racist world of comparative philology the only kind of change likely to be amenable to scientific study—the only kind of change that would manifest lawlike regularity—was change that took place behind the backs of human beings, that mimicked, as far as was possible, the dumb and purposeless regularities of nature. The 'reasonableness' of analogy, which, in an earlier age, was a sign of language's harmony with the divine plan, was now the source of unpredictability. Change motivated by analogy, change which apparently instilled regularity where there had been disorder, was, from the historical point of view, itself the source of disorder.

The Neogrammarian revolution that began in 1878 was, in some respects, a modern revival of the older view. Neogrammarian linguists argued that analogy was not only a normal feature of the evolution of language, but was in fact the very basis of grammar, of all regularity and system in language. Analogy did not muddy the clear waters of earlier grammatical structures, because those structures had also been made by analogy.[13] Bréal concurred:

> It is hard to understand why the parent language should be more perfect than its offspring, since it itself, made up of the remains of still older languages, would have been subject to ordinary conditions as they were, and thus could have exhibited neither the perfection nor the symmetry of a work created at a single moment.[14]

In the Neogrammarians, Saussure noted approvingly, 'the legitimacy and universality of this phenomenon is for the first time clearly accepted and declared'.[15] But acknowledging the centrality of analogy had implications for Saussure far beyond what the Neogrammarians might have suspected. George Wolf has noted that when Saussure lauds the Neogrammarians, he claims that they were the first to adopt a truly historical perspective on language, a claim that—given the emphasis by Bopp, Schleicher, and the rest on constructing language trees and families—is

---

[12] Hassler, 'Analogy', 163.

[13] Thus Osthoff and Brugmann, in the 1878 Preface: 'Second, since it is clear that form association, that is, the creation of new linguistic forms by analogy, plays a very important role in the life of the more recent languages, this type of linguistic innovation is to be recognized without hesitation for older periods too, and even for the oldest' ('Preface', 204). The belief that the same principles of development apply to all moments in the history of language, that there is *not* a distinctive stage in which the earliest Indo-European languages were shaped, has been called 'uniformitarianism', on analogy (!) with a principle that had been established in geology. See Morpurgo Davies, *Nineteenth-Century Linguistics*, 190–1, 231–3; Amsterdamska, *Schools of Thought*, 181–4.

[14] Bréal, 'Language and Nationality', 202–3.

[15] Ferdinand de Saussure, *Saussure's Second Course of Lectures on General Linguistics (1908–1909)*, ed. Eisuke Komatsu, trans. George Wolf (Oxford: Pergamon Press, 1997), 93a.

clearly false if we understand 'historical' in the usual way.[16] What Saussure is actually saying, according to Wolf, is that you can only think of language in properly historical terms if you treat it as an artefact of 'human' history, as the product and medium of human collectivities and their interaction, and you can only do this, if, like the Neogrammarians, you believe (in theory at least) that the study of modern languages is as important, maybe more important, as the study of ancient ones.[17] Assigning analogy its rightful place meant understanding that the very structure of language, the patterns of its syntax and morphology, are the consequence of some kind of collective interaction, and it was in that sense that the Neogrammarians had made language something historical. As Wolf has put it: 'as historical development was seen as the natural mode of existence of a collectivity of persons, history and collectivity could be taken to be in a relationship of mutual implication'.[18] Analogy was the historical product of collective interaction and assigning it its rightful place amounted to a reconceptualization of the nature of language change and language as such. For our purposes, we should go one step further: making analogy central to the orderliness of language, to its structuring, meant making the human collectivity responsible for that structure, at the very moment when European society is worrying about how its collectivities, organized in nations and empires, are going to maintain any structure or order at all.

In what was deemed the theoretical bible of Neogrammarianism, Hermann Paul's *Principles of the History of Language*, analogy and not just analogical change, was a crucial topic. Paul describes how the human mind grouped and classified the words and various morphological units of a language. Language didn't exist in the mind as a lexicon on the one hand, and a set of grammatical rules on the other, but took the form of what he calls 'proportion-groups' or analogical formations by which the mind systematizes the substance of a language. The linguistic mind doesn't contain the word *cow* and then a rule by which plurals were produced by the addition of *-s*, but a grouping of words *cow : cows = dog : dogs = pig : pigs*, which makes concrete the relationship between sounds and meanings. These analogies were what made language systematic, what lay at the basis of grammar itself. Proportion-groups, Paul remarks 'are of supreme importance for all linguistic activity, and for all development of language. It is unjust to this important factor in the life of language to neglect to take it into any account, until it produces an actual change in the use of language.'[19] For *all* linguistic activity: the point being that analogy is relevant not only when it results in the introduction of new forms, but whenever speakers create utterances. It was analogy that allowed speakers to hold in their memory the vast wealth of forms that constituted a language and it was analogy that made it possible

---

[16] George Wolf, 'A Glance at the History of Linguistics: Saussure and Historical-Comparativism', in Sheila Embleton, John E. Joseph, and Hans-Josef Niederehe (eds.), *The Emergence of the Modern Language Sciences, Vol. 1: Historiographical Perspectives* (Amsterdam: John Benjamins, 1999), 129–37.

[17] Recall Osthoff and Brugmann (1878 Preface): 'Language fields like Germanic, Romance and Slavic are without doubt the ones where comparative linguistics can most securely acquire its methodological principles' (200–1).

[18] Wolf, 'History of Linguistics', 135.   [19] Paul, *Principles*, 97.

to produce grammatical forms and sentences which one had never heard before—to create speech and not just reproduce it. Most of the sentences we utter, Paul insists, are not 'learnt by heart', but 'composed on the spur of the moment', and it was the working of analogy that made this possible.[20] Speakers did not have to hear *pigs*, or the sentence *I love to watch pigs* in order to utter it, because they could form the word on analogy with *dogs* and the sentence on analogy with *I hate to eat cows*. Paul, in effect, made a first stab at explaining the phenomenon that seventy years later Noam Chomsky claimed was the central question of linguistic theory. For Chomsky observed that while '[a] speaker of a language has observed a certain limited set of utterances in his language', on this basis 'he can produce an indefinite number of new utterances which are immediately acceptable to other members of his speech community' and he 'can also distinguish a certain set of "grammatical" utterances, among utterances that he has never heard and might never produce'.[21] How is it we can produce an infinite number of sentences when we have heard only a finite number of them? This was the mystery Paul was solving.

Or, to put the matter in Saussurean terms, Paul explained how the freedom of *parole*, the ability to create new sentences, depended on the systematic nature of language. Of course, Paul did not realize he had explained this: that is why Saussure had to expend so much effort in order to 'show the linguist what he is doing'. Paul did not understand what he was doing because he believed that the science of language depended on a marriage between psychology and physics: psychology to explain the association of ideas inside people's heads and physics to explain how sound moved the ideas from one head to another. Paul had committed the 'unforgivable error', as Saussure would put it in a manuscript of 1891, of believing 'that the psychological side is the *idea*, while the physical side is the *sound*, the *form*, the *word*'.[22] But Paul's very own explanation of analogy showed that the sound only became significant sound, sound as part of language, when it became part of a proportion-group. The 'formal' proportion-group (to use Paul's term) that systematically contrasted *cow : cows/dog : dogs/pig : pigs*, is what made *-s*, coming at the end of a word, into something linguistic, into more than an accidental buzzing or lisping. Perhaps more importantly, the very same proportion-group made the *absence* of the *-s* also meaningful, as the mark of a singular noun. This would chime with Saussure's famous claim that in language there were only differences, and not positive terms. But it also meant that sound itself could not be a proper object of linguistics, that the only proper object would be sound allied to meaning, and that '[t]here is one domain, interior, psychic, where both sign and meaning are to be found, bound indissolubly one to the other'.[23]

The workings of that domain would be the object of Saussure's new 'synchronic' or 'static' linguistics, which would focus not on sound changes that were beyond

---

[20] Paul, *Principles*, 98.
[21] Noam Chomsky, *The Logical Structure of Linguistic Theory* (Chicago: University of Chicago Press, 1985), 61.
[22] Ferdinand de Saussure, 'On the Dual Essence of Language', in *Writings in General Linguistics*, 41.
[23] Saussure, 'On the Dual Essence', 6. In this manuscript Saussure will use the term 'sign' to designate the acoustic image, that is, what he will later call the 'signifier'.

the ken of language users, but on the 'instantaneous' mental order that gave shape to sound and meaning, an order Saussure would eventually name *la langue* and which he would insist should be the starting point for linguistics. In the 1891 manuscript I've just alluded to (apparently no more than a sheaf of papers contained in an envelope labelled 'On the Dual Essence of Language') Saussure rails against those who will confuse a momentary state of language with the historical changes in sound or meaning that bring it into being. Phonetic change, which arcs across different moments in the history of language, is—as philology had insisted— unconscious and unwilled and, for that very reason, irrelevant to the order that defines a language. To add to the 'unforgivable error' mentioned above Saussure will complain about the 'continual, disastrous commingling of what is *sequential* or retrospective with what is momentary or present'.[24] If 'we see language as a mechanism for allowing the expression of thought', then 'the historical approach to forms is of no consequence whatever to us'.[25] This rather brutal sounding dismissal is not aimed at historical linguistics per se but at the confused manner in which linguistics had imagined history (as a succession of individual elements, not a succession of orders). In the search for the correct object of linguistics Saussure has no patience for those who, looking for the shiny object at the bottom of the depths, only succeed in making the water around it murkier.

By extending the principle of analogy to the whole of language, Paul unwittingly makes it coterminous with 'consciousness'. Henceforth the only criterion of 'what is real is what speaking subjects have some awareness of, however small; all they are aware of and nothing but what they can be aware of'.[26] In the purely descriptive science that follows from this doctrine, existing states of awareness or consciousness are decisive and '[w]e do not need to worry about where this feeling originates'.[27] But the new position leaves its own share of murkiness as well. For if language is coterminous with the awareness of a speaking subject, then it's unclear in what sense that language could be understood as something collective. Another problem, related to this: if language exists as consciousness, if its production is an exercise of conscious faculties, then is the exercise of language also the exercise of reason, individual or collective? Can something be conscious and beyond reason at the same time?

For most of the nineteenth century, the ideological figure of the organism dominated accounts of language. Morpurgo Davies has divided the legacy of organicism in linguistics into three claims: that a language was the organic expression of a people or nation; that each language was an organic whole composed of mutually dependent parts; and that, like a biological organism, languages developed autonomously and spontaneously (having a birth, death, flowering, and so on).[28] In its most extreme form, as in the works of August Schleicher, this claim identified languages with living

---

[24] Saussure, 'On the Dual Essence', 30.   [25] Saussure, 'On the Dual Essence', 27.
[26] Saussure, '[Morphology]', dated 1894–5, in *Writings in General Linguistics*, 125.
[27] Saussure, '[Morphology]', 126.
[28] See Morpurgo Davies, 'Historicism, Organicism and the Scientific Model', in *Nineteenth-Century Linguistics*, 83–97.

organisms and linguistics with the natural scientific study of them. In this context, the collective character of language was never in doubt, as individuals within the relevant polities were—aside from the odd Goethe or Shakespeare—simply swept along in the tide of the evolving language.

This conception was among the primary targets of the Neogrammarian revolution. The Neogrammarians insisted that linguistics was a historical, not a natural science: the changes charted by linguists were ultimately rooted in the physical and psychic features of human beings, in the physiology of their speech organs, in the physics of sound and hearing and in the psychology of individuals.[29] The psychology of *individuals*: Paul, in his introductory comments to the *Principles*, dismisses the *Völkerpsychologie* of Lazarus and Steinthal as having no real object, as psychology deals with the laws governing a psychic life that can only belong to individual people. The real object of any historical account of language would be not what has been spoken or written which 'has no development', but the 'psychical organisms' that speak and write.[30] The action which ultimately results in sound changes such as those I've described above or in analogical innovations takes place within the bounds of these organisms or as a consequence of intercourse amongst them. So while languages—German, Gothic, French, Persian—are still the object, they dissolve into myriad acts of individuals who speak and write, that infinite complexity we spoke of in the previous chapter: 'the entire sum of the products of the linguistic activity of the entire sum of individuals in their reciprocal relations'.

In theory at least. In practice, the Neogrammarians seemed to ignore 'the entire sum' in favour of more or less the same kind of linguistic work that their predecessors did. They may have claimed in the 1878 Preface to the *Morphological Investigations* that 'the comparative linguist must turn his attention from the original language to the present if he wants to arrive at a correct idea of the manner in which language is maintained', but when push came to shove, they (in the words of Morpurgo Davies) 'in fact spent most of their working life dealing with "Specialforschung", i.e. with minute problems of historical morphology or phonology'.[31] Olga Amsterdamska as well has observed that while Neogrammarian theory made possible the 'philosophical equalization' of ancient and modern we mentioned earlier, in practice Neogrammarian linguists 'continued to ignore the spoken and literary idioms of contemporary England, France and Germany'.[32] The Neogrammarian legacy consists of books written in familiar genres (Hermann Paul's history of the German language, Brugmann's *Grundriss der vergleichenden Grammatik der indogermanischen Sprachen* (1886–93)), and sound laws couched in familiar terms (Verner's, Siever's). While the claim that the real object of linguistic inquiry was the individual psychical organism seemed radical, in fact the psychical organism was derived from the language. The Neogrammarian linguist 'in practice

---

[29] Obviously, there is ambiguity if not paradox or contradiction here: linguistics is an historical science, but the physiology of speech organs introduces a 'natural', not historical element.
[30] Paul, *Principles*, 7.
[31] Osthoff and Brugmann, 'Preface', 200; Morpurgo Davies, *Nineteenth-Century Linguistics*, 237.
[32] Amsterdamska, *Schools of Thought*, 140.

extrapolated the mental processes from linguistic behaviour'.[33] 'Linguistic analogy', as one historian of the movement has put it, 'attracted psychology', so that many years later the behaviourist Leonard Bloomfield could quite reasonably complain that '[t]he only evidence for these mental processes is the linguistic process; they add nothing to the discussion, but only obscure it'.[34]

In short, the Neogrammarian movement produces two versions of language, which, while not necessarily incommensurable, leave us with the question of how it is possible for both to be the case. Insofar as language is a product of individual psychology, it stands as 'the entire sum of the products of the linguistic activity of the entire sum of individuals in their reciprocal relations'—a domain with no natural order, and even the suggestion of possible chaos (for why should the sum not amount to a jumble of individual initiatives and misfires?). In their research practice, on the other hand, the Neogrammarians produce a version of language with an even more rigorous order than before. One can explain this paradox by reference to institutional inertia, as Amsterdamska does when she describes Neogrammarianism as a conservative 'revolution from above', or by pointing out that working through the new insights depended 'on the rejection of other beliefs which effectively blocked the new development'.[35] But maybe things are simpler than that. Maybe there is nothing in fact to explain and no need to think about 'other beliefs' that block the inexorable development of a synchronic linguistics, in which 'language' is embodied in a collective practice or awareness. Maybe the Neogrammarians don't realize that analogy implies synchronic linguistics because they're not looking for synchronic linguistics. Franco Moretti has described how new literary techniques (the clue in detective stories, stream of consciousness in modernist literature) establish themselves in accordance with the laws of evolution, according to which successful 'traits' don't arise as part of a master plan, with the intent of solving an ecological issue for the organism in question, but as random mutations which turn out to be useful. Conan Doyle uses clues as a way to elaborate on the marvellous deductive powers of Holmes, not realizing he has stumbled upon a brilliant device for detective narrative; stream of consciousness begins as a way to describe the disorientation of a character or as a means to delay action: only with Joyce and Woolf will it become a focal point of narrative itself.[36] Naturally, we're apt to think that intellectual history is a different kettle of fish. New concepts, new paradigms, insights that drive our grasp of the world forward arise when intellectuals hit on a successful solution to a problem that confronts them. But sometimes the insight arises to solve a local

---

[33] Morpurgo Davies, *Nineteenth-Century Linguistics*, 247.
[34] Kurt Jankowsky, *The Neogrammarians: A Re-evaluation of their Place in the Development of Linguistic Science* (The Hague: Mouton, 1972), 153. The quotation of Bloomfield is from his *Language* (New York: Henry Holt and Company, 1933), 17.
[35] Amsterdamska, *Schools of Thought*, 135, 181.
[36] For the discussion of clues, see Franco Moretti, 'The Slaughterhouse of Literature', *Modern Language Quarterly* 61.1 (2000): 207–27; on the evolution of stream of consciousness, see 'Excursus: Stream of Consciousness – Evolution of a Technique' in Franco Moretti, *Modern Epic: The World System from Goethe to García Marquez*, trans. Quintin Hoare (London: Verso, 1996), 168–81.

issue that, in the grander scheme of things, turns out not to be the main point, and this may just be one of those cases.

Hermann Paul and his colleagues argue for analogy's historical persistence, for its normality, so that they can disburden linguistics of the need to reconstruct an original, purer language, so that they can 'equalize' the modern languages with the ancient ones (an important and useful task if you're a Germanist or Romance philologist), and so that they can argue for the centrality of the psychical mechanism in the production of language. But once analogy is presented as a psychological principle, as something that happens within the individual mind, then the difference between an innovation made in the language as a whole (such as the creation of Latin *honor* and its displacement of Latin *honos*) and an innovation made by an individual (such as the child who figures out that the plural of *pig* is *pigs*) disappears, and analogy becomes the way speakers do what linguists thought only *they* did: segment language into meaningful morphemes, arrange and establish patterns of declension, conjugation, and word-derivation. The linguistic positions that were supposed to rid us of dreams of a perfectly lucid Indo-European parent language end up by making the history of language irrelevant for its functioning in the present.

ANALOGY AND SOCIAL ORDER

Saussure recognized this. In the first set of lectures he gave on general linguistics in 1907, having reminded his students that a language 'which is following its natural course' will change continually, Saussure goes on to distinguish between 'the side of the language where everyone is at home, which each person has immediate sense and control of' and the side 'many people don't even suspect: the entire historical side of the language'.[37] He then describes the phonetic changes which deliver a state of language to speakers without their knowing how, before launching into his long account of analogy, described at this point as the '*general principle of the creations of the language*' [*principe général des créations de la langue*].[38] In order to understand this principle, however, we must take care to distinguish two separate moments: '1) the comprehension of the relationship of forms which are compared among themselves (generating, inspiring forms) and 2) the product which they imply, the engendered, inspired form which is the *x* of the proportion'.[39] First, we realize that we could make the analogy *pig* : *pigs* = *cow* : *cows*, at a moment, say, when the usual plural for the animal is *kine*—this is the instance of *langue*, when we comprehend the ordering of language at a particular moment; then we say '*cows*' instead of *kine*—who knows why?—and set the process of replacement in motion with our act of speaking, with *parole*.

Why is it so important to keep these aspects separate, to wall off the moment of comprehension from the conclusion that is drawn in speech? We'll explore that

---

[37] Saussure, *First Course*, 3a, 27a.   [38] Saussure, *First Course*, 63a.
[39] Saussure, *First Course*, 64a.

shortly. For the moment, the key is what follows after that distinction is made, which is worth quoting at length:

> All the facts of language, especially the evolutionary facts, force us to come face to face with speech on the one hand and on the other with the reservoir of forms in the mind or known by the mind. An unconscious act of comparison is necessary not only to create but to comprehend the relationships. Any word succeeds in expressing something to the mind only because it is immediately compared with everything which could mean something slightly different (*facias: faciam, facio*). If it is true that we always need the fund of the language in order to speak, conversely everything which enters the language was first essayed in speech a sufficient number of times for a durable impression to have resulted: the language is only the sanctioning of what has already been evoked by speech.[40]

Analogy is not just responsible for occasional innovations. As the 'general principle of the creations of the language' it is responsible for the entire 'reservoir of forms in the mind', which is one more of Saussure's many attempts to characterize *langue*, the language system. But *langue* is not merely a reservoir: it is also the 'unconscious' comparisons necessary to relate each unit in the reservoir to the next, comparisons which are made not just when we create new forms but whenever we use existing ones (as Hermann Paul had argued). Analogy thus becomes the principle behind the system of language, the way in which units of sound and meaning—what, two lecture courses later, Saussure will call 'signs'—acquire their identity. Outside the operations of comparison entailed by analogy, sound is just noise and concepts an amorphous mess. Four years later, when delivering the third course of lectures on general linguistics, Saussure will barely mention analogy by name, but will describe the same process of comparison first as 'relative arbitrariness' and finally as the 'associative relations' that structure *langue* in one's 'memory'.[41] Saussure doesn't discover the idea of comparing forms in the mind, of a 'state of language' in his first set of lectures: as John Joseph has demonstrated, you can find the idea more than twenty years earlier, in notes written for a course on Gothic phonology in 1884–5.[42] Rather, 1907 is the moment when Saussure brings the idea to fruition by drawing the conclusion that Paul was unable to draw.

Saussure, however, inherits more from Paul than a brilliant insight. He also inherits the unresolved business, the murkiness, that accompanies the insight. For if 'language' is 'the entire sum of the products of the linguistic activity of the entire sum of individuals in their reciprocal relations' then it's not at all clear how this object can be captured in thought. And the epistemological problem reflects an ontological one. Paul meant it when he said the 'sum of individuals': meant that the activity was grounded in individual psychology and that language as a whole was the mere aggregate of that activity, without an independent reality of its own. But then what

---

[40] Saussure, *First Course*, 65a.

[41] Saussure, *Third Course*, 132a. The discussion of relative arbitrariness takes place in the lecture on 9 May 1911 (85a–87a); the discussion of associative relations in the mind takes place in the final two lectures, on 27 and 30 June 1911 (127a–137a).

[42] Joseph, *Saussure*, 319–27; see also John E. Joseph, 'Saussure's Value(s)', *Recherches sémiotique/ Semiotic Inquiry* 34.1–2–3 (2014): 199–200.

holds it all together, what ensures that there is a language, and not utter chaos? Are individuals simply making strategic judgements, refined through trial and error, about what utterances work and how?

Saussure would initially adopt this sense of the buzzing, potentially chaotic world of discourse as his own, describing, as we noted in the previous chapter, language as a field of activity: the 'combined or isolated *actions* of physiological, physical, or mental forces'. In the first course he would stay on board with the idea that the 'language system' was a feature of the psychology of individuals ('the sphere of speech is the more social, the other sphere is the more completely individual').[43] But, as Joseph has shown in some detail, soon after this series of lectures Saussure switched to a more sociological understanding of the language system. Saussure had his own reasons, peculiar to his time and place, but these are, I think, the crests of the wave. For this new and strange object, 'language in general' or 'language as such' posed, in an acute form the very problem of social order, which seemed no longer to be able to rely on race or national spirit—now banished from 'the language'—to unify it. Synchronic linguistics created, at a stroke, a new object, and a new problem.

It was not, it goes without saying, a problem unique to linguistics. In the Introduction I used a phrase from Pierre Rosanvallon: the nineteenth century witnessed the extension and 'unleashing' of the political. This is what happens when the shaping of society, its institution and representation, loses the anchoring it had in a natural order of things.[44] When the old society of estates and status, the old corporatist model of the social whole, is overthrown by a society that is a 'sum of individuals', society's own institution, its own shape, becomes the concern of politics. Lacking an independent source of authority, religious or regal, 'the political is called upon to be the agent that "represents" a society to which nature no longer gives immediate form'.[45] Paul describes language as the sum of all activity conducted by the sum of all individuals, a formula that emphasizes the ceaselessly mobile and active nature of language and its apparent disunity. But this could easily stand for—I guess I am saying it *does* stand for—the social world of many nineteenth-century European nations, which now also appeared to be no more than a sum of individuals. Capitalism was dissolving older economic bonds, destroying the moral economy (in the eighteenth-century sense of the term described by E. P. Thompson), freeing economic activity from the political and social categories that had organized it previously, leaving in its wake the atomistic 'civil society' that worried Hegel and stimulated Marx.[46] The national revolutions that swept across Europe likewise installed the citizen endowed with rights and, if *he* were lucky, the franchise, at the

---

[43] Saussure, *First Course*, 65a.

[44] For Jacques Rancière, politics begins when the principle of government is separated from a natural order; see 'Politics, or the Lost Shepherd', in *Hatred of Democracy*, 33–49.

[45] Rosanvallon, 'Towards a Philosophical History of the Political', in *Democracy Past and Future*, 61.

[46] E. P. Thompson, 'The Moral Economy of the English Crowd in the Eighteenth Century', *Past and Present* 50 (1971): 76–136. Probably most writing on social questions in the nineteenth century evokes or describes this process, either with regret or enthusiasm or (as in the case of Marx) both. But if the reader wants a vibrant contemporary account, you could do worse than *The Communist Manifesto*.

centre of the polity. The political equalization this entailed had, as its corollary, the abstraction of the social body, which was now a 'sum of individuals'.

What I've described are, of course, ideal types or trends, in some respects images or fantasies of the social whole that—depending on where you stood—either inspired or terrified Europeans. The reality included a persistent *ancien régime* (which, as Arno Mayer has famously argued, retained much of its power until the mid-twentieth century), a severely limited franchise, widespread feudal economic arrangements, and the continuing existence of monarchies, constitutional and otherwise.[47] For much of the nineteenth century the bourgeoisie and their allies dreamed of a liberal polity in which a restricted franchise, a vigorous public sphere of debate and discussion, and the rule of law would establish the conditions for a stable but dynamic capitalist social formation. These arrangements were typically described as 'republican' or as 'representative government', and sharply distinguished from the 'democracy' that had existed in classical Greece.[48] But, as we know, things did not work out as planned, and democracy gradually established itself as both a sociological principle—the putative equalization of all citizens and the destruction of aristocratic distinctions of rank and status—and as an ideal of government, the embodiment of some form of popular sovereignty.

But democracy was also a problem, in two critical respects. First, and most obviously, because it endowed the popular masses, peasants and industrial workers, with political rights and the ability to organize. The fear this engendered in ruling elites can be described as 'the tension between number [i.e., majority rule, *PR*] and reason', that is, the ruling class conviction that the 'lower orders' were incapable of reason and would therefore be ruled by impulse, instinct, or the leadership of mindless demagogues.[49] Liberalism, with its faith in public assemblies and open political debate, had promised emancipation from royal and religious superstition, but that had depended on restricting the terms of that debate. As Jürgen Habermas showed many years ago, the expansion of the public sphere under pressure for popular sovereignty led to its evisceration in both theory and practice.[50]

'Number', however, posed a particular kind of problem on its own: 'a tension exists between the modern idea of emancipation, which implies a desire for individual autonomy (with an emphasis on rights), and collective participation in the project of self-government (which makes politics the priority)'.[51] How to hold all these newly autonomous citizens together? What social glue would replace the old corporatist model, legitimated by feudal ideologies?

National feeling, the 'deep, horizontal comradeship' of which Benedict Anderson has spoken, was clearly one possible answer, and in comparative philology it found

---

[47] Arno J. Mayer, *The Persistence of the Old Regime: Europe to the Great War* (New York: Pantheon, 1981).

[48] Pierre Rosanvallon, 'Democratic Universalism as a Historical Problem', Books & Ideas.net, http://www.booksandideas.net/Democratic-Universalism-as-a.html?lang=fr (accessed 10 April 2012), 6.

[49] Rosanvallon, 'Democratic Universalism', 13.

[50] Habermas, *Structural Transformation of the Public Sphere*, chapter 15, 'The Ambivalent View of the Public Sphere in the Theory of Liberalism (John Stuart Mill and Alexis de Tocqueville)'.

[51] Rosanvallon, 'Democratic Universalism', 13.

a significant source of intellectual ballast.[52] But it had competition in the shape of internationalist and class-based movements (communism, the cooperative movement, anarchism) and was fractured from within by severe disagreements over the substance of the nation itself. 'Race' was clearly another possible answer, often intertwined with nationalism, and buoyed by the use of linguistic theories to make arguments for the intellectual and cultural superiority of European languages. Léopold de Saussure, Ferdinand's younger brother would become a significant player in this debate, arguing strongly against attempts to educate the colonized Vietnamese in French, on the basis that innate racial characteristics would ensure that the Vietnamese would not and could not become French in cultural terms.[53]

Ferdinand, however, would have none of it. What's interesting about 'language as such' is precisely its break with national and racial distinctions, its insistence that the forces that animate, and perhaps confuse, language are active in the same way throughout all its manifestations. Individual linguists (and, as we'll see in later chapters, individual philosophers and literary critics as well) maintained their prejudices, of course, but their object, language itself, acquired a power that didn't depend on locale. Pierre Bourdieu has, as I mentioned earlier, described this ideology as a naïve linguistic communism, which of course it is. But it also contained an appeal to language, a dream or wish-content. For, after all, people spoke, listened, communicated successfully: somehow, it appeared language 'worked' in the midst of societies riven by conflict and individualism. What was its secret?

Hermann Paul had, in effect, dodged the question. In theory, the object of the linguist was the general condition of the life of language, its existence as a constant linguistic activity carried on by a sum of individuals having 'reciprocal relations'. In practice he and the other Neogrammarians studied the traces this activity left in the form of the familiar litany of European and Asian languages. Some of the centrifugal possibilities, so to speak, eventually to be given theoretical recognition by Mikhail Bakhtin, were acknowledged by the rise of dialectology, and in particular in the work of linguists like Hugo Schuchardt, which cast doubt on the spatial or territorial unity of the objects of linguistics.[54] But, generally speaking, the focus on historical linguistics, which remained resolute throughout the Neogrammarian moment, allowed linguists to not worry overmuch about the problem they had discovered.

---

[52] Benedict Anderson, *Imagined Communities: Reflections on the Origin and Spread of Nationalism*, revised edn. (London: Verso, 1991), 7.

[53] On Léopold's language theory, see Joseph, *Saussure*, 441–5; John E. Joseph, 'Language and "Psychological Race": Léopold de Saussure on French in Indochina', *Language & Communication* 20 (2000): 29–53; Robert Young, 'Race and Language in the Two Saussures', in Peter Osborne and Stella Sanford (eds.), *Philosophies of Race and Ethnicity* (London: Continuum, 2002), 63–78.

[54] On the emergence of dialectology, see Morpurgo Davies, *Nineteenth-Century Linguistics*, 287–90. See also Hugo Schuchardt, 'On Sound Laws: Against the Neogrammarians', in Theo Venneman and Terence H. Wilbur (eds.), *Schuchardt, the Neogrammarians, and the Transformational Theory of Phonological Change* (Frankfurt: Athenäum Verlag, 1972), 39–72.

ANALOGY AND THE COLLECTIVE WILL: WHETHER SPEAKERS THINK

Saussure, despite the ostensible confidence of some of his pronouncements, worried about it. Although he was certain that the Neogrammarians had opened the door to places they didn't necessarily wish to go to, he had to admit that there was something slippery and tricky about the object itself. Thus even the second of his courses on general linguistics begins with the admission that '[a] language [*langue*] offers the most troubling contrasts and paradoxes to anyone who wishes to get hold of it from one side or another'.[55] The idea of the language system was meant to install some kind of order into this otherwise amorphous world of actual linguistic activity: it was precisely this orderliness that distinguished, in his writing, *langue* from *langage*. But even though Saussure knew this orderliness made conventional signs possible, he realized that positing what he once called an 'immobile ensemble of facts', within or athwart a sphere of linguistic activity driven by 'physiological, physical, or mental forces', entailed excluding something, perhaps the forcefulness of language itself.[56]

The problem would play itself out in a conflict within the theory of analogy itself, which would eventually spread to the concept of *langue*, the language system, that had been erected on its foundation. The normalizing of analogy had entailed a radically new idea, that of a synchronic 'mental order' which endowed conventional signs with identity and stability, but it wasn't immediately clear how such an order could be *shared* (being a matter of awareness or consciousness) and why one wouldn't be able to alter such conventions at will. In 1907, Saussure made what must have seemed the obvious distinction between the necessarily individual and inward consciousness that made analogies possible and the outward act of speech that made them actual, with some measure of creativity and passivity awkwardly distributed between the two. It had been, of course, the 'deliberateness' of false analogy that led comparative philologists in the early part of the century to limit its scope: to them it represented a human intrusion, a moment of historical activity, within what was supposed to be something akin to a natural-historical process. Saussure's task was to insist on the historical character of language and language change, while finding a way to neutralize the danger of deliberate collective action.

One possible solution was to experiment with the medium of consciousness itself, to suggest that it had significant degrees or variations that affected what one could do within it. Yes, the test of what belonged to language was what a speaker was aware of, but the relevant forms were perhaps 'sensed merely in half-consciousness'.[57] But a better solution seemed to lie in a sharp distinction between the analysis involved in comparing existing forms with one another and the moment of creative insight, which would be assigned to the conscious production of speech:

---

[55] Saussure, *Second Course*, 1a.
[56] This very early formulation is taken from the abovementioned notes on Gothic phonology; see Joseph, *Saussure*, 320.
[57] Saussure, *First Course*, 64a.

> On the internal side (sphere of the language) there is never premeditation nor even meditation, reflection on forms outside of the act, of the occasion of speech, save for an unconscious, almost passive, in any case not creative, activity: the activity of classification.[58]

Analogy is creative, therefore, but the creative moment takes place in the world of speech, where speakers *intend*, not in the language, which exists as a kind of semi-conscious state.

By the time Saussure had to deliver that second course on general linguistics, in 1908–9, 'the role of the unconscious mind in insulating language from deliberate change was taken over by the force of the social group', as John Joseph has put it.[59] By this point the concept of the language system had, so to speak, grown up and left home: it was no longer presented as a generalization of the phenomenon of analogy and was no longer forced to live within the boundaries of some kind of consciousness. The new framework for thinking about *langue* was the convention or agreement: Saussure made the system stable by simply insisting that change within it had to win the assent of the community. This appears to be a very democratic sentiment, which it is, although this democracy is permitted on the condition that those granted it don't think too hard. In terms of the theory, we therefore find the same kind of nervous fiddling with the idea of an agreement as we did before with the idea of consciousness—Saussure needs an agreement that is willed, but not deliberate:

> We thus take the language to be a legislation in the manner of the 18th-century *philosophes*, as depending on our will. A language, however, even more so than legislation, must be accepted much more than created; there is in the language a minimum of initiative. The moment in which we agree on signs does not really exist, is only ideal; and even if it did exist it wouldn't be worthy of consideration next to the regular life of the language.[60]

This is the static square peg being forced into the historical round hole. Language is historical, the creation of human beings, 'a set of necessary conventions adopted by the social body', as Saussure put it in one of his most lucid formulations, but the creative process has to be unwilled, even when its effect is to systematize, to make more rational the language system (as when speakers began to make the plural of *cow*, 'cows', thereby bringing it into line with the most common form of English plurals).[61]

And yet Saussure knows perfectly well that although life is full of habitual or absent-minded comment, generally when we speak we intend to say something. The solution is therefore to concede that when we make analogies in speech we may be doing something wilful or creative, while insisting that the spread of the innovation into the language system—the moment of agreement or legislation—relies on some unreasoned process. In notes for one of the courses he will remark that 'once

---

[58] Saussure, *First Course*, 65a–66a.
[59] John E. Joseph, 'The Unconscious and the Social in Saussure', *Historiographia Linguistica* 27.2–3 (2000): 328.
[60] Saussure, *Second Course*, 11a.   [61] Saussure, *Second Course*, 4a.

the sign system belongs to the community nothing guarantees that an internal reason, a reason borne of individual reasoning, will continue to govern the relationship between sign and idea [signifier and signified in the later terminology, KH]'.[62] He follows this up with the ship metaphor I referred to in the previous chapter:

> *Langue*, or indeed any semiological system, is not a ship in dry dock, but a ship on the open sea. Once it is on the water, it is pointless to look for an indication of the course it will follow by assessing its frame, or its inner construction as laid out in an engineer's drawing.[63]

What, then, governs the relationship between sign and idea once the ship has left port? In the *Cours* itself, we find a fairly unambiguous answer: 'Before Latin *honor* could become a rival able to replace *honos*, a speaker had first to improvise it, and others to imitate it and repeat it, until it became accepted usage.'[64]

Imitation! It is, according to an excellent article by Barthes rarely cited in English-language scholarship (and to some degree the inspiration for this chapter), the key to Saussure's universe and it places him securely within the ambit of the French sociologist Gabriel Tarde.[65] 'Grammar, for example,' Saussure said in the second course, 'can only be studied in the crowd', so if you want to understand how the systematic, synchronic element of language evolves, you have to understand crowds, and Tarde was clearly the man for the job.[66] Even to bring up Tarde, however, is to plunge into some of the roughest waters of Saussure scholarship, for Tarde was not the only option for thinking about community and collectivity, and his great rival, Émile Durkheim, seems to have left traces in Saussure's work as well.

Durkheim and Tarde fought a pitched intellectual battle throughout the 1890s over the nature of sociology.[67] The issue was the one that concerns us here: how societies were bound together. Durkheim argued that a collective consciousness, an entity beyond the individual, constrained or gave shape to the individual consciousness. Tarde claimed that social conventions were an effect of the operations of individual psychology, principal among them being the 'laws of imitation' by which ideas and fashions spread through the social world. In an article which became a topic of strikingly heated discussion, Witold Doroszewski claimed he had been told by someone who knew Saussure well (it turned out to be Louis Caille, a former student of Saussure) that Saussure had followed the dispute carefully.[68] There is, however, no mention of either sociologist in Saussure's work

---

[62] Saussure, 'Sign systems – Community', in *Writings in General Linguistics*, 202.
[63] Saussure, 'Sign systems – Community', 202.
[64] Saussure, *Course in General Linguistics* (1983), 167.
[65] Roland Barthes, 'Saussure, the Sign, Democracy', in *The Semiotic Challenge*, trans. Richard Howard (Oxford: Basil Blackwell, 1988), 151–6.
[66] Saussure, *Second Course*, 111a.
[67] A very readable summary of the debate can be found in Wolf Lepenies, *Between Literature and Science: The Rise of Sociology*, trans. R. J. Hollingdale (Cambridge: Cambridge University Press, 1988), 47–59.
[68] W. Doroszewski, 'Quelques remarques sur les rapports de la sociologie et de la linguistique: Durkheim et F. de Saussure', *Journal de Psychologie normale et pathologique* 30 (1933): 82–91. The initial article did not mention Doroszewski's source, which was revealed in 1957; see the Addendum to Godel, *Les sources manuscrites*, 282.

and on this basis E. F. K. Koerner has argued that there is no evidence of Saussure's interest in the matter.[69]

That said, the concepts are there in the work for all to see. It's possible that the phrase 'collective consciousness', a staple of Durkheimian theory that makes its way into the third course of lectures on general linguistics and thence into the published version, was, as Joseph has suggested, taken from Saussure's student, Antoine Meillet, who both wrote for *L'année sociologique* (edited by Durkheim) and kept in relatively close contact with his teacher.[70] And it is certainly true that as the idea of the language system slowly crystallizes in the succeeding sets of lectures, its coercive force, the degree to which legislation 'must be accepted much more than created', is identified with its social nature. At the same time, in the first course of lectures Saussure, discussing whether phonetic changes are like changes in fashion, says: 'But no one has explained changes in fashion; they depend on the laws of imitation which exercise philosophers a great deal'—about as explicit a reference to the author of *The Laws of Imitation* as one could hope for.[71]

Imitation: could there be a balder attempt to discredit the continuous pressure for democracy? Saussure wants, it would seem, to formulate a kind of social consensus that is, on the one hand, spontaneous, and, on the other hand, unreasoned: an agreement which entails no actual decision to agree and certainly no discussion over whether one *should* agree. One must therefore insulate the social contract that is language from wilfulness or debate. But analogy, which provides the basis for the grammar which must be shared, teeters on the edge of reason: when Saussure speaks of analogy in 1891, he contrasts the '*mechanical* operations' that deliver phonetic change from 'the other *intelligent* operations [of analogy, KH], in which it is possible to make out an aim and a meaning'.[72] As we have seen, Saussure spends some of the next twenty years backing away from this commitment. And one is tempted to claim that the more analogical formations are identified with the social aspect of language, the less reason he wishes to attribute to them.

Imitation provides a possible second line of defence. Once the sign belongs to the community, 'internal reason' no longer governs it; which could mean that even if we allow that analogies entail the exercise of reason, they do so only at the moment of necessarily individual innovation, in a moment of speech—their spread into the language system, their acceptance or agreement depends on mere imitation, whatever their origin may have been. It is in this respect interesting to note that this is not quite the position Tarde himself took. In *The Laws of Imitation* Tarde proposes to make imitation the central process by which a society is formed and maintained, and he systematically contrasts the sharing of beliefs and values

---

[69] E. F. K. Koerner, *Ferdinand de Saussure: Origin and Development of His Linguistic Thought in Western Studies of Language* (Braunschweig: Vieweg, 1973), 59–61.

[70] Joseph, *Saussure*, 508, 535. Saussure seems to have first used the concept rather late in the day, when defining static linguistics in a lecture of 16 June 1911 (Saussure, *Third Course*, Lecture of 16 June 1911, 120a). From there it finds its way into the published version: Saussure, *Course in General Linguistics* (1983), 98.

[71] Saussure, *First Course*, 41a.

[72] Saussure, 'Second lecture at the University of Geneva, November 1891', in *Writings in General Linguistics*, 106.

through imitation with the merely individualizing principle of exchange. Society is, he claims, 'far more a system of mutually determined engagements and agreements, of rights and duties, than a system of mutual services'.[73] By imitation he means any way in which one person comes to adopt a custom, value, or practice present in another person, whether 'through spontaneous and unconscious or artificial and deliberate imitation'.[74] *The Laws of Imitation* therefore distinguishes between 'logical' and 'non-logical' causes of imitation, the former covering operations in which 'an individual prefers a given innovation to others because he thinks it is more useful or more true than others'.[75]

If grammar lived in the crowd, then Tarde, one of the leading exponents of crowd theory, made sense as a source. But Tarde clearly did not go far enough. Or, to be exact, at that point in time he had not gone far enough, for later he would go a bit further. As the 1890s progressed, Tarde began to focus on the particular operations of imitation in the formation of public opinion, where he found there were further significant distinctions worth making. In an article entitled 'Opinion and Conversation' he argued that ideas can take the form of tradition, reason, or opinion.[76] The first was self-explanatory: it referred to those domains (the Church above all) where ideas acquired their strength and power by virtue of long-established authority, embodied in historical institutions. But 'reason' was now cordoned off from the social world as a whole, deemed a powerful force only in particular secular institutions like the law, science, and the universities. That left 'public opinion', a sphere of belief and value which depended less on deliberation than on the power of conversation and the power of that peculiarly modern medium of speech, the mass-circulation press. Public opinion, a cohesive and unifying social phenomenon, depended not on arguments but on the sheer velocity of discourse.

Tarde's interest in public opinion wasn't capricious: it was impelled by the central drama of French public life in the 1890s, the Dreyfus affair. It was not just the vitriolic spread of anti-Semitism that got Tarde's (horrified) attention, it was also the means by which the vitriol was spread, through the untiring propaganda of papers like Édouard Drumont's *La libre parole*, where the case of 'High Treason' was first announced in November 1894 and the idea that it was part of a Jewish conspiracy was announced a few days later.[77] Saussure had also paid attention to Dreyfus, although his views on the matter are somewhat tricky to disentangle. A draft of a letter to *La libre parole* from November 1894 has been found in one of his notebooks: the draft speaks of Jews as 'swarms of parasites' and 'colonies of usurers'. One the other hand, three years later, Saussure drafts another letter in which he describes himself as a 'convinced Dreyfusard' and it is well known that three of the French linguists to whom he was closest—Bréal, Gaston Paris, and

---

[73] Gabriel Tarde, *The Laws of Imitation*, trans. Elsie Clews Parsons (New York: Henry Holt, 1903), 61.
[74] Tarde, *Imitation*, 2.   [75] Tarde, *Imitation*, 141.
[76] Gabriel Tarde, 'Opinion and Conversation (1898)', in *On Communication and Social Influence: Selected Papers* (Chicago: University of Chicago Press, 1969), 297–318.
[77] See Jaap van Ginneken, *Crowds, Psychology, and Politics, 1871–1899* (Cambridge: Cambridge University Press, 1992), 203–22.

Louis Havet—were leaders in the pro-Dreyfus movement. It's been suggested that this indicates a happy evolution towards reason in Saussure's position, but Joseph, who claims there is not an inkling of anti-Semitism to be found anywhere else in Saussure's writings, suspects the earlier draft letter is actually the work of Ferdinand's brother Léopold, who was far more sympathetic to racism.[78]

The power of imitation, the way in which an idea uttered from a single source in *parole* (Drumont? Zola?) could spread like wildfire through the social body and become an established convention, had been witnessed first-hand by Tarde and Saussure (whatever the latter's views were on Dreyfus). Should we be surprised that Saussure appealed to the same principle to explain the spread of analogies through the social body? We shouldn't have been surprised if Saussure had appealed to it, but, in fact, Saussure didn't appeal to it. Although the line '[...] and others to imitate it and repeat it' appears in the published *Cours*, Saussure is not responsible for it. It is one of many phrases—helpfully listed in Robert Godel's study of the source manuscripts—that Saussure's colleagues invented and added when they put together the *Cours* from Saussure's manuscripts and student notes of the lecture series.[79] What Saussure did say was that *phonetic* changes spread via 'imitation', but these changes were always deemed unconscious, physiological, mechanical.[80] As to how and why analogical changes, first hazarded in the 'conscious' and 'deliberate' world of speech, might have been taken up by others, this remained opaque.

Which is to say that while Saussure does not specify how the moment of individual inspiration turns into a social agreement, he does specify how it does *not* happen. Recognizing that analogy is, as he put it, 'a very delicate point in the distinction between synchronic and diachronic' (for if the synchronic structure *motivates* a diachronic change, then the wall Saussure had carefully built would have been breached), he enlists the discussion of analogy in a larger campaign against deliberation in language.[81] So, for example, what follows 'analogy' in the first course of lectures (and in the published *Cours*) is a polemic with so-called popular etymology, the practice whereby an 'incorrect' segmenting analysis of a word leads to change. Saussure's example: German *Abenteuer* ('adventure'), which derives from French *aventure* is misanalysed as *Aben/teuer*, as if the former meant 'evening' (*Abend*), and so the word is changed to *Abendteuer* In the lectures this popular etymology, the incorrectness of which should not matter a whit given Saussure's theory, is deemed a 'very restricted province of analogy'.[82] By the time of the published version, however, the two phenomena are 'essentially different, and must be carefully distinguished'.[83] Why? Because there is no question about the deliberateness of popular etymology, which must therefore be separated from the unwilled process of analogy.

---

[78] The argument that Saussure's views evolved is found in Michael Lynn-George, 'The Crossroads of Truth: Ferdinand de Saussure and the Dreyfus Affair', *Modern Language Notes* 121 (2006): 961–88. For Joseph's view, see *Saussure*, 414–17. Roy Harris insisted on the anti-Semitism in the *Times Literary Supplement*, 30 January 2004.
[79] Godel, *Les sources manuscrites*, 118.
[80] Saussure, *Third Course*, Lecture of 29 November 1911, 35a.
[81] Saussure, *Second Course*, 58a.   [82] Saussure, *First Course*, 98a.
[83] Saussure, *Course in General Linguistics* (1983), 174.

And then there is Saussure's *bête noire*: no, not 'writing', but 'literary language'. Writing is too stable and durable: its apparent continuity disguises subtle shifts of sound and usage that are taking place in actual discourse. Literary language, on the other hand, is the fruit of deliberate effort: 'a product of literature and of national will', it is where the *form* of language is consciously fussed over, reflected on and judged (its sins, as we shall see in Chapter 4, are precisely what the Russian Formalists considered its virtues).[84] Saussure, Joseph informs us, was an avid composer of poetry in his youth, so it's not as if he had some philistine aversion to the finer achievements of the literary vocation. His objection was to the illusions nurtured by attention to literary language at the expense of spoken discourse. Again, Saussure reveals a deeply democratic sensibility: literary language, often taken to be the exemplar of a national tongue is systematically contrasted with the natural state of a language, which displays a different dynamic.

But for Saussure the distinction is not so much a social one—after all, the regular life of language is manifest in the conversation of the educated folk who probably also form the audience for 'literature'—as a contrast between the spontaneity of conversation and the reflectiveness of literary composition.[85] Literary language is artificial and is therefore somehow unreal, even though Saussure has made perfectly clear that the study of language is a historical and not a natural science. It's as if language had a natural course, a kind of slow and unpredictable change, which could only be interrupted by something extra-linguistic, which would include anything that today we would call metalinguistic or metasemiotic: discussions of how one should speak or write, analyses and characterizations of how people speak in reportage or literature, dictionaries and grammars. The argument is, of course, circular: any hint of reflection is extra-linguistic because the genuinely linguistic has been defined as the absence of reflection.

Let's say all I have said is accepted by the reader, who even finds it mildly interesting. It turns out that Saussure, in formulating his ideas about the nature of language, was profoundly influenced by the ideas of his time, by sociology, psychology, political events, and so forth, just as the philologists who preceded him were influenced by German Romanticism, Darwin, and so on. Is that surprising? Is it in any way a problem? In fact, shouldn't we applaud Saussure for the extent to which he was able and willing to incorporate advances in cognate fields into his work? Would we not, in today's intellectual world, congratulate him for being interdisciplinary?

All that is true enough. Nevertheless, there are good reasons for paying close attention to precisely how and why Saussure is drawing on cognate fields. The first is that the 'ideas of his time' that were implanted in the theory of language ended up leading a strange afterlife. Saussure dies, the *Cours de linguistique générale* is assembled by Bally and Sechehaye, is widely reviewed and celebrated and becomes enormously influential within linguistics. But then, in the late 1940s, Saussure's

---

[84] Saussure, 'Notes for the Third Course (1910–1911)', in *Writings in General Linguistics*, 218.

[85] Thus Saussure will speak of '*real language* (by which I mean the language of educated conversation)': 'Second lecture, November 1891', in *Writings in General Linguistics*, 105.

theory takes on a new and quite different role: it becomes a model for other fields, first anthropology in the work of Lévi-Strauss, then for the analysis of literary and mass cultural objects in the work of Roland Barthes. Soon, it has given birth to 'structuralism' and acquires a niece nicknamed 'post-structuralism'. And in the course of this transformation, in which linguistics finds its lessons taken up by literary critics, anthropologists, historians, and political theorists, we discover that 'language', that modest but ever-present human institution, has implications for the way we think about culture, about society, and about politics. Which can hardly be a surprise if ideas about culture, society, and politics were embedded in that model of language in the first place.

Secondly, the view I've just described proceeds as if language were a stable object which Saussure was simply sizing up. Ideas from other fields that crept into his theorizing could then either help him understand language (if they were correct) or hinder him (if they were mere ideology, like racial theory). But Saussure himself knew things were not so simple. The doubts he articulates about apprehending language in any objective fashion are present in his earliest musings on general linguistics. In the 'Dual Essence' manuscript of 1891 he admits at the outset—in fact dwells on the matter at some length—that '*the object* in linguistics does not exist to start with, is not predetermined in its own right. Hence to speak of an object, to *name* an object, is nothing more than to invoke a particular point of view'.[86] The need to 'approach this object from one side or another, which will never be the whole of language' remains a cornerstone of his writing until the very end: there is no panchronic perspective, there is only 'synchronic' and 'diachronic' linguistics, *langue* and *parole*, external and internal linguistics, with no happy synthesis.[87] Something will always be squeezed out. Saussure does not say—because it is obviously ludicrous—that 'literary language' and other conscious interventions in discourse are not part of language: merely that they are bizarre, atypical, or misleading. He will worry 'about the manifold conclusions only too readily drawn from the way a language has been obliged to adopt a word like *telegraph*' because *telegraph*, something reflectively, consciously coined, is an aberration.[88] For sure, Saussure wants to justify certain viewpoints, like the one that leads to synchronic linguistics, as somehow more scientifically fruitful than others (because synchronic linguistics will yield order, and science needs an orderly object). But he knows that this fruitfulness can't be read off the facts of language, which display no preference for one viewpoint over another. As Paul Feyerabend has pointed out repeatedly, scientific progress, the creation of fruitful new theories often depends on ignoring the 'facts'.[89]

The linguistic turn within linguistics is therefore both exquisitely self-conscious—Saussure knows that he will have to choose, create an object out of the massively complex and heterogeneous world of uttered speech—and surprisingly naïve. Saussure is not drawn to language from some other discipline or intellectual region: he is already committed to comparative philology, therefore the problem of language

---

[86] Saussure, 'On the Dual Essence', 8.   [87] Saussure, 'On the Dual Essence', 7.
[88] Saussure, 'Notes for an article on Whitney', in *Writings in General Linguistics*, 147.
[89] Paul Feyerabend, *Against Method* (London: New Left Books, 1975), 55–68.

will appear to him as something methodological, as the need to 'show the linguist what he is doing' and to define the object in a way that will make disciplinary progress possible. In the course of showing the linguist what he is doing, however, Saussure ends up producing a new and strange object, *langue*, the system of language, which for him is the form taken by 'language in general'. Every language system is a body of conventions shared by its speakers and held together by nothing except their agreement and consent (it is merely mutual agreement that determines whether we say *dog* or *chien*), which makes language a striking image of a successful social order. Striking, but, of course, misleading, in two important respects. First, because order has been made coterminous with agreement: language succeeds because speakers have agreed to the conventions that are its basis, but language *cannot fail* because anything that did not rely on agreement, that failed to receive the 'social sanction', as Saussure called it, would not be part of the language.[90] Secondly, as Saussure's contortions over analogy demonstrate, it is hard to describe how this agreement is established and maintained without the use of human reason, how consent can be both unforced and unargued for. Reflection is excluded from the consent that underlies the system of language precisely because reflection implies the possibility of disagreement and the need for arguments.

Saussure's linguistics are, in this way, a powerful demonstration of how a conception of language can stand metonymically for the larger problem of collective order, at a time when European societies think democracies cannot be held together by reason alone. For Saussure, the metonymy is obvious and direct: he can't explain how language works without invoking the social body of speakers *as* a social body. For those working in other fields, however, the issue will be the intrusion of language itself into their concerns.

---

[90] Saussure, *Second Course*, 3a.

3

The Ship of Logic on the High Seas of Discourse

(Gottlob Frege, Bertrand Russell, Ludwig Wittgenstein, a little Gilbert Ryle)

Such will be the case for philosophy. Philosophy, obviously, had an interest in language from its very birth, when it defined itself against the prevailing science and craft of language, rhetoric. But at the end of the nineteenth and the beginning of the twentieth century, language intruded on the progress of reason in a new way. Philosophy's interest expressed itself initially as a critique of language in the name of logic. Advances in mathematics had prompted the establishment of a new, logically more rigorous system of symbols, more sharply defined than natural language. The old logic, inherited from Aristotle and refined over the centuries, depended on the categories of natural language grammar (such as subject and predicate), which somehow managed to express and obscure logical claims simultaneously. Gottlob Frege therefore took it upon himself, in the final quarter of the nineteenth century, to invent a new language, the so-called *Begriffsschrift* or 'Concept-script' with which one could make clear and unambiguous arguments. The new concept-script would help philosophy 'to break the domination of the word over the human spirit'.[1]

What's at stake can be illustrated with an example borrowed from Frege's most important English-language champion, Michael Dummett. The sentence 'Everybody envies somebody', although grammatically simple, is ambiguous from a logical point of view. Does it mean that it is true of every person that they envy some one other person or that there is a particular someone that everyone envies?[2] Frege's concept-script would prevent such ambiguities. It featured a series of carefully defined signs, explicit syntactic rules, and a hierarchical branching format that ensured we understood the structure of any assertion; within it, as Frege put it, '*nothing is left to guesswork*'.[3] This distillation of ordinary language was made possible by a resolute focus on only what could be asserted (as opposed to commanded, wished for, mused about, wondered at, and so on). 'I called what alone

---

[1] Gottlob Frege, *Begriffsschrift: a formula language modeled upon that of arithmetic, for pure thought* (1879), trans. Stefan Bauer-Mengelberg, in *Frege and Godel: Two Fundamental Texts in Mathematical Logic*, ed. Jean van Heijenoort (Cambridge, MA: Harvard University Press, 1970), 'Preface' (7).
[2] Michael Dummett, *Frege: Philosophy of Language* (London: Duckworth, 1973), 10–13.
[3] Frege, *Begriffsschrift*, §3 (12).

mattered to me the *conceptual content* [*begrifflichen Inhalt*]', Frege noted; 'all those peculiarities of ordinary language that result only from the interaction of speaker and listener—as when, for example, the speaker takes the expectations of the listener into account and seeks to put them on the right track even before the complete sentence is enunciated—have nothing that answers to them in my formula language'.[4] Making clear meant paring down, purging language of the elements that muddied the conceptual content.

Even a distilled language was, however, language: the *expression* of the 'conceptual content' in an arrangement of signs. Frege would therefore spend a considerable amount of time thinking about, and reconfiguring, this content. In the article 'On Sense and Reference' from 1892, conceptual content was reconceived of as the 'sense' of an utterance, to be distinguished from its 'reference' (roughly speaking, how an utterance presented something conceptually as opposed to the actual thing presented).[5] In 1918, a lecture on 'Thoughts' insisted that the 'thought' within an assertion was what could be true or false in it; the 'thought' contained within an utterance was therefore distinguished both from the 'judgment' that it was true—that is, the act by which one acknowledged (or denied) its truth—and from 'the manifestation of this judgment—assertion'.[6] Assertion was to be the moment one went public, so to speak, claiming the truth of a thought *to* someone else. But the public world was, yet again, full of hazards and circumstances that could insinuate themselves into the expressed sentence, becoming confused with the thought being asserted. Actual sentences had, as a result, constituents that were 'hard to avoid, even for one who sees the danger connected with them'.[7] Among these were elements 'meant to act on the feelings and the mood of the hearer, or to arouse his imagination' and what 'serves to aid the hearer's understanding'.[8]

In this manner Frege initiated a dialectic of 'language as such' that would both frame and galvanize the stream of analytic philosophy we focus on in this chapter: the search for a conceptual structure within the sentence, purer than actual speech, which nevertheless had to be expressed in linguistic signs and which could only be imagined as a ghostly version of a sentence. 'Language as such' was here divided against itself: it was simultaneously the absolutely clear 'thought' within actual utterances, pure and unsullied, and language's annoying habit of becoming distracted by the 'interaction of speaker and listener'. In the previous chapter we argued that Saussure made language social, a matter of consent and convention, but had to subtract rational debate from consent to make his linguistics work: he embedded language in the crowd, but at the price of excluding reason. In the current chapter we will see how analytic philosophy drew reason and language together

---

[4] Frege, *Begriffsschrift*, Preface (6), §3 (12).
[5] Gottlob Frege, 'On Sense and Meaning', trans. Max Black, in *Translations from the Philosophical Writings of Gottlob Frege*, 3rd edn., ed. Peter Geach and Max Black (Oxford: Basil Blackwell, 1980), 56–78. The translation of *Bedeutung* is a matter of dispute; I prefer 'reference', as less ambiguous in English.
[6] Gottlob Frege, 'Thoughts', in *Logical Investigations*, trans. P. T. Geach and R. H. Stoothoff (Oxford: Basil Blackwell, 1977), 7.
[7] Frege, 'Thoughts', 9.   [8] Frege, 'Thoughts', 8, 9.

(in the form of the ideal 'proposition'), but at the price of excluding the crowd. Crowds without reason, or reason without crowds: Saussure's linguistics and early analytic philosophy are not mirror images of one another, but one could describe them as—to paraphrase Adorno—the torn halves of an integral democracy, to which however they do not add up.

That crowd will not appear in the flesh in the pages of this chapter ('the people' make a brief appearance in Frege, but we discuss it in Chapter 6). In the analytic philosophers considered here the crowd appears in the guise of intersubjective features of language, which threaten to cloud the pure thought that philosophy wants to extract from it. Frege will not claim that the 'thoughts' expressed in his concept-script are private: they are commonly available entities that do 'not need an owner', graspable by minds, but in no sense contained in them.[9] What he did claim was that the lucidity of their expression depended upon a razor-sharp focus on 'assertion', conceived of as a distinctive kind of public utterance, which was made without considering the expectations or mindset of listeners, the possibility of acting on their feelings, or the appropriateness of a particular style or vocabulary: in short, everything that we might classify as the *rhetorical* aspect of speech. The place and time of the utterance might matter, but only insofar as indexical features of the sentence (the use of *I* or *you*, expressions like *here* and *now*, the tense of verbs) relied on them to fill in the blanks of what was being asserted.[10] In the public use of reason, precision was opposed to persuasion. It's in the exclusion of rhetoric, of the endless and difficult task of public persuasion and argument, that we find the newly enfranchised citizens of Europe. It might look like a replay of a very old quarrel, begun in Athens, except that rhetoric itself had been dissolved into a multitude of fields: into elocution, linguistics, public opinion, crowd psychology, stylistics, and so on. What remains is the idea that the need to persuade impinges on the lucid articulation of thought, and that the clear articulation of thought is not only a necessary but a sufficient cause of public reason.

Frege will claim that what concerns him is 'a certain softness and instability of language, which nevertheless is necessary for its versatility and potential for development', and he'll liken the difference between natural language and his concept-script to the difference between a hand and an artificial instrument.[11] As we examine the emergence of an analytic style of philosophy between 1879 (the date of the *Begriffsschrift*) and the mid-1930s, we'll therefore focus on why philosophers believe that clarity in language requires specialized artificial instruments rather than generally available linguistic faculties. Bertrand Russell will perfect one such instrument when he devises a procedure for translating ordinary sentences into analytically clear 'propositions', but he will never be entirely happy with it. Wittgenstein will polish and refine the instrument in his notes on logic from the

---

[9] Frege, 'Thoughts', 17.

[10] See Frege, 'Thoughts', 10–13. On Frege's thinking about indexical expressions see Edward Harcourt, 'Frege on "I", "Now", "Today" and Some Other Linguistic Devices', *Synthese* 121.3 (1999): 329–56; Robert May, 'Frege on Indexicals', *Philosophical Review* 115. 4 (2006): 487–516.

[11] Gottlob Frege, 'On the Scientific Justification of a Conceptual Notation', in *Conceptual Notation and Related Articles*, trans. and ed. Terrell Ward Bynum (Oxford: Clarendon Press, 1972), 86.

1910s and the book that draws them together, the *Tractatus Logico-Philosophicus* of 1921, but the intersubjectivity he systematically excludes will reappear as an ironic sense of the instrument's limits, of its narrow horizons. And when finally, in the period between 1929 and 1936, Wittgenstein decides that language as a whole can be perfectly clear, he'll make sure its clarity is divorced from anything that looks like public argument. As for Wittgenstein's next steps, which take him to the 'late' work of the *Philosophical Investigations*, these we'll examine in the final chapter, in which the analytic project is reconfigured as the so-called defence of ordinary language. Our focus here will be on the search for a perfectly lucid language, the specialized instrument that will serve as a substitute for the messier business of public debate. Of course, in contextualizing lucidity, I don't mean to question its importance: a university professor would be the last person to argue that all writing and speech is equally lucid. But lucidity in non-fiction prose is a bit like realism in fiction: writers tend to conflate the goal with a particular means, with a particular historical style that 'does the job' in a specific place and time.[12] We want to understand the analytic search for clarity as a historical project, which, like the other projects considered in this book, thinks it is simply exploiting the inner resources of language as such.

HUNTING THE SNARK: THE PROPOSITION WITHIN THE SENTENCE

Frege had not started off with an interest in language; he had particular logico-mathematical issues in mind. Nevertheless, he became caught up in language, although not language in the ordinary sense. Many years later, after philosophers had learned to see this predicament as something interesting and desirable, a symposium was staged in Oxford on the central question 'Are All Philosophical Questions Questions of Language?' Stuart Hampshire, a proponent of what was by then called 'linguistic philosophy', noted that philosophers meant something odd and unusual, remote from common usage, by 'question of language'.[13] '[I]n ordinary use', observed Hampshire, 'one would be inclined to say that what one means by a question of language is precisely a question which can be answered, and which perhaps can *only* be answered, by reference to lexicon, grammar or observation of people's normal linguistic habits.'[14] When philosophers contrasted 'questions of language', however, to 'questions of fact', in the belief that the former was a philosophical topic, they were talking not of language as something with empirical, historical

---

[12] The classic argument was made by Roman Jakobson, whom we'll encounter several times in these pages: 'On Realism in Art', in *Language in Literature* (Cambridge, MA: Harvard University Press, 1987), 19–27.

[13] Stuart Hampshire, 'Are All Philosophical Questions Questions of Language?', *Proceedings of the Aristotelian Society, Supplementary Volume* 22 (1948): 31–78. Hampshire's contribution was reprinted in Richard Rorty (ed.), *The Linguistic Turn: Recent Essays in Philosophical Method* (Chicago: University of Chicago Press, 1967), 284–93.

[14] Hampshire, 'Questions of Language', 35.

traits but of 'language with a capital L'.[15] To enmesh philosophy in language was understandable, even worthy, so long as it was 'language with a capital L'.

Let us return to the engineers intent on perfecting the ship of logic. Bertrand Russell took up Frege's cause but steered it in a slightly different direction. The key moment is the article 'On Denoting' from 1905, in which Russell proposed his theory of descriptions.[16] Described as 'a paradigm of philosophy', the theory, and 'On Denoting' more generally, not only seemed to solve a central problem for the new philosophy, but also established a new style and structure for philosophical scholarship, which would serve as a model for years after.[17]

The problem 'On Denoting' intends to solve is summed up in a notorious sentence: 'The present king of France is bald'. The sentence was obviously not true, but it was also neither false, strictly speaking, nor self-evidently nonsense. The phrase 'the present king of France', insofar as we could understand it, insofar as we understood that it referred to something that did not exist, referred to *something*, but it was not clear what kind of something. Russell solved the problem by distinguishing between the sentence and the 'proposition' itself, which lay, like thought, within the folds of the sentence expressing it. The sentence may have looked like a subject (the present king of France) with something (baldness) predicated of it. But this was not the actual proposition expressed in the sentence: it had another form entirely. To uncover it Russell had to rearticulate the sentence so that rather than being a statement about an attribute of a particular existing thing named by a descriptive phrase, it would be a statement containing mathematical variables—the xs and ys of algebraic equations—and so-called 'quantifiers' drawn from Frege's system, so that whatever the statement containing the variable was, it would be 'always true', 'always false', 'not always true', or 'not always false' (i.e., sometimes true). This produced the following translation of 'The present king of France is bald', which I take from Peter Hylton: 'It is not always false of x that x is the king of France and that x is bald and that "if y is the king of France then y is identical with x" is always true of y.'[18] The first half of the statement secures the claim that if there is a present king of France, he'll be bald, while the latter half tells us that if there is a king of France there will be only one of them (this would mark the difference between saying '*The* present king of France is bald' and '*A* present king of France is bald').

The article is traditionally understood as sorting out what is going on with tricky 'denoting phrases' like 'the present king of France'. But Hylton has argued that Russell had in fact already solved that problem with an earlier and somewhat different theory.[19] The real aim was to establish the importance of rephrasing propositions

---

[15] Hampshire, 'Questions of Language', 35.
[16] Bertrand Russell, 'On Denoting', *Mind* 14.156 (1905): 479–93.
[17] Described so by Frank Ramsey, 'Philosophy', in *The Foundations of Mathematics and other Logical Essays* (London: Kegan Paul, Trench, Trübner & Co., 1931), 263 n1.
[18] Peter Hylton, 'The Significance of "On Denoting"', in C. Wade Savage and C. Anthony Anderson (eds.), *Rereading Russell: Essays on Bertrand Russell's Metaphysics and Epistemology* (Minneapolis: University of Minnesota Press, 1989), 98.
[19] Peter Hylton, 'The Theory of Descriptions', in *Propositions, Functions, and Analysis* (Oxford: Clarendon Press, 2005), 200.

as statements with variables that were either always true, always not true, and so on. As Russell would put it later, he thought it was methodologically wise that, whenever possible, one should substitute 'logical constructions' ('it is not always false of x that x is the King of France') for inferred 'entities' ('the present King of France').[20] And the real achievement of 'On Denoting' was that it made clear that in order to render a proposition philosophically perspicuous in this way, one had to set aside its apparent grammatical form and structure. 'There comes to be a sharp break', says Hylton, 'between the grammatical form of the sentence and the form of the proposition it expresses—logical form, to anticipate a later terminology.'[21] The question of to what 'the present king of France' referred was only a question if you segmented the sentence according to its surface grammar. In the analysis of the sentence Russell produces there is no such phrase and therefore no question to answer. The distinction between the lucidity and rigour of logical argument and the softness of natural languages was in a sense a distinction within sentences rather than between them, for what made the sentences of everyday language meaningful was a deeper, elusive structure, which could be brought to the surface by means of logical analysis.

'On Denoting' thereby opened up one possible path for analytic philosophy: translating sentences of natural language into a logically clearer and more rigorous form. Russell's article, however, had another significant but unintended consequence. As Hylton points out, the very idea that a system of symbolism could be so misleading, that the difference between its apparent and actual structure could be so marked, compelled Russell to accept that philosophers had to be particularly self-conscious about the symbols they used and therefore particularly attentive to questions of language. Furthermore, the fact that logical analysis so drastically rewrites the sentences it examines means we can never be certain that successive stages of analysis are getting us incrementally closer to the 'real' form of the proposition. Once articulated, every form that was once deep comes to the surface, with no guarantee that it will itself remain forever undisturbed—how would one know one had arrived at the final analysis? Hylton therefore draws the conclusion that Russell can't quite bring himself to draw: 'The proposition itself, whose form is given by the final stage of analysis, becomes inaccessible, and our attention is focused on stages of analysis that may be short of the final stage. But all that we have at these stages are *sentences*.'[22]

Sentences it would be and sentences it would remain: analytic philosophy was destined to be at once suspicious of them and forever bound to them. Practitioners of logical analysis could insist that entangled in the dense, opaque brush of actually existing sentences were orderly propositions waiting for philosophers to find them. But it's hard to hunt the snark when you don't know in advance what it looks like. Over time this would lead some analytic philosophers to give up the hunt entirely.

---

[20] See Bertrand Russell, 'Logical Atomism' (1924), in *Logic and Knowledge: Essays 1901–1950* (London: Allen & Unwin, 1956), 326.
[21] Hylton, 'The Significance of "On Denoting"', 98.
[22] Hylton, 'The Significance of "On Denoting"', 104.

In a 1929 article, 'Are There Propositions?', Gilbert Ryle, the soon-to-be leader of Oxford philosophy, concluded that while there are facts and there are sentences in which the facts are stated, there are no 'propositions' interposed between them, no ideal form of the sentence we need to reveal first.[23] But Ryle and others would continue to maintain, whether they believed in propositions or not, that there were clearer and less clear versions of these sentences and that it was the responsibility of philosophers to formulate the clearer ones and to devise appropriate protocols of translation.

The exercise of philosophical reflection had always had to contend with something alien to its efforts: the material world, the flux of sense-impressions, an unknowable sphere of the divine, plain old *doxa*. But philosophers designing the ship of logic faced a different, thornier problem, for language was both the thing that made reflection possible and the thing standing in its way.

The structures of language were, to borrow a phrase from Jürgen Habermas, weakly or quasi-transcendental: they were unavoidable, enabling conditions of articulate and logical thought, and at the same time something empirical, with their own history and evolution.[24] Sentences had a logical structure, for sure, but they were also creatures of that complicated world of *parole*, where the 'combined or isolated *actions* of physiological, physical, or mental forces' produced a disorderly and somewhat unpredictable succession of acts of speech. Paraphrases and translations, no matter how pure the logical heart behind them, were destined to be acts of speech as well.

Russell hoped to sidestep the problem by having philosophy mimic the physical sciences, in method and thus in exactitude.[25] Its object, however—whether characterized as propositions, judgments, or sentences—remained intractable and out of focus. After several unsuccessful attempts to pin propositions down, Russell therefore decided to do without them altogether, shifting, as Thomas Ricketts has put it, 'from a metaphysics of propositions to a metaphysics of facts'.[26] It's as if Russell concluded that to avoid being entangled in the snares of actual language he had to avoid talking about propositions at all. But the way in which he stopped talking about them, or rather the terms in which he chose to talk about the kinds of things which he used to describe as propositions, is instructive. The sentences we produced would now be described as 'judgments' and these judgments would be effectively collocations of the various objects involved. If we believed, to use Russell's example, that 'Othello loves Desdemona', then the objects would be, accordingly, 'Othello', 'Desdemona', and 'loves'. And one other object, curiously unlike the others: the 'logical form' of the judgment itself, that is, the form that determined

---

[23] Gilbert Ryle, 'Are There Propositions?', *Proceedings of the Aristotelian Society* 30 (1929–30): 91–126.
[24] See Jürgen Habermas, 'What is Universal Pragmatics?', in *Communication and the Evolution of Society*, trans. Thomas McCarthy (London: Heinemann, 1979), 21–5.
[25] See Ray Monk, *Bertrand Russell: The Spirit of Solitude* (London: Jonathan Cape, 1996), 282.
[26] Thomas Ricketts, 'Truth and Propositional Unity in Early Russell', in Juliet Floyd and Sanford Shieh (eds.), *Future Pasts: The Analytic Tradition in Twentieth-Century Philosophy* (Oxford: Oxford University Press, 2001), 101.

how the three objects could be combined, ensuring that the end result was 'Othello loves Desdemona' rather than, say, the nonsensical 'loves Desdemona Othello'.[27]

Which is to say that here the syntax of the judgment, its structure, is demoted to the status of a logical object with which we are acquainted, in the same way we are acquainted 'with redness or the taste of a pineapple'.[28] The very articulation of the sentence—after all, the judgment still looks like a sentence—is immobilized or petrified, cast as something to be perceived rather than understood. Russell's theory of descriptions had argued that what looked like a name—'the present king of France'—was the surface form of an elaborate description. When he shifted his attention from propositions to judgments he took the reverse position: what had looked like a description (a proposition) in fact had the form of a simple name.

But there was a problem with this motley array of objects, which included both Othello and the logical form aRb (an a is in some relation to a b). If you weren't supposed to *think* about them, it wasn't clear how you would know that the logical form was a logical form, Othello an individual, 'loving' a relation and so forth, never mind those cases where one of the objects of a judgment was itself a judgment (as in the judgment 'He wrongly believed that the earth revolved around the sun'). Russell's proposed solution was to create another layer in his theory of judgment, the so-called theory of types, which would define the different kinds of objects and tell us what could fit where. But this solution was rapidly overtaken by events. To wit, the arrival of Russell's 'ferocious German' (actually an Austrian), Ludwig Wittgenstein.[29]

WITTGENSTEIN TURNS THE PROBLEM ON ITS HEAD

Wittgenstein had come to Cambridge in 1911, pestered Russell relentlessly, and assumed the burden of pushing the new work on logic and propositions forward. In 1913, coincidentally the year of Saussure's death, he told Russell in a series of letters that he had been barking up the wrong tree. Russell was trying to solve the problem with a new theory, which would classify the objects used in his sentences; Wittgenstein countered that the problem had to be solved, so to speak, *within* the sentence itself, as a matter of grammar. '[A]ll theory of types', Wittgenstein announced in January of that year, 'must be done away with by a theory of symbolism showing that what seem to be *different kinds of things* are symbolised by different kinds of symbols'.[30] That there were different kinds of objects or things combined in a

---

[27] I've drawn this account of Russell's 'multiple relations theory of judgment' from chapter 8 of Peter Hylton, *Russell, Idealism, and the Emergence of Analytic Philosophy* (Oxford: Clarendon Press, 1992), although what I say here is a very crude summary of his own account.

[28] Bertrand Russell, *The Principles of Mathematics, Vol. I* (Cambridge: Cambridge University Press, 1903), 'Preface', v.

[29] Bertrand Russell, Letter to Ottoline Morrell, 16 November 1911, in Ray Monk, *Ludwig Wittgenstein: The Duty of Genius* (London: Vintage, 1991), 40.

[30] Ludwig Wittgenstein to Bertrand Russell, January 1913, Letter 10 in Ludwig Wittgenstein, *Cambridge Letters: Correspondence with Russell, Keynes, Moore, Ramsey and Sraffa*, ed. Brian McGuinness and G. H. von Wright (Oxford: Blackwell, 1995), 25.

proposition was not something you could say in a theory, but something that became clear by virtue of the logic and form of the proposition itself. 'That M is a *thing* can't be *said*; it is nonsense: but *something* is *shewn* by the symbol "M".'[31] You could tell that Othello and Desdemona were objects because 'Othello' and 'Desdemona' were names, and you could tell 'Othello' and 'Desdemona' were names because they could fill the empty spaces provided by the function or predicate 'loves', in a way that, say, another function, 'is bald', could not (it would give you the nonsensical 'Is bald loves'). There was thus no need to say or no point in saying that Othello was an object or 'Othello' a name because the internal grammar of the proposition showed you that it was.

Over the next six years Wittgenstein would explore the ramifications of this insight, writing a series of notes and fragments that would eventually be codified in the *Tractatus Logico-Philosophicus* (completed in 1918, published in German in 1921 and in English translation a year later). On the one hand, the *Tractatus* would continue along the path Russell had begun to establish, making the case that statements in ordinary language were in need of a clarifying, logical analysis. On the other hand, Wittgenstein took a turn no one could have predicted, which ended up giving sentences and their syntax a larger role than Russell had ever envisaged.

'Different kinds of things are symbolised by different kinds of symbols': this meant that the way in which something was symbolized demonstrated something about the thing itself—the symbol in some way *resembled* or was similar to the thing symbolized. More precisely, it would resemble it in the manner in which it fit, syntactically, with other symbols in a proposition: the symbol's syntactic role would correspond to a formal feature of reality itself. Wittgenstein would neatly encapsulate the idea in the claim that a proposition 'pictured' the reality it signified: 'A picture represents a possible situation in logical space.'[32] Just as the internal arrangements of a visual picture corresponded to the arrangement of the situation it presented, so the internal structure of the proposition, its form, mirrored a possible state of affairs. Possible: because the picture was something like an experimental arrangement, which put forth a state of affairs that could be but might not be the case.[33] Propositions were bipolar—they could correspond to the facts or not. But the essential point was that in order to make sense at all, to even count as something that could be true of the world, a proposition had to have a certain form, which corresponded to the form of the world. 'We can quite well give a spatial representation', Wittgenstein said, 'of a set of circumstances which contradict the laws of physics, but not of one contradicting the laws of geometry.'[34] The logical structure of language was the world's geometry.

---

[31] Wittgenstein, 'Notes Dictated to G. E. Moore in Norway, April 1914', in *Notebooks 1914–1916*, 2nd edn., trans. G. E. M. Anscombe (Chicago: University of Chicago Press, 1984), 109.

[32] Ludwig Wittgenstein, *Tractatus Logico-Philosophicus*, 2nd edn., reprinted with corrections, trans. D. F Pears and B. F. McGuinness (London: Routledge & Kegan Paul, 1974), 2.202.

[33] Wittgenstein likened this experimental arrangement to 'when in the law-court in Paris a motor-car accident is represented by means of dolls, etc.' (Note of 29 September 1914, in *Notebooks 1914–1916*, 7e).

[34] Wittgenstein, Note of 21 May 1915, *Notebooks 1914–1916*, 49e.

Wittgenstein had a different way of putting the point: the world, according to the second line of the *Tractatus*, 'is the totality of facts, not of things'; it had a fact-like shape.[35] And facts, Wittgenstein had concluded in even his earliest notes on logic, 'are symbolised by facts, or more correctly: that a certain thing is the case in the symbol says that a certain thing is the case in the world'.[36] But when propositions, or other kinds of pictures, are described by Wittgenstein as facts (*Tractatus* 2.141: 'A picture is a fact') he does not mean, as he might have, that it is a fact of discourse, something someone has said or read at a discrete point in time—it is not a historical fact (as the states of affairs it describes might be). It is a fact by virtue of having a certain structure which, we're asked to assume, extends beyond any particular enunciation. In this respect it is like Saussure's idea of *langue*, the language system, which exists, but not as a moment of communication: rather, it exists through communication. A fact was a connection of elements, a structure with a logic or syntax—better yet, a 'logical syntax'—built into it.[37]

The insistence on the 'factual' nature of the proposition had a polemical point: it was aimed at the belief that the facts could be *named*. The *Tractatus*'s elaborate numbered, tree-like structure (it has a skeleton of statements 1–7, each of which has subheads like 2.01, 2.012, 2.0121. 2.1 and so forth) is meant to indicate the relative 'logical importance of the propositions'.[38] Yet tucked away in 4.0312 is Wittgenstein's claim that his 'fundamental idea' is 'that there can be no representatives of the *logic* of facts'. Russell had suggested that one of the objects we grasped in a judgment was the syntax of the relevant logical form (such as *aRb* in 'Othello loves Desdemona'). Against this Wittgenstein objected that '[t]here is no thing which is the form of a proposition, and no name which is the name of a form.'[39] Names could only be correlated with objects, or, to be more exact, they *meant* objects, for '[o]bjects can only be *named*'.[40] This absolute distinction between names/objects on the one hand and propositions/facts on the other has been neatly characterized by Alain Badiou:

> The opposition between *nomination* (representation without thought of objects by a sign) and *description* (signifying picture of the combinations of objects in a proposition) is completely disjunctive: that which can be named (the substantial atomic object) cannot be described, and that which can be described (the combination of objects or states) cannot be named.[41]

Even this, however, leaves out a critical element of the distinction. For the relationship between proposition and fact is one of 'picturing' or, we could say, analogy: 'The fact that the elements of a picture are related to one another in a determinate way represents that things are related to one another in the same way.'[42] By contrast,

---

[35] Wittgenstein, *Tractatus*, 1.1.
[36] Wittgenstein, 'Notes on Logic' (1913), in *Notebooks 1914–1916*, 96.
[37] Wittgenstein first mentions the idea of a 'logical syntax' in the *Tractatus*, 3.325.
[38] Wittgenstein, *Tractatus*, 7n.   [39] Wittgenstein, 'Notes on Logic', 105.
[40] Wittgenstein, *Tractatus*, 3.221.
[41] Alain Badiou, *Wittgenstein's Antiphilosophy*, trans. Bruno Bosteels (London: Verso, 2011), 100.
[42] Wittgenstein, *Tractatus*, 2.15.

the names within the proposition—the 'elements of a picture'—that refer to objects have a more intimate relationship with the reality they designate. The 'correlations of the picture's elements with things' are 'as it were, the feelers of the picture's elements, with which the picture touches reality'.[43] If we think of descriptions as a stencil, Wittgenstein says, 'the names pin it to the world'.[44]

But who does the pinning? Wittgenstein uses the idea of the name to glue the proposition to the facts it mirrors, but there is no subject to apply the glue. The name guarantees that propositions somehow hook onto reality, although it does not take up the activity of hooking, the 'factual' reality of making the utterance itself. Wittgenstein will be neither the first nor last figure to ask the name to do so much work, for names are continually cast as the parts of speech that reach out to, make direct contact with, the reality signified in language. Anticipating some of what we'll discuss later, we can say that names will be characterized by a mythic entanglement with the object-world: mythic in the sense that they 'touch' their objects, acquire some of their substance and, most importantly, in that they are connected to their objects through a ritualized form of action. This will persist even into the further reaches of analytic philosophy: when Saul Kripke famously takes issue with Russell's argument that names are condensed descriptions, his case will be that names depend upon what he calls an initial 'baptism', a ritualized human procedure by which a particular name is assigned to an individual, establishing and guaranteeing its identity.[45]

This direct contact, and the bipolar proposition it made possible, took place, however, at the smallest imaginable level: a level of 'atomic facts' or 'states of affairs' that would account for reality like a fine mesh.[46] All larger facts—those which might engage material objects of the sort we encounter in everyday life—would be effectively sums of the atomic ones. The world, such as it appears in the *Tractatus*, is the 'totality of true propositions', which, in its turn, 'is the whole of natural science (or the whole corpus of the natural sciences)'.[47] If there is a model for this world, it is the one provided by Heinrich Hertz's mechanics, which imagines the world as a series of connected space-time locations (Hertz's own philosophy of scientific symbolism would be a significant inspiration for Wittgenstein as well).[48] As for everything else we think of as the world—human relationships, feelings, ethics, art, religion, politics, and so on—these were not liable to picturing and were, in that sense, unworldly. This unworldliness would be characterized in a series of denials and claims that begin with 6.373 and continue through the 'mystical' section of the

---

[43] Wittgenstein, *Tractatus*, 2.1514, 2.1515.
[44] Wittgenstein, Note from 31 May 1915, in *Notebooks 1914–1916*, 53e.
[45] Saul Kripke, *Naming and Necessity* (Cambridge, MA: Harvard University Press, 1980), 96–7.
[46] 'State of affairs' and 'atomic fact' are the two translations that have been offered for the German *Sachverhalt*: the first in the translation by D. F. Pears and B. F. McGuinness (which I have used in this chapter), the second in the earlier 1922 translation by C. K. Ogden, about whom we will hear much more below.
[47] Wittgenstein, *Tractatus*, 4.11.
[48] See Gerd Grasshoff, 'Hertz's Philosophy of Nature in Wittgenstein's *Tractatus*', in Davis Baird, R. I. G. Hughes, and Alfred Nordmann (eds.), *Heinrich Hertz: Classical Physicist, Modern Philosopher* (Dordrecht: Kluwer, 1998), 243–68.

Tractatus: 'The world is independent of my will' (6.373); 'ethics cannot be put into words' (6.421); 'the good or bad exercise of the will [...] can alter only the limits of the world, not the facts—not what can be expressed by means of language' (6.43); 'God does not reveal himself *in* the world' (6.432); 'It is not *how* things are in the world that is mystical, but *that* it exists' (6.44).

Where did that leave the discourse of the *Tractatus*, that is to say, philosophy itself? On the one hand, Wittgenstein appeared dedicated to the 'critique of language' in Russell's terms, demonstrating that below the surface of ordinary language lay a logical syntax that philosophers should bring to light.[49] But whereas Russell thought he was bringing the rigour of science to bear on ordinary language, Wittgenstein thought the critique depended on making an absolute break with science. There was agreement that the aim of philosophy was 'the logical clarification of thoughts'.[50] The issue was how the clarification proceeded: Russell assumed philosophy pursued it by making propositions of its own—Wittgenstein insisted that '[p]hilosophy does not result in "philosophical propositions", but rather in the clarification of propositions.'[51]

So, *Tractatus* 4.12: 'Propositions can represent the whole of reality, but they cannot represent what they must have in common with reality in order to be able to represent it—logical form.' One could not make the symbols and logical forms used to describe the world into objects themselves without using the very logic and symbolism one was trying to pin down. In Wittgenstein's words: 'It is impossible to *say* what these properties [of language, KH] are, because in order to do so, you would need a language which hadn't got the properties in question, and it is impossible that this should be a *proper* language. Impossible to construct [an, LW] illogical language.'[52] But this, of course, was precisely what Russell and similar logicians had thought they were doing: creating a scientific theory of logical forms. Russell had imagined logic as a doctrine that spoke of things and relations 'as such', logic as having a domain of objects and forms different from ordinary objects and forms by virtue of their extreme generality. As Wittgenstein put it (speaking critically), 'it comes to seem as if logic dealt with things which have been deprived of all properties except thing-hood, and with propositions deprived of all properties except complexity'.[53]

But though philosophy could not, Wittgenstein argued, be a *theory* of logical forms and objects, it could nevertheless serve as their display case. One could, he had claimed, *see* logical form if you made a proposition clear and grasped it as a kind of picture: clearly designed propositions would '*show* the logical form of reality'.[54] Logical propositions, in turn, could help the process along, not by saying anything about forms, objects, and structures, but by displaying the 'logical syntax' of ordinary propositions in a particularly sharp and striking manner. In fact, logical propositions didn't say anything about anything, in the sense of making a claim

---

[49] Wittgenstein, *Tractatus*, 4.0031.   [50] Wittgenstein, *Tractatus*, 4.112.
[51] Wittgenstein, *Tractatus*, 4.112.
[52] Wittgenstein, 'Notes Dictated to G. E. Moore in Norway, April 1914', 108.
[53] Wittgenstein, 'Notes on Logic', 107.   [54] Wittgenstein, *Tractatus*, 4.121.

that could be true or false. When they were true, they were tautologies, when false, self-contradictory, because they merely articulated the logical rules of sense and of the world itself. If you recognized they were true—which you could do simply by examining the proposition—you simply understood something about how signs could be used and what they meant. 'Logical so-called propositions *shew* [the] logical properties of language and therefore of [the] Universe, but *say* nothing. This means that by merely looking at them you can *see* these properties; whereas, in a proposition proper, you cannot see what is true by looking at it.'[55] In that way, '[t]he propositions of logic describe the scaffolding of the world, or rather they represent it'.[56]

So while it looked like Wittgenstein was at one with Russell, aiming at the 'logical clarification of thoughts', he was subtly altering the course the latter had set. Clarity was his avowed aim, but it was not the clarity achieved by science. The latter was methodical and systematic, and it was progressive in character, a means towards the systematic mastery of nature. The clarity aimed at by Wittgenstein was different in aim and in affect. We need to think about it in more detail, but first we need to step back and consider from another point of view what this clarification of sentences amounted to. The work of the linguist Émile Benveniste will be helpful.

CLARITY AND INTERSUBJECTIVITY

Benveniste, writing in the wake of Saussure's transformation of linguistics, acknowledged that language depended on the structure Saussure had called *langue*, but he noticed that many of the elements within that structure owed their signifying power not to the structure itself, but to the 'reality of discourse'.[57] Tense in verbs, the personal pronouns *I* and *you*, deictic terms like *here* and *there*, may have appeared to receive their meaning from the differential system of language, but they were in fact 'instances of discourse' within that system, the hooks that allowed one to embed a 'semiotic' structure within the 'semantic' web of ongoing intersubjective communication. The interesting ambiguity of language, essential to its functioning, lay in the way these two dimensions were intertwined. From the semiotic point of view, for example, the first and second person pronouns received their meaning by virtue of their differential relations with the third person pronouns: they 'produce the impression of three coordinated persons'.[58] From the semantic point of view, the point of view of 'discourse', however, the three persons don't constitute a unitary class, because the first and second person pronouns have a function wholly distinct from that of third person pronouns. The first person pronoun 'signifies

---

[55] Wittgenstein, 'Notes Dictated to G. E. Moore in Norway, April 1914', 108.
[56] Wittgenstein, *Tractatus*, 6.124.
[57] Émile Benveniste, 'The Nature of Pronouns' (1956), in *Problems of General Linguistics*, trans. Mary Elizabeth Meek (Coral Gables, FL: University of Miami Press, 1971), 218.
[58] Benveniste, 'The Nature of Pronouns', 221.

"the person who is uttering the present instance of the discourse containing *I*".[59] This immediate reference to the one who speaks is, in fact, essential to language, Benveniste argues, for it makes possible 'the conversion of language into discourse'.[60] By means of the first and second person pronouns (coordinated with the various forms of the verb, which almost always relate the time of the event to the time of the utterance, and indicators like *today*, *tomorrow*, *there*, and so on) the 'sign is thus linked to the *exercise* of language and announces the speaker as speaker. It is this property that establishes the basis for individual discourse, in which each speaker takes over all the resources of language for his own behalf.'[61]

For the early analytic philosopher, the linguistic elements Benveniste picks out have to be purged to reach the actual propositional content of a sentence. All that is required to turn language into discourse—the set and costumes, the backstory, the *dramatis personae*, the props, the desires, passions and plots—must be excluded to avoid the taint of psychologism and to ensure the public and objective nature of the proposition.[62] It's significant that two of the ordinary sentences Russell sought to clarify in 'On Denoting'—'The present King of France is bald' and 'I met a man'—display 'instances of discourse' that bind them to a communicative situation (the adjective 'present' in the first case, the first person pronoun and past tense verb in the second); in both cases these are wiped out by the analysis. Russell was aware of the issue and dismissive of discourse's needs: 'The occurrence of tense in verbs is an exceedingly annoying vulgarity due to our preoccupation with practical affairs.'[63] Tyler Burge has described the legacy this left to analytic philosophy:

> As an approach to understanding language, the tradition's method of replacement was calculated to ignore certain aspects of language use as detrimental to scientific purposes. Thus, vagueness, ambiguity, indexicality, singular reference, implicature, intensionality, and so on, were ignored (by one writer or another) because of preconceptions about well-behaved logical systems or about the needs of science.[64]

Despite the aspirations, elements of intersubjectivity occasionally seeped into the new language. When Frege first began to formulate his logical concept-script, a trace of intersubjectivity remained in the form of what was called the 'judgment stroke'.[65] That symbol signified the conversion of a thought into an assertion,

---

[59] Benveniste, 'The Nature of Pronouns', 218.
[60] Benveniste, 'The Nature of Pronouns', 220.
[61] Benveniste, 'The Nature of Pronouns', 220.
[62] My theatrical metaphors inevitably bring to mind the early twentieth-century theorist of symbolism who insisted on a 'dramatistic' concept of language: Kenneth Burke. I don't discuss Burke—he falls outside the geographical limits of this study—but I wish I could, as his eclectic amalgam of theory of language, rhetoric, literary criticism, and social theory would fit neatly into my principal concerns.
[63] Russell, 'The Philosophy of Logical Atomism' (1918), in *Logic and Knowledge*, 248.
[64] Tyler Burge, 'Philosophy of Language and Mind: 1950–1990', *The Philosophical Review* 101.1 (1992): 14.
[65] Frege, *Begriffsschrift*, §2 (11–12); Frege discusses the difference between 'the act of judging and the formation of a mere assertible content' in 'On the Aim of the "Conceptual Notation"', in *Conceptual Notation and Related Articles*, 94. The judgment stroke was controversial from the outset and did not survive into modern symbolic logic.

understood as a public and external moment. The structure and content of a proposition would dictate what was to be said, but Frege thought it necessary to create a symbol for the moment of asserting it, which would, of course, mean asserting it to someone (in some context, for some reason). Wittgenstein would condemn this concession to discourse in the *Tractatus*, dismissing the judgment stroke as 'logically quite meaningless' and not really a 'component part of a proposition'.[66] In a sense, of course, he was right: for the moment of assertion could not be reduced to being a mere 'part of the proposition'. As something both in and beyond the sentence, it resisted the formalization Frege sought to impose on it.

Thus the clarifying paraphrases aimed at by logical analysis implied one could make sentences using only the resources of the semiotic system itself. This was what Benveniste deemed impossible, a kind of category mistake in its own right, insofar as what was at stake was not two different kinds of language, but two necessary and complementary aspects of communication: 'with the sentence we leave the domain of language as a system of signs and enter into another universe, that of language as an instrument of communication, whose expression is discourse'.[67] The grammar and lexis that constituted a semiotic system were not enough to make speech, which required a variety of semantic props to communicate a definite content. In fact, the severe formalization of the semiotic system implied by the idea of 'logical syntax' was only half the story, for philosophy's aspiration to produce knowledge that was absolute, infallible, and axiomatic meant that the syntax it uncovered had to possess 'necessity' as well. In the *Tractatus* Wittgenstein would claim that '[t]he only necessity that exists is *logical* necessity', insisting that all physical laws were forever hypotheses.[68] The systems Benveniste described were formal, but liable to change, necessary as the horizon of language, but 'quasi-transcendental'. But logical syntax had to be immune to change or revision (and the same across all possible natural languages): the geometry, not the physics of speech. The engineers designing the ship of logic (Wittgenstein, it's worth recalling, had been trained as an engineer) were, *pace* Saussure, intent on thwarting the pressure of the seas on which it would sail: this ship would move in a straight line, and only trained professionals would be permitted to alter its course.

Scientifically trained professionals, that is. As I've mentioned a few times, when philosophers like Russell decided language needed a clarifying analysis or paraphrase, their ideal was a mathematized, scientific discourse, epitomized by the new symbolic logic that he and Frege had established. It was not just a question of philosophy approximating the rigour and formality of science: philosophy's task was to purge discourse at large of its fuzziness and imprecision, to establish formalized reasoning as the model for knowledge in general and to guard against the dangers posed by the awkwardness of natural languages. The latter, as Wittgenstein put it, 'disguises thought. So much so, that from the outward form of the clothing it is impossible

---

[66] Wittgenstein, *Tractatus*, 4.442.
[67] Émile Benveniste, 'The Levels of Linguistic Analysis', in *Problems of General Linguistics*, 110.
[68] Wittgenstein, *Tractatus*, 6.37.

to infer the form of the thought beneath it, because the outward form of the clothing is not designed to reveal the form of the body, but for entirely different purposes.'[69]

Wittgenstein didn't specify what these 'entirely different purposes might be', but they sound a lot like the 'practical affairs' Russell associated with the vulgarities of tense in verbs. It's tempting to think these practical affairs consisted of the day-to-day business of ordinary language: the sphere, in short, of intersubjectivity, in which people make arrangements, negotiate agreements, give and follow orders, make jokes, and fall in and out of love. But practical affairs and purposes operate at the macro level as well as the micro one, and the drive to make discourse scientific had a looming significance in public life.

A CULTURE OF SCIENCE

Jürgen Habermas's analysis of the 'structural transformation of the public sphere' focused attention on how the function of public opinion and public discourse shifted in response to the widening of the franchise in Britain and the emergence of an articulate and organized labour movement. In the beginning of the nineteenth century the public sphere was valued as a place that made a rational-critical testing of government policies possible; as the century wore on, the rational testing of political claims by public discussion gave way to fear of majoritarian tyranny, to 'purposive opinion management' and to the administrative and bargaining practices of bureaucracies and special-interest associations.[70] The public sphere had dangled the gem of disinterested objectivity before the eyes of the citizenry: it promised that relatively open public debate would bring affairs of state before the tribunal of reason, reason that was objective because, and to the extent it was public. Its slow transformation into an arena for bargaining and public acclamation left that objectivity stranded.

There were, however, other developments within the sphere of objectivity. In *Trust in Numbers: The Pursuit of Objectivity in Science and Public Life*, Theodore Porter has described the displacement of elite professional judgment by quantitative analysis.[71] In Britain, France, and the United States political institutions turned, over the course of the nineteenth century, to the impersonal authority of statistics and quantification to legitimate their decisions. Where once the cultivated judgment of professionals had been allowed to guide policy, now government bureaucracies desired the security of numbers, calculations of costs and benefits, to justify public projects. 'Rigorous quantification is demanded in these contexts', Porter claims, 'because subjective discretion has become suspect.'[72] The numbers themselves did not fall from the sky: as Porter points out, the production of statistics

---

[69] Wittgenstein, *Tractatus*, 4.002.
[70] Habermas, *The Structural Transformation of the Public Sphere*, 196.
[71] Theodore M. Porter, *Trust in Numbers: The Pursuit of Objectivity in Science and Public Life* (Princeton, NJ: Princeton University Press, 1995).
[72] Porter, *Trust in Numbers*, 90.

required massive institutional structures and their interpretation was left not to the common man or woman, but to a new kind of bureaucratic expert. Indeed, public opinion itself came to be something measured and interpreted by statisticians: no longer the result of coffee-house debate, but an artefact of institutional data-gathering and 'expert' analysis. In this context the use of mathematics 'provided evidence of disinterestedness as well as expertise'.[73]

It was not mathematics in general that provided the numbers, but statistics in particular. In Britain the late nineteenth century witnessed the rise of statistical societies with an interest in social reform, i.e., government or otherwise public programmes to alleviate a host of social ills. Although the use of figures implied a new impersonality in decision-making, it signalled a transformation of, rather than an end to the class relations that structured British politics. For one thing, impersonal information was deemed useful only insofar as its targets themselves lacked individuality: as Porter puts it, 'averages must always appear less meaningful when drawn from a population of strong and interesting personalities'—the objects of measurement were the huddled, indistinct masses.[74] But quantification also entailed a change in the composition and training of the governing elites. The disinterest of cultivated aristocrats was to be replaced by the disinterest of trained, middle-class statisticians.

Among those middle-class statisticians, Porter rightly singles out Karl Pearson, the first professor of statistics at University College London and indeed in the UK as a whole. Pearson was not only the creator of much in the way of statistical method, but also the new discipline's most passionate champion.[75] An avid eugenicist, Pearson was keen to demonstrate the immediate relevance of his discipline to public policy, conducting, for example, a study that—to his mind—conclusively demonstrated that Jewish immigrant children in London were intellectually deficient compared with those of native stock.[76] Two features of Pearson's intellectual position make him particularly relevant to what we're interested in here.

The first is Pearson's conviction that, in Porter's words, 'all science is fundamentally statistical'.[77] Porter cites this as evidence of Pearson's 'descriptivism', which can be summarized as the conviction that science is better off focusing on the mathematical description of measurable states than searching for underlying causes, mechanisms, or objects. An earlier proponent of such descriptivism was Heinrich Hertz, whose theoretical commitments find a strong echo in the *Tractatus*, which

---

[73] Porter, *Trust in Numbers*, 118.   [74] Porter, *Trust in Numbers*, 77.
[75] See Theodore M. Porter, *Karl Pearson: The Scientific Life in a Statistical Age* (Princeton, NJ: Princeton University Press, 2004); Bernard J. Norton, 'Karl Pearson and Statistics: The Social Origins of Scientific Innovation', *Social Studies of Science* 8.1 (1978): 3–34.
[76] Karl Pearson and Margaret Moul, 'The Problem of Alien Immigration into Great Britain, Illustrated by an Examination of Russian and Polish Jewish Children, Part 1', *Annals of Eugenics* 1.1 (1925): 5–54. Obviously, the article is racist nonsense. But I cannot pretend to be disinterested: halfway through reading it I realized that my own grandfather was probably one of the Jewish children Pearson measured for the research.
[77] Theodore M. Porter, 'The Death of the Object: *Fin-de-Siècle* Philosophy of Physics', in Dorothy Ross (ed.), *Modernist Impulses in the Human Sciences 1870–1930* (Baltimore: Johns Hopkins University Press, 1994), 149.

urges the reader to give up metaphysical ideas like causality, law of nature, and explanation in preference for a web of descriptive propositions. The second conviction is that scientific method, as exemplified by statistics, provides the model for the objectivity demanded of the modern citizen.

In 1892 Pearson published *The Grammar of Science*, a printed version of lectures he had given in London the year before.[78] For the most part the book concerned issues of scientific method and scientific language: it was a long argument for the kind of descriptivism mentioned in the previous paragraph. Its Introduction, however, broached more general issues. 'The wide extension of the franchise in both local and central representation', Pearson observed

> has cast a greatly increased responsibility on the individual citizen. He is brought face to face with the most conflicting opinions and with the most diverse party cries. [...] He is called upon to form a judgment apart from his own feelings and emotions if it possibly may be—a judgment in what he conceives to be the interests of society at large.[79]

How would this newly enfranchised citizen sort things out, given the raised political temperature? For it was obvious, was it not, that his judgment (this was thirty-five years before *her* judgment was considered franchise-worthy) 'can only be based on a clear knowledge of facts, an appreciation of their sequence and relative significance'. What was needed was a sphere where this kind of thing was already common practice, and which therefore could serve as 'one of the best training grounds for citizenship'. Needless to say, Pearson had something in mind:

> The classification of facts and the formation of absolute judgments upon the basis of this classification—judgments independent of the idiosyncrasies of the individual mind—is peculiarly the *scope and method of modern science*. The scientific man has above all things to aim at self-elimination in his judgments, to provide an argument which is as true for each individual mind as for his own. [...] The scientific method of examining facts is not peculiar to one class of phenomena and to one class of workers; it is applicable to social as well as to physical problems, and we must carefully guard ourselves against supposing that the scientific frame of mind is a peculiarity of the professional scientist.[80]

Pearson's concession at the end—his democratizing of the scientific frame of mind—should fool no one: we are a long way from the public sphere. The latter guaranteed the objectivity of politics by fostering an open debate, in which participants had to support claims with arguments and evidence. In place of this Pearson suggested scientific method itself would purge the subjectivity of politics, that training could do the work that had been entrusted to public debate. What Pearson wanted was not for each man to become a scientist, but for training to inculcate in him a respect for science and deference to the scientific authority wielded by

---

[78] Porter, *Karl Pearson*, 198.
[79] Karl Pearson, *The Grammar of Science* (London: Walter Scott, 1892), 6–7.
[80] Pearson, *The Grammar of Science*, 7–8.

people like Pearson (for then the citizen would learn, among other things, about the science of eugenics and 'the struggle of race with race, and the survival of the physically and mentally fitter race').[81]

We will encounter this belief in the political virtues of science again later on. But to make clear what we are dealing with here we should distinguish between the practice of science itself—for which the empirical work of the comparative philologists could stand as a useful example—and what I'll call *the culture of science*. The culture of science treats the field as a series of virtues and values rather than as a definite form of practice. It extols cool-headedness, objectivity, sober description of states of affairs, and the incomparable beauty of mathematical formulae. Natural science itself, of course, had provided one of the earliest successful examples of a public sphere (although it gets short shrift in Habermas's account), in which open communication through societies and print publication had made possible the public testing of claims and arguments.[82] But this was not what Pearson had in mind. He recommended science as a method in which one could be trained: it was to be a modernized version of the *Bildung* (cultivation) that had been central to the formation of earlier European elites. Only this can explain his otherwise incomprehensible suggestion that Baden-Powell's *Aid to Scouting* could serve as a guide to scientific method.[83]

In short, the culture of science promised a new form of objectivity, reliant on education and training, that could substitute for the objectivity of the public sphere. The decisions made by a more democratic Britain could retain their claim to reason if they were guided by scientific cool-headedness and statistical knowledge, or, to be more exact, by cool scientific heads and statisticians. Of course, claiming that the new social sciences were the home of political reason meant sidelining the emerging alternative: what has been described as the 'proletarian public sphere', which would include the central social and political institutions of the labour movement (its political parties, social clubs and friendly societies, libraries and theatres).[84]

Bertrand Russell's political commitments and activities were famous: he has been described as England's last great radical.[85] Wittgenstein's politics are a source of constant puzzlement (on the one hand, aristocratic snobbery and the conservative tone of some of the philosophy; on the other, explicit sympathy with left-wing

---

[81] Karl Pearson, *National Life from the Standpoint of Science*, 2nd edn. (London: Cambridge University Press, n.d. [1901?]), 21.

[82] For a concise account, see Adrian Johns, 'Coffeehouses and Print Shops', in Katherine Park and Lorraine Daston (eds.), *The Cambridge History of Science, Vol. 3: Early Modern Science* (Cambridge: Cambridge University Press, 2006), 320–40. This sort of public sphere was not what Pearson had in mind.

[83] Pearson, *National Life*, 38.

[84] Oskar Negt and Alexander Kluge, *Public Sphere and Experience: Toward an Analysis of the Bourgeois and Proletarian Public Sphere*, trans. Peter Labanyi, Jamie Owen Daniel, and Assenka Oksoloff (Minneapolis: University of Minnesota Press, 1993).

[85] Alan Ryan, 'Russell: The Last Great Radical?', *Philosophy of the Social Sciences* 26.2 (1996): 247–66.

causes and a notable predilection for Communist and left-wing friends).[86] In their early philosophical writing, however, they share a commitment to the objectivity of science and to science as the only source of objectivity. Russell had been open about wanting philosophy to mimic the precision, style, and mathematical form of science. Wittgenstein had leaned heavily on Hertz's 'descriptionist asceticism' in the *Tractatus* and equated knowledge of the world with natural science itself.[87] The identification of objectivity with science, however, could lead in two different directions. In Russell's hands, it meant science should be a cultural model, a paradigm for clear thinking with broad application. In Wittgenstein's perspective, it appeared to entail the denigration of the worldly affairs that science captured. True clarity would be found not in science, but in grasping what can be 'shown' by philosophy and not 'said' by science.

'NEW WITTGENSTEINIANS' TAKE A LITERARY SLANT

That, at least, was a common understanding of what Wittgenstein was up to until the emergence of the so-called 'new Wittgensteinians' in the 1980s, who had a very different idea of what Wittgensteinian clarity entailed. Cora Diamond and James Conant, the earliest and most prominent of the group, took their cue from the Preface and the closing comments of the *Tractatus*.[88] In 6.54, the penultimate section of the *Tractatus*, Wittgenstein would describe the propositions of the text itself as 'elucidations in the following way: anyone who understands me eventually recognizes them as nonsensical, when he has used them—as steps—to climb up beyond them. (He must, so to speak, throw away the ladder after he has climbed up it.)'. The propositions within the *Tractatus* that correspond to the ones I have just mentioned, for instance, 4.121 where propositions are said to '*show* the logical form of reality', should therefore be understood as senseless, clarifying insofar as they allow us to realize that we should stop asking questions about 'objects' or 'relations' or even 'propositions' in general, because there is nothing to ask about. As Cora Diamond has put it: 'Really to grasp that what you were trying to say shows itself in language is to cease to think of it as an inexpressible *content: that which* you were

---

[86] On Wittgenstein's friends on the Left, see Brian McGuinness, ' "It Will Be Terrible Afterwards, Whoever Wins" ', in Brian McGuinness (ed.), *Approaches to Wittgenstein* (London: Routledge, 2002), 43–52.

[87] 'Descriptionist asceticism' is Theodore M. Porter's term for Hertz's philosophy of science; 'Death of the Object', 135.

[88] James Conant distinguishes between the frame of the *Tractatus*, which instructs us in how to read it, and the bulk of the text in 'The Search for Logically Alien Thought: Descartes, Kant, Frege, and the *Tractatus*', *Philosophical Topics* 20.1 (1991): 159–60. This distinction between the frame and the body of the *Tractatus* has become canonical for the new Wittgensteinians and is the source of a great deal of controversy. For a (to my mind, entirely persuasive) critique of the distinction see P. M. S. Hacker, 'Was He Trying to Whistle It?', in Rupert Read and Alice Crary (eds.), *The New Wittgenstein* (London: Routledge, 2000), 353–88.

trying to say.'[89] What you are shown is not 'the logical form of reality', as if this were a structure invisible to the naked eye, but only the fact that a phrase like 'the logical form of reality' has no sense.

New Wittgensteinians accuse old Wittgensteinians of 'chickening out' from the consequences of Wittgenstein's insistence that his own sentences are senseless.[90] The notionally philosophical sentences of the *Tractatus* don't mean in some special way, don't show us a sense that we aren't allowed to articulate directly: they are just 'sentence-like structures' that don't function in the only way sentences can function, which is to mean something that is true or false by virtue of its relationship to states of affairs.[91] They're a kind of halfway house for people addicted to metaphysics; there you use the old philosophical terms—'necessity', 'possibility', 'object'—in order to learn that you don't really need them, because whatever necessity and objectivity there is, is reflected in the *use* we make of non-philosophical sentences.

At first glance it appears that it is the new Wittgensteinians who take Wittgenstein's linguistic turn more seriously (they like to describe themselves as 'resolute' readers of Wittgenstein).[92] They believe that Wittgenstein's teaching should lead us to accept that there is nothing behind or beyond our language and that that is just fine; we should not, to quote James Conant, be 'making the space of thought wider than the space afforded by the logical structure of language'.[93] More to the point, we should not *want to*: in 1933 Wittgenstein will say that the difficulty of philosophy is 'not the intellectual difficulty of the sciences, but the difficulty of a change of attitude'.[94] The experience of accepting language for what it is, of surrendering the wish to go beyond its boundaries, should be—we'll return to this in Chapter 8— satisfying, even, in a way, pleasurable.

Accepting the constraints of language with good grace, however, does not entail *knowing* those limits. The new Wittgensteinians like to remind everyone that however much Wittgenstein might have broached 'meaning' as a topic, he refused to provide a philosophical explanation or theory of it, because such an explanation would imply 'the idea of a perspective on language as if from outside'.[95] The argument is paralleled in the later work of Richard Rorty, who had enthusiastically embraced the linguistic turn in philosophy, but had come to the conclusion that talk of 'language' led to metaphysics as surely as talk of essences had. Thinking that we were somehow 'within' language was really only useful as a route to think yourself out of the metaphysics of '*representation in general*'; about language itself,

---

[89] Cora Diamond, 'Throwing Away the Ladder', *Philosophy* 63 (1988): 24.
[90] Diamond, 'Throwing Away the Ladder', 7.
[91] Diamond, 'Throwing Away the Ladder', 18.
[92] On the notion of a 'resolute' reading see James Conant, 'Mild Mono-Wittgensteiniansim', in Alice Crary (ed.), *Wittgenstein and the Moral Life: Essays in Honor of Cora Diamond* (Cambridge, MA: MIT Press, 2007), 32 and 111–12n4.
[93] Conant, 'Logically Alien Thought', 151.
[94] Ludwig Wittgenstein, *The Big Typescript: TS 213*, ed. and trans. C. Grant Luckhardt and Maximilian A. E. Aue (Oxford: Basil Blackwell, 2005), 300e.
[95] Alice Crary, 'Wittgenstein's Philosophy in Relation to Political Thought', in Crary and Read, *The New Wittgenstein*, 137.

he decided, one could say and should say very little.[96] As he put it in *The Consequences of Pragmatism*:

> One can use language to criticize and enlarge itself, as one can exercise one's body to develop and strengthen and enlarge it, but one cannot see language-as-a-whole in relation to something else to which it applies, or for which it is a means to an end.[97]

By the end Rorty had concluded that the turn itself was no more than 'an unnecessary detour'.[98] It made sense to insist on language if the by-product was a different, more rhetorical conception of the philosopher's role, but 'there is nothing useful to say about the relation between two large entities called "Language" and "World"'.[99]

The challenge for the new Wittgensteinians is to explain comments such as the following, which Wittgenstein makes in a famous and oft-quoted letter to the poet Ludwig von Ficker, apparently in 1919. In it Wittgenstein says that he ought to have included the following in the preface to the *Tractatus*:

> My work consists of two parts: the one presented here plus all that I have *not* written. And it is precisely this second part that is the important one. My book draws limits to the sphere of the ethical from the inside as it were, and I am convinced that this is the ONLY *rigorous* way of drawing those limits. In short, I believe that where *many* others today are just *gassing*, I have managed in my book to put everything firmly into place by being silent about it.[100]

This would appear to be an ominous and meaningful silence. For Alain Badiou, such sentiments are evidence of what he calls Wittgenstein's 'antiphilosophical' position, which subordinates the enunciation of truth to the acting out of a unique ethical position.[101] Certainly the passage looks like an act of renunciation: a circumscribing of what one can say in language that at the same time devalues language for the very limits one has placed upon it. It's as if 'language as such' were condemned to banality, but could point, indirectly, to something important. For Conant and Diamond, however, the renunciation is illusory and the ominousness a mirage. Wittgenstein is illustrating the temptation of the mystical; in Conant's words, 'the idea that there are limits here confining one is the central idea that one needs to learn how to throw away'.[102] Wittgenstein isn't being silent because words would

---

[96] Richard Rorty, 'Ten Years After', in *The Linguistic Turn*, 2nd edn. (Chicago: University of Chicago Press, 1992), 368.

[97] Richard Rorty, 'Introduction: Pragmatism and Philosophy', in *The Consequences of Pragmatism (Essays 1972–1980)* (Minneapolis: University of Minnesota Press, 1982), xix.

[98] Richard Rorty, 'Wittgenstein and the Linguistic Turn', in *Philosophy as Cultural Politics: Philosophical Papers, Volume 4* (Cambridge: Cambridge University Press, 2007), 166.

[99] Rorty, 'Wittgenstein and the Linguistic Turn', 173.

[100] Letter from Wittgenstein to Ficker, in G. H. von Wright, 'The Origin of the *Tractatus*', in *Wittgenstein* (Oxford: Basil Blackwell, 1982), 83n32.

[101] Badiou, *Wittgenstein's Antiphilosophy*, 75–82.

[102] James Conant, 'Must We Show What We Cannot Say?', in Richard Fleming and Michael Payne (eds.), *The Senses of Stanley Cavell* (Lewisburg, PA: Bucknell University Press, 1989), 254.

befoul some ethical ideal, but is just telling us that, as Diamond has put it, 'there are not ethical problems whose solutions are thoughts'.[103]

About ten years after this letter Wittgenstein will deliver his 'Lecture on Ethics', where he claims that although those who continue to talk the talk, to speak nonsense by trying to speak about ethics, 'run against the boundaries of language', the tendency to do so is one he 'cannot help respecting deeply'.[104] Is Wittgenstein telling us, sympathetically, that people should stop banging their heads against the walls of language, or is he implying there is some interest or advantage in doing so? Diamond, interestingly enough, suggests we can have it both ways: ethical talk will be nonsensical, but worthwhile. For while nonsense is nonsense, there are occasions when speaking nonsense is important. Ethical statements, in which we ascribe a good or evil will to others, Diamond will designate 'attractive' nonsense, which we can use so long as we bear in mind what we are doing.[105] One is therefore *allowed* to speak nonsense, to use language in nonsensical ways, on condition that one acts as a 'self-aware user of nonsense'.[106] One is almost tempted to say that 'language as such' permits its own misuse.

It looks like an odd compromise, coming from a resolute reader who holds, in her own words, an 'austere view of nonsense' (which means there is no meaningful, 'showing' nonsense, just nonsense).[107] Why turn the ethical away from the house of language and then let it in by the back door? Part of the reason is that Diamond is herself an advocate for an ethics that depends less on arguments and evidence than on acts of imaginative identification and description, on the kinds of language use she believes are found in literary writing.[108] Another part of the reason is that Diamond realizes that Wittgenstein refuses to settle for scientific objectivity: while he insists that talk of ethics will inevitably be 'just *gassing*', he also insists that his work is ethical. Diamond's solution is to describe literary writing as an imaginative nonsense that one has to take seriously, and to imagine that Wittgenstein has provided a model of such imaginative nonsense in the *Tractatus* itself. Diamond is half-right: the *Tractatus*'s engagement in ethics should be thought of in literary terms. The problem is that she has chosen the wrong literature to compare him with: it's modernism that shows us how one can express the ethical without any 'gassing'.[109]

---

[103] Cora Diamond, 'Wittgenstein, Ludwig [Josef Johann] (1889–1951)', in Lawrence C. Becker and Charlotte B. Becker (eds.), *Encyclopedia of Ethics, Vol. II* (New York: Garland, 1992), 1321.

[104] Ludwig Wittgenstein, '[Lecture on Ethics] Established text of the Lecture', in *Lecture on Ethics*, ed. Edoardo Zamuner, Ermelinda Valentina Di Lascio, and D. K. Levy (Oxford: Wiley Blackwell, 2014), 51.

[105] Cora Diamond, 'Ethics, Imagination and the Method of Wittgenstein's *Tractatus*', in Richard Heinrich and Helmuth Vetter (eds.), *Bilder der Philosophie: Reflexionen über das Bildliche und die Phantasie* (Vienna: R. Oldenbourg, 1991), 55–90.

[106] Diamond, 'Ethics', 75.   [107] Diamond, 'Ethics', 60.

[108] An early statement of her case is Cora Diamond, 'Having a Rough Story about What Moral Philosophy Is', *New Literary History* 15.1 (1983): 155–69.

[109] As will become clear, I therefore define modernism differently from Stephen Mulhall, who claims Diamond for it in his 'Realism, Modernism and the Realistic Spirit: Diamond's Inheritance of Wittgenstein, Early and Late', *Nordic Wittgenstein Review* 1 (2012): 7–33.

Jürgen Habermas once characterized the *Tractatus* as leaving 'no middle ground between the coercion of deductive representation and the pathos of unmediated intuition'.[110] Diamond sets up Literature's camp precisely on that middle ground. In her 1991 essay on the *Tractatus* she claims that Wittgenstein's sense of good and evil—as attitudes to the world as a whole (itself something strictly unthinkable)—requires us to set 'talk about such evil apart from talk about how things go in the world, this way or that'.[111] Literary texts—her examples are two fairy tales collected by the Brothers Grimm and a Hawthorne short story—are able to ascribe this global evil to characters by an act of imagination: 'I have treated such ascriptions as cases of understanding a person as saying in his heart something that makes no sense, but something that we have the imaginative resources to grasp as attractive'.[112] In an essay on Martha Nussbaum two years later Diamond is more expansive, contrasting the deadness of moral philosophy, its preference for the detached investigator to literature's view of moral thinking as that which will 'not lie still to be investigated, but is made anew, and shaped in new ways, in our imaginative responses to life'.[113] Literature is not sense-making precisely because it exchanges the true-and-false game of deliberation for the 'shaping of the language of particularity', a language which conveys a deep sense of the value of a way of life and its specific possibilities.[114]

All of which might sound rather familiar to the English-language literary scholar. As Danièle Moyal-Sharrock has shown, Diamond's conception of imagination and individual responsiveness aligns her closely with the early twentieth-century, but profoundly anti-modernist critic F. R. Leavis, who, like Diamond, thought the moral force of literature lay in its ability to convey the thick texture and particularity of life.[115] Her notion of the literary is accordingly bound to Romantic conceptions of the imagination and her literary preferences—Wordsworth, Dickens, James, de la Mare—deeply nineteenth-century and conservative.[116]

The riposte to this particular way of valuing literature was made sixty years ago by Leavis's most penetrating critic, Raymond Williams. Williams pointed out that the very definition of Literature as the domain of a peculiarly imaginative and cultivated use of language, which takes place in the nineteenth century, had depended on the drastic narrowing of broader social and political claims for a creative and fulfilling life.[117] The touchstones of nineteenth-century literary value—responsiveness to individual experience, imaginative range and power, complexity

---

[110] Jürgen Habermas, *On the Logic of the Social Sciences*, trans. Shierry Weber Nicholsen and Jerry A. Stark (Cambridge, MA: MIT Press, 1988), 122.

[111] Diamond, 'Ethics', 88.   [112] Diamond, 'Ethics', 84.

[113] Cora Diamond, 'Martha Nussbaum and the Need for Novels', *Philosophical Investigations* 16.2 (1993): 144.

[114] Diamond, 'Martha Nussbaum', 153.

[115] Danièle Moyal-Sharrock, 'Cora Diamond and the Ethical Imagination', *British Journal of Aesthetics* 52.3 (2012): 223–40.

[116] See also, for a different take on the matter, Charles Altieri, *Reckoning with the Imagination: Wittgenstein and the Aesthetics of Literary Experience* (Ithaca: Cornell University Press, 2015).

[117] The argument is made in Raymond Williams, *Culture and Society, 1780–1950* (London: Chatto & Windus, 1958). See in particular the chapter 'The Romantic Artist' (30–48) and the comments on Leavis (252–63).

of feeling—were extolled as a specialized alternative to the social values that had overwhelmed Britain as a consequence of industrial capitalism. Dickens could make fun of the Gradgrinds of the world (and Diamond can endorse his criticism), but he made fun of them in the name of the 'cultural' values embodied in books, not an alternative social order. Literary writing, 'culture', was thus valued as imaginative, responsive, full of complex feeling precisely to the extent that it was contrasted with "'society" [...] often seen as essentially general and abstract: the summaries and averages, rather than the direct substance, of human living'.[118] Those summaries and averages included not only the statistical world discussed above, but the mechanisms and procedures of mass democracy itself, which were seen as levelling and quantitative. To escape this specializing cubby-hole, this Literary insistence on a narrow, purely bookish 'culture', Williams argued one had to turn precisely to those who had forced their way into public political life, to the working-class culture that had established itself in the same period. But even to see that culture as 'culture' one had to understand that working-class culture 'is primarily social (in that it has created institutions) rather than individual (in particular individual or imaginative work)'. Acknowledging that would, in turn, allow one to recognize 'the collective democratic institution, whether in the trade unions, the cooperative movement or a political party' as a 'very remarkable *creative* achievement [emphasis mine]'.[119] Diamond's intention is to take Wittgenstein's side, against the extravagant claims of the culture of science, but the claim for literature as 'attractive nonsense' ends up in the same specializing place. For the distinction between the 'imaginative' use of language in literature and 'talk of how things go in this world, this way and that' occludes the 'collective democratic institution' or proletarian public sphere as surely as Pearson's scientific professionalism did. In place of public debate and collective will, we have individual sympathy and complex ethical feeling.

MODERNIST IRONY

Wittgenstein had no faith in the collective democratic institution, either; he expresses his ethical dissatisfaction in stylistic and literary terms. The relevant literature, though, isn't Dickens or Wordsworth, but the modernism that had transformed the literary field itself by the time of the *Tractatus*. His friend Paul Engelmann once claimed Wittgenstein thought literature patrolled 'the border between genuine and sham emotion'.[120] The worry about sham emotion was a common one, fuelled by fear of the late-Romantic inflation of subjectivity on the one hand, and the sensationalism of the new mass culture on the other. It drew on the fear that the emotions and feelings communicated through public performance and the newer

---

[118] Raymond Williams, 'Literature', in *Marxism and Literature* (Oxford: Oxford University Press, 1977), 45.
[119] Williams, *Culture and Society*, 327.
[120] Paul Engelmann, *Letters from Ludwig Wittgenstein, With a Memoir* (Oxford: Basil Blackwell, 1967), 86.

media—newspapers and magazines in particular—were inauthentic, that they were the result of our old friend 'imitation' and its cousin, 'fashion'.

As Peter Nicholls has argued, modernism responded to the fear of repetition and imitation, to the perceived falseness of Romantic pathos, by means of irony.[121] The red-haired beggar girl Charles Baudelaire writes about might seem to incarnate a natural, unaffected beauty, but the poem's 'second, more devious voice will force upon the reader the unsentimental and cruelly ironic recognition that in fact she is nothing without the artifice of his poem to commemorate her'.[122] Flaubert will ridicule the literary clichés that organize Emma Bovary's life, while his 'countervailing model of verbal precision—the novel itself—tacitly proposes a "genuine" aesthetic as a ground of critical distance'.[123] For an emerging modernism, legitimate aesthetic feeling will be borne by the perfection of an ironizing literary style 'rather than by an act of imaginative identification'.[124]

Von Ficker, the addressee of Wittgenstein's comments on ethics and silence, was the editor of a German avant-garde periodical to which Wittgenstein had donated a tidy sum in 1914. It's true that Wittgenstein wasn't enthusiastic about all the writers von Ficker supported (although he was keen enough on Georg Trakl and Rainer Maria Rilke) and that his own artistic tastes—particularly when it came to the fundamental art for him, music—were conservative rather than avant-garde.[125] But, as John Holbo has observed, there's a disjunction between what Wittgenstein said about the arts and the practice of his own craft: arguments for his conservatism tend to quote liberally from the private comments contained in the collection *Culture and Value* at the expense of the texts he composed.[126] For those texts display a commitment to a modernist expressiveness distant from the nineteenth-century models on which Diamond relies. Nor is Wittgenstein unaware of what he's about, for in a slightly earlier letter to von Ficker he'll claim of the *Tractatus* that 'the work is strictly philosophical and at the same time literary: but there's no gassing in it'.[127] Literary, but with no gassing in it: as neat a definition of modernism as one is likely to find.

Hostility to 'gassing' could take several forms and have a variety of objects: it could be Flaubert's ironizing of the aspirations of his characters, Joyce's open parody

---

[121] Peter Nicholls, *Modernisms: A Literary Guide* (London: Macmillan, 1995), 'Ironies of the Modern', 5–23.

[122] Nicholls, *Modernisms*, 2.   [123] Nicholls, *Modernisms*, 20.

[124] Nicholls, *Modernisms*, 20.

[125] Wittgenstein's donation to von Ficker and his interest—or lack thereof—in the writers von Ficker helped with the donation are described in Monk, *Wittgenstein*, 106–10. An interesting account of Wittgenstein's appreciation for Trakl's poetry is Charles Altieri and Sascha Bru, 'Trakl's Tone: Mood and the Distinctive Speech Act of the Demonstrative', in Sascha Bru, Wolfgang Huemer, and Daniel Steuer (eds.), *Wittgenstein Reading* (Berlin: de Gruyter, 2013), 355–72.

[126] John Holbo, review of John Gibson and Wolfgang Huemer (eds.), *The Literary Wittgenstein*, Notre Dame Philosophical Reviews, 2 June 2005 (http://ndpr.nd.edu/news/24797-the-literary-wittgenstein/, accessed 23 July 2013). As Holbo puts it: 'Therefore, there is reason to suspect that reading his *modernist* masterpieces—*Tractatus, Philosophical Investigations*—in the light of the likes of *Culture and Value* risks fostering a misleading sense of the latter's place and function.'

[127] Letter from Wittgenstein to Ficker (October 1919?), in von Wright, 'The Origin of the *Tractatus*', 81n30.

of Irish nationalism, or critiques of political rhetoric by Ezra Pound and Wyndham Lewis.[128] Closer to Wittgenstein's Viennese home, it could be the satire of Johann Nestroy (whose work Wittgenstein knew well and who provides the epigraph for the later *Philosophical Investigations*) or the mocking sarcasm of Karl Kraus, whom Wittgenstein admired deeply and named as an influence in later life.[129] Where overblown rhetoric was the object, the sometimes implicit, sometimes explicit accusation was that, whether commercial, social, or political, it lived off imprecision, fuzziness, words untethered from meanings and things; the modernist retort was characteristically an emphasis on sharpness and clarity, exemplified in acts of immediate perception. 'The point', as Wittgenstein would himself put it in a New Year's Day conversation in 1931, 'is seeing, not proving'.[130] Seeing, which is, of course, the flip side of showing: when you grasp something that can only be shown, indicated indirectly, you grasp it in the form of an immediate perceptual experience—at once, without the need for interpretation. Logical sentences display or show the properties of language and '[t]his means that by merely looking at them you can *see* these properties'.[131] Merely by looking at them, and, in a sense, *only* by looking them. Seeing therefore manifests what Roman Jakobson, the Russian Formalist theorist of literature, will call in a pamphlet published the same year as the *Tractatus*, a 'set' or 'orientation' towards expression, i.e., towards the immediate and graspable surface of the discourse.[132]

It's a different theorist of literature who, however, provides the most telling and profound comparison with Wittgenstein: his Central European contemporary, Georg Lukács. Lukács was destined for a very different life than Wittgenstein and the intellectual commitments from which he started would have been alien to Wittgenstein, but in 1914–15, not yet a Marxist literary critic and political activist, he was composing *The Theory of the Novel*. Lukács's starting point was the rationalization of the modern world that Weber had written about: the novel was an attempt to recreate the totalizing force and reach of the classical epic in 'an age in which the extensive totality of life is no longer directly given, in which the immanence of meaning in life has become a problem, yet which still thinks in

---

[128] On modernist attitudes to rhetoric, see Matthias Somers, 'Modernism and Rhetoric: Literary Culture and Public Speech, 1900–1940' (PhD dissertation, Katholieke Universiteit Leuven, 2015), particularly the Introduction and Chapter 2.

[129] On the significance of Nestroy for Wittgenstein, see David G. Stern, *Wittgenstein's Philosophical Investigations: An Introduction* (Cambridge: Cambridge University Press, 2004), 56–71.

[130] Ludwig Wittgenstein, *Wittgenstein and the Vienna Circle: Conversations Recorded by Friedrich Waismann*, trans. Joachim Schulte and Brian McGuinness (Oxford: Basil Blackwell, 1979), 146.

[131] Wittgenstein, 'Notes Dictated to G. E. Moore in Norway, April 1914', 108.

[132] Roman Jakobson, *Noveishaia russkaia poeziia: nabrosok pervyi* [Contemporary Russian Poetry: An Initial Outline] (Prague: Politika, 1921), 10. Like many of the Russian Formalists, Jakobson was an avid reader of Husserl, whose philosophy had also depended on the refusal of depth and a focus on the things themselves, via the so-called 'bracketing' of the world depicted by signs (see §§31–2 in Edmund Husserl, *Ideas: General Introduction to Pure Phenomenology*, trans. W. R. Boyce Gibson (New York: Collier, 1962)). On Jakobson's debt to phenomenology, see Elmar Holenstein, *Roman Jakobson's Approach to Language: Phenomenological Structuralism* (Bloomington: Indiana University Press, 1977); Peter Steiner, *Russian Formalism: A Metapoetics* (Ithaca: Cornell University Press, 1984), 201–3; Dušan Radunović, 'Debates on Form in Russian Studies of Language and Art (1915–1929): Theoretical and Institutional Dynamics' (PhD dissertation, University of Sheffield, 2008), chapter 2.

terms of totality'.[133] The modern world fit together, but according to a formal, means-orientated rationality that left the meaning or significance of every action in abeyance. If novels nevertheless aimed to represent such a world as meaningful—which they would have to do, to fulfil their aesthetic vocation—the task could hardly be straightforward. Merely representing the world as if it were held together by some higher principle or force, as if it were something besides, as Wittgenstein put it, 'a totality of facts', would be to provide it with an arbitrary subjective coating. To simply record the events and facts as purposeless but related, would, on the other hand, leave us with something that would hardly be recognizable as a world at all. '[T]he objectivity of the novel is', as a consequence, 'the mature man's knowledge that meaning can never quite penetrate reality, but that, without meaning, reality would disintegrate into the nothingness of inessentiality'.[134]

This maturity takes the form of an overarching, complete irony. That is, the novelist not only ironizes the protagonist's inevitably failed search for meaning, but makes their own reflection on the matter, the novel's search for meaning in a world of facts, so to speak, an object of the same irony.[135] Irony is 'the objectivity of the novel' in the sense that the prose text must represent at once the effort to render the novelistic world meaningful in its details and as a whole, and its failure. The *Tractatus*, too, takes it as given that the world is meaningless, although coherent. It consists of the totality of facts, but this totality is structured by logical relations: larger ('molecular') propositions are summaries of the results of atomic propositions (so that proposition A is true when propositions a and b are true, or if a is true and b false, etc.). As a consequence, the world itself is a sphere of accident, the mere concatenation of facts: 'In the world everything is as it is, and everything happens as it does happen.'[136] Wittgenstein does not, however, leave the matter at that:

> If there is any value that does have value, it must lie outside the whole sphere of what happens and is the case. For all that happens and is the case is accidental.
>
> What makes it non-accidental cannot lie *within* the world, since if it did it would itself be accidental. It must lie outside the world.[137]

If there is a 'sense' beyond the world, it cannot be like the protagonist's search for meaning, merely within the world, but must be like the novelist's, the very condition of that world's objectivity. It *must* lie outside the world, but *does* it? Here is where the reflective irony comes in. For Wittgenstein says both that one can't 'assert' that the world is a meaningful whole, as if that could be a fact (which can only be claimed within the world), and that he feels compelled nevertheless to assert this in the form

---

[133] Georg Lukács, *The Theory of the Novel*, trans. Anna Bostock (Cambridge, MA: MIT Press, 1973), 56.

[134] Lukács, *Theory of the Novel*, 88.

[135] For an account of Lukács's concept of irony, see the chapter 'Transcendental Dialectic: Irony as Form', in J. M. Bernstein, *The Philosophy of the Novel: Lukács, Marxism and the Dialectics of Form* (Minneapolis: University of Minnesota Press, 1984), 185–227. Interestingly enough, while Bernstein does not explicitly invoke Wittgenstein as a comparison, he twice quotes him without attribution in his account of the reified, rationalized world that Lukács sees as the novel's raw material (though the quotations are referred to in the index entry under 'Wittgenstein').

[136] Wittgenstein, *Tractatus*, 6.41.   [137] Wittgenstein, *Tractatus*, 6.41.

of ethics. Lukács will interestingly describe this ambiguous position as 'demonic', an irrational force with the aspirations, but not the power of divinity. Mere acceptance of the world can only be countered by a demonic ethical impulse:

> [T]he indolent self-complacency of this quietly decaying life would be the only power in the world if men did not sometimes fall prey to the power of the demon and over-reach themselves in ways that have no reason and cannot be explained by reason, challenging all the psychological or sociological foundations of their existence. Then, suddenly, the God-forsakenness of the world reveals itself as a lack of substance, as an irrational mixture of density and permeability.[138]

It's the same irrational 'overreaching' that Wittgenstein can neither rationalize nor resist, the running 'against the boundaries of language' that is simultaneously hopeless and admirable. The logically coherent world given form by the *Tractatus* is at once exquisite in its detail and its order ('crystalline' is the word Wittgenstein uses to describe it in the *Philosophical Investigations*) and yet valueless: only the ethical impulse that encompasses it, without altering its details, can endow it with meaning.[139] Good or bad willing, Wittgenstein points out, makes the world 'an altogether different world. It must, so to speak, wax and wane as a whole.'[140] Nor does it really matter that 'all that happens and is the case' in the *Tractatus* is the world described by natural science, not sociology. For Wittgenstein's Tractarian philosophy assumes that the social world can only be factual (and therefore logically coherent) insofar as all values, indeed all beliefs, are considered external to it (he will notoriously refuse to think that belief-sentences—e.g., 'He thought Jews were responsible for the German defeat in World War One.'—are bearers of truth and falsity like other propositions).[141]

But is this so different from what the New Wittgensteinians propose? Doesn't claiming that the *Tractatus* undermines its own propositions, revealing, gradually, that what look like statements are actually examples of the nonsense we must give up, make it an instance of irony, of serious claims appearing somewhat ludicrous in the rear-view mirror of the text? Some recent accounts of irony have even suggested that irony entails an 'imaginary scene' in which the speaker contemplates taking seriously a statement which is then undercut or mocked, which would seem to echo Diamond's interpretation of Wittgenstein's text.[142] But Diamond and Conant believe that Wittgenstein's self-undoing points to a solution, not a deadlock, providing a way out of philosophical perplexity and confusion. But a solution is only possible if the problem is philosophy, rather than the world it is entangled with: to the extent there is a deadlock, for Diamond and Conant, it's a philosophical deadlock, which, granted, can't be solved by pointing to an answer, but can be resolved by means of Wittgenstein's self-ironizing discourse.

---

[138] Lukács, *Theory of the Novel*, 90.
[139] Wittgenstein, *Philosophical Investigations*, §107 (51e).
[140] Wittgenstein, *Tractatus*, 6.43.   [141] Wittgenstein, *Tractatus*, 5.541–5.542.
[142] Louis de Saussure and Peter Schulz, 'Subjectivity out of Irony', *Semiotica* 173.1–4 (2009): 397–416, especially 400. See also Deirdre Wilson and Dan Sperber, 'On Verbal Irony', *Lingua* 87 (1992): 53–76.

I've been arguing, though, that at this historical moment problems of language stand metonymically for social and political problems that have become acute. Doesn't the New Wittgensteinian reading simply brush such considerations aside? In fact, Diamond ends up confronting them in a revealing way. In a more recent reading of the *Tractatus* (which appears to be a revision of her earlier 'Ethics, Imagination and the Method of Wittgenstein's *Tractatus*'), Diamond explains how Wittgenstein's philosophical writing transforms our perspective on the world, even though it can make no argument about the world as such. But that world as such, the world of everything that is the case, as established by propositions, is described in the most interesting terms:

> Prior to the transformation that can be effected by philosophy, we are similarly in the midst of things, immersed in seeings and doings and sayings in the world. We investigate whether things stand this way or that; we do things to bring about this or that effect; we say that things stand thus-and-so.[143]

In three respects this looks quite different from the world Wittgenstein portrays. First, there is no mention here (or elsewhere in Diamond's chapter) of the limitation of the sphere of propositions to natural science; 'seeings and doings and sayings of the world' would appear to cover a wider range. Second, here propositions are bound up with practice—'we do things', having investigated and spoken, as if the propositional reasoning was instrumental and practical. Finally, while it is not explicitly articulated, it certainly sounds like 'we say that things stand thus-and-so' to *someone*: being in 'the midst of things' entails an intersubjective give-and-take. Let us take one more, admittedly speculative, interpretative step: this world looks like a public sphere attached to civil society, in which investigations and claims are made, practical solutions sought, and matters—whether 'things stand thus-and-so'—are debated.

Philosophy and art, in this account of the *Tractatus*, bring about a 'transformation in our relation to all that is accidental', such that we respond to it with satisfaction rather than discontent, and this is its ethical achievement. But if 'all that is accidental' is a world arrived at through 'seeings and doings and sayings' then regarding it with satisfaction doesn't seem much of a stretch: being 'in the midst of things' looks almost too good to be true. Because, of course, it is too good to be true. Diamond's world, in which we investigate, do stuff, and say things, is far more comfortable and habitable than the world of natural science conveyed in the *Tractatus*. It isn't hard to imagine being satisfied with it, because Diamond has used Wittgenstein's sphere of natural scientific propositions as a metonym for what looks like a fairly peaceable version (there is doing and saying, but no struggling or fighting) of our ordinary practical life.

But 'all that is accidental' is not arrived at in the *Tractatus* through anything responsive and active—as even Diamond's use of gerunds (seeings, doings, sayings) implies—but by something that looks a lot more like solitary measurement (when

---

[143] Cora Diamond, 'The *Tractatus* and the Limits of Sense', in Oskari Kuusela and Marie McGinn (eds.), *The Oxford Handbook of Wittgenstein* (Oxford: Oxford University Press, 2013), 258.

Wittgenstein introduces the idea of picturing reality, he says that the picture 'is laid against reality like a measure').[144] It's tempting to read the *Tractatus* as simply reserving truth and knowledge for science—exemplified by Hertz's mechanics—and pushing ethics and aesthetics into the place usually occupied by religious contemplation ('what is mystical' in Wittgenstein's description).[145] But the first object of the *Tractatus*'s irony is science itself or, to be more precise, certain mythic versions of science: science as that which, through the discovery of a network of natural laws, explains the world around us. It is surely no accident that the passages which precede the 'mystical' section of the *Tractatus* (6.373–6.54)—where Wittgenstein discusses will, God, death, and the problem of life's sense—are dedicated to the debunking of scientific myth. At 6.3 Wittgenstein makes an opening gambit—'outside logic everything is accidental'—and from there insists that there is no causal, empirical necessity, no natural laws in the inherited sense of the term and no *explanation* of nature. The conclusion to this short series of remarks rebukes the 'whole modern conception of the world' for 'the illusion that the so-called laws of nature are the explanations of natural phenomena'. 'Thus', Wittgenstein argues, 'people today stop at the laws of nature, treating them as something inviolable, just as God and Fate were treated in past ages.'[146]

If we think about the *Tractatus* as analogous to the novels described by Lukács, we could say that the protagonist of the work—the voice that analyses the scientific proposition—discovers that the world is meaningless, but *not* because it is ruled by science. It discovers that the totality of facts isn't even meaningful *as* science. The totality of facts is not a whole stretching from axioms through natural laws down to the tiniest empirical details, but a combination of sheer form and empirical happenstance. That the world is a comfortable and meaningful domain of empirical happenings is the first illusion to be shattered. The 'novelist' of the work, who wants to make something meaningful out of the *Tractatus* itself, then demonstrates that that meaning cannot be rescued by the discourse of the work itself, for it wants to say 'the inexpressible', but can't (to say it would amount to mere 'gassing'). It can only express 'the second part', the 'important' part of the book indirectly, by 'making itself manifest' [*zeigt sich*] in the form of irony.[147]

Let's put the matter more pointedly, if also somewhat crudely: the irony in Wittgenstein's text is the revenge of the semantic and the intersubjective. What is 'made manifest' or 'shown' is visible only as distance between the act of enunciation (the 'instance of discourse', in Benveniste's terminology) and the enunciated proposition. Much of the *Tractatus* is written in a voice we might call the ponderous indicative (from '1 The world is all that is the case' to '7 What we cannot speak about we must pass over in silence') and its elaborate numbered hierarchy implies

---

[144] Wittgenstein, *Tractatus*, 2.1512.   [145] Wittgenstein, *Tractatus*, 6.522.
[146] Wittgenstein, *Tractatus* 6.371–2. There is nothing particularly original about this diagnosis, which was shared by numerous scientists of the time, including Karl Pearson: see Porter, *Karl Pearson*, 198–204.
[147] Wittgenstein, *Tractatus*, 6.522 I have borrowed 'the inexpressible' from the translation by C. K. Ogden (*Tractatus Logico-Philosophicus* [London: Routledge, 1981]); 'making itself manifest' is an adaptation of the Pears/McGuinness translation.

tightness of structure and articulation. But the saying of all this from one person to another, the enunciation of the work, 'shows how little is achieved when these problems are solved'.[148] Science has taken the place of Madame Bovary.

AN AESTHETIC OF CLARIFICATION

Wittgenstein did not speak of irony—he transposed the elements I've described as ironic into an aesthetic of clarification, which, in attenuated form, came to be shared by analytic philosophers in his wake. When philosophers offered more logically perspicuous paraphrases or translations of ordinary sentences, the changes they made merely clarified or brought to the surface a logic already at work in ordinary language. But why do it? What was the 'added value' of the clearer translation? Frege and Russell, as we've seen, thought they were perfecting a more precise and exacting instrument for thought, which would bring philosophy closer to science. Wittgenstein, on the other hand, believed that 'clarity, transparency is an end in itself. I am not interested in erecting a building, but in having the foundations of possible buildings transparently before me.'[149] His irony had the shape of taking clarity too seriously.

He was not alone in this. In the avant-garde art contemporary with him, the constructivist wing of modernism attempted to make functionality, objectivity, and mechanism into aesthetic values: the clarity with which an object displayed its workings was a measure of its aesthetic worth.[150] Wittgenstein's main contact with this kind of modernism was through the architect Adolf Loos, author of the modernist architectural manifesto, 'Ornament as Crime', whom Wittgenstein would meet in 1914 (when Wittgenstein made his own debut as an architect in 1926–8, he would design a home of the most austere functionalist sort for his sister).[151] Edward Harcourt has suggested that Wittgenstein's hostility to decorative notation

---

[148] Wittgenstein, *Tractatus*, Preface, 5.

[149] Wittgenstein, 'Sketch for a Foreword', MS 109: 204, 6–7 November 1930, in *Culture and Value*, revised edn., trans. Peter Winch (Oxford: Basil Blackwell, 1998), 9e. A good current example of the instrumental attitude is provided by Timothy Williamson: 'The rise of modern logic from Frege onwards has provided philosophers with conceptual instruments of unprecedented power and precision, enabling them to formulate hypotheses with more clarity and to determine their consequences with more reliability than ever before.' Timothy Williamson, 'Past the Linguistic Turn?' in Brian Leiter (ed.), *The Future for Philosophy* (Oxford: Clarendon Press, 2004), 127.

[150] There were various versions of this, stretching from Pound's Imagism to Soviet Constructivism. The version that makes the tidiest comparison to Wittgenstein is probably the *Neue Sachlichkeit* (New Objectivity) of Germany and Austria. An expansive and classic description is found in John Willett, *The New Sobriety, 1917–1933: Art and Politics in the Weimar Period* (London: Thames and Hudson, 1978); but see also Peter Wollen's account of the machine aesthetic, 'Modern Times: Cinema/Americanism/The Robot', in *Raiding the Icebox: Reflections on Twentieth-Century Culture* (London: Verso: 1993), 35–71.

[151] Loos makes an appearance in Wittgenstein's notorious 1931 list of influences; see *Culture and Value*, 16e. Interestingly, the two major English-language biographies of Wittgenstein offer radically different accounts of Wittgenstein's reaction to meeting the great Viennese architect. Brian McGuinness notes his disappointment (*Wittgenstein: A Life—Young Ludwig, 1889–1921* (Berkeley: University of California Press, 1988, 281)) while Ray Monk reports enthusiasm (*Wittgenstein*, 108). On Wittgenstein's architectural exploits see Paul Wijdeveld, *Ludwig Wittgenstein, Architect* (Amsterdam:

is akin to Loos's hostility to 'useless' ornament.[152] But Lukács (whose modernist preferences, even in 1914, were quite different) provides a model that better explains not only the form this clarity takes, but the pathos associated with it. Clarity is an end in itself when it culminates in the properly ironic attitude towards the God-forsaken world, what Lukács calls at various points in *The Theory of the Novel* the 'mature man's knowledge', a 'virile maturity', or '[t]he melancholy of the adult state'.[153] Clarity yields, on this reading, 'genuine' rather than 'sham' emotion, a melancholy pleasure derived from using language beyond its literal, propositional sense, in the knowledge that its literal sense breeds illusion.[154]

The analytic style of philosophy that followed Wittgenstein and Russell echoed the concern with clarification, while ditching Wittgenstein's melancholy resignation. To some extent philosophers were simply making themselves at home in the culture of science I described earlier. The philosopher who did most to make the lodgings comfortable was Russell himself, who argued that philosophy was in all essential respects continuous with science. 'A scientific philosophy such as I wish to recommend', intoned Russell, 'will be piecemeal and tentative like other sciences'. Science's success depended, above all else, on the 'possibility of successive approximations': 'to transfer this possibility to philosophy is to ensure a progress in method whose importance it would be almost impossible to exaggerate'.[155] This meant philosophy should make analysis, the decomposition of matter into constituent parts and relations between them, its mode of operation. This was, in the first case, a matter of ontology: when Russell broke with idealism, it was on the basis of what he would later call 'the apparently piecemeal and higgledy-piggledy nature of the world' (which was constituted of objects with external relations among them).[156] But it was also a matter of method; in a world built of separate parts, falsified propositions could be jettisoned without endangering the theory as a whole.

But science was also a way of life, with the virtues Pearson had attributed to it. Russell's 1945 *History of Western Philosophy* ended with an encomium for 'scientific truthfulness, by which I mean the habit of basing our beliefs upon observations and inferences as impersonal, and as much divested of local and temperamental

---

The Pepin Press, 1993). On the wider context of his asceticism, see Brian McGuinness, 'Asceticism and Ornament', in *Approaches to Wittgenstein*, 17–26.

[152] Edward Harcourt and Richard Marshall, 'Wittgenstein's Ethical Enterprise and Related Matters' (Interview with Edward Harcourt), *3:AM Magazine*, 19 November 2016, http://www.3ammagazine.com/3am/wittgensteins-ethical-enterprise-related-matters/, accessed 21 June 2017.

[153] 'The novel is the art-form of virile maturity', Lukács, *Theory of the Novel*, 71. The 'melancholy of the adult state', 86.

[154] Diamond claims that if our attitude to the world remains one of 'resignation', as I've suggested here, we have not gone through the final change of perspective the *Tractatus* demands of us (Diamond, 'The *Tractatus* and the Limits of Sense', 261–3). The final step is the moment when one realizes there is nothing to be resigned about—then one is apparently satisfied. I'll just say that the satisfaction one arrives at here is a very attenuated version of happiness, precisely the kind one is 'resigned to'.

[155] Bertrand Russell, 'On Scientific Method in Philosophy' (1914), in *Mysticism and Logic and Other Essays* (London: Longmans, Green and Co., 1918), 113.

[156] Bertrand Russell, 'Philosophy in the Twentieth Century', *The Dial* 77 (October 1924): 283, or *Sceptical Essays* (London: Allen & Unwin, 1928), 70.

bias, as is possible for human beings'.[157] Impersonality as a cure for local bias: it's a substitute for the other, somewhat more difficult cure—a democratic public sphere. If the former removes bias by something akin to surgical intervention—involving technical equipment (logical vocabulary) and highly skilled personnel—then the latter depends on more amorphous, but ultimately more far-reaching changes to the 'lifestyle' of a political community: to wit, the institution of procedures for the kind of open public debate that should ensure only the best argument will win.[158]

Analytic philosophy by and large followed Russell's lead. As Juliet Floyd has put it, Russell was influential

> [n]ot because he offered correct views or an exact philosophy satisfactory in all details, or bequeathed several different conceptions of what analytic method could achieve, but because he invented the *idea* of scientific philosophy with which many of us now live: the brief article, the piecemeal approach, the opportunistic use of results of contemporary science, the problem- and solution-oriented thinking, the engagement with social issues, the concern to debunk religion in favor of naturalism (if only by way of a naturalism at times only halfway embraced).[159]

To this one can add (in J. J. Ross's words) a style that 'placed emphasis on the colleague rather than the master' and which 'rejected the dramatic style which sought striking examples to intensify what we see and feel'.[160] In this way philosophy availed itself of scientific virtues, without having much to do with natural science itself. When the journal *Analysis* was launched in 1933, its statement of editorial policy insisted its main concern would be 'the elucidation or explanation of facts, or groups of facts, the general nature of which is, by common consent, already known; rather than with attempts to establish new kinds of fact about the world, of very wide scope, or on a very large scale'.[161]

The facts to be clarified were varied. They were not usually, in England at any rate, scientific facts (unlike the philosophers on the continent inspired by the *Tractatus*—the so-called Vienna Circle or 'logical positivists'—who aimed to turn philosophy into a logic of science). Much of the elucidation was turned inward, towards problems and puzzles generated by philosophy itself. In a lecture on 'The Justification of Analysis' given by G. E. Moore in 1933, Moore dismissed the idea that analysis made a significant clarifying difference to either our everyday use of language or even to our practices of argument: analysis was only of significant use in solving philosophical puzzles (by showing they were often based on

---

[157] Bertrand Russell, *History of Western Philosophy and its Connection with Political and Social Circumstances from the Earliest Times to the Present Day* (London: George Allen & Unwin, 1946), 864.

[158] Jürgen Habermas has argued, often and at length, that in modern societies the objective validity of claims depends on particular procedures of argument (which seek to guarantee that the best argument will be successful). Democratic will-formation relies on the institutionalization of these procedures: see, for example, Chapter 7, 'Deliberative Politics: A Procedural Concept of Democracy', in *Between Facts and Norms*, trans. William Rehg (Cambridge: Polity Press, 1997), 287–328.

[159] Juliet Floyd, 'Recent Themes in the History of Early Analytic Philosophy', *Journal of the History of Philosophy* 47.2 (2009): 179.

[160] J. J. Ross, 'Analytic Philosophy as a Matter of Style', in Anat Biletzki and Anat Matar (eds.), *The Story of Analytic Philosophy: Plot and Heroes* (London: Routledge, 1998), 61.

[161] 'A Statement of Policy', *Analysis* 1.1 (1933): 1.

nonsensical questions).[162] Others, however, had bigger plans. Gilbert Ryle claimed his analysis of the distinction between 'knowing how' and 'knowing that' was aimed at an 'intellectualist' confusion that afflicted arguments made throughout the social sciences, in trade as well as academic texts.[163] In an infamous exchange with his student and friend Norman Malcolm in 1939, Wittgenstein was horrified to hear him use the phrase 'national character', so horrified that five years later he referred back to the incident, telling Malcolm it had made him consider 'what is the use of studying philosophy [...] if it does not improve your thinking about the important questions of everyday life, if it does not make you more conscientious than any... journalist in the use of *dangerous phrases* such people use for their own ends'.[164] Clarification was unquestionably good—but there wasn't unanimity over what it was good for.

Nor was clarification destined to retain its exalted significance: W. V. O. Quine would deal it a serious blow in 1951, when he attempted to bury the distinction between the truth of empirical scientific propositions and the analytical truth of philosophical ones (if all propositions were, at some remove or another, elements of an empirically testable theory, then the difference between philosophical clarification and scientific investigation thinned considerably).[165] As the linguistic turn began to run out of steam a few years later (which we will talk about nearer the end of this book), when Hilary Putnam noticed that something called 'analytic metaphysics' was appearing on the philosophical agenda, clarification had to cede pride of place to the establishment of metaphysical truths, which were certainly 'new kinds of fact about the world'.[166] The rise and fall of clarity's fortunes were tied not to pressing problems and confusions in science, politics, or everyday life, but to the linguistic turn itself. For, as Karl-Otto Apel has pointed out, thinking of the Vienna Circle, in the first instance: 'This "analysis", however, which is considered so revolutionary, is not applied to the objective facts of science, but rather to the sentences of science, i.e. not to things, but to the language that speaks of these things.'[167] Clarification, as the method and aim of philosophy, depended on the idea that

---

[162] G. E. Moore, 'The Justification of Analysis', *Analysis* 1.2 (1934): 28–30.

[163] Gilbert Ryle, 'Knowing How and Knowing That: The Presidential Address', *Proceedings of the Aristotelian Society*, New Series 46 (1945–6): 1–16. Ryle claimed that 'knowing how' constituted a kind of skilled practice that did not depend on the 'intellectualist' belief that one had to know something propositionally before doing anything intelligently. That this 'intellectualist' fallacy was widespread in the period around the war and was thus not merely a matter of philosophical interest has been established by Michael Kremer in a fascinating article: 'Ryle's "Intellectualist Legend" in Historical Context', *Journal for the History of Analytical Philosophy* 5.5 (2017): 16–39.

[164] Letter from Wittgenstein to Norman Malcolm, November 1944, quoted in Norman Malcolm, *Ludwig Wittgenstein: A Memoir* (London: Oxford University Press, 1958), 39. The original incident is recounted on p. 32.

[165] See W. V. O. Quine, 'Two Dogmas of Empiricism', in *From a Logical Point of View*, 2nd edn. (Cambridge, MA: Harvard University Press, 1980), 20–46. A telling, but not fatal blow because at the time there were arguments against Quine, because clarification maintained its prestige in some quarters, and because you could fairly describe much of what Quine himself did as 'clarification'.

[166] Hilary Putnam, 'A Half Century of Philosophy, Viewed from Within', *Daedalus* 126.1(1997): 188–9.

[167] Karl-Otto Apel, *Analytic Philosophy of Language and the Geisteswissenschaften* (Dordrecht: D. Reidel, 1967), 2.

philosophy should be preoccupied with 'language with a capital L', because language (with a capital L) was itself responsible for things being unclear.

Lack of clarity was described, persistently, as nonsense: not fuzziness, ambivalence, or evasiveness. Just as there was disagreement over what needed to be clarified, there was disagreement over the sources of nonsense: philosophers like Frege and Russell, and later A. J. Ayer and the Vienna Circle, believed it originated in the confusions of everyday language, in ethical talk or in existentialist philosophy; philosophers like Wittgenstein, and later J. L. Austin, thought it was the result of people trying to do philosophy in the first place. But local disputes over whom to blame and where the rot was worst masked the deeper consensus, the conviction that nonsense was ultimately the result of, as Wittgenstein famously put it, 'the bewitchment of our understanding by the resources of our language'.[168] This meant that the nonsense in question was structural and formal: not the effusion of a delirious mind or a playful manner, but something that issued spontaneously from language as such. In fact, the nonsense that language produced was the consequence of the very same mechanism that produced linguistic sense: this was nonsense that closely resembled sense, resembled it so closely that we needed skilled, trained philosophers to weed it out. Frege, Russell, Wittgenstein, and the rest weren't bothered by nonsense which anyone could recognize as such, but by phrases, sentences, and expressions that *misled* those who read or heard them, leading them to imagine the words had significance when they didn't. To put it this way, however, is to acknowledge that language could not be nonsensical on its own. As Stuart Hampshire shrewdly noted, 'Strictly it is not language which is clear or muddled, but we who are clear or muddled.'[169] Muddled, apparently, because we understood similar-looking phrases and sentences to have similar meanings: we thought that 'M is an object' must mean something like 'X is an apple'.

Or did we? To become confused by syntactic and grammatical similarities, language users would have to interpret statements as if language were a fixed, 'semiotic' structure, a code in which context and intention would make no difference to what a statement meant or how it was shaped. Which is to say they would have to understand everyday language as if it were a formally consistent, consciously designed language like Frege's concept-script, rather than the sediment of countless instances of the 'reality of discourse', acts of speech or *parole* in which users adapted or modified existing forms to serve their purposes. When Saussure had performed his balancing act between *langue* and *parole*, linguistic system and acts of speech, he'd insisted both that language was systematic and that its system was modified by the somewhat unpredictable use of it in speech. He was well aware of who might find this disturbing. 'What philosophers and logicians have missed here', he'd pointed out in 1894, 'is that *with the action of time* a system of symbols *independent* of the

---

[168] Wittgenstein, *Philosophical Investigations*, §109 (52e). Here, as elsewhere, I use the most recent translation, a modification of the original G. E. M. Anscombe translation by P. M. S. Hacker and Joachim Schulte. Here, as will occasionally be the case, the result is somewhat unfamiliar: the better known translation is 'the bewitchment of our intelligence by means of language' (*Philosophical Investigations*, 2nd edn., trans. G. E. M. Anscombe [Oxford: Blackwell, 1997], 47e).

[169] Hampshire, 'Questions of Language', 42.

designated objects is itself bound to undergo shifts which *the logician cannot calculate* [emphases, Saussure]'.[170] But ordinary language users were not literal-minded—they sometimes adapted existing forms for new purposes by making analogies, by thinking metaphorically or metonymically, by using tropes or playing with syntax and grammar. They didn't, therefore, necessarily think that being an object was like being an apple or that 'he buys apples' was like 'the waiter expects a tip'. They knew that the subject of a sentence is not necessarily the agent of an action, that 'is' has a variety of functions, that 'everybody envies somebody' means every person envies another person, and so forth, without having to translate anything into its 'logical form'.

That language users could so competently navigate the troubled seas of discourse caused some awkwardness for analysis, exemplified in the contortions of Gilbert Ryle, who confronted the question of misleadingness head-on in his 1932 article, 'Systematically Misleading Expressions'.[171] Ryle admitted at the outset that the expressions that troubled him—such as 'Carnivorous cows do not exist' or 'Virtue is its own reward'—were clearly understood by ordinary speakers and listeners. But even if such expressions 'occur perfectly satisfactorily in ordinary discourse', one could argue that they are *systematically misleading*, that is to say, that they are couched in a syntactical form improper to the facts recorded and proper to facts of quite another logical form than the facts recorded'.[172] This amounted to saying that one had chosen the wrong form to express certain ideas, believing, for instance, that 'Carnivorous cows do not exist' was a statement analogous to 'Analytic philosophers do not meditate'. When people took syntactic form too literally, imagining carnivorous cows before imagining them out of existence, the solution was a notation that would change the form, so that misleading formal similarities were replaced by deeper formal dissimilarities and the correspondence of form and meaning would be restored. But the obvious question was why this mattered, given that no one was actually confused about the statements themselves. These were misleading expressions that, in actuality, didn't mislead anyone. To make that the criterion, however, would be to admit—Hampshire, once more—that 'the test of whether the adoption of a certain rule for the use of a familiar expression is helpful or misleading is an empirical test—does it in fact mislead?'[173]

The abiding commitment to clarification was not, therefore, a pragmatic response to a spate of pressing confusions, but something at once more scattershot and more formal. That very first issue of *Analysis* contained, on the one hand, a short article by A. J. Ayer arguing that the philosophical expression 'atomic proposition' was meaningless and nonsensical and, on the other hand, an even shorter piece by Gilbert Ryle setting out the different uses of the ordinary preposition 'about': both

---

[170] Saussure, 'Notes for an article on Whitney', 145.
[171] Gilbert Ryle, 'Systematically Misleading Expressions', *Proceedings of the Aristotelian Society*, New Series 32 (1931–2): 139–70.
[172] Ryle, 'Systematically Misleading Expressions', 143.
[173] Hampshire, 'Questions of Language', 42.

might be confusions, but they were of very different kinds.[174] But the aim of analytical clarification was not, appearances notwithstanding, an impersonal and logically unambiguous form of discourse. The *Analysis* editorial began with a commitment to the 'elucidation or explanation' of already accepted facts, but it continued by invoking something quite different. Having observed that '[m]ost philosophers probably receive a good deal of stimulation from conversation on philosophical topics', the editors suggested that '*Analysis* will be a means of supplementing, and perhaps connecting, the oral discussions which go on where philosophy is studied systematically, or by groups of people, and that it will, to some extent, supply those who are out of reach of these discussions with a substitute for them.'[175] Conversation, not the perfectly transparent and formalized language of logic, was supposed to supply the model for philosophy. Analytic philosophy would accordingly stress the short article, couched in an engaging, unbuttoned style, shot through with intersubjective cues and twists, and would encourage continual acknowledgment of the views of one's interlocutors (articles would expend considerable space anticipating possible objections, and the pages of *Analysis* were littered with 'Replies to...'). When Ryle later wrote a philosophical book, *The Concept of Mind*, its reviewer in the *Times Literary Supplement*, J. L. Austin, used his final long paragraph to enthuse about the writing, which was 'racy, untechnical and idiosyncratic' and filled with decent jokes, making the book 'intelligible to many outside the fold of philosophy'.[176] '*Le style, c'est Ryle*', Austin concluded with a flourish.

He could have been bolder: the style was not just the man, but the school of philosophy itself. For in the early going, analytic philosophers did not so much ape the formality of science as make it one half of a strange but remarkably effective dialectic. The substance of their discussion, in the sense of its goal and content, was the refining and clarification of language, its transformation into an impersonal, formally consistent tool. But the form of their discussion was strikingly informal and conversational: the 'personality' of their discourse, its social dimension was embedded in the form, not its 'content'. As Ross has put it, its address was to the colleague, not the master or their disciples. It had, one might say, the form of the classic, civic, public sphere, but shorn of its political purposes. The form, and maybe also the substance of that civic public sphere, if one thinks that the pleasure gained in talk, the sense of social solidarity produced by informal conversation on serious matters, should be thought of as more than a mere happy by-product of 'rational-critical' discourse. Had the coffee-house migrated to the Senior Common Room? Wittgenstein had claimed in the *Tractatus* that philosophy was 'not a body of doctrine but an activity'; as analytic philosophy picked up steam in the 1920s and 1930s, it looked more and more like a new style republic of letters, an activity circumscribed by style and manner.[177]

---

[174] A. J. Ayer, 'Atomic Propositions', *Analysis* 1.1 (1933): 2–6; G. Ryle, "'About'", *Analysis* 1.1 (1933): 10–12.
[175] 'A Statement of Policy', *Analysis*, 1.
[176] J. L. Austin, review of Ryle, *The Concept of Mind*, *Times Literary Supplement*, 7 April 1950, 220.
[177] Wittgenstein, *Tractatus*, 4.112.

ANALOGY, THE ALTERNATIVE

What was the feature of 'language with a capital L' that gave rise both to sense and nonsense?: it was our old friend, analogy. Analogy, and its correct application, held the key to twentieth-century concerns about linguistic and logical form. In fact, it had been an issue since Kant. In an earlier, but proleptic attempt to separate metaphysics from natural science, Kant argued that when making transcendental arguments one had to speak metaphorically, applying concepts derived from experience, from the sphere of the phenomenal, to the metaphysical or noumenal, as if, there, too, one could speak of facts and causes. When speaking of the relation of the Supreme Being to the world, while we cannot speak anthropomorphically, assuming the Maker has the attributes of a person, we could 'allow ourselves a *symbolic* anthropomorphism, which in fact concerns language only and not the object itself'.[178] By means of what Kant calls 'cognition of analogy', we 'are compelled to consider the world *as if* it were the work of a Supreme Understanding and Will'.[179]

This is precisely the ground Wittgenstein refused to concede in the *Tractatus*: whatever you 'said' analogically was vacuous.[180] Sentences modelled on empirical propositions but dealing with metaphysics—with 'objects' as such, with 'existence', with the relationship between language and the world—could not have cognitive value, because they couldn't be true or false. But in 1929, when Wittgenstein had returned to Cambridge and to philosophical work, he was less sure. In the 'Lecture on Ethics' he delivered in November to the Cambridge Heretics (we'll hear more about them later), Wittgenstein observes that 'in ethical and religious language we seem constantly to be using similes'.[181] When we claim that the world is God's creation, that we feel absolutely safe in God's hands or that we feel absolutely guilty on account of God's disapproval, we use similes to express analogies. Except in these cases, 'as soon as we try to drop the simile and simply to state the facts which stand behind it, we find that there are no such facts. And so, what at first appeared to be a simile, now seems to be mere nonsense.'[182] There is no literal rendering of these ethico-religious experiences, but only similes, which appear to make sense, but cannot, given what Wittgenstein requires of sense. As observed earlier, Wittgenstein concludes that while such expressions exhibit a tendency 'to run against the boundaries of language', the tendency is one 'which I personally cannot help respecting deeply'.[183]

Soon enough, 'analogy' would become a flashpoint in his conception of language. There is debate within Wittgenstein scholarship over what happens after 1929: whether what he writes after that point is continuous with the writing of the

---

[178] Immanuel Kant, *Prolegomena to Any Future Metaphysics*, trans. James W. Ellington and Paul Carus (Indianapolis: Hackett Publishing, 1977), 97.
[179] Kant, *Prolegomena*, 97.
[180] As Apel has pointed out, once you insist that structures of meaning have a logical form, cognition by analogy—expressed by the use of metaphor—is impossible: *Analytic Philosophy of Language and the Geisteswissenschaften*, 8–9.
[181] Wittgenstein, 'Lecture on Ethics', 49.   [182] Wittgenstein, 'Lecture on Ethics', 49.
[183] Wittgenstein, 'Lecture on Ethics', 51.

Tractatus or a critique of it; and, if a critique, whether it is a radical critique or a partial one; and, if a partial one, what exactly is criticized and when the critique is brought to bear. When the New Wittgensteinians launched their campaign, they argued that the change was the refinement of Wittgenstein's no-nonsense position in the *Tractatus*, but they kept to the received periodization. The options were, in the words of Mauro Luiz Engelmann, that Wittgenstein 'either had *one dramatic* or he had *one subtle* change of mind', but in either case the change took place around 1929.[184] Engelmann argues the choice is not nearly so simple: there are many changes of mind between the writing of the *Tractatus* and the eventual composition of the *Philosophical Investigations* in the late 1930s. But which change is the critical one and when does it take place? Engelmann believes it is the abandonment of what he calls the 'calculus' conception of language and the adoption of a 'genetic' method and an anthropological perspective that is decisive, and that the decisive time is late 1933, when Wittgenstein is figuring out what's wrong with the 'Big Typescript' he has just composed (and the economist Piero Sraffa is telling him); but this is just one of a dazzling array of options. Oskari Kuusela claims the key is the recognition that all one can do is offer 'models' of language that are useful as points of comparison but don't capture an essence, and that the epiphany takes place in 1930–2; Wolfgang Kienzler thinks the Big Moment is 1931–2, Wittgenstein's *Wiederaufnahme*, when in one of his manuscript notebooks he begins to use his new method to criticize the *Tractatus* itself; Nikolay Milkov says that the 'Big Typescript' is the thing and the moment, because there Wittgenstein sees that philosophy is a matter of will and courage rather than knowledge; David G. Stern believes that the critical moment is later, around 1936, when Wittgenstein shifts to a 'practical holism' and a decidedly dialogical manner of exposition.[185]

Many options, many views, and at least one straightforward explanation for the ensuing mêlée. Wittgenstein didn't publish any of the material under discussion, but just kept writing notebooks and reorganizing the comments within them; it's only over the last twenty years or so that the huge *Nachlass* has become readily available. If Wittgenstein could never really impose order and hierarchy on his writing, why should readers be unanimous when they try? What the mêlée has given us, however, is a new period: 'middle period' Wittgenstein, from 1929 till 1936 (give or take a year), when the sands shift, the style changes, the ideas slowly morph and something quite different looking emerges at the end. It's hard not to

---

[184] Mauro Luiz Engelmann, *Wittgenstein's Philosophical Development: Phenomenology, Grammar, Method, and the Anthropological View* (Basingstoke: Palgrave Macmillan, 2013), 1.

[185] See Engelmann, *Wittgenstein's Philosophical Development* and Mauro Luiz Engelmann, 'Wittgenstein's "Most Fruitful Ideas" and Sraffa', *Philosophical Investigations* 36.2 (2013): 155–78; Oskari Kuusela, 'From Metaphysics and Philosophical Theses to Grammar: Wittgenstein's Turn', *Philosophical Investigations* 28.2 (2005): 95–133; Wolfgang Kienzler, 'About the Dividing Line between Early and Late Wittgenstein', in Gianluigi Oliveri (ed.), *From the Tractatus to the Tractatus and Other Essays* (Frankfurt am Main: Peter Lang, 2001), 125–30; Nikolay Milkov, 'Wittgenstein's Method: The Third Phase of Its Development (1933–36)', in António Marques and Nuno Venturihna (eds.), *Knowledge, Language and Mind: Wittgenstein's Thought in Progress* (Berlin: de Gruyter, 2012), 65–79; David G. Stern, 'How Many Wittgensteins?', in A. Pichler and S. Säätelä (eds.), *Wittgenstein: The Philosopher and his Works* (Frankfurt am Main: ontos Verlag, 2006), 205–29.

think that Saussure's comment on his own project—that 'language can only be understood with the help of four or five principles, intertwining constantly'—applies equally to Wittgenstein and that the fact that neither Saussure nor Wittgenstein could ever arrive at a definitive ordering of their thoughts on language is no coincidence. Or perhaps this style of work—endless note-writing and reorganizing, refusal of the old modes of arranging an argument, postponement of the final text—is linked to the linguistic turn itself; after all, it seems to afflict a high proportion of the figures treated in this book: Wittgenstein, Saussure, Walter Benjamin and the *Arcades Project*, Bakhtin and his notebooks. It's as if having entered the maze of language, they can never quite find their way out. In the remainder of this chapter, let us watch Wittgenstein negotiate the maze in the mid-1930s; we will talk about where he ends up, which we'll identify with the *Philosophical Investigations*, in the final chapter of this book.

Saussure's gambit had been to admit language was amorphous and then claim that within it lurked an object orderly enough for science, a knowable object: *langue*, the language system. Wittgenstein began with the conviction that *some* statements within language—those of natural science—were orderly and therefore amenable to logical analysis, and then discovered in this middle period that there was a 'logic' to language that went far beyond what could be captured by the notation he refined in the *Tractatus*. The example which illustrated this (and to which he would return until the end of his life) was colours: to say something could not be red and green at the same time, or even to say 'red is a colour' was not an empirical claim within language but an account of the logic of colours themselves, a description of the rules that allowed us to speak of colours.[186] This meant that ordinary language had an orderliness he had not considered before and what he had claimed was characteristic of logical propositions—that they showed you something that could not be asserted (said)—was characteristic of a much larger class of what he now called 'grammatical' statements. The change is represented in Wittgenstein's systematic substitution of 'grammar' and 'grammatical' for 'logic' and 'logical' from 1930 onwards (aided by his portmanteau terms in the *Tractatus* 'logical grammar' and 'logical syntax').[187] 'Grammar' had always represented one aspect of order in language, but Wittgenstein stretches the term considerably, so that it covers not only the usual rules of syntax and morphology, but also a range of quasi-logical constraints on what we can say, constraints beyond the formal distinctions of logic. So if logic alone prevents us from making sense when we say 'This pitch is a semitone higher and not a semitone higher than that one', what Wittgenstein calls the 'grammar' of our language ensures it is nonsense to say, as he put it in the *Philosophical Remarks* (1930), 'of a colour that it is a semitone higher than another'.[188]

---

[186] Wittgenstein, addendum to discussion of 30 December 1929, *Wittgenstein and the Vienna Circle*, 63–4.
[187] Wittgenstein, *Tractatus*, 3.325.
[188] Ludwig Wittgenstein, *Philosophical Remarks*, trans. Raymond Hargreaves and Roger White (Oxford: Basil Blackwell, 1975), 53.

The extension of grammar did not please or persuade everyone: G. E. Moore, sitting in on Wittgenstein's classes in the early 1930s, thought it was unwarranted.[189] In effect, Wittgenstein had laid waste to the distinction Noam Chomsky would articulate in *Syntactic Structures* in 1957: while the sentence, 'Colorless green ideas sleep furiously' was nonsensical for semantic reasons, it was, Chomsky argued, grammatically correct.[190] By contrast, Wittgenstein's grammar extended to semantic matters as well: in the language we use, something cannot be colourless and green at the same time, and ideas cannot be green or sleep, either calmly or furiously. Which is to say that all the rules determining which combinations of words were meaningful and which were nonsense should be considered part of a language's grammar, not just those that insist that, for instance, every sentence has a subject and a predicate. Having acknowledged this, logic should wake up from the dream of an ideal language and devote itself to 'the analysis of something we have, not of something we don't have', that is, the grammar of our ordinary language, 'no matter what idiom it may be written or expressed in'.[191] '[T]he syntax of logical constants', he now realized, 'forms only part of a more comprehensive syntax', to which philosophy should devote itself.[192] In a class delivered at Cambridge in February 1930, Wittgenstein will thus describe grammar in the very same terms that he had once reserved for logic: 'Grammar enables us to express true and false propositions; and that it does so tells us something about the world. What can be expressed about the world by grammar being what it is cannot be expressed in a proposition.'[193] Similarly, the newly conceived 'grammar' could be seen in the structure of actual propositions or grasped in 'grammatical' statements that displayed the logic of language without actually asserting anything, in sentences like 'blue is a colour' or 'bodies have volume'.

It's a widening of focus, and in its course some of the things that are supposed to remain the same—the hostility to metaphysics, the distinction between what can be said and what can be shown—inevitably take on a new aspect. That 'cognition of analogy' was not really cognition at all, that it was precisely this confusion that led to metaphysics, remained the central polemic, although it now led not only to metaphysics but also to a host of other misunderstandings and illusions. That philosophy was therefore predicated on a certain kind of seeing, a seeing that led to insight while not being cognition, remained the central methodological point. But now the very thing you saw was whether a certain analogy worked or not. For it turned out that sometimes when we were seeing things we were only 'seeing things'. As Wittgenstein remarked in September of 1930: " 'This proposition has a sense" sounds like "This man has a hat" '.[194] It is this faulty seeing that produces

---

[189] G. E. Moore, 'Wittgenstein's Lectures in 1930–33', in Wittgenstein, *Philosophical Occasions, 1912–1951*, 69.
[190] Noam Chomsky, *Syntactic Structures* (The Hague: Mouton, 1957), 15.
[191] Wittgenstein, *Philosophical Remarks*, 52, 51.
[192] Ludwig Wittgenstein, discussion on 2 January 1930, in *Wittgenstein and the Vienna Circle*, 76.
[193] Ludwig Wittgenstein, *Wittgenstein's Lectures: Cambridge, 1930–1932, from the Notes of John King and Desmond Lee*, ed. Desmond Lee (Oxford: Basil Blackwell, 1980), 9.
[194] *Wittgenstein's Lectures*, 108.

metaphysical nonsense, which, Wittgenstein claims, 'always arises from forming symbols analogous to certain uses, where they have no use'.[195]

In the so-called 'Big Typescript', composed in 1932–3, he will therefore title one chapter with the claim that 'Philosophy Points out the Misleading Analogies in the Use of our Language'.[196] 'If I rectify a philosophical mistake', Wittgenstein goes on to say, '[…] I must always point out an analogy according to which one had been thinking, but which one did not recognize as an analogy'.[197] Analogy derives from a kind of mistaken seeing and it leads us to assume that every verb names an activity, that 'having' always indicates a kind of physical possession, that to say blue is a colour is like saying the sky is blue, and so on. These mistaken uses of words arise from making analogies that, in the end, don't work.

Analogies could lead to nonsense and confusion; but they also led to language itself. In answer to a query about the meaning of a word Wittgenstein recommended we merely list its various uses and say 'I don't know how to state it in a sentence—but surely you see many analogies.'[198] And from 1930 onwards, the making of analogies itself becomes Wittgenstein's own preferred method for philosophy, which exchanges the bald, if ironic claims of the *Tractatus* for a series of comparisons: language is like a game, its order is created by something like rules, concepts are held together by family resemblances, metaphysics is like wheels spinning idly, language is like a city, and so on. Many of the most quotable bits of the later Wittgenstein corpus are the analogies, and the most important methodological precept is the axiom that one must always bear in mind that they are only analogies.[199] Remember Wittgenstein's discomfort with the need to speak in similes when dealing with ethics and religion. A few years later, he seems to have had a change of heart: 'Usually, we think of similes as second-best things, but in philosophy they are the best thing of all.'[200]

Saussure had assigned analogy more or less the same role, although the analogies that worried him were different in form, four-part 'proportions' that concerned morphology rather than logical syntax. If one follows the progress of his three courses in general linguistics, from 1907 to 1911, however, it becomes clear that the idea of the language system (*la langue*) evolves as an extension and elaboration of analogy. In the end, the grammar of language was systematic precisely to the degree that it was analogical (Saussure would claim in 1891 that 'any language at any moment is nothing more than a vast web of analogical formations').[201] He wasn't the first to make this connection. As early as 1836 Wilhelm von Humboldt had

---

[195] Moore, 'Wittgenstein's Lectures in 1930–33', 67. [196] Wittgenstein, *Big Typescript*, 302e.
[197] Wittgenstein, *Big Typescript*, 302e. [198] Wittgenstein, *Big Typescript*, 55e.
[199] Oskari Kuusela has argued that the big shift (which he dates to 1931) concerns the status of Wittgenstein's models: in the *Tractatus* period he treats them as idealizations which convey the essence of every concrete instance; after that he understands them as objects of comparison that are useful in bringing out a feature of the target object, but in no way their ideal, abstracted form. See his 'From Metaphysics and Philosophical Theses to Grammar'.
[200] From Wittgenstein's dictations to Francis Skinner (1933–1941), quoted in Yasemin J. Erden, 'Wittgenstein on Simile as the "Best Thing" in Philosophy', *Philosophical Investigations* 35.2 (2012): 128.
[201] Saussure, 'Second Lecture at the University of Geneva', 107.

said that language was 'a coherent web of analogies'.[202] Roughly forty years later the Neogrammarians who trained Saussure had declared that the creation of analogical formations, far from being a source of misguided evolution, was itself part of the regular life of language; Saussure merely took this insight to its logical conclusion. It's not surprising, therefore, that in Wittgenstein's middle period analogy and grammar stride to the front of the stage hand in hand. When the meaning of a word is 'the position of the word in grammatical space' and language itself is compared to a calculus, analogy becomes the means by which words acquire a location.[203]

But how then does one distinguish between the correct analogies and the misleading ones, given that one *sees* both kinds of resemblance? Could it be as simple as avoiding the analogies that, as one critic put it, 'mislead philosophers to add entities beyond what the facts really warrant'?[204] Wittgenstein himself seemed to zero in on analogies that suggested entities or processes having an 'occult character', as if this were a reliable guide to their appropriateness.[205] But other writers taking the linguistic turn—and often turning at the same time to analogy—didn't assume that 'occult' or metaphysical entities would be its first victim. Walter Benjamin, an almost exact contemporary of Wittgenstein, believed that language held the key to the reinvention of European society.[206] His account of language would, like Wittgenstein's, develop over the course of his life, but it will do for now to say that in his earliest writings on language (such as the essays 'On Language as Such and Human Language' and 'The Task of the Translator'), language is identified with naming and translation, while later texts focus on the idea of a 'mimetic faculty' from which language emerges. In the course of these later writings—they date from 1934—Benjamin will describe language as an 'archive of nonsensuous similarity', a typically complicated phrase that I think, in the end, means language is a tissue of analogies.[207]

But Benjamin has no investment in ordinary language. On the contrary: his own writing and his aesthetic preferences speak of a man with esoteric ideals. This makes Benjamin a much different read than Wittgenstein and a poor model for anyone interested in analytic clarity. But Benjamin's chromatic melodies are a revealing counterpoint to Wittgenstein's plainchant. He also assembles reminders that make analogies perspicuous: how else would one describe the hoard of short remarks and quotations that make up the *Arcades Project*, the method of which he

---

[202] Von Humboldt, *On Language*, 235.   [203] Wittgenstein, *Big Typescript*, 26e.
[204] Dudley Shapere, 'Philosophy and the Analysis of Language', in Rorty, *The Linguistic Turn*, 272.
[205] Ludwig Wittgenstein, 'The Blue Book', in *The Blue and Brown Books*, 2nd edn. (Oxford: Basil Blackwell, 1969), 5.
[206] In the various curricula vitae Benjamin composed in his short life the critic of literature, media, and urban space repeatedly describes his focus as the philosophy of language. In the 'Curriculum Vitae (VI): Dr. Walter Benjamin' in the English *Selected Works*, dated 1939–40, Benjamin claims 'From the outset, my primary interest has been the philosophy of language, along with the theory of art.' (This at a time when reflections on the concept of history and the Arcades Project are dominating his time.) *Selected Writings: Volume 4*, 381.
[207] Walter Benjamin, 'Doctrine of the Similar', in *Selected Writings: Volume 2, 1927–1934*, trans. Rodney Livingstone and others (Cambridge, MA: Harvard University Press, 1999), 697.

describes as 'literary montage. I needn't *say* anything. Merely show.'[208] But in this instance the practical or everyday form is not distorted by the abstract analogy, but made comprehensible by it. Thus Benjamin will claim, with typical extravagance, that the nineteenth century 'conceived the residence as a receptacle for the person, and it encased him with all his appurtenances so deeply in the dwelling's interior that one might be reminded of the inside of a compass case, where the instrument with all its accessories lies embedded in deep, usually violet folds of velvet'.[209] The analogy is strict and not a metaphor. For one can only understand the bourgeois dwelling when and if one thinks of it as a casing for the individual, when one invests such 'ordinary' features of modern urban life with this kind of force.[210] In this perspective, the extravagant analogy, the understanding of 'casing' as both literal and metaphorical, is the one we have to hold on to in order to understand the world correctly; literalism is the misuse of language.

When M. M. Bakhtin insisted we understand Rabelais in the context of medieval and Renaissance carnival, it was to draw out the analogies that gave such ordinary, earthly activities as eating, drinking, and defecating a 'universal' or 'philosophic' significance. The realism of 'grotesque realism' (his term for Rabelais's style) lay in the way excrement could be 'an essential moment [...] in the struggle between life and death' or eating could serve as the triumph of the body 'over the world, over its enemy'.[211] In notes made while revising this notorious study, Bakhtin went even a little further, insisting that what looked like ordinary physical directions like 'up' and 'down' were, and should have been, filled with a metaphysical, 'topographical' significance.[212]

Wittgenstein's retort to all this would be that the metaphysical employment of certain words makes no sense, and that one can *see* that they make no sense when one illustrates this use through fictional examples. One of the most marked changes of middle period Wittgenstein will therefore be methodological and stylistic: the increasing use of a conversational idiom which asks the reader to imagine the

---

[208] Walter Benjamin, *The Arcades Project*, trans. Howard Eiland and Kevin McLaughlin (Cambridge, MA: Harvard University Press, 1999), convolute N1a, 8 (460). Further references list the convolute and then the page number.

[209] Benjamin, *Arcades Project*, I4, 4 (220).

[210] Perhaps the most explicit indication of Benjamin's reliance on analogy is his frequent recourse to a particular grammatical construction, the '*Wie...so...*' (in English: 'Just as..., so...'). On this see Peter Buse, Ken Hirschkop, Scott McCracken, and Bertrand Taithe, *Benjamin's Arcades: an unGuided tour* (Manchester: Manchester University Press, 2005), 162–3.

[211] M. M. Bakhtin, *Tvorchestvo Fransua Rable i narodnaia kul'tura srednevekov'ia i renessansa* [*The Work of François Rabelais and the Popular Culture of the Middle Ages and Renaissance*] (Moscow: Khudozhestvennaia literatura, 1990), 248, 312. Translated into English in *Rabelais and His World*, trans. Hélène Iswolsky (Cambridge, MA: MIT Press, 1968), 224, 282–3.

[212] 'The image in Shakespeare always senses that under it is hell and above it heaven (i.e., it senses the actual topography of the stage), it is profoundly topographical and liminal. His similes either materialize/give body to the phenomenon (a bodily topography) or cosmicize it (a world topography), they extend it to the limits of the world, from pole to pole, they turn their play into a play among the elements (as in Aeschylus), everything small is drawn out into something great, something at the very limit (as compared to similes where both elements are of the same scale).' 'Dopolneniia i izmeneniia k "Rable"' ['Additions and Amendments to *Rabelais*'], in *Sobranie sochinenii, tom 5: raboty 1940-x— nachalo 1960-x godov* (Moscow: Russkie slovari, 1996), 91–2. English translation: 'Additions and Changes to *Rabelais*', trans. Sergeiy Sandler, *PMLA* 129.3 (2014): 530.

saying of certain words in certain contexts. Alois Pichler, one of the editors of the Wittgenstein *Nachlass*, has catalogued the phrases responsible for this idiom in manuscript 107, from 1929, which is liberally peppered with the locutions that would become the hallmark of Wittgenstein's late style: 'I want to say', 'One cannot say', 'It seems to me', 'In this case one can certainly say', and so on.[213] The shift in style entails the reintroduction of the context of enunciation, the 'reality of discourse' that Benveniste had been so keen to emphasize, with an intention similar to Benveniste's: to demonstrate that the structure of sentences alone is not enough to make them meaningful. 'What happens', Wittgenstein will therefore ask in *The Blue Book* of 1933–4, 'if from 4 to 4:30 A expects B to come to his room?'[214] Wittgenstein will use the imaginary scenario to demonstrate that though 'expecting' sounds like something we do, it is neither an activity (we aren't continually expecting for 30 minutes and it seems nonsensical to even think about it that way) nor a sensation.

LANGUAGE ALWAYS WORKS

As Wittgenstein became more and more convinced that language was structured by analogies all the way down, so to speak, what had been the bedrock of significant language—the propositions of natural science—dissolved into a more variegated landscape. There was no longer a 'general form of a proposition', like the one Wittgenstein specified in statement 6 of the *Tractatus*, but a range of heterogeneous possibilities. Language as such began to look more like the patchwork system Saussure had imagined, and philosophy began to look more like the descriptive linguistics Saussure was designing. This heterogeneity meant the old test of whether a statement had sense—whether it could be true or false, according to the facts it pictured—no longer did the job. How, then, would we know what had sense and what not? How would we know, when doing philosophy, how far to take an analogy (like the analogy we might make between 'expecting' and 'running')? Wittgenstein's new method of doing philosophy, centred on the testing of analogies and the dramatization of acts of speech, seemed to rely on an intuitive grasp of when particular utterances made sense and when they seemed to fail. But this method demands what Simon Jarvis has shrewdly called, 'the assumption, so powerfully prevalent in so much study of language, that language, in the default situation, *works*'.[215] Language in the 'default' situation—which means 'as such', when language is left to its own devices. Even if one can't *know* language, it seems one can rely on it, because simply using it will show us what properly belongs to it and what can be jettisoned as metaphysics. It may well be, as Rorty insisted, that there is no

---

[213] Alois Pichler, 'Wittgenstein's Later Manuscripts: Some Remarks on Style and Writing', in Paul Henry and Arild Utaker (eds.), *Wittgenstein and Contemporary Theories of Language*, Wittgenstein Archive Bergen Working Papers No. 5 (1992), 219–51.
[214] Wittgenstein, *The Blue and Brown Books*, 20.
[215] Simon Jarvis, 'There is No Science of Language' (review of Jean-Jacques Lecercle, *A Marxist Philosophy of Language*). *Radical Philosophy* 146 (2007): 50.

stepping back from language, no position from which one can attribute properties to it or examine its relation to the world. But the "'social practice" view of language' to which this apparently leads relies on a language that functions smoothly, that works well in practical terms, its valves well-oiled and its broken parts quickly mended.[216]

The metaphor is, of course, borrowed from middle and late Wittgenstein, who continually figured language as something mechanical, as a railway engine with its multiple levers, or as an engine which is merely 'idling' in philosophy, but—we are left to assume—purrs like a Ferrari otherwise.[217] Language would work when words 'are geared with something', or when they 'meshed gears with us', and when it would fail, it would not so much stall, as 'run in neutral' or go '*on holiday*' (that is—*stop trying to work*).[218] Indeed, the more intensely language is characterized as a social practice, as an activity or labour of discourse, inextricably meshed with human action, the more unthinkingly is it assumed that the labour or practice is naturally successful. You can work, or you can fiddle around, but you can't work poorly (or engage in industrial sabotage). See language as a social practice and the relation between subject and the world it inhabits becomes, in Rorty's revealing words, 'as unproblematic as that between the ball and the socket, the dove and the light air it cleaves'.[219]

Such conceptions constitute, as Jarvis puts it, 'an evaluation masquerading as a description', in which the success of language in practice is never in doubt.[220] Writing about Wittgenstein's penchant for describing language as a tool, Hilary Putnam pointed out that '[i]f language is a tool, it is a tool like an ocean liner, which requires many people cooperating (and participating in a complex division of labor) to use.'[221] This implies that *parole*—the use of language—is not a random force battering the ship of language from outside, but a matter of cooperative direction. But why assume that in language, unlike every other human social institution, cooperation is immediately available and continuously effective? Isn't it more likely that in the effort to make, use, and maintain a language we find a mix of cooperation, conflict, incompetence, misfires, unintended consequences, and the like? It isn't a question of whether there is a struggle over the sign, as some theorists have suggested, or whether we need a model of language as *agon* rather than consensus.[222] It isn't a matter, to adapt Putnam's simile, of whether the ship endures a mutiny now and then (for mutinies assume successful cooperation among the mutineers). The question is why we assume that the ocean liner goes forward at all,

---

[216] Rorty, 'Wittgenstein and the Linguistic Turn', 172.
[217] Wittgenstein, *Philosophical Investigations*, §132 (56e).
[218] Wittgenstein, *Big Typescript*, 6e; Wittgenstein, *Philosophical Investigations*, §38 (23e).
[219] Rorty, 'Ten Years After', 365.   [220] Jarvis, 'There is No Science of Language', 50.
[221] Putnam, 'A Half Century of Philosophy', 196.
[222] The classic statement of this doctrine is the 'social *multiaccentuality* of the ideological sign', in V. N. Voloshinov, *Marksizm i filosofiia iazyka*, 2nd edn. (Leningrad: Priboi, 1930, reprinted The Hague: Mouton, 1972), 27 [*Marxism and the Philosophy of Language*, trans. Ladislav Matejka and I. R. Titunik (Cambridge, MA: Harvard University Press, 1986), 23]. For a contemporary version see Louis-Jean Calvet, *Language Wars and Linguistic Politics*, trans. Michel Petheram (Oxford: Oxford University Press, 1998).

why the ship of Saussure's and Putnam's imaginings is *guaranteed* to work. Of course, languages often work: people exchange ideas, give orders, play games, fall in love, and the rest of it. But not always. People sometimes lack the words, or cannot find the 'subject position' they need, to do what they want to do; or they find that they are meaning something they did not intend to mean and thereby doing something they did not intend to do; or they find themselves beset by anxiety and confusion because they cannot express feelings, needs, or responses requiring expression. Nor is it clear that a given language works for everyone equally well—perhaps the difficulties and misfires are unevenly distributed? In the 'Big Typescript' Wittgenstein will warn us not to say that " 'Without language we couldn't communicate with each other" ', because it creates a false analogy with devices like the telephone. 'But', he'll argue, 'we can say: Without language we couldn't influence people. Or console them. Or build houses and machines.'[223] The point is not that one can do terrible things with language—humiliate people as well as console them—in addition to decent things, although that's worth bearing in mind. It's that we can easily fail to console someone or fail to influence them, or try to do one and do something quite different, and that we shouldn't imagine the failure as always separate from the language.

But is this assumption something distinctively modern? There had been conceptions of a perfect language before the twentieth century, but linguistic perfection had either been something remote, located in a distant and inaccessible past or a specialized language of logic or mathematics. Fantasies of a lost Edenic language (which we will encounter when we discuss Benjamin in earnest) habitually counterposed the necessary perfection of Adam's naming with the confusion of human language after Babel.[224] When that fantasy lost its force, the Edenic language found a substitute in the perfect languages of antiquity: in Greek, Latin, and Sanskrit, perhaps Proto-Indo-European, all of which represented an original correspondence between sound and idea, or grammar and structure, that was later lost due to the endless pressure of human usage. These examples of perfection were typically, however, examples of perfect naming: language worked because linguistic forms corresponded to ideas and things. It's only with the advent of twentieth-century linguistic turns that we encounter the assumption that *all* human language works, because at that point the perfection of language resides in its conventionality: the very existence of any language is evidence that it is working, because a language is nothing other than a 'set of necessary conventions adopted by the social body' (Saussure) or a shared and necessary grammar (Wittgenstein). Not every linguistic turn will make this claim: as we'll see in later chapters, for writers like Ernst Cassirer, 'language' works well, but not as well as theoretical physics, because both are still

---

[223] Wittgenstein, *Big Typescript*, 148e. I prefer this formulation of the comment to that set out in *Philosophical Investigations*, §491 (145e).
[224] On disputes as to the nature of the original language, see Maurice Olender, *Languages of Paradise: Race, Religion and Philology in the Nineteenth Century* (Cambridge, MA: Harvard University Press, 1992).

tied to the project of representation and knowledge.[225] Likewise, for writers excited by or scared by linguistic myth and magic, language will tend to look like something that isn't working nearly as well as it should, either because it needs some magic to revivify it or needs to expel magic so that it can become more precise and analytic.

To assume language always works is not to ignore the fact that it's a social institution, but to imagine it as a perfectly functioning social institution or even the one functioning social institution that makes every other social institution possible. It protects language from the idea, hazarded at one point by Benjamin, that it is 'a single great experiment that is conducted in as many laboratories as there are peoples', and prone, one would therefore suppose, to error and failure as much as success.[226] Perhaps most importantly, to assume that language always works is to fence off 'actually existing language' from the unpredictable and violent human history around it. The failures in which language may be implicated—when the consoling doesn't work, when expressive resources are inadequate, when political exhortations produce unintended effects—are blamed on something beyond language, thereby protecting and preserving language's innocence. None of which means that we have to sacrifice the idea of language as 'social'; rather, we have to recognize that the identification of language with a shared grammar or convention, the particular way in which we think of it as public, produces a vision of an innocent social institution that always does what is expected of it.[227]

Of course, if one had a concept of what language was *for*, there would then be criteria for judging whether it was working or not, whether it was succeeding or failing. But both Saussure and Wittgenstein define language in a way that rules out in advance the possibility of failure. For Saussure, the language system is precisely what is shared by the mass of speakers, so any failure to communicate, any difference within the language, is automatically deemed an externality. When Wittgenstein

---

[225] While the focus of this study is on the historical consequences of the belief that 'language works', that, if left to its own devices, it expresses our thoughts, unites communities, coordinates harmonious human action, builds consensus, and so on, it's worth pointing out that there are substantial philosophical arguments that make failures of language parasitic on an essential success. Habermas, whose discourse ethics places an enormous political burden on the pragmatic structures of language (making them, in effect, a substitute for Marx's conception of the universal class), has acknowledged that his theory demands an explanation of why, for example, lying and deception are 'parasitic' on honesty and plain dealing in language; see his *The Theory of Communicative Action, Volume I: Reason and the Rationalization of Society*, trans. Thomas McCarthy (Boston: Beacon Press, 1981), 286–95. According to Habermas, J. L. Austin's distinction between illocutionary and perlocutionary acts allows us to show 'that the use of language with an orientation to reaching understanding is the *original mode* of language use, upon which indirect understanding, giving something to understand or letting something be understood, and the instrumental use of language in general, are parasitic' (288).

[226] Walter Benjamin, 'A State Monopoly on Pornography', in *Selected Writings: Volume 2*, 72.

[227] If the reader is looking for an inkling of what an 'unconventional' theory of language as a social art might look like, it's worth consulting some of the later work of Donald Davidson or the highly polemical work of Roy Harris (who conducted a lifetime campaign against the idea of language as a fixed code). See Davidson's 'Communication and Convention', *Synthese* 59.1 (1984): 3–17 and 'A Nice Derangement of Epitaphs', in Ernest Lepore (ed.), *Truth and Interpretation: Perspectives on the Philosophy of Donald Davidson* (Oxford: Basil Blackwell, 1986), 433–46. A representative work by Roy Harris is 'On Redefining Linguistics', in Hayley G. Davis and Talbot J. Taylor (eds.), *Rethinking Linguistics* (London: Routledge/Curzon, 2003), 17–68.

makes language as such his concern, one of his first, and most far-reaching, analogies sets language side-by-side with games, a comparison that will make it impossible for there to be such a thing as an error, systematic weakness, or flaw within it:

> Why don't I call the rules of cooking arbitrary; and why am I tempted to call the rules of grammar arbitrary? Because 'cooking' is defined by its end, whereas speaking a language isn't. Therefore the use of language is autonomous in a certain sense in which cooking and washing aren't. For anyone guided by other than the correct rules when he cooks, cooks badly; but anyone guided by rules other than those for chess plays *a different game*, and anyone guided by grammatical rules other than such and such doesn't as a result say anything that is false, but is talking about something else.[228]

Language always works, and it works effortlessly. It's a system that constrains those who use it but without the least exercise of force. You can make mistakes, but the mistakes simply leave you outside of language itself, which embodies an unconscious consensus of the population at large.

As is often the case, a comparison with nineteenth-century conceptions is revealing. For then the belief that language manifested an unforced consensus served as a major prop for nationalist doctrines, which wished to transform agreement over the forms of language into deep-seated spiritual fellowship and ideological conviction. Bréal—something of a hero in these pages, you may have noticed—was characteristically sceptical of this gambit. 'It makes little difference', he wryly noted, 'that a people's language is the same if its speakers think differently; the ease of communication only points up more effectively the divergence in attitudes.'[229] The consensus embodied in a national language, however, was limited to those who embodied 'the nation', that is, the minority who owned property, received formal education, and were permitted to vote. The majority of every European country was outside the consensus of the learned and the franchised: they did not participate in what Bourdieu has called 'the legitimate language'.[230] With the gradual democratization of the concept of 'the national language' in linguistics, so well charted by Carita Klippi, the boundaries of the consensus were extended, while the substance of it was transformed.[231] Saussure had no time for the so-called 'genius of a language', which he contemptuously said was 'worth *nothing* compared with a single fact such as the dropping of a final *o*'.[232] In fact, it was the randomness and breadth of linguistic interactions, the fact that the language system was used not only by a literary minority, but also by a 'speaking mass' that guaranteed that it would always remain something of a patchwork affair. But if the patchwork system of *langue* did not guarantee ideological homogeneity, it was nevertheless the index of a functioning community, whose consensus was embodied in it. It was, I want to say, a potentially unruly consensus: unpredictable and, in theory,

---

[228] Wittgenstein, *Big Typescript*, 187e.   [229] Bréal, 'Language and Nationality', 214–15.
[230] Pierre Bourdieu, 'The Production and Reproduction of Legitimate Language', in *Language and Symbolic Power*, 43–65. On the reproduction of this language in France see also Balibar and Macherey, 'On Literature as an Ideological Form'.
[231] See p. 10 of the Introduction, above.
[232] Saussure, 'Notes for an article on Whitney', 151.

uncontrollable—a grammar of the crowd. But it was also an unreasoned but *unenforced* consensus and, for this reason, there was nothing to fear.

Language works—if you leave it alone. Problems only arise when people—let's call them 'intellectuals', for short—interfere with its functioning. In Saussure's writing the instances of language not working correctly can be subsumed under the rubric of the 'artificial'. When intellectuals create and enforce the forms of a literary language, when 'the people' act like intellectuals and engage in false etymologies, when clever individuals create words like *telegraph*: all this is artificial and, while it succeeds briefly, it is at best a temporary holding back of the tide of natural language. In Wittgenstein the ranks of interfering intellectuals are whittled down to the philosophers alone, who take words that work perfectly well and, by disengaging them from 'ordinary' use, create absurd metaphysical misfires.

There are many issues to deal with here, and the stage is already a little too crowded for the action to proceed. We can deal with Benjamin and Bakhtin in Chapter 5, when the issue of the historical force of language is the topic, and both again when 'word magic' will be considered. Cassirer can wait as well, until Chapter 7. For now we need to think more intently about this new sense of 'language as such'. With Saussure, Wittgenstein (but also Benjamin and Bakhtin) we find a new sense of language as a medium that at once creates a 'world'—in the sense that there is no access to objects, ideas, or feelings independent of it—and a community of language users, a 'speaking mass', coextensive with a population bound together by that language and in some obscure sense responsible for it. Language as such appears to engender a new kind of consent, one with an imaginary origin and a spontaneous, unconscious form. To maintain this consent, sacrifices had to be made: in both Saussure and Wittgenstein, the price of consent is a weakening of the force of argument, which neither establishes that consent nor can question it. One can make clear the structure of language, one can seek to rid it of intellectual excrescences ('metaphysics', 'folk etymology', 'errors' brought on by writing and literary language), but the structure itself, which seems at once to float on the surface of society, buoyed by its passive consent, and serve as its foundation, is beyond critical scrutiny. One can, at best, mimic, ironize, or exploit the analogies that constitute that structure.

Weren't these versions of 'language as such' a model, or perhaps more precisely, a vision, of community and social order at a moment when social order seemed to have no rationale or basis? Did they not provide a model that accepted the atomistic individualism of European society and showed how it might nevertheless be bound together by a system? And was not that system a marvellous synthesis of democracy and political quiescence? For 'language' in Saussure and Wittgenstein was, on the one hand, democratic and self-invented—everyone had a hand in framing it and nothing beyond grounded it—and, on the other hand, immune to public argument, insofar as one could not offer *reasons* for changing it. At a time of crisis, it was an image of social equilibrium.

Their optimism may have owed something to their personal histories. Saussure was a citizen of the republic of Geneva and the Swiss Federation, one of the most stable liberal societies in Europe (though it had its own political struggles, in which

Saussure was involved, as John Joseph has shown).[233] Wittgenstein's Austria was not at all like that—it was the centre of an empire, then a nation, then an annexed nation—but he left it for Britain in 1929, and avoided the worst (though his family did not, as Ray Monk has shown).[234] In other places, the very basis of society was in question. Would 'language as such' seem more pliable to change in a society that was consciously remaking itself? Or would it manage to float above the fray, as Saussure himself prophesied? The issue was taken up in earnest by writers and linguists in the Soviet Union in the 1920s, and Saussure was their guiding light. Their battles reveal the fissures in his writing.

[233] Joseph, *Saussure*, 608–23.   [234] Monk, *Wittgenstein*, 389–400.

4

Saussure and the Soviets

(S. I. Kartsevskii, G. O. Vinokur, L. Iakubinskii)

Binding language to the speaking mass, making linguistics an historical science rather than a natural one, wasn't a Saussurean novelty: the Neogrammarians had already decided to put language in the hands of its speakers. Saussure's achievement lay in showing the Neogrammarian linguist 'what he is doing', or rather, what he had done, when phonetic change was linked to the psychology of interconnected individuals. For if the collective had no supra-individual existence, if it couldn't be embodied in national spirit or divinely implanted reason, then any will or consciousness it possessed would be a disorderly, irrational affair, the patchwork consequence of unpredictable and random interactions. This wasn't a matter of aristocratic snobbery. *No* conscious individual innovation was guaranteed a place in a collectively agreed language, whether it was the jargon of a thief or an Academician ensuring the *clarté* and purity of his native tongue. A language that rested on no more than the agreement of those who spoke it was democratic and undirectable, a herd of cats that no one could control. On the one hand, Saussure would claim language was simply a body of conventions, a contract struck and renewed by speakers and thus entirely within their demesne. On the other hand, the nature of their interaction and of the conventions themselves excluded 'the possibility of any general or sudden linguistic change'.[1] This, despite the fact that this apparently random interaction produced linguistic *systems*, which were not only elegant internally, but also the building blocks for our most fine-grained and complex reasoning.

My point in this chapter is simple: it took the Russian Revolution and the linguists who responded to it to 'show Saussure what *he* was doing'. Lacan is not going to play much of a role in this book, but in this particular case he provides the perfect terminology. Russia was, in effect, Saussure's Big Other, the destination of his utterance, from which Saussure would have received the true meaning of his discourse. Or it is, if you prefer Darwin to Lacan, a classic instance of evolution, in which a mutation that appears to solve one problem—the status of phonetic sound change and the laws that describe it—turns out to have surprising and unexpected relevance in a new 'ecosystem'. Saussure thought defining the sign as a conventional association of sound and meaning would put to rest the traumas of a linguistics

---

[1] Saussure, *Course in General Linguistics* (1983), 72.

obsessed with sound laws: but 'arbitrariness' opened the Pandora's Box of democracy. Or, rather, it unlocked the box, and 1917 opened the lid.

Soviet linguists believed that they had a special relationship with Saussure: they've claimed that in Russia 'one found the most fruitful soil for the comprehension and evaluation of Saussurean theory', more fruitful soil, they imply, than in Western Europe.[2] The soil was hospitable in part because of native linguistic traditions (the work of Baudouin de Courtenay and N. S. Trubetskoi was strikingly similar) but more importantly because in the Soviet Union the '[a]ttention of many linguists was directed in this period towards the solution of practical tasks of cultural-linguistic construction'.[3] At a time when collective reinvention was the order of the day, when the remaking of the politics and culture of Soviet nations was the focal point of intellectual life, linguists wished to play their part in creating a language fit for Soviet citizens. It was Saussure who insisted that linguistic material was human, historical, *institutional*, thus letting politics in the back door, however tidy he might have kept the front hall.

But politics wasn't the only force ensuring a warm welcome for Saussure's theory. The idea of a systematic recreation or remaking of language had also been raised explicitly within twentieth-century Russian Futurist poetry. For rather than explore and deploy the resources of the existing language, for which they felt an 'insurmountable hatred', Futurist writers declared—in the endless manifestos they couldn't resist publishing—their commitment to the 'enlargement of the *scope* of the vocabulary by the addition of arbitrary and newly produced words (word-innovation)'.[4] The methods of enlargement turned out to be perhaps even more varied than the manifesto-writers first implied: a few months after the above had been published ('A Slap in the Face of Public Taste', 1912), Kruchenykh, Khlebnikov, Mayakovsky and a host of others declared they had not only 'made syntax loose and rickety' and realized 'the role of prefixes and suffixes', but also 'gave content to words according to their graphic and *phonic characteristics*', 'rejected orthography', and understood 'vowels as time and space (having the character of thrust) and consonants as colour, sound, smell'.[5] The poetry of which these declarations spoke was full of not only neologisms generated 'grammatically', but also the notorious

---

[2] N. A. Sliusareva and V. G. Kuznetsov, 'Iz istorii sovetskogo iazykoznaniia: rukopisnye materialy S. I. Bernshteina o F. de Sossiure' ['From the History of Soviet Linguistics: Manuscript Materials of S. I. Bernstein on F. de Saussure'], *Izvestiia Akademii Nauk, Seriia literatury i iazyka* 35.5 (1976): 441.

[3] A. V. Desnitskaia, 'Frantsuzskie lingvisty i sovetskoe iazykoznanie v 1920–1930 godov' ['French Linguists and Soviet Linguistics in the years 1920–1930'], *Izvestiia Akademii Nauk, Seriia literatury i iazyka* 50.5 (1991): 475.

[4] D. Burliuk, Aleksandr Kruchenykh, V. Mayakovsky, and Viktor Khlebnikov, 'Poshchechina obshchestvennomu vkusu' ['A Slap in the Face of Public Taste'], in D. Burliuk et al, *Poshchechina obshchestvennomu vkusu: v zashchitu svobodnago isskustva* (Moscow: G. L. Kuz′min, 1912), 3; Getty Research Institute digital library: http://www.getty.edu/research/tools/guides_bibliographies/russian_avant_garde/index.html. English translation: Anna Lawton (ed.), *Russian Futurism through Its Manifestoes, 1912–1928*, trans. Anna Lawton and Herbert Eagle (Ithaca, NY: Cornell University Press, 1988), 51–2.

[5] David Burliuk et al., Untitled manifesto, in *Sadok sudei* [*A Trap for Judges*], Vol. 2 (St Petersburg: Zhuravl′, 1913), 1–2; Getty Research Institute digital library: http://www.getty.edu/research/tools/guides_bibliographies/russian_avant_garde/index.html. English translation: Lawton, *Russian Futurism*, 53–4.

заумный язык (*zaumnyi iazyk*, 'transrational language') which seemed set on defying the ordinary morphology of Russian. All this, however, was done in the name of a desire 'that language must first of all be *language*' and the belief that 'the word as such' had resources the inner development of which had to be unshackled from the manacles of thought or spirit.[6] That the revolution in language was the driver of a larger revolution, social or cultural, hardly needed to be said.

And as if to prove the point, it would be politics, not the internal community of linguistic scholarship, that brought Saussure to the Soviet Union. In 1906 a young man named S. I. Kartsevskii was arrested for his activity in the Socialist-Revolutionary movement; he wisely emigrated to Geneva shortly afterwards, not because there were linguists there—he didn't know that and may not have cared if he had—but because there were Socialist-Revolutionary exiles there.[7] But once he arrived he found the linguists, Saussure included, and became one of their number, though when the tide turned in 1917, he returned to Russia and began presenting Saussure's theory to linguists at home.[8]

This initially took the form of a series of lectures on the distinctive grammatical features of the Russian verb, which—though activists, by definition, need verbs—was itself a topic fairly remote from political work. The lectures were delivered at meetings of the Moscow Dialectological Commission between December 1917 and May 1918, an organization within Moscow University that, though its own focus was on the collection of data on Russian dialects, songs, and folktales, was also the cradle in which the Moscow Linguistic Circle (MLC)—a very different organization, with great ambitions, a brilliant cast, and a broad range of interests—would be nurtured. Kartsevskii may have brought a copy of the Book with him, although Vinokur, who was present at these initial meetings, claimed in 1923 that there were only two or three copies of the *Cours* circulating in Moscow and the first copy to reach St Petersburg apparently arrived from Paris only in 1923.[9] Not everyone, of course, was equally impressed. S. I. Bernshtein, one of the founders of the Petersburg OPOIaZ (the Society for the Study of Poetic Language, the formal name for the Petrograd wing of the Russian Formalists) commented in some notes made from that sole St Petersburg copy that 'In general Saussure's work is no more than a brilliant exposition and an excellent systematizing of terms for conceptions

---

[6] A. Kruchenykh and V. Khlebnikov, *Slovo kak takovoe* [*The Word as Such*] (Moscow, 1913), 10; Getty Research Institute digital library: http://www.getty.edu/research/tools/guides_bibliographies/russian_avant_garde/index.html. English translation: Lawton, *Russian Futurism*, 55–6.

[7] N. S. Pospelov, 'O lingvisticheskom nasledstve S. Kartsevskogo' ['On the Linguistic Legacy of S. Kartsevskii'], *Voprosy iazykoznaniia* 6.4 (1957): 46.

[8] According to Jindřich Toman, Kartsevskii took only a course in Sanskrit from Saussure himself (which means he did not attend any of the series of lectures on general linguistics) in 1911–12 and took the majority of his courses with Charles Bally, Saussure's student and eventual editor of the *Cours de linguistique générale*. See Jindřich Toman (ed.), *Letters and Other Materials from the Moscow and Prague Linguistic Circles, 1912–1945* (Ann Arbor: Michigan Slavic Publications, 1994), 33.

[9] See G. Vinokur, 'Kul'tura iazyka: zadachi sovremennogo iazykoznaniia' [The Culture of Language: Tasks for Contemporary Linguistics'], *Pechat' i revoliutsiia* 5 (1923): 105n1 and Sliusareva and Kuznetsov, 'Iz istorii sovestskogo iazykoznaniia', 443. Vladimir Alpatov claims Kartsevskii arrived in Moscow after the February Revolution of 1917 and brought a copy of the *Cours* with him (Author's interview with Vladimir Alpatov, 13 October 1999, University of Sheffield, Sheffield, England).

and views that have been familiar for a long time.'[10] Nor can we be certain that Saussure was the only, or even primary source, for the kind of sociological ideas about language Russians thought of as 'Saussurean'. Antoine Meillet's *Linguistique générale et linguistique historique* has been described as one of the standard texts for new Soviet linguists in the 1920s, and Meillet, a contributor to Durkheim's *L'année sociologique*, helped Saussure move towards the more 'sociological' position he assumed in the final two sets of lectures on general linguistics.[11]

But though their topic was technical, Kartsevskii's lectures are reported to have provoked 'great arguments about the morphology of the Russian verb' that pushed the MLC towards a more generally theoretical stance.[12] Saussure wasn't the only, or even the most important figure in the theoretical arguments that defined the Circle from 1919 until 1924, when it was effectively wrapped up: avant-garde poetry, embodied in the presence of Mayakovsky and Pasternak and ever-present in the minds of the more 'Formalist' members of the Circle, and the work of the phenomenologist Gustav Shpet, who joined in 1920 and ended up pulling much of the Circle along in his wake, were more decisive. But the Circle was, from the beginning, a group of linguists (rather than literary critics, as was the case with OPOIaZ), so it became the place where Saussure's text was worked through, in works by members of the Circle and in a notable session on 5 March 1923, when G. O. Vinokur gave a lecture on the *Cours* which drew long and sustained comment.[13]

SAUSSURE OPENS PANDORA'S BOX: THE SOCIAL SIDE OF LANGUAGE

The shape and direction of the reaction was revealing. The 'arbitrariness' of the sign, though noted, wasn't treated as an occasion for grand philosophical conclusions. Instead, it was the distinction between synchrony and diachrony, perhaps the most sharply polemical of Saussure's innovations, that attracted the most attention and the most sceptical comment. For while the value of the distinction wasn't in doubt, it led to historical conclusions members of the Circle didn't like. First, Saussure had securely embedded phonetic change in the unpredictable, random world of diachrony. Secondly, and perhaps more profoundly, Saussure had thereby fenced

---

[10] S. I. Bernshtein, 'Zametki o de Saussure' [NB: 'de Saussure' is in Roman alphabet in original, KH. 'Notes on de Saussure'], in Sliusareva and Kuznetsov, 'Iz istorii sovestskogo iazykoznaniia', 448.

[11] Desnitskaia, 'Frantsuzskie lingvisty', 474. On Meillet's influence on Saussure, see Joseph, *Saussure*, 534–5.

[12] So claims Boris Gornung is his memoirs; see Boris Gornung, 'Zapiski o pokolenii 20-x godov' ['Notes on the Generation of the 1920s'], in *Pokhod vremeni: stat 'i i esse* [*The Path of Time: Articles and Essays*] (Moscow: Russian State University for the Humanities, 2001), 365.

[13] Detailed minutes of the session, which I've drawn on for the following discussion, are reprinted in E. A. Toddes and M. O. Chudakova, 'Pervyi russkii perevod "Kursa obshchei lingvistiki" F. de Sossiura i deiatel'nost' moskovskogo lingvisticheskogo kruzhka' ['The First Russian Translation of F. de Saussure's *Cours de linguistique générale* and the Activity of the Moscow Linguistic Circle'], *Fedorovskie chteniia* 1 (1978), 242–5.

off the systematic nature of language—an emphasis that played very well in Moscow—from the history of the language, ensuring that the latter could only intrude upon or interrupt the fine web of synchrony. Linguists who were generally sympathetic to Saussure—Rozalia Shor, M. N. Peterson, A. I. Romm—thought there ought to be a distinction between changes that were random in nature and those conditioned by systemic relations.[14] It was a proleptic suspicion that by the end of the decade would become a full-blown thesis when Jakobson and Iurii Tynianov suggested, in their 'Problems in the Study of Literature and Language' (1928), that systems, too, might evolve: 'Pure synchrony proves to be an illusion: every synchronic system has its past and its future as inseparable structural elements of the system.'[15]

Suspicions about the nature of the synchronic system played themselves out in a striking interpretative recasting of it. Saussure had presented *langue* itself as an abstraction from the buzzing and ceaseless activity of discourse that was 'concrete' insofar as it was coercive or imperative, forcing the individual speaker to fall in line with its structures. The members of the Circle could see this didn't quite work, either as a characterization of the system or as a description of how one arrived at it methodologically. They therefore took their cue from a comment made almost in passing by Saussure in the chapter 'Immutability and mutability of the sign' (about which I'll say a good deal more below), when he described the language sign as knowing 'no other law than that of tradition'.[16] To describe *langue* as tradition was to give it a very different status than the one it has for the most of the *Cours*: tradition requires the authority of the past and, in some understandings of it, the unreasonable, 'meaningless' authority of the past. It therefore also implies that there could be challenges to that authority and grounds for challenges, and this seems to be just what the MLC membership had in mind. Rather than perceive the linguistic system as an instantaneous abstraction from an incessantly changing discourse, it was cast as tradition which would naturally be prone to deviations and challenges: a system which had resistance to change built into it, as a structural feature, even if this resistance was never completely successful.

But the refusal to think of the linguistic system as no more than an averaging or abstraction from actual language use, with no evaluative component, also had methodological consequences. In the second lecture of Saussure's final course on general linguistics, he claimed one arrived at knowledge of the true object of linguistics, the language system or language in general, by abstracting from the particular languages one studies.[17] But something more radical was at work, and this was

---

[14] A. I. Romm, comment, Protocol of the meeting of the MLC on 5 March 1923, in Toddes and Chudakova, 'Pervyi russkii perevod', 244.

[15] Roman Jakobson and Iurii Tynianov, 'Problemy izucheniia literatury i iazyka', *Novyi LEF* 12 (1928, reprinted Mouton: The Hague, 1970): 36.

[16] Saussure, *Course in General Linguistics* (1983), 74. This is, of course, a clause from one of Saussure's most brilliant formulations: 'It is because the linguistic sign is arbitrary that it knows no other law than that of tradition, and because it is founded upon tradition that it can be arbitrary.'

[17] Saussure, *Third Course*, Lecture of 4 November 1910, 9a–10a.

immediately obvious to the members of the Circle. Romm saw in Saussure's theories 'a profound contradiction between their true meaning and the empiricist manner of exposition'; although he 'frequently fell into a vulgar empiricism', the 'principles he discovered—like that of arbitrariness, and associative and syntagmatic connections—are purely theoretical and universal'.[18] To find 'a more profound meaning' in Saussure's theory, M. M. Kenigsberg remarked, 'we have to go beyond and against de Saussure'.[19] Like so many scientific discoveries, Saussure's was in part a leap in the dark, a bold theory that reconceptualized its object and the problems of its analysis, not an incremental step grounded in interesting new data. Its principles, embodied in the notorious series of oppositions Saussure introduced, had made language a different kind of object, not a mere abstraction. To be fair, Saussure himself was aware of the ambiguity. In the 1891 passage we cited in the Introduction, he had claimed that 'language can only be understood with the help of four or five principles, intertwining constantly', and to make sure the principles are grasped, each paragraph had to be 'set like a solid object planted firmly in the marsh, marking the route both forwards and backwards'.[20] None of the principles were prior to the others because Saussure had not arrived at them piecemeal but virtually all at once, as struts in a new linguistic framework that would only stand on its own when—like the language system it describes—it managed to hang together by itself.

In these respects, Soviet linguists were able to inflect a notionally 'descriptivist' theory in the direction of a practical, or even avant-garde approach to language. They could see, however, that there were obstacles and that the 'tradition' of the linguistic system would not give way easily. In fact, the very chapter where Saussure's remark on tradition is found plays a strange role in the *Cours*. It is based on a lecture delivered near the end of the third set given in 1910–11. Saussure had been motoring along through lectures devoted to the nature of the linguistic sign and the nature of linguistic units, and he had just explained what would turn out to be the critical distinction between unmotivated signs and relatively motivated signs. On 19 May 1911 he began with a review of the lectures that pertained to *la langue* and the sign, quickly introduced two very useful new terms, 'signifier' and 'signified', and then suggested that his students insert a new third chapter into their notes on the 'Immutability and mutability of the sign', which would take up this and the following lecture.[21] It's as if, having discussed the arbitrariness of the sign, Saussure was afraid that his conventionalism would be taken as an invitation to reshape language consciously. Thus he opened with the claim that while it appears that the terms of signification are freely chosen, '[i]n relation to the human society called upon to employ it, the sign is not free but imposed, and the corporate body

---

[18] A. I. Romm, comment, Protocol of the meeting of the MLC on 5 March 1923, in Toddes and Chudakova, 'Pervyi russkii perevod', 245.
[19] M. M. Kenigsberg, comment, Protocol of the meeting of the MLC on 5 March 1923, in Toddes and Chudakova, 'Pervyi russkii perevod', 245.
[20] Saussure, 'On the Dual Essence', 65.   [21] Saussure, *Third Course*, 93a.

[of speakers, KH] is not consulted'.[22] In the published chapter based on these lectures, Bally and Sechehaye neatly compile the various reasons Saussure adduces to justify the claim that the linguistic sign 'eludes the control of our will'.[23] There are too many signs for one thing, and the system is too complex to be altered. And even if one could grasp the mechanism 'people use their language without conscious reflexion'.[24] But two justifications stand out and both would become central to the way in which the *Cours* was reinterpreted in the Soviet Union: one is that arbitrariness itself ensures there is no criterion on which one could make a case for linguistic change. 'No reason', Saussure intoned, 'can be given for preferring *sœur* to *sister*, *Ochs* to *bœuf*, etc.'[25] The second relates to the 'collective inertia' of the body of speakers themselves, an inertia which derives from the way in which the collectivity interacts, for, unlike those institutions which are governed by a few who labour in concert, '[a] language, on the contrary, is something in which everyone participates all the time, and that is why it is constantly open to the influence of all. This key fact is by itself sufficient to explain why a linguistic revolution is impossible.'[26]

The year before the meeting of the Moscow Linguistic Circle when Saussure had been discussed, Romm had begun work on a Russian translation of the *Cours de linguistique générale*. The translation was never completed and publishing arrangements never finalized, although the roughly eight chapters that Romm finished circulated through Moscow (Gustav Shpet became acquainted with Saussure through them). The translation apparently involved only a few indigenous amendments, supplementary examples of the phenomena Saussure discussed taken from Russian. But the position taken in 'Immutability and mutability of the sign' prompted Romm to add the following telling observation:

> The truthfulness of these words is underlined with particular sharpness by the Russian Revolution. Compare the radical shifts it produced in all social institutions and relations with those negligible changes which it introduced into the Russian language. In fact, its system remained completely untouched. The single innovation was some thousands of new compound abbreviations (of the type represented by 'Glavton', TsUS, and so on). But such words existed even earlier (like 'Ropit', 'Instiblium', etc.) and as their current distribution is not broad, they constitute a negligible percentage of words in the Russian language and are subject to all its already existing laws, both phonetic and grammatical.[27]

The Revolution had put Saussure's conservatism to the test, and it had not been found wanting.

---

[22] Saussure, *Third Course*, 94a.
[23] Saussure, *Course in General Linguistics* (1983), 71. I have, however, followed the lead of John Joseph and Wade Baskin, Saussure's first English translator, in translating the title for this chapter; see *Course in General Linguistics* (1974), 71.
[24] Saussure, *Course in General Linguistics* (1983), 72.
[25] Saussure, *Course in General Linguistics* (1983), 73.
[26] Saussure, *Course in General Linguistics* (1983), 73, 74.
[27] A. I. Romm, quoted in Toddes and Chudakova, 'Pervyi russkii perevod', 235.

KARTSEVSKII TRIES TO CLOSE THE BOX: LANGUAGE AND REVOLUTION

Romm was not the only linguist to think of the Revolution as a testing ground for the new systematic linguistics. Jakobson, one of the founders of the Circle, and its most well-known representative, had discussed the question in a review of a French book on the topic written in Czechoslovakia.[28] But it was Kartsevskii himself, who had proposed a Russian translation of the *Cours* in 1916 that never got off the ground, who took the lead.[29] As one of the only Soviet linguists with a politically revolutionary past, he was well placed to register the challenge the Soviet experience might pose to the linguistics he was now advocating.[30] And to his credit, he faced the challenge head-on, in a book entitled *Language, War and Revolution*, published in Berlin (for he was also shrewd enough to know Socialist-Revolutionaries shouldn't hang around in Soviet Russia) in 1922. *Language, War and Revolution* is about the question Saussure thought he had answered: is a linguistic revolution possible? Is language the kind of material that renders a revolution possible? The explicit answer is straightforward. Recognizing the enormous changes to Russian that followed in the wake of the revolutions of 1905 and 1917, Kartsevskii claims that '[w]ithout doubt, there is a "language of revolution". But, on the other hand, there are no grounds for speaking of a "revolution of language".'[31] To make the case, Kartsevskii made a distinction between the creation of new words, however extravagant in number and method, and changes that altered the systematic, grammatical structure of the language, arguing that 'the "spirit of a language" is found in its grammar and its formal elements, not in its vocabulary' and that revolutions, to qualify as such, had to touch on this spiritual core.[32]

Of course, Saussure had explicitly opposed the claim that languages had an animating or structuring 'spirit', but this was really the index of a deeper and more pervasive difference between the Swiss linguist and his Russian interpreter, a difference that in fact would slowly chip away at the foundations of Kartsevkii's support for Saussure's position. Although Saussure insisted that 'there is no reason for preferring *sœur* to *sister*, *Ochs* to *bœuf*', that the arbitrary character of the sign made conscious reflection and evaluation of it pointless, he had himself opened a crack in this absolute position in the lectures that immediately preceded his discussion

---

[28] Roman Jakobson, 'Vliv revoluce na ruský jazyk (Poznamky ke knize André Mazona, *Lexique de la guerre et de la révolution en Russie*)', *Nové Atheneum* 2 (1920–1): 110–14, 200–12, 250–5, 310–18.

[29] A few historical studies have suggested that Romm's was the first attempted translation of the *Cours* into Russian (this is the claim behind the article by Toddes and Chudakova, for example), but in a letter of 27 May 1916 to an unknown recipient, Kartsevskii says that he intends to translate the *Cours* into Russian with Bally's help; see Letter no. 7, from S. Kartsevskii, in Toman, *Letters and Other Materials*, 34–5.

[30] Vladimir Alpatov points out that Kartsevskii was one of the only linguists in Russia who was politically active and committed before the Revolution. See V. M. Alpatov, 'Filologi i revoliutsiia' ['Philologists and Revolution'], *Novoe literaturnoe obozrenie* 53 (2002): 199–216.

[31] S. I. Kartsevskii, *Iazyk, voina i revoliutsiia* (Berlin: Russkoe universal'noe izdatel'stvo, 1923), 64–5.

[32] Kartsevskii, *Iazyk*, 55.

of immutability in May 1911. Having established the arbitrary character of the sign the week before—May 1911 may have been Saussure's busiest month, theoretically—he now added a deadly qualification: 'we must distinguish between what remains radically arbitrary and what can be called relative arbitrariness'.[33] Signs like *Ochs* and *bœuf*, which could, in theory attach different sounds to the same concept, were radically or absolutely arbitrary, whereas a sign like *poirier* (French for pear-tree), Saussure pointed out, was only relatively so, insofar as its meaning depends on the combination of two constituent elements (*poire* for pear and the ending *-ier*). Another of Saussure's examples is the numerical combination *vingt-neuf*, twenty-nine, a rather obvious case which underplays the significance of relative arbitrariness or 'motivation'. For as Saussure himself noted when he made the point, '[e]verything that makes language a system or an organism needs to be approached [...] as a *limitation on arbitrariness* in relation to the idea'.[34] Relative arbitrariness will apply to every regular compound and every regular grammatical construction—from 'wallpaper' and 'authoritarian' to 'runs', 'dogged', and 'lightly'— which is to say that it is more or less equivalent to the entire range of syntagmatic constructions. In other words, what Saussure will call the 'mechanism' of language, the nuts and bolts of its system, ensures that motivation and relative arbitrariness are inevitable and apply from the details of morphology to the sphere of syntax.

Kartsevskii makes 'motivation' the central piece in his argument against linguistic revolution. Most of the new words arising in and after the revolution are, he claims, 'motivated', recombinations of the existing lexical and grammatical material that amount to no more than a reshuffling of the linguistic deck. They maintain—in fact, depend on—the systematic structure of the language and thus can hardly be deemed 'revolutionary'. But a closer examination reveals that Kartsevskii gives 'motivation' an expressive twist it doesn't have in Saussure's usage, a twist that in the end makes his professions of faith in systematic linguistics a lot less convincing.

In Saussure's account, the systematic nature of *langue* and the arbitrariness of the sign are two sides of the same coin, the system ensuring the stability of a sign that has no natural 'glue'. It's because language is systematic that signs can be defined by negative, differential relations. But that didn't mean that the arrangement of the system itself was arbitrary, or that arbitrariness might not decrease as one ascended the levels, from phonology to morphology to syntax. As has often been pointed out, when one translates between languages—an obvious test of their arbitrariness—it is easier to work from the sentence down, from the unit that is less arbitrary, to the word-units that are more so. That the building blocks were arbitrary did not mean that the final edifice would be. Or to put it slightly differently: the notorious absence of syntax from the *Cours* was reflected in its theory of the structure, which, in effect, treats syntagms as mere aggregates of the conventional signs that constitute them.

Kartsevskii took a different tack, with motivation at its centre. At the very opening of *Language, War and Revolution* he conflates Saussure's use of the term with two

---

[33] Saussure, *Third Course*, Lecture of 9 May 1911, 85a.
[34] Saussure, *Third Course*, Lecture of 9 May 1911, 87a.

very different interpretations of it, in effect rotating the concept on its axis so that it comes to represent the basic principle of a 'connection between the signifying and its signified'.[35] Motivation refers not only to cases where words are composed of smaller significant units, but also to onomatopoetic words (where an iconic or mimetic relation obtains) and to names that are also descriptions (an English equivalent to his example would be 'sunflower'). Motivation isn't, then, understood as arising from the systematic nature of the linguistic structure, but from an expressive tendency within language itself: 'This active, emotional and subjective relation to language leaves its mark on language, hindering its transformation into a nomenclature of labels.'[36] Instead of seeing convention as the starting point of language, as the imaginary welding of sound-image to meaning, he interprets it as what happens to language when its 'expressive' aspect has been worn out by habit. From there, it is but one step to a conception of language in which arbitrariness is the enemy against which speech always struggles:

> The drive towards expressivity and in general a subjective relation to language leads to the fact that we continually resort to metaphors, we in all ways describe instead of define. Thanks to this, the imageness in words is maintained. [...] A living language in general does not like unmotivated words and where a previously existing connection between a word and a concept has disappeared, or where it never even existed for us, like, for example, in loanwords, it strives to establish motivation.[37]

Thus, Kartsevskii notes, when the population get hold of an absolutely arbitrary word, such as the borrowing 'boulevard' from French, they 'strive to motivate' it, to ensure that it is more than a mere label or name, by endowing it with semantic resonance, in this case by a subtle change from the borrowing бульвар [*bul'var*] into гульвар [*gul'var*], a word recalling the Russian verb гулять [*guliat'*], to 'walk around'.[38]

This expanded understanding of motivation appeared to draw on the avant-garde belief that the 'word as such' possessed a native metaphorical energy that was slowly dissipated by habit, that the poetic word, as opposed to the 'word-label' (Kartsevskii's term), drew on resources and energies that were stored up and endlessly renewed in language itself. But it wasn't just Kartsevskii who saw 'motivation' as the wedge with which one could lever open the semiotic model of language. Romm, in the fateful discussion of March 1923, noted that Saussure's examples of relative arbitrariness (more plentiful in the book than in the notes we have of the lectures) 'patently relate the concept of relative arbitrariness to the concept of inner form, more precisely, the figural inner form according to [Anton] Marty'.[39] Inner form was an idea first hazarded by Humboldt, then developed by various nineteenth-century followers, such as Steinthal and the Swiss phenomenologist Marty, and developed in Russia primarily by Gustav Shpet and Aleksandr Potebnia,

---

[35] Kartsevskii, *Iazyk*, 6.   [36] Kartsevskii, *Iazyk*, 10.
[37] Kartsevskii, *Iazyk*, 11.   [38] Kartsevskii, *Iazyk*, 11.
[39] A. I. Romm, comment, Protocol of the meeting of the MLC on 5 March 1923, in Toddes and Chudakova, 'Pervyi russkii perevod', 243.

who had made it central to their respective philosophies of language.[40] The inner form of language determined how its meanings were conveyed in a particular lexis and grammar, and it implied that linguistic systems were not the heterogeneous constructions Saussure implied, but structures with a certain internal coherence and patterning.

If the forms of language possessed this kind of structure, a structure with determinate effects on the kinds of meanings one could convey with a language, then there *would be* a reason to prefer—or not—*Ochs* to *bœuf*. Kartsevskii manages to ward off this danger, because he believes that for the most part the creation of new expressions in Soviet Russia has not altered the inner form of the language but moved straight along the tracks laid for it. But there was one sphere where this play of expression and motivation led Kartsevskii to wonder, where the linguistic innovations produced are 'revolutionary and [...] deserving of special attention', and this is the distinctive phenomenon of Russian institutional 'abbreviation'.[41] We have already seen this phenomenon broached, and dismissed, by Romm, but it's worth pointing out how widely it was recognized as something distinctive in the Soviet period. What was at issue was the emergence of that vast series of abbreviated expressions that designated the new institutions of Soviet society, such things as 'СССР' (for the USSR), НЭП [*NEP*], Наркомпрос [*Narkompros*], ОПОЯЗ [*OPOIaZ*], and Политбюро [*Politburo*] (the first and last of these are my own 'modernized' examples)'.[42] Kartsevskii notes that these abbreviations work on different principles: some—СССР—use the names of the first letters of each word (just as we pronounce 'USSR', or, for that matter, 'USA'); some—NEP—use the sounds of the first letters of each word, New Economic Policy (the beginning sounds are the same in Russian, and one says 'nep', rather than naming the constituent letters); and some use the initial syllable of each word, Нар/ком/прос [*Nar/kom/pros*, explained below]. But there are mixed forms as well: ОПОЯЗ [*OPOIaZ*], which names the 'Society for the Study of Poetic Language', mixes initial sounds with syllables—the sound 'O', for Общество [*Obshchestvo*, 'society'], followed by the syllables ПО [*Po*], for поэтического [*poeticheskogo*, 'poetic'], and Яз [*Iaz*] for языка [*iazyka*, 'language']. And Политбюро [*Politburo*] mixes the initial syllables of политическое [*politicheskoe*, 'political'] with the entire word бюро [*biuro*,

---

[40] On the influence of Anton Marty, see Craig Brandist, 'Voloshinov's Dilemma: On the Philosophical Roots of the Dialogic Theory of the Utterance', in Craig Brandist, David Shepherd, and Galin Tihanov (eds.), *The Bakhtin Circle: In the Master's Absence* (Manchester: Manchester University Press, 2004), 97–124. Shpet exerted a great deal of influence over some members of the Circle (Gornung, Buslaev, Kenigsberg, Vinokur), who would eventually launch a critique of Jakobson that split the Circle; on this see Radunović, 'Debates on Form in Russian Studies of Language and the Arts (1915–1929)', Chapter 3.

[41] Kartsevskii, *Iazyk*, 49.

[42] Soviet abbreviations had already been the topic of two lectures delivered at the Moscow Linguistic Circle, one on 2 May 1919 titled 'On Abbreviations in Factory Terminology (using material from a single enterprise)', delivered by S. B. Gurvitz-Gurskii, and one on 24 October 1920 on 'Contemporary Words Constituted from Abbreviations', delivered by one of the Circle's founders, B. A. Kushner. See A. B. Krusanov, *Russkii avangard, 1907–1932, tom 2(1): Futuristicheskaia revoliutsiia, 1917–1921* [*The Russian Avant-Garde, Volume 2(1): The Futurist Revolution, 1917–1921*] (Moscow: Novoe literaturnoe obozrenie, 2003), 455, 464.

'bureau']. Kartsevskii's interest in these types focused on the extent to which the abbreviations were motivated words, or not. The first two types (CCCP and NEP) produce, in Kartsevskii's view, 'word-labels', unmotivated *names* the internal parts of which retain no meaning.[43] The final three categories (Narkompros, OPOIaZ, Politburo), however, are different, for there syllables acquire the significance of what Kartsevskii calls 'themes', that is, significant, meaningful parts within the word, which thereby becomes a different, motivated, complex sort of name, in essence, a description (by themes he may have meant what we call 'stems'). Such complex names would constitute a grammatically unique, distinctive feature in Russian, something akin to the patterns of German word-formation. Perhaps more interestingly, the semantic layering of Soviet abbreviations reflects certain functional requirements. Insofar as Soviet abbreviations name institutions of the government's administrative apparatus, and this apparatus is a '*system* of institutions, found in relations of subordination and authority', 'the names of administrative institutions cannot be a simple nomenclature, a catalogue of word-labels, but must reflect these hierarchical relations'.[44] All these considerations will lead Kartsevskii to conclude, finally, that 'for the replacement of words by initial sounds or even syllables to become an ordinary technique in the Russian language [...] sounds and syllables would at once have to acquire a completely different significance than they had in the rest of the inflecting languages'; this would, he concedes, be a 'revolution, as a result of which the Russian language would leave the family of Indo-European languages'.[45]

Having surrendered the '*Ochs* to *bœuf*' argument, Kartsevskii is forced to retreat to Saussure's second line of defence, the argument that the interactions that constitute the linguistic community are too random and complex for any wilful intervention to succeed. If it turns out abbreviations constitute something revolutionary, nevertheless they are doomed by their 'artificial, far-fetched character'.[46] Being the 'individual and always deliberate creation' of intellectuals, abbreviations are, Kartsevskii claims, alien to ordinary conversational, popular language and destined—is this a prediction or a hope?—to disappear with the state institutions they name.[47] When Kartsevskii takes this line, he concedes language can be rationally manipulated and resorts to the Saussurean argument that when this happens to language, *it isn't really language*, because an absence of conscious reflection, a certain model of unselfconscious speech interaction defines 'language as such'. A linguistic revolution is no longer impossible, just improbable on this account. And, to be perfectly frank, Kartsevskii had made it much less improbable when he reinterpreted the very phenomenon of motivation along expressivist lines, turning the desire to shape language into something that made cognitive sense to its ordinary users. When Kartsevskii spoke of the 'striving' for motivation, of the way in which speakers reorganize language in order to render its elements less arbitrary, he made arbitrariness less the default condition of language than a problem that speakers try to overcome, and which they often succeed in overcoming.

---

[43] Kartsevskii, *Iazyk*, 50.   [44] Kartsevskii, *Iazyk*, 53.   [45] Kartsevskii, *Iazyk*, 69.
[46] Kartsevskii, *Iazyk*, 52.   [47] Kartsevskii, *Iazyk*, 66.

VINOKUR: SAUSSURE AND LINGUISTIC POLITICS

The second line of defence could not hold. Could not hold because it had, according to the linguists who followed in Kartsevskii's wake, already been breached in Soviet society (and pre-revolutionary poetry) and it was only necessary to acknowledge the fact. Grigorii Osipovich Vinokur was not the only linguist who made Saussure an ally of the project of linguistic revolution, but he was certainly the most thorough, adventurous, and intently focused on the issues Saussure had raised but dodged (Jakobson was just as committed to the structuralist project and interested in many of the same issues, but less interested in a practical theory aimed at wholesale linguistic reconstruction). He had been present at Kartsevskii's lectures in 1917 and 1918 and had delivered the opening speech at the MLC's session on the *Cours de linguistique générale*.[48] He was in many respects a typical member of the humanist intelligentsia of the time, trained as a linguist but with an equal commitment to the world of Russian poetry and to Russian avant-garde poetry in particular. As was the case with so many of his colleagues, that commitment took the form of an irresistible attraction to both the poetry and person of Mayakovsky, whom he met in 1917, who for a while was a regular attendee at meetings of the MLC, and 'in whose "orbit" I remained for a very long time', in Vinokur's own words.[49]

Kartsevskii conceded that Russian word-creation was wilful and rational, a motivated and expressive response to the existing language, but denied that it constituted actual change, or very much change, at any rate. You could say that Vinokur put the argument into reverse, starting with word-creations which definitely constituted change, but which were less obviously rational or systematic. In fact, the linguistic inventions of Futurism, which aspired to remould the Russian language, announced their irrationality, their offence against common sense; the poets who created them thought that if language was to be 'first of all *language*', they had to steer the ship of language towards the far-off lands of myth and spontaneous creativity. Whether or not these inventions made sense—literally—had already been a source of furious debate within Russian critical circles before Vinokur arrived on

---

[48] For the details of Vinokur's biography, see R. M. Tseitlin, *Grigorii Osipovich Vinokur* (Moscow: Izd. Moskovskogo universiteta, 1965) and 'Slovarnaia avtobiograficheskaia zametka' [Autobiographical Note'] and 'Iz vospominanii moei iunosti' ['From Reminiscences of my Youth'] in G. O. Vinokur, *Vvedenie v izuchenie filologicheskikh nauk* (Moscow: Labirint, 2000), 105–7, 110–15.

[49] Vinokur, 'Iz vospominanii', 113. Mayakovsky's presence at the Moscow Linguistic Circle was clearly important, although there is a pronounced difference of opinion on its ultimate significance. According to Krusanov, Mayakovsky first attended on 2 May 1919; (Krusanov, *Russkii avangard*, 455). B. V. Gornung, a participant in the Circle from early 1919, has written scathingly of his influence on the likes of Jakobson in his memoirs: 'But the most important thing was the aphorisms flung down in passing by Mayakovsky, who was in continual attendance at the MLC. From each such aphorism Jakobson, Brik and Vinokur constructed a theory, which Jakobson later argued for in print' (Gornung, 'Zapiski o pokolenii 20-x godov', 369). On the other hand, Jakobson has written proudly of Mayakovsky's presence (along with other poets) at the Circle's sessions; see Roman Jakobson, 'Moskovskii lingvisticheskii kruzhok', *Philologica* 3.5/7 (1996): 367. Vinokur's response lies interestingly in the middle: he clearly valued Mayakovsky highly, like Jakobson, although he came to share Gornung's aversion to Formalism. Gornung's and Jakobson's differences are indices of a deeper dispute over the achievement of the Moscow Linguistic Circle.

the scene. The critics who later became OPOIaZ (the 'Russian Formalists') argued that this kind of play with pure sound qualities was a way of 'making strange' ordinary, communicative language, but these claims were met with suspicion by critics working on or familiar with the new linguistics, who knew there was no such thing as pure sound, only 'phonemes', i.e., sounds that acquired significance and identity within a linguistic system.[50]

Vinokur brought Saussure into the equation. The point of bringing him into the equation was to show that a genuine act of word-creation was, by definition, a 'social fact', creating a much desired link between the adventures of Futurist poetry and the larger cultural revolution. His initial foray into the field was made in the journal of the 'Left Front in Arts', *LEF*, founded by Mayakovsky and Osip Brik as a place where avant-gardism could prove its socialist bona fides and socialism would recognize its cultural image in experimental (rather than realist) art. *LEF*'s initial issue therefore included not only Vinokur's article 'The Futurists: Language Builders' but also an editorial by Mayakovsky and Brik on 'Our Verbal Work', which cast writers as engaged in the shaping of common linguistic material, in 'the making precise of linguistic expressiveness' through their verses.[51] Vinokur argued that Futurism's experiments were unlike the esoteric efforts of Symbolism because '[n]ot the "magic of words" but the internal mechanism of words attracts the Futurists'.[52] Soviet ideology was, of course, obsessed with mechanisms and engineering as tropes for human transformation, but in this case the reference probably passes through Saussure, who had devoted a few lectures (and a chapter of the *Cours*) to 'Mécanisme de la langue', which described the interplay of associative and syntagmatic relations that produces meaningful units. The Futurist poets understood intuitively what Saussure had demonstrated theoretically—that language was a system, and that new meanings could be generated by the rational manipulation of the possibilities offered by the system. For Futurism this meant the generation of new signs by the extensive use of analogy, our old ambiguous friend, by playing with the phonological resources of Russian and by fanciful or 'poetic' etymologies. Thus the underlying systematicity of language became a reflexive element of it; otherwise inert speech, in Vinokur's words, 'is transformed into a conscious intervention in the system of language, when the utterance finds itself in conditions which require the speaker to use his linguistic faculties rationally and purposefully'.[53]

Futurist poetry was rational when its word-creation was 'not so much *lexicological* as *grammatical*', hewing to the inner structures of the system.[54] And when it was *zaumnyi*, that is, transrational, drawing on sound combinations and morphemes

---

[50] In this respect it's significant that one of the first linguists to use the concept of the phoneme, the Polish linguist Baudouin de Courtenay (who taught at St Petersburg University and was often credited with having invented local equivalents to Saussure's insights), attacked the Futurists in 1914 on exactly these lines. See Gerald Janecek, 'Baudouin de Courtenay versus Kručenych', *Russian Literature* 10 (1981): 17–30.

[51] V. V. Mayakovsky and O. M. Brik, 'Nasha slovesnaia rabota' ['Our Verbal Work'], *LEF* 1 (1923): 41.

[52] G. Vinokur, 'Futuristy – stroiteli iazyka' ["The Futurists: Language Builders'], *LEF 1* (1923): 212.

[53] Vinokur, 'Futuristy', 204.   [54] Vinokur, 'Futuristy, 208.

alien to the Russian language, 'there remains for it a purely *nominative* role, and such a role it can successfully fulfil in the field of social nomenclature'.[55] As Vinokur observed, the strange warblings of Kruchenykh's transrational verse— дыр бул щыл [*dyr bul shchyl*], which means nothing in Russian, either—were no odder-sounding than the loanwords and other concoctions used to name cinemas in the Soviet Union or consumer items like cigarettes. In fact, the sounds used for names, 'not only can be, but ought to be, meaningless', he suggested: they served their function better when they were in no way motivated, when they stood askew the phonological and grammatical system of the common language.[56]

For linguistic interventions were possible when the speaker had to use his linguistic faculties not only 'rationally', but also 'purposefully'. The following issue of *LEF* contained another article by Vinokur, one which went straight to mass linguistic usage. 'On Revolutionary Phraseology' applied avant-gardist norms to the world of political slogans, arguing that the latter had also to be made strange (although he didn't use this term) because 'when the form of the word ceases to be sensed as such, when it does not force its way to perception, *then the meaning also ceases to be sensed*'.[57] But much of the article was devoted to the '[q]uestion of the possibility of linguistic politics' understood as 'the question of the possibility of the conscious, organizing action of society on language'.[58] Although Vinokur was apt to describe this action as the work of a 'technologist', a merely objective knowledge of the language system was not enough: interventions had to be guided and calculated according to a goal or purpose that was internal to language itself.[59] The model for such goal-orientated language had been the distinctively poetic language so intensively examined in Russia that it had a society named for it— OPOIaZ: the Society for the Study of Poetic Language. To round off his campaign, Vinokur published a third article in *LEF*, 'Linguistics Poetics Sociology', which confronts Saussure head-on with his ambiguities. Saussure had brilliantly separated the messy, inchoate stuff of language into *langue* and *parole*, the former understood by Vinokur (and others from the MLC) as having the nature not of a neutral average but of a 'certain legitimate norm' that puts pressure on individual speech and which can be maintained despite speech's actual minute variations.[60] But it was the other side of the equation that received the most severe revision. For where Saussure saw the wilful side of language as individual, creative, and arbitrary, Vinokur saw it as *style*, as language driven not by individual, capricious wills, but by functions that determined how utterances were put together.

---

[55] Vinokur, 'Futuristy', 212.   [56] Vinokur, 'Futuristy', 212.
[57] G. Vinokur, 'O revoliutsionnoi frazeologii (odin iz voprosov iazykovoi politiki)' ['On Revolutionary Phraseology (One of the Questions of Linguistic Politics)'], *LEF* 2 (1923): 111.
[58] Vinokur, 'O revoliutsionnoi frazeologii', 104.
[59] Vinokur never shook off the technical conception. Thus: 'Only by starting from the concept of a linguistic system will the linguist-technologist learn in detail how to distinguish all the innumerable nuts and bolts that make up the linguistic machine. Only in this way will he learn how to take it apart and put it back together again, after changing the useless parts.' Vinokur, 'Kul′tura iazyka', 106.
[60] G. Vinokur, 'Poetika Lingvistika Sotsiologiia' ['Poetics Linguistics Sociology'], *LEF* 3 (1923): 105.

This was more than a mere socializing of the 'wilful' side of language, for 'the very concept of stylistics is fundamentally connected with the concept of a goal'.[61] Saussure's model treated subjectivity as an arbitrary force, embodied in *parole*, that was moderated or tamed by the social side of language: whatever one wanted to do in and with language, one had to communicate with others, participate in the 'social convention which is the language'.[62] If this was the case, if language's expressive purposes were always subordinate to communicative ones, then there was indeed 'no reason to prefer *Ochs* to *bœuf*' and no 'practical' bent within linguistics. But if language didn't mean 'in general' but meant functionally, in accord with a particular *telos* or goal, then one could evaluate the relative value of different forms for achieving the task at hand.

When Saussure had made his mid-course correction in the third series of linguistics lectures, adding the chapter on 'immutability and mutability', he also added a striking new element to the system of language: for '[i]n order for there to be a language, there must be a body of speakers [*masse parlante*] using the language'.[63] Up till that point the existence of speakers had not, of course, been in doubt and, in keeping with the Neogrammarian inheritance, their importance for the development and maintenance of the language was always central: *langue*, after all, only existed in their minds. But only when Saussure needed to assure himself of language's irrationality did he introduce speakers *en masse*, as a collective body with a certain shape. That shape did not allow for any kind of collective will, which Saussure thought impossible. When Vinokur and his colleagues got hold of Saussure's theory, they had a somewhat different model of the social body or speaking mass in front of them. But more than that, they still believed that what had been cast—and castigated—as national or collective 'spirit' in the nineteenth century could not be dissolved into the merely interior psychic life of individuals. Vinokur, too, believed that the 'spirit' of a language was hidden in its grammatical arrangements, in objectified form.

'Linguistics Poetics Sociology' was, to some extent, a polemic with the Russian Formalists who thought 'language as such' had essentially one function or shape, barely visible in practical language but brought into the foreground in poetic language. The point agreed on was that language had a shape; the point of difference was Vinokur's claim that the shape was multiform and that '[p]oetics, thus understood, is only a part of stylistics'.[64] Let us look at one more article, 'The Culture of Language', published in late 1923 in the Communist Party journal *Press and Revolution*. After describing the revolution introduced by Saussure's 'static' method, Vinokur remarks that it's not a matter of transforming language into a consciously deployed instrument—of, so to speak, poeticizing it—but of recognizing the ordinariness of such deployment:

> Whether we write a chancellery document or a scholarly treatise, whether we speak with a friend or a boss, we are always compelled to manoeuvre with our linguistic

---

[61] Vinokur, 'Poetika', 108. [62] Saussure, *Second Course*, 4a.
[63] Saussure, *Third Course*, Lecture of 30 May 1911, 101a. [64] Vinokur, 'Poetika', 108.

faculties in different relationships, with the goal of the fullest, actively goal-orientated use of the possibilities stored in our speech. Our speech must be *constructed* to a certain degree. It is the object of cultural *overcoming*, it demands a definite *organization from without*.[65]

Promoters of 'linguistic culture' (as he first dubs it here) or of 'linguistic technology' (as he calls it later in the article—an interesting contrast) should therefore direct their attention to 'the kind of linguistic field where its bearers are already to a certain degree conscious of it as a system, as an organization, as a machine'.[66] And to ensure that this consciousness is not identified with a 'poetic' feeling for language, the field chosen should not be poetry—the Futurists are clearly no longer the ideal of the linguistic politician. One needs, instead, 'a linguistic system which would not be distant from practical language according to its function, but at the same time would be conscious of itself precisely as a system'.[67] This field will be 'extra-artistic literature', represented in this particular article by the newspaper.

Thus in late 1923 there is a slight recoil from the belief that poetic invention is the model for conscious linguistic intervention. Then, in early 1924, there is a kind of reverse Damascene moment when, as Vinokur put it, he 'experienced a very sharp disenchantment with "Formalism" and Futurism and I went to Leningrad, as it happens, intending to "clarify relations" with the Leningrad Formalist school and to show myself "in a new light"'.[68] The clarification was expressed not only in discussions with colleagues (including a tortured correspondence with Jakobson, who seemed wholly unsympathetic to his friend's change of heart), but also in print.[69] There was a pointed renunciation of Futurism and its poetics ('This generation took shape in the atmosphere created by Futurism. The destructive tendencies of this trend were in essence anti-cultural tendencies.');[70] there was a pointed embrace of 'philology' as an alternative to the 'linguistic' approach to language;[71] there was enthusiasm for the doctrine of inner form articulated by the philosopher Gustav Shpet (who had attracted a sizeable number of the MLC *aktiv* over to his side, leading to a split within the group).[72] When Vinokur's articles on 'linguistic politics' were drawn together as parts of a substantial book, *The Culture of Language: Studies in Linguistic Technology* in 1925, the preface (dated August 1924) announced that some of the chapters had been extensively reworked because 'on a series of points

---

[65] Vinokur, 'Kul'tura iazyka', 105.   [66] Vinokur, 'Kul'tura iazyka', 107.
[67] Vinokur, 'Kul'tura iazyka', 107.
[68] G. Vinokur, 'Neskol'ko slov pamiati Iu. N. Tynianova' ['A Few Words in Memory of Iu. N. Tynianov'], in *Vospominaniia o Iu. Tynianove* (Moscow: Sovetskii pisatel', 1983), 66.
[69] Letter from G. O. Vinokur to R. O. Jakobson, 18 August 1925, in S. I. Gindin, 'Druz'ia v zhizni—opponenty v nauke: Perepiska R. O. Jakobsona i G. O. Vinokura' ['Friends in Life—Opponents in Scholarship: The Correspondence of R. O. Jakobson and G. O. Vinokur'], *Novoe literaturnoe obozrenie* 21 (1996): 90–4.
[70] Anon. (but presumed to be Vinokur), Preface, in G. Vinokur and Filipp Vermel', *Chet i nechet: al'manakh poezii i kritiki* (Moscow: authorial publication, 1925), 5.
[71] 'My path is to philology in the authentic sense of this term, in that sense in which it is opposed to linguistics by Porzhensinskii in his "Introduction".' Letter to Jakobson, 18 August 1925, 'Druz'ia v zhizni', 92.
[72] See Vinokur's review of Shpet, *Esteticheskie fragmenty*, in *Chet i nechet*, 44–6.

they no longer correspond to my current point of view'.[73] That point of view was changing so rapidly that in a letter to Jakobson on 18 August 1925 he complained that 'when I see my name already (!!) in bibliographies or in other places with references to the first edition of *The Culture of Language* it has become painful and repulsive to me, I am horrified'.[74] But it couldn't have been that painful: in 1929 a second, somewhat revised edition of the book was published.

The project itself, however, was maintained even in the face of such impassioned disillusionment; perhaps because from the start it had a certain degree of flexibility built into it, being alternately described as the creation of a 'linguistic technology', 'linguistic politics', and 'linguistic culture'. Did one take political positions *within* language? Use it like a tool? Cultivate it self-consciously? These were different ways to think about the conscious shaping and use of linguistic material: maybe they were all necessary. Just as, at the very same moment, physicists accepted that light and matter behaved sometimes like a wave, sometimes like particles, so it might be that the organization and direction of language was technological, political, and cultivating in different moments. Or maybe 'language as such' was a solution so powerful that these distinctions dissolved within it.

The Culture of Language—the book of 1925—applied the final turn of the screw. In the initial celebration and critique of Saussure, the *langue/parole* distinction is again redrawn as the distinction between *language in general* and *style*, and *langue* is again a social norm. But Vinokur has by this point decided that the very philology Saussure's linguistics broke with has to be brought back into play and that Saussure's concept of a linguistic system will be understood as a 'linguistic structure' once we acknowledge the need for a 'restitution of philology and its methods'.[75] Why the change? Because 'language is a kind of system which is meaningless outside of a definite environment that regards the given system as some kind of norm, as a tradition'.[76] It sounds similar to the claims made in the earlier articles, but something has shifted in the interim: 'norm' here means not just a system with coercive force, but a system with a purpose. Which means that style is not a new way of thinking about *parole*, a way of de-individualizing it and giving it purpose, but a new way of thinking about *langue*, the linguistic system (or structure) itself. Of course, *parole* and *langue* were never supposed to be different phenomena: merely two ways of objectifying *langage* (as a series of historical performances, or as the order which made the performances possible). So in this new disposition 'language in general' exists as a kind of intersection or amalgamation of the various functional systems or styles in which the whole is realized, styles which are traditions not only in the sense that they are forceful, but in the sense that they contain or embody cultural values that give the norms a point:

---

[73] G. Vinokur, *Kul'tura iazyka: ocherki lingvisticheskoi tekhnologii* [*The Culture of Language: Studies in Linguistic Technology*] (Moscow: Rabotnik prosveshcheniia, 1925), 3.
[74] Vinokur, Letter to Jakobson, 18 August 1925, in 'Druzia v zhizni', 92.
[75] Vinokur, *Kul'tura iazyka*, 17n1. [76] Vinokur, *Kul'tura iazyka*, 18.

Stylistics looks at language, i.e., at that which Saussure calls *la langue*, as material which can be used, interpreted by a speaking individual, as a normative scheme, a tradition, within which individual linguistic activity, individual linguistic *creation*, finds a place for itself.[77]

At which point the link with philology, the study of language as an element of culture, has been satisfactorily re-established.

The re-establishment of philology was not bloodless, and Futurism was its most prominent casualty. It makes an appearance near the end of the book in a chapter where the Futurists' fatal mistake is to '*struggle* with the linguistic tradition', that is, to look on language as material, as merely a grammatical system, rather than recognize it as norm-laden tradition.[78] Futurist word-creation, once celebrated for its grammatical orientation, is now condemned as the 'hypertrophic, at times pathological development of grammatical analogies',[79] with the result that it is characteristically 'only *formal* and not *substantive*'.[80] An avant-garde interest in 'throwing Pushkin, Dostoevsky, etc. off the ship of modernity' is not likely to elicit much sympathy from a critic who has decided language takes the form of tradition. But Vinokur's deeper point is that the Futurists are kidding themselves. Because they fail to realize that 'new words grow only from new cultural concepts', from linguistic expressiveness and functionality, in practice their lexical inventions remain within the bounds of existing tradition: insofar as they rely on the existing grammar, they do no more than reshuffle, with a certain theatrical flair, the linguistic deck.[81]

It's not a mistake made by the general populace or by those engaged in 'extra-artistic literature'. They also want to play with language, to invent new forms and new words, but they do so by shedding language's grammatical baggage. After *The Culture of Language* lays out its theoretical case, it proceeds to an examination of the vagaries of popular usage during the time of the New Economic Policy (which had begun in 1921). 'The language of NEP', according to Vinokur, is characterized not by this or that grammatical feature, not by an infusion of loanwords, say, or the emergence of some new syntactical pattern, but by 'the striving of the speaking collective towards the consciousness of and organization of their linguistic experience', that is, by an infusion of precisely the kind of self-reflexiveness that Saussure had deemed artificial, alien to 'language as such'.[82] Vinokur, though, is not quite finished with his manhandling of Saussure's theory. His original claim had been that Saussure made language amenable to conscious transformation by revealing its systematicity, by making it a matter of nuts and bolts that could be grasped and turned. The transformations charted by Kartsevskii had followed this logic, however much Kartsevskii might have wished to underplay their significance: neologisms were

---

[77] Vinokur, *Kul'tura iazyka*, 20. It's worth noting that Saussure's student and editor, Charles Bally, would become the first Professor of Stylistics at the University of Geneva. See p. 128, below.
[78] Vinokur, *Kul'tura iazyka*, 191.   [79] Vinokur, *Kul'tura iazyka*, 192.
[80] Vinokur, *Kul'tura iazyka*, 193.   [81] Vinokur, *Kul'tura iazyka*, 192.
[82] Vinokur, *Kul'tura iazyka*, 62.

conscious to the extent they were rational and they were rational to the extent that they relied on a tacit knowledge of the linguistic system, to the extent that they were tightly motivated. Vinokur's examples of conscious transformation follow the opposite logic: they are conscious to the extent that they endow sounds and syllables with a meaning which *defies* the systematicity of language. It is when the speaking collective endows linguistic elements with a signifying life of their own, escaping from or transforming the context which originally gave them life, that they take control of their language.

As if to make the contrast complete, Vinokur's examples are the *same examples* as those instanced by Kartsevskii: he, too, is fascinated by the emergence of what Kartsevskii called 'themes', the '*new* compositional elements' from which Soviet abbreviations are formed: the нар [*nar*], ком [*kom*], and прос [*pros*] which, for example, in combination signified the 'People's Commissariat of Enlightenment', Напкомпрос [*Narkompros*].[83] These elements transfer the signification of a word onto its initial syllable, but in the process something changes: the link to the words they abbreviate—in this case народный [*narodnyi*], комиссариат [*kommissariat*], and просвещение [*prosveshchenie*]—'has lost almost any grammatical character and becomes only referentio-semantic'.[84] Evidence that elements had broken out of the prison-house of grammar took a variety of forms. Vinokur points out that Soviet abbreviations often put their themes in the wrong order, grammatically speaking, or that they freely omitted elements, thus gradually weakening the motivation that supposedly explains and justifies the abbreviation. They openly defied the existing rules of Russian grammar in order to maintain their independence—as when the theme авиа [*avia*, as in aviation] refused to exchange its final 'a' for the traditional 'o' when combining with other morphemes, or when the abbreviations for People's Commissariat—нарком [*narkom*]—and for People's Commissar—also нарком—were differentiated by simply adding the -ат [*–at*] syllable (which does not correspond to any existing suffix) of the former, creating наркомат [*narkomat*], in effect a sign made out of the first and final syllables of an existing word. To give you some sense of an equivalent move in English, we have to turn to Orwell's *Nineteen Eighty-Four*, which mimics Soviet abbreviations in Newspeak: it's as if the Ministry of Truth and the Minister of Truth were both 'Minitrue' and the populace improvised by making the former 'Minirytrue'.

Vinokur wants to stress the point: the speaking mass improvises. 'In fact', he remarks, 'it would be difficult to deny that all this free play with themes is based on a particular kind of inventiveness'.[85] That they can do so, that free play is possible, brings us back to the liberating force of the arbitrariness discovered by Saussure. For while there is 'no reason to prefer *Ochs* to *bœuf*' there is no reason to prefer '*bœuf* to *Ochs*', either, meaning language is 'defenceless' against any change supervening on it.[86] Thus once themes escape the domestic grasp of the words that 'gave birth to them' and strike off on their own, they are free to acquire meanings that could not have been predicted from the circumstances of their upbringing and

---

[83] Vinokur, *Kul'tura iazyka*, 63.
[84] Vinokur, *Kul'tura iazyka*, 63.
[85] Vinokur, *Kul'tura iazyka*, 64.
[86] Saussure, *Course in General Linguistics* (1983), 76.

to mix with other words from all walks of life.[87] This newfound autonomy is notable for two reasons. First, because it means that the speaking collective directs language most impressively when its coinages defy grammar in the service of its 'linguistic needs'. Secondly, because of what may look like a fundamental irony: it is when the theme becomes 'referentio-semantic', in effect, a *name*, that it becomes pliable and flexible. Its maturity is, if you like, of the bourgeois kind, defined not by a rigid adherence to its object, but by a willingness to compromise. Of course, the irony is only apparent, only a consequence of the 'pre-Saussurean' tendency to understand names as labels for things. In reality, the more the sign approaches the status of a name, the closer it comes to what Žižek calls the 'signifier without the signified', which points not only to an object, but also to its own act of designating an object, to the act of enunciation itself.[88]

It's surely no accident that Vinokur acknowledges this paradox when the topic of discussion is not the abbreviated name of this or that Soviet institution, but the abbreviated name for the historical moment itself: НЭП [*NEP*], a theme in its own right that arises not as a syllable in an abbreviation but as the acronym for the Новая экономическая политика [*Novaia ekonomicheskaia politika*], the New Economic Policy of the Soviet government (the chapter title itself, 'The Language of НЭП' is thus uncannily self-reflexive). NEP starts life as mere shorthand, but it rapidly outgrows its roots, becoming semantically flexible and therefore relatively unmotivated. For while the New Economic Policy remained a publicly endorsed programme, NEP became a signifier of the policy's bad underside, and like many other themes, with maturity it gave birth to its own progeny, among them the class of detested and reviled 'Nep-men', whose greed and amorality testified to the corruption of Soviet ideals. Vinokur calls this swerving of NEP 'an emotional and ethical colouring', as if it were an added subjective coating to the objective reference of the term.[89] In fact, NEP, freed from the need to designate its object, had become a way of pointing to the situation of enunciation itself, in which one could not talk about the New Economic Policy soberly or objectively, so that the effects of the policy were, discursively, separated from the policy itself.

Whatever their differences, Vinokur and Kartsevskii were Saussure enthusiasts; they thought they were drawing logical conclusions from Saussure's work. The full weight of Saussure's ambiguities, however, become clear when we see that one could echo Vinokur's arguments for linguistic politics and yet claim Saussure's theory was an *obstacle* to them. Thus Lev Iakubinskii, originally a Russian Formalist and, like Vinokur, an advocate of linguistic politics, attacked Saussure as an opponent rather than an ally in a mean-spirited article the title of which conveys the essential point: 'F. de Saussure on the Impossibility of Linguistic Politics'.[90]

---

[87] Vinokur, *Kul'tura iazyka*, 63.
[88] Slavoj Žižek, *The Sublime Object of Ideology* (London: Verso, 1989), 99.
[89] Vinokur, *Kul'tura iazyka*, 61.
[90] L. Iakubinskii, 'F. de Sossiur o nevozmozhnosti iazykovoi politiki' ['F. de Saussure on the Impossibility of Linguistic Politics'], in N. Ia. Marr (ed.), *Iazykovedenie i materializm*, 2 (Moscow: Gosudarstvennaia sotsialno-ekonomicheskaia izdatel', 1931), 91–104.

Published in 1931, but based on a lecture given in 1929, the piece is obviously part of the Stalinist campaign against 'bourgeois intellectuals' launched in that year, though it has little to do with the Marrism that eventually would engulf Soviet linguistics (Marrism is a set of linguistic doctrines, promulgated by the Soviet scholar Nikolai Ia. Marr and embraced by the party, according to which human language emerged initially in the Caucuses and developed on a class rather than national basis; though Marr was in some respects an able and intelligent scholar, the doctrines themselves were largely speculative and eventually repudiated in the USSR). But Iakubinskii, however unfortunate his involvement in this effort, was no fool, and he shrewdly alights on the very features of Saussure's text we discussed earlier.[91] That an active participant in Soviet life would dispute Saussure's key claim that social collectivities are naturally inert can hardly come as a surprise. But Iakubinskii also has a clever linguistic argument against the claim that the complexity of the language system defuses all efforts at change. For while it may be the case that one cannot hope to replace one language system in its entirety by another, 'the existence of different systems, or, more precisely, the existence of collectivities with different linguistic systems to a great degree makes possible the clarification of these systems for their speakers and thus provides the basis for their transformation'.[92] And the proof of the pudding lies in its having been eaten: for, indeed, one can witness, *pace* Saussure, many instances in which 'widespread mass linguistic catch-phrases' with systematic features, have been invented.[93]

But the most telling of all Iakubinskii's criticisms is the one aimed at an assumption in Saussure's theory that is both casually made—without a shred of evidence—and yet in many respects central to his claims for linguistic inertia. Early in the chapter on immutability Saussure describes language as 'the most striking proof' that 'the rules a community accepts are imposed upon it, and not freely agreed to'.[94] Fine, language is a matter of fate, but Saussure goes on to claim we hug our chains. 'For, in any case,' Saussure says, 'linguistic facts are rarely the object of criticism, every society being usually content with the language it has inherited.'[95] The first half of that sentence is so obviously false that it requires no comment, but the second may be even more significant. For it echoed, in a particularly vivid way, the assumption I referred to earlier, 'that language, in the default situation, *works*'. But for Iakubinskii 'it is clear that Saussure's assumption is false';[96] people have 'an abundance of motives for preferring one signifier to another', which testifies to their dissatisfaction with language.[97] In an article notable for rhetorical

---

[91] Iakubinskii's hostility to Saussure was not confected or opportunistic, even if the terms in which he attacked him were discreditable, and Iakubinskii himself was an accomplished and original thinker. On some of his achievements, see Viktoria Gulida, 'Theoretical Insights and Ideological Pressures in Early Soviet Linguistics: The Cases of Lev Iakubinskii and Boris Larin', in Craig Brandist and Katya Chown (eds.), *Politics and the Theory of Language in the USSR, 1917–1938* (London: Anthem Press, 2011), 53–68.
[92] Iakubinskii, 'F. de Sossiur', 102.   [93] Iakubinskii, 'F. de Sossiur', 102.
[94] Saussure, *Course in General Linguistics* (1983), 71.
[95] Saussure, *Course in General Linguistics* (1983), 73.
[96] Iakubinskii, 'F. de Sossiur', 99n1.   [97] Iakubinskii, 'F. de Sossiur', 99.

overkill, Iakubinskii makes the point rather delicately. For couldn't one argue that language, the contract one inherits but has never agreed to, is for many not a source of satisfaction, but of frustration, anxiety, resentment, less the locus of successful communication than of lost opportunities, missed connections, fatal misunderstandings, inexpressible wants? Wouldn't that give the people who speak a reason to change the language they use? And didn't they, in fact, do that? What Saussure did not realize and what it took Soviet linguists to reveal was that once he had made language an historical and social institution, there was no turning back. The matter was out of his hands.

5

On the Diversity—and Productivity— of Language

(M. M. Bakhtin, Walter Benjamin, Saussure)

Language was protected from the forces of reason not by walls, but by 'soft power'—by the inertia of complacency, the complexity of the system, the force of traditionalism, and the arbitrariness of signs. Or so it had seemed until the likes of Vinokur and Iakubinskii showed that revolution could be fomented from within. Iakubinskii pointed to the discontent that was brewing within the citadel of discourse, and both could point to islands of linguistic use, different linguistic subsystems or social dialects, where one's discourse was guided by reflection and where, as Vinokur put it, 'we make a choice from among the possibilities that grammar gives us'.[1] These indigenous movements nevertheless required some external help to find their feet, which duly arrived in the Trojan horse named 'stylistics'. Stylistics had been the brainchild of Saussure's editor and student, Charles Bally, who published two books on the topic in 1905 and 1909, and who ascended to the world's first chair in the subject at Geneva in 1912, with Saussure's help.[2] But stylistics at that point was the study of the 'affective' side of what was still an 'unconscious' language system. It was left to Vinokur to render style conscious and reflective.

But making the leap required a critical amendment to the concept of *langue*: the idea that a natural language is *functionally* differentiated. There were plenty of reasons to make the leap at that moment. Many within linguistics had become sceptical of the very concept of a unified language bound to a homogeneous speech community: in part because regional dialects were no longer regarded as corrupt deviations from a national norm, leading to rich studies in dialectology, and in part because even dialects were beginning to be interpreted as fictions of homogeneity, masking the fact that language always consisted of an overlapping series of features (phonetic, grammatical, lexical, syntactical).[3] Linguistics could also look to the new discipline

---

[1] Vinokur, *Kul'tura iazyka*, 51.

[2] Joseph describes the machinations leading to the establishment of the chair and the disputes over the meaning of 'stylistics' that accompanied it in *Saussure*, 611–15.

[3] On the assault on the idea of a homogeneous language and a homogeneous speech community, see Morpurgo Davies, *Nineteenth-Century Linguistics*, 287–90. The assault was led by Hugo Schuchardt, who founded the study of pidgins and creoles, and scholars of dialectology. Among the most important were Jules Gilliéron, whose work culminated in a dialect atlas of France, and Louis Gauchat, who showed that even the dialect of a village was divided on various social lines. On Gauchat, see the homage

of sociology, which made the functional specialization and differentiation of roles one of the defining features of modern (and urban) life. And within pre-Soviet and Soviet Russia there was the intense examination of literature as precisely a language made distinct and particular by virtue of its functional uniqueness. Jakobson had led that charge, and he remained focused on literary language, but he recognized the more general significance of what had taken place. A plan for a never-published book included the following telling remark:

> So long as linguistics was a principally genetic, and not functional science, it could not have an authentic practical application. There was no bridge from historical grammar to a school textbook, and active intervention in linguistic development could only take the form of a groundless reactionary purism. Functional linguistics allows one to construct a school grammar informed by scholarship, it opens the possibility, furthermore, of a teleological critique of linguistic development, it makes the participation of linguistics in active linguistic culture necessary.[4]

When linguistics only charts linguistic change, Jakobson is arguing, the only *practical* thing a linguist can do is try to prevent or hinder that change, insofar as he or she cannot promote a change that is necessarily unpredictable. Interventions by historical linguists are thus bound to be 'purist', no matter what the feelings or ideology of the linguist in question. The 'functional' point of view, by contrast, gave linguistic subsystems a purpose, thereby making internal criteria of evaluation possible.

Vinokur had made the point at great length in the chapter of *The Culture of Language* entitled 'On Purism'. Purist attacks on current vocabulary or usage, he contended, were distinguished by their 'uselessness', because they inevitably took the form of a protest or reaction against an existing linguistic usage: 'Like any form of reaction, purism always arrives too late, because it cannot predict its enemies, cannot know in advance when and against what it will be necessary to struggle.'[5] And yet, after ridiculing purists for the usual reasons, Vinokur makes the surprising claim that purism, 'as an *idea*, as a *principle*, is *not bad*'.[6] In fact it can be quite good—if it is erected 'on the basis of a thoughtful, strict and scientific knowledge of language'.[7] A true purism would 'pay exclusive attention to matters of *style*'.[8] Instead of railing helplessly against neologisms and changes in grammar, the scientific purist makes the evaluative moment a moment of stylistic judgment, ensuring that the choices that create *parole* are not arbitrary but guided by a sense of what kind of language will suit the situation and the goals embedded within it. Purism would be reborn as the culture of language, more precisely, the culture of a functionally differentiated language.

(a prefatory article and translation) by J. K. Chambers, Sarah Cummins, and Jeff Tennant, 'Louis Gauchat—Patriarch of Variationist Linguistics', *Historiographia Linguistica* 35.1/2 (2008): 213–74 (thanks to Nigel Vincent for calling my attention to Gauchat). Gilliéron's dialect studies would serve as a model for Soviet linguists like Viktor Zhirmunskii, who took the model of the regional dialect and applied it to variations arising from social differentiation. See Craig Brandist, 'Marxism and the Philosophy of Language in Russia in the 1920s and 1930s', *Historical Materialism* 13.1 (2005): 63–84.

[4] Attachment to a letter from Jakobson to Viktor Shklovskii, 26 February 1929 (no. 15), in Toman, *Letters and Other Materials*, 66–7.
[5] Vinokur, *Kul'tura iazyka*, 34.   [6] Vinokur, *Kul'tura iazyka*, 48.
[7] Vinokur, *Kul'tura iazyka*, 48.   [8] Vinokur, *Kul'tura iazyka*, 50.

The critical point is that differentiation was meaningful less because of the multiplicity it revealed than on account of the new features it assigned to that which had been split. For Vinokur the fact that there were linguistic subsystems revealed the functionality of language; one could, so to speak, see the heterogeneity of linguistic subsystems only when one attributed more finely-grained sets of goals to language than simple communication (or, if you wish, a more finely-grained sense of what it means to 'communicate'). It's an interesting move and, as it turns out, an exemplary move. For although it might seem that an interest in language as such and an interest in the diversity of actual languages point in opposite directions, in the early decades of the twentieth century they walk hand in hand. Saussure, for many the very model of a modern language unifier, begins his third course of lectures with the acknowledgment that though 'language' (*langue*) might be our ultimate object, 'what is given is not only the language but languages'.[9] 'As far as linguistics is concerned', he admits, 'the diversity of languages is indeed the fundamental fact.'[10] But the fundamental fact does not lead where you might expect: it does not lead to maps and family trees, peoples and migrations, to the distinctions of national spirit and culture so dear to the nineteenth century. The linguistic turns of the twentieth century pivot on the fundamental fact and interpret it as the outward sign of something very modern, rather than the residue of something very ancient. For Saussure, Walter Benjamin, and M. M. Bakhtin—three writers who make diversity central to their linguistic doctrines—what appears to be a matter of 'spatial' differentiation (the coexistence of different natural languages, dialects, and registers) is in fact the mark of the historical, productive side of language, the side of language that leads to constant innovation and change. Saussure will be explicit: what looks like the differentiation of language in space, the division of language as such into geographically distinct languages and dialect forms, is, in fact, a consequence of language change over time, language's historical tendency. Walter Benjamin will make the Babel-like confusion of tongues the very thing that points towards a utopian 'language as such', which is not simply a single natural language elevated to ideal status, but a productive forcefulness that can only appear within and through the interference of different languages. Finally, Bakhtin, whose name is indelibly linked (at least in Western Europe and the Americas) with the idea that language takes the form of 'heteroglossia'—the stratification of language 'not only into linguistic dialects in the strict sense of the word (according to formal linguistic markers, for the most part phonetic ones), but, more importantly for our purposes here, into socio-ideological languages: the languages of social groups, professions, genres, generations and so on'—will use the differentiation of language as a tool for the moulding of a new, modernist and historical conception of language.[11]

---

[9] Saussure, *Third Course*, Lecture of 4 November 1910, 9a.
[10] Saussure, *Third Course*, Lecture of 8 November 1910, 12a.
[11] M. M. Bakhtin, 'Slovo v romane: K voprosam stilistiki romana' ['Discourse in the Novel: On Issues in the Stylistics of the Novel'], in *Sobranie sochinenii, tom 3: teoriia romana (1930–1961 gg)* (Moscow: Iazyki slavianskikh kul′tur, 2012), 25; English translation: 'Discourse in the Novel', in *The Dialogic Imagination*, trans. Michael Holquist and Caryl Emerson (Austin, TX: University of Texas Press, 1981), 271–2.

Saussure's journey from comparative philology to 'language in general' was, as we have seen, somewhat reluctant. Benjamin invested 'language as such' with magical force from his earliest work until the *Arcades Project*. For Bakhtin the interest in language was sudden and abrupt, and the resulting conception correspondingly wild and dramatic.

BAKHTIN: DIVERSITY AND PRODUCTIVITY IN THE NOVEL

At first glance Bakhtin's essays on the style of the novel make him appear like a less sober, more militant version of Vinokur. The latter thought that conceiving of language as style made linguistic politics, a kind of specialized science of language use, possible; the former writes as if conceiving of language as style makes everything possible, as if novelistic style constituted a politics in its own right. Thus the novel is responsible for 'a radical revolution in the fate of human discourse: the essential liberation of cultural-semantic and expressive intentions from domination by a single and unitary language'; drawing its strength and its tactics from 'the social life of discourse outside the cloistered artist, in the spaces of public squares, streets, cities and villages', it undermines every trace of traditional authority, makes language democratic and free, and lays the basis for a scientific and realistic approach to the world.[12]

Why would Bakhtin invest so much in style, or in any form of language? What makes Bakhtin's case particularly interesting is the decisiveness with which he made the investment. From 1918 until the late 1920s, Bakhtin worked on a systematic ethical philosophy that only occasionally touched on the nature of language, even when examining artistic works and aesthetic experience. In an article written by Bakhtin in 1924—'The Problem of Form, Content and Material in Verbal Artistic Work'—he in fact polemicized at great length with the Formalist claim that literature arose from the reforming or deforming of linguistic material. Language was the material of literature, just as marble might be the material of sculpture, but no scrutiny of the grammar and syntax of a work could reveal the source of its cognitive, ethical, or aesthetic force. The Formalists had burdened language with a lot of excess baggage:

> By endowing the word with everything that belongs to culture, i.e., with all cultural properties—cognitive, ethical and aesthetic—one easily comes to the conclusion that there is nothing to culture besides the word, that all culture is nothing but a phenomenon of language, that the scholar and the poet to the same degree deal only with the word.[13]

---

[12] Bakhtin, 'Slovo v romane'/'Discourse in the Novel', 122/367, 10–11/259.

[13] M. M. Bakhtin, 'K voprosam metodologii estetiki slovesnogo tvorchestva: I. Problema formy, soderzhaniia i materiala v slovesnom khudozhestvennom tvorchestve' ['On Methodological Issues in the Aesthetics of Verbal Creation: I. The Problem of Form, Content, and Material in Verbal Artistic Work'], in *Sobranie sochinenii, tom 1: Filosofskaia estetika 1920-x godov* (Moscow: Russkie slovari, 2003), 299. English translation: 'The Problem of Content, Material, and Form in Verbal Art (1924)',

The 1924 article is one of three long texts Bakhtin wrote in the early 1920s. Those texts—the other two are known as 'Towards a Philosophy of the Act' and 'Author and Hero in Aesthetic Activity'—made a particular brand of ethical or moral philosophy the key to the rescue of a devastated Europe. Bakhtin's argument was that a scientific and legalistic view of morality, founded on an individualistic model of the human being, had made the evasion of moral responsibility simple and convenient. The idea that we should love others as we love ourselves, that we should simply generalize our self-love or universalize our maxims, was based on a fundamental and fatal misunderstanding. Ethical responsibility would only be compelling when we acknowledged the fundamental 'architectonic' distinction between *I* and *other*, that is, the fact that we experience our own thoughts, feelings, bodies, and lives in a register completely different from our experience of the thoughts, feelings, bodies, and lives of others. Moral feelings only made sense given this distinction, for we are unable to love ourselves or to find fulfilment or contentment in life we experience as *I*, which is necessarily shapeless and perpetually on the move, even unto death. Only the *other*, whom we experience as part of worldly time and space, as an outward body and as verbal and gestural expression, could be loved: moral feelings were a *response* to others, not the result of feeling what someone else felt. The end result of this doctrine is 'a uniquely deep synthesis of *ethical solipsism*, of infinite severity towards one's own self, i.e., a disinterested and pure relation to oneself, with *ethical-aesthetic kindness* for the other'.[14] Or to put it more simply: this was a phenomenology, an analysis of the structure of experience, that led to a kind of Christian ethics and to an emphasis on *conscience*, not law or moral reasoning, as the motive force for moral action.

Fortunately, one didn't have to engage in phenomenological analysis to recognize the architectonic split and feel the weight of its consequences: it was also manifest in the relation of 'authors' and 'heroes' in prose. Heroes were *others* whose subjectivity, whose *I*-ness was captured, held in tension, by the prose writer whose gift of form placed them in a complete, external, fulfilled world. Bakhtin's philosophy was therefore shadowed almost from the very beginning by work on Dostoevsky, finally issuing in a book, *Problems of Dostoevsky's Art*, published in 1929, shortly after Bakhtin had been arrested for participating in a 'counter-revolutionary' discussion group.[15] But it might be more accurate to say the research led to two books, for although *Problems of Dostoevsky's Art* is a single volume, it looks and reads like two books spliced together, a fact acknowledged by its formal division into two parts, each comprising four chapters. Part One, 'The Polyphonic Novel of Dostoevsky',

---

trans. Kenneth Brostrom, in *Art and Answerability: Early Philosophical Essays by M. M. Bakhtin* (Austin, TX: University of Texas Press, 1990), 291.

[14] Bakhtin, 'Avtor i geroi v esteticheskoi deiatel'nosti', in *Sobranie sochinenii* 1, 133; English translation: 'Author and Hero in Aesthetic Activity (ca.1920–1923)', in *Art and Answerability*, 56.

[15] In a letter to his friend Matvei Kagan in 1922, Bakhtin says 'Now I am writing a work on Dostoevsky, which I hope to finish very soon'; Letter from M. M. Bakhtin to M. I. Kagan, 18 January 1922, in Iu. M. Kagan, 'O starykh bumagakh iz semeinogo arkhiva (M. M. Bakhtin i M. I. Kagan'['On Old Papers from a Family Archive: M. M. Bakhtin and M. I. Kagan'], *Dialog Karnaval Khronotop* 1 (1992): 72. A description of the arrest, interrogation, and eventual sentencing can be found in S. Konkin, 'Arest i prigovor' ['Arrest and Sentencing'], *Sovetskaia mordoviia*, 26 March 1991, 3.

continues, with some interesting variations, the discussion of the relationship of author to hero that Bakhtin analysed in the spirit of ethical philosophy. By contrast, the four chapters gathered in Part Two, 'Discourse in Dostoevsky', look brand new. They don't discuss the asymmetry of authors and heroes, or any aspect of their relationship: they talk about style—parody, irony, so-called *skaz* narration (the use of a markedly oral narrator), 'hidden dialogue'. Instead of focusing on the features of the Dostoevskian hero, they offer a complex classification of styles, of which the centrepiece is clearly those styles described as 'double-voiced'. Two parts, and it's as if Bakhtin, having written a book on Dostoevsky, decided to write a different one—in fact some scholars think that is exactly what happened.[16] But if the book is literally ambivalent, its place in Bakhtin's trajectory is not. After 1929, 'authors' and 'heroes', *I* and *other*, make regular appearances, but Bakhtin's project is in the main devoted to the stylistic analysis of the novel, to a searching analysis of the features and effects of its distinctive mode of language.

This linguistic turn is not only relatively easy to see—it corresponds more or less to the turn of the page that brings us to Part Two of the Dostoevsky book—but also relatively easy to date. In 1925 Bakhtin's friend and colleague V. N. Voloshinov began his stint as a doctoral researcher at the Institute for the Comparative History of the Literatures and Languages of the West and East (known by its acronym ILIaZV and home to Iakubinskii among others), where he did the work that would eventually lead to his book on Freudianism and to *Marxism and the Philosophy of Language*.[17] The research led Voloshinov to texts by many of the most important philosophers of language of the day (Marty, Bühler, Croce, Bally, and so on), and to at least two volumes of Ernst Cassirer's *Philosophy of Symbolic Forms*, the fruit of a slightly earlier linguistic turn (which I discuss in Chapter 7). Records show that in 1928-9 Voloshinov was working on, or at least planned to work on, a translation of two parts of Cassirer's *Philosophy*. In a précis of the book *Marxism and the Philosophy of Language* from 1928, Voloshinov claims that in neo-Kantian philosophy of language—of which Cassirer is the greatest representative—'the "word" becomes a *mediating point* between transcendental significance and concrete actuality, like a "third realm"' and this means that '[t]hrough the mediation of *the inner forms of language (which are, so to speak, half-transcendental forms)* movement and historical becoming are introduced into the petrified kingdom of transcendental-logical

---

[16] This hypothesis is the one advanced by N. I. Nikolaev, in his article '"Dostoevskii i antichnost'" kak tema Pumpianskogo i Bakhtina (1922–1963)' ['"Dostoevsky and Antiquity" as a Theme in Pumpianskii and Bakhtin (1922–1963)'], *Voprosy literatury* 3 (1996): 115–27. Nikolaev argues that an initial version of the Dostoevsky book, without the idea of polyphony and the categories of discourse, was completed by 1925. The thesis has received an extended and sympathetic discussion in S. G. Bocharov's commentary on *Problems of Dostoevsky's Art* in the *Collected Works*; see the notes and commentary to *Problemy tvorchestva Dostoevskogo* in M. M. Bakhtin, *Sobranie sochinenii, tom 2: 'Problemy tvorchestva Dostoevskogo', 1929; stat 'i o L. Tol'stom, 1929; zapisi kursa lektsii po istoriii russkoi literatury, 1922–1927* (Moscow: Russkie slovari, 2000), 431–506.

[17] On ILIaZV, one of the most important Soviet centres for work on language, see Craig Brandist, 'Sociological Linguistics in Leningrad: The Institute for the Comparative History of the Literatures and Languages of the West and East (ILJAZV) 1921–1933', *Russian Literature* 63 (2008): 171–200.

categories'.[18] These passages didn't make the final cut—you can't find them in the published text of *Marxism and the Philosophy of Language*. But it's difficult not to think that they would have struck Bakhtin as a promising alternative to phenomenology, a different way to secure a connection between concrete actuality and the Kantian categories (in interviews near the end of his life Bakhtin singled out the *Philosophy of Symbolic Forms* as one of the most remarkable products of neo-Kantianism).[19] Voloshinov had blazed the path, in any case, writing an article—never published as such, but forming the basis for part three of *Marxism and the Philosophy of Language*—on 'The Problem of the Transmission of the Speech of the Other', which demonstrated how the author/hero dialectic might be translated into linguistic analysis.[20] I'd said Bakhtin's turn was decisive and immediate: if that requires a discrete moment in time, you could do worse than presume the moment is the summer of 1928, which Voloshinov—having just completed a draft of *Marxism and the Philosophy of Language*—spent at a dacha with the Bakhtins on the Karelian isthmus.[21] It's all there, so long as we're willing to accept the fact that Bakhtin might have learned a thing or two from his Marxist friends.

Motivations aside, the real question is what was lost, and gained, in translation. If we compare the two parts of *Problems of Dostoevsky's Art*, we see Bakhtin trying to make the shift as literal as possible. Bakhtin's stated object in Part One was to explain Dostoevsky's 'revolutionary innovation in the field of the novel as an artistic form'.[22] Although Dostoevsky's heroes were often ideologues, it was not the ideology they spouted that was important: what was significant was the way in which these ideologies seemed to leap off the page, to confront the reader directly, as if each hero was not a character in a plot, but 'the full-valued bearer of his own discourse, with equal rights to those of the author'.[23] In Dostoevsky's hands, the novel was not so much a context for the subjectivity of the heroes as an arena, in which the point was to 'touch a raw nerve of the hero, provoke him, interrogate him, even

---

[18] 'Lichnoe delo V. N. Voloshinova' ['Personal File of V. N. Voloshinov'], transcribed by N. Pankov, *Dialog Karnaval Khronotop* 2 (1995): 87, 87–8. The reference to the Cassirer translation is found on 75. It's interesting to compare this to the role Cassirer will play in Habermas's linguistic turn forty years later, in which Cassirer is the philosopher who rightly focuses on language and symbol, but does so ahistorically. See Habermas, *On the Logic of the Social Sciences*, 6–10. I discuss Habermas's take on Cassirer in Chapter 7.

[19] *M. M. Bakhtin: Besedy c V. D. Duvakinym* [*M. M. Bakhtin: Conversations with V. D. Duvakin*] (Moscow: Soglasie, 2002), 48. Bakhtin's enthusiasm for Cassirer did not, unfortunately, end there: he would later plagiarize his work for the Rabelais book. See Brian Poole, 'Bakhtin and Cassirer: The Philosophical Origins of Bakhtin's Carnival Messianism', *South Atlantic Quarterly* 97.3–4 (1998): 537–78.

[20] A précis of the article can be found in Pankov's transcription of Voloshinov's ILIaZV file; 'Lichnoe delo V. N. Voloshinova', 79–80.

[21] See V. M. Alpatov, *Voloshinov, Bakhtin i lingvistika* [*Voloshinov, Bakhtin, and Linguistics*] (Moscow: Iazyki slavianskikh kul'tur, 2005),91–2, 110–18. As Alpatov makes clear, in the Bakhtin Circle it was Voloshinov who had expertise in linguistics.

[22] M. M. Bakhtin, *Problemy tvorchestva Dostoevskogo* (Leningrad: Priboi, 1929), 4. English translation: Mikhail Bakhtin, *Problems of Dostoevsky's Poetics*, trans. Caryl Emerson (Manchester: Manchester University Press, 1984), 276. The English translation is of a later edition of the book, but there is substantial overlap and some excised passages (like this one) are reproduced in an appendix.

[23] Bakhtin, *Problemy tvorchestva Dostoevskogo*/*Problems of Dostoevsky's Poetics*, 8/5.

polemicize with him and mock him; everything must be addressed to the hero himself, must be turned to him, must be felt as *a discourse about someone present*.[24]

It sounds like a recipe for a 'liberal' justification of the novel, and this is often the way it has been understood, by those enthusiastic about Bakhtin and those sceptical of him.[25] Dostoevsky's technique, the argument goes, exemplifies and encourages the open conversation we need to have, the free exchange of opinions essential to a liberal polity, and so on.[26] But for Bakhtin that would be politics, not art: he doesn't admire Dostoevsky for representing a clash of world-views that will lead to a more rational outcome, but for representing a clash of world-views that *won't*, that *can't* lead to a rational outcome. The ideological passion of Dostoevsky's heroes drives the narrative forward, of course, but it also significantly raises the stakes: if the hero is someone 'present' then the hero's ideology has broken the confines of the plot. As Bakhtin puts it in the book's conclusion, Dostoevsky's heroes no longer intersect according to the exigencies of plot or within a defined time and space, but 'directly on the ground of ultimate questions'.[27]

Ultimate questions. And, by virtue of this, unanswerable questions. The permanent discontent of Dostoevsky's characters, which is not merely a personality trait, but a distinctive feature of their style—looping, endlessly self-reflexive, unsettled—renders their discourse *nezavershennyi*, unfinished or unfinalized. Not in the banal sense that it may always be added to or reinterpreted at a later date; it's unfinished in the sense that it articulates a point of crisis, a moment where the hero can go neither forward nor back. When Bakhtin briefly returned to the study of Dostoevsky in the mid-1940s, he noted that Dostoevsky had a spatial figure for this crisis: the 'threshold'—those doorways and frames over which his characters perpetually hover.[28] But what makes Dostoevsky's prose artistic is its determination not to resolve the crisis (in which case it would be merely ethical or political writing) but to intensify it, to make it as clear as possible—without ever stating the matter directly—that the crisis could only be resolved by making the leap into Christian faith (faith being not the 'resolution' of the ultimate questions, but the only manner in which one can successfully respond to them).

---

[24] Bakhtin, *Problemy tvorchestva Dostoevskogo/Problems of Dostoevsky's Poetics*, 70/64.
[25] Enthusiastic: Katerina Clark and Michael Holquist, *Mikhail Bakhtin* (Cambridge, MA: Harvard University Press, 1984), 242–3. Sceptical: Franco Moretti, *The Way of the World: The Bildungsroman in European Culture* (London: Verso, 1987), 150–1.
[26] When I say liberalism, I mean liberalism (not 'liberal democracy'). Because belief in the power of open discussion, which requires a free press and some kind of elected parliament among other things, is a liberal idea, separable from belief in democracy, i.e., in the rule of the people at large. It is possible, therefore, for a critical-rational public sphere to exist in the absence of an extended franchise and institutions for mass political participation. Nineteenth-century liberals believed passionately in parliamentary and public debate, but with a highly restricted, 'undemocratic' franchise. It was Habermas's great achievement to demonstrate, in what he called his theory of 'discourse ethics', that the aspirations of that public sphere required democracy for their fulfillment.
[27] Bakhtin, *Problemy tvorchestva Dostoevskogo/Problems of Dostoevsky's Poetics*, 240/280.
[28] 'All action, all events take place *on the threshold*', in M. M. Bakhtin, 'K voprosam samosoznaniia i samootsenki...', in *Sobranie sochinenii 5*, 74. English translation: 'On Questions of Self-Consciousness and Self-Evaluation', *Slavic and East European Journal* 61.2 (2017): 221.

The project of representing a hero in crisis sutures together the 'author and hero' half of the book with the half entitled 'Discourse in Dostoevsky'. What Bakhtin finds in the defensive, hectoring, and argumentative style of the Underground Man and Raskolnikov is an 'inner dialogism', that is, a discourse that is not merely aimed at making its case but at defending itself against objections and anticipating attacks (both from within and beyond the diegetic plane, that is, attacks both from other characters and from the reader as well). The 'presentness' of Dostoevsky's heroes finds expression in the dual orientation of their language: they have a topic to address and they are provoked by the author—which means, in actuality, by the narrative itself—and they respond by always speaking with the shadow of that provocation upon them. The discourse can never therefore only say what it wants to say, never justify itself or find rest, because it is permanently engaged in a dialogue which, Bakhtin claims, takes place *within* the line of discourse. Whether this internalized 'dialogism' can fully assume the role Bakhtin has assigned it is another matter. The 'internally dialogized' discourses of Dostoevsky's heroes certainly contribute to the sense of crisis, but they only contribute to it; they cannot place the hero on a threshold by dint of style alone. If Dostoevsky's heroes debated less weighty issues with themselves—not, say, the existence of God, or the morality of killing, but where they might go on holiday or whether they should ask the boss for a promotion—it seems unlikely that the dialogical style would propel them to the existential precipice on its own.

And if the kinds of intense dialogism Bakhtin finds in Dostoevsky can't single-handedly push characters to the point of crisis, it's even less obvious that parody, stylization, or *skaz* could. That, however, is precisely what the argument of that important second section, 'Discourse in Dostoevsky', seems to entail. The opening lines of the section set the scene for Dostoevsky's entrance with the observation that '[t]here exists a group of artistic-speech phenomena which have begun at the present time to attract particular attention from investigators. They are the phenomena of stylization, parody, *skaz* and dialogue.'[29] United by their 'dual directedness to both the object of speech, like ordinary discourse, and to *the words of an other*, to *alien speech*', these diverse phenomena eventually find themselves classified into distinct genera and species by means of a notoriously elaborate diagram.[30] At one end stands 'discourse immediately directed at its object' with no shade of the other's influence, at the other end the 'active type' of double-voiced discourse, in which the influence of the *other* is most insistent. Compare the diagram with the remainder of the book and one thing becomes absolutely clear: the species of double-voiced style that Dostoevsky uses to dramatize the conflicts experienced by his heroes— 'hidden inner polemic', 'polemically coloured autobiography and confession', 'the word with a sideward glance', 'hidden dialogue'—are all members of this last genus. Parody and stylization, the intermediate, 'weaker' manifestations of the dialogical principle, hardly figure at all. Which makes one wonder whether their deployment

---

[29] Bakhtin, *Problemy tvorchestva Dostoevskogo/Problems of Dostoevsky's Poetics*, 105/185.
[30] Bakhtin, *Problemy tvorchestva Dostoevskogo/Problems of Dostoevsky's Poetics*, 105/85. The diagram is found on 127/199.

in a prose work could possibly create the kind of crisis that is the artistic point of Dostoevskian discourse.

In the 1930s, though, when 'dialogism' moves from the cramped quarters of Dostoevskian prose to the altogether grander, more expansive Hotel Romanza, it is precisely stylization and parody that exemplify it. The examples of dialogical discourse Bakhtin selects in his studies of the novel are typically drawn from the comic prose of Dickens or the light-touch social irony of Pushkin. And the texts in which these techniques are employed do not produce watered-down versions of Dostoevskian crisis; according to Bakhtin, they pick up steam, embodying a kind of world-historical 'becoming' that destroys everything in its path. Did Bakhtin discover something in parody he had missed earlier?

More likely, he hadn't really looked at parody and stylization much at all. Voloshinov had been studying reported speech since 1927. The Formalist Boris Eikhenbaum had developed the theory of *skaz* and Iurii Tynianov had been writing about parody.[31] Bakhtin looked at these techniques, looked at what Dostoevsky was doing, and realized he could cram them together into a category that implied they shared some ethical substance or tendency. It may not have been out of simple expediency; but the force of what he was then calling dialogism came from the kind of inner polemic one found in Dostoevsky, and the implicit claim that something like this might be found in other kinds of what he called 'refracted' discourse was, in effect, no more than a gamble.

One which paid off handsomely, if not in the currency Bakhtin expected. 'Novelistic discourse', as Bakhtin described it in the essay 'Discourse in the Novel', written and rewritten in 1930–6, showed little interest in the kind of existential crises that 'Discourse in Dostoevsky' helped dramatize, nor was it inclined to spend much time on the 'ultimate questions'. Its preferred habitat was precisely that thicket of 'existing social forms' and 'socially concrete flesh' that Dostoevsky's dialogism aimed to transcend.[32] Dialogism was now the generic technique of making the 'heteroglossia' of language, its inner social divisions, explicit and conscious (turning 'heteroglossia "in-itself"' into 'heteroglossia "for-itself"', as Bakhtin said at a curiously Hegelian moment):[33] through stylization and parody one divided the shared national language into a world of intersecting 'socio-ideological languages', each of which aligned a certain syntax, vocabulary, and pronunciation with a specific function or world-view. Within the frame provided by the novel, all meaning would be refracted, would be expressed in discourse which 'not only represents, but is itself represented', made heroic and worldly, so that, as Bakhtin put it in a characteristically vivid phrase '[e]ach word tastes of the context and contexts in

---

[31] Eikhenbaum introduced the idea of *skaz* in two articles: 'Illiuziia skaza' ['The Illusion of *skaz*'], *Knizhnyi ugol* 2 (1918) and the famous 'Kak sdelana "Shinel'" Gogolia' ['How Gogol's "The Overcoat" was Made'], in O. Brik et al., *Poetika: sborniki po teorii poeticheskogo iazyka* (Petersburg: n.p., 1919), 151–65. On parody see Iurii Tynianov, 'Dostoevskii i Gogol: K teorii parodii' ['Dostoevsky and Gogol: Towards a Theory of Parody'] (1921), in *Arkhaisty i novatory* (Leningrad: Priboi, 1929, reprinted Ann Arbor, MI: Ardis, 1985), 412–55.

[32] Bakhtin, *Problemy tvorchestva Dostoevskogo*/*Problems of Dostoevsky's Poetics*, 241, 240/280.

[33] Bakhtin, 'Slovo v romane'/'Discourse in the Novel', 155/400.

which it has lived its socially intense life'.[34] The novel produced effects as forceful as the crises of Dostoevsky's heroes, but it must have had a new strategy for doing so.

But a careful reading of 'Discourse in the Novel'—or any of the writings on the novel produced in the period between 1930 and 1946—reveals that there was no strategy. The frustration many readers experience when reading Bakhtin's theory of the novel stems from this lack of explicitness, from the fact that novelistic discourse is endowed with a power at once murky and impressive. Parody is more than mere mockery, stylization more than simple stereotyping, we're assured, to the extent that it 'draws its energy, its dialogized ambiguity, not from individual disagreements, misunderstandings or contradictions (even if they are tragic and deeply grounded in the fates of individuals)' because 'in the novel this double-voicedness is deeply rooted in a fundamental, socio-linguistic heteroglossia and multi-languagedness'.[35] But where does the energy come from? More explicitly than with any of the linguistic turns we've discussed to this point, Bakhtin's turn to language is simultaneously a turn to the social world, conceived of as first and foremost a socially differentiated world. The result, however, is a short circuit: a simple and immediate overloading of language with the 'energy' of social life.

Perhaps Bakhtin was simply disguising his underlying intentions, which remained metaphysical, religious, and precise. But he had done his homework when making his turn, and it's hard to believe he ploughed through Cassirer, through Leo Spitzer's study of Italian colloquial language, through Viktor Zhirmunskii's and Iakubinskii's studies of urban dialects and national language, simply to make his disguise more persuasive.[36] It makes far more sense to suppose that Bakhtin identified language with a conception of social life that he clarified for himself through the medium of the novel. 'Discourse in the Novel' therefore contains a few different hypotheses explaining the energy of heteroglossia. At some points Bakhtin simply borrows the familiar notion that class struggle is the motor of history, suitably expanding it so that the 'struggle among socio-linguistic points of view' that moves things forward reflects a broader range of social conflicts.[37] At other points heteroglossia is identified strongly with 'the social life of discourse beyond the cloistered artist, in the spaces of public squares, streets, cities, and villages', as if its energy was derived from the random collisions of urban life itself.[38] The eventual winner, however, has to do with time rather than place: it is the identification of the novel with modernity, argued for in the final chapter of the essay, a history of the evolution of the novel which dates its flowering to the European Renaissance and which makes it the unique bearer of a modern, contemporaneous culture. It takes Bakhtin roughly a decade to work out the details: in the lecture-turned-essay 'The Novel as

---

[34] Bakhtin, 'Slovo v romane'/'Discourse in the Novel', 90/336, 46/293.
[35] Bakhtin, 'Slovo v romane'/'Discourse in the Novel', 79/325–6.
[36] On Iakubinskii and Zhirmunskii see Vladislava Reznik, 'From Saussure to Sociolinguistics: The Evolution of Soviet Sociology of Language in the 1920s and 1930s' (PhD dissertation, University of Exeter, 2004), 141–8. Bakhtin's notes on Spitzer and Cassirer have been published in Volumes 2 and 4.1 of the *Collected Works*, respectively.
[37] Bakhtin, 'Slovo v romane'/'Discourse in the Novel', 27/273.
[38] Bakhtin, 'Slovo v romane'/'Discourse in the Novel', 10–11/259.

a Literary Genre' of 1941 (known in English as 'Epic and Novel'), the modernity of novelistic discourse is its central feature, brought into relief by contrast with its epic cousin. The epic is not merely 'of' the past—it relies on a certain sense of the 'absolute past'. The novel, by comparison, is the genre of 'contemporaneity', drawing its strength from 'the spontaneity of an unconsummated present', that is, not merely the present, but a certain kind of present: the present as something 'in principle and essentially unconsummated; it demands continuation by its essence, it moves into the future'.[39]

Bakhtin meant more than that life just goes on. The 'inconclusive contemporaneity' that the novel embodies is in fact itself ambivalent, manifest in two quite different kinds of change in time, two different ways in which the present could be orientated to the future.[40] On the one hand, this contemporaneity took the form of the ceaseless 'becoming' of heteroglossia, the way in which every style seemed to reach beyond itself in pursuit of a goal or purpose immanent to it. But it was also inconclusive in a more drastic sense, the open-endedness of the novel implying (as Bakhtin put it in a slightly later fragment on Flaubert) '[n]ot changes within the limits of a given life (progress, decline), but the possibility of a life different in principle, with different scales and dimensions'.[41] Change could take the form of dramatic reversal and sudden transformation, the negation of an existing identity or ideology: precisely the change brought on by the application of ridicule, satire, and parody in the upside-down world of carnival, when kings and priests were brought low and the poor made regal. Writing about satire for the *Soviet Literary Encyclopedia* in 1940, Bakhtin claimed that '[t]he satirical moment introduces into every genre the corrective of contemporary actuality.'[42] But Bakhtin's argument actually runs in the reverse direction. Rather than show how satire introduces contemporary actuality, the time of 'becoming', into the novel, Bakhtin demonstrated that a novelized, modernized version of satire, by its powerful negations and reversals, made 'becoming', the irresistible forward movement of contemporary actuality, possible in the first place.

A novelized version of satire: because Bakhtin takes this classical category and refunctions it, so that satire's critical force does not merely lay bare the vices of the time, but the fragile and fluid nature of modern social roles and identity itself. The connection is hinted at in a short section of 'Discourse in the Novel' that ties the creation of heteroglossia to the dramatic practice of 'the rogue, the clown and the fool', whose parodic, unserious speech is the very model of an assumed, 'acted' identity (what, in Judith Butler's terms, we would call performative identity).[43] These figures have a proleptic function, not only in relation to the modern, but to

---

[39] M. M. Bakhtin, 'Roman, kak literaturnyi zhanr' ['The Novel as a Literary Genre'], in *Sobranie sochinenii 3*, 631n, 633. English translation: 'Epic and Novel', in *The Dialogic Imagination*, 27, 30. Bakhtin's usual term for the novel's peculiar historical consciousness in this essay is 'contemporaneity' [*sovremennost'*]. But in this part of the essay he once calls it the 'indestructible modernity' [*neistrebimaia modernistichnost'*] of the novel (633n31), using an unusual loanword to describe it.
[40] Bakhtin, 'Roman, kak literaturnyi zhanr'/'Epic and Novel', 641/39.
[41] M. M. Bakhtin, 'O Flobere' ['On Flaubert'], in *Sobranie sochinenii 5*, 132.
[42] M. M. Bakhtin, 'Satira' ['Satire'], in *Sobranie sochinenii 5*, 12.
[43] Bakhtin, 'Slovo v romane'/'Discourse in the Novel', 160/405.

Bakhtin's work itself, which in the late 1930s will drastically expand their role in the creation of the novel by means of an elaborate study of Rabelais and carnival culture.[44] Carnival, in Bakhtin's interpretation, is a world in which the principles of roguishness, clowning, and foolery overwhelm the entire social space. The 'uncrowning' central to it is the cultural equivalent of satire and parody, a moment of sudden and dramatic transformation in which the subject changes its form without any intermediate steps. When, in 'Discourse in the Novel', Bakhtin designates the public square as the place 'where all "languages" were masks and there was no such thing as an authentic, uncontentious linguistic face', he connects the dots between parody and a peculiarly modern conception of the human subject.[45] All languages are masks, because a modern subject is never coincident with its identity or its place in a symbolic order; its being subjective is not a sign of its independence but of the way in which—to use some psychoanalytic language—it is always derailed, compelled to move forward, in some fundamental sense incomplete. The modern subject is, for Bakhtin, a kind of permanent crisis state. And this permanent crisis compels the subject to be ethical, in the sense that it forces the subject to act in the absence of tradition or a defining role, to produce action out of its own willing and self-invention. It is this crisis state that makes language productive and is thereby responsible for the energy of heteroglossia.

That the stylized languages of the novel 'express' an ideology and that they are 'represented', exhibited, undercut by the novel's dialogical frame are therefore two sides of the same coin. Subjectivity, embodied in the historical becoming or evolution of a 'socio-ideological language' can only exist for Bakhtin as something parodied, stylized, caught, to borrow the terminology of Lacan, in the grip of a big Other or Symbolic Order that reinterprets its meanings and disturbs its self-sufficiency. This isn't as clear as it ought to be because Bakhtin describes the novel as a dialogue between these socio-ideological languages and a super-identity, an authorial voice or meta-language that alters their course. But there is no super-identity, because the subjective voice as such, 'the speaking person and his discourse' relates not to some larger meta-voice but to the symbolic order instantiated in a novel or in the heteroglot world itself.[46] In a striking passage in 'Discourse in the Novel' Bakhtin describes novelistic pathos as 'the discourse of a preacher without a pulpit, a terrifying judge without judicial or punitive authority, a prophet without a mission, a politician without political power, a believer without a church, and so forth', as if a merely symbolic, mask-like identity had no real authority.[47] But masks, symbolic form, are what furnish modern subjects with force and power—every

---

[44] The study will be embodied in a dissertation Bakhtin will complete in 1940 and defend officially in 1946, 'Fransua Rable v istorii realizma' ['François Rabelais in the History of Realism']. The dissertation was revised for publication in 1965, becoming the book known in English translation as *Rabelais and His World*.

[45] Bakhtin, 'Slovo v romane'/'Discourse in the Novel', 26/273.

[46] 'The fundamental, defining theme of the novel as a genre, which creates its stylistic uniqueness, is the *speaking person and his discourse*'; Bakhtin, 'Slovo v romane'/'Discourse in the Novel', 86/332.

[47] Bakhtin, 'Slovo v romane'/'Discourse in the Novel', 150/394–5.

role mentioned by Bakhtin is an example of the 'empty place of power' described by Claude Lefort—not something that weakens or compromises it.[48]

This explains why the account Bakhtin offers of political power seems so flimsy. Power, in his view, depends on the delusion of a non-symbolic identity, on the gamble that one can make the tide of signification stop. In those passages where Bakhtin describes the symbolic universe of the 'crowned' and the powerful, he makes clear that the monumental and commemorative discourse they rely on is a kind of language turned against itself. In these conditions, all one has to do is assert the symbolic nature of any political mandate and the walls will come tumbling down.

The productivity and inventiveness of language, its creative power, is therefore identified with its 'democracy'. 'We live, write, and speak in a world of free and democratized language' Bakhtin claimed, without irony, in 1940.[49] But what is interesting from the perspective of linguistic turns is not the wide-eyed optimism of the claim, but its tautological nature: for Bakhtin language as such is free and democratized. One can go one step further: language as such is productive *because* it is free and democratized—subjects that wear their masks provisionally are the sources of linguistic becoming. In which case, the productivity of language is in no way a threat to the social consensus, for that very consensus relies on the interactions of subjects who are not quite hooked onto the language they speak, not quite coincident with their identities.

SAUSSURE: THE PRODUCTIVITY OF SOCIAL LIFE

Diversity within language is therefore the mark not of some division of spirit or function within the community but of an irrepressible forward motion within language itself. It's an interesting idea, but even more interesting is the fact that it was shared by such different writers on language as Saussure and Walter Benjamin. With one signal difference: whereas Bakhtin shifts the productivity of 'spirit' *into* language, Saussure and Benjamin struggle to liberate this creative force from its entombment in a false conception of language, to wit, the famous account of linguistic diversity known as comparative philology. The key moment for Benjamin is not, therefore, his attack on the Babel of actual human speech, launched in the 1916 'On Language as Such and Human Language'. His substantive struggle with linguistic diversity comes under a different heading: it is the battle waged in the *Arcades Project* with what he calls the 'narcotic historicism' of the nineteenth century.[50] That cultural practice, embodied in the museums, panoramas, *feuilletons*—and, yes, arcades—endows the utopian impulses of modernity with a backward, mythic form.

---

[48] See Claude Lefort, *The Political Forms of Modern Society: Bureaucracy, Democracy, Totalitarianism* (Cambridge: Polity Press, 1986), 303–4.
[49] M. M. Bakhtin, 'Iz predistorii romannogo slova', in *Sobranie sochinenii 3*, 540. English translation: 'From the Prehistory of Novelistic Discourse', in *The Dialogic Imagination*, 71.
[50] Benjamin, *Arcades Project*, K1a, 6 (391).

But this narcotic historicism has an immediately linguistic form, comparative philology, and Benjamin and Saussure make it their business to liberate the historical movement of language from its grasp.

Marx had accused the political economy of his day of a lack of historical sense, of treating the circumstances and relations particular to the capitalist mode of production as eternal. Benjamin's ideology critique has a different target: it aims at the historical obsessions of the nineteenth century, which take the form of both a particular historiographical doctrine—Leopold Ranke's injunction to render the past 'as it really was'—and a practice of historical representation.[51] The latter is exemplified by the rise of the great museums and their collections, by the historicist inclinations of nineteenth-century architecture, and by the emergence of commercial historiography in the form of panoramas and wax museums. These practices placed a premium on the empirical precision with which they could render the fine details of the past. But they were not monuments to positivism alone. One could not understand the museums for what they were, 'dream houses of the collective', Benjamin argued, without emphasizing 'the dialectic by which they come into contact, on the one hand, with scientific research and, on the other hand, with "the dreamy tide of bad taste"'.[52] The historicism that lulled Europe into its deep nineteenth-century sleep was a form of passion and longing, equal parts realism and kitsch.

Saussure was well acquainted with the ways of this historicism: he had been trained as a comparative philologist at the discipline's most central institution, the University of Leipzig, where he studied with its most eminent representatives.[53] His 1879 *Mémoire* was a brilliant contribution to the reconstruction of the Indo-European vowel system, a comparative philological project on a time-honoured theme, and his teaching, until he was compelled by circumstances to do general linguistics, was on similarly familiar topics.[54] There's heated debate over his ultimate relation to this tradition: some see the new synchronic linguistics as a rejection of German comparative philology in the name of French Enlightenment traditions, while others think his general linguistics created an escape route from the corner into which comparative philology had painted itself.[55] But you miss something if

---

[51] In fact, as H. D. Kittsteiner has shown, Benjamin's critique appears to have conflated two different historiographical targets: Ranke's empathetic reconstruction of the past, and the progressivist ('Whiggish', in British terms) idea that history was a tale of eternal and incremental improvement; see his 'Walter Benjamin's Historicism', *New German Critique* 39 (1986): 179–215.

[52] Benjamin, *Arcades Project*, L1a, 2 (406).

[53] On Saussure's education and relationship to the comparative philological establishment, see Joseph, *Saussure*, 184–99.

[54] Saussure was happily teaching Sanskrit and the like until the sudden retirement of the chair in general linguistics at Geneva forced him to lay his theoretical cards on the podium, so to speak. See Joseph, *Saussure*, 489–91.

[55] The case for Saussure's hostility to comparative philology is made vehemently by Hans Aarsleff in *From Locke to Saussure* (Minneapolis: University of Minnesota Press, 1982). Anna Morpurgo Davies, however, in the Conclusion (324–6) to *Nineteenth-Century Linguistics*, claims twentieth-century linguists were simply solving the problems their predecessors left them. Olga Amsterdamska makes the interesting argument that the Neogrammarian philologists who trained Saussure had effectively pointed the way forward but were blocked by certain philosophical assumptions; Saussure's theory was

you restrict the argument to the history of linguistics. For if comparative philology partakes in that 'thirst for the past' that so fascinated Benjamin, then its critique will not reject its historical impulse but reconfigure it.[56] And that is what happens: just as the *Arcades Project* 'liberates the enormous energies of history that are bound up in the "once upon a time" of classical historiography', Saussure awakens the nineteenth century from its slumbers, by a modernist recuperation of the energies petrified by historicism.[57]

That is to say that while it's true Saussure is responsible for putting the so-called 'synchronic' perspective front and centre and that, as we've seen, he continually harps on the need to separate this viewpoint from the historical perspective of the language scholar, he is well-nigh obsessed with the historical productivity of language, with the incessant and, to his mind, inevitable process of metamorphosis to which every language is liable. Saussure creates an orderly object for linguistics, worthy of scientific attention, and he goes to great lengths to ensure that change in language is seen as beyond any kind of deliberation. At the same time, he wants to insist on the fact of that change itself, on the fact that every language state is a human creation. It's worth bearing in mind that the inventor of synchronic or static linguistics spent nearly all his academic time on the historical description and reconstruction of particular languages. But the apparent irony dissipates if we think of his career not as an attempt to dismiss the history of language but as a continuous effort to rescue the force of history from the historians of language.

This would explain why after Saussure declares in November 1910 that the diversity of languages is the fundamental fact, he then devotes the next seven lectures to an attack on the geographical conception of diversity, on the belief that diversity is a consequence of the scattering of languages across territories. Such conceptions assume that the original language—called Proto-Indo-European—is created in one place and then moves in order to produce difference: 'and this transport of the language presupposes a displacement of peoples, and this displacement implies the idea of nationality'.[58] But it isn't movement that produces diversification, it's the action of time, as he illustrates with a local example:

> The Saxons and the Angles, the day after landing, spoke the same language as they had done the day before on the continent. It is a kind of figure of speech which allows us to attribute divergence to geography [...] the action of time alone is responsible for the difference.[59]

Time alone: it's an odd but telling phrase. In one respect it is clear enough what Saussure means: while it's true that people migrate and their armies conquer new lands and meet new people, to put it politely, this isn't why language changes. For even if the Angles and Saxons had stayed put the language they spoke would have

---

therefore both a logical development from and philosophical break with comparative philology; see her *Schools of Thought*, 176–251.

[56] Benjamin, *Arcades Project*, L1a, 2 (407). [57] Benjamin, *Arcades Project*, N3, 4 (463).
[58] Saussure, *Second Course*, 97a.
[59] Saussure, *Third Course*, Lecture of 15 November 1910, 21a.

changed simply because they kept speaking it (although it might have changed in a different way than it did on the island that would become Great Britain).

But it obviously isn't time that introduces phonetic and grammatical changes into a language, replacing *d-* with *t-* or reorganizing the system of case endings, but speakers who do so *over* time. Individual speakers, who then, in a fashion that remains mysterious even to Saussure, work in concert to change the collective institution of language. When they change it, they can change it however they like, because language is only a convention. And yet:

> The postulated act by which, at a given moment, names were assigned to things, the act by which a contract was completed between ideas and signs, between the signifying and signified elements, this act is purely imaginary. It is an idea inspired by the feeling we have of the arbitrariness of the sign, but belongs to no recognizable reality. Never has any society known its language other than as a product more or less perfected by preceding generations and to be taken just as it is. In other words, we recognize a *historical fact* at the origin of every language state.[60]

The act is 'imaginary', the historical fact that inspires it, actual. We can see language change after the fact, as accomplished history, but we can't see the actual making of it. It's as if language was made by speakers without subjectivity, so that one may as well say that time alone is responsible for linguistic innovation. But what we are probably witnessing is a case of reverse-engineering, where Saussure has deduced the nature of linguistic subjectivity, or rather the absence of linguistic subjectivity, from the patchwork state of its products, the lack of any organizing principle or, if one can still use this phrase in serious conversation, intelligent design, in the language system. 'The "genius of a language", we can recall Saussure insisting, 'is worth *nothing* compared with a single fact such as the dropping of a final *o*'. For how could a coherent inner process, a guiding spirit or logic, lead to the kind of senseless and unpredictable innovations that distinguished linguistic change? When the language romantics of the nineteenth century bound national peoples to national languages they had to infuse the languages themselves with some inner logic, identifying the presence, for example, of inflectional paradigms with a certain European intellectual sophistication. But if languages are the ramshackle things Saussure thinks they are, then there is nothing interesting for a people or race to bind itself *to*. Hence the kitsch quality of linguistic nationalism, which finds itself forced to transform consonant sounds or the details of verb conjugation into signs of national virility or intellectual prowess.

Bakhtin should be called a modernist because he made 'the spontaneity of an unconsummated present' the inner principle of language as such, counterposing it to the mythic investment in the past. Saussure's modernism is similar in character, but aims at a different target, responding to nationalist kitsch rather than myth. Instead of overloading specific alterations in the history of a language with Meaning, he looks on the inevitability of mutation as a continual 'making it new' with no other

---

[60] Saussure, *Third Course*, Lecture of 19 May 1911, 94a.

purpose than to disrupt the system, forcing it to constantly reorganize—often, through analogy. Language is constantly productive and productive in an unpredictable manner, but unlike the products of artistic modernism—most of them, at any rate—it's a collective, the body of speakers, that's innovating, not an individual, because the true moment of linguistic innovation is the moment of collective agreement to a new mutation (a mutation that arises in the discourse of one speaker, but never catches on, is simply random noise). Collective coherence, and productivity: Saussure seems to have found an ideal kind of 'institution' for modern societies. But he's reticent, almost shy about his discovery. Instead of describing the institution, he will compare it to 'a ship on the open sea'. But were speakers really to be likened to waves and tides? While there is no explicit alternative on offer either in the *Cours* itself or from the lectures, there are several competing characterizations of the 'body of speakers' or collective, all distinctively modern and all, as it happens, quite Parisian (or at the minimum, French). For it's worth recalling that Saussure's earliest attempts at general linguistics—set forth in lectures and notes for a book at the beginning of the 1890s—followed his decade in Paris, where he taught at the École des Hautes Études and played a major role in the Société de Linguistique de Paris. Paris in the 1880s was wedged between the destruction of the Commune and the Dreyfus affair: how could anyone there avoid thinking about what made collections of individuals cohere?

We have already discussed some of these half-conscious models. There is the republican paradigm, represented in Saussure by his hedged references to language as a social contract or as something legislated, an idea he admits is drawn from the eighteenth-century *philosophes*.[61] There are the theories of imitation drawn from Tarde and 'collective consciousness' drawn from Durkheim. There is the economic market, subject of the most explicit comparisons Saussure makes, which provided a useful model of ceaseless activity married to peaceful equilibrium.[62] The final three—imitation, sociology, the market—share two significant features: all share 'the aspiration to discover a way of dedramatizing the confrontation of individuals, to drain their relations of passion, to minimize the hidden violence of power relations', as Pierre Rosanvallon has put it.[63] They are conceptions of social order in which struggles over ideology are tamed and declawed, but they pay a price, revealed in

---

[61] Saussure, *Second Course*, 11a: 'We thus take the language to be a legislation in the manner of the 18th-century *philosophes*, as depending on our will.'

[62] Saussure does not directly invoke the market, but he invokes the principles of exchange and value that depend on market relationships and the science of economics as the means of their analysis: Saussure, *Course in General Linguistics* (1983), 79–81, 112–16. We do not know what the precise source for Saussure's knowledge of economics was, but it is worth pointing out that the theory of general economic equilibrium, and the marginalist theory of value, were pioneered by Léon Walras, teaching at the University of Lausanne in the late nineteenth century. John Joseph has suggested that Saussure learned about the economic concept of value from lectures delivered at the University of Geneva by Henri Dameth: see Joseph, 'Saussure's Value(s)'. Not everyone, however, is convinced that the idea of 'value' was imported from economics; see Sylvain Auroux, 'Deux hypothèses sur l'origine de la conception saussurienne de la valeur linguistique', *Travaux de linguistique et de littérature* 23.1 (1985): 295–9.

[63] Pierre Rosanvallon, 'The Market, Liberalism, and Anti-Liberalism', 151.

the second feature: all leave unclear how social orders might create or produce new forms or arrangements. They are theories of agreement, not of production.[64] So is, for the most part, Saussure's. As Fredric Jameson suggested long ago, '*langue* is not so much the power to speak as it is the power to understand speech', a tool for consuming rather than producing language.[65]

But Paris did not merely put models of collectivity into circulation: it was itself a model of collectivity, and a peculiarly modern one at that. Saussure's offhand remark that '[g]rammar, for example, can only be studied in the crowd' had implied a distinctive and specific physiognomy for the linguistic collective, the physiognomy that Benjamin would focus his own recuperative attention on twenty years later, when Paris became the focus of his investigations. For Benjamin takes from Baudelaire the conception of urban crowds as those who 'do not stand for classes or any sort of collective; rather, they are nothing but the amorphous crowd of passers-by, the people in the street'.[66] And, probably without intending to, Saussure endows the 'body of speakers' or '*mass parlante*' with the attributes of just such an 'amorphous crowd of passers-by'. Their interactions are, for one thing, spontaneous and random, and it is that randomness that guarantees that no collective will or initiative can ever be exercised. When Saussure uses the complexity of the system and the 'influence of all' as factors standing in the way of deliberate change, he assumes not only that everyone participates in language, but also that there are endless and unpredictable combinations of speakers and listeners. Were these combinations stable and ritualized, we would have precisely the kind of linguistic subsystems that Iakubinskii rightly said could be open to conscious intervention. But urban social life is unpredictable—at least when one is out on the street—and this immunizes it against schemes and directives. Franco Moretti has pointed out that when the modern metropolis (Paris and London) became the matrix for narrative, the narrative arc acquired a new feature: the redirection of plans and the confusion of heroic aims created by the intervention of a new 'Third' mediating force, neither hero nor villain.[67] In urban narratives the road from A to B requires a detour through C, a mediating character, institution, or place whose intervention redirects the hero's aspirations and path. The city is the place where dreams are frustrated, because to achieve them one must enter a network of streets and contacts that lead to endless detours, new paths, revised plans, and so on. Individual will dissolves in the city, as it dissolves in language.

But the frustration of dreams has a flip side. Yes, the randomness built into urban interaction frustrates the dreams one arrives with, but if you wander through the amorphous crowd with the right attitude, your reward is endless possibility,

---

[64] I take the claim that neoclassical economics is a theory of consumption rather than production from Philip Mirowski, *More Heat than Light: Economics as Social Physics, Physics as Nature's Economics* (Cambridge: Cambridge University Press, 1989), 280–334.

[65] Fredric Jameson, *The Prison-House of Language: A Critical Account of Structuralism and Russian Formalism* (Princeton, NJ: Princeton University Press, 1972), 26. Jameson credits A. I. Smirnitskii with this insight.

[66] Walter Benjamin, 'On Some Motifs in Baudelaire', in *Selected Writings, Vol. 4*, 320–1.

[67] Franco Moretti, *Atlas of the European Novel, 1800–1900* (London: Verso, 1999), 105–10.

dreams at once unfocused (because they have no particular, stable object) and multiform (because a chance meeting could lead to romance, to fame, to fortune). A good deal of Benjamin's *Arcades Project* is devoted to anatomizing this attitude, the 'intoxication' and aimlessness required of the urban *flâneur*, who has to sacrifice single-mindedness and discipline for an alertness to the sudden correspondence or the significant chance encounter. It is precisely this attitude that Saussure liberates from narcotic historicism when he insists, ironically, on the primacy of the synchronic point of view. Comparative philology appears to be interested in historical change, but it actually embalms it: its emphasis on written examples of language (which Saussure angrily criticized) privileges the dead and finished letter, while its obsession with codifying laws of sound change (which Saussure insisted weren't really laws) transformed spontaneous and unpredictable events into something regular, caused, and explicable.[68] Conversely, although Saussure appears less interested than his predecessors in historical change, his insistence that we privilege the synchronic, instantaneous perspective on language has precisely the reverse effect: it endows even past states of language with 'presence', by making that state, in the most literal sense, contemporary.

This is bound to sound strange to anyone who has read Saussure: his descriptions of the language system invariably emphasize its stability and orderliness (as when he likens it to a dictionary and a grammar).[69] The reason is clear: he wanted to contrast the orderliness of the object he had crafted for linguistics with the messiness of the 'combined or isolated *actions* of physiological, physical, or mental forces'. His scientific ambition thus keeps the contemporaneity he has uncovered in check. But he glimpses the Promised Land—language as ceaselessly productive; a series of often unpredictable leaps into the future; a delicate combination of individual initiative and collective direction; something based on the collectivity of cities rather than nations or races—even if it is left to others to settle it and make it fruitful.

BENJAMIN: FROM PURE LANGUAGE TO THE CITY

It's tempting to think of Benjamin as playing Joshua to Saussure's Moses. After all, he writes his first essay on language—the notoriously difficult 'On Language as Such and Human Language'—in the very year, 1916, that the *Cours* is published, and his conception of 'language as such' points to a creative spontaneity peculiar to the linguistic. But it doesn't work, and not just because Benjamin takes a swipe at the apparently 'bourgeois' conception that the word is 'a sign for things (or knowledge of them) agreed by some convention'.[70] The deeper difference is that Benjamin's earliest meditation on language treats the diversity of actual languages—the 'human language' of the title—as a symptom of language that has 'fallen' into

---

[68] On Saussure's criticism of writing, see *Third Course*, Lecture of 6 December 1910, 40–7a; for the critique of the 'sound law', see *Second Course*, 46a.
[69] See Saussure, *Third Course*, Lecture of 28 April 1911, 71a: 'we can say in short that a dictionary and a grammar give an acceptable, appropriate image of what is contained in the language'.
[70] Benjamin, 'On Language as Such and the Language of Man', in *Selected Writings, Vol. 1*, 69.

communication: 'man makes language a means, [...] and therefore also, in one part at any rate, a *mere* sign; and this later results in the plurality of languages'.[71] Benjamin has not yet discovered the city, or encountered the Surrealism that will reveal its revolutionary potential. His conception of the magical element of language remains tethered to theology; it isn't yet connected to the kinds of experience that a distinctively modern urban life will make possible, or to any kind of sociability.

So it's no accident that the first decisive step in this direction—his prefatory essay, 'The Task of the Translator'—is occasioned by a translation of Baudelaire, the poet who serves as Benjamin's first guide to both Paris and modernity.[72] Benjamin is still making few explicit concessions to the semiotic conception of language, but on one critical point he agrees with Saussure. For the historical mutability of languages is now cast as their essential trait, although this ceaseless transformation has been given a kind of high Romantic twist, such that it is no longer understood as random and meaningless, but as an unfolding or manifestation of spirit. But to see linguistic transformations in this light, one has to take a certain distance from their conventional surface, to extract the element of 'pure language' that resides in every actual language and makes itself evident in their changes, but is somewhat veiled or hidden. So while 'in the various tongues that ultimate essence, the pure language, is tied only to linguistic elements and their changes', one can only grasp this creative, historical force by establishing a distance within each language between its universal vocation and its particular semiotic structure.[73] Or to put it in the terms of Benveniste, one has to open the gap between the semantics of the language— what Benjamin would have called language as naming—and its conventionalized, semiotic organization.

I put it this way in order to make clear that Benjamin's theory is not just some alchemical mix of Romanticism and Jewish mysticism. The idea that linguistic change might issue from some kind of creative intelligence, and thus have both rhyme and reason, was hardly novel and it didn't have to take the form of nationalist faith in French clarity or German *Kultur*. Bréal had coined the term 'semantics' precisely so he could display the phenomenon of linguistic change in a more rationalist light. His alternative history of language sought to chart 'the intellectual causes which have influenced the transformation of our languages' in the belief that the history of language was the history of an instrument honed and gradually perfected.[74] Likewise, the distinction between a semantic core of language and its surface semiotic structure didn't require belief in a linguistic Fall or Babel moment, as Benveniste would demonstrate. But Benjamin believed that while this pure,

---

[71] Benjamin, 'On Language as Such', 71.
[72] Walter Benjamin, 'The Task of the Translator', in *Selected Writings, Vol. 1*, 253–63. According to the editors, the essay was written in 1921 and published in 1923.
[73] Benjamin, 'Task of the Translator', 261.
[74] Bréal, *Semantics*, 5. Of course, the risk entailed by any claim that language change is directed and progressive is that it will end up making distinctions between more and less advanced languages, even when those languages are contemporary. Bréal did not manage to avoid this problem: he believed there were 'gradations in the educative power of the world's languages'; see 'Language and Nationality', 211–12.

creative language was evident in the fact of linguistic change, in actual utterances or texts it was hidden by the vulgar need to communicate.

It could be uncovered, however, by translation. While the language of an original text is burdened with the task of reference, of symbolizing things beyond itself, for the translator every text is effectively a work of fiction, in the sense that their interest lies not in what is being referred to but in the language itself as expression, an expressiveness the translator seeks to abstract and convey in the new language. By releasing language from the task of reference, the translator is able 'to release in his own language that pure language which is exiled among alien tongues'.[75] A translation, Benjamin argues, 'instead of imitating the sense of the original, must lovingly and in detail incorporate the original's way of meaning, thus making both the original and the translation recognizable as fragments of a greater language, just as fragments are part of a vessel'.[76] Translation thus takes an utterance in which linguistic energy is caged by the task of reference, and 'turn[s] the symbolizing into the symbolized itself', in effect distilling 'language as such' from its admixture with representation.[77]

Saussure liberated what was conventionally called the 'spirit' of a language by insisting on the randomness of the changes it engendered: he made it spontaneous by unbinding it from the nation. Benjamin takes aim at the same philological target, but from a different direction. In a later essay on the sociology of language (that never actually discusses the sociology of language) he notes that although 'the conservative stance which is frequently encountered in philology [...] seems mostly to go hand-in-hand with the high-mindedness and human dignity so movingly exemplified by the Grimm brothers', nevertheless, 'regressive', 'nationalist' tendencies seem to haunt the modern study of language.[78] Nineteenth-century philologists like the Grimms recognize linguistic spirit, the creative work done by language in comprehending and shaping a world, but it is easy—particularly in 1935, when Benjamin writes—to confuse it with the immediate grammatical and lexical structure of a particular national language. But the universal or semantic, intelligent moment of language isn't and can't be identified with the semiotic structure of a particular language (and by extension, with the culture of a particular 'people'): that it exists at all only becomes clear when one language is thrown into relief by another in translation. You can recover, Benjamin argues, the historical energy of the evolving language system from a particular text—from a piece of *parole*—but only by forcing it through the sieve of an alien tongue.

Benjamin did not abandon this line of argument, or his faith in a pure or divine state of language, after his attention was captured by Marxism, Surrealism, and Parisian modernity. A fragment from 1933, titled 'Antitheses Concerning Word and Name', shows him drawing the links between the doctrines from 'On Language as Such' and newer ideas about an indigenous 'mimetic faculty', which we will

---

[75] Benjamin, 'Task of the Translator', 261. [76] Benjamin, 'Task of the Translator', 260.
[77] Benjamin, 'Task of the Translator', 261.
[78] Walter Benjamin, 'Problems in the Sociology of Language: An Overview', in *Selected Writings: Volume 3, 1935–1938*, trans. Edmund Jephcott, Howard Eiland, and others (Cambridge, MA: Harvard University Press, 2002), 80.

explore in Chapter 7.[79] But though language as such was still a vehicle of revelation, the form and pattern of revelation had changed: it was now modelled on the 'profane illumination' of the Surrealists—sudden, discontinuous, unexpected and, as such, requiring what Benjamin will call *Geistesgegenwart*, 'presence of mind' or receptiveness.[80] The 'games that have run through the whole literature of the avant-garde for the past fifteen years' are not, Benjamin observes, just games, but 'magical experiments with words'.[81] It's a different, much more modern magic, though: not enchantments and spells, but the rabbit out of a hat or the woman who disappears in a puff of smoke.

It is, to Benjamin's mind, urban magic. That cities presented an assault on the senses, a sphere of remarkable coincidences, the juxtaposition of high and low, comic and serious, was already established. The artistic consequences had been drawn before by novelists and poets; in Benjamin's time, Georg Simmel drew the theoretical ones. But for Simmel the constant stream of stimuli had to be warded off by the adoption of 'the blasé attitude'; the urban subject needed a protective shell to preserve their independence and possibly their sanity.[82] The Surrealist innovation was to present the random shocks and juxtapositions of urban life as productive, as opportunities for profane illumination. They in turn, however, presented Benjamin with an opportunity. For Surrealism turned out to be the spark that closed the circuit between the forces of language and the modernity of Paris: their avant-garde linguistic experiments could be made to appear as a deciphering of Parisian modernity. In his essay on Surrealism Benjamin insists that 'the writings of this circle are not literature but something else—demonstrations, watchwords, documents, bluffs, forgeries if you will' because 'the writings are concerned literally with experiences'.[83] And the kind of experience the writings are concerned with is Paris, for 'no face is surrealistic to the same degree as the true face of a city'.[84]

Benjamin had always been interested in experiences of 'intoxication', moments when, in Axel Honneth's words, 'instrumental attention recedes to give way to a state of lower concentration or half-wakefulness'.[85] These were, Honneth claims, secular versions or equivalents of the religious experience Benjamin had appealed to early on: what united hashish use, *flânerie*, the moment of awakening, Proustian remembrance, and childhood experience was the dissolution of the subject/object distinction; 'in different contexts he would again and again attempt to prove with these examples that to experience sometimes truly can only mean suddenly

---

[79] Walter Benjamin, 'Antitheses Concerning Word and Name', in *Selected Writings, Vol. 2*, 717–19.
[80] Walter Benjamin, 'Surrealism: The Last Snapshot of the European Intelligentsia', in *Selected Writings, Vol. 2*, 207–21. The category of 'profane illumination' is introduced on 209. 'Presence of mind' figures throughout Benjamin's career; an excellent elucidation of it is found in his Surrealist-inspired 'One-Way Street', *Selected Writings, Vol. 1*, 482–3.
[81] Benjamin, 'Surrealism', 212.
[82] Georg Simmel, 'The Metropolis and Mental Life' (1903), in *On Individuality and Social Forms* (Chicago: University of Chicago Press, 1971), 329–30.
[83] Benjamin, 'Surrealism', 208.   [84] Benjamin, 'Surrealism', 211.
[85] Axel Honneth, 'A Communicative Disclosure of the Past: On the Relation between Anthropology and Philosophy of History in Walter Benjamin', *new formations* 20 (1993): 86.

experiencing the world as a social field of analogies and correspondences'.[86] But Benjamin had not appealed to religious experience of the immediate kind, to mystical visions, the experience of prayer, or religious ritual—his appeal had been to revelation that was encoded or veiled in language, and which could be coaxed out of its hiding place by the right kind of criticism. It was in language that subjectivity lost its foothold and that the world appeared as a magical community of things. 'Languages', Benjamin had said, 'therefore, have no speaker, if this means someone who communicates *through* these languages'.[87] Conversely, '[t]here is no event or thing in either animate or inanimate nature that does not in some way partake of language'.[88]

The profane illuminations of the Surrealists likewise depended on a 'loosening of the self'.[89] They were able to 'pick up' the 'signal of true historical existence' that lurked in the arcades and winter gardens, the railways stations and street names, only by making their individual will take a back seat.[90] But in this case the loss of subjectivity proceeds from social circumstances. The civic subject that takes initiative may succeed on the surface, but they will miss the point of the city (and, by extension, of the modern): the utopian core of urbanity, the promise of a world made pleasurable by the presence of others in built space, is only available to those who lose themselves in the crowd. There were, of course, other models for dissolving the individual into the social or collective, offered up by the likes of Jung and Jünger.[91] But Benjamin condemns them as archaic, which in this context has a socio-political as well as an historical meaning. For subsumption of the individual into the nation or *Volk* is subsumption into a mythic image of the collective, in which technology can only play a destructive role (as the handmaiden of war) and in which knowledge and experience have to give way to amorphous feelings. For the modern collective, one had to look to Paris, and to language.

Benjamin makes the equation himself: '[E]very city', he remarks in the *Arcades Project*, 'is beautiful to me (from outside its borders), just as all talk of particular languages having greater or lesser value is to me unacceptable'.[92] But the beauty is only made visible to the one who loses herself in the city, just as the beauty of language is only available when one gives up on reference and luxuriates in the spontaneous analogies and similarities that emerge in its contemplation. One loses oneself in language by doing something—translating, philosophizing, criticizing— and one loses oneself in the city not by staying at home in one of those interiors Benjamin so despised, but by getting out and about. Just as in Saussure speakers have to take the initiative—they have to speak for there to be language, but with the consciousness that a larger collective process holds sway—so Benjamin proposes schemes for a loss of subjectivity that nevertheless depends on particular

---

[86] Honneth, 'Communicative Disclosure', 85.
[87] Benjamin. 'On Language as Such', 63.
[88] Benjamin, 'On Language as Such', 62.
[89] Benjamin, 'Surrealism', 208.
[90] Benjamin, *Arcades Project*, K1a, 6 (391).
[91] On Jung's archaic version of the collective, see Convolute K of the *Arcades Project*, 6.1–6.4 (399–400). On Ernst Jünger's nationalist fantasies see Benjamin's 'Theories of German Fascism', *Selected Writings, Vol. 2*, 312–21.
[92] Benjamin, *Arcades Project*, N1, 6 (458).

kinds of activity. Žižek has described what he calls '*states that are essentially produced by the big Other*'—love and respect are his examples—as by-product conditions, which you cannot achieve by direct pursuit (you can't decide to fall in love or to be respected) but which might befall you in the pursuit of other, well-defined goals.[93] For Saussure and Benjamin, true historical existence is a state essentially produced by the big City.

The medium of that state is language. No one doubts that Benjamin liked a bit of a wander, but dialectical images were his quarry and 'the place where one encounters them is language'.[94] The 'open sky of cloudless blue'[95] under which the *Arcades Project* commenced, was, after all, not an actual sky but the ceiling of the Bibliothèque Nationale in Paris, for it was there that Benjamin could lose himself not only in the city but in the '[t]ens of thousands of volumes [...] dedicated solely to the investigation of this tiny spot on the earth's surface'.[96] Isn't the *Project* a kind of exercise in translation, where the texts so liberally quoted throughout are supposed to surrender the pure language within by virtue of the context in which they appear? In a late fragment on translation, Benjamin insisted a successful one 'acknowledges its own role by means of commentary and makes the fact of the different linguistic situation one of its themes', which is as good a description of the form of the *Arcades Project* as any.[97] When Benjamin speaks of 'the revolutionary energies that appear in the "outmoded" ',[98] doesn't the outmoded include the vast array of conservative writers, French and German, whose effusions on Paris are scattered throughout what's supposed to be a radical text?[99]

What is potentially liberated in the dialectical image, in the translation of an image of Paris by the *Arcades Project* itself, is therefore a creative power that has debts both to language as such and to a utopian urbanity. Once again, we see language serve as a metonym for a far-reaching social transformation. In Benjamin, however, that social transformation is itself modelled on the idea of pure language: the social order is one in which the magical experiences made possible in language have somehow become part of the substance of social life itself.

In the writings of Bakhtin, Saussure, and Benjamin, linguistic diversity is evident to the traveller and to the city-dweller, whose presence in market squares and public spaces exposes them to (Bakhtin again) 'the languages of social groups, professions, genres, generations and so on'. But the significance of the diversity is not some kind of linguistic relativism or delight in variety, but—for the creators of language as such—the implication that language is productive. Productive, it turns out, in a quite particular and quite urban way. The urban crowd has some striking advantages for those trying to imagine modern forms of collective life. For it combines two features that seemed at odds in the nineteenth century: cohesiveness,

---

[93] Slavoj Žižek, *Looking Awry: An Introduction to Jacques Lacan through Popular Culture* (Cambridge, MA: MIT Press, 1992), 77.
[94] Benjamin, *Arcades Project*, N2a, 3 (462).   [95] Benjamin, *Arcades Project*, N1, 5 (457).
[96] Benjamin, *Arcades Project*, C1, 6 (82–3).
[97] Walter Benjamin, 'Translation – For and Against', in *Selected Writings, Vol. 3*, 250.
[98] Benjamin, 'Surrealism', 210.
[99] On Benjamin's use of conservative sources, see Buse et al., *Benjamin's Arcades*, 126–30.

and creative spontaneity. But the compromise that seemed to work so well in 'amorphous crowds of passers-by' was necessarily unsteady, for crowds could easily lose that amorphousness and become something more compact, directed, and threatening. Benjamin would remind us of the story in which the revolutionary Blanqui watched his army parade before him on the Champs-Elysées, hidden in the crowd.[100] The anonymity and amorphousness of crowds could both defuse collective action and enable it.

SOME CONCLUDING REMARKS OF A PROVISIONAL SORT

The linguistic turns we have examined in Saussure and his Soviet interpreters, in the emerging practices of analytic philosophy, in Bakhtin and Benjamin, embed the problems of a democratizing social order in language, distilled into the form of 'language as such'. For the ambiguities of the crowd were the symptoms of more general issues of political order and consent. The quantitative extension of the franchise and the new forms of political and cultural activity that accompanied it—new political parties, new kinds of unionism, new forms of urban proletarian culture—were not simple enlargements of a liberal public sphere. They made both the consent of the governed and the mechanisms of collective political debate and decision more complex and tangled. The nineteenth century had secured an identification of languages with 'peoples'. As those 'peoples' became the substance of political societies, and as politics itself gained responsibility for establishing and maintaining order in those societies, discussion about the nature of linguistic order and consent was invested with particular urgency.

What should we take away from the discussions we've examined so far? We should start with Saussure's claim that the use and maintenance of language depends on the consent, the agreement of its users, which he establishes as the underlying principle of his version of language as such, *langue*. On the one hand, this seemed to liberate language from attempts to bind it to naturalized or given features, such as national or racial characteristics: language had become the sphere of collective self-invention, where order was manufactured by the people organized through it. But the nature of that consent and agreement remained a constant source of ambiguity and even anxiety. Was it consciously sought or given? Could it be the result of deliberation or debate? We've seen the ruses Saussure came up with in order to keep the democratic, self-inventing genie in the bottle (no reason to prefer *Ochs* to *bœuf*, language is too complicated, the body of speakers is too amorphous, everyone is satisfied with their language anyhow...) and how his Soviet interpreters demonstrated the effort was doomed, allowing for deliberation at the very core of language. In the new linguistics language as such was presented as an institution that kept order without ever giving orders, buoyed by an ambiguous consent.

---

[100] Benjamin, *Arcades Project*, V9, 1 (617).

But then there were questions about that deliberation itself, about how the exercise of reason contended with the linguistic medium itself, questions raised forcefully and persistently in the emerging world of analytic philosophy. In Frege, Russell, and early Wittgenstein, 'language as such' is a problem for rational argument, a problem because it is systematically, formally unclear and illusory. They will seek to make it clear by means of radical translation: the paraphrase or replacing of an utterance by a statement rendered in a distinctive notation, different in syntax and vocabulary. The philosophers who launch 'analysis' do not seek to clarify what is vague or ambiguous by means of further conversation in the existing idiom, but by a drastic change of idiom, as if the existing language were afflicted by confusion at its root. What's remarkable in this proposal is the degree to which the problems of actually existing language are identified with intersubjectivity, with those features of language that Benveniste called an 'instance of discourse', embedding the sentence within a specific occasion of speech. Clarity in language was to be achieved by filtering out intersubjectivity: one had to purge the exercise of argument from the rhetorical aspect of speech, which adjusts linguistic elements to the task of persuading a particular audience.

But, as we pointed out in Chapter 3, the translation of sentences by logical analysis led, in the end, to new sentences, which might themselves be analysed and translated again. It was as if these philosophers would not be satisfied until linguistic form and meaning were in perfect, unshakeable alignment, as if they were set on building a ship that could resist any challenge the ocean of discourse might throw at it. To make clarity dependent on this new specialized system of symbols—rather than further discussion or meta-linguistic commentary—was to make lucid argument and deliberation the province of trained professionals, in keeping with the culture of science articulated by Pearson in his public lectures. Culture of science: because these philosophers were not scientists (though Russell, to be fair, was familiar with science's progress and achievements), but drew on its style to decouple what Habermas had called rational-critical argument from an ever-expanding and diversifying public sphere. But only part of its style: for the emphasis on conversation as the central medium of analytic philosophy reintroduced the rhetorical aspect of that public sphere through the back door, so to speak.

A doubting Thomas, however, was within their midst. For while Wittgenstein agreed with the project of logical analysis, he did not buy into the accompanying culture of science. The clarity of sharply formulated propositions was flawed: true clarity arrived only when one 'saw the world rightly' and acknowledged the barrenness of what scientific propositions could say. Because he could not imagine language as something other than a formal system, the intersubjectivity of language, its rhetorical aspect, took the shape of an irony that cast a shadow over the whole of his *Tractatus*, showing 'how little has been achieved' by scientific clarity.

Wittgenstein's melancholy resignation was not shared by the philosophers he inspired. But his conception of nonsense was, and this paved the way for a route to a quite different conception of language as such. The notion that language generated expressions that were systematically misleading, analogies that might be taken too far or too seriously, led to a conception of language as a web of analogies, which then had to be weighed, evaluated, and put to use in 'instances of discourse' (which Wittgenstein, from 1929 onwards, became adept at picturing). We are thus led back to the vision of language as a sphere of practice kept afloat by the consent of its users, with no anchor in the structure of the world or the shapes of things. Like Saussure, Wittgenstein will not ground this consent in any kind of deliberation or debate: speakers will know when an analogy works and when it generates nonsense simply by testing it out in practice or by testing it in the dramatizations of possible practice that Wittgenstein provides in his examples. It sounds eminently practical, and it is, so long as we are happy to go along with the myth that language always works, that any failure associated with it is an externality, at best parasitic on the smooth functioning of this marvellous social institution. If one wanted an image of a spontaneous social order that required no coercion, language—in the first decades of the twentieth century—was the place to look. And yet, 'if we wish to demonstrate that the rules a community accepts are imposed on it, and not freely consented to, it is a language which offers the most striking proof' (Saussure).[101]

Language as consent or agreement, language as a practice defined by its success: aren't these useful models, possible metonyms for societies that are no longer sure just what it is that makes them societies? Polities that have to invent their own social order, that must literally 'constitute' themselves (as Mazower has pointed out, constitution-making was the rage after the First World War), run enormous risks. The risks are significantly less if that constitution takes the form of an unconscious or even half-conscious consent, of spontaneous agreement about what 'works' and what doesn't, if it can avoid open dispute over the social bond itself.

But the linguistic turns take their distance from ideas of consent anchored in those strange mixtures of biology and culture called 'nationality' and 'race'. There were echoes. Thomas Akehurst has carefully catalogued and analysed the nationalist cultural politics of analytic philosophy, in which the bracing habit of analysis was often identified with a distinctively British empiricism and contrasted with the murkiness and fanaticism of European, particularly German metaphysics.[102] Wittgenstein himself agonized over his Jewishness in racial terms and the consequences that might have for his manner of thought, in 1931, at a critical moment in his changing philosophy.[103] We've reviewed Saussure's ambiguous feelings about the Dreyfus affair. Yet for all that, what's noticeable is how alien language as such is to ideas of nation and race. Simple matters of personal history and geography may have played a role: Saussure and Wittgenstein, after all, were citizens of multilingual and multinational polities, the Swiss Federation and the Austro-Hungarian Empire respectively. But, as we've observed in the current chapter, often language as such appears as an almost open polemic with nationalistic or racist conceptions of

---

[101] Saussure, *Course in General Linguistics* (1983), 71.
[102] Thomas L. Akehurst, *The Cultural Politics of Analytic Philosophy: Britishness and the Spectre of Europe* (London: Continuum, 2010).
[103] There's a substantial literature on Wittgenstein and Judaism, some of which assigns the latter a major role in his thought. For perceptive treatments, see Monk, *Wittgenstein*, 313–17, and David G. Stern, 'The Significance of Jewishness for Wittgenstein's Philosophy', *Inquiry* 43 (2000): 383–402.

language.[104] For one thing, the appeal to language as such is by character absolute and universalist: it captures language as a force or process that pushes against the structure and detail of any actually existing language. The distinguishing features of particular languages appear accidental and contingent and so can't be invested with national spirit as had been the case in the nineteenth century (even in Benjamin's theory, where each language has its distinctive profile, spirit as such only emerges in translation between languages or in their poetic or philosophic distortion). But even more importantly, the varieties of language as such we've examined have no room for collective spirit at all, if by that we understand a directing or guiding force. Not only is deliberation on the future of language ruled out of court, wilful change itself is barred. Creativity in language, innovations in form, depend on an absence of will, whether this is a consequence of Benjamin's urban intoxication, the loosening of subjective identity in Bakhtin, or the randomness of *parole* in Saussure.

It's an interesting moment for the linguistic turns, which underscores the ambiguity of all appeals to collectivity. For the latter comes in all shapes and sizes. It can be defined historically, as grounded in a continuous tradition, or as a creature of the present. It can move into the future with intent, or blindly, or by virtue of some unpredictable combination of forces. The linguistic turns discussed in this Part insisted on the collective, social being of language, but made language consensual without being deliberate, spontaneous but still orderly. Where deliberation and reason were allowed, they were carefully limited to the language of a professional caste.

Language as such brooks no collective reason and therefore no collective will. But there was another possibility: collective will embodied in language that was not reasonable, not argumentative, but mythic. This possibility is the topic of our second Part.

---

[104] This isn't to claim there was no possible overlap between racism and the new form of general linguistics. Christopher Hutton has shown how the assumption of a mother tongue, implicit in Saussure, contributed to the explicitly racist linguistics of Nazi Germany; *Linguistics and the Third Reich: Mother-Tongue Fascism, Race and the Science of Language* (London: Routledge, 1999).

PART II
MYTH

6

Do They Believe in Magic? The Word as Myth, Name, and Art

(C. K. Ogden and I. A. Richards, Frege, George Orwell, Bakhtin, Saussure)

Let's begin with two lectures, each delivered before the First World War in front of a self-consciously radical audience. The first was given by C. K. Ogden, then a student at Cambridge, before the Heretics Society on 19 February 1911. It may be a stretch to call the Heretics radical: the society had been formed by Ogden and others in 1909 to foster open discussion about religion, philosophy, and art. At the inaugural session, the anthropologist Jane Harrison stressed that 'heresy' was rooted in the idea of a bold, self-conscious choosing, and the society's founding 'Laws' insisted its members reject 'traditional a priori methods of approaching religious questions'.[1] But, as one historian has observed, '[d]espite their flamboyant name, the Heretics were quite at the centre of university respectability [...] Of the fifteen original members two were professors and four others became heads of houses.'[2]

Ogden's lecture, 'The Progress of Significs', complained about the 'incalculable confusion produced by our neglect of clear conceptions of the functions of language, of the use of words, as bearers of meaning, and of conscious attempts at a reasonable method of conveying that meaning', at the same time noting that the last decade had witnessed the publication of a striking number of volumes that had tried—unsuccessfully, in Ogden's view—to address the problem.[3] The source of the confusion was an outdated, no doubt 'traditional' view of language, based on the mystical conception of the name: 'Barbarous ideas about the properties of the name can, I believe, be shown to have a far wider significance than is generally admitted.'[4] The solution lay in Victoria Welby's work on 'significs', which distinguished between the sense, meaning, and significance of words, and which would

---

[1] Damon Franke, *Modernist Heresies: British Literary History, 1883–1924* (Columbus, OH: Ohio State University Press, 2008), 25, 45 table 1.

[2] William C. Lubenow, *Liberal Intellectuals and Public Culture in Modern Britain, 1815–1914* (Woodbridge: Boydell Press, 2010), 23.

[3] C. K. Ogden, 'The Progress of Significs', in W. Terrence Gordon (ed.), *C. K. Ogden and Linguistics, Vol. I: From Significs to Orthology* (London: Routledge/Thoemmes Press, 1994), 2.

[4] C. K. Ogden, 'Appendix: Significs & Logic/Definition' [to 'The Progress of Significs'], in *C. K. Ogden and Linguistics I*, 39.

prevent us from assuming every word named some kind of substance.[5] This was the first salvo Ogden would fire in a lifelong war against the confusion caused by the magical theory of names.

The second lecture was delivered at around one in the morning on 23 December 1913, at the Stray Dog Café, an avant-garde hangout in what was then called Petrograd. The speaker was Viktor Shklovskii, then, like Ogden, a university student, and his topic, as in Ogden's case, was words, in particular 'The Place of Futurism in the History of the Language'. Shklovskii was as unhappy as Ogden with the use being made of words, but his objection was that '[t]he word has been chained by habit, it is necessary to make it strange so that it touches the spirit, so that it interrupts things'. The avant-garde linguistic experiments of Russian Futurism were therefore not pointless, aestheticist ravings, but the means towards the 'renewal of the word'. Shklovskii believed in the magic of words: 'We will', he boldly claimed, 'remove the muck from the precious stones, we will [wake] the sleeping beauty.'[6]

Ogden's obsession with the dangers of 'word magic' would lead to many polemics on the subject, to a new Science of Symbolism, and eventually to his campaign for a new universal language, Basic English. Shklovskii's desire for magical words would lead to Russian Formalist criticism in the first instance and to what we think of as modern literary theory in the long run. In manner, style, and intellectual background they were very different and they held diametrically opposed views on the value of word magic. But they agreed word magic was possible and that its existence within language was not a merely stylistic matter, but something crucial to European society. Ogden and Shklovskii were not the only intellectuals worried about this—they are two points in a constellation that emerges vividly in the early morning of the twentieth century, held together by anxiety or excitement about the forcefulness of linguistic myth and magic. The force itself was given several different names in the period: word magic or myth, metaphysics, an aesthetic 'imageness' built into language, or the power of the Name itself. In every case, however, what agitated the writer was a force invested in certain words or phrases, words and phrases that stuck out from the everyday flow of discourse and which gave rise to strong feelings and dramatic actions. The excitement and anxiety was not merely aesthetic: it was fuelled by excitement and anxiety over the possibilities of mass democracy itself, which seemed to be developing its own distinctive rhetorical forms, described, by those unimpressed with them, as charisma or demagoguery.

The constellation of linguistic turns centred on myth thus constituted a distinctive class. Here the turn was not to language as a model of consensus or social order, but to language as the source of a magical power that could disrupt and reorganize the social whole. Here fascination with language was impelled by the sense that it spontaneously generated disturbing, powerful words, whether for good or ill. The 'force' of word magic is therefore different in kind than the productive force of language we encountered in Part I. There language spontaneously produced new

---

[5] See V. Welby, 'Sense, Meaning, and Interpretation', *Mind* New Series 5.17 (1896): 24–37.
[6] Viktor Shklovskii, notes for 'The Place of Futurism in the History of Language', in *Gamburgskii schet: stat 'i—vospominaniia—esse (1914–1933)* (Moscow: Sovetskii pisatel', 1990), 487.

forms throughout its range, reshaping itself continuously. In the case of myth and magic, however, the force of language is concentrated in specific words and phrases: it retains, even in its modern form, a distinction between the sacred and magical on one hand, and the profane and everyday on the other.

A crude way to distinguish the class of linguistic turns we're about to consider is to say that they approach language as the bearer of passion and enthusiasm rather than reason and consent. Language is a worry for the writers discussed in Part II because it spontaneously gives rise to moving, forceful words and phrases that inspire and direct, and that may convince without argument. As we'll see, for some this capacity to inspire is something to be feared, because it signals the death of rational political decision-making: myth will inspire democratic crowds, but at the expense of the older forms of liberal argument. For others, those older forms of liberal argument—based on a restricted electorate—are already dead and we need magic to inject some life into the common language. But if Part I featured a motley crew of intellectuals, the constellation assembled in Part II may test even the most generous reader's patience. We have the leader of the Italian Communist Party and a Russian Futurist poet, Oxbridge philosophers and a Syndicalist theorist, Russian literary critics devoted to the avant-garde, an English novelist devoted to plain speaking, and whatever it is we wish to call C. K. Ogden. What unites this disparate collection of intellectuals is the idea that 'language as such' has an inner propensity to words and phrases that acquire a magical substantiality: whether this magic is cause for joy or alarm, whether it is a necessary ingredient of democracy or a threat to its proper functioning, is one of the questions that distinguishes the various positions.

Sometimes the political and social stakes are discussed openly, and sometimes there is no interest in political consequences at all. In every case, however, the mythic propensity of language as such has an inner link to the politics of democratizing societies, because myth is not something that spurs random individuals to action, but a force that both creates collectives and rouses their passions. If we wanted to draw a sharp contrast between the social theory at work in this Part of the book and the kind hazarded in Part I, we could say that in Part I collectives are formed as part of the internal order of language, and in Part II collectives are formed when they are united by the passions articulated in myths. But that implies another critical distinction: the collectives in Part I are typically unifying—the internal order of language is a metonym for an orderly, consensual polity; the collectives aroused by myths, on the other hand, are typically partial, even divisive—they are either groups that threaten the order and wholeness of the polity, or polities that are defined by some kind of particularism—religious, ethnic, or national. The collectives organized around magical words and phrases divide societies, often along class lines, but sometimes along religious or ethnic lines. For that reason, word magic will, more often than not, be described as particularly tempting to newly enfranchised, usually proletarian or plebeian, members of political society. Naturally enough, some of the characters in our drama welcome these new collective movements: if they lead to dramatic political change, so much the better. Others will see these same movements as a threat to democracy and will devise strategies for defusing myth and integrating the newly enfranchised into the political status quo.

There are, finally, two other lines of demarcation that define this constellation, beyond the individual idiosyncrasies of its elements. One is the relationship of myth to language itself. Is myth an ineliminable feature of language or an excisable excrescence, a rival form of symbolism or a force lurking within language but only occasionally expressing itself? In Ogden's writing, for example, myth stems from outdated attitudes to language: word magic is first and foremost a matter of primitive attitudes towards language, a misunderstanding about how language works that leads to confusions about what language is doing. In Cassirer, by contrast, myth is an independent form of symbolism, distinct from language, that intersects and overlaps with it. For Benjamin, the power of the name resides in the inner recesses of language, from which it can be occasionally coaxed out by poetry, philosophy, and translation. For Shklovskii the magical power of words is a birthright that has been hastily given away for the pottage of modernity.

The second line of demarcation concerns the historical coordinates of myth, the question of whether word magic is a primitive relic or atavism, which has survived the onslaught of modernity, or a modern phenomenon in its own right, perhaps mistakenly given a label borrowed from the past. Is this magic an inheritance from a distant past, deriving its power from the sacred and pagan and thus living on borrowed time? Is myth the adaptation of a sacred force for modern political ends? Or is it something genuinely new, a force that is generated by the dynamic of modern social and political life itself?

Let's begin with those who thought that myth was a danger, whether it was intrinsic to language as such or not, whether it was ancient or modern in origin. That group will include C. K. Ogden and I. A. Richards, George Orwell, Mikhail Bakhtin, Gottlob Frege, and, to a degree, Saussure. We'll devote the next chapter to those who welcome language's mythical inclinations: Ernst Cassirer, Viktor Shklovskii and Roman Jakobson, the Russian Futurists, and Walter Benjamin. An excursus following that chapter accounts for two figures, Sorel and Gramsci, who, in a sense, put our argument into reverse: their political positions are informed by theories of language rather than the other way round. We'll conclude this Part by returning to analytic philosophy, in the persons of Wittgenstein and J. L. Austin, whose battle against metaphysics—which I will argue is myth in philosophical attire—in the name of 'ordinary language' provides language as such with what may be its most complex and ambiguous elaboration.

WORD MAGIC, SCIENCE OF SYMBOLISM

Ogden's position on myth was, at least on the surface, consistent and clear. In his address to the Heretics, he asked about the source of the current linguistic confusion, and he located it firmly in the past: in a mystical view of 'names' dating back to the Hebrew Scriptures, which endows names with exceptional powers and which has somehow survived in various forms into the twentieth century. For a young Heretic, this would seem to be the natural position to take—word magic depended on a traditional authority, which would crumble when subjected to the force of modern reason. In this Ogden was already deviating from Welby's writing, even if most of his programme, including its name, echoed Welby's work.[7]

From the late nineteenth century onwards, Welby had taken aim at the persistence of linguistic ambiguities in our speech, particularly the misuse of metaphor and analogy. The problem was the 'tyranny of misfitting Expression' in all fields of human endeavour; the solution was 'the drastic critique of imagery and the resulting acquirement of more fitting idioms, figures, and expressive forms in general'.[8] She insisted that this was a problem with enormous consequences and brought to its solution a striking moral zeal. The 'moral basis of speech-life' was, she argued:

> Significance and lucidity. These are not merely accomplishments, they are ethically valuable. We owe it to our fellows to assimilate truth and to convey it to them unalloyed by needless rubbish of the senseless, the meaningless, the confused and the contradictory.[9]

Welby accordingly called for a 'linguistic conscience', on analogy with the social conscience some Victorians thought they should have.[10] But the key to this programme of reform wasn't a direct change in the signs themselves. That is to say, Welby didn't simply argue for sharper, more careful definitions of words and strict attention to our use of metaphor. She thought the lasting solution lay in a sharper meta-linguistic understanding, one which would, among other things, disentangle the confusions surrounding terms like 'meaning' and 'sense', which often conflated literal meaning, intended meaning, and the import or significance of our words (this project had a significant overlap with that of C. S. Peirce in the United States, with whom she had a substantial correspondence). Ogden seemed to share Welby's zeal, her conviction that linguistic ambiguity had enormous social consequences, and the belief that the ultimate solution lay in a more scientific understanding of signs. An early manuscript shows him warning of the 'tyranny of Language' and concurring in the need for a meta-linguistic, not just a linguistic intervention: 'As Lady Welby has so often urged to be content with mere reform of articulate expression would be fatal to the prospect of a significantly adequate language.'[11] But whereas for Welby, linguistic ambiguity seemed to arise from a general lack of care and laxness in keeping our meanings up-to-date, from the outset Ogden had a more focused opponent: word magic.[12] When he returned to his theme in 1920, it looked at once more modern and more menacing.

---

[7] For a detailed account of the relationship between Ogden and Welby, see Susan Petrilli, *Signifying and Understanding: Reading the Works of Victoria Welby and the Signific Movement* (Berlin: De Gruyter Mouton, 2009), 731–47.

[8] Victoria Lady Welby, *Signifcs and Language: The Articulate Form of Our Expressive and Interpretative Resources* (London: Macmillan and Co., 1911), 4, 38.

[9] Welby, 'Sense, Meaning, and Interpretation', 30.

[10] Welby, 'Sense, Meaning and Interpretation', 30.

[11] C. K. Ogden, untitled draft for a lecture (estimated date, 1914), Box 126, Folder 1, C. K. Ogden Archive, McMaster University Library, Hamilton, Ontario, unpaginated. At one point in the manuscript Ogden describes the programme as a 'Eugenics of Language'.

[12] Petrilli notes that Ogden and Welby disagreed about the role of classical antiquity and suggests this was their first significant parting of the ways: Welby thought the classical writers were models of conscientious writing, Ogden thought they were early proponents of word magic. See Petrilli, *Signifying and Understanding*, 741–2.

Ogden had spent the war period editing *The Cambridge Magazine*, which became infamous for its translation of a wide range of foreign press sources and for its pacifist stance on the war itself. In reward, Ogden's offices were ransacked on Armistice Day by chauvinist thugs. In reward: because the cunning of history was at work, and it arranged for I. A. Richards to be standing outside Ogden's offices as the plunder happened. The two met, the two talked, the two discovered they harboured the same anxieties about language and how it was understood, and the two embarked on a long, intellectually sophisticated campaign to make things right.[13]

The campaign was launched in *The Cambridge Magazine* in 1920, in a series of articles that attacked the problem from both the historical point of view—a further, more elaborate history of the attitudes that fostered word magic—and the theoretical point of view—a proposal for a new 'Science of Symbolism'. Although Ogden and Richards announced they had 'secured the co-operation of a body of specialists', the body of specialists turned out to be mostly Ogden and Richards writing under a series of pseudonyms and altered initials (Ogden appeared as 'C. K. Ogden', 'C. M.', 'Adelyne More', 'C. K. O.', and anonymously).[14] As was the case earlier, word magic was in essence meta-linguistic, stemming not so much from language itself as from '*habitual attitudes towards words, and lingering assumptions due to theories no longer openly held but still allowed to guide our practice*'.[15] Word magic had its origins in a variety of ancient and primitive religions, more precisely in 'the magical theory of the name as part of the thing, the theory of an inherent connexion between symbols and referents'.[16] In ancient religion names were endowed with an extraordinary force: they were not so much symbols of gods and spiritual forces as elements of the gods and spiritual forces themselves, which, given the proper ritual, could conjure up the thing or spirit named. When one spoke the name, one drew on the 'inherent connexion'. According to Ogden, the magical theory of names survived the death of the gods themselves, refusing to acknowledge its outdatedness by hanging around in the form of metaphysics (for intellectuals) and propaganda (for everyone else). But as word magic was a matter of attitudes towards language, rather than language as such, the dissolving of these attitudes through argument was the surest way to do battle with it; Richards accordingly supplied a new theory of symbolism in his 'What Happens When We Think'.[17]

---

[13] The details of the events vary somewhat from account to account. Ogden's biographer, W. Terrence Gordon, claims the shop was wrecked by 'angry rioters'; see *C. K. Ogden: A Bio-Bibliographical Study* (Metuchen, NJ: Scarecrow Press, 1990), 12–20. I. A. Richards, on the other hand, describes the offenders as '[m]edical students, flown with the spirits of the occasion' (i.e., the signing of the Armistice); see his 'Co-Author of the "Meaning of Meaning": Some Recollections of C. K. Ogden', in P. Sargent Florence and J. R. L. Anderson (eds.), *C. K. Ogden: A Collective Memoir* (London: Elek Pemberton, 1977), 97.

[14] Unsigned [C. K. Ogden], 'The Linguistic Conscience', *The Cambridge Magazine* (Summer 1920), 31.

[15] Unsigned [C. K. Ogden], 'Thoughts, Words and Things', *The Cambridge Magazine*, Decennial Number, 1912–1921, 29.

[16] Ogden, 'Thoughts, Words and Things', 29.

[17] I. A Richards, 'What Happens When We Think', *The Cambridge Magazine*, Decennial Issue, 1912–1921, 32–41.

That new theory was essentially a loose behaviourism, modified by associationist psychology.[18] The fundamental claim was that signs came into being when we were able to recall an element of a situation we had experienced—Richards's example was the striking of a match—and use it to evoke another element of the situation we had experienced. The sound of the striking thus stood for the appearance of the flame. The polemical crux of the theory was that the sign only attached itself to a referent, acquired a meaning, by virtue of this situation, and that it was in the mind that the associations were forged. Names had no inherent connection to things named: the link between them was always mediated by the human mind and by the vagaries of human experience. Richards would formalize the claim in a famous diagram, depicting a triangle with 'Symbol', 'Thought', and 'Referent' at its corners: while the symbol (match-striking, or a word) could cause the 'thought', and the thought could summon up the referent or thing, between the symbol itself and the thing there was not an 'inherent connexion', but only an indirect, 'imputed' relation.

The theory struck a chord: Ogden and Richards brought their work together in the book *The Meaning of Meaning* in 1923, and the text went through ten editions in the following twenty-five years.[19] The triangular account of symbolization was frequently reproduced, and the appendix on so-called primitive languages, provided by the anthropologist Bronislaw Malinowski, also attracted a fair share of attention. But achieving popularity is not the same thing as achieving success and you could argue that, far from stopping theories of word magic in their tracks, the book ended up making theories of word magic even more pervasive. Malinowski had been brought on board on account of his interest in magic in the Melanesian societies he studied. But, as has been pointed out by historians of pragmatics like Brigitte Nerlich and David Clarke, Malinowski promoted magic from a special case of language use to the primary form of all language. 'Magic', as they have put it, 'is obviously the domain in which language really seems to be doing something, to have some effect and some sort of force.'[20] It was a short step from this to Malinowski's conclusion in 1935 that 'the main function of language is not to express thought, not to duplicate mental processes, but rather to play an active pragmatic part in human behaviour'.[21] The force of magic was just a concentrated version of the general pragmatic force of all language, which, in the second half of the century, would become a subfield of linguistics and a live topic in analytic philosophy (where it would travel under the name of 'speech acts').

The ironic impact of *The Meaning of Meaning* could be chalked up to the haphazard nature of intellectual evolution, which rarely moves in a straight line.

---

[18] George Wolf has described the theory as indebted both to Watson's behaviourism and to Russell, who added the mental image to the causal account of meaning; see his 'C. K. Ogden', in Roy Harris (ed.), *Linguistic Thought in England, 1914–1945* (London: Duckworth, 1988), 85–105.

[19] C. K. Ogden and I. A. Richards, *The Meaning of Meaning: A Study of The Influence of Language upon Thought and of The Science of Symbolism* (London: Kegan Paul, Trench, Trubner & Co., 1923).

[20] Brigitte Nerlich and David D. Clarke, *Language, Action, and Context: The Early History of Pragmatics in Europe and America, 1780–1930* (Amsterdam: John Benjamins, 1996), 321.

[21] Bronislaw Malinowski, 'An Ethnographic Theory of Language and Some Practical Corollaries', in *Coral Gardens and Their Magic, Vol. 2: The Language of Magic and Gardening* (London: Allen & Unwin, 1935), 7.

But it was partly the fault of Ogden and Richards themselves, for their Science of Symbolism did not quite hit the magical target at which it was aimed. The fusing of name and thing was certainly central to word magic. But word magic was not defined only by the *form* of the connection it made between word and thing, but also by the nature of the things themselves. The things conjured up by mythical and magical names were never mere 'things'; they were animated with a peculiar spiritual force or power, set off from the rest of the world as sacred or supernatural. If the striking of a match were to be absorbed by word magic, if, say, it were to be surrounded by magical ritual (as fire-making arguably still is in some modern religious ceremonies), the referent would no longer be the simple physical event of fire, but fire as the manifestation of a force pervading the ordinary world, fire as something to be summoned rather than caused. 'Fire' might then even become the name of a corresponding deity—as historically has been the case in several cultures.

Perhaps Ogden and Richards were aware of all this and thought that match-striking was a clever modern way of taking mythical fire down a peg. For at other points in their writing they make clear that magic attaches itself to certain sorts of words and things, that it is not a mere formal error in the understanding of language. When, for example, they choose to discuss contemporary forms of word magic, their attention is immediately drawn to modern versions of the ancient deities. The following biblical parody, published under a pseudonym in the opening fusillade of articles in 1920, makes the matter clear:

> And when Homo came to study the parts of speech, he wove himself a noose of Words. And he hearkened to himself, and bowed his head and made abstractions, hypostasising and glorifying. Thus arose Church and State and Strife upon the earth; for oftentimes Homo caused Hominem to die for Abstractions hypostasised and glorified: and the children did after the manner of their fathers, for so had they been taught. And last of all Homo began also to eat his words.[22]

'Abstractions hypostasised and glorified': these were the modern equivalents of the old gods—not just any old thing, but a peculiar type of thing. A more dangerous sort of thing as well: in 1911 the 'bandying of large imposing names and abstract qualities' by Cambridge students was merely an annoyance—now people were dying for them.[23]

Nor would any old abstraction do. Also part of the initial fusillade was a short discussion of 'The Cause and the Cure', which approached the problem of symbolism in a slightly different manner than Richards's account of match-striking. Instead of a descriptive account of how symbols emerge, it proposed 'certain Canons or Rules, six in number, which govern the proper use of Symbols'.[24] Of these canons, Canon I—'*One Symbol refers to one and only one Referent*'—and Canon III—'*The referent of a contracted symbol is the referent of that symbol expanded*'—would prove the most consequential.[25] For they explained both how abstractions hypostasized

---

[22] C. M. [C. K. Ogden], 'What is What?', *The Cambridge Magazine* (Summer 1920), 40.
[23] Ogden, 'Progress of Significs', 2.
[24] C. K. Ogden and I. A. Richards, 'Symbolism', *The Cambridge Magazine* (Summer 1920), 34.
[25] Ogden and Richards, 'Symbolism', 34.

and glorified emerged (by ignoring the rules) and how to prevent them (by following them). And when Ogden and Richards discussed the regrettable consequences of ignoring the rules, which led to the 'hypostatization of contracted symbols', they pointed to abstractions that had played an outsized role in the conflicts of their time: 'Virtue, Liberty, Democracy, Peace, Germany, Religion, Glory', all, they conceded, 'invaluable words, indispensable even, but able to confuse the clearest issues, unless controlled by Canon III'.[26]

The modern version of the sacred was, in short, politics, for there was where one found abstractions worth dying and killing for. Ogden and Richards were well aware of this substitution, even if they did not draw all the necessary conclusions. In *The Meaning of Meaning*, published after the concession of adult male suffrage in 1918 and in the midst of the campaign for women's suffrage (of which Ogden was a consistent supporter), they noted that word magic had now an enlarged field of action: 'New millions of participants in the control of general affairs', they remarked, 'must now attempt to form personal opinions upon matters which were once left to a few'.[27] Just before the theory of symbolism was launched, Ogden acknowledged in *The Cambridge Magazine* that 'we are about to enter on an era in which the Press is destined to play a part in the life of the community in the formation of public opinion second only to that of the Movies themselves'.[28] The press and the movies: no one could accuse Ogden of not being aware of what was happening around him.

Similarly, when it came time to talk about the spheres in which word magic was deadliest, Ogden's attention shifted, as if by some unconscious knowledge, from universities and poetry to the public sphere. In his first diatribe on 'The Power of Words' in 1920, he claimed that '[b]etween the attitude of the early Egyptian and that of the modern poet there would appear at first sight to be but little difference'.[29] Three years later, an expanded disquisition on the same topic changed the focus (Ogden would continue polemics with word magic into the 1930s, and *The Meaning of Meaning* advertised an entire book on the subject—which never appeared—on its title page).[30] Having described 'logocracy' in ancient Greece and Eastern 'logolatry', Ogden turned to a consideration of 'Modern Methods', 'More Modern Methods', and 'Most Modern Methods'. The paradigm of the modern in this case turned out to be the English chauvinist Horatio Bottomley, whose

[26] Ogden and Richards, 'Symbolism', 36.
[27] Ogden and Richards, *The Meaning of Meaning*, xxix.
[28] Unsigned [C. K. Ogden], 'Another Jungle Story', *The Cambridge Magazine* 9.14 (1920), 193.
[29] Ogden and Richards, 'Symbolism', 32.
[30] The pattern of the obsession is interesting. A 45-page article on 'The Power of Words' (cited below), appeared in 1923, and the initial edition of *The Meaning of Meaning* reproduced much of this in a 68-page chapter. When understandable editorial pressure gradually reduced the discussion of word magic to a mere 24 pages by the 6th edition in 1944, Ogden responded by publishing a 105-page article on the topic in his own journal *Psyche* ('Word Magic', *Psyche* 18 (1938–52): 9–126). Ogden's archive includes a table of contents for the Word Magic book that never appeared (Box 130, folder 5). Its first two parts, on 'The Power of Words' and 'Towards Orthology' (Ogden's new name for the science of symbolism), go over the same territory as the earlier chapters and articles. As for 'The Principles of Orthology' which were to complete the book, we can only guess they would echo the already established canons of symbolism.

warmongering speeches were 'an example of the exploitation of the power of symbols without parallel in ancient or modern times'.[31] '[I]t was', Ogden coldly observed, 'by words, and words alone, words as empty and insincere as any ever spoken or penned by a public idol, that this linguistic adept maintained his influence with the masses whom he so magnificently duped'.[32]

'[A]ny symbolic apparatus which is in general use', Ogden and Richards claimed, 'is liable to incompleteness and defect': it remained unclear whether language had a formal defect that led, in the absence of exceptional vigilance, to word magic or if it was merely an instrument which could be misused when careless or malevolent people were allowed to play with it.[33] This ambiguity mapped onto the question of word magic's primitivism, for if word magic were indeed just a consequence of an antiquated understanding of a linguistic mechanism with no inherent fault or defect, then a healthy dose of modern science should finish it off. The Science of Symbolism did not, however, finish it off. Then again, the Science of Symbolism was not actual science: it entailed no experiments, no empirical data, no hypotheses testable under controlled conditions. In comparison with the highly developed protocols of comparative philology, it looked like mere introspection mixed with philosophy. What Ogden and Richards provided was an attenuated version of the 'culture of science', in which the rhetoric of hard-headed, tough-minded objectivity, combined with behaviourist talk of causes and effects, was supposed to sweep away misty ideas drawn from religion. It was, in the end, one more attempt by a *soi-disant* 'body of specialists' (Ogden's description of his intellectual team in *The Cambridge Magazine*) to make a democratic people reasonable by educating them in the ways of science.

FREGE GRAPPLES WITH THE PUBLIC

The Meaning of Meaning had opened with a dismissive wave of the hand, which assured the reader that all previous writing on the topic of signs—by Bréal, Saussure, and so on—had somehow missed the mark. Among those cursorily dismissed was Frege (he gets a page and a half in the Appendix), whose famous article 'On Sense and Reference' would at first glance seem close to the concerns of Ogden and Richards. For Frege, too, had distinguished carefully between the external thing referred to in discourse and the 'sense' of the expression that did the referring (the most famous example was the equation of the 'morning star' and the 'evening star', which referred to the same star but with different senses). And Frege, too, railed against the imperfections of natural language, because it spontaneously generated phrases and words that seemed to make sense but which actually referred to nothing,

---

[31] [C. K. Ogden], 'The Power of Words', *The Cambridge Magazine* (Early Spring, Double Number (1923), 32.
[32] Ogden, 'The Power of Words', 32.
[33] Ogden and Richards, *The Meaning of Meaning*, 26.

phrases which thereby gave shape and apparent substance to imaginary entities, which would take on a life of their own in speech.

And Frege, too, experienced a kind of undertow towards politics when discussing these unfortunate abstractions. Having complained about the emergence of meaningless entities in mathematics, Frege suddenly steers the conversation towards uncharted political waters:

> This lends itself to demagogic abuse as easily as ambiguity—perhaps more easily. 'The will of the people' can serve as an example; for it is easy to establish that there is at any rate no generally accepted meaning for this expression.[34]

Thirty-one years after this article Frege would make clear, in a personal diary, just how politically conservative he was, but in his published work he stuck to strictly logical matters. Or at least he tried to, for his choice of examples tells a slightly different story. 'On Sense and Reference' often has to illustrate its arguments with sample sentences and these, in the first half of the article, are of the sort you'd expect: everyday observations about the morning and evening star, something about Homer and Odysseus, a bit about the astronomer Kepler. But the offhand comment about demagogues who might exploit the apparently meaningless 'will of the people' sets off a torrent of political reference, for after that Frege's examples concern Napoleon's tactics at Waterloo, August Bebel's views on the fate of Alsace-Lorraine, and the dispute between Prussia and Denmark over Schleswig-Holstein. If clarity in expression seemed at first to be aimed at better mathematics and astronomy, by the end Frege is exploring a rather different application.

Rather different, and rather more complicated. For the rush of politically themed examples coincides with Frege's turn to the logical analysis of what come to be called belief sentences, that is, sentences that describe what someone believes or thinks. 'Bebel fancies that the return of Alsace-Lorraine would appease France's desire for revenge' is tricky from the logician's point of view because the truth or falsity of its subordinate clause does not—as it should in ordinary factual sentences—contribute to the truth or falsity of the whole.[35] Maybe the return of Alsace-Lorraine would appease France, and maybe it wouldn't: it's a matter of opinion. But whether it would or not makes no difference to the truth of the claim that August Bebel believes it would (it's a problem that will bedevil the logical analysis of language for quite a while, reminding it of its limits).[36]

It's a matter of opinion—to be more precise, a matter of 'public opinion'. August Bebel was not a random individual, and sovereignty over Alsace-Lorraine was not a private question: the sentence concerned the intervention of a prominent political leader, and noted orator, on a politically explosive issue. Bebel had set out to influence

---

[34] Gottlob Frege, 'On Sense and Meaning', in *Translations from the Philosophical Writings*, 70. As in Chapter 3 I have changed the translation of *Bedeutung* from 'meaning' to 'reference', which is particularly appropriate when comparing Frege with Ogden and Richards.
[35] Frege, 'On Sense and Meaning', 76.
[36] As Karl-Otto Apel has pointed out, the logical analysis of language will always come up against the intersubjectivity of language itself, which it cannot adequately explain or account for; see his *Analytic Philosophy of Language and the Geisteswissenschaften*, chapter II.

public opinion, this strange new beast that roamed the now half-democratized expanses of the nineteenth century. All of which makes Frege's slightly earlier comment on the fictitiousness of 'the will of the people' even more provocative. For one thing, Frege cites the very fact that there is no 'generally accepted meaning' for the expression as evidence that the expression has no meaning, which amounts to making the will of the people the criterion for whether 'the will of the people' exists. More telling, however, is that Frege complains not only that 'the will of the people' has no reference—that there is no such thing, just a series of words that work grammatically, but not logically—but also that the existence of this meaningless phrase itself may lead to demagoguery, that is, to attempts to create the very popular will he insists is impossible.

Frege knows that 'the will of the people' does not exist, and yet is afraid that someone might bring it into being—he is caught in what Žižek calls 'fetishistic disavowal', believing unconsciously in what he knows cannot be the case consciously.[37] The intellectual awkwardness, though, is just the symptom of a larger discomfort: the feeling that the abstractions that language might hypostasize are not mere logical errors, but the mark of some worrying transformation in the nature of signs themselves. What bothers Frege and Ogden about the will of the people is precisely the way it chases after, gets inflamed by, *believes* in such apparently reference-less phrases as 'the will of the people'. Word magic seen from this perspective isn't just some primitive meta-linguistic prejudice, but a phenomenon rooted in modern democratic political life. The solution both arrive at is rules: either the rules that define an artificial extension of the language (Frege's *Begriffsschrift*) or the Canons of Symbolism that constrain how we use the existing language. Rules will channel the waters of discourse, ensuring that the ship moves forward on a constrained path, protected against the dangers of the high seas.

It was possible, however, to acknowledge such strange beasts as public opinion and the will of the people without taking fright. Gabriel Tarde, whom we discussed in Chapter 2, described public opinion as a 'storm' or 'wind' that bends parliaments and governments to its will, but not as something either necessarily irrational or rational.[38] In the articles he wrote about Opinion at the end of the 1890s and early 1900s—i.e., at the very height of public debate over the Dreyfus affair—he insisted on the modernity of public opinion, arguing that it only took shape when a nationwide press was able to stimulate the views of a private reading public. The public itself is 'the social group of the future', because it depends on several features of modern life:[39]

> It is not meetings of men on the public street or in the public square that witness the birth and development of these kinds of social rivers, these great impulses which are presently overwhelming the hardest hearts and the most resistant minds, and which are now being consecrated as laws or decrees enacted by governments and parliaments.

---

[37] Slavoj Žižek, *For They Know Not What They Do: Enjoyment as a Political Factor* (London: Verso, 1991), 241–53.
[38] Tarde, 'Opinion and Conversation', 318.
[39] Tarde, 'The Public and the Crowd' (1901), in *On Communication and Social Influence*, 281.

> The strange thing about it is that these men who are swept along in this way, who persuade each other, or rather who transmit to one another suggestions from above—these men do not come in contact, do not meet or hear each other; they are all sitting in their own homes scattered over a vast territory, reading the same newspaper. What then is the bond between them? This bond lies in their simultaneous conviction or passion and in their awareness of sharing at the same time an idea or a wish with a great number of other men.[40]

Tarde will later qualify the description: the men [*sic*] who read newspapers engage in 'conversation' as well, a distinctly sociable discourse that provides the glue for this public. But leaving conversation to one side for the moment, we can't help but notice that public opinion is premised here on a form of mass communication—the printed mass newspaper—and, perhaps even more significantly, that it entails a significant element of self-reflexivity (the members of the public not only share the same idea, but they are aware that they do so).

It was this self-reflexivity that discomfited Frege: it made the strict formalization of language impossible (a different kind of reflexivity would lead to Russell's Paradox, which proved Frege's logical project was doomed to failure). Public opinion and the will of the people were more than the sum of individual wills and perspectives, more than mere 'simultaneous conviction', precisely to the extent that these wills recognized themselves and each other in public accounts of popular will and opinion (in speeches, in the press, and even, of course, in opera, where Public Opinion made a striking entrance in 1858).[41] One could say that the will of the people not only lent itself to demagogic abuse, it depended on it. For the awareness of which Tarde spoke was not a matter of individual psychology but of public utterance: it took the shape of invocations of public opinion and popular will that were ratified when the public or the people recognized themselves in them.

But public opinion could not have had the force it did, could not be a storm or river of discourse, if it reflected on itself with complete equanimity. The conversation which drew the public to one another was, as Tarde put it, 'the apogee of the *spontaneous attention* that men lend each other' and 'consequently, the strongest agent of imitation, of the propagation of sentiments, ideas, and modes of action'.[42] The public did not merely know themselves to be united in agreement—they felt it. 'It is rightly said of a good conversationalist', Tarde agreed, 'that he is a *charmer* in the magical sense of the word'.[43] The reflexivity of public opinion was not that of a meta-language, of a discourse which takes discourse as its object, but of a discourse that understands, so to speak, its role and purpose, that is aware that the views it enunciates flow into the current of public opinion. Public or popular will was no mere abstraction; it had a magic all its own.

---

[40] Tarde, 'The Public and the Crowd', 278.
[41] In Jacques Offenbach's *Orfée aux enfers* [*Orpheus in the Underworld*], a full-length operetta first performed in 1858, L'Opinion Publique is incarnate as a character voicing its disapproval of the fallen morals of the protagonists.
[42] Tarde, 'Opinion and Conversation', 308.   [43] Tarde, 'Opinion and Conversation', 309.

Tarde insisted this magic was a creature of modernity. Conversation, the mass press, and the nation—the three essential ingredients of public opinion—had been inherited from the past, but had come together in a distinctive way in the late nineteenth century. Ogden and Richards, at least on the surface, remained resolute in their conviction that magic was a matter of outdated attitudes to language, and that science was accordingly an adequate response. While language was clearly in need of reform, they were sure 'that no practical value would attach to such an attempt if the outcome involved extensive changes in the ordinary modes of speech'.[44]

INVENTED LANGUAGES: THEIR PLUSES AND MINUSES

Nevertheless, both Ogden and Richards spread their bets. Richards installed 'practical criticism' at the centre of the Cambridge English course, hoping that rigorous training would inculcate better linguistic habits. In the late 1920s Ogden concluded that, despite the earlier assurances, theoretical enlightenment was not enough—the defeat of word magic required a direct intervention in linguistic conventions, which would take the form of a new, somewhat artificial language, Basic English. Basic English was justified to a great extent as a possible *lingua franca* that would grease the wheels of international commerce and international scientific understanding. At the same time, however, Basic English was described as the 'most valuable exercise in the understanding of word-behaviour that has yet been devised'; it had a role to play in the fight against word magic.[45] This was not merely because Basic was a language stripped of what were regarded as unnecessary, merely stylistic overgrowths; it was mainly due to the way in which Basic exploited the 'analytic tendency' embedded in English.[46] By this Ogden meant the fact that English used word order and auxiliary words like prepositions to accomplish what other languages achieved by means of inflection: it was the analytic quality of English that, in Ogden's mind, made it a better candidate for a universal language than inflected Esperanto (though English chauvinism was probably a powerful consideration).

It's worth dwelling, if only for a moment, on the difference between these two projects for a universal language. For while both were ostensibly motivated by the need for a means of common international discourse, a substance to smooth the course of communication between peoples, beneath this surface lay a significant disagreement about what a language should do. L. L. Zamenhof, the idealistic creator of Esperanto, nursed great hopes for his linguistic creation: Esperanto contained an 'internal idea', the dream of universal brotherhood (maybe sisterhood as well). It was to be not merely a means of communication, but the medium in

---

[44] Ogden, 'The Linguistic Conscience', 31.
[45] C. K. Ogden, *Debabelization* (London: Kegan Paul, Trench, Trubner & Co., 1931), 37.
[46] C. K. Ogden, *Basic English: A General Introduction with Rules and Grammar*, 3rd edn. (London: Kegan Paul, Trench, Trubner & Co., 1932), 25. In claiming that English was peculiarly 'analytic', Ogden was relying on an established form of linguistic classification; see Morpurgo Davies, *Nineteenth-Century Linguistics*, 72–5.

which a new, ethical people would grow and flourish.[47] In effect, Zamenhof took the Herderesque, Humboldtian concept of language as the bearer of a national spirit and stretched it onto an international frame—Esperanto was not intended to neutralize national feeling, but to thin it out and spread it across the globe.[48] Ogden's project could not have been more different. Basic English didn't deal in magical abstractions like the human spirit: it improved its speakers by equipping them with the analytical habits they needed.

The Ogden scholar W. Terrence Gordon has explained how the earlier Canons of Symbolism provided the basic framework for the construction of Basic English, which was premised on the reinterpretation of words as collocations of smaller units of meaning.[49] This analytic tendency manifested itself most clearly in Basic English's attack on the 'essentially contractive nature of the verb'.[50] Verbs were classical instances of the contracted symbols Ogden and Richards had spoken of before and Basic English was the way one could ensure their necessary expansion. The 'operators', 'directives', and 'names' that Basic English offered instead of verbs and nouns forced speakers to acknowledge that

> a verb is primarily a symbolic device for telescoping an operation and an object or a direction (*enter* for 'go into'). Sometimes an operator, a directive, *and* a name are thus telescoped, as in the odd word 'disembark' (*get*, *off*, a *ship*); Latin goes so far as to throw in a pronoun, and a tense auxiliary [...][51]

In this way Basic English became a practical means of compelling people to think scientifically. Its 'practical analytic tendency', Ogden suggested, '[...] in two respects at least has reflected modern scientific developments (a) away from the Word-magic which induced a reverence for linguistic forms and rituals; (b) away from specific and towards general names'.[52] Basic English compelled its speakers and writers to translate hypostasized abstractions into a collocation of more modest real constituents. As Ogden himself put it, in characteristically un-Basic language:

> If, as we maintain, manipulation of the minimum vocabulary gives practice in the analytic habit of mind which is essential to scientific thinking, and if the Basic words point to the concrete constituents of those fictional statements by which the sophisticated no less than the untutored mind is so frequently misled, its relevance at every phase of the educational curriculum cannot be questioned. By placing emphasis on these aspects of the system, it would be possible to use Basic as a technique for achieving control of the language-machine [...][53]

---

[47] On the connection between Esperanto and a new ethical people see Esther Schor, 'L. L. Zamenhof and the Shadow People', *Language Problems & Language Planning* 34.2 (2010): 183–92.

[48] Thus enthusiasm for Esperanto was easily alloyed with larger social and political commitments. See Roberto Garvía, *Esperanto and its Rivals: The Struggle for an International Language* (Philadelphia: University of Pennsylvania Press, 2015), 103–28.

[49] W. Terrence Gordon, 'From "The Meaning of Meaning" to Basic English', *Et cetera* (1991): 165–71.

[50] Ogden, *Basic English*, 20.   [51] Ogden, *Basic English*, 19–20.

[52] Ogden, *Basic English*, 28.

[53] C. K. Ogden, 'Basic English and Grammatical Reform', in W. Terrence Gordon (ed.), *C. K. Ogden and Linguistics, Vol. II: From Bentham to Basic English* (London: Routledge/Thoemmes Press, 1994), 214–15.

In the case of 'disembark' this amounted to a relatively harmless economy; but the absence of 'democracy' from the Basic word-list, and its reduction to elements of the 'minimum vocabulary', surely had profounder intentions and profounder consequences.

Did Orwell connect the dots? It's hard not to think that when he invented 'Newspeak' in *Nineteen Eighty-Four* (i.e., in 1946–8), he was satirizing the project of Basic English, of which he was well aware and to which he even seemed mildly sympathetic earlier in the decade.[54] The inventors of Newspeak, like Ogden, speak with enthusiasm about the way in which elements of English deemed surplus to requirements are stripped away: 'We're destroying words—scores of them, hundreds of them, every day', exults Symes, the compiler of the Newspeak dictionary's Eleventh Edition.[55] Like Basic English, Newspeak cuts 'the language down to the bone' by replacing words with morphological compounds that, in effect, analyse them—'disembark' becomes 'get off a ship'; 'very bad' becomes 'doubleplusungood'.[56] Both Basic English and Newspeak are planned, artificial versions of English, which pride themselves on their rational construction and on the ruthlessness with which they eliminate sources of linguistic ambiguity: these ships are so well engineered, the theory goes, they will withstand any possible challenge the sea of discourse has in store.

Judging by the parallels, Orwell smelled a political rat and set a trap for it—he would reveal the totalitarian potential of Ogden's high-minded, well-meaning project. Look in a little more detail, however, and bear in mind Orwell's other forays into the 'politics of language', and the business becomes much murkier. It's not just that Ogden is much more relaxed about allowing 'irregularities of form and idiom' to persist—he doesn't propose to replace 'bad' with 'ungood' or 'men' with 'mans'—or that he openly accepts that once in circulation Basic English will acquire a larger vocabulary.[57] Nor is it that Newspeak, far from steering clear of politics, has an entire vocabulary, called the B vocabulary in *Nineteen Eighty-Four*'s Appendix, devoted to political words. More telling and more significant is the fact that these political words, far from being sharply and narrowly defined (like the words used for everyday Newspeak, the so-called A vocabulary), are described as 'a sort of verbal shorthand, often packing whole ranges of ideas into a few syllables'.[58] Although Newspeak 'presents as' rational, structured, even skeletal, it is, in Orwell's

---

[54] While working for the BBC's Indian Section, Orwell had commissioned a radio talk on Basic English, delivered on 2 October 1942. In a letter to Ogden afterwards (16 December 1942), he says that he had hoped 'to follow this up sometime later by a series of talks giving lessons in Basic English which could perhaps afterwards be printed in India in pamphlet form', but the project had met with severe opposition at the BBC; 'To C. K. Ogden' (item 1746), in *The Complete Works of George Orwell, Vol. 14: Keeping Our Little Corner Clean, 1941–1942* (London: Secker & Warburg, 1998), 239. In his 18 August 1944 'As I Please' column for *Tribune*, he notes, approvingly, the claim that Basic English 'can act as a sort of corrective to the oratory of statesmen and publicists': *The Complete Works of George Orwell, Vol. 16: I Have Tried to Tell the Truth, 1943–1944* (London: Secker & Warburg, 1998), (item 2534) 338.

[55] George Orwell, *Nineteen Eighty-Four* (Harmondsworth: Penguin, 1954), 44.

[56] Orwell, *Nineteen Eighty-Four*, 44.   [57] Ogden, *Basic English*, 26.

[58] Orwell, 'Appendix: The Principles of Newspeak', in *Nineteen Eighty-Four*, 244.

own description, a mechanism for the production of meaningless discourse and an incitement to the very word magic Basic English is designed to prevent.

This isn't to say that Ogden's project had no political leaning at all. In Ogden's 1911 speech on 'Significs', he singles out 'Socialism' as a magic word, and it is hard not to interpret the hostility to abstractions, and the implicit analogy between old religion and new politics, as a subtle argument for some species of Liberalism.[59] Some critics have argued that any project for an artificial language, intended for ordinary, not specialized use, is politically suspect.[60] But the larger point is that the resemblance between Basic and Newspeak is for the most part a matter of style: the trademark surface feature of each is the use of morphological compounds in place of words deemed merely idiomatic (it's hard to discuss style in Newspeak at any other scale, because *Nineteen Eighty-Four* doesn't contain any actual spoken sentences in the language).[61] Similarity of technique, however, disguises a difference in function and intention.

For Basic English aims at rerouting the forcefulness of words, depriving them of any aura or magic, so that the resulting prose has a certain dryness and austerity. Its *bête noire*, from beginning to end, was the mythical word, derived from religion and repurposed for the modern age. The vice of Newspeak, however, is not austerity or dryness, but lack of originality and tendency to *cliché*. Orwell sounds like Ogden when he tells us—in the essay 'Politics and the English Language', composed in 1945—that 'the worst thing one can do with words is to surrender to them'.[62] But surrender here means not endowing words with an independent force, but letting the 'language-machine' run on automatic. 'Orthodoxy, of whatever colour', Orwell claimed, 'seems to demand a lifeless, imitative style.'[63] The paradigm of such orthodoxy is not, however, the brief snippets of dry Newspeak we encounter in the pages of *Nineteen Eighty-Four*. When Winston Smith receives instructions from his superiors, conveyed 'in the abbreviated jargon—not actually Newspeak, but consisting largely of Newspeak words—which was used in the Ministry for internal purposes', the language is 'bureaucratic' and lifeless, certainly, but not imitative.[64] The substance of the instructions may be noxious—Smith is being instructed to rewrite history—but they are articulate and original. It's when Winston overhears someone parroting the Party line in a cafeteria, when we're told the spoken language is 'jerked out very rapidly and, as it seemed, all in one piece, like a line of type cast solid' (a clever riff on the concept of the *cliché*, which was a metaphor drawn from the printing process), that we encounter the orthodoxy that forever annoys

---

[59] Ogden, 'The Progress of Significs', 18.

[60] See, for example, Michael Silverstein, 'From the Meaning of Meaning to the Empires of the Mind: Ogden's Orthological English', *Pragmatics* 5.2 (1995): 185–95.

[61] It is surely significant that when the novel wishes to present us with examples of ideological language, we get not Newspeak (which remains a source of vocabulary only), but the kinds of sloganeering ('Ignorance is Strength') and rambling argument Orwell associated with twentieth-century 'totalitarianism'. O'Brien the torturer does not speak Newspeak or attempt to compel Winston Smith to speak it: his energies are focused on Smith's 'will'.

[62] George Orwell, 'Politics and the English Language', in *The Complete Works of George Orwell, Vol. 17: I Belong to the Left, 1945* (London: Secker & Warburg, 1998), 429.

[63] Orwell, 'Politics and the English Language', 427.   [64] Orwell, *Nineteen Eighty-Four*, 34.

Orwell.[65] It's in this Newspeak of the political 'B vocabulary' that ideology does its work. But while there is no doubt that this kind of Newspeak—summed up, as Syme the lexicographer tells us, in the word *duckspeak*—is imitative to the highest degree, it's not lifeless, and that is Orwell's problem.

Accordingly, in 'Politics and the English Language' Orwell condemns the inflated, 'purple' prose of so much contemporary writing in the name of clarity and liveliness. Orwell hates big words, large abstractions, stale metaphors, and prolixity of every kind. What he wants in its stead, however, is not just clear and unambiguous language, though that is the article's declared aim. He also pines for the 'fresh, vivid, home-made turn of speech', a phrase which is far more revealing than Orwell would have probably liked.[66] The man who later that year would say his primary goal as a writer was to 'make political writing into an art' aimed for a distinctive kind of rhetoric, however much he might have praised the virtue of transparency.[67] Freshness was a traditional literary virtue, as was vividness; but to insist a figure of speech was 'homemade' was more than praise of originality. It's set not only against '*phrases* tacked together like the sections of a prefabricated henhouse' (the poultry-themed predecessor to duckspeaking).[68] It also evokes English hearth and home, signifying a local and rooted originality.

Francis Mulhern has spoken of how Orwell 'looked beyond the contraries of highbrow and masses toward an authentically national popular culture, and strained to image it in a normative English prose style'.[69] Vivid, homemade turns of speech—turns of speech like the simile of the prefab henhouse—are supposed to be the hallmark of this style. But the language this style opposes is vivid in its own prefabricated way, and this upsets Orwell's tidy binary. In this respect, it's telling that Orwell rails not against dead metaphors, which he thinks are fine in their way, but 'dying' ones, metaphors which are recognizably figural, but which have become part of the ordinary arsenal of speech. Metaphors such as 'toe the line' or 'stand shoulder to shoulder with' are used, Orwell, complains, because they 'save people the trouble of inventing phrases for themselves'.[70] That said, there is no denying their force or effectiveness: indeed, if Orwell weren't quite so committed to a Romantic sense of originality, we could look on these dying metaphors as ordinary instruments of the rhetorical toolbox which, effectively deployed, can play a significant role in eloquent political discourse. Orwell knows this, for *Nineteen Eighty-Four* is, among other things, a story about prefabricated eloquence.

Dying metaphors: perhaps undead metaphors would be a more precise and fresher description (isn't 'dying metaphor' itself a dying metaphor?). In a very different context Eric Santner has talked of how an excess of want and desire can be sculpted by fantasy into a kind of defensive posture, '*rigid*', as Santner cleverly puts

---

[65] Orwell, *Nineteen Eighty-Four*, 46.   [66] Orwell 'Politics and the English Language', 427.
[67] George Orwell, 'Why I Write', in *The Complete Works of George Orwell, Vol. 18: Smothered Under Journalism* (London: Secker & Warburg, 1998), 319.
[68] Orwell, 'Politics and the English Language', 423.
[69] Francis Mulhern, *Culture/Metaculture* (London: Routledge, 2000), 42.
[70] Orwell, 'Politics and the English Language', 423.

it, '*with energy*'.[71] 'Undeadness' is Santner's word for this defensive channelling of unconscious energy, an excessive investment or animation that renders the subject less responsive to his or her world. That seems like an apt characterization of the language, imitative but not lifeless, that Orwell can't quite get a handle on. The undead turn of phrase evokes a passion in excess of its meaning, it's the familiar phrase that awakens a fervour that is connected with its content but not wholly explicable in terms of it.

The critique of language in *Nineteen Eighty-Four* and 'Politics and the English Language' thus misfires. Both the novel and the essay hope to identify a poor style with authoritarian politics, but the equation doesn't work. The dry rationalism of Newspeak seems only important as a kind of bureaucratic shorthand, while the heavy ideological lifting is done by the populist ranting of Big Brother et al. (in this respect, it is probably important that the other source of inspiration for Newspeak was the so-called 'cablese' used for internal communications at the BBC).[72] The pretentious, inflated style condemned in the essay is not really similar to the propaganda Orwell loathes which is, in any case, not as lifeless as he would like.

BAKHTIN, MODERNITY AND MYTH

But Orwell was hardly alone in his belief that hostility to democracy led to a certain style of language, that there was a politics of style itself. Mikhail Bakhtin could hardly be more different than Orwell in his intellectual formation, his political beliefs, his cultural preferences, or his own manner of writing, yet the evolution of his own critique of language echoes the paradoxes of Orwell's. In Chapter 5 I described how Bakhtin's linguistic turn transformed a project for an ethical philosophy into a stylistic analysis of the novel. This turn naturally changed the way in which Bakhtin conceived of the forces that opposed his ethical vision as well.

In his philosophical work of the early and mid-1920s, Bakhtin's ethical, 'architectonic' philosophy was presented as an alternative to a dominant 'theoreticism' (first described in the essay fragment 'Toward a Philosophy of the Act').[73] Theoreticism was a broad tendency, insinuating itself into the intellectual culture of Europe at several points. In ethical thought it was manifested in the Kantian belief that morality stemmed from a lawlike, universalizing impulse, summed up by the empty, formal shape of the Categorical Imperative. It was against this formalism, which Bakhtin believed was intertwined with an individualist conception of the self, that architectonic philosophy set itself. Moral action didn't stem from the conviction

---

[71] Eric L. Santner, *On the Psychotheology of Everyday Life* (Chicago: University of Chicago Press, 2001), 20.
[72] Jean-Jacques Courtine, 'A Brave New Language: Orwell's Invention of "Newspeak" in *1984*', *SubStance* 15.2 (1986): 71.
[73] M. M. Bakhtin, 'K filosofii postupka', in *Sobranie sochinenii 1*, 7–68; the term 'theoreticism' first appears on 15, as a label for the orientation Bakhtin has been discussing since the beginning of the fragment. English translation: M. M. Bakhtin, *Toward a Philosophy of the Act*, trans. Vadim Liapunov (Austin, TX: University of Texas Press, 1993), 11.

that individuals should treat others as they would want to be treated, because it was the basic gap, the fundamental distinction in experience, between *I* and *other* that founded all moral feeling and action.

The critique of theoreticism survived Bakhtin's initial linguistic turn. In *Problems of Dostoevsky's Art* the theoreticist framework is renamed 'monologism', but it retains its basic shape and emphasis. The monologic belief in a universal consciousness 'is not', Bakhtin insists, 'a theory created by this or that thinker; no, it is a profound structural feature of ideological creation in modernity, determining all its outer and inner forms'.[74] This was in keeping with what he had argued a few years earlier, when he made clear that theoreticism was 'a specific feature of modernity, one could say a feature of the nineteenth and twentieth centuries'.[75]

On the surface, Bakhtin was offering Dostoevsky's revolutionary dialogism as an alternative to the dry rationalism of Enlightenment thought; in fact, this was one of many similar reactions to the imperialism of twentieth-century positivism, which could only understand personalities on the same terms as physical things and discourse as analogous to natural phenomena. It's the ideology which is manifest in the A vocabulary of Newspeak, which promises to introduce the rigour and precision of natural science into language. But although this strand of hostility to natural science would persist in one form or another throughout his career, almost immediately after the Dostoevsky book was published, Bakhtin both recast the role of ideological villain and rewrote the story of the villain's ascent.[76]

In the essay 'Discourse in the Novel', which Bakhtin began writing in 1930, the 'dialogism' of the novel is at first opposed to the monologism of 'poetry', a contrast that has understandably confused and annoyed many critics otherwise sympathetic to Bakhtin. In fact, this contrast turned out to be short-lived, not even lasting until the end of the essay. When in the latter half of the essay Bakhtin comes to write the history of the novel, he opens by presenting it as 'the expression of a Galilean linguistic consciousness', a remark implying that natural science is no longer the problem and modernity no longer the moment of ideological decline.[77] At the end of this history, which traces a steady progression of novelistic development, Bakhtin lays his (newly dealt) cards on the table:

---

[74] Bakhtin, *Problemy tvorchestva Dostoevskogo/Problems of Dostoevsky's Poetics*, 79/82.

[75] Bakhtin, 'K filosofii postupka'/'Toward a Philosophy of the Act', 12/8.

[76] I say hostility because from the 1950s onwards Bakhtin treats monological discourse, exemplified by natural science and, in the humanities, linguistics, as something necessary and appropriate within its own sphere. The problem is not so much monologism/theoreticism per se, as the application of natural scientific method to the objects of the human sciences. Ten years ago, I would have directed the reader to a discussion of the difference between the precise and the human sciences in Bakhtin's late collection of notes, 'K metodologii gumanitarnykh nauk' ('Towards a Methodology of the Human Sciences'). We now know that this collection and the similar 'Notes Made in 1970–71' were concoctions made by one of Bakhtin's editors, without Bakhtin's authorization; they were selections made from a much longer set of unedited working notes. As a result, I have to direct the reader to 'Tetrad 4' [Notebook 4] of the 'Rabochie zapisi 60-x – nachalo 70-x godov' ['Working Notes of the 1960s and early 1970s'], in *Sobranie sochinenie, tom 6: 'Problemy poetiki Dostoevskogo', 1963; raboty 1960-x—1970-x gg.* (Moscow: Russkie slovari, 2002), 423. English translation: 'Toward a Methodology of the Human Sciences', in M. M. Bakhtin, *Speech Genres and Other Late Essays*, trans. Vern W. McGee (Austin, TX: University of Texas Press, 1986), 161.

[77] Bakhtin, 'Slovo v romane'/'Discourse in the Novel', 121/366.

For the epoch of great astronomical, mathematical, and geographical discoveries, which destroyed the completeness and self-enclosedness of the old Universe and the completeness of mathematical quantity, which disturbed the boundaries of the old geographical world, for the epoch of the Renaissance and Protestantism, which destroyed medieval verbal-ideological centralization—for such an epoch only a Galilean linguistic consciousness, embodied in the novelistic discourse of the Second Stylistic Line, is adequate.[78]

To the destruction of these ancient world-views corresponds 'the destruction of the absolute intertwining of ideological meaning and language that defines mythological and magical thinking'.[79] Our old friend again! What had been called monologism, the '[a]bsolute intertwining of discourse with concrete ideological meaning', is now described as myth, that is, as part of the past.[80]

This radical change in the historical coordinates of Bakhtin's argument gains momentum as his case for the novel is elaborated. In the lecture/essay 'The Novel as a Literary Genre' ('Epic and Novel' in the current English translation), delivered in 1941, Bakhtin will contrast the traditionalism of epic form with the contemporaneity of the novel, now celebrated as the 'leading hero in the drama of the literary development of modernity', a position it occupies because 'it best of all reflects the *tendency to becoming* in the new world, it is the only genre born of this new world and in every way of the same nature as it'.[81] From this point onwards Bakhtin will describe dialogism and novelistic discourse as a liberation from ancient cultural constraints.

But it isn't just the historical narrative that changes. The enemy, one could say, acquires a human face. Monologism or theoreticism, by definition, lacked a face: they stood for the hegemony of 'consciousness in general', for which, as Bakhtin shrewdly pointed out, 'the only principle of cognitive individualization [...] is *error*'.[82] When Bakhtin shifts his angle of approach in 1930, the problem is not the faceless language of modernity, but what he will call at first 'authoritative discourse (religious, political, moral, the discourse of fathers, adults, teachers, and so forth)'.[83] This kind of language is 'inextricably knitted together with an external authority—with political power, with an institution, with a person'.[84] It's the language given satirical expression in the discourse of the Party and of Big Brother in *Nineteen Eighty-Four* and in the B vocabulary of Newspeak.[85] Thus Bakhtin no longer draws the critical boundary between the abstract, lifeless language of science and bureaucracy and the vital language of human interaction: the key distinction lies between different kinds of human interaction.

---

[78] Bakhtin, 'Slovo v romane'/'Discourse in the Novel', 170/415.
[79] Bakhtin, 'Slovo v romane'/'Discourse in the Novel', 123/369.
[80] Bakhtin, 'Slovo v romane'/'Discourse in the Novel', 123/369.
[81] Bakhtin, 'Roman, kak literaturnyi zhanr'/'Epic and Novel', 612/7.
[82] Bakhtin, *Problemy tvorchestva Dostoevskogo/Problems of Dostoevsky's Poetics*, 77/81.
[83] Bakhtin, 'Slovo v romane'/'Discourse in the Novel', 95/342.
[84] Bakhtin, 'Slovo v romane'/'Discourse in the Novel', 97/343.
[85] It's important to point out that, according to Bakhtin, such authoritative discourse can only be given satirical or parodic expression in the novel: the style of the genre means it portrays or represents authoritative discourse, but cannot serve as its vehicle.

Myth, monologism, authoritarian discourse, epic: the name keeps changing, as if Bakhtin was circling his prey, unsure of how best to attack it. It's a frequent and reasonable complaint about Bakhtin that he dealt in binaries, presenting cultural history as a struggle to the death between two mutually opposed, but mutually defining tendencies. Perhaps unsurprisingly, the shape-shifting villain in this struggle tends to be less well defined, so that we often have to infer its features by inverting the characteristics of the more elaborately described positive term (the novel, dialogism, and so on). The one moment when Bakhtin seems willing to add grey to his cultural sketch is in the early 1940s, when, writing about Rabelais, the binary pits the positive 'culture of laughter', developed in ancient and medieval carnival, against what he dubs 'official seriousness'.

'Official seriousness': it's easy to assume the title contains a little redundancy, because official life abhors comedy and irony, and seriousness tends naturally to legalism and formalism. And there is little in the text that announced the term—known in English by the brief title *Rabelais and His World* (and in Russian by the verbose one, *The Work of François Rabelais and the Popular Culture of the Middle Ages and Renaissance*)—to disturb the equation. 'Seriousness' is associated with the official culture of medieval Europe precisely insofar as that culture depended on law, prohibition, and fear:

> In contrast to laughter, seriousness was infused from within with elements of fear, weakness, humility, resignation, falsehood, hypocrisy or, conversely, with elements of violence, fear, threat, and prohibition. In the mouths of power seriousness frightened, demanded and forebade; in the mouths of the subordinated it trembled, submitted, lauded, glorified.[86]

As a term for conveying the force of a certain kind of language, 'seriousness' is, at first glance, an odd term. It is, in ordinary English usage, a subjective personal quality, an attitude or approach to life and work, and Bakhtin's word is *ser'oznost'*, that is, a transliteration of the English adjective with a Russian nominalizing suffix added. In typical fashion, Bakhtin extrapolates from the local meaning of the term, to the point that 'seriousness' both designates and characterizes an entire sphere of cultural forms. The paradoxical nature of the expansion is neatly summed up in a paragraph devoted to '*The problem of seriousness*' in a text written by Bakhtin in the early 1940s, by which point he seems to have decided that seriousness required more serious attention.

Having announced the problem, Bakhtin lists (without much in the way of syntax) seriousness's various features, starting with the elements of its expression: 'scowling eyebrows, terrifying eyes, tensely furrowed wrinkles and creases, etc.— the elements of fear or fright, preparation for attack or defence, a demand for

---

[86] M. M. Bakhtin, 'Fransua Rable v istorii realizma' (1940) ['François Rabelais in the History of Realism'], in *Sobranie sochinenii, tom 4.1: Fransua Rable v istorii realizma (1940g); materialy k knige o Rable (1930–1950-e gg.); kommentarii i prilozheniia* (Moscow: Iazyki slavianskikh kul'tur, 2008), 87. As ever, things are complicated in Bakhtin. I'm quoting from the first version of this text, Bakhtin's doctoral thesis: completed in 1940, examined in 1946, published in revised form in 1965, published in its original form only in 2008. The lines appear in almost identical form in the better known 1965 text (and its translation): *Rabelais and His World*, 94.

obedience <?>, the expression of inevitability, of iron necessity, categoricalness, peremptoriness, etc'.[87] Seriousness is thus both a subjective attitude and the iron law of history, just as the undead ravings of the Party in *Nineteen Eighty-Four* are simultaneously 'objective claims'—'Ignorance is Truth', '2 + 2 = 5'—and fervour-inspiring calls to arms. The sternness, the fear, the submissiveness depends on identification with this iron necessity, on the conviction that the future is somehow predetermined. It's a style with philosophical and political content. But can mere language contain all that?

To be fair, this will not be Bakhtin's wager alone—stylistics as such takes the same gamble. If we look, for example, at Erich Auerbach's magisterial *Mimesis*, written almost simultaneously with the texts of Bakhtin we are discussing, we can see the same conviction that stylistic detail has the deepest philosophical repercussions. When Auerbach expresses his fundamental convictions about the nature of historical reality (which he openly takes from German Historicism), when he insists we must understand past and present as 'incomparable and unique, as animated by inner forces and in a constant state of development; in other words, as a piece of history whose everyday depths and total inner structure lay claim to our interest both in their origins and in the direction taken by their development', he tells us that to comprehend this reality 'the separation of styles, the exclusion of realism from high tragedy' must be overcome, an emphasis borne out by the constant attention to details of vocabulary and syntax in the many literary analyses in the book.[88]

Although Auerbach's conception of reality sounds much like Bakhtin's, the corresponding aesthetic, which stressed the mixture of styles and the fusion of high rhetorical technique with everyday concerns and language, had a different slant. In fact, Bakhtin himself was introducing nuance into the original distinction of comic and serious, when, in other fragments and notes from the 1940s, he suggested that '[b]esides official seriousness, the seriousness of power, terrifying and intimidating seriousness, there is also the unofficial seriousness of suffering, fear, fright, weakness, the seriousness of the slave and the seriousness of the sacrificial victim (as opposed to the priest)',[89] to which he would add the '*serious* courage of tragedy'[90] and 'a new historical seriousness'.[91]

These refinements, however welcome, do not affect the main issue, which is Bakhtin's identification of this force within language, this species of word magic, with political domination. In Bakhtin's hands the power of 'serious' discourse is not the consequence of some contingent linguistic malfunction, which is then

---

[87] M. M. Bakhtin, 'K filosofskim osnovam gumanitarnykh nauk' (1940) ['Towards Philosophical Bases for the Human Sciences'], *Sobranie sochinenii 5*, 10.

[88] Erich Auerbach, *Mimesis: The Representation of Reality in Western Literature*, trans. Willard R. Trask (Princeton, NJ: Princeton University Press, 2003), 444.

[89] Bakhtin, 'Dopolneniia i izmeneniia k "Rable"'/'Additions and Changes to *Rabelais*', 81/524–5.

[90] Bakhtin, Archival fragment, quoted in notes and commentary to 'Ritorika, v meru svoei lzhivosti…', in *Sobranie sochinenii 5*, 463. English translation: 'Rhetoric, to the Extent That It Lies…', *Slavic and East European Journal* 61.2 (2017): 215n1.

[91] Bakhtin, Archival fragment, quoted in notes and commentary to 'Dopolneniia i izmeneniia k "Rable"', in *Sobranie sochinenii 5*, 481.

appropriated for political purposes. The power or aura of certain words dictates their social role. That said, it's not entirely clear—in fact it is *systematically* unclear—whether or not seriousness is a force generated from within language or some odd, almost inexplicable distortion of it. In all Bakhtin's writing about language, from the 1930s till 1975, the negative term, be it monologism, myth, epic, or official seriousness appears as a form of language that denies the truth of language, that acquires its power and force by ignoring its dependence on a context lying beyond it. In 'Discourse in the Novel' myth arises when language is bound immediately to meaning, as if there were no dialogical context (earlier words, existing forms, utterances to which one was implicitly responding) that gave it sense, and when the novel arrives on the scene, its contextualization of mythic discourse robs it of its power. While the novel can therefore stage a mythic, epic, or serious form of discourse, within its dialogizing bounds it is robbed of its force, having been transformed into 'the discourse of a preacher without a pulpit, a terrifying judge without judicial or punitive authority', and so forth.

In that respect, Bakhtin's account of word magic mirrors Ogden's: word magic works when we ignore the context (the sign situation in Ogden, the dialogical situation in Bakhtin) that signs depend on—it's what happens when mistaken views of language somehow infiltrate the functioning of language itself. But aren't the contexts that bring forth 'official seriousness' just different sorts of context? If dialogue is ever-present as a matter of theoretical fact, then did Bakhtin not have to admit that dialogue is not per se liberating, egalitarian, comic, and so forth, that some dialogues entail fear and obedience, but are no less 'dialogical' for all that? In which case, the solution to word magic, novelistic discourse, is perhaps another kind of magic and not just the smooth functioning of the linguistic mechanism.

In Bakhtin's writing, he swings to and fro between these positions. Thus in one of his ruminations on seriousness, he describes how the powerful seek to escape the vicissitudes of the historical process by building monuments and having themselves heroicized in verse: 'The thirst for glory and immortality in the memory of one's descendants, for one's *proper name* (and not nickname) in people's mouths; concern about one's memorial.'[92] He will go on, in a wholly characteristic way, to contrast the serious 'proper name', with the familiar, comic 'nickname', arguing that the first, by virtue of its very form, entails an ultimately false conception of the individual. It seems a stretch, however, to exile the proper name itself from language's territory.

In turning to 'the name' Bakhtin calls up not one debate, but a series. It's the theory of the name, after all, which Ogden holds responsible for word magic; it's 'the name' that Benjamin will turn to (as we'll see in Chapter 7) in his attack on semiotics, and names will become a favourite and vexed topic in analytic philosophy. For the name seems to occupy a borderline space in our discussions of language: not just a category of speech, but a form that implies an ontology, that seems almost necessarily mythic in its operation. The flame that results from match-striking in Ogden and Richards's account remains part of a symbol, restrained and controlled,

---

[92] Bakhtin, 'Dopolneniia i izmeneniia k "Rable"'/'Additions and Changes to *Rabelais*', 84/526.

so long as we bind it to the situation in which we perceive it. But a language is, according to Saussure, 'not a ship in dry dock, but a ship on the open sea'. Match and flame might start off as a mere sign, but once lit it could spread in unforeseeable directions, with more force and range than anyone expected. Striking the match could make a sign, or be the spark that sets off an uncontrollable conflagration.

Saussure himself saw the problem, in a passage devoted to myth in his 1894 'Notes for an article on Whitney'. Speaking of the Indian fire-god, he noted that:

> As long as the word *agni* refers to both—hence confusion—everyday fire and the god *Agni* [...] we can never make *Agni* or *Djeus* a figure comparable with *Varuna* or Ἀπόλλων [*Apollon*], whose names characteristically do not refer simultaneously to any other earthly thing.
>
> If there is a precise moment when *Agni* stops figuring [as 'fire', KH]...that moment consists in nothing other than the accident which brings about a break between the *name* and the perceivable object, such as fire: an accident which is at the mercy of any event occurring in a language, and not necessarily related to the sphere of mythological ideas.[93]

Suppose another word came to mean 'fire', breaking the link between the name of the god and the common noun? The result would be a kind of divine promotion, for 'at that moment the god *Agni*, just like the god Ζευς, will INEVITABLY be promoted to the rank of untouchable deities such as *Varuna*, instead of running around in the lower circles of deities like *Ushas*'.[94] The god with a proper name always trumps the god with a common one, but the god gets the proper name as a result of a '*purely linguistic*' event: the word is therefore 'the instigator and final cause of a new deity'.[95]

Saussure agrees with Ogden and Richards: mythological entities are the consequence of a kind of linguistic short-circuit, when the link between a name, the context in which it arose (its place in the system of common nouns) and its reference is elided, when it appears that the signifier *Agni* conjures up its own meaning from the divine ether. Saussure disagrees with Ogden and Richards: this short-circuit is not a misfire or a confusion, but part of the normal operation of language, where signs shift because the system containing them shifts. The magic of words arises from deep within language itself, and knowing this is so doesn't mean one can—or should—stop it.

---

[93] Saussure, 'Notes for an article on Whitney', 154–5.
[94] Saussure, 'Notes for an article on Whitney', 155.
[95] Saussure, 'Notes for an article on Whitney', 155.

7

Myth You Can Believe In

(Ernst Cassirer, Viktor Shklovskii, Velimir Khlebnikov, Roman Jakobson, Benjamin)

For every writer who thought myth was a dangerous flaw in language, there was another who thought it was language's gift to the twentieth century, a buried resource that, properly exploited, would rejuvenate language and, with it, social and political life in Europe. There was agreement, that is, on the 'fact' of myth and word magic, agreement that language as such endowed certain of its words and phrases with an extraordinary force and aura. To those writing about the presence of magic and mythical language, language as such tended to disequilibrium, a disequilibrium which might then be regarded as a problem to be corrected or as a situation to be exploited. The disequilibrium might be a sign of incomplete modernity, of a mythic residue in language that had yet to be dissolved, or it might be a consequence of modernity itself. Given the importance of that question, and in the interests of symmetry, we should probably return to Shklovskii and his speech at the Stray Dog Café, for that speech, published the following year (1914) as 'The Resurrection of the Word', drew a straight line from ancient magic to the Russian avant-garde. But we're going to make Shklovskii wait for a little while.

We are going to make him wait in order to clarify what is at stake in this discussion. When we read the work of writers like Ogden, Frege, Orwell, and Bakhtin—who turn their attention to language precisely in order to combat word myth, magic, or monologism—myth and its equivalents appear as an obstacle to the smooth functioning of language, an obstacle which can be overcome either through sober science (Ogden), a new concept-script (Frege), a style at once artistic and homespun (Orwell), or the ironic, stylizing discourse of the novel (Bakhtin). In Frege's case, the desired language is a specialized instrument, better than ordinary natural language (which is liable to all kinds of illogical mischief), but for the other three ordinary language contains everything it needs to be an effective vehicle of what Bakhtin called 'internally persuasive discourse' but what we should probably call 'rhetoric'.[1] Language 'works', which for Ogden means it is naturally analytic, for Orwell that it can be vivid and fresh, for Bakhtin, that it is dialogical; let it work and we will get intelligent, persuasive public speech and a functioning democracy.

---

[1] On Bakhtin's idea of 'internally persuasive discourse' (and its antithesis, 'authoritative discourse'), see Bakhtin, 'Slovo v romane'/'Discourse in the Novel', 95–104/341–9.

All three assume a tight metonymic relation between the right kind of language and the right kind of politics.

But they differ over what the right kind of politics is. Ogden and Orwell are worried about the clarity of language in the institutions of the public sphere: in public speeches and in the press. When they discuss what is wrong and what could be right about language, they take language to be a metonym for the political 'superstructure' (to use Marx's much derided term). By contrast, Bakhtin understands the struggle between dialogical 'novelistic' prose and monological or mythic language as a metonym for a more diffuse but, in a sense, more extensive struggle between the 'popular-carnivalesque' and the 'official-serious'. It's tempting to describe this as a struggle between cultures, which bypasses formal political institutions—a struggle below the superstructure, in the sphere of civil society, if not actually the economy—but this would understate both the radicalism and the strangeness of Bakhtin's argument. For Bakhtin identifies 'official-serious' culture, which relies on and encompasses the mythic discourse we've been discussing, with the sphere of institutionalized political power as such. It's worth recalling what we observed about Bakhtin in Chapter 5: his linguistic turn transformed an ethical philosophy into a theory of style or discourse, and that ethical philosophy took aim at morality based on law and at morality based on roles, i.e. on institutionalized responsibilities. When he speaks of the 'specific inflection of sobriety, simplicity, democracy and freedom that inheres in all modern languages' he is therefore claiming (or hoping) that the democratic style of modern languages is a metonym not for a better form of the political superstructure, but for a kind of social life superior to formal politics, for civil society *against* the political superstructure as such.[2]

We will discover similarly ambitious claims in the writers covered in this chapter. They see the mythic element in language as neither ornament nor defect, but as the index of a vivid force within language, which creates new forms and drives language forward. Language is thus reimagined as a dynamic system, which transforms itself, which contains the seeds of its own development, and which not only represents and analyses the existing, but also makes and creates. To think of language as spontaneously creative in this sense demands, of course, an entirely different sense of orderliness and system. In the theory of Saussure or of the analytic philosophers, the order of language is static, held together either by consensus (Saussure), the laws of human thought (Frege), or the unrepresentable structure of the world (Wittgenstein): it is a condition of thought, the territory of human thinking and willing. By contrast, for writers like Cassirer, Khlebnikov, Shklovskii, and Benjamin, it's as if language does the thinking and willing itself.

Their belief in language, however, differs from nineteenth-century convictions about national spirit or culture being embodied in German or English or ancient Greek. For the stars in this part of our constellation think the creative spirit issues

---

[2] M. M. Bakhtin, 'Tetrad' 2' ['Notebook 2'], 'Rabochie zapisi 60-x – nachala 70-x godov', 389. English translation: 'From Notes Made in 1970–71', in *Speech Genres and Other Late Essays*, 132. As noted in Chapter 6 (note 76), the English translation is of a text that we now realize was an editorial creation, unauthorized by Bakhtin, although the actual notes are genuine.

from language itself rather than some determinate group of people (Sorel will be a notable exception here, although his people are defined by class rather than nation). The form of a language does not borrow its shaping ideology from a national culture—no more strong German verbs mimicking German nobility!—but is itself deemed the principle underlying an alternative kind of social order. Nor is language an instrument that, depending on its shape, can be more or less adequate to the purposes that animate it (as seems to be the case in Orwell and Ogden). We've already had a hint of this in Wittgenstein's comments in the 'Big Typescript' when, comparing the rules of language and other 'games' to the rules of cooking, he claims that insofar as 'speaking a language' isn't defined by some goal or end external to it, 'anyone guided by rules other than those for chess plays *a different game*, and anyone guided by grammatical rules other than such and such doesn't as a result say anything that is false, but is talking about something else'.[3] Language generates its own order.

In this respect what we're describing resembles the twentieth-century formation that Francis Mulhern has memorably dubbed 'metaculture'. By metaculture Mulhern means a discursive position in which the idea of culture itself provides not only subject matter, but also a position from which one speaks: the metacultural writer speaks of modern society—critically, and sometimes contemptuously—*in the name of* culture and as a moment of it. 'Culture' is thus not just what one writes about: it is presented 'as the necessary, unregarded truth of society, whose curse is the inadequacy of the prevailing form of social authority, *the political*'.[4] In its early twentieth-century variant metaculture rejects politics as such and offers culture as an 'imprescriptable moral reality which might regain at least something of its rightful authority'.[5]

The writers in this chapter have equally great ambitions for 'language as such', enlivened by mythic forces: the kind of social order promised by mythically charged language is a challenge to the existing political order, to the whole apparatus of state, law, and government summed up in the term 'official'. The focus of their ambitions, however, is slightly different. Language as such, when its inner tendencies are given room to flourish, becomes a source of not only social order and ethical authority, but also, in some cases explicitly, a truer form of 'justice' than is available in the official spheres of law and parliament. Metaculture attempts to dislodge and displace politics—language as such wants to encroach on its territory. But just as metaculture both speaks of culture and embodies it, so the 'just' order that language can bring into being is often evoked in the very language used to argue for it. The claims that Shklovskii and other members of the Russian avant-garde will make for the 'word as such' or the 'self-valuable word' will read like attempts to draw the force of language out of its lair. Walter Benjamin's refocusing of myth and the magical force of language will be cast in a prose—legendary for its densely figurative style—that claims to fan a messianic spark latent in language past and present. Georges Sorel's championing of social myth urges and declaims.

---

[3] Wittgenstein, *Big Typescript*, 187e.   [4] Mulhern, *Culture/Metaculture*, xix.
[5] Mulhern, *Culture/Metaculture*, 21.

If you believe in the magic of words, your proof takes the form of conjuring it up: you can't argue for its existence—you have to make the rabbit come out of the hat yourself.

CASSIRER'S STRUGGLE WITH MYTH

Let's start, though, with the writer who appears to be the soberest of the lot, the one who takes myth on carefully and systematically, and yet manages to misjudge it at the crucial moment: the philosopher Ernst Cassirer. Cassirer will make a fine-grained and philosophically rigorous argument for the enduring importance of myth as a cultural form in careful, systematic prose. In a series of philosophical works written in Germany in the 1920s, he will argue that we both cannot and should not imagine a world in which myth has no role or force. And yet during the Second World War, having escaped to the United States, Cassirer will confess that when he saw the beast face-to-face he was taken by surprise:

> When we first heard of the political myths we found them so absurd and incongruous, so fantastic and ludicrous that we could hardly be prevailed upon to take them seriously. By now it has become clear to all of us that this was a great mistake.[6]

The irony is that in 1924 Cassirer had himself upbraided those who thought myth was something fantastic and incongruous, who believed 'that myth is founded not on a positive *force* of configuring and forming but on a type of *affliction* of the mind, that we must see in myth a "disease" required by language'.[7] It's the linguist Max Müller who exemplifies this confusion for Cassirer, but Ogden, and even Saussure, take a similar position. In a seminar after the war Cassirer will describe *The Meaning of Meaning* as an instance of the 'destructive theory of language', obsessed with language's tendency to foment illusion and idolatry.[8] Saussure's mythological gods, as we saw in Chapter 6, accrue their power as a consequence of changes in the language system. For Ogden and Saussure, when the form of language asserts itself, the result is ontological confusion. Cassirer, however, thinks that mythical belief in the power of words, in the 'objective character and objective force of the sign', is acknowledgment of a linguistic forcefulness one has to understand and value.[9]

On the face of it, myth and Cassirer were an unlikely pair. In the 1900s and 1910s Cassirer was known as a leading philosopher of science and ardent neo-Kantian, who thought philosophy's job was to explain and justify the achievements of modern natural science, physics in particular. In his book *Substance and Function* (1910) he

---

[6] Ernst Cassirer, *The Myth of the State* (New Haven, CT: Yale University Press, 1946), 296.
[7] Ernst Cassirer, 'Language and Myth: A Contribution to the Problem of the Names of the Gods' (1924), in *The Warburg Years (1919–1933)*, trans. S. G. Lofts and A. Calcagno (New Haven, CT: Yale University Press, 2013), 134.
[8] Ernst Cassirer, 'Seminar on Symbolism and Philosophy of Language, Vorlesung New Haven 1941/1942', in *Nachgelassene Manuskripte und Texte*, Band 6 (Hamburg: Felix Meiner Verlag, 2005), 202.
[9] Ernst Cassirer, *The Philosophy of Symbolic Forms, Volume 2: Mythical Thought*, trans. Ralph Manheim (New Haven, CT: Yale University Press, 1955), 24.

argued for a new understanding of scientific concepts, in which they would be construed not as abstractions from our sensuous experience—the names of properties or parts of objects—but as something akin to mathematical functions, which generate a series of particulars in the form of produced values. It was, in many respects, a bolder and more ambitious—and therefore riskier—version of the logical arguments Frege and Russell had been making. Instead of the model proposition having the form: 'This ball is red' (or 'This ball has x mass') the model would be something like '$2x = 6$', where 2 would be understood as the function 'doubling'; 6, the 'particular', would fall under the functional concept 'doubling', because the function of doubling could generate it. 'Redness' was a substantial concept, because it names an attribute; 'doubling', a functional one, because it produces a series of specific values (not just 6, but 8, 10, 12, and so on, each of which would be thereby related to one another). To think of concepts in this way was to think of objects differently as well: not as 'things' with a discrete number of abstractable, nameable properties, but as points at which the values of various functions intersected.

Of course, the functions that interested Cassirer were not simple ones like doubling and the mathematics that interested him was calculus, not the maths-for-dummies kind I've used as an example. He was concerned with the complex functions and equations used to frame the laws of modern chemistry and physics and with the way in which these physical laws reconstructed the objects of those sciences. The founding figure of this kind of science was Galileo, insofar as he had been the first to mathematize physics thoroughly, to recast it as a series of mathematical laws that accounted for the particulars of the physical world. But it was in Heinrich Hertz's *Principles of Mechanics*—which we have already mentioned in connection with Wittgenstein—that this reconstruction attained a self-reflective and conscious form. Hertz had demonstrated that certain substantial notions in physics like 'energy' and 'force' were chimerae: fictions that had been proposed as causes of motion and change, but which could be dispensed with when mechanics understood its symbols in a more functional, descriptive manner.[10] Cassirer thought this change in the nature of concepts was illustrated by the shift in physics from 'atomism' to 'energism', the former implying a substantial object with properties, the latter not a thing but a '*unitary system of reference* on which we base measurement', a way of quantifying and relating phenomena to one another.[11] In chemistry, which begins as a science of substances, the struggle between substance and function was

---

[10] See Heinrich Hertz, *The Principles of Mechanics Presented in a New Form*, trans. D. E. Jones and J. T. Walley (London: Macmillan & Co., 1899), 1–41 ('Introduction'), where he discusses whether the best 'image' for mechanics should include 'force' or 'energy', and concludes that the concepts of 'space', 'time', and 'mass' can do the job without them. On Hertz's critique of the use of unperceivable entities in physical and chemical theory, see Michael Heidelberger, 'From Helmholtz's Philosophy of Science to Hertz's Picture-Theory', in Baird, Hughes, and Nordmann, *Heinrich Hertz*, 9–24. In the *Philosophy of Symbolic Forms, Mythical Thought*, Cassirer will note that the concept of 'force' must free itself from a 'semimythical hypostasis', a blurring of the substantial and the functional (59).

[11] Ernst Cassirer, *Substance and Function*, trans. William Curtis Swabey and Marie Collins Swabey (New York: Dover, 1953), 191. Cassirer discusses Hertz explicitly in *Substance and Function* at 170 and in the supplement, *Einstein's Theory of Relativity Considered from the Epistemological Standpoint*, at 399–400.

articulated in the fate of the 'atom' itself, which first 'appears as a fixed substantial kernel, from which different properties can be successively distinguished and separated out', but over time becomes a '"virtual" point' that draws together and organizes a number of different physical laws, without having any substantial reality of its own (think, in this respect, of how it becomes progressively more difficult to picture the atom, to visualize it as a 'thing').[12]

Hertz had been able to ironize our use of 'energy' and 'force' because he'd realized that the signs used in science did not have to refer (in the Fregean sense) to anything, but captured reality by articulating the laws responsible for the nature and shape of what we experienced. The form we give to 'images or symbols of external objects', he noted, is 'such that the necessary consequents of the images in thought are always the images of the necessary consequents in nature of the things pictured'.[13] So long as those images, when combined, produced the correct results (i.e., images which were verified experimentally), then it 'is not necessary that they should be in conformity with the things in any other respect whatever'.[14] For Cassirer, calculus provided the sharpest illustration of this use of symbols. Gregory B. Moynahan has shown that he was following the lead of his teacher and mentor Hermann Cohen, whose 1881 book *The Infinitesimal Method and its History* argued for the significance of the concept of the 'infinitesimal' in calculus. More precisely:

> As products of mathematics that define "reality" yet cannot be directly intuited as insular or discrete elements of being, the infinitesimal epitomizes the relation of thought, intuition and the transcendental imagination which in Cohen's view is to characterize all of modern science.[15]

More bluntly: the infinitesimal didn't 'represent' anything, didn't imitate or copy a thing in the world, but did the job that had to be done in mathematics. Calculus had another signal advantage: its particulars were not static points but points in motion, so to speak, vectors of change and movement. For Cassirer, this was what was necessary to capture a world the individual sensory moments of which were not objects but motions or movement, as exemplified, in crude experiential terms, in moving objects, in sensations of (changing temperature), in the movement of touching. To understand particulars in this way was to see that 'phenomena that are sensuously different from another, such as a falling stone, the movement of the moon, and that of the earth and tide, have been for us, since Newton, under one and the same physical concept'.[16] Natural science *formed* the world as a web of universal laws: a world of mathematical relations, points of force, atoms, valences and so forth, in which the individual was 'a particular element in an ordered manifold'.[17] In this exact sense, science was creative and its symbols forceful.

---

[12] Cassirer, *Substance and Function*, 210. See Gregory B. Moynahan's excellent summary of this in his *Ernst Cassirer and the Critical Science of Germany, 1899–1919* (London: Anthem Press, 2013), 134–7.
[13] Hertz, *Principles of Mechanics*, 1.   [14] Hertz, *Principles of Mechanics*, 1–2.
[15] Moynahan, *Ernst Cassirer*, 51.
[16] Ernst Cassirer, 'The Concept of Symbolic Form in the Construction of the Human Sciences' (1923), in *The Warburg Years (1919–1933)*, 95–6.
[17] Cassirer, *Substance and Function*, 231.

What would lead a philosopher of this kind to myth? What possessed Cassirer, having gone to great lengths to escape the confusion of names and substances, to visit the primeval forests of '[w]ord and name magic'?[18] At first glance, it looks like the result of two epiphanies. The first took place in 1917, during the First World War, which Cassirer spent in Berlin, reviewing and redacting French newspapers for the German censor's office (as has been observed, the job gave him first-hand exposure to the kind of bellicose mythmaking that so incensed Ogden).[19] According to his friend and colleague Dmitri Gawronsky, 'just as he entered a street car to ride home, the conception of the symbolic forms flashed upon him; a few minutes later, when he reached his home, the whole plan of his new voluminous work was ready in his mind, in essentially the form in which it was carried out in the course of the subsequent ten years'.[20] The second took place when the war had ended, and Cassirer found himself with a post at the newly established University of Hamburg, in the city that boasted the library of the Renaissance scholar Aby Warburg.[21] Warburg was interested in the 'afterlife of antiquity', the survival into the Renaissance and after of cultic ritual, of gestures and images, and of what he called 'pathos formulae', drawn from ancient European and American societies. His extensive private library accordingly divided its holdings into those concerned with 'image', 'word', 'orientation', and 'action', so that ancient texts sat cheek-by-jowl with modern ones, and one could trace the recurrence of historic motifs over time.[22] For Cassirer, this way of arranging the material had philosophical significance. In the words of Fritz Saxl, the Warburg's librarian, who had given Cassirer an introductory tour of the library in 1920: 'It came as a shock to him, therefore, to see that a man whom he hardly knew [Aby Warburg, KH] had covered the same ground, not in writings, but in a complicated library system, which an attentive and speculative visitor could spontaneously grasp.'[23]

Mythic formulae and patterns persisting over time, in different guises, and the notion that there might be different 'symbolic forms' at play in the world: these were the ideas that led Cassirer, in the 1920s, to compose and publish a *Philosophy of Symbolic Forms* in three volumes (a fourth was planned, but published posthumously) as well as a number of articles on the same topic. It is, from the perspective of the present book, one of the most dramatic linguistic turns of the period: an entire philosophical system erected on the idea of the symbol. But it wasn't clear at first what the different symbolic forms were going to be and how they would relate to one another. According to Edward Skidelsky, the initial candidate to accompany science was probably art, as the concept of symbolic form first surfaces explicitly in

---

[18] Cassirer, *Philosophy of Symbolic Forms, Mythical Thought*, 40.
[19] Moynahan, *Cassirer*, 36–7.
[20] Dmitry Gawronsky, 'Ernst Cassirer: His Life and Work', in Paul Arthur Schilpp (ed.), *The Philosophy of Ernst Cassirer* (LaSalle, IL: Open Court, 1949), 25.
[21] On the establishment of the University, see Emily J. Levine, *Dreamland of Humanists: Warburg, Cassirer, Panofsky, and the Hamburg School* (Chicago: University of Chicago Press, 2013), 72–92.
[22] See John Michael Krois, 'The Pathos Formulae of Mythic Thought', in Paul Bishop and R. H. Stephenson (eds.), *The Persistence of Myth as Symbolic Form* (Leeds: Maney Publishing, 2008), 1–17.
[23] F. Saxl, 'Ernst Cassirer', in Schilpp, *The Philosophy of Ernst Cassirer*, 49.

a 1920 article with the revealing title 'Goethe and Mathematical Physics'.[24] A 1920 book on *Einstein's Theory of Relativity* concluded by proposing that 'there occur also, over against the whole of *theoretical* scientific knowledge, other forms and meanings of independent type and laws, such as the ethical, the aesthetic "form"'.[25] Two years later Cassirer wondered whether it was 'a mere metaphor to speak of a nonscientific logical formation' and what it would mean to say that each of the spiritual forms, 'language and myth, religion and art [...] possesses its own particular task and justification'.[26]

The eventual catalyst for the philosophy of symbolic forms seems to have been language, or, to be more precise, Humboldt's theory of language. In a 1923 essay, 'The Kantian Elements in Wilhelm von Humboldt's Philosophy of Language', Cassirer presented Humboldt as the man who showed us how the Kantian framework could be extended, so that a series of additions could be made to the original edifice. Kant's argument that science was productive rather than passive, a matter of forming and articulating experience rather than registering patterns built into experience, was paralleled in Humboldt's contention that 'language is itself not work (*ergon*) but an activity (*energeia*)', or, as Cassirer wanted to put it, a 'production', a '*process* in which spiritual signification itself becomes and emerges'.[27] Humboldt's concept of the 'inner form of language' referred to the way in which linguistic form and meaning were intertwined and reciprocally determined. 'Thus', Cassirer observed, 'the concept of the inner form of language obtains for the domain of the philosophy of language what the general concept of form achieved for the critical theory of knowledge.'[28] But the idea of inner form added a significant twist: it proposed that *different* languages had different inner forms, so that, in Cassirer's words, 'this very individuality of the "inner form of language" was grounded not only in a certain direction of feeling and fantasy but also in a *particular* intellectual lawfulness'.[29] When Cassirer finally got round to describing the '*particular* intellectual lawfulness' of myth, he therefore claimed to be analysing the '"inner form" of mythology'.[30]

Myth had to wait its turn, however: the first volume would be devoted to 'language' itself as a symbolic form. John Michael Krois has discovered that when Cassirer submitted the manuscript for the first volume of his project in 1923, it was not called 'the philosophy of symbolic forms': the study of 'Linguistic Thought' was presented as a contribution to the 'phenomenology of knowledge', focusing on

---

[24] Edward Skidelsky, *Ernst Cassirer: The Last Philosopher of Culture* (Princeton, NJ: Princeton University Press, 2008), 80–3.
[25] Cassirer, *Einstein's Theory of Relativity Considered from the Epistemological Standpoint* (supplement to *Substance and Function*), 446.
[26] Ernst Cassirer, 'The Form of the Concept in Mythical Thinking' (1922), in *The Warburg Years (1919–1933)*, 7, 6.
[27] Ernst Cassirer, 'The Kantian Elements in Wilhelm von Humboldt's Philosophy of Language' (1923), in *The Warburg Years (1919–1933)*, 119.
[28] Cassirer, 'Humboldt's Philosophy of Language', 123.
[29] Cassirer, 'Concept in Mythical Thinking', 7.
[30] Cassirer, *Philosophy of Symbolic Forms, Mythical Thought*, xviii.

the 'spiritual expressive forms'.[31] Krois suggests that the eventual change in title came about because Cassirer realized that language didn't quite deserve the billing he was about to give it: it wasn't *primus inter pares* in the symbolic forms and, as we shall see, it was not even the primary or original form. And one can see, throughout the volume, the awkwardness of trying to describe the '*particular* intellectual lawfulness' of language itself. For, on the one hand, Cassirer assumed that each symbolic form was lawful in a different way, had a distinctive internal logic that governed the formation of its symbols. But, on the other hand, the very idea of an intellectual lawfulness, of 'a positive *force* of configuring and forming', was drawn from Cassirer's model of natural science and its distinctively functional concepts. Could a symbolic form be lawful without being aimed at the construction and formulation of natural laws?

At least one philosopher thinks not. Jürgen Habermas has argued that Cassirer tries to cram everything into a space designed for science alone. Cassirer's unwillingness to break with a basically Kantian epistemology lands him on the horns of a dilemma: '[...] Cassirer cannot assert both of the following at the same time: that the different symbolic languages are incommensurable, and that they can nevertheless be at least partially translated into one another'.[32]

The argument of the first volume seems to bear out Habermas's worry. For in many respects language is here portrayed as a kind of table-setter for natural science, organizing a relatively stable world of objects and establishing an initial, fuzzy yet distinctive template for the formal activity that will characterize science. The story of language will be the story of intellect coming to grasp the world in its own terms, of language 'achieving its inner freedom': beginning with a mimetic reproduction of the sensory world—what we often call onomatopoeia; passing through an analogical representation of the world—what C. S. Peirce called iconicity, where the language pattern resembles the thing it designates (as when we say: 'that took a *loooooooooong* time'); and eventually landing in symbolic expression, in which language, now wholly conventional, gains the '*distance* from immediate reality' that reason demands.[33] Focusing on space, time, and number, Cassirer will trace the evolution of linguistic categories from relatively concrete forms, tied to sensuous experience—deictic spatial terms ('there' and 'here'), numerical terms tied to the physical activity of counting—to abstract forms, like those verbs of motion which, through the use of affixes, inflections, and prepositions, designate the source, direction, goal, and nature of movement (Russian verbs of motion, with their notorious proliferation of forms that differentiate between going on foot or by vehicle, frequently or once, as a completed action or a continuing one, and whether to, from, past, up to, or out of a place, furnish a good illustration).

---

[31] John Michael Krois, 'The Priority of "Symbolism" over Language in Cassirer's Philosophy', *Synthese* 179 (2011): 12–13.

[32] Jürgen Habermas, 'The Liberating Power of Symbols: Ernst Cassirer's Humanistic Legacy and the Warburg Library', in *The Liberating Power of Symbols: Philosophical Essays*, trans. Peter Dews (Cambridge: Polity Press, 2001), 21.

[33] Ernst Cassirer, *The Philosophy of Symbolic Forms, Volume 1: Language*, trans. Ralph Manheim (New Haven, CT: Yale University Press, 1955), 190, 189.

Central to the story of language's transformation into 'an organ, a living tool of reason as well as the critique of reason' is the creation of complex grammar and syntax.[34] For the making of grammatical distinctions and the creation of grammatical functions is, for Cassirer, the moment in which form asserts itself in language. Following Humboldt, he thinks of the 'matter' as language's conceptual content, the meanings words have, and 'form' as the way a particular language organizes and classifies its words grammatically. Grammar abstracts language from the sensuous world—grammatical categories don't correspond to anything sensuous—and it is responsible for establishing relations between the conceptual contents of language, just as in modern linguistics one can distinguish between so-called lexical morphemes, which have variable content, and grammatical morphemes (affixes and words like prepositions and conjunctions), which establish relationships. So, for example, Cassirer will argue that when a language has evolved a definite article ('the' in English), 'its manifest purpose is to constitute a representation of substance, while its origin unmistakably pertains to spatial representation', i.e., it moves from the sensuous to the abstract.[35] He'll be impressed by what current linguists call grammaticalization, that is, the transformation of content words into grammatical functions, exemplified for modern linguists (and Cassirer as well), by the evolution of the German adjectival suffix *-lich* from the Proto-Germanic word **līkom*, meaning 'body'. In Cassirer's words: 'The history of language shows that a great number of these suffixes originated in words of material signification, which gradually cast off this initial character and became transformed into terms of general relation.'[36]

And, of course, Cassirer will want to call attention to our old friend, analogy, which stands here, as before, for the operation of reason, though now it is credited with far more philosophical depth than in Saussure. In fact, Cassirer is intrigued by so-called 'false analogy', by the fact that even where suffixes owe their origin to a 'linguistic "misunderstanding"', as he calls it, they 'represent *progress* to a new formal view, a development from substantial expression to the expression of pure relation'.[37] His example will be the creation of the German suffix *-keit*—as in *Sachlichkeit* ('objectivity')—from combinations such as *ewic-heit*, in which 'the final *c* of the stem blended with the initial *h* of the suffix, so as to form a new suffix which was propagated by analogy'.[38] Analogy stands as a spiritual, formative moment in language, because it uses phonetic and morphemic material to establish formal relationships between terms: the relationship between plurals and singulars, between verbs and their derivative nouns (*educate/education*), between verb tenses (*ring/rang/rung* and the analogous *swim/swam/swum*). In analogy we see the mind making comparisons and connections amongst the sounds and meanings of a language.

[34] Cassirer, 'Humboldt's Philosophy of Language', 105.
[35] Cassirer, *Philosophy of Symbolic Forms, Language*, 204.
[36] Cassirer, *Philosophy of Symbolic Forms, Language*, 307.
[37] Cassirer, *Philosophy of Symbolic Forms, Language*, 308.
[38] Cassirer, *Philosophy of Symbolic Forms, Language*, 308. An English equivalent would be the 'false' analogy mentioned in Chapter 2: the suffix *-ician*, which results from what linguists call 'reanalysis'. Words like *electrician* (*electric* + *-ian*) and *logician* (*logic* + *-ian*) become, by analogy, the template for words like *beautician* (*beauty* + *-ician*) or *mortician* (*mort* + *-ician*). The new ending is created from the old suffix and what was part of the stem of the older word.

All of this testifies to the 'fundamental tendency of language', which is to be '*at once* a sensuous and an intellectual form of expression'.[39] Of course, if language as such is animated by a tendency, it's to be expected that some languages will embody it more than others, and this is certainly the case in Cassirer's account. It relies continually on a contrast between 'primitive languages', characterized by terms that are still mired in concreteness, by parataxis in sentence and word construction, and by the relative absence of the grammatical features that excite Cassirer, and 'highly developed' languages, distinguished by complex patterns of subordination in sentence construction, by a thoroughly abstract system of number, and by, of course, an elaborate system of inflections and derivational affixes. Even those highly developed languages, however, appear to be impressive as spiritual creations precisely to the extent that they approach the functional, relational form of science. The particular intellectual lawfulness of language is an etiolated version of the lawfulness of science.

The introduction of myth into the equation complicated matters. In Cassirer's first work on the topic, 'The Form of the Concept in Mythical Thinking', based on a talk he gave in 1921, language still occupied a somewhat privileged position, although the essay was largely devoted to totemism and astrology.[40] But in the next couple of years myth asserted itself. In the second volume of the *Philosophy of Symbolic Forms*, published in 1925, and in his 1924 essay on 'Language and Myth', mythical thought is set out as primary, as the original form of human consciousness, from which language will have to detach itself. This marked a significant turn. Up to that point Cassirer had opposed his vision of creative, forceful science to the empiricism of philosophers like Ernst Mach, who argued that the only reality we could grasp was the chaotic flux of raw sensations and that the patterns and regularities we established among them were pragmatic instrumental constructions: science was *useful*. Now Cassirer was at pains to emphasize that science had not arisen through a historical confrontation with the chaos of sensation, because the very notion of bare and chaotic sensation was a product of scientific abstraction itself. What science confronts historically is myth: 'Before self-consciousness rises to this abstraction,' Cassirer notes, 'it lives in the world of the mythical consciousness, a world not of "things" and their "attributes" but of mythical potencies and powers, of demons and gods.'[41] In the essay 'Language and Myth' Cassirer makes an even stronger claim: none of the symbolic forms 'immediately emerges as a separate, independent, and recognizable configuration, but each gradually detaches itself from the common mother earth of myth'.[42]

At the very beginning, this mythic spirit is diffuse, centrifugal, and undisciplined. This, we could say, is when we find myth in a sort of pre-natal state, when it is not yet a subject and thus unnameable:

---

[39] Cassirer, *Philosophy of Symbolic Forms, Language*, 318, 319.
[40] On the essay, see Stefanie Hölscher, 'Ernst Cassirer's *Die Begriffsform im mythischen Denken* and the Beginnings of his Friendship with Fritz Saxl and Aby Warburg', in Bishop and Stephenson, *The Persistence of Myth as Symbolic Form*, 71–83.
[41] Cassirer, *Philosophy of Symbolic Forms, Mythical Thought*, xvi.
[42] Cassirer, 'Language and Myth', 168.

Every single factor in intuitive reality has magical traits and connections; every occurrence, however ephemeral, has its magical-mythical "meaning". A whispering or rustling in the woods, a shadow darting over the ground, a light flickering on the water: all these are demonic in their nature and origin; but only gradually does this pandemonium divide into separate and clearly distinguishable figures, into personal spirits and gods. [...] Everything is connected with everything else by invisible threads; and this connection, this universal sympathy, itself preserves a hovering, strangely impersonal character.[43]

The historical break or rupture that transforms this situation gives birth, simultaneously, to language, to myth, and to the sacred. When an individual, confronting this strange and unnameable force, 'is, on the one hand, completely given up to a momentary impression and "possessed" by it' and when 'external being is not simply considered and perceived but suddenly overcomes man in its sheer immediacy with the affect of fear and hope, terror or wish fulfillment, then, as it were, a spark jumps across, the tension finds a release, as the subjective excitement objectifies itself and presents itself before man as god or daemon'.[44] The first mythical image is, according to Cassirer, fixed at the same moment and in the same gesture as the word—in this case, as the name of this momentary god or daemon—and it's this movement that creates both the sphere of sacred names and the first mythic entity.

This confusion of name, thing, and sacredness was, for Ogden, an outdated attitude that had, for reasons he could not explain, persisted into the modern world. Cassirer's claim will be that it typifies a distinctive symbolic form, which cannot be dissolved theoretically and which will evolve and develop in its own way, according to a logic of 'images'. Just as the 'functional' nature of scientific concepts distinguishes science as a symbolic form, so the mythical image will be marked and distinguished by its confusion of the ideal and the substantial, of meaning and existence. Thus, on the one hand, in myth all properties, qualities, concepts, and names are not abstractions, but substances, real parts of the things to which they were attributed. In alchemy, for example, every similarity between things, every common property or attribute of empirical objects, 'is ultimately explained by the supposition that one and the same material cause is in some way "contained" in them'.[45] Likewise, spiritual and even moral attributes are 'in this sense regarded as transferable substances'.[46] The soul itself is endowed with the plasticity and firmness of objects, as if it were a real physical force. But the most important aspect of this distinctive mythical logic is that names and signs are deemed part of the objects they signify. In the universe of myth, Cassirer noted, 'the basic presupposition is that word and name do not merely have a function of describing or portraying but contain within them the object and its real powers'.[47] Hence in the religious rite, what takes place 'is no mere imitative portrayal of an event but is the event itself': words

---

[43] Ernst Cassirer, *The Philosophy of Symbolic Forms, Volume 3: The Phenomenology of Knowledge*, trans. Ralph Manheim (New Haven, CT: Yale University Press, 1957), 71–2.
[44] Cassirer, 'Language and Myth', 160.
[45] Cassirer, *Philosophy of Symbolic Forms, Mythical Thought*, 66.
[46] Cassirer, *Philosophy of Symbolic Forms, Mythical Thought*, 56.
[47] Cassirer, *Philosophy of Symbolic Forms, Mythical Thought*, 40.

and action don't serve to represent something else, but are woven into the reality they seem to represent.[48] Word magic is not only ineradicable—it is the signal achievement of the mythical image.

Can one describe this as a particular intellectual lawfulness? For the logic of myth seems to be an unlawful one, depending on the connection of particular to particular, substance to proximate substance, rather than abstract formula to particular value. Language at least aspired to become more like science—myth seems wholly alien to science. But just as the lawfulness of science is not simply an achieved state in Cassirer's account, but a tendency, a pressure at work within language and within science itself, so myth—if we are willing to follow its evolution—also has a distinctive tendency: it will begin with momentary daemons and culminate in religion and art.

The mythic god therefore acquires greater definition and self-confidence over time, a story which Cassirer relates in detail in the 'Language and Myth' essay. That essay was subtitled 'A Contribution to the Problem of the Names of the Gods'; like so many of Cassirer's works, it was in effect a philosophical reinterpretation of a work of science, in this case Hermann Usener's 1896 *Names of the Gods*. Accordingly, it followed the progression of gods Usener mapped out—momentary gods, gods of activity, personal gods—and described the philosophical significance of each. Thus:

> To the extent that the human being's own *action* gradually extends itself to an ever-larger sphere and orders and organizes itself within this sphere, a progressive organization, an ever more determined "articulation" of the mythical as well as the linguistic *world* will also be achieved. In the place of the gods of the moment now arise the gods of activity [...][49]

The new gods require new names, and new activities require new words, so language develops in harness with myth. But the new words don't label things, for they 'come about in accordance with activity, not according to the "objective" similarity of things, but according to the way in which the contents are grasped through the medium of activity'.[50] We therefore get gods named for the activities they govern. Each particular activity—making fire, hunting, cooking, and so on—is comprehended not by a concept but as 'an intuitive whole [...] embodied in an independent mythical figure'.[51]

The next moment in the story should sound familiar, because Usener echoes a claim we have encountered in Saussure already. When the link between the name of a god and an activity is broken—when 'Agni' no longer means 'fire', in Saussure's example—and the name thereby becomes a proper name, the god changes once again; it becomes a 'personal god', and its spirit begins to acquire the trappings of 'personality'. But there is one more necessary step for myth to be able to express its power fully: the moment of monotheism and the emergence of creator gods. For now a wholly new conception of spirit becomes available:

---

[48] Cassirer, *Philosophy of Symbolic Forms, Mythical Thought*, 39.
[49] Cassirer, 'Language and Myth', 162.   [50] Cassirer, 'Language and Myth', 164.
[51] Cassirer, *Philosophy of Symbolic Forms, Mythical Thought*, 204.

The further mythical feeling and thinking progress in this direction, the more distinctly the figure of a supreme *creator god* is singled out from among the mere specialized gods and from the throng of individual polytheistic gods. In him all the diversity of action seems, as it were, concentrated in a single summit: the mythical-religious consciousness is now oriented not toward an aggregate, an infinite number of particular creative powers, but toward the pure act of creation itself, which like the creator is apprehended as one.[52]

What matters here is not merely the abstractness of the creator god itself, but the manner in which it creates the world. For, unlike those religious narratives in which the world is moulded in an artisanal manner—as if God were a craftsman—, in monotheistic consciousness creation is *ex nihilo*, or from formless chaos. The religious spirit 'must negate and destroy the being of things in order to arrive at the being of pure will and pure action', embodied in the creative act.[53] That pure will, however, takes shape as speech:

> The act of creation is no longer designated by a single material image; now the creator uses no instrument other than the power of his will, which is concentrated in that of his voice and his *word*. The word forms the power which produces the gods themselves, which produces heaven and earth. Once language and word are thus conceived as instruments of world creation, the act of creation itself acquires a new, purely spiritual significance.[54]

We see this illustrated in the first of the Genesis creation stories, in which 'it is the word of God that divides the light from the darkness, that lets heaven as well as earth emerge from himself'.[55]

The emergence of pure action and will—we could say 'action as such' and 'will as such'—in the creator gods has repercussions for the human subject. For here Cassirer pulls a kind of reverse Feuerbach: rather than claim the gods are projections of human agency heavenwards, he argues that 'it is rather through the figure of his gods that man first *finds* this self-consciousness'.[56] In other words, it is by arriving at the idea of the pure creator god—untethered to any particular activity, embodying pure wilfulness—that humanity discovers its own capacity for willing and creation, its capacity for ethical life, embodied in symbols.

Monotheistic religion is, then, the most 'developed' form of myth, but it can never quite escape its mythic origins: it is caught in a permanent dialectic of spirit and substance. Religion differs from pure myth in that it acknowledges that sensuous images and signs are just that—signs that bear a transcendent meaning. It regards them as 'a means of expression which, though they reveal a determinate meaning,

---

[52] Cassirer, *Philosophy of Symbolic Forms, Mythical Thought*, 206.
[53] Cassirer, *Philosophy of Symbolic Forms, Mythical Thought*, 212.
[54] Cassirer, *Philosophy of Symbolic Forms, Mythical Thought*, 210.
[55] Cassirer, 'Language and Myth', 200. It's worth mentioning that the second creation story in Genesis (2:4–2:24), from the so-called 'J source', is quite different: there God's creative power is presented in terms of distinct physical actions. This would, according to Cassirer, rely on a less developed conception of creation.
[56] Cassirer, *Philosophy of Symbolic Forms, Mythical Thought*, 211.

must necessarily remain inadequate to it', being merely earthly.[57] But the religious consciousness cannot abandon the substantial and earthly entirely. Thus, 'the conflict between the pure meaning it embraces and the image in which it is expressed is never resolved but bursts forth anew in every phase of development'.[58] However, Cassirer does provide an alternative ending for this tale in the *Philosophy of Symbolic Forms*: at the very end, he briefly implies that in art myth finds a cultured, tamed fulfilment, in which the image is acknowledged as such and played with.

The story of myth is compellingly told by Cassirer, but it ends ambiguously. For it is never quite clear whether the particular intellectual lawfulness of myth is to be found only in its most developed forms, like religion and art, or whether its original impulse has some enduring and necessary contribution to make to human society. Stephen Lofts has rightly emphasized a central ambivalence in Cassirer's writing about myth and religion, which sometimes wants to capture both in the single category of the 'mythico-religious', as in the second volume of the *Philosophy of Symbolic Forms*, and at other times implies that religion breaks away from or transcends its mythic origins.[59] Is religion, like modern physics, the culmination of a symbolic form, from which there is no turning back, or does myth remain an ineradicable feature not only of religion, but of every other symbolic form as well—science, art, language—perpetually threatening their progressive achievements? The waters are muddied further by the third volume of the *Philosophy of Symbolic Forms* (1929), which, subtitled 'The Phenomenology of Knowledge', is not so much an independent treatment of science as a summarizing of the whole project. For there Cassirer lines up the symbolic forms in an evolutionary order, as if each—myth, language, science—were a stepping stone to the next, while each is also taken to correspond to a different kind of symbolism—expression, representation, and signification, respectively—as if their contributions were accumulative. It is a classic instance of what Skidelsky has called Cassirer's 'peculiar fusion of teleological and centrifugal motifs'.[60] In the discussion of 'expression' Cassirer himself will ask whether myth could still have a point '[o]nce the day has dawned, once the theoretical consciousness and theoretical perception are born'.[61] The answer will be to reclassify myth as an ancient incarnation of the spiritual function of 'expression', which continues to play a role in the modern world. Quite a substantial role, it turns out. 'As a matter of fact,' Cassirer observes, 'this territory can be designated with perfect precision: it is that form of knowledge by which the reality not of natural objects but of other subjects is opened up to us.'[62] Myth is the earliest form assumed by the vast sphere of intersubjectivity.

In the twenty pages that follow this provocative claim, Cassirer will explore its philosophical ramifications. Most of the discussion will focus on the need to understand expressive form as *sui generis*, as a primary kind of symbolism, exemplified by human expressions, rather than as object-forms with subjective meaning added on. Cassirer, it's worth pointing out, is hardly alone in emphasizing this point.

---

[57] Cassirer, *Philosophy of Symbolic Forms, Mythical Thought*, 239.
[58] Cassirer, *Philosophy of Symbolic Forms, Mythical Thought*, 251–2.
[59] S. G. Lofts, *Ernst Cassirer: A 'Repetition' of Modernity* (Albany, NY: SUNY Press, 2000), 126–7.
[60] Skidelsky, *Cassirer*, 107.   [61] Cassirer, *Philosophy of Symbolic Forms, Knowledge*, 78.
[62] Cassirer, *Philosophy of Symbolic Forms, Knowledge*, 79.

He'll draw extensively on Max Scheler, the phenomenologist of sympathy (and a key influence on Bakhtin) for much of his argument, and we now know that the young Emmanuel Levinas was making a similar case in regard to Husserl's theory of intentional objects in the dissertation he was writing at this time; this would eventually become the primacy of ethics over ontology in Levinas's philosophy.[63] The philosophical discussion is pointed and acute—but it isn't a philosophical interpretation of some concrete historical phenomenon. Having made myth the grandparent of all intersubjectivity, Cassirer is singularly disinclined to examine the fate of its progeny. There is no discussion of any concrete form of ethical life: no politics, no law, no culture. In this account, there is myth in the past, forceful but antiquated, and 'expression' in the present, modern but empty.

A multitude of forms, a claim about lawfulness that seems to fit some better than others, and a glaring absence of any sustained interest in the ethico-political dimension of human experience and society: what looks like a philosophical system from one point of view looks like a bit of a mess from another. But the circle can be squared if we see the 'theoretical consciousness' typical of science as itself already ethical, which is the claim made by a few of Cassirer's more recent interpreters. Moynahan has argued that the 'neutral functionalist critique contained in works such as *Substance and Function* had broad implications for the social sciences and politics', which Cassirer developed in his work *Freedom and Form* of 1916.[64] Skidelsky's study of Cassirer as the 'last philosopher of culture' claims that *Substance and Function* is not only a justification of modern science, it's also a display of 'the *pathos* of rationalism: a stirring vision of the autonomous intellect confronting and overcoming the world of inert sensation'.[65] In Skidelsky's view, the architecture of Cassirer's philosophy of science had already made space for the extensions that would later be erected. The shift to 'symbolic form' was simply the building permit that allowed construction to proceed:

> The same productive spontaneity ascribed by Kant to the purely rational faculties is now housed in a more basic symbolic capacity, embracing art, language, and myth alongside science. These other symbolic forms thereby acquire something of the intellectual dignity of science, while science for its part acquires something of their human warmth.[66]

That pathos is occasionally on display in the *Philosophy of Symbolic Forms*, particularly in the passage from the planned Volume 4 that was to conclude the entire work:

> In this act of becoming conscious and of making himself conscious we do not find the power of fate which governs organic processes. Here we attain the realm of freedom. The true and highest achievement of every "symbolic form" consists in its contribution to this goal; by means of its resources and its own unique way, every symbolic form works toward the transition from the realm of "nature" to that of "freedom."[67]

---

[63] See Max Scheler, *The Nature of Sympathy*, trans. Peter Heath (London: Routledge & Kegan Paul, 1954). Levinas's critique of Husserl can be found in his dissertation, published in 1930; the English translation is *The Theory of Intuition in Husserl's Phenomenology*, trans. André Orianne (Evanston, IL: Northwestern University Press, 1973).
[64] Moynahan, *Cassirer*, xxix. [65] Skidelsky, *Cassirer*, 64. [66] Skidelsky, *Cassirer*, 83.
[67] Ernst Cassirer, 'On the Metaphysics of Symbolic Forms' (1928), in *The Philosophy of Symbolic Forms, Volume 4: The Metaphysics of Symbolic Forms*, trans. John Michael Krois (New Haven, CT: Yale University Press, 1996), 111.

But the most radical and provocative version of this thesis is surely Almut Shulamit Bruckstein's. In her view, the ethical force of the symbolic forms is grounded in the religiosity of the Jewish prophets, who give testimony, in Cassirer's own words, 'to the power, to the purity, and to the autonomy of the human spirit'.[68] The pathos of rationalism one finds in Cassirer is in fact inherited from Hermann Cohen, who derives his concept of 'the fundamental idea of spontaneity, the sovereignty of the human spirit whose freedom is predicated upon no external factor' (Cassirer on Cohen, again) from Jewish literary sources that Cassirer is only aware of second-hand.[69] If this is right, then the story of myth we've recounted, leading from rustling in the woods to the single creator God, is self-reflexive: it explains the origin, the animating spirit behind the very text in which it appears. To grasp the various forms of culture—myth, religion, art, science—as 'symbolic form' is to grasp the 'productive *force* of configuring and forming' that makes them comprehensible. But to grasp that force is, according to Bruckstein's reading of Cassirer, to recognize the ethical human will at work, because a force that is purely creative, aimed at an undetermined future, is ethically responsible for what it does.

The 'sovereignty of the human spirit' is a marvellous sounding phrase and, in many contexts, it is only a marvellous sounding phrase, a substitute for politics rather than a form of it. In this case, however, the matter is more complicated. One of the elements of religiosity Cassirer acknowledges borrowing is the 'negative theology' of Nicholas de Cusa and Moses Maimonides, according to which God can be known not directly, but only in its activity. We find that reflected in an argument Cassirer foregrounds throughout his discussions of scientific consciousness, from *Substance and Function* onwards: human spirit can only grasp the world indirectly, through the mediation of forms and symbols that do not imitate or reproduce what they represent:

> We find that all theoretical determination and all theoretical mastery of being require that thought, instead of turning directly to reality, must set up a system of signs and learn to make use of these signs as representatives of objects. [...] The retreat into the world of signs forms the preparation for that decisive breakthrough, by which thought conquers its own world, the world of the idea.[70]

The insistence on the 'mediate grasp which characterizes "reason"'—and, conversely, on the apprehension of spirit only in mediated form—is not, however, just a matter of symbols and symbolism.[71] In 'Language and Myth' Cassirer makes the identical argument about the human grasp of the world in action, which, as it develops historically, depends on the mediation of tools:

---

[68] Ernst Cassirer, 'Hermann Cohen', *Korrespondenzblatt des Vereins zur Gründung und Erhaltung einer Akademie für die Wissenschaft des Judentums* 1 (1920): 9; translated in Almut Sh. Bruckstein, 'Practicing "Intertextuality": Ernst Cassirer and Hermann Cohen on Myth and Monotheism', in Jeffrey A. Barash (ed.), *The Symbolic Construction of Reality: The Legacy of Ernst Cassirer* (Chicago: University of Chicago Press, 2008), 178.
[69] Cassirer, 'Hermann Cohen', 9; translated in Bruckstein, 'Practicing "Intertextuality"', 179.
[70] Cassirer, *Philosophy of Symbolic Forms, Knowledge*, 45.
[71] Cassirer, *Philosophy of Symbolic Forms, Language*, 181.

The will must seemingly distance itself from its goal in order to reach it; instead of appearing to move the object into its circle through a simple, almost reflexive sort of action, the will must differentiate its doing, distribute it to a larger sphere of objects in order to realize through the union of all acts, through the application of diverse "means", the purpose that it sets before itself.[72]

The symbols that science uses to establish a kind of mastery-through-distance are analogous to the technical, material tools one uses to achieve particular worldly ends. Cassirer will make the analogy explicit in his essay on 'Form and Technology' (1930), which celebrates the 'double act of "grasping"—"comprehending" reality in linguistic-theoretical thought and "gripping onto it" through the medium of efficacy'.[73] Aud Sissel Hoel has summed up the analogy concisely: '[...] it is only by virtue of the distance introduced by symbols and tools that the life complex becomes a knowledge complex. Human existence is a peculiar existence because it is *mediated in principle.*'[74]

Applied to ethics, this means that ethico-political achievements do not issue directly from acts of will, but also depend on a kind of mastery-through-distance, in this case the indirection provided by laws, rule-governed institutions, and constitutional arrangements. For Cassirer these are not constraints on autonomous action, but the only way in which the human spirit can attain sovereignty at all. Just as a speaker exerts their will by framing and using the rules—the inner form of a particular language, embodying certain principles—so the citizen of a state exerts its will through rules and procedures that reflect and make possible the citizen's political activity.

It therefore shouldn't be surprising that although Cassirer does not discuss politics or law in the *Philosophy of Symbolic Forms*, at the very time he is completing this work he delivers an address on 'The Idea of a Republican Constitution' at the University of Hamburg, in celebration of the ninth anniversary of the declaration of the Weimar Republic. The speech itself is known primarily for its attempt to Germanize the ancestry of the republic, by tracing the idea of natural rights back from the French and American revolutions, through Blackstone and Christoph Wolff to its foundation in Leibniz (thereby avoiding Rousseau). But it also shows us that the political embodiment of symbolic form will be found in constitution- and law-making, in which human will creates a social order 'predicated on no external factor'—no naturally given political arrangements, no divine authority, no racial or ethnic belonging—but at the same time 'mediated in principle'. A constitution would be, for Cassirer, the supreme achievement of political will, insofar as it depends on a moment of political self-invention and establishes the rules, procedures, and ideas that make further ethical progress possible. Cassirer accordingly speaks of the 'inner form of the state as a totality', as if rules of state and the rules

---

[72] Cassirer, 'Language and Myth', 180.
[73] Ernst Cassirer, 'Form and Technology', in Aud Sissel Hoel and Ingvild Folkvord (eds.), *Ernst Cassirer on Form and Technology: Contemporary Readings* (Basingstoke: Palgrave Macmillan, 2012), 24.
[74] Aud Sissel Hoel, 'Technics of Thinking', in Hoel and Folkvord, *Ernst Cassirer on Form and Technology*, 72–3.

of language shared a similar logic.[75] Making political orders and institutions into symbolic forms would provide European society with a desirable combination of stability and openness, cohesion and dynamism. By cannily drawing together the progressivism of science, the messianism of the Jewish prophets, and the institutional form of language, Cassirer had come up with a political model that ticked most of the boxes for a democratizing Europe.

Most, but not all. The two missing ingredients were 'justice' and 'public opinion', or, to be more precise, 'injustice' and 'public opinion'. Justice itself was present in Cassirer's insistence on natural rights and on the egalitarian claim that 'only such laws will be sanctioned as could arise through the unified will of the whole nation'.[76] Justice was the endpoint towards which the constitutional symbolic form moved, the horizon of the future that made ethical and political action possible. Justice was therefore what made it possible for Kant and Goethe to see the historical events of their time, most notably the French Revolution, and 'interpret them intellectually and understand them symbolically'.[77] In Goethe's case that meant that 'a concrete, momentary experience could suddenly take off into a global event, into a world of human fate and the destiny of peoples'.[78] In the case of the French Revolution, Goethe grasps the inner form of a decisive battle, in which the new French Revolutionary Army defeated the invading Prussians: 'He had found such a "concise point" with the cannonade at Valmy: in one swing, the unmediated present became pregnant with the future for him'.[79]

Pregnant with the future: this sounds very much like Walter Benjamin's famous claim that the critical historical moment has a messianic spark, which the revolutionary critic, interested in justice, must fan. But with this crucial difference: for Benjamin messianic energies are inspired 'by the image of enslaved ancestors rather than by the ideal of liberated grandchildren'.[80] It was, after all, injustice needing to be undone, sin in need of redemption, that inspired the messianic fury of the Hebrew prophets.[81] Goethe can see the cause of justice in a famous military victory—that is the symbolic talent Cassirer identifies in him. But the Weimar Republic was founded in the wake of military *defeat*, and here it was the Nazis who stepped in to provide a symbolic interpretation: the 'stab in the back' (spineless political leaders betraying the army), the humiliation of Versailles. What Cassirer's theory can't explain is the cause of justice made visible by historical loss and catastrophe, as a wrong that must be righted, as misery that must be redeemed. Symbolic form can find the present pregnant with the future, but not defeat pregnant with the future.

---

[75] Ernst Cassirer, 'The Idea of a Republican Constitution', trans. Seth Berk, *Philosophical Forum* 49.1 (2018): 13.
[76] Cassirer, 'Republican Constitution', 13.   [77] Cassirer, 'Republican Constitution', 14.
[78] Cassirer, 'Republican Constitution', 14.
[79] Cassirer, 'Republican Constitution', 14. Note the chapter on 'symbolic pregnance' in *Philosophy of Symbolic Forms, Knowledge*, 191–204.
[80] Walter Benjamin, 'On the Concept of History', in *Selected Writings, Vol. 4*, 394.
[81] 'Ah, Jerusalem has stumbled / And Judah has fallen / Because by word and deed / They insult the Lord', Isaiah 3:8; trans. *The Jewish Study Bible (Tanakh Translation)*, ed. Adele Berlin and Marc Zvi Brettler (Oxford: Oxford University Press, 2004).

And this turned out to be a fatal weakness, one that the opponents of the Republic, of constitutionalism in general, were able and willing to exploit.

For the fascists military defeat would be redeemed by revived German greatness, embodied in a powerful state and a renewed national will, which brings us to the second missing ingredient, public opinion. The 'unified will' of which Cassirer spoke in 1928 was unified 'indirectly', through, one could say, the technologies of the constitutional republic—its laws, procedures, and institutions. Compared to this the Nazi *Volk*, united by race and land, by their 'rootedness' and shared culture, was sheer mythic immediacy, an intuition confirmed by the cult-like rituals that defined its public expression. It's revealing, in this respect, that those philosophers who argued for the renewal of mythic presence also opposed myth to technology and the modern. In what was intended as the philosophical, but polemical conclusion to the *Philosophy of Symbolic Forms*, Cassirer takes aim at the work of Ludwig Klages and Jacob von Uexküll. Klages is presented as the most 'radical defender' of the 'romantic thesis of the unbridgeable gulf between the creative ground and the world of *cogitatio*, between "life" and "geist"'.[82] For Klages, the world of cognition is 'in the end [...] impotent and incapable of any genuine productive energy'.[83] Von Uexküll was an older colleague of Cassirer's at the University of Hamburg and the founder of what is today called biosemiotics. He distinguished between the immediacy of an animal's response to its environment, which was shaped by its own, unique physical organization, and the diffuse character of human perceiving and acting, not determined by direct needs. The *Umwelt* or 'environment' that an animal's internal organization dictates is not just a fact—for Uexküll it is also a haven in heartless world, a utopia lost to the technicized, mechanized, mediated world of modernity. In the words of Frederik Stjernfelt, Uexküll's 'far right-wing position' leads him 'to highlight the tragedy of man being estranged from his natural state by the ever-growing thicket of intermediary constructions of culture and technology, so as to form a pessimist, conservative version mirroring Cassirer's enlightened optimism'.[84]

Klages and von Uexküll, in the short run, turned out to have backed the right political horse—both supported, with some reservations, the Nazi regime and survived the war—but they were as confused about politics as Cassirer was. Because the fascism that overwhelms the Weimar Republic combines some of those intermediary constructions of culture and technology—radio, film, weaponry—with an appeal to the mythic immediacy of 'the people', in a way that none of these philosophers can comprehend. In fact, modern technology turns out to be central to creating this mythic immediacy, as is most graphically demonstrated in what may be the most famous Nazi work of myth, Leni Riefenstahl's *The Triumph of the*

---

[82] Cassirer, *Philosophy of Symbolic Forms, Metaphysics*, 23.
[83] Cassirer, *Philosophy of Symbolic Forms, Metaphysics*, 24.
[84] Frederik Stjernfelt, 'Simple Animals and Complex Biology: Von Uexküll's Two-Fold Influence on Cassirer's Philosophy', *Synthese* 179 (2011): 174. Of course, one could adduce Uexküll's semiotizing of biology as one more case of a linguistic turn in the period. For a brief account of Uexküll's politics, see Torsten Rüting, 'History and Significance of Jacob von Uexküll and of his Institute in Hamburg', *Sign Systems Studies* 32.1–2 (2004): 35–71.

Will (1935), an elaborately staged film of an elaborately staged Nazi Party Congress. The title could not be more apt, from our point of view: it presents political will as a bodily presence endowed with what Cassirer calls 'magical desire and efficacy'.[85] In 'Form and Technology', Cassirer claims that '[t]he will can never succeed in its application simply by making itself stronger'; the mythical fascist claim is precisely the opposite.[86] *The Triumph of the Will* is intended as a demonstration of the claim— its multiple evocations and invocations of the people, who are both represented within the film and present in the film as its intended, addressed audience, aim to install in them that sense of magical omnipotence, of direct willing, that defines the mythical. As we know from Cassirer's later account, this combination of 'magical desire and efficacy' with 'technological will and accomplishment' came as a complete shock to him. The new political myths, he observed in 1942, 'are not wild fruits of an exuberant imagination. They are artificial things fabricated by very skilful and cunning artisans.'[87] That political myths 'can be manufactured', that there is 'a new technique of myth' made no sense in the philosophy of symbolic forms, where technique was the antithesis of mythic intensification.[88]

Gabriel Tarde, whose theory of public opinion we discussed in Chapter 6, had already grasped this possibility. You'll recall that the 'social rivers, these great impulses which are presently overwhelming the hardest hearts and the most resistant minds' do not arise from 'meetings of men on the public street or in the public square'. The men 'who persuade each other, or rather who transmit to one another suggestions from above [...] are all sitting in their own homes scattered over a vast territory, reading the same newspaper'. Public opinion does not gather its mythic force by mimicking ancient ritual, but by the interweaving of private opinion through a public technology: the newspaper, the film, today, the internet. But its force is also mediated in a different sense, for the impulse doesn't become great merely by aggregating individual perspectives; it is not, to use the kind of mathematical analogy Cassirer might appreciate, an arrangement of points or vectors or even the trajectory they define. Its force depends on the kind of self-consciousness and reflexivity media technology makes possible. The bond of those who share a will, Tarde had argued, 'lies in their simultaneous conviction or passion and in *their awareness of sharing at the same time an idea or a wish with a great number of other men*' (my emphasis).

Cassirer had thought that in art he found the modern home of the mythical image: Goethe's grasping the republican cause in the image of Valmy seemed modern enough for him. But Goethe may have been part of the problem, rather than the solution. Cassirer's investment in him looks quixotic, when you consider how the culture around him was finding new ways to draw together magical efficacy and technological accomplishment. When Cassirer was writing *The Philosophy of Symbolic Forms*, art could mean the cultivated irony of Thomas Mann or the spontaneity of Dada, the organicist pessimism of Spengler or the constructivist fantasy of El Lissitsky. Art that adhered to the distanced, mildly self-reflexive forms that Cassirer

---

[85] Cassirer, 'Form and Technology', 25. [86] Cassirer, 'Form and Technology', 29.
[87] Cassirer, *The Myth of the State*, 282. [88] Cassirer, *The Myth of the State*, 282.

valued was just one of the options. As Sascha Bru has shown in his shrewd and careful analysis of politics and avant-gardism, the instability of democratic arrangements in the time made the border between politics and art permeable and encouraged new, dramatic, experimental kinds of cultural-political intervention.[89]

MAKING STRANGE AS DEMOCRATIZED MYTH: FUTURISTS AND FORMALISTS IN RUSSIA

Which brings us, finally, back to that fateful night at the Stray Dog, where the young Shklovskii proposed a very different kind of culture, in which the magic powers of the word were revived by 'technique'. You could say that Shklovskii, Khlebnikov, and Jakobson redeemed the promise Cassirer had made at the end of his volume on myth, where he claimed that in art one found a reflexive, self-conscious version of the mythical image, which preserved its force and vividness without depriving the subject of its will. But the art that accomplished this looked nothing like the art Cassirer had in mind. When Shklovskii published his late-night talk in a slightly revised version a few months later, 'The Resurrection of the Word' opened with the following claim:

> The most ancient poetic creation of humanity was the creation of words. Now words are dead, and language is like a graveyard, but the newly-born word was alive, was an image. Every word is fundamentally a trope.[90]

In this account, mythic words don't evolve into art—they start as art and gradually fade away. But this opening gambit, echoing a common idea of language-as-metaphor, turns out to be just an opening gambit, for the rest of the article isn't concerned with tropes at all.[91] Its focus will be on what Russian Formalism will eventually call the 'deformation' of language, the conscious reshaping of sound and grammar to make language strange and unfamiliar. Poetry is not defined by the figurative use of language—a semantic affair—but by the foregrounding of properties of the signifier. '"[A]rtistic" perception', Shklovskii argues, 'is perception in which form is experienced' and in order to make sure the form of words is experienced we need to 'crumple up and break up words so that they strike the ear'.[92]

In intention and effect this was a manifesto for the 'transrational language'—*zaumnyi iazyk*—of Russian Futurist poetry. But it was by no means the first or last such document, for the Futurists were not only prolific poets, but prolific writers of manifestos, some of which we discussed briefly in Chapter 4. In 1912 and the

---

[89] Sascha Bru, *Democracy, Law and the Modernist Avant-Gardes: Writing in the State of Exception* (Edinburgh: Edinburgh University Press, 2009).
[90] Shklovskii, *Voskreshenie slova*/'The Resurrection of the Word', 3/41.
[91] See, for example, Friedrich Nietzsche, 'On Truth and Lying in a Non-Moral Sense', in *The Birth of Tragedy and Other Writings*, trans. Ronald Spiers (Cambridge: Cambridge University Press, 1999), 141–53.
[92] Shklovskii, *Voskreshenie slova/* 'The Resurrection of the Word', 4/42, 13/46.

years following they produced several, each insisting that Futurist poetry was the exploitation, the blossoming of the 'the word as such'.

The manifestos—variously labelled 'The Word as Such', 'Declaration of the Word as Such', 'A Slap in the Face of Public Taste', 'New Ways of the Word', 'The Liberation of the Word', and so on—didn't argue for the gentle transformation of poetic culture.[93] The break with previous verbal art—even, or especially that of the decade before (the poetry of Russian Symbolism)—was sharp and uncompromising. One had to '[t]hrow Pushkin, Dostoevsky, Tolstoy, etc., etc. off the Ship of modernity' and acknowledge not only the sterility of earlier literature, but the sterility of its aesthetic aspirations and models.[94] For up till the present verbal art had been shackled either by its *subordination to meaning*, its interest in psychology or philosophy, or its concern with representing some external reality.[95]

The new Futurist verbal art would make no such mistake: its guiding light was 'the word as such'. To expect artful language to be 'clear, pure, honest, melodious, pleasing (delicate) to the ear, expressive (striking, colourful, rich)' was to make a category mistake, attaching the language to something beyond it: 'We think that language should above all be *language*, and if it reminds us of something else, let it be a saw or the flying arrow of a savage.'[96]

Of course, the claim begs the question of what the defining features of 'language' are. The Futurists did not have a single answer to this. It was clear what the word was not—or maybe, more precisely, was *not only*: it was not, or not only, a vehicle for the representation of external reality or inner psychological states. This could be cashed out as the relatively modest claim that words did not merely 'copy' the world and that an experimental poetry, stuffed with difficult metaphor and the occasional neologism, would be a better showcase for language's unique talents. But the more extreme answer was that 'the word as such' had to be unchained from representation entirely for its virtues to shine. This distance from things was not the same as the distance Cassirer had championed: words didn't need to back up from reality to make possible a 'mediate grasp' of it—words aimed for complete detachment, so they themselves would have the quality of an immediate, present object. In practice, this usually entailed the combination of Russian sounds—sometimes phonemes, sometimes morphemes—to create words that had no obvious signification, although sometimes the nonsense words were strategically scattered within syntactically correct clauses and sentences: 'Bobe-obi sang the lips/Ve-e-omi sang the gazes...' (Khlebnikov).[97] But beyond the implication that words should

---

[93] For English translations of all of these, see Lawton, *Russian Futurism Through Its Manifestoes*.
[94] Burliuk et al., 'Poshchechina obshchestvennomu vkusu'/'A Slap in the Face of Public Taste', 3/51.
[95] A. Kruchenykh, 'Novye puti slova', in V. Khlebnikov, A Kruchenykh, and E. Guro, *Troe* (St Petersburg: Zhuravl', 1913), 24; Getty Research Institute digital library: http://www.getty.edu/research/tools/guides_bibliographies/russian_avant_garde/index.html. English translation: 'New Ways of the Word', in Lawton, *Russian Futurism Through its Manifestoes*, 70.
[96] Kruchenykh and Khlebnikov, *Slovo kak takovoe*/*The Word as Such*, 10 /60, 61.
[97] Velimir Khlebnikov, [Untitled poem], *Sobranie sochinenii, tom 1: literaturnaia avtobiografiia, stikhotvoreniia 1904–1916* (Moscow: IMLI RAN, 2000), 198. English translation: *Collected Works of Velimir Khlebnikov, Vol. 3*, trans. Paul Schmidt (Cambridge, MA: Harvard University Press, 1997), 30.

be jarring or grating, that they should 'strike the ear', it wasn't clear what they did and how they were to do it.

Sometimes the case for a successful transrational language was made by an analogy with the new, Cubist-inspired, visual art; several of the poets had, in fact, been painters also and in 1913 some adopted the name 'Cubo-Futurist'. Thus:

> Futurist painters love to use parts of the body, cut into sections, while the Futurist word-creators use hacked-up words, half-words, and their fantastic, cunning combinations (transrational language). By this they achieve the very greatest expressiveness, and precisely this distinguishes the language of speeding modernity, which has annihilated the earlier petrified language [...][98]

The new visual language of art would provide the model for a new kind of verbal language which, would, in Velimir Khlebnikov's phrase, 'paint by words'.[99] Just as the abstract properties of paint, colour, line, and space made a new kind of painting possible, so exploitation of the word's phonic, graphic, and morphological properties would make a new literariness possible. In fact, often the commitment was not merely to an analogy between the two arts but to their merging. Futurist poems were not only published in booklets or pamphlets lavishly illustrated and inventively designed by Russian avant-garde artists; the poems themselves were frequently occasions for graphic invention and experiment.[100]

The analogy with visual modernism, while suggestive, was bound to fail. Charles Altieri has argued that the conception of the modernist poem as an 'aesthetic object', modelled on the abstract painting, has blinded us to the rhetorical core of poetic practice, which subsists even when it is denied.[101] But, in any case, the emphasis on the word, and sometimes the individual sound (in practice, phoneme) as the privileged expressive unit had no obvious correlate in the painterly universe.

What did the word as such express? One obvious possibility was human emotion: this, for example, was what Ogden and Richards settled on when they acknowledged that not all language had cognitive intent; there were 'emotive' as well as 'symbolic' uses of words. But this was clearly too individualistic and subjectivist an interpretation for the Futurists, who felt they were liberating an expressiveness secreted in language, not expressing personal feelings in sounds. And didn't that explanation, in any case, do exactly what Cassirer had warned against, when discussing the mythic-expressive function of language? In mythic images expressiveness 'is not a subjective appendage that is subsequently and as it were accidentally added to the objective content of sensation; on the contrary, it is part of the essential fact

---

[98] Kruchenykh and Khlebnikov, *Slovo kak takovoe*/*The Word as Such*, 12/61.
[99] The poem 'Bobeobi', from which I quoted above, was described by Khlebnikov as a sound-painting (звукопись/*zvukopis*), drawing correspondences between letters and colours. See Khlebnikov, Note of 25 October 1921 from 'Iz zapisnykh knizhek' [From the Notebooks], in *Sobranie proizvedenii, tom 5* (Leningrad: Izdat. Pisatelei v Leningrade, 1933), 269.
[100] See Susan P. Compton, *The World Backwards: Russian Futurist Books, 1912–16* (London: British Library, 1978) and Marjorie Perloff, *The Futurist Moment: Avant-Garde, Avant Guerre, and the Language of Rupture* (Chicago: University of Chicago Press, 1986).
[101] Charles Altieri, 'What Theory Can Learn from New Directions in Contemporary American Poetry', *New Literary History* 43.1 (2012): 65–87.

of perception'.[102] The meaning of transrational poetry could not be traced back to the intentions of a subject—it had the 'hovering, strangely impersonal character' typical of mythic expression.

The opportunity was therefore open for nationalist *Geist* to fill the void, and it was taken up, sometimes with enthusiasm. Kruchenykh would mischievously claim of his notorious poem 'дыр бул щыл' [*Dyr bul shchyl*]—the sounds are recognizably Russian, but meaningless—that 'in this five-line poem there is more Russian national feeling than in all the poetry of Pushkin'.[103] When discussing lexical choices in 'New Ways of the Word', he contrasted the dullness of the obviously imported гладиаторы [*gladiatory*, 'gladiators'] with the colour and vitality of the obviously Russian мечари [*mechari*].[104] For a while he had a reliable ally in Khlebnikov, who forced Kruchenykh to exclude foreign loanwords from their jointly written manifestos and who devoted much of his extraordinary energy to generating neologisms with the help of Russian's endless supply of derivational affixes.[105] But Khlebnikov's interest in Russianness was unusually supple and complicated.

It has sometimes been described as 'pan-Slavic', implying that Khlebnikov regarded Russia as merely the largest of a broader ethnic-racial grouping, held together by the usual mélange of history, culture, and dodgy biology. The political dramas of his time certainly encouraged this kind of sympathy. Khlebnikov understood the Balkan Wars of 1911–12 as Germanic (i.e., Austro-Hungarian) assaults on Slavic (e.g., Bosnian and Herzegovinian) peoples and he responded with a number of anti-German polemics. Pan-Slavism also inflected the lexical substance of his poetry, which enjoyed seasoning its Russian with words drawn from various, sometimes obscure Slavic languages and dialects. But when Khlebnikov complained about the narrowness of Russian writing, his grievance had a cosmopolitan and imperial flavour—he thought it should draw on all the cultures operating within the borders of the Russian Empire (and later, Soviet Union), whether Slavic or not. In this sense, Harsha Ram's description of his position as 'futurist Eurasianism' seems more on point.[106] In 'On enlarging the boundaries of Russian letters', published in a Slavophile journal in 1913, Khlebnikov complains that Russian writing ignores not only the cultural contributions of Polabian Slavs and various Russian legends, but also the Persians, Mongolians, and Jews who have lived within and on the borders of the Russian landmass. The nation's 'mind', he concludes, should not be 'merely Great Russian', but ought to be 'continental'.[107]

---

[102] Cassirer, *Philosophy of Symbolic Forms, Knowledge*, 73.

[103] Kruchenykh and Khlebnikov, *Slovo kak takovoe/The Word as Such*, 9/60. 'Dyr bul shchyl'' is taken by many as the archetypal transrational poem. For a detailed analysis, see Gerald Janecek, *Zaum* (San Diego: San Diego University Press, 1996), 49–69.

[104] Kruchenykh, 'Novye puti slova'/'New Ways of the Word', 25/71.

[105] Gerald Janecek, 'Kručenych and Chlebnikov Co-authoring a Manifesto', *Russian Literature* 8 (1980): 483–98.

[106] Harsha Ram, 'The Futurist Eurasianism of Roman Jakobson and Velimir Khlebnikov', in Mark Bassin, Sergey Glebov, and Marlene Laruelle (eds.), *Between Europe and Asia: The Origins, Theories, and Legacies of Russian Eurasianism* (Pittsburgh: University of Pittsburgh Press, 2015), 137–49.

[107] Velimir Khlebnikov, 'O rasshirenii predelov russkoi slovesnosti' (1913), in *Sobranie sochinenii, tom 6, kniga 1: stat'i (nabroski), uchenye trudy, vozzvaniia, otkritye pis'ma, vystuplieniia, 1904–1922* (Moscow: IMLI RAN, 2005), 67. English translation: 'Expanding the Boundaries of Russian Literature',

The tensions in this world-view might have been exacerbated when, the following year, the Italian Futurist Filippo Marinetti paid Russia a visit. Although the visit received an impressive amount of publicity, it was also the occasion for a vigorous airing of differences. This was in part over matters of poetic technique, but also over matters of ideology: the Italian Futurist obsession with technology and war, and its national chauvinism in particular, did not sit well in Moscow and St Petersburg.[108] Khlebnikov himself circulated a leaflet at Marinetti's talk in St Petersburg, accusing his supporters of placing 'the noble name of Asia beneath a European yoke'.[109] In an open letter about Marinetti's speech composed the next day, he suggested that someday the two should 'meet, amongst the cannon fire, for a duel between the Italo-German union and the Slavs on the Dalmatian coast'.[110]

The reaction was, of course, itself chauvinist in character, even if Khlebnikov's claims were made in the name of a kind of Eurasian version of the Slavic peoples. His fellow avant-gardist, Benedikt Livshits, who co-signed the leaflet attacking Marinetti, was interestingly circumspect about it. After a dinner with the Italian Futurist at which they argued vehemently, Livshits mused:

> Something else was bothering me... the political core of Italian Futurism, one which was so different from our radical convictions and our anarchic rebelliousness...'[111]

What bothered Livshits in particular was the possibility that what was explicit in Italian Futurism—the link between nationalist political ideology and avant-gardism—might be merely unacknowledged in the Russian version. It was possible that different causes had led to the same Futurist outcome, or that there was no necessary link between politics and art, but it was also possible that the same effect (Futurism) had the same cause in both cases and that there were elements of nationalism and patriotism in Futurism that the Russians were simply disavowing.

But there's something novel about a nationalism that's expressed by avant-garde poetry: the playful, technical aspect of the poetry and the magical, mythical nature of nationalism make them strange bedfellows. In an interesting note from 1915, Khlebnikov claims the Futurist—he uses the Slavic name for such avant-gardists, *budetlianin*—'is Pushkin in the light of the world war, in the cloak of the new century, asserting the right of the century to "laugh" at the Pushkin of the nineteenth century'.[112] Was this to be a more distanced, sober kind of nationalism? The choice of verb was significant: Khlebnikov's most notorious example of *zaumnyi*,

in Khlebnikov, *Collected Works, Vol. 1: Letters and Theoretical Writings*, trans. Paul Schmidt (Cambridge, MA: Harvard University Press, 1987), 254.

[108] On Marinetti's politics in the prewar period, see Bru, *Democracy, Law and the Modernist Avant-Gardes*, 41–54.

[109] Velimir Khlebnikov and Benedikt Livshits, Leaflet, in Khlebnikov, *Collected Works, Vol. 1*, 87 n1.

[110] Velimir Khlebnikov, '"Bezdarnyi boltun!..." <Otkrytoe pis'mo v sviazi s priezdom Marinetti v Rossiiu>' (2 February 1914) ['"Talentless chatterbox!" Open Letter in connection with Marinetti's visit to Russia'], in *Sobranie sochinenii, 6/1*, 223. English translation: *Collected Works, Vol. 1*, 87–8.

[111] Benedikt Livshits, *The One and a Half-Eyed Archer*, trans. John Bowlt (Moscow: The State Russian Museum, n.d.), 128.

[112] Velimir Khlebnikov, 'Mysli i zametki <1915>' ['Thoughts and Notes'], in *Sobranie sochinenii, tom 6, kniga 2: doski sud'by, mysli i zametki, pis'ma i drugie avtobiograficheskie materialy, 1897–1922* (Moscow: IMLI RAN, 2006), 84.

transrational poetry was 'Incantation by Laughter', composed entirely of words derived from the combination of the Russian root смех/*smekh*, 'laughter', with a generous selection from Russian's seemingly boundless reservoir of affixes. In fact, this kind of creative derivational morphology was responsible for most of Khlebnikov's neologisms. Kruchenykh had taken as his basic material the phonological resources of Russian, recombined in forms that were allusive, recognizably Russian, but in the end something like sound-pictures without definite sense. For Khlebnikov the basic linguistic substance seemed to be Russian morphemes (both bound and free, in formal linguistic terms), the roots and affixes that composed so much of the Russian lexicon. And this meant that Khlebnikov's word-creation, a prominent feature of his poetry and his theory, relied on—what else?—analogy.[113]

In 'A sample of word-innovation in language', written in 1909, Khlebnikov, discussing what should be the nominative form of the verb летать/*letat'*, which means 'to fly', runs through a series of analogies in order to produce a variety of nouns that designate a 'fly-er', to use a rough English translation:

> *Letatel'* is convenient for ordinary expression, but for a statement about a particular flight it is better to offer *poletchik* (*perepletchik*) [KH, a flight-taker (migratory bird)], and similarly, others, each having their own specific shading, for example, *neudachnyi letun* (*begun*) [a failed flyer (runner)], *znameniityi letai* (*khodatai, oratai*) [a celebrated flyer (a petitioner, orator)].[114]

Khlebnikov begins with the usual Russian suffix for deriving nominative agents from verb forms, -тель/-*tel'* (a reasonable English equivalent would be the suffix -*er*) and then riffs on a series of ever more distant analogies, which create words from the root лет-/*let*- ('fly') by using terms for migratory birds, for runners, for public speakers, as their templates. The implicit argument is that Russian provides the resources necessary for finely-grained distinctions between different kinds of things-that-fly and that these resources should not be left unmined.

This kind of inventiveness looks like a conscious and reflective form of the analogizing that Saussure insisted was never premeditated. But with this difference: Saussure saw analogy as unpredictable because it was unreasonable—speakers could and did reanalyse words 'incorrectly' (*electr*/*ician*), and the end result was a patchwork version of language, without a guiding 'genius'. Khlebnikov assumes, in common with linguists like Kartsevskii or Vinokur, that the 'spirit of a language' resides in its grammar, that it has a 'genius' (as discussed in Chapter 1) or 'inner form' (as discussed in this chapter) that dictates the shape and direction of its future development, though he does not use those terms.[115] Nevertheless, Khlebnikov takes pains to emphasize the ordinariness of the process, as if his innovations were

---

[113] Thus the vast bulk of the neologisms catalogued in Natalia Pertzov's *Slovar' neologizmov Velimira Khlebnikova* [*Dictionary of Velimir Khlebnikov's Neologisms*] (Vienna: Wiener Slawistischer Almanach, 1995) is taken up with 'morphologically interpreted words', as she describes them, although she also records neologisms that are instances of 'sound-painting' or the manipulation of letters and syllables.

[114] Velimir Khlebnikov, 'Obrazchik slovonovshestv v iazyke' (1909, 1912), in *Sobranie sochinenii*, 6/1, 28.

[115] S. I. Kartsevskii, *Iazyk, voina i revoliutsiia*, 55; G. O. Vinokur, 'Futuristy – stroiteli iazyka', 208.

simply a sped-up version, a time-lapse film, of the general progress of linguistic evolution. In a revealing passage, he compares the creation of new words to the inventiveness of the Russian mathematician Lobachevsky, the creator of non-Euclidean geometry:

> And if the living language, in the mouths of the people, can be likened to the geometrical measure of Euclid, then cannot the people permit themselves the luxury, unavailable to other peoples, of creating language—a likeness of the geometrical measure of Lobachevsky, of this phantom of other worlds? Do not the Russian people have the right to this luxury?[116]

Khlebnikov was merely helping the language along and, in the process, helping the Russian people as well. But he was not content to mimic the procedures of actual linguistic evolution—he thought he could take matters a few steps further.

The currency of analogy was morphemes: combinations of phonemes, or basic sound structures, which were invested with meaning. Khlebnikov decided to drill down further, to the level of what he called the 'simple names' of language, represented by letters or single sounds, which he then claimed were invested with even more fundamental or basic meanings than their combination. But what might look like a simple quantitative extension of the principle of analogy was in fact a qualitative leap, catapulting Khlebnikov into a quite different, possibly mythic space.

On the one hand, Khlebnikov went small: associating meaning with individual sounds (which he took to be identical with the letters representing them), he violated one of the tenets of modern linguistics—that the morpheme is the smallest unit of meaning and that sounds (phonemes) have no meaning outside their combination. On the other hand, he went big: the meaning captured by these sounds was strikingly abstract, depending upon a series of extraordinary—and, to their credit, imaginative—analogies to make sense.

In the 1915 essay, 'On the simple names of language'—not his first experiment of this kind, but one of the most systematic and detailed—he insists that the initial letter of words contains a meaning that controls the whole. Thus, of the letter *M* he says (with English translations of the Russian M-words in square brackets):

> With it begin the names of the smallest members of certain multiplicities.
>
> The world of plants: *mokh* [moss] (a toy forest), *murava* [grass] (relative to trees)
>
> The world of insects: *moshka* [midge], *mukha* [fly], *mol'* [tiny moth], *muravei* [ant] (compare the dimensions of beetles and birds)
>
> The world of animals: *mys'* (squirrel), *mysh'* [mouse] (relative to: elephants, elks), among fish—a little fish is *men'*
>
> The world of seeds: *zerna maka* [a poppy-seed]
>
> The world of fingers: the smallest—*mizinets* [the pinky]
>
> The world of time: *mig* [a moment]—the smallest division of time—and *makh* [a stroke]
>
> The world of words about the word: *molvit'* [to utter] (to say once)

---

[116] Velimir Khlebnikov, 'Kurgan Sviatogora' (1908–9) ['Sviatagor's Tomb'], in *Sobranie sochinenii*, 6/1, 25. English translation: 'The Burial Mound of Sviatagor', *Collected Works, Vol. 1*, 234.

In the multiplicity of abstract qualities: *malyi, makhon'kii, men'shii* (from *men'*), *melochi, melkii* [small, tiny, smaller (from 'little'), trifles, petty things]

In these 19 words beginning with *M*, we see one and the same concept wandering about—the smallest quantity of the member of a given field.[117]

All of which leads Khlebnikov to a conclusion that seems obvious to him: 'If we reduce the content of M-names to one form, then this concept would be the action of division.'[118] This demonstration is followed by similar ones showing how 'V' signifies the action of subtraction, 'K' addition, and 'S' multiplication. The mathematical cast of these meanings is not accidental, for at the same time that Khlebnikov is writing brilliant avant-garde poetry and manifestos for the word as such, he is elaborating arguments for a mathematical understanding of history, according to which significant historical events recur at exact and calculable intervals. It's the myth of maths, in which particular numbers acquire substantive properties.[119]

Boris Gasparov has made an interesting argument: he believes that Khlebnikov's justification of word-creation, bizarre as it might seem initially, finds itself reinvented in Roman Jakobson's phonological discovery, the theory of 'distinctive features'. For Khlebnikov's examples, in which the substitution of a single letter transforms one word into another, look a great deal like the so-called 'minimal pairs' used to illustrate basic distinctions in phonology (say, for example, *bus* and *buzz*, in which the voicing of the final sibilant makes all the difference). Khlebnikov, he claims, sees language as a continuous field of meaning riddled with gaps, as a result of which 'speakers remain oblivious to the interconnectedness of all meanings inherent in language'.[120] His word-creation seeks to fill the gaps and to make of language a more finely and densely woven web. In a late, programmatic essay called 'Our Fundamentals', Khlebnikov had noted:

> How often does the spirit of a language allow for a direct word, the simple alteration of a consonant sound in an already existing word, but instead of it everyone uses a complex and brittle descriptive expression, and thereby adds to the squandering of world reason by the time devoted to thinking it through. Who travels from Moscow to Kiev by going through New York?[121]

Khlebnikov's endless analogizing was the solution: 'Having substituted one sound for another in an old word, we immediately create a path from one valley of language

---

[117] Velimir Khlebnikov, 'O prostykh imenakh iazyka', in *Sobranie sochinenii* 6/1, 117. English translation: *Collected Works, Vol. 1*, 299–300.

[118] Khlebnikov, 'O prostykh imenakh iazyka'/'On the Simple Names of Language', 119/301.

[119] The various calculations and explanations are laid out in Khlebnikov's *doski sud'by* ['tables of fate'], reprinted in *Sobranie sochinenii*, 6/2, 9–72; English translation: 'Excerpt from The Tables of Destiny', *Collected Works, Vol. 1*, 417–33. In fact, Cassirer discussed the mythic notion of numbers, which precedes their mathematical formalization; see *Philosophy of Symbolic Forms, Mythical Thought*, 140–51.

[120] Boris Gasparov, 'Futurism and Phonology: Futurist Roots of Jakobson's Approach to Language', in François Gadet and Patrick Sériot (eds.), *Jakobson entre l'Est et l'Ouest 1915–1939*, Cahiers de l'ILSL No. 9 (Lausanne: Presses Centrales de Lausanne, 1997), 114.

[121] Khlebnikov, 'Nasha osnova' (1920) ['Our Fundamentals'], in *Sobranie sochinenii* 6/1, 167. English translation: *Collected Works, Vol. 1*, 376.

to another and, like a railway engineer, blaze a communication trail in the territory of words through the mountain range of linguistic silence.'[122] He thereby, as Gasparov points out, dissolves language into its primary elements, a project that provides 'a first glimpse into the future utopian state of language, when all potential links between the primary language elements will be realized and their meaning will be revealed in its totality'.[123] Roughly two decades later, Jakobson will present 'distinctive features' as the 'ultimate elements into which the whole structure of language could be dissolved'.[124]

The whole structure, that is, of *any* language. The focus on distinctive features rather than phonemes as building blocks universalizes the resource base of language, so that every particular language is a realization of universal phonetic possibilities. Likewise, when Khlebnikov simultaneously drills down to single consonant sounds and ascends upwards to meanings conceived in terms of mathematics and physics—elsewhere letters will be linked to relations of forces and surfaces—when he in effect drives the Saussurean poles of sound pattern and concept as far apart as possible, Russian seems less and less the vehicle of a specific culture. This may explain what he meant when, in a note from 1908–10, he remarked 'I will think as if no other language existed than Russian.'[125] Russian becomes the earthly embodiment, perhaps chosen by an accident of birth and upbringing, of the word as such, no longer defined by a specific shape or inner form, but capable of a universal expressiveness.

Khlebnikov claimed there was 'a path to make transrational language rational', with the implication that he was the one blazing the trail.[126] But one might just as well describe what he was doing as the reverse: making the rational transrational, turning the logical structure of language into a magical space. In fact, Khlebnikov's conception of language bears an uncanny resemblance to the world of astrology, as Cassirer analysed it in the 1920s.[127] For astrology, as Cassirer understood it, was a strange mixture of science and myth: on the one hand, astrology tried 'to think of the totality of the world as a lawful unity, as a self-contained causal structure'; on the other hand, '[t]his unity, even where it appears as the expression of the causal and dynamic, has its origin and fundamental significance in an always statically substantial unity'.[128] In Khlebnikov's hands, language itself becomes the meaningful cosmos, a world of sound inhabited by a spirit with a 'hovering, strangely impersonal character'. Its rich and complex interconnection of sounds mimics the seamless but static mathematical order of history—the analogizing just fills in the gaps, never creating anything truly new. Khlebnikov's word-creation would then be not so much a process of rational, considered innovation as the way in which

---

[122] Khlebnikov, 'Nasha osnova'/'Our Fundamentals', 168/377.
[123] Gasparov, 'Futurism and Phonology', 115.
[124] Gasparov, 'Futurism and Phonology', 119.
[125] Velimir Khlebnikov, 'Mysli i zametki <1908–1910>' ['Thoughts and Notes'], in *Sobranie sochinenii*, 6/2, 78.
[126] Khlebnikov, 'Nasha osnova'/'Our Fundamentals', 174/383.
[127] In 'Concept in Mythical Thinking', and, extensively, in *The Individual and the Cosmos in Renaissance Philosophy* (1926), trans. Mario Domandi (New York: Dover Press, 2000).
[128] Cassirer, 'Concept in Mythical Thinking', 31, 37.

a mystically ordered language, the word as such, manifests itself. Is this order democratic? No, insofar as there is no moment of discussion or decision in it, no public sphere, no institutions of popular sovereignty, unofficial or official. It is a world of fate, not ethical action. Yes, however, in the sense that the source of all legitimate meaning is a collection of peoples occupying a particular landmass—coinciding with Imperial Russia!—and that it is their ordinary activity that maintains and renews this cosmos. Khlebnikov's role as poet is analogous to that of the Rousseauean legislator, who is merely the externalized, conscious figure that proposes systemic rules for assent by the people at large.

The Futurists wrote poetry, and the occasional manifesto. The Formalists wrote *about* poetry. Historical commentary on Formalism has emphasized the looseness of the grouping, the heterogeneity of the positions taken by its putative members, and has wondered whether one can justifiably call it a critical school or movement.[129] Part of the confusion stems from the way in which writers identified with Formalism sought to present their criticism as scientific, principled, and rigorous, while at the same time extolling the magical power of literary language. Shklovskii began, as we've seen, with tales of sleeping beauties; but to move further along he would have to make contact with the new linguistics. He did this in the most literal way possible: having delivered his speech at the Stray Dog, he brought a printed copy to Baudouin de Courtenay, professor of linguistics at St Petersburg University and one of the most important advocates of the new synchronic linguistics (Jakobson would claim Saussure's work was warmly welcomed in Russia because Baudouin de Courtenay had anticipated his discoveries). Baudouin de Courtenay had a sceptical view of the new poetry—he would eventually denounce it, after an unfortunate evening in February 1914—but introduced Shklovskii to his linguistics student, the young Lev Iakubinskii (whose older, Marrist self we met in Chapter 4).[130] Iakubinskii and Shklovskii met and, in Shklovskii's excited words 'We became a duo.'[131] Another linguist, Evgenii Polivanov, was brought on board and Russian Formalism was launched in the first of three anthologies devoted to the study of poetic language.

For 'poetic language' was the key concept—or perhaps it would be appropriate to say, the movement's talisman, at the beginning. Shklovskii, Iakubinskii, Polivanov, and Osip Brik produced collections devoted to the 'theory of poetic language', in 1916, 1917, and 1919 and finally christened their association the 'Society for the

---

[129] See, for example, Peter Steiner's discussion 'Who is Formalism? What is She?', in his *Russian Formalism*, 15–43.

[130] Futurist poetic evenings needed an official sponsor, and the liberal Baudouin de Courtenay generously agreed to act as such on a few occasions. At the 'Evening for the New Word' held in February 1914, however, his patience with avant-garde scandal wore thin and he stormed out, having declared that 'We need a psychiatrist here.' See A. P. Chudakov, 'Dva pervykh desiatiletiia' ['The First Two Decades'], in Shklovskii, *Gamburgskii shchet*, 11. Baudouin de Courtenay's consequent polemics with Futurism are described in Janecek, 'Baudouin de Courtenay versus Kručenych'.

[131] From an unpublished chapter of *Third Factory*, quoted in A. P. Galushkin, Notes to *Voskreshenie slova*, in Shklovskii, *Gamburgskii shchet*, 487.

Study of Poetic Language'—OPOIaZ—in October 1919.[132] In Shklovskii's article for the first of the three anthologies (reprinted in the third), 'On Poetry and Transrational Language', he noted that some people claimed they could represent their emotions by meaningless sounds and asked 'whether this means of displaying one's emotions is a peculiarity of a small coterie or is a general phenomenon of language, but one not yet understood'.[133] The remainder of the collection was a long argument for the latter possibility.

The claim was parallel to the one made in Futurist manifestos: releasing the word from the burden of signifying something made it possible to assert and display what was called its 'autonomous value' [*samostoiashchaia tsennost'*]. Iakubinskii put the argument in the sharpest terms: in '*practical language*', aimed at communication, 'linguistic features (sounds, morphological units, etc.) do not have autonomous value and are only a *means* of communication'; in verse language, by contrast, these features are valued in themselves.[134] However, Iakubinskii did not discuss syntax or morphology, but only how sound in verse language 'focuses attention on itself', citing a variety of examples and, interestingly, moments when a novelistic narrator comments on the significance of some verbal tic or detail of pronunciation.[135]

It's a familiar avant-garde claim: the artist, rather than pursue extrinsic goals drawn from some *Weltanschauung*, explores the properties of his or her medium, be it the flat surface of the canvas, the exhibition space, or the sounds of language. It's also a complex claim, for, as T. J. Clark has pointed out, 'flatness' itself, or any other empirical property or technical fact of a medium, has to be seen *as* something, metaphorically, to bear some kind of value. In avant-garde practice, Clark notes, 'there was no fact without the metaphor, no medium without its being the vehicle of a complex act of meaning'.[136] How could we place a value on sound without reference to something else?

In fact, Iakubinskii could not do it. In 'On the Sounds of Verse Language', despite his promises, sounds only acquire value by serving as means or technique for some external significance, either by being invested with emotion or used to complement the existing semantic thrust of this or that poem. In this respect, the linguistically untrained Shklovskii was more inventive. He argued that a nonsensical emphasis on sound was not merely the province of conscious and intentional art, but could also be found in children's games, popular ditties, the experience of foreign languages, formulae for exorcisms, and in what Wilhelm Wundt had dubbed *Lautbilder* (sound-images, like 'splash') in ordinary language. Even pure

---

[132] *Sborniki po teorii poeticheskogo iazyka, vypusk 1* [Anthologies on the Theory of Poetic Language: Issue 1] (St Petersburg: n.p., 1916); *Sborniki po teorii poeticheskogo iazyka, vypusk 2* (Petrograd: n.p., 1917); *Poetika: sborniki po teorii poeticheskogo iazyka* (Petrograd, n.p.: 1919). The 1919 publication reproduced most of the articles in the first two.
[133] Viktor Shklovskii, 'O poezii i zaumnom iazyke' ['On Poetry and Transrational Language'], in *Poetika* (1919), 14–15. English translation: 'On Poetry and Trans-sense Language', trans. Gerald Janecek and Peter Mayer, *October* 34 (1985), 6.
[134] L. Iakubinskii, 'O zvukakh stikhotvornogo iazyka' ['On the Sounds of Verse Language'], in *Poetika* (1919), 37.
[135] Iakubinskii, 'O zvukakh', 39.
[136] T. J. Clark, 'Clement Greenberg's Theory of Art', *Critical Inquiry* 9.1 (1982): 152.

zaumnyi iazyk was found not only in Futurist poetry, but also in the glossolalia of Russian mystics.

The example of glossolalia was particularly revealing. Shklovskii had drawn his knowledge of this strange speech phenomenon from a study of religious ecstasy written by Dmitri Konovalev, who had applied William James's psychological account of religious feeling to Russian mystical sects. A review of the study in 1915 (which Shklovskii may have read, although he cites directly from Konovalev) had, in fact, compared the ravings of Russian Khlysts with those of Symbolist and Futurist poets.[137] For Shklovskii a marriage between religious ecstasy and modernist poetry would have been perfect. For the mystical sound has an 'autonomous value', as the immediate embodiment of a spiritual force, without having a meaning or a distinct signification: it draws on myth as an alternative to language as a sign-system. But the tidiness of this possible solution only throws into relief the general messiness of Shklovskii's comparisons, which were strikingly heterogeneous. There were all sorts of situations in which the sounds of words became detached from or ungoverned by meanings. But that didn't amount to establishing a new kind of 'autonomous value' for sound itself, to be epitomized in poetic language.

What the various examples of nonsensical language practice shared was, in fact, simply what they negated: sense, or meaning. But that suspension of meaning turned out to be the crucial point in Shklovskii's next major statement, his contribution to the 1917 'Poetics' anthology, 'Art as Technique' (*priem*, also sometimes translated as 'device'). For now it turned out that the deadness of words was just the index of a larger deadness, which afflicted every sphere of life. The process of habit, 'automatization', Shklovskii argued, 'eats away at things, at clothes, at furniture, at our wives, at the fear of war'.[138] We were endowed with art, therefore, 'in order to restore the sensation of life, to make us feel things, in order to make a stone feel stony'.[139] Art did this by means of techniques that made the perception of objects difficult or laborious: narrators who don't recognize or understand familiar things and activities, the use of difficult tropes, phonetically striking language, the use of dialect words. It was, however, the sensation that counted: 'the thing made [by art, KH] is not important'.[140] Words that didn't make immediate sense didn't get their value from sound alone, but from the more difficult route they provided to sense.

While 'Art as Technique' provided a broad rationale for the technical business of Formalist criticism, it also introduced ambiguities that would plague Formalism and its theoretical progeny for decades to come. There was, on the one hand, ambiguity over what it was that needed to be experienced freshly, by means of some 'estranging' gesture or device. Was it language and its formal structures, or was it

---

[137] See Alexander Etkind, 'James and Konovalev: *The Varieties of Religious Experience* and Russian Theology between Revolutions', in Joan Delaney Grossman and Ruth Rischin (eds.), *William James in Russian Culture* (Lanham, MD: Lexington Books, 2003), 184.

[138] Viktor Shklovskii, 'Isskustvo, kak priem' ['Art as Technique'], in *Poetika* (1919), 105. This is a reprint of the piece in the 1917 collection. English translation: 'Art as Device', in *Viktor Shklovsky: A Reader*, trans. Alexandra Berlina (London: Bloomsbury, 2017), 80.

[139] Shklovskii, 'Isskustvo, kak priem'/'Art as Device', 105/80.

[140] Shklovskii, 'Isskustvo, kak priem'/'Art as Device', 105/80.

the world that language could signify through its structures? Following on that, there was the question of *why* it was important to feel or sense whatever it was that had been automatized, whether war or the words used to signify war. One possible reading of the ambiguities was that it was language that had to command our attention so that we would understand its role in constituting the world beyond it: the screen had to be muddied so we would stop thinking of it as a window. Poetic discourse luxuriated in the density of its own language, whether for pleasure or edification.

This line of interpretation would pass through what became known as structuralism, and a kind of structuralist interpretation of Formalism. Which means, in a way, it had to pass through Roman Jakobson, who would come to represent an alternative pole of this same movement, centred in Moscow and the members of the Moscow Linguistic Circle and committed formally to the analysis of linguistic structures.

The Circle itself had begun, in 1915, as a group of students and faculty devoted to dialectological analysis and Jakobson initially characterized poetic language itself as a social dialect. Like Shklovskii, Jakobson was part of the Futurist milieu at the time, even contributing two poems to a Futurist collection called Заумная гнига/*Zaumnaia gniga* ('Transrational boog', because *kniga* would be 'book' and '*gnig*' means gnat).[141] And like Shklovskii, Jakobson was interested in popular language with mythic force: when he first met Khlebnikov at the Stray Dog in 1913, he gifted him a collection of spells and exorcisms he had collected. But it was not till 1917 that Jakobson would travel to Petrograd and meet with the members of what would become OPOIaZ, thus setting in motion the movement that would become modern literary theory.[142]

Already a committed Futurist, Jakobson was in accord with Shklovskii on several key points—the belief that art depends on the breaking of habitual associations, the idea that artworks are defined by the deployment of particular techniques or devices—but shaded them with his own linguistic views. Perhaps unsurprisingly, he set out his stall in a discussion of Khlebnikov, the central Futurist as far as the critics were concerned, first presented as a lecture in 1919 and published as *Contemporary Russian Poetry: An Initial Outline* in 1921.[143] Italian Futurism was condemned at some length and used as contrastive background for the Russian variety. The centrality of technique was assured: 'If the science of literature wants to be a science, it must recognize "technique" as its unique "hero".'[144] But for Jakobson techniques drew their force from the immanent laws of language itself: the autonomously valuable word was one in which the formal properties of language were exploited. '[P]oetry,' he would famously declare, 'which is nothing other than

---

[141] Kruchenykh, Aliagrov, *Zaumnaia gniga* (Moscow: n. p.: 1916), http://www.getty.edu/research/tools/guides_bibliographies/russian_avant_garde/index.html. Jakobson's two poems were published under the pseudonym Aliagrov.

[142] So, yes, the claim is that literary theory as such originates in Eastern Europe. For a brilliant exposition of this argument, see Galin Tihanov, 'Why Did Modern Literary Theory Originate in Central and Eastern Europe? (And Why Is It Now Dead?)', *Common Knowledge* 10.1 (2004): 61–81.

[143] Jakobson, *Noveishaia russkaia poeziia*. English translation: 'The Newest Russian Poetry: V. Xlebnikov', in Roman Jakobson, *My Futurist Years*, trans. Stephen Rudy (New York: Marsilio, 1997).

[144] Jakobson, *Noveishaia russkaia poeziia*/'The Newest Russian Poetry', 11/179.

an utterance with an orientation to expression, is ruled by what we would call immanent laws'.[145] There was no question here of what form drew attention to: it was language, and language alone. But this focusing of attention on the medium itself was also presented as the very essence of the aesthetic, which consisted, in every field, of a cultivation of the qualities and properties of the medium:

> If pictorial art is the form of the self-valuable material of visual representations, if music is the form of self-valuable sound material, and choreography the same for the self-valuable material of gesture, then poetry is the formation of the self-valuable, "self-living", as Khlebnikov put it, word.[146]

Nor was this merely the project of the avant-garde. The essay opened with a discussion of Pushkin, who appeared in the guise of an earlier technician, in effect the Khlebnikov of the nineteenth century (Jakobson would not be the only one to make the comparison). Pushkin may have been classicized over time, but to his contemporaries, Jakobson pointed out, his verse was strange and deformed, as defamiliarizing in its time as Futurist verse was in the present. But now that Pushkin's innovations were habit-forming, artists had to do something else to bring 'expression' into focus.

In a lecture delivered in 1933 entitled 'What is Poetry?', Jakobson argued that while 'the content of the concept of *poetry* is unstable and temporally conditioned' the 'poetic function, *poeticity*, is, as the "formalists" stressed, an element sui generis'.[147] That function was 'present when the word is felt as a word and not a mere representation of the object being named or an outburst of emotion': language could express what it expressed by virtue of its delicate internal machinery and poetry was a matter of putting the machinery on show.[148] One could only see the gears turn, however, by suspending the spell of meaning and signification, by producing some kind of nonsensical parallelism or structural feature that would 'fail' to mean and would thus appear, as Jakobson continually put it, 'deformed'. As Jakobson, and Shklovskii as well, pointed out, literary works would frequently disguise the technical feature, the moment of deformed nonsense, as the intrusion into the text of some pathological moment, a disturbance of ordinary consciousness producing nonsense: the use of the technique would be 'logically justified by means of pathologies'—*motivated* was the preferred term—by 'dreams, ravings and other pathological phenomena'.[149]

Shklovskii had crafted his theoretical position on the basis of Futurist poetry, but he rapidly applied it, by analogy, to the workings of narrative prose (the move is made explicit in his 1919 article, 'The connection of techniques of plot construction to stylistic techniques in general').[150] Not only as a critic: his memoirs of these

---

[145] Jakobson, *Noveishaia russkaia poeziia*/'The Newest Russian Poetry', 10/178.
[146] Jakobson, *Noveishaia russkaia poeziia*/'The Newest Russian Poetry', 10–11/179.
[147] Roman Jakobson, 'What is Poetry?', in *Language in Literature*, 378.
[148] Jakobson, 'What is Poetry?', 378.
[149] Jakobson, *Noveishaia russkaia poeziia*/'The Newest Russian Poetry', 15/182, 14/180.
[150] Viktor Shklovskii, 'Sviaz´ priemov siuzhetoslozheniia c obshchimi priemami stilia', in *Poetika* (1919), 115–50. English translation: 'The Relationship between Devices of Plot Construction and

formative years—*Third Factory* (covering 1914–17), *Sentimental Journey* (1917–22), and *Zoo, or Letters not about Love*—are notorious for their episodic construction and general refusal to toe a narrative line.[151] His interest was captured by the ways in which prose could put the machinery of narrative on show, the various techniques of plotted disorder, temporal slowing or speeding up, distension and concentration that, many years later, would be catalogued by structuralist narratologists like Gerard Genette. Both he and Jakobson imagined an art defined by continuous technical innovation, exploiting the structural possibilities of language and narrative discourse. They seemed to promote the means to the status of an end in itself.

When Jakobson tried to explain the point of the poetic function in the abovementioned 'What is Poetry?' this, indeed, looks like his line of argument:

> Why is it necessary to make a special point of the fact that sign does not fall together with object? Because, besides the direct awareness of the identity between sign and object (A is A_1), there is a necessity for the direct awareness of the inadequacy of that identity (A is not A_1). The reason this antinomy is essential is that without contradiction there is no mobility of concepts, no mobility of signs, and the relationship between concept and sign becomes automatized. Activity comes to a halt and the awareness of reality dies out.[152]

The poetic function is, so to speak, absorbed back into language itself. In Jakobson's formulation, poetry is assigned a surprisingly modest role, as if it were no more than the self-cleaning button on the linguistic oven, to be pressed intermittently. No doubt part of the explanation lies in Jakobson's debt to 'finalist' theories of evolution, which, *contra* Darwin, held that evolutionary changes were motivated by the organism itself.[153] When Jakobson assimilated Saussure, his principal critique was aimed at the idea of historical change as random and blind; in its stead he proposed the idea of a language as a dynamic system, evolving lawfully in accord with its native structural constraints. This entailed, however, 'the substitution of a teleological approach for the mechanical view': one could only understand language by regarding it as a whole, the parts of which were functionally integrated.[154] This 'means-ends model of language' made it possible to understand—and in fact, to evaluate—how various linguistic features worked, but it also seemed to subordinate poetry to the larger needs of language itself.[155]

Of course, everything depends on how one construes those larger needs, on what is contained or implied by Jakobson's claim that, without the distance poetry

General Devices of Style', in *Theory of Prose*, trans. Benjamin Sher (Normal, IL: Dalkey Archive Press, 1991), 15–51.

[151] Viktor Shklovskii, *Tret'ia fabrika* (Moscow: Krug, 1926); *Sentimental'noe puteshestvie: vospominaniia, 1917–1922* (Moscow: Gelikon, 1923); *Zoo, ili Pis'ma ne o liubvi* (Berlin: Helikon, 1923).

[152] Jakobson, 'What is Poetry?', 378.

[153] See Patrick Sériot, 'The Impact of Czech and Russian Biology on the Linguistic Thought of the Prague Linguistic Circle', in *Travaux du Cercle linguistique de Prague* 3 (Amsterdam: John Benjamins, 1999), 15–24.

[154] Roman Jakobson, 'The Concept of the Sound Law and the Teleological Criterion' [1928], in *Selected Writings, Vol. I: Phonological Studies* (The Hague: Mouton, 1962), 2.

[155] Roman Jakobson, 'Efforts Toward a Means-Ends Model of Language in Interwar Continental Linguistics', in *Selected Writings, Vol. II: Word and Language* (The Hague: Mouton, 1971), 523.

introduces between the sign and the object, 'activity comes to a halt and the awareness of reality dies out'. There's a hint here of something that will only be unfolded much later, when theorists like Paul de Man will claim that 'the introduction of linguistic terminology in the metalanguage about literature' disturbs our ordinary convictions about reference.[156] In 'The Resistance to Theory' de Man will point to literature 'as the place where this negative knowledge about the reliability of linguistic utterance is made available', making literature the exposer of language's dark secret.[157] You can see language as principally referential, and then understand poetry as simply a way to keep the referential machinery in working order. Or you can understand literature as, in its way, the truth of language, insofar as it ensures a certain looseness in relationship to things, a form of engagement with the world in which reference plays only a partial role. Poetry would then be the avant-garde of language, rather than its supply line.

Jakobson tended to choose the more conservative path, burying the magic potency of poetic language in the sands of the linguistic system as a whole: in the end, the autonomous value of the word was subordinate to the presumed autonomous value of language itself. If he was the great, consistent systematizer in Formalism, Shklovskii was its loose cannon, a 'scandalist', as some of his fellow writers put it, for whom consistency, the accurate quotation of sources, and reliable footnotes were cumbersome burdens.[158] It was unsurprising, therefore, that in his hands the various techniques and devices of literary art do much more than the linguistic housekeeping. The literary artist 'always incites insurrections among things' by cutting them free from their normal or inherited web of associations.[159] Technical novelties serve avant-garde aesthetic ends that are not simply functions of language. But though Shklovskii speaks in the early twentieth-century idiom of energy and sensation, it's hard not hear the echo of myth in his description of literary experience.[160] The objects or phenomena that literary techniques made strange were, as a consequence, cut loose, isolated from—as Cassirer had put it—'the whole of common, everyday experience' and it was this sudden isolation that produced a sense of 'sheer immediacy' when 'as it were, a spark jumps across'.[161] Shklovskii's artistic moment arrives when the spark jumps across again, as if literature is tasked with the continuing recreation of the original, evanescent linguistic-mythical moment.

But Shklovskii doesn't call it myth, and for good reason. For one thing, he wanted to separate the extraordinary moment from its sacred trappings: he was confident

---

[156] De Man, 'The Resistance to Theory', 8.   [157] De Man, 'The Resistance to Theory', 10.
[158] Shklovskii's nickname in the post-revolutionary writers group, the Serapion Brothers, was 'Brother Scandalist'. See Vladimir Berezin, *Viktor Shklovskii* (Moscow: Molodaia gvardiia, 2014), 129.
[159] Viktor Shklovskii, 'Stroenie rasskaza i romana', in *Razvertyvanie siuzheta* (Petrograd: OPOIaZ, 1921), 10. English translation: 'The Structure of Fiction', in *Theory of Prose*, 62.
[160] Shklovskii's aesthetic ideas are couched in terms of the economy of energy: artistic speech is laboured, difficult, impeded, while practical language requires a minimum of effort. In thinking of feeling in energetic terms, he is following the shift beautifully described by Enda Duffy in 'Energy, Stress, and Modernist Style', in Gregory Castle (ed.), *A History of the Modernist Novel* (Cambridge: Cambridge University Press, 2015), 211–30.
[161] Cassirer, 'Language and Myth', 160.

that the magical element of art, the moment of surrender and possession, could be separated from the mythology of priests and extraordinary people that mystified it. The Russian Symbolists, with whom Futurism had a relationship best described as Oedipal, had argued for the magic of words, but they thought '[s]ymbolism in modern poetry is the first vague reminiscence of the holy language of high priests and magi'.[162] Technique was the democratizing substitute for this pseudo-priestly insight: art was a skilled response to historical circumstances, not a negotiation with fate or higher spiritual powers. But the estranged object or situation was also immediate in a different way from the mythic object. It was isolated, vivid, not because it stood above the ordinary course of life, as sacred to profane, but because it had been set adrift, unmoored from its usual associations: it was presented as something without a defining use or purpose—a meeting that was confused and pointless, a jar or wheelbarrow that contained nothing important, a classical building sitting in a desert. The object of estrangement appeared, to use Frege's language, like a referent that had no sense, no obvious meaning.

In his 'Letter to Roman Jakobson', published in 1922, Shklovskii famously claimed: 'We now know how life is made and how *Don Quixote* is made and how an automobile is made'.[163] It was a clever riff on the titles of two Formalist articles—'How *The Overcoat* is Made' by Boris Eikhenbaum and 'How *Don Quixote* is Made' by Shklovskii himself—but it was, on another level, entirely serious, for Shklovskii really did know how automobiles were made. He had served as an instructor in an armoured division for the First World War and was an occasional mechanic as well, then and in the civil wars that followed.[164] He knew how tanks were made and he knew 'the laws of war' and how the latter 'reshapes things in its own way', compelling people to make fires with pianos and books and forcing tank mechanics to improvise.[165] War, insofar as it affected everyone and penetrated every sphere, was a 'democratic' crisis, which destroyed the coherence and patterning of everyday life. As a crisis, it detached objects from their original functional context and meaning, in effect estranging them, which is how particular objects become reconfigured as bare, uncomprehended, *merely* sensory 'things'.

The thinly-disguised parallel between wartime exploits and literary technique was cemented in two other texts written in the early 1920s. In Shklovskii's pamphlet on Rozanov he noted that 'when there is a change of literary schools the inheritance passes not from father to son but from uncle to nephew'.[166] The genius

---

[162] Viacheslav Ivanov, 'The Testaments of Symbolism', in *Selected Essays*, trans. Robert Bird (Evanston, IL: Northwestern University Press, 2001), 39.

[163] Viktor Shklovskii, 'Pis'mo k Romanu Iakobsonu', *Veshch/Objet/Gegenstand* 1–2 (Berlin: Skify 1922; reprinted Baden: Verlag Lars Müller, 1994), 5. English translation: 'A Letter to Roman Jakobson (1922/1990)', in *Viktor Shklovsky: A Reader*, 120.

[164] Shklovskii's biographer, Berezin, has emphasized how Shklovskii's early experiences with 'technical people' kept him supplied with a full arsenal of technical metaphors and analogies; *Viktor Shklovskii*, 55–6.

[165] Viktor Shklovskii, 'Samovarom po gvozdiam' ['Samovars as nails'], *Khod konia* [*The Knight's Move*] (Moscow: Gelikon, 1923; reprinted Orange, CT: Antiquary, 1986), 42. English translation: 'Driving Nails with a Samovar', *Viktor Shklovsky: A Reader*, 154.

[166] Viktor Shklovskii, *Rozanov* (Petrograd: OPOIaZ, 1921; reprinted Letchworth: Prideaux Press, 1974), 5. English translation: 'Literature without a Plot: Rozanov', *Theory of Prose*, 190.

does not beget another genius: literary evolution follows a crooked path, in which new techniques depend on improvisational borrowing from uncanonical sources, from the 'new forms [that] are being created in a lower stratum'.[167] Two years later he would christen this pattern 'the knight's move' in a collection with that title. In its preface he gave the gambit an ethico-political spin:

> One more thing: do not think that the knight's move is the move of a coward.
>
> I am not a coward.
>
> Our winding path is the path of the bold, but what are we to do when with our own two eyes we see more than honest pawns and loyal, single-minded kings.[168]

Viktor Shklovskii was certainly no coward. Decorated in the war, seriously injured at least once, plotting an uprising, he again and again put himself at physical risk either for Russia itself or his preferred version of social democracy (he was an active, militant supporter of the Socialist Revolutionary Party at the time of the Revolution and afterwards).[169] He was also, by all accounts, not lacking in charisma. But though conscious of his virtue, Shklovskii takes pains to distinguish it from the official form of courage, in which responsible traditional authorities ('loyal, single-minded kings') lead gullible, obedient masses to victory: his was the unofficial path of the improvising middleman, who fashions something forceful from what circumstances have given him. To grasp an object immediately, to see the stoniness of the stone, required an alertness to the new possibilities of the object, the presence of mind to see the thing outside its usual function, and a certain boldness and sense of initiative.

This boldness, and that of the art it mirrors, can be set in relief if we compare it with a contemporary attempt to rationalize the power and charisma inherited from myth. Max Weber's two lectures, 'Science as a Vocation' and 'Politics as a Vocation' were delivered in late 1918 and early 1919 and their context was revolutionary Germany. In the first he declared the world disenchanted: 'precisely the ultimate and most sublime values have withdrawn from public life', replaced by rational

---

[167] Shklovskii, *Rozanov*, 6/190.
[168] Shklovskii, 'Pervoe predislovie' ['First preface'], *Khod konia*, 11. English translation: 'Preface One', *Viktor Shklovsky: A Reader*, 154.
[169] Shklovskii has described his wartime exploits in *Third Factory* (covering the First World War) and *Sentimental Journey, 1917–1922*, the first part of which had been published as *Revolution and the Front*. It's enough to say he was in military service, with intervals, from 1914 till 1921, fighting on a striking variety of fronts and for a striking number of different outfits. On Shklovskii as a 'war writer', see Galin Tihanov, 'Politics of Estrangement: The Case of the Early Shklovsky', *Poetics Today* 26.4 (2005): 665–96, and Jan Levchenko, 'Towards the Formalist Dimension of War, or how Viktor Šklovskij used to be a Soldier', *Studies in East European Thought* 66 (2014): 89–100.

That said, Shklovskii has been accused of cowardice: for submitting to 'self-criticism' in 1930, when he published what has been viewed as a partial recantation of Formalist positions, 'Pamiatnik nauchnoi oshibke' ['Monument to a Scholarly Error'], *Literaturnaia gazeta* (27 January 1930), 4. For a discussion of the complexities of this recantation, see Richard Sheldon, 'Introduction: Viktor Shklovsky and the Device of Ostensible Surrender', in Shklovsky, *Third Factory*, trans. Richard Sheldon (Ann Arbor: Ardis, 1977), xxiii–xxvii. In an interview with Marietta Chudakova, Shklovskii claimed that he only became afraid in 1937, when he realized he could no longer see the danger coming ('Before that', he says, 'I used to have a sense of my own back'): Marietta Chudakova, 'Conversation with Viktor Borisovich Shklovsky, January 9, 1981', *Poetics Today* 27.1 (2006): 241–2.

calculation and progress.[170] In the second he nevertheless insisted that political leadership required not just a sober appreciation of circumstances, but also a form of passion that evolved from religion and magic. The very idea of a 'calling' or 'vocation' was rooted in a charismatic leadership embodied in two exemplary figures: the magician or prophet of ancient times and the modern elected demagogue, whose personality inspired democratic citizens. Modern passion takes the form of a commitment to a *Weltanschauung* that cannot be justified by reason: 'Passion in the sense of *objectivity*, a passionate surrender to an "object", to the god or daemon that is its master.'[171] Irrational passion would then be complemented by a sense of responsibility—the ability to calculate and weigh consequences—and a sense of proportion, both of which require a distance from men and things that prevents passion from overwhelming the polity.

Weber is dreaming of an ideal political leader; Shklovskii is arguing that moments of boldness and genius depend on a certain distance from the official and the canonical. Both insist that, in modern times, the successful myth must account for the force of circumstances, but in interestingly different ways. For Weber thinks of circumstances as a causal web complicating one's political aims, a balance of political forces and mesh of institutional arrangements through which one's passions must be filtered. Shklovskii, on the other hand, sees circumstances as what must be accounted for to generate a passionate attachment to objects in the first place. The artist surveys the field and realizes they can use something unregarded—the conventions of detective fiction, the genre of the letter—as a device to reinvigorate sensation and excite the passions.[172] For Shklovskii, the power of myth demands not coolness and rationalizing restraint, but an alertness to altered possibilities.

This draws our attention to a final feature of Shklovskii's position. Although it appeared he opposed art, as genuine sensation, first of all to life, as automatized perception, that simple dyad was always complicated by the presence of older, classicized literature, so familiar it could no longer discharge its aesthetic duties. In the essay on plot construction Shklovskii says:

> Let me add as a general rule: a work of art is perceived against the background of and by association with other works of art. The form of the work of art is determined by its relationship to other, pre-existing forms.[173]

Those new forms being created in the lower cultural depths thus appear against the background of the 'forms of older art,' Shklovskii remarks in the Rozanov essay, 'which are no more consciously felt than are grammatical forms in speech, and have

---

[170] Max Weber, 'Science as a Vocation', in *The Vocation Lectures*, trans. Rodney Livingstone (Indianapolis: Hackett Publishing, 2004), 30.

[171] Weber, 'Politics as a Vocation', in *The Vocation Lectures*, 76 (translation altered).

[172] Shklovskii had turned private correspondence into public art when he wrote his open letter to Jakobson (which was published in three different journals) and then again when he published *Zoo, or Letters not about Love*, a series of notionally personal letters to Elsa Triolet. On his use of letters see Asiya Bulatova, '"I'm writing to you in this magazine": The Mechanics of Modernist Dissemination in Shklovsky's Open Letter to Jakobson', *Comparative Critical Studies* 11.2–3 (2014): 185–202.

[173] Shklovskii, 'Sviaz´ priemov siuzhetoslozheniia'/'Plot Construction and Style', 120/20.

gone from being elements of an artistic orientation to official, unfelt phenomena'.[174] It's the official, not the everyday, that has to be worked around. Not formlessness, but forms that work all too well are the real problem. It might, therefore, make more sense to say that Shklovskii expects avant-garde art not to 'wake the sleeping beauty', but to wake the 'sleepwalking beauty', who thinks and feels *as if* she were awake, but is not.

BENJAMIN, THE DIVINE AND THE MYTHIC

This, of course, recalls the narcotic historicism against which Walter Benjamin battled: the waking dream states of the European bourgeoisie which he thought might be unsettled by a sudden 'moment of awakening'.[175] Like Shklovskii, Benjamin hoped the language of the avant-garde could appropriate the force of myth, but realized at an early point in his career that the reconfiguration would be complicated. As with Shklovskii, Benjamin's polemic initially aims at the wrong target—at language as a mere practical, communicative instrument—before bending its efforts towards separating out the positive from the negative within mythic force, the revolutionary from the somnambulant.

Which is to say that an idea of myth is also the source for Benjamin's belief in the force, the creative power of language; he will only gradually realize that he cannot appropriate this force wholesale, but must acknowledge its inner fissuring. In July of 1916, shortly before Benjamin composes 'On Language as Such and Human Language', Gershom Scholem claims that 'Benjamin accepted myth alone as "the world". He said he was still not sure what the purpose of philosophy was, as there was no need to discover "the meaning of the world": it was already present in myth. Myth was everything [...].'[176] In a letter to Martin Buber written at the same time Benjamin would say 'I can understand writing as such as poetic, prophetic, objective in terms of its effect, but in any case only as *magical*, that is as un-*mediated*.'[177]

What the 'Language as Such' essay tells us is that this magical power is a gift from God and that God's power is uniquely available in language. To persuade us that our human language contains an unacknowledged magic potency, Benjamin engages the most archaic of devices: the language origin story, in this case based on a reading of Genesis. Here it is not the imitation of natural sound by humans, or their expressive cries and singing that gets the ball rolling, but the divine 'Let there be':

> In this 'Let there be' and in the words 'He named' at the beginning and end of the act, the deep and clear relation of the creative act to language appears each time. With the creative omnipotence of language it begins, and at the end language, as it were, assimilates the created, names it.[178]

---

[174] Shklovskii, *Rozanov*, 6/190.   [175] Benjamin, *The Arcades Project*, N18, 4 (486).

[176] Gershom Scholem, *Walter Benjamin: The Story of a Friendship* (London: Faber and Faber, 1982), 31.

[177] Walter Benjamin, Letter to Martin Buber, July 1916, in *The Correspondence of Walter Benjamin, 1910–1940*, trans. Manfred R. Jacobson and Evelyn M. Jacobson (Chicago: University of Chicago Press, 1994), 80.

[178] Benjamin, 'On Language as Such', 68.

This is the same story Cassirer discusses in the *Philosophy of Symbolic Forms*, in which pure creative will is identified with language—God speaks the world into being. But whereas Cassirer made this moment of creative will, embodied in language, a climax, for Benjamin this is the beginning of a tale of decline, the progressive weakening of language's initial forcefulness. Benjamin, therefore, continues on to Adam. When God creates Adam, he endows him with language and impels him to employ it: God brings the newly created animals and birds 'to the human to see what he would call it, and whatever the human called a living creature, that was its name'.[179] The creative power of God's word, 'relieved of its divine actuality, became knowledge'.[180] 'All human language', therefore, 'is only the reflection of the word in name'.[181]

Names lack the creative, magical force of the divine word—but they are not, in Benjamin's reckoning, merely reflections of or labels for their objects, for naming is also 'the translation of an imperfect language'—what Benjamin will call 'the unspoken nameless language of things'—'into a more perfect one, and cannot but add something to it, namely knowledge'.[182] Naming isn't a matter of subsuming sensuous particulars under abstract concepts—it has some of the immediacy of myth, the sense that the name participates in or is part of the object. What the name 'adds' is an explicit articulation of the natural order God has created and a relationship to the one who speaks the name.

As we know, this will not be the end of Benjamin's linguistic story. The Fall 'marks the birth of the *human word*, in which name no longer lives intact'.[183] 'In stepping outside the purer language of name', Benjamin observes, 'man makes language a means [...], and therefore also, in one part at any rate, a *mere* sign; and this later results in the plurality of languages'.[184] The final step is the 'enslavement of language in prattle' and the Babelian confusion that is its correlate.[185] Its mythic force dissipated through the world's several thousand tongues, language finds itself reduced to a conventional means of communication. This will leave us with the situation we observed when we discussed Benjamin earlier. There is, on one hand, language as such, pure language, in which we find 'the residue of the creative word of God'.[186] In a letter to his friend Herbert Belmore written near the end of 1916, he insists that '[t]o criticize [...] is not the concern of language.[...] Language resides only in what is positive, and completely in whatever strives for the most fervent unity with life.'[187] On the other hand, there is 'human language', actually existing language, in which the name, the magical force of language sits dormant, perhaps only occasionally rising to the surface. Benjamin's task as a writer is to call our attention to every manifestation of this residue, to point out how the discourse

---

[179] Genesis 2:19, trans. Robert Alter, *The Five Books of Moses* (New York: W. W. Norton, 2004), 22.
[180] Benjamin, 'On Language as Such', 68. [181] Benjamin, 'On Language as Such', 68.
[182] Benjamin, 'On Language as Such', 70. [183] Benjamin, 'On Language as Such', 71.
[184] Benjamin, 'On Language as Such', 71. [185] Benjamin, 'On Language as Such', 72.
[186] Benjamin, 'On Language as Such', 74.
[187] Walter Benjamin, Letter to Herbert Belmore, late 1916, in *The Correspondence of Walter Benjamin*, 83–4.

of his community has strayed from the path language makes available, and to urge the cause of language as such by example as well.

Benjamin will eventually turn to the city, to modernity, and to Surrealism for help. But before that his analysis of bourgeois soullessness would take a dramatic and original turn. In the words of his biographers Howard Eiland and Michael W. Jennings:

> His writings in the period 1919–1922 were concerned above all to reveal the ways in which the present moment was infiltrated by myth: in the essays "Fate and Character," "Critique of Violence," and "Goethe's Elective Affinities," myth emerges as the power that dominates and disorients human relations.[188]

Eiland and Jennings have a persuasive explanation for this change of tack: the works of Hermann Cohen, in particular *Religion of Reason Out of the Sources of Judaism*, which had been published, posthumously, in 1919. We have met with Cohen's influence once already, as a philosopher of science and as an interpreter of the messianic element in Judaism, presented as the antidote to the mythic worldview that makes fate, rather than ethics, the basis of human action.[189] We know Benjamin had read and thought about Cohen, because Scholem's diaries recount their joint complaints about Cohen's rationalist neo-Kantianism. We know Cohen is relevant to these three texts in particular, because he merits a positive mention in each. And we can guess that, complaints aside, Cohen made a difference, because in these texts the writer who a few years earlier thought 'myth was everything' now thinks that when myth is everything, ethics and justice are nothing.

But Benjamin does not, like Cassirer, present the ethical, messianic, and divine as something evolved from myth: he splits the mythical power secreted in speech down the middle, dividing it into the force of divine justice on one hand, and that of mythical fate, on the other. When nature is invested with mythic power, humans feel themselves under the rule of an inscrutable fate, which exacts misfortune and retribution unpredictably but also endlessly. The admixture of meaning and material that distinguishes myth makes nature expressive, even beautiful, but also systematically ambiguous. Myth is always a matter of reading nature as a set of signs, but nature never actually speaks: there is no moment of revelation. The result is permanent guilt and anxiety, guilt not tied to responsibility for a specific action or decision, but the 'natural guilt of human life', as Benjamin calls it in 'Fate and Character'.[190]

But because myth figures as the antithesis, rather than the ancestor of divine justice, because each is archaic in its way, Benjamin does not have to explain why and how myth survives into a modern, disenchanted present—myth is identified not with an antiquated past but with the bourgeois present. Alison Ross has demonstrated in a shrewd and perceptive essay that Benjamin's 1924–5 study of

---

[188] Howard Eiland and Michael W. Jennings, *Walter Benjamin: A Critical Life* (Cambridge, MA: Harvard University Press, 2014), 151–2.
[189] Hermann Cohen, *Religion of Reason Out of the Sources of Judaism*, 2nd edn., trans. Simon Kaplan (Atlanta: Scholars Press, 1995).
[190] Walter Benjamin, 'Fate and Character', in *Selected Writings, Vol. 1*, 206.

Goethe's *Elective Affinities* 'identifies "fear" as both the symptom and the motive force of bourgeois life' and bourgeois civility as a false reconciliation.[191] The two slightly earlier pieces make an ostensibly more outlandish equation: in 'Fate and Character' and 'Critique of Violence' myth is identified with that most central institution of modernity, *law*. Law, Benjamin argues, may have the appearance of clarity and reasonableness, but, like myth, it is ultimately grounded in the inscrutable, and thus terrifying sphere of fate: like the anger of the gods, the punishments meted out by law are comprehensible, but not inevitable, threatening yet not ultimately predictable. More to the point, legal violence, like mythic violence, is a 'manifestation' of political power, not just its tool (just as episodes of mythic violence are manifestations of the gods). As Benjamin puts it in 'Critique of Violence', 'Lawmaking is powermaking, assumption of power, and to that extent an immediate manifestation of violence.'[192]

This reshuffling of the modern deck means Benjamin can no longer play the card of reason against myth. Not that he would have wanted to: in a 1925 letter to Hugo von Hofmannsthal, he remarked that, having read Cassirer's book on myth, he 'remained unconvinced that it is feasible not only to attempt to present mythical thought in concepts—i.e., critically—but also to illuminate it adequately in contrast with what is conceptual'.[193] What opposed myth would be the divine, as understood in the messianic Jewish tradition Benjamin had absorbed from Cohen and Scholem. It's as if the Old Testament struggle between myth and monotheism was being rerun, only with the antagonists in modern dress. 'In its present state', Benjamin claimed, 'the social is a manifestation of spectral and demonic powers'; the divine manifested itself in 'revolutionary force' and in 'perception oriented toward revelation and, first and last, in language, sacred language above all'.[194]

You could describe the remainder of Benjamin's career as an attempt to align those two supposed manifestations of the divine: revolutionary force, on the one hand, and what he continued to call 'the magical side of language', on the other, each of which, however, explicitly excluded 'the social', which had been colonized by 'demonic powers'.[195] The catalyst would be avant-garde art. In Berlin in 1922 he had come into contact with the modernists and constructivists of the 'G Group'.[196] In 1924, having escaped to Capri, he met someone who would be for him the literal incarnation of revolutionary avant-gardism, Asja Lacis. Above all, from 1925 onwards he would become enamoured with the Surrealists, who would reveal to him the 'revolutionary energies of the outmoded' and set the stage for his long, somewhat tortured work on the *Arcades Project*.

---

[191] Alison Ross, 'The Distinction between Mythic and Divine Violence: Walter Benjamin's "Critique of Violence" from the Perspective of "Goethe's *Elective Affinities*"', *New German Critique* 41.1 (2014): 117.
[192] Walter Benjamin, 'Critique of Violence', in *Selected Writings, Vol. 1*, 248.
[193] Walter Benjamin, Letter to Hugo von Hofmannsthal, 28 December 1925, in *The Correspondence of Walter Benjamin*, 287.
[194] Walter Benjamin, 'World and Time', in *Selected Writings, Vol. 1*, 227.
[195] Walter Benjamin, 'Reflections on Humboldt', in *Selected Writings, Vol. 1*, 424.
[196] Eiland and Jennings, *Walter Benjamin*, 170–2.

Surrealism would provide Benjamin with some of the vocabulary he needed to rejig his project; Marxism would provide the rest. Myth, which had stood for the inscrutable powers of nature, was the first in line for an update. Benjamin had already marvelled over Georg Lukács's *History and Class Consciousness*, which would have taught him to regard the products of capitalism as a 'second nature'.[197] (He had himself described capitalism as 'a purely cultic religion' in 1921.)[198] The transposition of mythic force from nature to capitalist society therefore just needed a terminological bridge, and Surrealism was there to provide it. In a 'Gloss on Surrealism' written in 1925 and published in 1927 Benjamin identified the kitsch of the late nineteenth century, 'worn through by habit and patched with cheap maxims' with dreams, citing Breton and Aragon as sources.[199] Shortly thereafter, he would read Louis Aragon's *Paris Peasant* (1926), which presented itself as a mythology of the modern and was set in a decaying, soon to be demolished arcade. It was an opportunity to think of dreams as not merely infusing the luxury objects of consumer capitalism, but as, in the most literal way possible, housing the human race itself, enclosing it in what Benjamin would call the '[d]ream houses of the collective: arcades, winter gardens, panoramas, factories, wax museums, casinos, railway stations.'[200] An entry in the *Arcades Project* confirmed the shift in terminology: 'Capitalism was a natural phenomenon with which a new dream-filled sleep came over Europe, and, through it, a reactivation of mythic forces.'[201]

But, as earlier, the plan was not to extinguish mythic darkness with the light of conceptual reason. It's a telling point that for Benjamin it is illumination, not darkness, that characterizes the dream-states of the nineteenth century, and what deludes its denizens is not the fogginess or murkiness of ideology, but naturalism and attention to historical detail. That is why so much of the *Arcades Project* is devoted to the 'art of the dazzling illusion' produced by street-lighting, mirrors, panoramas (each of which merits a Convolute to itself), shop displays, and so on, for the illuminated object, presented in museums, shop windows, exhibitions, and, of course, arcades is the ideological form par excellence.[202] If this is the stuff dreams are made of, then clearly no amount of light will disturb them.

The route out was the profane illumination we discussed earlier. But Benjamin would have to make one crucial adjustment to Surrealist 'magical experiments with words', which he spells out in one of the methodological comments sprinkled throughout the *Arcades Project*:

> Delimitation of the tendency of this project with respect to Aragon: whereas Aragon persists within the realm of dream, here the concern is to find the constellation of awakening. While in Aragon there remains an impressionistic element, namely the

---

[197] In a letter to Gershom [Gerhard] Scholem of 16 September 1924, Benjamin says that 'The book astonished me because these principles resonate for me or validate my own thinking'. *The Correspondence of Walter Benjamin*, 248.
[198] Walter Benjamin, 'Capitalism and Religion', *Selected Writings, Vol. 1*, 288. See Michael Löwy, 'Capitalism as Religion: Walter Benjamin and Max Weber', *Historical Materialism* 17 (2009): 60–73.
[199] Walter Benjamin, 'Dream Kitsch: Gloss on Surrealism', in *Selected Writings, Vol. 2*, 3.
[200] Benjamin, *Arcades Project*, L1, 3 (405).   [201] Benjamin, *Arcades Project*, K1a, 8 (391).
[202] Benjamin, *Arcades Project*, R1, 1 (537).

"mythology" (and this impressionism must be held responsible for the many vague philosophemes in his book), here it is a question of the dissolution of "mythology" into the space of history. That, of course, can happen only through the awakening of a not-yet-conscious knowledge of what has been.[203]

The constellation of awakening: meaning the moment in which something from the wakened present creates a kind of chemical reaction with a dream element from the past. For our purposes the important thing is that it is a *moment* of awakening, 'the flash of awakened consciousness', as Benjamin calls it, in which the magical force of a phrase, object, or building is clarified, in some respect transformed, but not dissipated.[204] Surrealism thinks the dream is itself real, the positivists (which would include Marx in this context) think the dream is just illusion, so Benjamin cleverly borrows the force of awakening from a somewhat different French source, Marcel Proust, who opens the novel Benjamin is translating in the 1920s with a moment that combines awakening and sharp, insightful remembrance.[205]

The terminological universe of the *Arcades Project*—in which the creative power of the name is seeded in the dream, bourgeois-mythical complacency is sleep, and translation is a moment of 'awakening'—has a signal advantage: it allows Benjamin to combine the idea of a sudden semantic change, the sudden breaking through of linguistic force, with the idea of historical recuperation, for it is semantic contents from the past that are awakened.[206] The dialectical image is 'that wherein what has been comes together in a flash with the now to form a constellation'.[207] But, of course, the dialectical image itself is a clever marriage of mythical force and immediacy with the discursivity of language. For Cassirer, for Shklovskii (the word 'was an image'), for Sorel (as we'll see very soon) the image is the defining form of myth: the image as something visually immediate, but also static, an iceberg in the flow of discourse. In Benjamin's text the image is composed of words, yet arrests their meandering forward movement: '[w]here thinking comes to a standstill in a constellation saturated with tensions—there the dialectical image appears'.[208] It is not supposed to be an argument, but a scene, drawn by Benjamin, that will change the meaning of things, or to recur to Benjamin's earlier terminology, will restore or revive 'the unspoken nameless language of things'.

The introduction of modernity, Marxism, and Surrealism into Benjamin's world demanded an updating of his theory of language as well: at some point in 1932 or early 1933, he began to play with a new and extravagant concept of similarity, which provoked his first attempt at a 'mimetic' theory of language in the short

---

[203] Benjamin, *Arcades Project*, N1, 9 (458).   [204] Benjamin, *Arcades Project*, K1, 2 (388).
[205] For a somewhat more detailed account of awakening and its sources, see 'Awakening' in Buse et al., *Benjamin's* Arcades: *An unGuided tour*, 105–12.
[206] On this see Jürgen Habermas's great essay, 'Walter Benjamin: Consciousness-Raising or Rescuing Critique', in *Philosophical-Political Profiles*, trans. Frederick G. Lawrence (Cambridge, MA: MIT Press, 1983), 129–64. Habermas points out that Benjamin commits himself to 'preserving an endangered semantic potential' (149) that modernity threatens to destroy; he regards the semantic energy of culture as an inheritance which one could conceivably exhaust, leaving one with a 'meaningless emancipation' (158).
[207] Benjamin, *Arcades Project*, N2a, 3 (462).   [208] Benjamin, *Arcades Project*, N10a, 3 (475).

piece 'Doctrine of the Similar'. According to a letter Benjamin wrote to Scholem at the end of February 1933, the four pages of this 'new theory of language [...] were formulated while I was doing research for the first piece of the *Berliner Kindheit*'.[209] It's hard not to think he meant the sketch 'The Mummenlehren', in which he describes how his childhood was dominated by what he calls 'the old compulsion to become similar and to behave mimetically'.[210] But mimesis is not quite what you would expect, for the young Benjamin seeks to become 'similar to dwelling places, furniture, clothes' and wants to resemble not his parents, but his parents' Chinese porcelain.[211] As Benjamin noted in 'Doctrine of the Similar': 'Children's play is everywhere permeated by mimetic modes of behavior, and its realm is by no means limited to what one person can imitate in another. The child plays not only at being a shopkeeper or teacher but also a windmill and a train.'[212]

The mimetic theory of language thus inherits the ambitions of the earlier theological one. It's not so much a theory of actually existing language as a theory of a larger, universal process that contextualizes what we ordinarily call language, so that the latter appears as, on one hand, the tip of a larger mimetic iceberg and, on the other hand, a confused amalgamation of 'mere signs' and a deeper form of communication (called 'naming' in the earlier theory and mimesis in the later one). A kind of middle point in this anthropological recasting of Benjamin's linguistic theory is found in a short piece dated a little while before, in 1932, in which he tries to explain astrology on the basis of this new idea of mimesis. In Benjamin's discussions of language, astrology plays the same mediating role it did for Cassirer: it is a halfway house between older, purely mythic forms of understanding, and newer, modern practices of reading. It was astrology that provided Benjamin with the 'constellation' as a model of a sudden grasping, a suddenly available concatenation of significant elements. In 1932 Benjamin approaches this mythic process and proposes to construct a 'rational astrology', 'from which the doctrine of magical "influences", of "radiant energies", and so on has been excluded'; he wants to re-imagine astrology so that it retains the immediate power of myth but without recourse to either magic or religion.[213] In exceptionally systematic fashion (systematic for Benjamin, that is), he argues that we should understand astrology as a historical

---

[209] Benjamin, Letter to Gershom Scholem, 28 February 1933, *The Correspondence of Walter Benjamin*, 402–3.

[210] Walter Benjamin, 'The Mummenlehren' [1932–1934 version], in *Berlin Childhood around 1900*, trans. Howard Eiland (Cambridge, MA: Harvard University Press, 2006), 131. It's not immediately clear what Benjamin meant by the 'first' piece in *Berlin Childhood around 1900*, as he was continually adding to and rearranging its sections. Scholem, in an editorial note to the above letter, can't see any connection between two possible candidates for 'first' position, but, if we just look for the most thematically relevant piece, 'The Mummenlehren' is the clear winner. See *The Correspondence of Walter Benjamin*, 404 n6. On the emergence of 'mimesis' in Benjamin's work see Beatrice Hanssen, 'Language and Mimesis in Walter Benjamin's Work', in David S. Ferris (ed.), *The Cambridge Companion to Walter Benjamin* (Cambridge: Cambridge University Press, 2004), 54–72.

[211] Benjamin, 'The Mummenlehren', 131.

[212] Walter Benjamin, 'Doctrine of the Similar', in *Selected Writings, Vol. 2*, 694.

[213] Walter Benjamin, 'On Astrology' (1932), in *Selected Writings, Vol. 2*, 685, 684. Astrology had a long history—Benjamin seems to have been invested in a particular Protestant version of it: see Jane O. Newman, 'Enchantment in Times of War: Aby Warburg, Walter Benjamin, and the Secularization Thesis', *Representations* 105 (2009): 133–67.

form of mimesis. To do so, we must understand that the resemblances we grasp daily, as coincidences, are 'nothing more than tiny prospects from a cosmos of similarity'.[214] This cosmos is the joint consequence of 'the effects of an active, mimetic force working expressly inside things' and of human subjects who are now capable not only of mimetic behaviour but of perceiving similarities, which they do when they 'read' entrails, the skies, runes, and texts. Finally, we must understand that mimesis has a history, that it undergoes transformations such that 'the mimetic force and the mimetic mode of vision may have vanished from certain spheres, perhaps only to surface in others'.[215] This transformation has affected astrology itself, which was once a kind of experience, and is now a kind of reading, in which we grasp a correspondence between constellations in the sky and human fates.

It's a bold attempt to separate the forceful kernel from the mythical chaff, but the ultimate point of it is to represent language as continuous with child's play and the reading of runes and stars. In the following year, Benjamin will produce two short accounts of the evolution of mimesis, of its voyage from astrology to human language: 'Doctrine of the Similar', earlier by a few months, is more comfortable with contextualizing language within magical practices; 'On the Mimetic Faculty' is more ascetic in this regard. In between the writing of these two he had written to Scholem, asking him for his copy of the 1916 'Language as Such' essay, which, upon receipt, he compared with his current musing on mimesis and similarity.[216] The result, the 'Antitheses Concerning Word and Name', set the two approaches side by side. So whereas the 'foundation of the name' in the earlier conception had been the 'communication of matter in its magic community', now Benjamin would say that '[t]he communication of matter in its magical community takes place through similarity.'[217]

To make the final jump to language, however, to close the loop containing writing, spoken discourse, astrology, and the reading of runes, Benjamin has to modify similarity itself. In 'Doctrine of the Similar', he will, accordingly, speak of astrology as 'mak[ing] comprehensible the concept of a nonsensuous similarity'.[218] The paragraph in which this counterintuitive and novel idea joins up all the dots is worth quoting in full:

> If, at the dawn of humanity, this reading from stars, entrails, and coincidences was reading per se, and if it provided mediating links to a newer kind of reading, as represented by runes, then one might well assume that this mimetic gift, which was earlier the basis for clairvoyance, very gradually found its way into language and writing in the course of a development over thousands of years, thus creating for itself in language and writing the most perfect archive of nonsensuous similarity. In this way, language is the highest application of the mimetic faculty—a medium into which the earlier perceptual capacity for recognizing the similar had, without residue, entered to such an extent that language now represents the medium in which objects encounter and

[214] Benjamin, 'On Astrology', 684.   [215] Benjamin, 'On Astrology', 684.
[216] Benjamin, Letter to Gershom [Gerhard] Scholem, 23 May 1933, in *The Correspondence of Walter Benjamin*, 414.
[217] Walter Benjamin, 'Antitheses Concerning Word and Name', in *Selected Writings, Vol. 2*, 717.
[218] Benjamin, 'Doctrine of the Similar', 696.

come into relation with one another. No longer directly, as they once did in the mind of the augur or priest, but in their essences, in their most transient and delicate substances, even in their aromas. In other words: it is to script and language that clairvoyance has, over the course of history, yielded its old powers.[219]

The nonsensuous similarity, which Benjamin elsewhere calls a 'correspondence', is not a matter of an idea resembling a thing, of an iconic relation between picture and real object. It's a substitute for the idea of 'meaning', insisting that the relationship between what words signify and the objects of the world (in semiotic terms, between the signified and its referents; in Fregean terms, between sense [*Sinn*] and reference [*Bedeutung*]) is a relationship between two ideas or 'essences', rather than an idea and a thing. In a different part of the essay Benjamin will point to the fact that words in different languages can refer to the same object. When Saussure pointed this out, in order to demonstrate the arbitrariness of signifiers (e.g., *Ochs* and *boeuf*), he had, as commentators noticed, also asserted the non-arbitrary nature of signifieds.[220] Benjamin's point is, so to speak, similar: for sure, mimesis must make its appearance in conventional semiotic material, but this presumes something non-arbitrary at its core, allowing all these words to refer to the same object, and it is this which Benjamin once called 'name' and now calls 'similarity'.

Those correspondences, those similarities, can be surprising, unexpected, esoteric: when children play and when Surrealists make art, they may discover that a bicycle seat is a bull's head, and the lid of a garbage can is a shield. And isn't Cassirer's observation that the movement of the moon and a falling stone express the same concept a matter of grasping similarities that aren't evident at first glance? The crucial difference, of course, is that mimetic reading, in children, Surrealism, and Benjamin, isn't a cognitive achievement, isn't the establishment—through patient experiment and theory-building—of a network of relations between objects, but a mode of response or openness to what Benjamin had called, in 'On Astrology', the 'active, mimetic force working expressly inside things'. It required observation—and, in Benjamin's case, extensive reading—but also the 'quick-wittedness' or 'presence of mind' (*Geistesgegenwart*) that allowed you to notice similarities and correspondences that everyday life might have masked. It's continuous, then, with Shklovskii's sense that improvisation can lead you to estrange and see the familiar object differently, except that Shklovskii presents that improvisation as the consequence of circumstances, as forced upon you by war and crisis, whereas Benjamin thinks it follows from the plasticity of childhood, the disorientation brought on by hashish, the dopiness of early morning, or the confusion of city streets.[221]

It's a theory meant to ground the striking analogies and comparisons we find in Benjamin's writing, the dialectical images that provoke awakening, but it has the

---

[219] Benjamin, 'Doctrine of the Similar', 697–8.
[220] On this see Sebastiano Timpanaro, who celebrates this moment of 'realism' in Saussure: 'Structuralism and its Successors', in *On Materialism*, trans. Lawrence Garner (London: New Left Books, 1975), 153–5.
[221] David L. Marshall has argued that we should understand *Geistesgegenwart* as a rhetorical category; see 'The Intrication of Political and Rhetorical Inquiry in Walter Benjamin', *History of Political Thought* 34.4 (2013): 726–8.

potential to account for the most ordinary linguistic accomplishments: the simple utterances whereby one asks someone to pass the salt, asserts that the weather is fine, or makes a date for coffee. These accomplishments, the argument would go, require something more than a set of agreed conventions, a system of language ready to be put in play by a willing subject. It's the mimesis present in all speech, our ability to mimic and to see and create analogies (at the level of sound, meaning, and gesture), that makes it possible for these conventions to signify anything in the first place; it's the desire for mimesis, the willingness to acknowledge and encourage the web of similarities that, according to Benjamin, explains language to begin with. Just as Benjamin admits that mimesis can work 'only in connection with something alien as its basis: precisely the semiotic or communicative element of language', so Benveniste, whom we discussed earlier, acknowledges that we always depend on a system of lexis and grammar founded on convention, the semiotic structure of language.[222] But the conventions themselves, the differential system of signs, don't reach the objects of the world: for that, the available signs must be engaged by subjects with intentions and set in a context; they must become an 'instance of discourse'. The moment of reference is indeed a 'moment', a 'flashing up', as Benjamin calls it, and there's a genuine sense in which the meaningfulness and forcefulness of the sentence depends on the instantaneous animation of its parts in discourse.[223]

For Benveniste it is the operation of language, the self-reference of the 'I' in a moment of discourse that allows the speaker to *become* a subject for that instant; but he writes as if discourse itself is the engagement of signs by a subject with a purpose.[224] Benjamin, by contrast, describes the same discursive fact in different terms, as a response to a situation and a willingness to be engaged by it: the astrologer is not really thinking, but is 'like the addition of a third element [...] to the conjunction of two stars'; similarities are not neutral facts that subjects contingently discover, but, 'fundamentally, stimulants and awakeners of the mimetic faculty which answers them in man'.[225] You might say that while we choose to speak at any particular instance, we don't choose to be linguistic in the first place—for Benjamin that follows from a mimesis in which we participate, willingly or not.

One can therefore use language purposively—in aid of getting the salt or the drink or learning about the weather—but this merely disguises the true vocation of language. That emerges when philosophizing enforces disinterestedness, when translation shifts our attention from the symbolized onto the symbolizing, and when art affords language the breathing space it needs to manifest itself. The conviction that language as such shows itself most vividly in literary art is, of

---

[222] Benjamin, 'Doctrine of the Similar', 697.

[223] If one had the space and the intellectual fortitude, this could be compared with the language theory of Donald Davidson, who is similarly sceptical of claims for the centrality of convention and insistent that communication depends on a kind of momentary act of understanding—what he calls, interestingly, a convergence of passing theories—between two subjects. See, in particular his 'Communication and Convention' and 'A Nice Derangement of Epitaphs'.

[224] Émile Benveniste, 'Subjectivity in Language', *Problems in General Linguistics*, 223–30.

[225] Benjamin, 'Doctrine of the Similar', 696, 695.

course, hardly unique to Benjamin: it's the fundamental plank not only of Formalist theory, which we discussed above, but also of the expressivist philosophy of language that flourished just before Benjamin, in the work of writers like Karl Vossler and Benedetto Croce. But Croce thinks of art in Romantic terms, as subjective self-expression, and his account of language follows suit.[226] Benjamin's paradigm is decidedly avant-garde and modern: 'To interrupt the course of the world—that was Baudelaire's deepest intention.'[227] The immediacy of mimesis, asserted in avant-garde art or the 'awakening' of the *Arcades Project*'s dialectical images, acts as a check on the purposive, instrumental, 'progressive' movement of ordinary discourse.

Axel Honneth has argued that Benjamin, in his final works, uses the experience of reality as magical and animated—mythical and mimetic—as a model for communication with the suffering, morally wronged victims of the past. Benjamin, he claims, aspires to 'a historiography that can disclose the past in such a way that the dead victims assume anew the form of animated beings'.[228] This is a shrewd and persuasive reading of the theses in Benjamin's 'On the Concept of History' (1940), which try to tie neatly together the force of dialectical images with the revolutionary project. There he characterizes the historical materialist as the one who can grasp 'a memory as it flashes up in a moment of danger', which is possible because 'like every generation that preceded us, we have been endowed with a *weak* messianic power, a power on which the past has a claim'.[229] But as Honneth notes, the project seems to fall short of the revolutionary promises Benjamin has made. At best the redemptive re-animating of history's victims offers them 'recognition' and moral standing rather than relief from past injustice. And if one hopes that the awakening of the past, the exercise of the weak messianic power, *leads* to political revolution (because it's the memory of enslaved ancestors that inspire the latter), then one instrumentalizes their suffering, and the coupling of past and present becomes a moment in the 'course of the world' rather than its interruption.

In Benjamin's later writings, divine justice finds its creaturely heir in the insurrectionist Louis-Auguste Blanqui, a revolutionary distinguished by his insatiable appetite for uprisings, his stoic ability to survive terms in prison, and his complete lack of interest in planning for the socialist future. In the *Arcades Project* he is explicitly twinned with Baudelaire, for both have as their aim the interruption of the course of the world—the first through writing, the second through insurrectionary action. 'The activity of a professional revolutionary such as Blanqui', Benjamin observes, 'does not presuppose any faith in progress; it presupposes only the determination to do away with present injustice.'[230] Blanqui's insurrection is divorced from any concern with the future at all, with the design or institutionalization of a better society; it's the modern version of divine violence.

---

[226] See Benedetto Croce, *Aesthetic as Science of Expression and General Linguistic*, trans. Douglas Ainslie (London: Macmillan & Co., 1909): 'Aesthetic and Linguistic, in so far as they are true sciences, are not two different sciences, but one single science' (234).
[227] Benjamin, *Arcades Project*, J50, 2 (318).
[228] Honneth, 'A Communicative Disclosure of the Past', 92.
[229] Benjamin, 'On the Concept of History', theses VI (391) and II (390).
[230] Benjamin, *Arcades Project*, J61a, 3 (339).

The split between divine and political is formalized in a disputed text of Benjamin's, the 'Theological-Political Fragment', written—according to Adorno and the editors of the English *Selected Writings*—around 1938, or—according to Scholem and the German editor Rolf Tiedemann—around 1920–1. The fragment may as well have been titled 'Theological-Political Fragmentation', for it suggests that all attempts to cash out the idea of divine justice in earthly institutions are doomed. Politics has one job—to strive for 'an eternal and total passing away', the eternally transient condition of happiness—and theology another (the erection of the Divine, just, Kingdom).[231] The contribution of the latter to the former can only be destructive and interruptive, while the former can urge the latter along asymptotically, but not directly.

We might therefore conclude by saying that while Benjamin allies language as such with the sphere of justice, he opposes both to 'institutions as such'. Language, as the immediate bearer of spirit, divine or otherwise, cannot be used to build anything in the world. To that extent Saussure's claim, borrowed from Whitney, that language is 'a social institution' would seem absurd to Benjamin: the social remains a sphere of demonic powers, occasionally interrupted by art and revolutionary violence. One interesting implication of this view is that language can be intersubjective in relation to the past—the dead for whom injustice must be redeemed, the writing on Paris that is rescued through Benjamin's commentary on it—but not in the present. Benjamin's conception of a 'just' present retains a mythic immediacy, as if communities were bound by the sacred and politics itself were corrupting. That would allow us to add Benjamin's anarchism to the list of movements that Pierre Rosanvallon claims strive for a wholly transparent social order, devoid of actual political debate and struggle.[232] Should we be surprised, then, that the moment when politics as intersubjectivity and discussion is explicitly broached in Benjamin's work is when he takes up the *technological* mediation of human culture, in the famous essay on 'The Work of Art in the Age of its Technological Reproducibility'?[233] For that is the text in which he most strikingly breaks with myth and ritual.

Benjamin's anarchism was not merely a consequence of theological conviction: there were actual revolutionaries and revolutionary theorists who believed in the revolution as an 'unalloyed means', that is, as an end in itself. Blanqui was one. Another, whose works Benjamin read in the run-up to his 'Critique of Violence'

---

[231] Walter Benjamin, 'Theological-Political Fragment', in *Selected Writings, Vol. 3*, 306. The dating is discussed on 306n1. Michael W. Jennings, the editor of the *Selected Writings*, has elsewhere pointed out that the term 'messianic' disappears from Benjamin's vocabulary between 1921 and 1938, and that its reappearance is triggered by Benjamin's reading of Scholem's *Major Trends in Jewish Mysticism*: see his 'The Will to Apokatastasis: Media, Experience and Eschatology in Benjamin's Late Theological Politics', in Colby Dickinson and Stéphane Symons (eds.), *Walter Benjamin and Theology* (New York: Fordham University Press, 2016), 93–109.

[232] In the essays, 'Revolutionary Democracy', 'The Market, Liberalism, and Anti-Liberalism', and 'Marx and Civil Society' (in *Democracy Past and Future*), Rosanvallon describes how Jacobinism, liberal political economy, and communism respectively imagine it is possible to avoid politics by means of a transparent form of social association.

[233] Walter Benjamin, 'The Work of Art in the Age of its Technological Reproducibility (Second Version)', in *Selected Writings, Vol. 3*, 101–33.

and some other unrealized plans for political writing, was Georges Sorel, critic of parliamentarianism and advocate for the myth of the General Strike.

Sorel was invested, like Benjamin, in the idea of a revolutionary image, more precisely, in the idea that 'image' and myth itself had a revolutionary force absent from discursive language. But he didn't invest these energies in a theory of language as such. The confrontation between the power of myth and the complexities of language took place in the writings of a very different revolutionary, Antonio Gramsci. We should briefly explore this intersection, the final attempt to corral the power of myth in revolutionary language, before moving back to the myth-busters across the Channel.

Excursus
Reversing Out—Sorel's Heroic Myth, Gramsci's Slow Magic

In a prison note devoted to Georges Sorel, the Italian Communist leader Antonio Gramsci enumerated 'all of Sorel's merits and all his flaws: he is tortuous, rambling, incoherent, superficial, profound, etc., but he provides or suggests original viewpoints, he discovers unthought-of connections, he compels one to think and to probe'.[1] It's a characteristically shrewd assessment of one of the Left's most eccentric figures by one of its most sober and careful ones. Sorel had been an enthusiastic and then disillusioned Dreyfusard, who then reacted strongly against parliamentary socialism, championed the cause of revolutionary syndicalism, briefly became a Royalist, and ended his days an enthusiastic supporter of the Bolshevik cause (and that is just a selection of his enthusiasms). His *Reflections on Violence*, a book edition of articles first published in 1908, which promoted the myth of the General Strike, inspired Benjamin as well as many activists on the Left, but was also admired by Mussolini and was selected by none other than T. S. Eliot as an exemplar of the classicist tendency in modern thought.[2]

No other twentieth-century writer, however, makes the case for the importance of political myth with the same panache or conviction. For just as Benjamin insists that only awakening guarantees the revolutionary nature of his discourse, so Sorel believes that myth is not merely a weapon or instrument of proletarian insurrection, but is its very substance. And though this myth is made from and in language, at the same time it is language's antithesis. Sorel was a writer, not a painter, but, again like Benjamin, he comes to the conclusion that in writing one must create an 'image' rather than a discursive argument. The first leads to revolution, the second only to parliamentary wrangling and compromise. In a nutshell:

> Thanks to these men, we know that the general strike is indeed what I have said: the *myth* in which socialism is wholly comprised, i.e. a body of images capable of evoking instinctively all the sentiments which correspond to the different manifestations of the war undertaken by socialism against modern society. Strikes have engendered in the proletariat the noblest, the deepest and the most moving sentiments that they

---

[1] Antonio Gramsci, *Prison Notebooks, Vol. II*, ed. and trans. Joseph A. Buttigieg (New York: Columbia University Press, 1996), Notebook 4, §31 (168).
[2] T. S. Eliot, 'The Idea of a Literary Review', *The New Criterion* 4.1 (January 1926): 5.

possess; the general strike groups them all in a coordinated picture and, by bringing them together, gives to each one of them its maximum intensity; appealing to their painful memories of particular conflicts, it colours with an intense life all the details of the composition presented to consciousness. We thus obtain that intuition of socialism which language cannot give us with perfect clearness—and we obtain it as a whole, perceived instantaneously.[3]

A 'body of images', an 'intuition of socialism', a 'coordinated picture', a 'composition': the myth of the General Strike, which alone promises the victory of socialism, has no length, no development, no extension in time, no trace of dialogic interaction. All such discursive process is identified with the rhetorical edifice of parliamentary politics, for which Sorel has only boundless disdain. 'Advocates of the general strike', he proudly announced, 'turn their backs on the preoccupations of the liberals of the past: the tribunes' oratory, the moulding of public opinion, the coalition of political parties.'[4] In Sorel's theory, form and content, style and political orientation, are one.

Such a complete melding of radical politics and mythic expression demanded a fairly drastic restructuring of myth itself. Sorel did not, however, have to start from scratch: as Dan Edelstein has shown, he inherited an already modernized conception of myth from the nineteenth century. In Balzac and Baudelaire what had been, for centuries, a narrative drawn from the ancient past was reworked as a static, image-like construction, now orientated to the future.[5] To this Sorel added his reading of Vico, who had made myth respectable in the early eighteenth century and who had insisted that the poetic wisdom it embodied was a condition and substratum of all human language. Vico's contention that a heroic language cast in 'imaginative universals' was periodically revived gave Sorel confidence that myth was not merely an option, but a constant possibility within language, a possibility Vico had called *ricorso*, the 'rerunning' of an earlier moment in the development of human language, a return to its mythical, image-dependent roots.[6]

Vico's 'imaginative universals' were typically gods or heroic figures incarnating virtues or principles: Achilles, Hercules, Jove, and so on. The general strike, however, was not a heavenly presence, but an actual political event, pursued energetically by the syndicalist movement at the end of the nineteenth century and the beginning of the twentieth. The Belgian general strike of 1893, aimed at universal suffrage, had set the tone; it was followed by general strikes across Europe, in (among other

---

[3] Georges Sorel, *Reflections on Violence*, trans. T. E. Hulme and Jeremy Jennings (Cambridge: Cambridge University Press, 1999), 118.

[4] Georges Sorel, 'On the barbarism of revolution' [an extract from *Matériaux d'une théorie du prolétariat* (Paris 1919)], in Richard Vernon, *Commitment and Change: Georges Sorel and the Idea of Revolution* (Toronto: University of Toronto Press, 1978), 112.

[5] Dan Edelstein, 'The Modernization of Myth: From Balzac to Sorel', *Yale French Studies* 111 (2007): 32–44; see also Dan Edelstein, 'The Birth of Ideology from the Spirit of Myth: Georges Sorel among the *Idéologues*', in Joshua Landy and Michael Saler (eds.), *The Re-enchantment of the World: Secular Magic in a Rational Age* (Stanford, CA: Stanford University Press, 2009), 201–24.

[6] Sorel published his 'Étude sur Vico' in 1896 in the socialist journal *Le Devenir social*. On Vico's influence on Sorel see John L. Stanley, 'Sorel's Study of Vico: The Uses of the Poetic Imagination', *The European Legacy* 3.5 (1998): 17–34.

places) Dublin, Barcelona, St Petersburg, and Finland. Sorel thus proposes not to use the imagination to create new entities, but to change the register, so to speak, in which we perceive historical ones. In that respect, too, Sorel and Benjamin seem to move in parallel: they believe that revolutionary energies are unleashed when the revolutionary (in Benjamin's words) 'blast[s] open the continuum of history', removing historical facts from the dull nexus of cause and effect, so that they can be reconstituted as images that will inspire their readers to great things.[7]

In place, therefore, of calculation and strategy, of the entire apparatus of consequences Weber took such pains to emphasize, Sorel puts forward the mythic immediacy of popular will, in which there is no gap between the moment of willed action and the achievement of its goals. As an 'expression of [...] convictions', myth cannot be falsified: those who support the General Strike 'always picture their coming action in the form of images of battle in which their cause is certain to triumph'.[8] As Edelstein has pointed out, in the modern myth 'its mythical qualities depend instead on its "fatefulness", or seemingly necessary connection to a *future* order of affairs'.[9] Events themselves are thus reinterpreted as portents or harbingers, such that workers 'see in each strike a model, a test, a preparation for the great final upheaval', rather than an event with causes and consequences.[10] It therefore 'matters little whether the general strike is a partial reality or simply a product of the popular imagination'.[11]

'Their cause is certain to triumph': therein lies the mythic core of Sorel's conception. Mythic immediacy, the older sense in which the name was part of and master of the thing named, is translated here into the notion of 'certainty', which makes the image a part of the willed political event itself. That certainty is the key criterion of myth is made clear in one of Sorel's early treatments of political myth, in which, discussing some of Marx's disputed 'laws', Sorel wonders 'if one should treat the theories that the *savants* of socialism no longer want to accept but which militants regard as "axioms beyond dispute" as myths'.[12] Myths, he goes on to say, might be the form we choose for theories that 'do not wish to deceive themselves or take themselves for science' while being 'necessary for modern revolutionary action': theories which must be treated as certain, not so that they can be 'used' as propaganda, but because belief in them ensures their efficacy.[13] It's also manifest in his insistence that the General Strike has no political plan for what comes after: it must make its moves immediately. 'As experience conclusively shows,' Sorel notes, 'the revolution does not know the secret of the future but proceeds in the same manner as capitalism, exploiting every opening that presents itself.'[14]

---

[7] Benjamin, 'On the Concept of History', thesis XVI (396).
[8] Georges Sorel, 'Introduction: Letter to Daniel Halévy, 15 July 1907', in *Reflections on Violence*, 29, emphasis added.
[9] Edelstein, 'The Modernization of Myth', 42.   [10] Sorel, *Reflections on Violence*, 110.
[11] Sorel, *Reflections on Violence*, 117.
[12] Georges Sorel, *Introduction à l'économie moderne*, 2nd edn. (Paris: G. Jacques, 1922), 376–7.
[13] Sorel, *Introduction*, 377.   [14] Sorel, 'On the barbarism of revolution', 114.

Such certainty requires outcomes painted in black and white, not shades of grey: victory or defeat in a great battle, not the measurable consequences of a social policy or initiative. Part and parcel of political myth is therefore the 'cleavage between the classes', in which the certainty of the proletariat separates itself completely from all institutionalized politics.[15]

How could the great theorist of 'wars of position', Antonio Gramsci, have the least sympathy for this? Interestingly enough, Gramsci's own belief in the institutional basis of the revolutionary process, in its complex layering, may have been derived directly from linguistics. For while most of the writers we've examined imported social and political ideas into conceptions of language as such, Gramsci put the gears into reverse: he took ideas from linguistics and imported them into social and political thought. That, at least, is the well-known argument of Franco Lo Piparo, Derek Boothman, Luigi Rosiello, and Tullio De Mauro, who claim that Gramsci's key political concepts emerge when ideas current in the Italian school of neolinguistics—which Gramsci absorbed as a young researcher—were transferred into the political field.[16]

Gramsci was, indeed, a rare creature and if he had not existed the present study would have tried to invent him. He would become leader of the Italian Communist Party and the most significant Marxist political thinker after Lenin, but from the beginning of his short life to the end 'language' remained an object of the utmost importance to him. At the University of Turin he immediately became a favourite of Matteo Bartoli, the linguist who was pioneering neolinguistics as an alternative to Neogrammarianism. Gramsci was charged with transcribing some of Bartoli's lectures and provided him with information about the Sardinian dialects he had grown up with (and which, by all accounts, he used throughout his life whenever possible).[17] Gramsci, however, ended his studies in 1918, turning to journalism and political organizing. Many years later, while in prison, he would express regret that he had disappointed Bartoli, who had expected him to become 'the archangel sent to destroy the neo-grammarians once and for all'.[18] But while he never completed his degree, nor a planned thesis in linguistics, he continued to engage systematically with questions about language. Alessandro Carlucci has observed that Gramsci was in Russia (and able to read Russian) at the very moments—1922-3 and 1925—when the debates we discussed in Chapter 4, on Saussure and linguistic politics, were at their height.[19] After 1926, when Gramsci was in prison, his

---

[15] Sorel, *Reflections on Violence*, 178.
[16] See Franco Lo Piparo, 'The Linguistic Roots of Gramsci's Non-Marxism', in Peter Ives and Rocco Lacorte (eds.), *Gramsci, Language, and Translation* (Lanham, MD: Lexington Books, 2010), 19–28. Lo Piparo makes the extreme case that the concept of hegemony is derived from the idea, central to neolinguistics, that linguistic features spread through the 'irradiation of prestige', i.e., when features used by social groups with prestige are imitated by groups in contact with them.
[17] Derek Boothman, 'Gramsci's Interest in Language: The Influence of Bartoli's *Dispense di glottologia* (1912–13) on the *Prison Notebooks*', *Journal of Romance Studies* 12.3 (2012): 10–23.
[18] Gramsci, Letter to Tania Schucht, 19 March 1927, in Antonio Gramsci, *Letters from Prison*, trans. Lynne Lawner (London: Jonathan Cape, 1975), 80.
[19] Alessandro Carlucci, *Gramsci and Languages: Unification, Diversity, Hegemony* (Chicago: Haymarket Books, 2014), 83–8.

reading included not only works of history and political theory but books on linguistics. Linguistics appears as a topic throughout the prison notebooks and is the sole focus of the final one, Notebook 29, composed in 1935 and titled 'Notes for an Introduction to the Study of Grammar'.[20]

Gramsci engaged with questions about language, but particularly with 'the language question', which could be summarized as: 'now that Italy is formed, how can the Italian language be created?'[21] The severe regionalism of Italy had been a pressing political and cultural issue since the Risorgimento. In the early twentieth century Italians still typically spoke and wrote in local idioms—call them dialects or languages as you wish—and often had a shaky grasp of 'standard' Italian itself (Giulio Lepschy suggests that Italian was not a first language for anyone until the 1950s; as of 1996 only 50 per cent of the population used it in conversation with colleagues and friends).[22] The European nations formed in the eighteenth and nineteenth centuries assumed a shared national language was part of the standard kit of nationhood, but in creating one they had to decide what its form would be, how it would be encouraged and spread, and what its relationship to an existing mass of dialects would be.

The novelist Alessandro Manzoni had tried his hand at solving the problem in the early nineteenth century, when he, in a phrase Gramsci quotes, 'rinsed his personal Lombard-influenced vocabulary in the River Arno', i.e., replaced Milanese with Florentine words in the 1840 reworking of his novel *I promessi sposi*; in 1868 he would head a commission that concluded that Italy needed an army of Tuscan teachers to spread the Florentine dialect.[23] Graziadio Isaia Ascoli, a fierce late nineteenth-century opponent of Neogrammarianism, disputed the efficacy and logic of this statist solution. While not doubting the need for a national idiom, Ascoli argued that it should evolve as the spontaneous product of increasingly dense national connections in communication and commerce. Gramsci would cite Ascoli's position in a polemic with Socialist proponents of Esperanto in 1918: 'the Italian language was being formed by itself and would be formed only in so far as the shared life of the nation gave rise to numerous and stable contacts between the various parts of the nation'.[24]

This kind of bottom-up, civil society approach to language change seems, in its form and timing, wholly antithetical to the immediate organizing force of political myth. But Ascoli was not the only linguistic source on which Gramsci drew. His teacher, Bartoli, had pioneered the neolinguistic, or areal linguistic, approach to

---

[20] As recorded in Gianni Francioni's account of the structure and composition of the Notebooks, *L'Officina Gramsciana: Ipotesi sulla struttura dei 'Quaderni del carcere'* (Naples: Bibliopolis, 1984), 146.
[21] Antonio Gramsci, 'A Single Language and Esperanto' [1918], in *Selections from Cultural Writings*, 26.
[22] Giulio Lepschy, *Mother Tongues and Other Reflections on the Italian Language* (Toronto: University of Toronto Press, 2002), 20, 41–4.
[23] Gramsci, *Selections from Cultural Writings*, Notebook 23, §40 (172).
[24] Gramsci, 'A Single Language and Esperanto', 28. On Gramsci's debt to Ascoli see Luigi Rosiello, 'Linguistics and Marxism in the Thought of Antonio Gramsci', 29–49 and Tullio De Mauro, 'Language from Nature to History: More on Gramsci the Linguist', 51–62, both in Ives and Lacorte, *Gramsci, Language, and Translation*.

the analysis of linguistic change. It argued that linguistic innovations spread—that is, were imitated—by 'irradiating' from centres of social and political power, when the source of the innovation had a prestige or social authority that encouraged others to imitate it.[25] Gramsci would use the idea as a model for political leadership. As Lo Piparo has pointed out, in a 1919 article Gramsci argued that the Socialist Party (the Italian Communist Party had not yet split from the Socialists), could be 'an incorporeal government that is transmitted through millions and millions of spiritual links; it is an irradiation of prestige'.[26] It's a precise application of a linguistic concept to a political problem.[27]

Was the interest in Sorel, then, a minor episode or passing enthusiasm? Not at all, for Gramsci imagines his political-intellectual project in terms inspired by Sorel. In the first note, from 1932, where Gramsci proposes the plan for a text entitled 'The Modern Prince', he says the following of the Machiavelli book that serves as his exemplar:

> Machiavelli's *Prince* could be studied as a historical example of the Sorelian "myth", that is, of a political ideology that is not presented as a cold utopia or as a rationalized doctrine but as a concrete "fantasy" that works on a dispersed and shattered people to arouse and organize its collective will.[28]

The modern Prince—the thing—will be the Communist Party; 'The Modern Prince'—the text—will establish the party as myth, that is, as the local god or daemon of political action.

This magical, mythical element of politics cannot, however, do its work in the instantaneous, immediate fashion Sorel imagines. In a note on Croce and Sorel, Gramsci observes that '[p]olitical will must have some other mainspring besides passion'.[29] Discussing *The Prince*, he claims that myth only works immediately, is only a directly effective catalyst for political action, when that action, 'is a "defensive" rather than creative type of action [...] based on the assumption that an already existing "collective will" has dispersed, lost its nerve, and needs to be regrouped and reinforced'.[30] For the kind of political innovation Gramsci has in mind, however, there is no royal road, no by-pass around the 'formidable complex of trenches and fortifications' Gramsci famously identified with the long-term ideological war of position.[31]

---

[25] About half a century later the American sociolinguist William Labov would propose something quite similar: phonetic innovations would be picked up if and when those who adopted them had social prestige. See 'On the Mechanism of Linguistic Change', in *Sociolinguistic Patterns* (Philadelphia: University of Pennsylvania Press, 1972), 160–82.

[26] Antonio Gramsci, 'The Party and the Revolution', in *Selections from Political Writings (1910–1920)*, trans. John Mathews (London: Lawrence & Wishart, 1977), 143 (translation slightly altered). The passage is also quoted in Lo Piparo, 'The Linguistic Roots of Gramsci's Non-Marxism', 26.

[27] Lo Piparo has argued that Gramsci was not a Marxist, and that his political ideas are translations of linguistic concepts.

[28] Gramsci, *Prison Notebooks, Vol. III*, ed. and trans. Joseph A. Buttigieg (New York: Columbia University Press, 2007) Notebook 8, §21 (246–7).

[29] Gramsci, *Prison Notebooks III*, Notebook 7, §39 (190).

[30] Gramsci, *Prison Notebooks III*, Notebook 8, §21 (247).

[31] Gramsci, *Prison Notebooks II*, Notebook 3, §49 (53).

The 'most notable and dynamic part' of this complex 'is the press in general: publishing houses (which have an implicit and explicit program and support a particular current); political newspapers; reviews of every kind—scientific, literary, philological, popular, etc.; various periodicals, including even parish bulletins'.[32] Dynamic: Gramsci, unlike Cassirer, understands how mythic passions might be built up through the mediation of cultural forms and he accordingly focuses relentlessly, in his prison years, on the contents of a striking variety of periodical publications (scientific, literary, philological, etc., although no parish bulletins, so far as I know). The relationship between press and public, however, has been made problematic in Gramsci. Gabriel Tarde, whom we have discussed a few times, described the journalist as someone who makes a collective, national force out of individually held sentiments. Hence the anti-Semite Drumont, enemy of Dreyfus, takes as his raw material anti-Semitism as a state of mind that was 'purely individual, with little intensity and even less contagion, unaware of itself' and creates from it 'a collective force, artificial perhaps, yet nonetheless real'.[33]

But things were not so simple in Italy, where, Gramsci complained, writers lacked a '"national educative" function: they have not and do not set themselves the problem of elaborating popular feelings after having relived them and made them their own'.[34] As a result, the Italian people 'feel more closely related to foreign intellectuals than to "domestic" ones' and their preferred reading is the secular, thoroughly nationalized literature that comes to them in translation from republican France.[35] For it is republican ideology and practice, not just conversation, which gives discourse the power of spontaneous attraction in France; Tarde's public is, in its form, already unified and nationalized. In Italy, by contrast, the public lacks the very medium in which it could become aware of itself. The Italian people are divided linguistically by dialect, Italian intellectuals are distant and cosmopolitan, and when the people attempt to articulate higher feelings, their only medium is an inflated 'operatic' style of expression, 'a theatrical rendering coupled with a baroque vocabulary'.[36] On this rocky and uneven terrain the cultivation of a collective will is difficult, if not impossible.

What France had in spades and Italy lacked, what Sorel detested and Gramsci thought essential was Jacobinism. Italy needed 'an effective "Jacobin" force—precisely the force that creates the national-popular collective will, the foundation of all modern states'.[37] But Jacobinism was more than the Communist's devotion to the hard and tedious slog of political organization: it was also 'intellectual and moral reform',[38] which entailed, Gramsci eventually concluded, the 'formation of a lively, expressive and at the same time sober and measured prose'.[39] To make the terrain

---

[32] Gramsci, *Prison Notebooks II*, Notebook 3, §49 (52–3).
[33] Tarde, 'The Public and the Crowd', 282.
[34] Gramsci, *Selections from Cultural Writings*, Notebook 21, §5 (207).
[35] Gramsci, *Selections from Cultural Writings*, Notebook 21, §5 (209).
[36] Gramsci, *Selections from Cultural Writings*, Notebook 14, §19 (380).
[37] Gramsci, *Prison Notebooks III*, Notebook 8, §21 (248).
[38] Gramsci, *Prison Notebooks III*, Notebook 8, §21 (249).
[39] Gramsci, *Selections from Cultural Writings*, Notebook 14, §72 (204).

of Italian public opinion arable, one had to establish a suitable linguistic medium in which the nation could converse.

It's Sorelian myth, but with a difference. For, on one hand, Gramsci identified the national-popular character of his desired form of Italian with the mythical and figurative side of language; while, on the other, he realizes this myth will be the endpoint of a long and complex political labour. Just as Sorel identified parliamentary reason with reformist treachery, so Gramsci sees the authoritarian side of liberalism in Manzonian proposals to unify Italian from above, by means of models and prescriptions. In Prison Notebook 29 (the one devoted to grammar), Gramsci, building on his earlier debt to Ascoli, remarks that while it makes sense to take steps to establish a unified national language, one mustn't 'imagine that the ends proposed will all be reached in detail, i.e. that one will obtain a *specific* unified language [...] What this language will be, one cannot foresee or establish.'[40] Planned interventions in a language can be more or less well thought out, rational in a tactical sense, but the actual path to a unified Italian depends upon establishing national channels of discourse—the press, education, conversation, and so on—that will, by means of 'a whole complex of molecular processes', nationalize the language in their own way.[41]

Gramsci's account of the 'diffusion of linguistic innovations' was clearly an elaboration of linguistic ideas he first encountered in Ascoli and Bartoli.[42] His originality lay in the conviction that a national-popular language would necessarily be an energetic language, and that an energetic language would necessarily be one in which myth played a central role. When Gramsci insisted that arguments addressed to the Italian people should be presented 'dramatically', avoiding 'cold ratiocination', he was not making a tactical point—as if the Italian people were incapable of abstract thought—but a point about the nature of political opinion.[43]

This might explain the kind and degree of attention Gramsci pays to Bukharin's *The Theory of Historical Materialism* (called the *Popular Manual* in the Prison Notebooks), a text to which Gramsci returns repeatedly. For the *Popular Manual* is not merely an abbreviated exposition of one kind of Soviet Marxism, but also a work of propaganda or popularization, and Gramsci appraises it as such, claiming that Bukharin aims at the wrong target and uses the wrong ammunition. So, Gramsci observes, Bukharin contrasts Marxism to other systematic philosophies, as if these were what stood in the way of the popular acceptance of Marxism, whereas his starting point should have been the 'critical analysis of the philosophy of common sense', that is, a critical approach to the existing, unsystematized ideas of his popular audience.[44] More striking, however, is an entry on the *Popular Manual* subtitled 'Metaphor and language', where Gramsci takes Bukharin to task

---

[40] Gramsci, *Selections from Cultural Writings*, Notebook 29, §3 (183).
[41] Gramsci, *Selections from Cultural Writings*, Notebook 29, §3 (183).
[42] Gramsci, *Selections from Cultural Writings*, Notebook 29, §3 (183).
[43] Gramsci, *Prison Notebooks III*, Notebook 8, §21 (249).
[44] Gramsci, 'Critical Notes on an Attempt at Popular Sociology', in *Selections from Prison Notebooks*, ed. and trans. Quintin Hoare and Geoffrey Nowell-Smith (London: Lawrence & Wishart, 1971), 419.

for calling attention to Marx's use of metaphor, as if such figures were poetic departures from rational argument. But, Gramsci insists:

> All language is metaphor, and it is metaphorical in two senses: it is a metaphor of the "thing" or "material and sensible object" referred to, and it is a metaphor of the ideological meanings attached to words in the preceding periods of civilization. [...] Language is transformed with the transformation of the whole of civilization, and it absorbs the words of previous civilizations and cultures as, precisely, metaphors. Nobody today thinks that "dis-aster" is related to astrology or claims to be misled about the views of those who use the word. The new metaphorical meaning spreads with the spread of the new culture, which moreover coins new words and gives a precise meaning to words acquired from other languages.[45]

It is precisely as mythic substitution and concentration that words arise, and they arise, and are remade, according to ideological needs, which means—for Gramsci—in accordance with the requirements and situations of a new kind of practice. There's a linguistic reference here, but it isn't, tellingly, to the usual suspects, Bartoli, Ascoli, or Croce: instead, Gramsci mentions the work of Michel Bréal, the linguist and Dreyfusard whose *Essai de Sémantique* made speakers the engine of linguistic change and innovation. To place semantics at the heart of linguistic change, was, in Bréal's view, to reveal its 'only true causes, which are human intelligence and will'.[46]

Bréal was proposing a thesis about language in general—Gramsci was thinking of what language would be like once it became the medium for national-popular collective will. Myth, in this context, itself stood for a practical, active moment in language, the moment when practical effort or energy produced a useful verbal instrument, so that the more engaged the public became, the more mythical its language would be. But this was a slow magic: not the lightning flash of the General Strike or the sudden *J'accuse!*, but the gradual construction of a style—lively, expressive, and at the same time sober and measured. It was magic adapted to the war of position that Gramsci thought was required in modern, complex, partly democratized nations, a steady and systematic struggle to conquer the various institutions of modern civil society and reshape them for the cause of the Left. More importantly, it was magic that was not filtered through the institutions of the press and the work of journalists, but created by them—in Tarde's apt words, 'a collective force, artificial perhaps, but nonetheless real'. It would owe its power to their mediation, because it was only through this writing, through the print media, that the collective would become aware of itself as a collective.

Lively, expressive, and at the same time sober and measured: the description of the style is also the description of the popular will it is supposed to embody, a will that blends mythic passions with a certain Weberian calculation. The democratic bloc Gramsci has in mind—which will have Communist leadership—requires both anger at injustice and a certain amount of self-distancing, the ability to grasp one's place in a political and social network. It is, finally, a formal description of the

---

[45] Gramsci, *Prison Notebooks III*, Notebook 7, §36 (187–8). [46] Bréal, *Semantics*, 6.

style and the will: not an account of specific political positions taken (which, in any case, Gramsci had to disguise), but of the medium within which popular-democratic politics would take place. Formal, but still political—because this lively and sober prose was meant to be contrasted with the baroque and 'operatic style of expression' that had made fascism possible and become its public face. If anyone had managed to make language an effective metonym, it was Gramsci.

8

High Anxiety, Becalmed Language
Ordinary Language Philosophy

(Wittgenstein, J. L. Austin)

In the preceding chapters myth has figured as the means by which some modern kind of collective will is created and maintained, whether that prospect is viewed with suspicion or enthusiasm. The contours and scale of that collective will vary from writer to writer: in Sorel it is the will of a class, in Gramsci (and, to a degree, in Shklovskii) something national-popular, in Ogden, Orwell, and Bakhtin, something national but demagogic, and in Benjamin and Khlebnikov something universal. But while it is always the vehicle for uniting some kind of political collective, it is not necessarily a principle of order. T. S. Eliot, Sorel's surprising supporter, famously called myth 'a way of controlling, of ordering, of giving a shape and a significance to the immense panorama of futility and anarchy which is contemporary history'; but Sorel himself saw it as the very way and means of anarchy.[1] As I've emphasized, some have regarded mythic entities and the passions they provoke with alarm, while others believed harnessing the power of myth was the only means by which modern people could be saved from fascism. It was, correspondingly, sometimes understood as a warping of language and sometimes as its magical secret.

What all these accounts of myth shared, however, was the conviction that what myth opposed was science: dry, rational, empirical argument. Science, in the shape of a 'science of symbolism' might be the necessary antidote to myth (Ogden); science, in the shape of sociology and parliamentary manoeuvring, might be the disease for which myth was the cure (Sorel); or science might be the force that pulls against myth, in a tug-of-war over the fate of language (Cassirer). The writers we've discussed for the most part shared Cassirer's characterization of the difference between the logical-conceptual mode of theoretical science and the mode of myth. In the latter, 'thought does not stand freely over against the content of intuition in order to refer and compare it to others in conscious reflection, rather here, it is, as it were, taken captive and held spellbound by this content as soon as it stands directly before it'.[2] Cassirer will describe the process by which myth is made from simple intuition as a '*thickening*', thereby contrasting it with the gossamer thinness

---

[1] T. S. Eliot, '*Ulysses*, Order, and Myth', in *Selected Prose of T. S. Eliot* (London: Faber and Faber, 1975), 177.
[2] Cassirer, 'Language and Myth', 159.

of objects in science, where '[e]verything individual is increasingly spun together [...] as if by invisible intellectual threads'.[3]

But what if it were science itself that generated mythical confusion? In the *Tractatus* Wittgenstein had suggested precisely that, by noting that 'people today stop at the laws of nature, treating them as something inviolable, just as God and Fate were treated in past ages'. After his 1929 return to Cambridge, the concern about science seemed to deepen. In his foreword to the material published as *Philosophical Remarks* (composed in 1929–30), Wittgenstein noted that the spirit of his book was 'different from the one which informs the vast stream of European and American civilization in which all of us stand'. '*That* spirit', he insisted, 'expresses itself in an onwards movement, in building ever larger and more complicated structures'; the alternative, which he was pursuing, expressed itself in 'striving after clarity and perspicuity in no matter what structure'.[4] In an earlier draft of the foreword he says that '[o]ur civilization is characterized by the word progress', which is 'its form'. In rejecting this, Wittgenstein is 'aiming at something different than are the scientists'.[5]

Progress and onwards movement were built into the functioning of science, necessary aspects of its structure, but Wittgenstein discusses these as expressions of a certain kind of 'spirit', which meant he, too, was thinking of a 'culture of science' and not just the actual practice. When this culture infected philosophers, when they thought of what they did as a kind of super-science, the result was the occult entities of metaphysics:

> Philosophers constantly see the method of science before their eyes, and are irresistibly tempted to ask and answer questions in the way science does. This tendency is the real source of metaphysics, and leads the philosopher into complete darkness.[6]

The classical form of this error was confusing philosophical statements with scientific ones and philosophical nouns with the names of things, such that one could ask questions like 'what is an object?' or 'does redness exist' as if they were empirical questions, open to investigation.

In fact, when confronted with the kind of thing Cassirer would have called mythology—the beliefs and practices of peoples outside the various forms of modernity—Wittgenstein turns the tables. Reading J. G. Frazer's notorious study of 'primitive' mythology, *The Golden Bough*, Wittgenstein defends the integrity and meaningfulness of these practices against Frazer's attempt to explain them 'scientifically'. You could, he comments, begin an anthropological study by looking at 'the life and behaviour of mankind throughout the world' and note that besides the basic biological functions, 'men also perform actions which bear a characteristic peculiar to themselves, and these could be called ritualistic actions'; but it would be 'nonsense for one to go on to say that the characteristic feature of *these* actions is the

---

[3] Cassirer, 'Language and Myth', 160, 159.
[4] Ludwig Wittgenstein, 'Foreword', *Philosophical Remarks*, 7.
[5] Wittgenstein, MS 109: 204, 6–7 November 1930, in *Culture and Value*, 9e.
[6] Wittgenstein, 'The Blue Book', 18.

fact that they arise from faulty views about the physics of things'.[7] The observation, made in 1931, will turn out to be significant: the actions which bear a 'characteristic peculiar to them' will soon be the elements of 'language games', a category which will eventually absorb the practice of science itself. When Wittgenstein selects from and orders his various post-1929 remarks for the 'Big Typescript' in 1933, he'll draw on his Frazer notes to make the case that an 'entire mythology is laid down in our language', but the exemplar of that mythology will be Frazer's modern language, not the supposedly primitive language of those he studies.[8]

It's the metaphysician who is captivated by the feeling that his or her objects—the proposition, thought, language, etc.—are something 'remarkable', 'unique', harbouring 'a peculiar depth', who believes naming is 'a *strange* connection of a word with an object'; in everyday discourse, by contrast, words work not by a mysterious attachment to things, but by being geared or meshed with one another, hooking onto reality indirectly.[9] And just as the mythical thinker thickens an ordinary object and so makes it sacred, so the metaphysical thinker is accused of taking the serviceable, ordinary word and employing it in such a way as to give it a false depth, a 'nimbus'.[10]

All that said, there is something different about the affective register in which Wittgenstein's mythology circulates. Cassirer's myth deals in awe and fear; Sorel's with feelings of sublime confidence. From the 1930s onwards Wittgenstein says metaphysical puzzles arouse in us 'deep disquietudes'; they trouble us, make us dissatisfied, uneasy, and 'profoundly anxious'.[11] At first glance this kind of dissatisfaction is bound to appear muted, philosophical, even professional, in comparison with the other passions aroused by myth. But the disquiet of metaphysics is called 'deep' for a reason, and the anxiety is profound rather than passing. Whatever the *Tractatus*'s conception of philosophy, it presented itself as the solution to intellectual problems, problems that had remained unsolved because 'the logic of our language is misunderstood'.[12] As James Klagge has pointed out, it had a self-consciously 'esoteric' air, assuming that only 'someone who has himself already had the thoughts that are expressed in it'—a small contingent of like-minded intellectuals—would understand it.[13] There's a dramatic shift in the way Wittgenstein characterizes resistance to his arguments after 1929. It's not just that now he figures himself as swimming against the tide of science-driven civilization. It's that the obstacles that stand in the way of clarity are no longer intellectual: 'What has to be overcome is not a difficulty of the intellect, but of the will'; the difficulty attending philosophy is not 'the intellectual difficulty of the sciences, but the difficulty of a change of

---

[7] Wittgenstein, 'Remarks on Frazer's *Golden Bough*', in *Philosophical Occasions, 1912–1951*, 129.
[8] Wittgenstein, *Big Typescript*, 317e.
[9] Wittgenstein, *Philosophical Investigations*, §93 (48e), §95 (48e), §89 (46e), §38 (23e).
[10] Wittgenstein, *Philosophical Investigations*, §97 (49e).
[11] Wittgenstein, *Philosophical Investigations*, §111 (52e); *Big Typescript*, 307e.
[12] Wittgenstein, *Tractatus*, Preface, 3.
[13] Wittgenstein, *Tractatus*, Preface, 3. James C. Klagge, 'Wittgenstein and his Audience: Esotericist or Evangelist?', in Nuno Venturinha (ed.), *The Textual Genesis of Wittgenstein's* Philosophical Investigations (London: Routledge, 2013), 52–64.

attitude'.[14] Attitude and will are ethical phenomena—the temptations that lead us into philosophical darkness are a matter of 'what most people *want* to see' (Wittgenstein will frequently signpost the road to perdition with 'We are tempted to say...').[15] The anxiety and discomfort that accompany linguistic mythology are not psychological irritants, but signs of ethical distress.

To relieve this anxiety a philosopher has to show us *that* 'language works', by showing us *how* 'language works'. They must describe how the phrase, word, or expression that's causing trouble is used, which Wittgenstein calls its 'grammar', and the relief comes not from learning that we were misusing the expression, but from learning that it has a grammar in the first place. Describing the method of his middle period philosophy, Wittgenstein asks himself why 'establishing a rule [for the use of the word, KH] helps us. Why it calms us after we have been so profoundly anxious.'[16] At different points the experience is compared to the relief afforded to an ascetic carrying a heavy ball who is set free when someone tells him to drop it or to 'show[ing] the fly the way out of the fly-bottle'.[17] Somewhat more dramatically, Wittgenstein claims that our problems are solved by 'the redeeming word'—*das erlösende Wort*—that frees us from the unease and frustration of a self-imposed burden.[18] But in every case we are made less anxious not because we learn the 'correct' use of an expression, but because to do so we must acknowledge the peculiar kind of order that characterizes language: '(Instead of turbulent conjectures and explanations, we want the calm ascertaining of linguistic facts.)'.[19] As we'll see, while the boundaries of this order blur and expand throughout the 1930s, its role, as testimony to the fact that language works, remains the same.

Wittgenstein's talk of anxiety and relief has fuelled the belief that his philosophy after 1929 (and maybe even before) is therapeutic in character: its goal is not a distinctive philosophical theory or doctrine, but merely the dissolution of the anxiety-creating urge to do philosophy. As Wittgenstein would say in the section of the *Philosophical Investigations* devoted to method, 'The real discovery is the one that enables me to break off philosophizing when I want to.'[20] On this reading, philosophy doesn't provide a theory of meaning or language; it simply illuminates what we mean by calling attention to how we use various words.[21] The therapeutic

---

[14] Wittgenstein, *Big Typescript*, 300e.   [15] Wittgenstein, *Big Typescript*, 300e.
[16] Wittgenstein, *Big Typescript*, 307e.
[17] Wittgenstein, *Philosophical Investigations*, §309 (110e).
[18] The redeeming word makes several appearances in Wittgenstein's writings. In a somewhat different translation: 'Everything we do consists in trying to find the liberating word'; from notes of a discussion on 2 January 1930 (with Schlick and Waismann), published in *Wittgenstein and the Vienna Circle*, 77. The phrase would reappear in *The Big Typescript*, 302e. Interestingly, Wittgenstein uses this same phrase in his early notebooks on logic as early as November 1914, on which see Ilse Somavilla, 'Wittgenstein's Coded Remarks in the Context of His Philosophizing', in Nuno Venturinha (ed.), *Wittgenstein After His Nachlass* (Basingstoke: Palgrave Macmillan, 2010), 41–2. In the available translation of the notebooks, the phrase appears as 'The key word', *Notebooks 1914–1916*, 39e.
[19] Wittgenstein, *Big Typescript*, 316e. The sentence apparently made it into the first version of the *Philosophical Investigations*, composed in late 1936, but disappeared thereafter.
[20] Wittgenstein, *Philosophical Investigations*, §133 (57e).
[21] For a brief description of the division between the 'therapeutic' school of Wittgenstein interpretation and the 'theory' school, see Stern, *Wittgenstein's* Philosophical Investigations, 29–37.

interpretation, however, misses something: what I called in Chapter 3 the melancholy pleasure Wittgenstein takes in conjuring up examples, articulating rules and establishing '*complete* clarity'.[22] The relief afforded by philosophy is not just the cessation of anxiety—it's a positive pleasure. Wittgenstein conceded as much when he sheepishly admitted to Rush Rhees that '[i]n my book I say that I am able to leave off with a problem in philosophy when I want to. But that's a lie; I can't.'[23] The problem is not that Wittgenstein never makes the discovery that allows him to stop doing philosophy when he wants to—the problem is that, when all is said and done, Wittgenstein never wants to stop doing philosophy. In this context, nothing seems more apt than Stanley Cavell's description of Wittgenstein's philosophizing as a 'resettlement of the everyday': it's a return to an existing and familiar order that both clarifies it and, if you will forgive the extravagant language, luxuriates in it.[24]

Analogies that worked could be *seen*: one of Wittgenstein's little dramatizations would reveal whether a particular analogy made sense or nonsense. How does one see a grammar? Thinking about how to describe the grammar of colours, Wittgenstein lit upon the example of the colour octahedron, in which the pure colours (red, green, yellow, blue) occupied the corners. 'Using the octahedron as a representation', he claimed in the *Philosophical Remarks*, 'gives us a *perspicuous* representation of the grammatical rules'—in this case, the rules that dictate that, for instance, something cannot be red and green at the same time.[25] *Übersichtliche Darstellung*: the 'perspicuous' or 'surveyable representation' that is lauded in the *Philosophical Investigations* as 'of fundamental significance for us', because it defines the distinct 'way we represent things, how we look at matters'.[26] It's lauded in the *Philosophical Investigations*—and everywhere else in Wittgenstein's *oeuvre* as well, which has led to a great variety of English translations: 'perspicuous representation', 'surveyable representation', 'clearly surveyable representation', and '*bird's eye view*'.[27]

The last translation—the one, as it happens, used in the translation of the *Philosophical Remarks*—is in some ways the most interesting and revealing, because it describes not just the quality of the seeing, but also the place from which the grammatical rules are seen. Does one grasp the grammar of an expression from above? Like so much else, it's a matter of dispute in Wittgenstein circles. Peter Hacker thinks grammar could be represented as a conceptual map or tabulation of rules, the interconnections of which would be made visible much as an ordinary

---

On why Wittgenstein doesn't have a theory of meaning as use, see Crary, 'Wittgenstein's Philosophy in Relation to Political Thought'.

[22] Wittgenstein, *Philosophical Investigations*, §133 (56e).
[23] Quoted in Stern, *Wittgenstein's* Philosophical Investigations, 53.
[24] Stanley Cavell, 'The Uncanniness of the Ordinary', in *In Quest of the Ordinary: Lines of Skepticism and Romanticism* (Chicago: University of Chicago Press, 1988), 176.
[25] Wittgenstein, *Philosophical Remarks*, 52. Translation modified, for reasons that will soon become clear.
[26] Wittgenstein, *Philosophical Investigations*, §122 (55e).
[27] Translations from Wittgenstein, *Philosophical Investigations*, 3rd edn. trans. G. E. M. Anscombe (Oxford: Basil Blackwell, 1967), §122; *Big Typescript*, 307e; *Big Typescript* 306e; *Philosophical Remarks*, 52. All further references to the *Philosophical Investigations* are, as earlier, to the 4th edition, in which Anscombe's translation and editing have been revised by Peter Hacker and Joachim Schulte.

map makes the relationship of one road, one geographical feature to another, visible. So, for example, a perspicuous grammar would show us that while 'running' and 'swimming' are generally analogous, they cannot be used in the same way as 'pondering' or 'considering'. But as Beth Savickey rightly points out, Wittgenstein's metaphors don't support this sense of perspective: when Wittgenstein discusses how he comes to see things, he prefers, to use a military distinction, 'ass in the grass' to 'eye in the sky'.[28] In the *Philosophical Investigations* he characterizes himself as a guide through a tangle of streets, working out the urban geography by hit and miss, and in the work's Preface he describes the remarks as 'sketches of landscapes which were made in the course of these long and meandering journeys'.[29] The clarifying gaze seems to remain at street level.

The problem is exacerbated by an important shift in what grammar itself governs. The *Tractatus*, you'll recall, had had problems with intentional propositions—statements of belief and wishing—but once Wittgenstein substituted the grammar of everyday language for the logic of scientific propositions statements about expecting, believing, and wishing were as ripe for investigation as any other. In fact, one of the striking features of Wittgenstein's middle and late works is the degree to which intersubjective statements become the preferred objects of discussion: the statements analysed in the *Philosophical Investigations* are statements made in teaching, statements expressing pain, statements about expecting or believing, and so on. Even when the discussion is of something as apparently neutral as the identification of colours, there is a marked change. In the *Tractatus* the identification of colour is objectivistic: there is a piece of paper and one says 'for each point on the sheet, whether it is black or white'.[30] In the *Philosophical Investigations*, we have a shopkeeper at §1 selling someone red apples, someone telling someone else 'That is called "sepia"' at §30, and someone exclaiming 'How blue the sky is!' at §275. The instance of discourse of which Benveniste spoke, the markers that hook a statement onto an intersubjective exchange, are ever-present. More than merely present: Wittgenstein's private language argument in §243–§271 of the *Philosophical Investigations*—where, for example, he discusses why we want to say things like 'Another person can't have my pains'—is focused precisely on how the instance of discourse, the requirements of the intersubjective exchange, sculpts our use of pronouns, deictic expressions, and the like.

Wittgenstein asks us to imagine such instances of discourse, so that we can determine what, in a working language—for Wittgenstein, of course, there is no other kind—is grammatical and what not. In the 'Big Typescript' he suggests that the endpoint of these investigations should be a picture of 'language and a grammar *as* a calculus, i.e. as a process that follows fixed rules'.[31] Given this, the philosopher's job is 'to remove the confusions and anxieties that stem from the difficulty of seeing the system all at a glance [*übersehen*]' by, roughly speaking, showing which analogies

---

[28] Beth Savickey, 'Wittgenstein and Hacker: Übersichtliche Darstellung', *Nordic Wittgenstein Review* 3.2 (2014): 99–123.

[29] Wittgenstein, 'Preface', *Philosophical Investigations*, 3e.

[30] Wittgenstein, *Tractatus*, 4.063. [31] Wittgenstein, *Big Typescript*, 203e.

make sense, which don't, and how they connect.[32] This 'calculus' conception of language, as it's been called, fits neatly with the 'bird's eye view' translation of *übersichtliche Darstellung*.

The problem with this conception is that the encounter with the rulebook, with the tabulation or map, is itself an intersubjective instance of discourse: we need rules to help us understand how to use these apparently objectified rules. Wittgenstein notes: 'But I could also invent a game in which I play with the rules themselves [...] *In this case I have yet another game and not a metagame.*'[33] The issue will blossom into one of the most important and memorable sections of the *Philosophical Investigations*, the discussion of what it means to 'follow a rule'. In an earlier version of the discussion, contained in the 'Big Typescript', Wittgenstein will ask us to imagine the rulebook as a kind of table we consult when reading something, and then he will anticipate the philosopher who wants to know how we know the table is a table and how we will know how to apply its rules (and that what it contains *are* rules), which will lead Wittgenstein to remark:

> And if we remember "that the table doesn't force us" to use it this or that way, nor to use it in the same way every time, then it becomes clear to everybody that our use of the word "rule" and the word "game" vacillates. (Blurs as it approaches the edges.)[34]

The table of rules, the conceptual map, then, may work as a guide, but it is itself an intersubjective encounter, for which there must be a grammar—the grammar of maps and tables. And yet, despite these complications, we follow rules, and language works. 'The chain of reasons', Wittgenstein concludes, 'comes to an end—to its end within this game.'[35]

The tilt towards intersubjectivity thus puts pressure on the very idea of a grammar consisting of rules, which we can see in the transition from middle Wittgenstein to late Wittgenstein, from the texts of the early 1930s (*Philosophical Remarks*, the 'Big Typescript', *Philosophical Grammar*, maybe the Blue and Brown Books) to the *Philosophical Investigations*. One might say: Wittgenstein knows that language works, but he is not quite sure why it works. It's not surprising, therefore, that even in the 'Big Typescript' there are hints of a complementary view of language, sometimes called 'anthropological', in which the rules are not systematic, in which they are bounded and secured in the end, not by other rules, but by what Wittgenstein eventually calls 'forms of life' (a concept which makes its debut in Wittgenstein in 1937).[36] At one point in the 'Big Typescript' Wittgenstein will conclude, after much toing and froing, that 'language functions as language only by virtue of the rules we follow in using it' and that, therefore, if a new sign is invented, 'a system, a rule, has to be invented'.[37] This appears to give 'language' itself sharp borders and definite criteria; but roughly a page later he will note that one can mean something by simply

---

[32] Wittgenstein, *Big Typescript*, 203e.
[33] Wittgenstein, *Wittgenstein and the Vienna Circle*, 120–1.
[34] Wittgenstein, *Big Typescript*, 140e.   [35] Wittgenstein, *Big Typescript*, 139e.
[36] The 'anthropological view' is described as such in Mauro Luiz Engelmann, *Wittgenstein's Philosophical Development*, 148–70.
[37] Wittgenstein, *Big Typescript*, 151e.

shrugging one's shoulders. How would we know the shrugging was *meant*? Not because some feeling or experience accompanied it (the usual explanation): 'Isn't it rather the entire *context* in which the movement is situated? What follows from it, so to speak'.[38] Rules are not mentioned in the brief discussion of this possible language of gestures that follows, although Wittgenstein will admit that 'shrugging one's shoulders is not so very different from a word, indeed a sentence'.[39] He'll stop the conceptual bleeding by claiming that '*primarily* it is the apparatus of our language, our word-language, that we call language; and only then do we call other things language, depending on their analogy or comparability to word-language' (even the word 'language' has rules for use).[40]

AN ART OF SEEING SENTENCES

There is, nevertheless, a significant moment when Wittgenstein takes flight. It's in August 1930, when he has been describing how art gives us a detailed and exalted view of the world. His friend Engelmann has told him how sometimes, rummaging around in a drawer, he looks at the manuscripts he has written and finds them 'glorious'; at other times they seem ordinary. Wittgenstein compares this to something he would find remarkable: 'seeing someone who thinks himself unobserved engaged in some quite simple everyday activity', or perhaps a theatrical version of the same—'surely', he says, 'this would be at once uncanny and wonderful'.[41] When Engelmann thinks his manuscripts splendid, 'he is seeing his life as God's work of art, & as such it is certainly worth contemplating, as is every life & everything whatever'.[42] '[O]nly the artist', he continues, 'can represent the individual thing so that it appears to us as a work of art'. Although, as it turns out, it is not only the artist who exalts the world and makes it wonderful:

> But now it seems to me too that besides the work of the artist there is another through which the world may be captured sub specie aeterni. It is—as I believe—the way of thought which as it were flies above the world and leaves it just as it is, contemplating it from above in its flight.[43]

A way of thought which leaves the world just as it is, but which sees it from above and under the sign of eternity: isn't this the bird's eye view of philosophy? In an article extolling the virtues of the calculated, yet naturalistic photographic practice of Jeff Wall, Michael Fried has suggested that this vision of art anticipates Wall's photography and that the way of thought Wittgenstein describes as artistic prefigures the idea of a 'perspicuous representation'.[44] In fact, it need not prefigure it:

---

[38] Wittgenstein, *Big Typescript*, 153e.   [39] Wittgenstein, *Big Typescript*, 155e.
[40] Wittgenstein, *Big Typescript*, 155e.
[41] Wittgenstein, MS 109: 28, 22 August 1930, in *Culture and Value*, 6e.
[42] Wittgenstein, MS 109: 28, 22 August 1930, in *Culture and Value*, 6e.
[43] Wittgenstein, MS 109: 28, 22 August 1930, in *Culture and Value*, 7e, translation slightly modified.
[44] Michael Fried, 'Jeff Wall, Wittgenstein, and the Everyday', *Critical Inquiry* 33 (2007): 495–526.

the passage Fried discusses and which we have quoted above appears in manuscript 6 months *after* the original manuscript instance of the passage where Wittgenstein calls the colour octahedron an *übersichtliche Darstellung*.[45] And note: the 'bird's eye view' contemplation about which Wittgenstein fantasizes is not merely calming—it generates enthusiasm for the 'uncanny and wonderful', more precisely, for the appearance of ordinary, everyday things as uncanny and wonderful.

The similarity between these kinds of vision, an artistic view from above, *sub specie aeterni*, and the perspicuous representation, is striking, and is supported by Wittgenstein himself, who noted '[t]he queer resemblance between a philosophical investigation (perhaps especially in mathematics <>) and one in aesthetics'.[46] The insistence on description, the pleasure taken in particularity, the concern with comprehending spontaneous unities of expression: these features distinguished aesthetic contemplation and Wittgenstein's philosophizing from generalizing, progressive science. The association itself, however, might have remained something abstract and general, asserted on occasion but never really cashed out, were it not for the fact that there was a sphere of art in which Wittgenstein had been, almost from birth, wholly engrossed, about which he was both exceptionally knowledgeable and practically able, and on which he pinned his highest cultural aspirations: music. The entwining of Wittgenstein's family with musical Vienna is well known: their residence was visited by the likes of Brahms, Mahler, and Bruno Walter; they were skilled musicians themselves and Wittgenstein's brother Paul was a noted concert pianist and—as a consequence of a war injury—the left-handed player for whom Ravel wrote his famous concerto.[47] That Ludwig should therefore have both a deep, impressive knowledge of the classical repertory and strong opinions about the fate of modern music should come as no surprise (his notebooks contain frequent comments on the latter). What has emerged relatively recently, thanks to the early inquiries of Brian McGuinness and the later research of Eran Guter, is something a little more surprising: in the late 1920s and early 1930s, Wittgenstein discussed an important body of music theory—the ideas of Heinrich Schenker—in a number of meetings with his nephew Felix Salzer, who would later become one of Schenker's most articulate advocates in postwar America.[48]

One can see the appeal, for Schenker—another Viennese Jew, whose work on music analysis and theory spans the first four decades of the twentieth century—combined the cultural pessimism to which Wittgenstein already subscribed (both thought the twentieth century had proved itself incapable of producing great music) with an analytic practice focused on 'perspicuous representation': Schenker's graphs of the masterworks of classical music purported to represent—in musical

---

[45] Transcription of Wittgenstein, MS 108: 89, entry on 23 February 1930, from the Wittgenstein Archive at the University of Bergen, http://wab.uib.no, accessed 30 November 2016.

[46] Wittgenstein, MS 116: 56, 1937, in *Culture and Value*, 29e.

[47] A description of the centrality of music in the Wittgenstein household is found in McGuinness, *Wittgenstein*, 19–21.

[48] Eran Guter, '"A Surrogate for the Soul": Wittgenstein and Schoenberg', in Enzo De Pellegrin (ed), *Interactive Wittgenstein* (Dordrecht: Springer, 2011), 118. Salzer would become famous in American music theory circles for his elaboration of Schenker's ideas in *Structural Hearing: Tonal Coherence in Music* (New York: Dover, 1962).

notation rather than words—the underlying rule-governed counterpoint of the eighteenth and nineteenth century's most complex, harmonically daring compositions.[49] In fact, musical themes—which could be thought of as the basic unit of musical syntax—had provided Wittgenstein with a usefully different picture of language, an alternative to the rigid, empiricist syntax of the proposition, for a long time. The analogy had struck him as early as February 1915, when he wrote that '[m]usical themes are in a certain sense propositions. Knowledge of the nature of logic will for this reason lead to knowledge of the nature of music.'[50] The interest or advantage of musical 'propositions' was that they made sense without relying on either an object world or a mental 'occult' entity; a tune was, as he observed a month later, 'a kind of tautology, it is complete in itself'.[51] It's hardly a surprise that when Wittgenstein began to think about propositions again in the 1930s and wanted to think of them as no longer relying on names, musical sentences again caught his philosophical eye. Late in the *Philosophical Investigations*, he observes that '[u]nderstanding a sentence in language is much more akin to understanding a theme in music than one may think.' Why? Because of what we might call the theme's 'tautological' features:

> Why is just *this* the pattern of variation in intensity and tempo? One would like to say: "Because I know what it all means." But what does it mean? I'd not be able to say. As an "explanation", I could compare it with something else which has the same rhythm (I mean the same pattern).[52]

In the 1934 manuscript where this remark first appeared it follows one devoted to 'intuitive thought' and to Mozart—who could grasp an entire composition in an instant—as its exemplary bearer.[53] Together the two remarks tell us that we understand musical themes by acquiring a feel for their rightness: the way in which the details of the theme fit together and fit the situation, the remainder of the composition, surrounding it. (What they don't tell us is that this conception works only for a narrow band of music: the 'pure', instrumental classical music of modern Europe and its attendant aesthetics.) In 1946 Wittgenstein will return to the issue of what 'following a musical phrase with understanding' amounts to, dismissing the idea that it means having some sort of inner experience, and focusing our attention on the kinds of things someone who understands musical phrases might say and do while listening to them with understanding.[54] He'll return to the topic in 1948: 'Someone who understands music will listen differently (with a different

---

[49] Excellent examples can be found in Heinrich Schenker, *Five Graphic Music Analyses* (New York: Dover, 1969).
[50] Wittgenstein, Note from 7 February 1915, in *Notebooks 1914–1916*, 40e.
[51] Wittgenstein, Note from 4 March 1915, in *Notebooks, 1914–1916*, 40e.
[52] Wittgenstein, *Philosophical Investigations*, §527 (151e).
[53] Wittgenstein, MS 116: 101–3, Wittgenstein Archives at the University of Bergen, http://wab.uib.no.
[54] Wittgenstein, MS 132: 51, 22 September 1946, in *Culture and Value*, 58e–9e. On this see also Oswald Hanfling, '"I heard a plaintive melody": (*Philosophical Investigations*, p. 209)', in A. Philips Griffiths (ed.), *Wittgenstein: Centenary Essays* (Cambridge: Cambridge University Press, 1991), 117–33.

facial expression, e.g.), play differently, hum differently, talk differently about the piece than someone who does not understand.'[55]

Does this resemble the ordinary understanding of sentences? No, the resemblance is to the philosophical understanding of sentences, that is, to the way in which we appreciate sentences as 'wonderful' once we have represented them perspicuously. In ordinary life, we express the rightness of a sentence by responding to it in the right way: following an order, replying to a query, consoling someone who suffers, sharing in someone's celebration, selling them the apples for which they asked. If I say 'I have a terrible stomach-ache', someone can acknowledge the appropriateness of the statement by sympathizing or offering a remedy. It's when the philosopher takes over, elucidating the rules governing a sentence's usage, clarifying our sense of how a sentence fits its situation by providing what Wittgenstein called 'intermediate cases', that we are in a position to see this rightness, to see the successful work of language as uncanny and wonderful. Thus Wittgenstein's remarks on expressions of pain show us that it would make no sense to say—in response to the complaint about the stomach-ache—'how do you know you have a stomach-ache?', or 'I have a stomach-ache, too, but it's a different one', and so on. Wittgenstein's perspicuous representations show us how the language works, and we cannot help but be impressed. To a great extent, this marvelling at language is a secularization of the idea Wittgenstein tried out in the 1929 'Lecture on Ethics', when he admitted that he was 'tempted to say that the right expression in language for the miracle of the existence of the world, though it is not any proposition *in* language, is the existence of language itself'.[56] Now the existence that is miraculous is that of the intersubjective and the everyday. But the everyday is not, as Cavell shrewdly pointed out, identical with its 'resettlement': our original absorption in a world has been replaced by something self-conscious, uncanny, and pleasurable.

Some of that pleasure is captured in Wittgenstein's description of how we learn a language through what he will call training. When describing how he would teach someone to use certain words, Wittgenstein emphasizes that 'I'll teach him to use the words by means of *examples* and by *exercises*'—and then describes the training: 'I do it, he does it after me; and I influence him by expressions of agreement, rejection, expectation, encouragement.'[57] The aim will be the mastery of the relevant grammar; the encouragement and agreement are rewards for mastery of the form itself, apart from its deployment in actual life. But no one, it seems, has invested more in this kind of training than Cavell, who has described how he encouraged his daughter, through the same kind of positive reinforcement, to learn the meaning of the word 'kitten':

> But although I didn't tell her, and she didn't learn, either what the word "kitty" means or what a "kitty" is, if she keeps leaping and I keep looking and smiling, she will learn both. I have wanted to say: "Kittens"—what we call "kittens"—do not exist in her world yet, she has not acquired the forms of life which contain them. They do not

---

[55] Wittgenstein, MS 137: 20b, 15 February 1948, in *Culture and Value*, 80e.
[56] Wittgenstein, 'Lecture on Ethics', 50.
[57] Wittgenstein, *Philosophical Investigations*, §208 (89e).

exist in something like the way cities and mayors will not exist in her world until long after pumpkins and kittens do; or like the way God or love or responsibility or beauty do not exist in our world; we have not mastered, or we have forgotten, or we have distorted, or learned through fragmented models, the forms of life which could make utterances like "God exists" or "God is dead" or "I love you" or "I cannot do otherwise" or "Beauty is but the beginning of terror" bear all the weight they could carry, express all they could take from us. We do not know the meaning of the words.[58]

There is a critical moment here, but it points to language we have not mastered, or mastered well; if we are irresponsible or loveless, it's because we have failed to learn or establish the appropriate form of life. But the moment of training, because it involves play, because it is to some degree distanced from the practical use of words, encourages the same kind of contemplative pleasure in the language as does the bird's eye view.

Cavell's critique is instructive. When he says that love and responsibility 'do not exist in our world' because we have failed to master the forms of life that give them meaning, he turns hate and irresponsibility into a failure of training and mastery, rather than a failure internal to the forms of life themselves. But this is in keeping with Wittgenstein's subtle insistence that language works. What we are asked to see, perspicuously, is the uncanny way our statements perform, whatever the intentions or consequences of their working-through or working-out in the empirical details of actual ordinary life. The romantic date you eagerly anticipated may have been a disaster: he wasn't what you expected at all, there were misunderstandings, feelings were hurt and you had to be consoled afterwards (the example cannot, alas, stretch to building houses and machines). Perspicuously represented, however, we see not the disaster but the grammar that makes the whole catastrophe possible and, in its way, comprehensible. It is not language that fails us—what we see is somehow always 'God's work' and never mere human disaster.

In a striking passage in the 'Big Typescript' Wittgenstein will contrast this contemplative, descriptive, kind of understanding—which 'leaves everything as it is'—with the scientific desire for a justification or grounding of every utterance, the desire that wants rules to explain the application of rules:

> We would like to give reason after reason after reason. Because we feel: so long as there is a reason, everything is all right. We don't want to stop explaining—and simply describe. How can *what is happening right now* be interesting? All that we're ever interested in is the justification, the why! It isn't mathematics, after all, to say what people do.[59]

To make what people do interesting: if what they do is somehow like music, that task will be a lot easier. But to secure the analogy between musical understanding and our comprehension of speech, we need to return to the tension in Wittgenstein's understanding of language. We need to return to the shrug of the shoulders that challenged the idea of a grammar based on rules.

---

[58] Stanley Cavell, *The Claim of Reason: Wittgenstein, Skepticism, Morality, and Tragedy* (Oxford: Oxford University Press, 1999), 172–3.
[59] Wittgenstein, *Big Typescript*, 139e.

GESTURES, MUSIC, AND A SIGNIFICANT COMPLICATION

One of the great Wittgenstein stories involves a gesture made by his colleague and friend Piero Sraffa, the Italian economist who, among other things, was a close friend and comrade of Antonio Gramsci. Wittgenstein had become friendly with Sraffa shortly after returning to Cambridge in 1929 and they would meet regularly for several years (although they would eventually fall out). Sraffa appears amongst the intellectual influences Wittgenstein listed in a 1931 manuscript, but when Wittgenstein writes the preface to the *Philosophical Investigations* in 1945, the others have fallen away. Frank Ramsey is mentioned in fond terms, but even his help is not as important as the criticism of Sraffa: 'It is to this stimulus that I owe the most fruitful ideas of this book.'[60] Some of that stimulus can be gauged from what we have of their correspondence and from Sraffa's annotated copy of the Blue Book. The storied moment is when Sraffa, responding to Wittgenstein's insistence on the centrality of grammar in language, made what has been described as a derisive Neapolitan gesture and asked Wittgenstein what the grammar of that was.

Mauro Luiz Engelmann has described the impact of this critique in depth.[61] The crux of the matter is that Wittgenstein is compelled to realize that he cannot explain all meaning as the consequence of a calculus, of a system of rules: primitive gestures do not have a grammar in the sense that word-language does. In which case, the claim that word-language has priority may be false and shrugging one's shoulders may have more to tell us about language than Wittgenstein had been willing to admit. But, as we've observed already, the 'Big Typescript' is not consistent, and Wittgenstein, as Engelmann has shown, takes on board Sraffa's criticism in a handwritten addendum, admitting that we may learn the meaning of 'foreign gestures' in 'the way we learned as children to understand the gestures and facial expressions of grown-ups—without explanation'.[62] Should we then be surprised that in 1946, when Wittgenstein again asks 'what does it consist in, following a musical phrase with understanding, or, playing it with understanding?' he ends up describing the musical phrase as a gesture and then concludes by saying that '[a] theme, no less than a face, wears an expression'?[63] The musical phrase, the gesture, the facial expression: these stand as forms of language that rest on something besides rules, though rules may come into play at some point. What is that something? In 1946 it is 'the whole field of our language games'.[64] Two years later the understanding of music will be 'a manifestation of human life', which can never proceed by explanation, but depends on becoming embedded in a peculiar form of that life.[65] David Stern has described this transformation with reference to three emblematic phrases of

---

[60] Wittgenstein, 'Preface', *Philosophical Investigations*, 4e.
[61] Mauro Luiz Engelmann, 'Wittgenstein's "Most Fruitful Ideas" and Sraffa'.
[62] Wittgenstein, *Big Typescript*, 8e.
[63] Wittgenstein, MS 132: 51, 22 September 1946, and MS 132: 59, 25 September 1946, in *Culture and Value*, 58e and 59e.
[64] Wittgenstein, MS 132: 59, 25 September 1946, *Culture and Value*, 59e.
[65] Wittgenstein, MS 137: 20b, 15 February 1948, *Culture and Value*, 80e.

Wittgenstein: 'Logic must take care of itself' (from the *Tractatus* notes); 'Language must speak for itself' (from the *Philosophical Grammar*); 'practice has to speak for itself' (from *On Certainty*).[66] As Stern notes, it isn't a simple widening of scope, but a progressive change in the conception of language's foundation. For the last step entails surrendering the bird's eye view in favour of making 'what people do' be interesting.

But just as we can misunderstand language, we can misunderstand music, and Wittgenstein found himself having to settle accounts on that score as well. He did so by invoking none other than Schenker, who, as Guter has discovered, finds himself hauled onstage for the briefest of cameos in the 'Big Typescript'.[67] The occasion is a critical discussion of Spengler, whose diagnosis of 'the West' seems sound to Wittgenstein, but whose method contains a basic flaw. Spengler presents his cultural periods as archetypes, and he then 'dogmatically attribute[s] to the object [various cultural phenomena] what should be ascribed only to the archetype'.[68] Archetypes are fine, but their role, according to Wittgenstein is to determine the form and direction of the investigation, not to serve as idealizations to which empirical cases must conform. For Oskari Kuusela, the decisive change in Wittgenstein's philosophy is precisely this: that archetypes, models, prototypes are to be understood as objects of comparison that may bring out certain features of language and are not generalized cases the features of which must be found in every sentence or proposition.[69] In the margins next to the claim that Spengler has committed just this error Wittgenstein has written: 'Schenker's way of looking at music'.[70]

Where did Schenker go wrong? He had described the 'masterworks of music' as elaborations of basic contrapuntal structures grounded on the major/minor tonality that governed European classical music from roughly the late seventeenth century onwards. His perspicuous representations, graphs that purport to reveal the *Ursatz*, or 'fundamental structure' of particular musical pieces, were transformed into a prescriptive grammar for music 'as such', as if the actual music had been derived and elaborated on the same basis as the analysis, but in, so to speak, reverse order.[71] In short, he objectivized the rules he had derived for the classical tradition, so that music appeared as the outgrowth of a system rather than a form of life (although Schenker himself continuously presented the rules of music as expressions of a form of life).[72]

But Schenker was not wrong about twentieth-century music and the failure of twentieth-century composers to produce works commensurate with those of the past. Wittgenstein, too, felt compelled '[to] approach what is called modern music

---

[66] Stern, *Wittgenstein's* Philosophical Investigations, 27.
[67] Guter, 'Wittgenstein and Schoenberg', 119, in particular n36.
[68] Wittgenstein, *Big Typescript*, 204e.
[69] Kuusela, 'From Metaphysics and Philosophical Theses to Grammar'. See also Oskari Kuusela, 'The Development of Wittgenstein's Philosophy', in Kuusela and McGinn (eds.), *The Oxford Handbook of Wittgenstein*, 597–619.
[70] Wittgenstein, *Big Typescript*, 204e n110.
[71] See Guter, 'Wittgenstein and Schoenberg', 120–3.
[72] For this reason Nicholas Cook has described Schenker's work as a project rather than a theory: see *The Schenker Project: Culture, Race, and Music Theory in Fin-de-Siècle Vienna* (Oxford: Oxford University Press, 2007).

with the greatest mistrust (without understanding its language)'.[73] And, like Schenker, he distrusted no one more than Gustav Mahler, whose music he described as 'worthless'.[74]

His music was 'worthless': although Mahler himself possessed '*a string of very rare talents*'; although Wittgenstein thought him a brilliant conductor; although he carried a picture of Mahler with him at all times.[75] This was not ordinary disparagement: when Mahler produced the kinds of simple tonal progressions that grounded the great tradition, Wittgenstein found them 'unbearable'.[76] His attitude, with its ambiguity, is summed up in a manuscript remark from 1931:

> A picture of a complete apple tree, however accurate, in a certain sense resembles it infinitely less than does the smallest daisy. And in this sense a symphony by Bruckner is infinitely more closely related to a symphony from the heroic period than is one by Mahler. If the latter is a work of art it is one of a *totally* different sort. (But this observation itself is actually Spenglerian.)[77]

What does this mean? It refers to the fact that Mahler seems to deploy the formal vocabulary, the habits of orchestration, and the tonal palette of the great nineteenth-century classics (the 'heroic period'), but in a manner that is false or inauthentic. He writes great symphonies, which pay explicit homage to the works of Beethoven and Brahms, but they are inauthentic, unoriginal, the form without the spirit. Guter points to the manner in which Mahler uses the tonal vocabulary of the nineteenth century—in effect, the chord progressions that define our sense of classical musical syntax—but doesn't use it to anchor the formal structure of his works, as had been the case with the works of the eighteenth and nineteenth centuries.[78]

But Wittgenstein does not accuse Mahler of being frivolous. For if, as Wittgenstein put it in a diary entry from 1931, music 'always appropriates certain maxims of the good and the right of its own time', if it is only understood as a manifestation of the life of which it is a part, then Mahler's problems reflect those of the modern form of life around him, the truth of which, Wittgenstein goes on to say, 'would sound *entirely* paradoxical to all people'.[79] Mahler's music is unbearable, and it is unbearable because it ironizes the 'heroic period', announces its end, demonstrates

---

[73] Wittgenstein, MS 109: 204, 6–7 November 1930, in *Culture and Value*, 8e. This MS is a sketch for a foreword, apparently intended for the *Philosophical Remarks*.

[74] Wittgenstein, MS 136: 110b, 14 January 1948, in *Culture and Value*, 76e.

[75] Wittgenstein, MS 136: 110b, in *Culture and Value*, 76e.

[76] Wittgenstein, diary entry 6 May 1931, in 'Movements of Thought: Diaries 1930–1932, 1936–1937', in *Ludwig Wittgenstein: Public and Private Occasions*, ed. James C. Klagge and Alfred Nordmann (Lanham, MD: Rowman & Littlefield, 2003), 93. My discussion is heavily indebted to incisive discussions of Wittgenstein's relationship to Mahler's music by Eran Guter and Béla Szabados: Guter, 'Wittgenstein and Schoenberg'; Eran Guter, 'Wittgenstein on Mahler', in Danièle Moyal-Sharrock, Volker A. Munz, and Annalisa Coliva (eds.), *Mind, Language and Action: Contributions to the 36th International Wittgenstein Symposium* (Austrian Ludwig Wittgenstein Society, 2013), 169–71; Béla Szabados, 'Wittgenstein Listens to Mahler: How to Do Philosophy and Compose Music in the Breakdown of Tradition?', *Dialogue* 46 (2007): 91–113.

[77] Wittgenstein, MS 154: 15v, 1931, in *Culture and Value*, 17e.

[78] Guter, 'Wittgenstein and Schoenberg', 128–33.

[79] Wittgenstein, diary entry of 27 January 1931, as quoted and retranslated in Eran Guter, 'The Good, the Bad, and the Vacuous: Wittgenstein on Modern and Future Musics', *Journal of Aesthetics and Art Criticism* 73.4 (2015): 426.

the impossibility of its continuation. It is, in fact, not quite art 'of a *totally* different sort', but a kind of artistic version of what Gramsci called 'passive revolution', marking the moment when the old forms are dying but no new form is there to replace them. Theodor Adorno remarks that in Mahler '[s]carcely a theme, let alone a whole movement, can be taken at face value. [...] Although the composer claims to love nature, he puts musical immediacy and naturalness in doubt and this doubt goes to the very core of his musical ideas.'[80] That the apple tree is pictured is therefore the *point* of Mahler. 'He had', Adorno adds later,

> no illusions about the inexorable decline of forms that behave as if their mere existence could establish a meaning which is no longer present in society. He perceived the direction this decline was taking and complied with it. Hence his power.[81]

Adorno's idiom is obviously different from Wittgenstein's, but they are pointing to the same thing: the way in which Mahler's ironic handling of inherited forms and tonal procedures announces the end of a certain kind of aesthetic culture. Wittgenstein, no less than Adorno, believes this is not just a matter of music, but of the form human life has taken in the early twentieth century. If music is a manifestation of human life, then its decline is an indication that something larger is amiss.

Hence, the complication. Music is supposed to be an analogue, a model for language. But language always works, and now music doesn't. Mahler's music fails in a manner that language is never allowed to, and the failure is not personal, but a matter of twentieth-century Europe's form of life.

Why the disjunction? The immediate temptation is to point out the difference between the arena in which language works for Wittgenstein and the arena in which music works: the former, throughout the writing of the 1930s and 1940s is local and interpersonal (consoling, building, feeling pain, teaching), whereas Mahler's music is a public occasion, in terms of its audience and its rhetoric. But it's not as if Wittgenstein couldn't apply his philosophical method to public affairs, or was unwilling to. Wittgenstein discussed his ideas about grammar with Sraffa; but he also discussed politics, and even the application of his ideas to politics. In notes he made for a discussion with Sraffa in 1934, he applied a prominent theme in his investigations—the critique of the belief that we have a private world of thoughts and sensations that doubles and drives our external actions—to a dispute he was having with Sraffa. The dispute was about fascism: whether it would spread to Austria and whether the German people had turned to it on account of their 'mentality' or national spirit:

> Now the fallacy which I want to point out is this,—to think every action which people do is *preceded by* a particular state of mind of which the action is the outcome [...] The fallacy could be described by saying that one presupposes a mental reservoir in which

---

[80] Theodor W. Adorno, 'Mahler', in *Quasi una Fantasia*, trans. Rodney Livingstone, (London: Verso, 1992), 83–4.

[81] Adorno, 'Mahler', 88. A longer and more technical account is found in Theodor W. Adorno, *Mahler: A Musical Physiognomy*, trans. Edmund Jephcott (Chicago: University of Chicago Press, 1992).

the real causes of our action are kept. Now this connects up with our first question because one is tempted to think of such a reservoir, *i.e.,* "the mentality of a people" and when one speaks of changes which the Government of a country might undergo one imagines this thing, the mentality, not to alter.[82]

The idea echoes what we looked at in Cassirer: the actions of a collective are not understandable in terms of a national will, some gaseous inspiration within that motivates action. In Wittgenstein's universe, calling a fascist leader a gasbag would have been not an *ad hominem* insult, but the cleverest and most apt of analogies. Wittgenstein's point is that the useless hypothesis of a national mentality masquerades as an explanation, but in fact does nothing except make a political situation look smoother and more stable than it actually is.[83]

Wittgenstein is able to clarify the meaning of the claim that the Germans 'are a monarchist people' or at least show why it is a false explanation.[84] But Mahler's music leaves him at a loss: he is able to condemn it, but not elucidate it. It may be uncanny, but it is decidedly not wonderful. Is the problem that its grammar is ironic? That seems unlikely, as Wittgenstein had himself produced an ironic masterpiece, the *Tractatus*, in many ways a philosophical version of a Mahler symphony, in which the grasping of the Holy Grail—the announcement that 'I therefore believe myself to have found, on all essential points, the final solution of the problems'—is followed by a confession of atheism—the declaration that 'anyone who understands me eventually recognizes them [the solutions, KH] as nonsensical'[85] (as Béla Szabados has pointed out, Wittgenstein, in the midst of all his suspicions, identifies with Mahler, both as someone unoriginal and as someone who might be doing something that is incomprehensible in traditional categories).[86] No, the problem is not capturing an ironic grammar, but the fact that Mahler is ironizing grammar itself. The music reveals not that the rules of musical style, of the classical tradition, work differently than one supposes, but that the rules don't work anymore—in the early twentieth century, they are empty, and there is nothing to replace them.

Wittgenstein would have denied that he had produced a characterization of language in general or language as such. Not only does he not outline a systematic account of language, he ridicules the very idea of doing so. 'We ask:', Wittgenstein says, '"*What is* language?", "*What* is a proposition?"', and it is clear that we would be

---

[82] Wittgenstein, 'Notes for P. Sraffa, [21.2.1934]', in *Wittgenstein in Cambridge: Letters and Documents 1911–1951*, ed. Brian McGuinness (Oxford: Blackwell, 2008), 225.

[83] More than once, Wittgenstein has been accused of conservatism in his writing (although his intellectual friendships—Russell, Keynes, Sraffa, Nikolai Bakhtin, George Thomson, Fanny Pascal—were overwhelmingly with men and women of the Left). See J. C. Nyíri, 'Wittgenstein's Later Work in Relation to Conservatism', in Anthony Kenny and Brian McGuinness (eds.), *Wittgenstein and His Times* (Chicago: University of Chicago Press, 1982), 44–69. But see also Hannah Fenichel Pitkin, *Wittgenstein and Justice* (Berkeley: University of California Press, 1972); Crary, 'Wittgenstein's Philosophy in Relation to Political Thought'; James Tully, 'Wittgenstein and Political Philosophy: Understanding Practices of Critical Reflection', in Cressida J. Heyes (ed.), *The Grammar of Politics: Wittgenstein and Political Philosophy* (Ithaca, NY: Cornell University Press, 2003), 17–42.

[84] Wittgenstein, 'Notes for P. Sraffa [21.2.1934]', 225.

[85] Wittgenstein, *Tractatus*, 'Preface' (4); §6.54.

[86] Szabados, 'Wittgenstein Listens to Mahler', 98, 102–4.

better off not asking such questions—which are unanswerable—at all.[87] One of the most persistent motifs of the *Philosophical Investigations* is that 'language' is not a '*super*-concept' and that if it has a use, 'it must be as humble a one as that of the words "table", "lamp", "door".'[88] The least inclination to search for 'the incomparable essence of language' should be held at bay.[89] But the very method of the *Philosophical Investigations* and much of the other middle and late work assumes not only certain characteristics, but that the reader shares the form of life that Wittgenstein needs to evoke. Yes, Wittgenstein claims that he is simply describing 'what people do'. But the rhetoric of description distracts us from the fact that Wittgenstein does not, in the *Philosophical Investigations*, actually describe anything, much less '*what is happening right now*'. Instead, we are treated to a series of invitations to *imagine* situations and what might be said in them, with what consequences. Beth Savickey has quite rightly described these descriptions as scripts or improvisational exercises, in which we are invited to see *what would happen*: if we were explorers in a country with a wholly alien language; if we blindfolded someone and guided them across a field; if we kept a diary in which we wrote down an 'S' every time we felt pain, and so on.[90] The so-called descriptions are, in Wittgenstein's own words, 'instruments for particular uses'.[91] But the reader must be already trained in the use of the instrument: the invitations to imagine what would make sense and what not depend on participation in a form of life, not a bird's eye view of it. The pleasure of the perspicuous representation is therefore a pleasure in revealing the form of life that is one's own. We might say (to borrow Wittgenstein's style of expression): it is indeed uncanny that forms of life exist and that language works. But it's an achievement, not a given; a concept of language that can't imagine failure or formlessness can't, arguably, truly appreciate success.

MEANWHILE, IN OXFORD

Wittgenstein enjoyed philosophizing more than he let on; J. L. Austin, on the other hand, made a point of enjoying himself thoroughly. He intended to enjoy himself, intended to put philosophy on a footing that would afford him 'what philosophy is so often thought, and made, barren of—the fun of discovery, the pleasures of co-operation, and the satisfaction of reaching agreement'.[92] Wittgenstein's philosophical pleasure involved taking flight and was always tinged with an ironic distance. Austin's involved other people and witty banter. His legendary 'Saturday morning meetings' in the 1950s were distinguished, according to those present,

---

[87] Wittgenstein, *Philosophical Investigations*, §92 (48e).
[88] Wittgenstein, *Philosophical Investigations*, §97 (49e).
[89] Wittgenstein, *Philosophical Investigations*, §97 (49e).
[90] Savickey, 'Wittgenstein and Hacker: *Übersichtliche Darstellung*', 112–13; Beth Savickey, 'Wittgenstein's Use of Examples', in Kuusela and McGinn, *The Oxford Handbook of Wittgenstein*, 676–7.
[91] Wittgenstein, *Philosophical Investigations*, §291 (106e).
[92] J. L. Austin, 'A Plea for Excuses' [1956], in *Philosophical Papers*, 2nd edn. (Oxford: Clarendon Press, 1970), 175.

by their informality, their collaborative ethos, and the telling of jokes. G. J. Warnock thought the Saturday mornings were 'enormously enjoyable'; the American George Pitcher claimed those attending Austin's sessions at Harvard felt 'like children at a party'.[93] Pleasure is also had in the wry, donnishly clever style of his prose and the fancifulness of his examples. Wittgenstein imagines people learning series of numbers and having toothaches; Austin imagines them shooting the wrong donkey and hearing bitterns at the bottom of their gardens.

The tonal differences are partly a matter of happenstance, though not entirely, as we'll see. They point, nevertheless, to a striking pattern of similarities and dissimilarities between these two moves towards 'ordinary language philosophy'. Austin claimed that he had come to his own position independently of Wittgenstein, whose works he did not apparently read till after the Second World War. They shared a debt to the 'common sense' positions of G. E. Moore who, nevertheless, never made a linguistic turn. Wittgenstein moved swiftly from his Tractarian devotion to logic to the belief that language was anchored in rules and forms of life between 1929 and about 1937; Austin's moves are harder to trace, because he published so little and talked so much, but by common consent he developed his position in the latter half of the 1930s and you can see it exemplified in his paper 'Other Minds' from 1940.[94] If language was a force field, you could say they entered it from different directions, but its pressures produced some significant homologies.

The projects were similar in three dimensions: the reconceptualization of language, the method by which one clarified the structure of language, and the ways in which one had to remodel the philosophical enterprise. And just as our three dimensions of space are shaped and defined by a fourth dimension of time, so these three dimensions were shaped by a shared polemical thrust, a persistent unhappiness with both the metaphysical habits of other philosophers and the endless strife that was a consequence.

'I'll teach you differences' was a line from *King Lear* that Wittgenstein thought might serve as a motto for his book, because, in contrast to Hegel, Wittgenstein claimed, 'my interest is in showing that things that look the same are really different'.[95] That is equally apt for Austin: the essay (posthumously edited from a lecture) 'Three Ways of Spilling Ink' is devoted to the distinction in language between doing something 'intentionally', 'deliberately', and 'on purpose'.[96] The drawing of fine distinctions in the ways we use words was central to his project and probably nowhere better in evidence than in the essay 'A Plea for Excuses', which proposed to distinguish between the various ways in which we excused untoward actions: we did it 'by mistake', 'by accident', 'inadvertently', and so on. There Austin would

---

[93] G. J. Warnock, 'Saturday Mornings', 39; George Pitcher, 'Austin: A Personal Memoir', 19; both in Isaiah Berlin et al., *Essays on J. L. Austin* (Oxford: Clarendon Press, 1973).
[94] See Isaiah Berlin, 'Austin and the Early Beginnings of Oxford Philosophy', in *Essays on J. L. Austin*, 1–16; J. L. Austin, 'Other Minds', in *Philosophical Papers*, 76–116.
[95] Monk, *Wittgenstein*, 536–7.
[96] J. L. Austin, 'Three Ways of Spilling Ink', in *Philosophical Papers*, 272–87.

produce his famous, somewhat Burkean justification for dwelling on the distinctions our language already included:

> [...] our common stock of words embodies all the distinctions men have found worth drawing, and the connexions they have found worth marking, in the lifetimes of many generations: these surely are likely to be more numerous, more sound, since they have stood up to the long test of the survival of the fittest, and more subtle, at least in all ordinary and practical matters, than any that you and I are likely to think up in our arm-chairs of an afternoon—the most favoured alternative method.[97]

The claim sounds less Burkean, and more interesting, when we realize that the distinctions made in language are not matters of sense or reference, but constitute the very texture of human action.[98] For 'to proceed from "ordinary language"' is to proceed 'by examining *what we should say when*'; more precisely, it is 'to examine [...] what words we should use in what situation'.[99] To understand when we say 'by mistake' rather than 'by accident' is to understand what it is to make a mistake, just as in Wittgenstein we realize what it is to 'expect' someone by examining what we do, and don't do, when we're in the business of expecting. Austin agreed with Wittgenstein that 'words are our tools' (though, characteristically, he would spend time canvassing the alternatives: 'instruments', 'utensils', 'implements', etc.) and that the question was how we used them.[100] To claim, therefore, that 'what we ordinarily say and mean may have a direct and deep control over what we can philosophically say and mean'—Stanley Cavell's neat summary—was to claim that philosophy had to reflect, in the first place, not on 'ordinary' things or people, but on what people did in and through language.[101]

To make the distinctions, to understand 'what we should say when' demanded imagination and a new method, or, rather, imagination *as* a new method. Imaginative recreation and improvisational drama, the staples of Wittgenstein's later writings, were required to ferret out the fine distinctions between uses. One had to narrativize language to establish what meant what:

> The more we imagine the situation in detail, with a background of story—and it is worth employing the most idiosyncratic or, sometimes, boring means to stimulate and to discipline our wretched imaginations—the less we find we disagree about what we should say.[102]

Hence, the donkey:

> You have a donkey, so have I, and they graze in the same field. The day comes when I conceive a dislike for mine. I go to shoot it, draw a bead on it, fire: the brute falls in

---

[97] Austin, 'A Plea for Excuses', 182.
[98] Accordingly, Austin would, in one of his first papers, attack 'the curious belief that all words are *names*' and with it the philosophical concept of 'meaning'; 'The Meaning of a Word' [1940], in *Philosophical Papers*, 61.
[99] Austin, 'A Plea for Excuses', 181, 182.
[100] Austin, 'A Plea for Excuses', 181. The time was spent with George Pitcher, discussing the *Philosophical Investigations*; see Pitcher, 'Austin: A Personal Memoir', 24.
[101] Stanley Cavell, 'Must We Mean What We Say?', in *Must We Mean What We Say?: A Book of Essays* (New York: Scribner's, 1969), 1.
[102] Austin, 'A Plea for Excuses', 184.

its tracks. I inspect the victim, and find to my horror that it is *your* donkey. I appear on your doorstep with the remains and say—what? "I say, old sport, I'm awfully sorry, &c., I've shot your donkey *by accident*"? Or "*by mistake*"? Then again, I go to shoot my donkey as before, draw a bead on it, fire—but as I do so, the beasts move, and to my horror yours falls. Again the scene on the doorstep—what do I say? "By mistake"? Or "by accident"? [103]

This is how one learns the difference, a difference with conceivably serious moral (and legal) consequences, between mistake and accident.

As scriptwriters, Austin and Wittgenstein had some unsurprising differences. For Austin the exercise had to answer the question: 'what do we say when we do *x*?' (e.g., shoot the wrong donkey). For Wittgenstein, drama answered the converse question: 'what do we do when we say *x*?' (e.g., when we say we are 'expecting' someone). They accordingly progressed in different ways. Austin's improvisations resembled the pattern of legal training, in which case after case is invented to determine exactly when certain concepts apply: the play was episodic in structure. By contrast, Wittgenstein's were extended by means of something like a Greek chorus, by the voice of the so-called 'interlocutor' (called so in Wittgenstein commentary, not by Wittgenstein himself), who would query the drama, insisting that the real action was not onstage, but inside the head of the actor.[104]

But the aim of the drama was the same: to demonstrate that everything was in clear view and that philosophical agreement was in essence clarification of what we already knew. We would know that shooting your friend's donkey was 'truly' a mistake, once we realized that that is what we call it afterwards. We would know that 'expecting' means 'I walk up and down the room, look at the clock now and then, and so on' once we realized that that is what we did when we were expecting someone.[105] The method of cases and reminders produced not just assent, but a particular kind of assent.

This new kind of agreement was crucial, for both men, to the remodelling of the philosophical enterprise. The first renovation was a devout incrementalism, a conviction that philosophy ought to aim at resolving a series of small questions rather than banging its head against the big ones. Austin wanted his audience to 'get going on agreeing about discoveries, however small, and on agreeing about how to reach agreement';[106] Wittgenstein looked forward to the time when '[p]roblems are solved (difficulties eliminated), not a *single* problem.'[107] The rhetoric of piecemeal advance, of course, was not entirely in earnest: when Austin began his campaign, his first efforts aimed to clarify the use of the words 'meaning' and 'know', that is, he aimed directly at the big beasts of the philosophical world and not at the donkeys.[108] Rather, the point was to turn the big questions into a series of small questions: to turn the matter of Necessity into the question of 'Ifs and Cans' (the title of another

---

[103] Austin, 'A Plea for Excuses', 185 n1.
[104] Stern, *Wittgenstein's* Philosophical Investigations, 3–4, 21–8.
[105] Wittgenstein, *Philosophical Investigations*, §444 (138e).
[106] Austin, 'A Plea for Excuses', 183.
[107] Wittgenstein, *Philosophical Investigations*, §133 (57e).
[108] J. L. Austin, 'The Meaning of a Word', 55–75, and 'Other Minds', 76–116, in *Philosophical Papers*.

Austin paper) or the question of the object of wishing and expectation into the question of how one behaves while waiting for a guest to arrive. Behind these moves lay the big substitution Wittgenstein had aimed at: '(Instead of turbulent conjectures and explanations, we want the calm ascertaining of linguistic facts.)'.

There was supposed to be some redundancy in that last phrase. If it was 'linguistic facts' one was after, this alone would guarantee a certain measure of composure in the search and discovery. For facts were per se out in the open, ready for collection: it wasn't mathematics, as Wittgenstein had quipped, to say what people do. In Austin's view this calm incrementalism had two other implications: a drive towards collaboration in philosophical work and an alignment of philosophy with the practice—calm, measured, progressive—of natural science. No one kidded themselves, of course, about who was *primus inter pares* when Austin convened his meetings of colleagues: Warnock claims he could not 'think of any comparable instance of personal authority so effortlessly exercised'.[109] Nevertheless, Austin was serious about his priorities: his prestige in British philosophy stemmed largely from teaching, lectures, and his participation in what were in some respects English versions of the Russian circles we discussed in Chapters 4 and 7.[110]

Wittgenstein, moody and remote, may have seemed like a throwback in comparison; Austin seemed to regard him that way. But it's worth recalling that he published even less than Austin in his lifetime, that his reputation was based on classes at Cambridge and the notes taken at classes (the Blue and Brown Books, among others), and that, in the end, he could only imagine philosophical insight in the form of a conversation. Where Wittgenstein and Austin differed substantially was over what to call the newly renovated space of philosophy. For Austin, the seminar room had become a scientific laboratory, and philosophy was becoming scientific. Linguistic facts were truly facts, to be systematically accumulated through collective observation and discussion. In the conclusion to 'Ifs and Cans' he compares philosophy to an 'initial central sun, seminal and tumultuous: from time to time it throws off some portion of itself to take station as a science, a planet, cool and well regulated, progressing steadily towards a distant final state'. 'Is it not possible', he dreamed, 'that the next century may see the birth, through the joint labours of philosophers, grammarians, and numerous other students of language, of a true and comprehensive *science of language*?'[111]

Does it matter that Wittgenstein imagined the new philosophical style differently? The difference has less to do with how he understood philosophical practice than with how he, and Austin, understood science. One of Ernest Gellner's complaints in his notorious critique of linguistic philosophy, *Words and Things*, was that

---

[109] Warnock, 'Saturday Mornings', 32.
[110] Isaiah Berlin has described the first of these circles, which met in his rooms from 1937 to 1939 and included Stuart Hampshire and Austin's philosophical rival and opponent, A. J. Ayer; Berlin, 'Austin and the Early Beginnings of Oxford Philosophy', 9–16; the second was the group who met on Saturday mornings in the 1950s, described in Warnock, 'Saturday Mornings'.
[111] J. L. Austin, 'Ifs and Cans', in *Philosophical Papers*, 232. It's worth pointing out how close this is to the conception of philosophy Jürgen Habermas set out in 'Philosophy as Stand-In and Interpreter', in *Moral Consciousness and Communicative Action*, trans. Christian Lenhardt and Shierry Weber Nicholsen (Cambridge, MA: MIT Press, 1990), 1–20.

the Oxford philosophers were not acquainted with, or terribly interested in natural science, as genuine philosophers should have been.[112] Wittgenstein had initially been orientated to science; Austin had been trained in classical philology. Yet Austin seemed to be fully committed to the culture of science I've discussed in earlier pages: not to a particular methodology, but to a certain kind of open, experimental discussion and to a sense of how one ought to treat the material, or what we could call the data, for that discussion.

His reasons were not, on the face of it, political. In an immediate sense, they seemed cultural: he wanted to make philosophy into an open, self-reflective examination of what we said when and, by extension, what we did when. The practice would require training, but not specialist knowledge and its field work (as he liked to call it) would take place in the world directly around the investigator.[113] That this kind of philosophy would be pleasurable as well was not, I suspect, a mere bonus: it was an important element of the culture he wished to foster.

Perhaps, though, it's a mistake to think of the aspiration in terms of *natural* science. Not because either Austin or Wittgenstein had any interest or meaningful contact with sociology or anthropology, but because of what the still emerging social sciences represented. In his 1969 article, 'Components of the National Culture', Perry Anderson argued that '*Britain—alone of major Western societies—never produced a classical sociology.*'[114] Anderson had made a habit of defining Britain by what it lacked, but the shrewdly made point was that the absence of something can be an historical event in its own right and, in this case, the absence of sociology signalled an unwillingness or inability to think of the social world in totalizing, analytical terms. In Anderson's view, F. R. Leavis's exaltation of literary criticism would step in to the void, installing culture where society ought to have been (that Britain's most original socialist intellectual would turn out to be Raymond Williams, deeply indebted to Leavis, confirmed the point). English philosophy was, unsurprisingly, condemned as a 'chloroforming ideology', hostile to innovation, technicist and self-enclosed.[115]

Austin's ordinary language philosophy was obviously not the totalizing discipline Anderson thought Britain needed. But there is a sense in which Austin imagines that the careful analysis of language is a means of covering the social field. His papers on 'Other Minds', 'Truth', and 'Unfair to Facts' would cover what and how we could know; 'A Plea for Excuses' and 'Three Ways of Spilling Ink' would cover the moral questions of what we should do ('Ifs and Cans' would fall somewhere in the middle).[116] The remaining papers (I'm leaving aside *Sense and Sensibilia* and *How to Do Things with Words*) dealt largely with method. But that simply underscored the degree to which Austin imagined himself as training people, rather than passing on a body of philosophical knowledge. Warnock describes the Saturday morning meetings as 'in some ways more like meetings of civil servants, seeking

---

[112] Ernest Gellner, *Words and Things* (London: Victor Gollancz, 1959).
[113] The reference to '*field work* in philosophy' is found in 'A Plea for Excuses', 183.
[114] Perry Anderson, 'Components of the National Culture', in Alexander Cockburn and Robin Blackburn (eds.), *Student Power: Problems, Diagnosis, Action* (Harmondsworth: Penguin, 1969), 219.
[115] Anderson, 'Components', 237.   [116] All are found in Austin, *Philosophical Papers*.

impersonally and anonymously to reach workable agreement on matters of common concern'.[117] Warnock was thinking of the style of what went on, but he has in fact touched on its substance. For ordinary language philosophy of the Austinian variety was in many respects the training of a democratic elite, who would draw on nothing but common practice around them, but add to it a clarifying gaze. In manner and by virtue of their collaboration, they were like civil servants; in technique the obvious comparison is to lawyers, who busy themselves with the application of concepts and principles—mistake, accident, knowledge—to specific cases and who draw their ammunition from precedent. Either way, Austin's community of philosophers resembled the educated elite of bureaucrats that worried people like T. S. Eliot, who wanted to place strict limits on what mere training or intelligence could do for English culture.[118] *De facto*, of course, they shared Eliot's class background; *de jure*, however, they were pushing towards something new.

For Austin, language was more or less equivalent to what others would call 'a way of life'. The job of education was not to intervene substantially in it, but to bring a kind of self-reflexive clarity to it. Philosophy was to be a language's civil service. Or, if you like, its political leadership.

Did European democracy need an effective civil service or an impassioned collective will? Did the discussions characteristic of parliament, of the press, of the bureaucracies that were flowering throughout the continent, drain democracy of its life or add to its collective power? No doubt Adorno's comment on avant-garde and popular culture—that they are the 'torn halves of an integral freedom, to which, however, they do not add up'—which I took advantage of earlier, applies here as well.[119] There was a world of ordinary language, containing, depending on which writer you read, strikingly fine moral distinctions, messianic force, the uncanny pleasures of successful discourse, the power of vivid expression and dialogue, or a keen analytical eye. It needed, however to be understood, clarified, valued, perhaps pruned or made self-reflexive. It's the common lot of political organization: a dialectic of massed forces and organizing leadership, though the leadership can take many different forms. Lively and expressive, but at the same time sober and measured: did the life come from ordinary language and sobriety from the leadership, or was some other division of democratic virtues possible? Our writers on myth explored the myriad possibilities.

---

[117] Warnock, 'Saturday Mornings', 43.
[118] See T. S. Eliot, *Notes Toward the Definition of Culture* (London: Faber and Faber, 1948), chapters 2 and 6.
[119] Theodor W. Adorno, Letter to Walter Benjamin, 18 March 1936, in Theodor W. Adorno and Walter Benjamin, *The Complete Correspondence 1928–1940*, trans. Nicholas Walker (Cambridge: Polity Press, 1999), 130.

Conclusion
Motorways and Cul-de-Sacs—What the Linguistic Turns Turned To

It ended not with a bang or a whimper, but with a book. The book was *The Linguistic Turn: Recent Essays in Philosophical Method*, edited by a young Richard Rorty, a collection of essays and selections from books that illustrated the case for what was then called linguistic philosophy. It was published in 1967: never had the Owl of Minerva chosen a more decisive moment to fly. For Rorty's book *named* the phenomenon in philosophy we've been examining in this book; although the phrase 'the linguistic turn' had been coined by Gustav Bergmann fifteen years earlier, it had lain more or less undisturbed, until Rorty brushed it off and used it for the title of his collection, after which it became the term of art it is today. But in naming the movement, attempting to describe it and to codify its various strands, Rorty was in fact writing not quite its obituary, but the kind of note one composes for a retiring colleague. The linguistic turn named by *The Linguistic Turn* was losing steam, its best moments in the rear view mirror, and while it might trundle along for a while longer, signs of its inevitable demise were clear.

Why an anthology at that point in time? Anthologies are useful teaching tools in a discipline devoted to the scholarly article: Rorty's was motivated in part by the needs of current graduate students.[1] There were already plenty of collections around in analytic philosophy, each with its own particular case to make on behalf of the discipline. In 1953 A. J. Ayer, Gilbert Ryle, and assorted English colleagues had teamed up to put together *The Revolution in Philosophy*, an anthology whose very title announced that analytic philosophy, like the modernist movements contemporary with it, was ready and willing to throw everything before it—from Descartes to McTaggart—off the ship of modernity.[2] A decade later *British Analytical Philosophy*, edited by Bernard Williams and Alan Montefiore, took it as read that analytic philosophy was a tradition and sought to build bridges to neighbours on the continent: it was an attempt by younger colleagues to explain 'British' philosophy to writers more inclined to phenomenology and existentialism.[3]

---

[1] On the genesis of *The Linguistic Turn*, see Neil Gross, *Richard Rorty: The Making of an American Philosopher* (Chicago: University of Chicago Press, 2008), 177–84.
[2] A. J. Ayer et al., *The Revolution in Philosophy* (London: Macmillan, 1956).
[3] Bernard Williams and Alan Montefiore, *British Analytical Philosophy* (London: Routledge & Kegan Paul, 1966).

Rorty knew from the outset that he wanted to do something slightly different. *The Linguistic Turn* would not simply describe, explain, or celebrate the linguistic method—it would raise 'metaphilosophical' questions about it, that is, the question of what justified doing this kind of philosophy rather than another. Accordingly, it featured articles and excerpts that focused either on the justification for linguistic philosophy or on its future direction, all prefaced by Rorty's introduction, 'Metaphilosophical Difficulties of Linguistic Philosophy'. If raising these sorts of questions looked like a way of keeping your distance, this was in keeping with Rorty's career to that date, which had been marked by a notably ambivalent attitude towards analytic philosophizing. He had accepted its value and embraced its methods, but on condition that linguistic philosophy not delude itself about what it was doing. In an article published at the time Rorty was planning the anthology, he insisted that the linguistic turn had to be justified pragmatically, not theoretically, as 'a practical answer' to the problem of how to avoid endless battle between philosophical world-views, something that would keep philosophy moving forward, even if one couldn't justify it by self-evident first principles.[4]

The metaphilosophical introduction to the anthology took this one step further. Rorty accepted that a 'linguistic revolution' had taken place in philosophy from which there was no turning back. From here on in, philosophy progressed because it realized 'that philosophical problems are problems which may be solved (or dissolved) either by reforming language, or by understanding more about the language we presently use'.[5] But he understood that revolutions create their justifications retrospectively, that is, they establish the grounds that justify them after they have triumphed: you can't therefore explain them as simple progress from what preceded. All appeals to the new philosophy as somehow more scientific than what it followed, as the result of careful and incremental progress in the discipline, perhaps depending on some discovery regarding 'language' or 'symbols', were thus misguided. Linguistic philosophy, he argued, had not put the discipline on the scientific footing it craved. It had triumphed because it had succeeded in discrediting the way of doing philosophy that preceded it. Successful philosophies are, in the end, simply 'better ways of talking' and philosophical progress was, in the end, just a matter of intellectual snakes shedding now useless verbal skins.[6]

At the time Rorty was writing, linguistic or analytic philosophy, true to its revolutionary creed, still had no history: as the radically new, it was destined to go about its business without worry about whatever errors had preceded it. It would be another twenty years until philosophers developed an interest in 'the history of analytic philosophy'.[7] In the 1990s the origins, roots, boundaries, and defining

---

[4] Richard Rorty, 'Realism, Categories, and the "Linguistic Turn"', *International Philosophical Quarterly* 2 (1962): 313.

[5] Richard Rorty, 'Metaphilosophical Difficulties of Linguistic Philosophy', in Rorty, *The Linguistic Turn*, 3.

[6] Rorty, 'Metaphilosophical Difficulties', 36.

[7] That was two decades ago. Today things have come to the point where one can even provide references for 'the history of the history of analytic philosophy'. See Juliet Floyd's excellent and comprehensive 'Recent Themes in the History of Analytic Philosophy' and Michael Beaney,

figures of the discipline became the subject of an impassioned debate, which can only mean that there was uncertainty over where it was headed and whether the party was over. But the issue, the subject of the debate, was 'analytic philosophy', not 'linguistic philosophy'. For one of the main stakes in the discussion was the relationship between the two, a relationship that, however happy it had been in the past, was obviously on the rocks.

That much was clear from the writing of and response to Michael Dummett's *Origins of Analytical Philosophy*, which, although it was not the first work to study the history, was one of the most provocative.[8] Dummett made two significant claims: that analytic philosophy was defined by the conviction that one could only analyse thought by analysing its expression in language and that this conviction had first been articulated in the works of Gottlob Frege. Both claims were controversial. Frege had designed a new symbolic notation for logic, his *Begriffsschrift*, and had shown, by doing so, how imprecise natural language was as a logical instrument. But the first claim came under heavy fire. For, as many pointed out, if analytic philosophy flowed from the linguistic turn, then its acknowledged sources—G. E. Moore, Bertrand Russell—weren't analytic philosophers.[9]

One didn't approach these issues *en bloc*: there were permutations available. You could agree that analytic philosophy had, at some point, taken the turn, but argue that the turn was taken by someone else (as Peter Hacker, Wittgenstein's most prolific commentator, would argue).[10] You could say that the revolution was initiated by Moore and Russell, when they became convinced that the business of philosophy should be the analysis of propositions and the understanding of their logical form, and that the turn was therefore just a moment or variation within the analytic movement (Ray Monk's position).[11] Or you could hold that Frege was indeed the fount, but had not taken the turn: he had brought mathematical logic into philosophy and so forced a rethinking of how philosophers went about their business, a rethinking that was logical rather than linguistic (Juliet Floyd).[12]

On one point, however, Dummett scored a direct hit. He had claimed that philosophers (Gareth Evans was his example) who proposed to analyse thought *without* recourse to its expression in language, were, by virtue of that fact, *not* analytic philosophers. To many this seemed preposterous: of course people like Evans were analytic philosophers. But there was agreement that he was not a linguistic philosopher. And as the 'history of analytic philosophy' picked up steam, the outlines of a significant consensus on a significant issue became clear. Philosophers were still doing analytic philosophy, but the linguistic turn was over: it had proved

'The Historiography of Analytic Philosophy', in Michael Beaney (ed.), *The Oxford Handbook of the History of Analytic Philosophy* (Oxford: Oxford University Press, 2013), 30–60.

[8] Michael Dummett, *Origins of Analytical Philosophy* (London: Duckworth, 1993).

[9] See, for example, Peter Hylton, review of Dummett, *Origins of Analytical Philosophy*, *Journal of Philosophy* 92.10 (1995): 556–63.

[10] P. M. S. Hacker, 'The Rise of Twentieth Century Analytic Philosophy', in Hans-Johann Glock (ed.), *The Rise of Analytic Philosophy* (Oxford: Basil Blackwell, 1997), 51–76.

[11] Ray Monk, 'Was Russell an Analytic Philosopher?', in Glock, *The Rise of Analytic Philosophy*, 35–50.

[12] Floyd, 'Recent Themes', 164–9.

to be something *historical*. In an article titled 'Past the Linguistic Turn?', Timothy Williamson argued that language had been superseded by the more capacious notion of mental 'representation' and this was all to the good.[13] Peter Hacker, responding to Williamson in 'Analytic Philosophy: Beyond the Linguistic Turn and Back Again', acknowledged the change and said this was all to the bad—analytic philosophers, having severed themselves from the turn, were now making the very mistakes Wittgenstein had made in the *Tractatus Logico-Philosophicus* and corrected in the *Philosophical Investigations*.[14] But there was agreement that analytic philosophy was moving on, and that the linguistic turn, having played its part, had left the stage, probably at some point in the 1960s or 1970s, leaving analytic philosophy to resume some metaphysical business, to take up the 'language of thought', and to recommence its pursuit of positive knowledge.[15]

When Rorty wrote of the 'linguistic revolution' in his Introduction, he knew some kind of restoration, a metaphysical 1660 or 1830, was in the works. The ambiguity is evident in the way Rorty tried, and failed, to use pragmatism as a hedge against the scientific pretensions of linguistic philosophy, pretensions he in part shared. Throughout his Introduction, Rorty claimed that the linguistic turn depended on a substantive thesis that one could not prove, 'methodological nominalism', the thesis that questions about concepts and natures—traditional philosophical questions—that aren't empirical and that 'can be answered in *some* way, can be answered by answering questions about the use of linguistic expressions, and in no other way'.[16] The arguments for accepting this thesis and its consequences were, Rorty further claimed, practical and not theoretical: 'They amount to saying to traditional philosophers: try doing it this way and see if you don't achieve your purposes more efficiently.'[17] Nevertheless, throughout the Introduction Rorty extols a version of philosophy indebted to the culture of science we discussed in Chapter 3: a philosophy in which arguments are stated so that one would both know what would count as evidence for or against it and be able to weigh that evidence, a philosophy that proceeds by careful piecemeal contributions and which is remote from 'subjectivity'. One attends to linguistic expressions because they are, to put it bluntly, observable: one has access to them and can measure them, as one cannot measure the concepts for which they supposedly stand.

If we now turn to an article Rorty published when he was writing his Introduction (an article celebrated as one of his great analytic achievements), one finds a similar claim made for 'better ways of talking'. In 'Mind-Body Identity, Privacy, and Categories', the issue is whether, *pace* the views of some linguistic philosophers, one could countenance replacing statements like 'I am in pain' with descriptions of

---

[13] Williamson, 'Past the Linguistic Turn?', 106–28.

[14] Peter Hacker, 'Analytic Philosophy: Beyond the Linguistic Turn and Back Again', in Michael Beaney (ed.), *The Analytic Turn: Analysis in Early Analytic Philosophy and Phenomenology* (London: Routledge, 2007), 125–41.

[15] Hilary Putnam has described this as the 'ontological style' that characterized analytic philosophy in the 1960s, a style that made it possible to be at once analytic and metaphysical; see 'A Half Century of Philosophy', 189.

[16] Rorty, 'Metaphilosophical Difficulties', 11.

[17] Rorty, 'Metaphilosophical Difficulties', 9.

the relevant brain-process (such as 'My C-fibers are firing').[18] Rorty's conclusion was that all talk of 'sensations' could be dumped in favour of brain-process talk, and might be someday, and that this dumping is analogous to replacing talk of demons by talk of hallucinations. Here, as in his discussion of the turn, his own talk is of the practicality of these substitutions, which make no claim to get closer to the essence of things but which work better than the terms they replace. Yes, they are more practical: but they are also, not coincidentally, more *scientific*. Rorty may say, hedging his bets, that the case for making the turn, for talking of hallucinations instead of demons, and for acknowledging the neurological basis of pain is not theoretical. But the bets he makes are *all* on science (which suggests that for all his Dewey-eyed rhapsodizing about pragmatism, the man who called the tune for him was Quine).

Ten years after *The Linguistic Turn*, Rorty would doubt that language itself was something one might turn to, and eventually he would reject the very idea that there were questions language itself posed to us ('I am no longer inclined,' he says in an afterword to the second edition of *The Linguistic Turn*, 'to think there is such a thing as "language" in any sense which makes it possible to speak of "problems of language".'[19]). Even in 1967 he could note, with some irritation, that philosophers who had made the turn and who should have known better were claiming 'to have discovered necessary truths about various sorts of entities (intentions, actions, sensations, thoughts, etc.)'.[20] In short, the enterprise of *analytic* philosophy now appeared separate from the linguistic turn, which might have helped it along at one point, might have served as a mediating point or pivot for an analytic project that really did hope to become scientific in form, but was now dispensable. Philosophers—Rorty included—tried analysis thinking it might be science, and they tried the linguistic turn thinking it would make philosophical prose clearer. He had been right: the linguistic turn was not evidence of scientific progress and its historical moment was passing. But the reasons were probably broader than even as imaginative a writer as Rorty would have thought.

Of course, Rorty spoke of *the* linguistic turn—in 1967 he didn't realize there had been several (he would try, in his own way, to synthesize some of them in his post-analytic writing from the 1980s onwards). They did not all end in the same way. Some, it seems, never actually took off. Cassirer finished the *Philosophy of Symbolic Forms*, debated with Heidegger, was forced to flee the Nazis and died in America: but though his work remained impressive and influential, no one picked up the torch (but for one notable disciple, Suzanne Langer).

The turn in analytic philosophy did not, as we now know, just plod along and then fizzle out. The period after the war was the true, self-conscious moment of linguistic philosophy, when Austin's influence was at its zenith and intellectual confidence (perhaps overconfidence) suffused the air. It's the period in which

---

[18] Richard Rorty, 'Mind-Body Identity, Privacy, and Categories', *The Review of Metaphysics* 19.1 (1965): 24–54.
[19] Richard Rorty, 'Twenty-Five Years After', in *The Linguistic Turn*, 2nd edn., 371.
[20] Rorty, 'Metaphilosophical Difficulties', 30.

Austin produced most of his essays, Ryle published *The Concept of Mind*, and Oxford philosophy seemed to carry all before it.[21] If Austin and his colleagues were indeed planning a revolution in philosophy, if the idea of a talented civil service of language was going to take hold, the 1950s promised success.

It was, however, a golden moment: by 1960, Peter Strawson was talking of a 'post-linguistic thaw' and looking wistfully back to the moment around 1950 when 'every new move was delightfully subversive and liberating'. Now, he had to confess, 'the revolutionary ferment had quite subsided' and philosophers seemed to be going about their business 'in a relatively traditional manner'.[22] After Austin died suddenly in 1960, his influence declined precipitously afterwards: the Oxford philosophy syllabus veered away from questions typical of ordinary language philosophy and though there were symposia and memorial volumes afterwards, no torchbearer for Austin emerged in his wake.[23] In fact, Austin's principal legacy turned out to centre on the William James lectures he had delivered at Harvard, published posthumously as *How to Do Things with Words*.[24] The text's terminology, constative and performative utterance, illocutionary and perlocutionary force quickly percolated not only into analytic philosophy, but also into literary criticism, deconstruction, and eventually and famously, gender studies.[25] Insofar as the lectures had tried to effect a major break with the descriptive fallacy, their influence shouldn't be surprising.[26] What's telling is that what survived Austin was not the practice of ordinary language philosophy he had defined and inspired, but a moment of conceptual innovation, a scientific moment, if you like, that redefined our sense of what language and speech accomplished in general terms.

---

[21] Gilbert Ryle, *The Concept of Mind* (London: Hutchinson, 1949). A good brief summary of the philosophy is the section 'Philosophy at Oxford, 1945–1970' in P. M. S. Hacker, *Wittgenstein's Place in Twentieth-Century Analytic Philosophy* (Oxford: Blackwell, 1996), 148–61. An excellent account of the overconfidence is Jonathan Rée, 'English Philosophy in the Fifties', *Radical Philosophy* 65 (1993): 3–21.

[22] Anonymous [P. F. Strawson], 'The Post-Linguistic Thaw: Getting Logical Conclusions out of the System', *Times Literary Supplement*, 9 September 1960, lx.

[23] This is not to say that Austin did not profoundly influence several important philosophers; merely that he did not leave a 'school'. One account of his influence is Stanley Cavell's 'Austin at Criticism', in *Must We Mean What We Say?*, 97–114.

[24] J. L. Austin, *How to Do Things with Words* (Oxford: Clarendon Press, 1962).

[25] Austin's immediate heir in analytic philosophy was John Searle, who codified and elaborated the ideas of the William James lectures in *Speech Acts* (Cambridge: Cambridge University Press, 1969). But the turn towards naturalism in analytic philosophy meant that Austin was most likely to inspire writers in other fields, and so it turned out. His work was taken up in literary criticism first by Mary Louise Pratt, in *Toward a Speech Act Theory of Literary Discourse* (Bloomington: Indiana University Press, 1981) and later by Shoshana Felman, *The Literary Speech Act: Don Juan with J. L. Austin, or a Seduction in Two Languages* (Ithaca, NY: Cornell University Press, 1983). But its most spectacular impact was on Jacques Derrida, who famously invoked it in the essay 'Signature Event Context', in *Margins of Philosophy*, trans. Alan Bass (Chicago: University of Chicago Press, 1982), 307–30, whence it passed to Judith Butler, in *Gender Trouble*.

[26] You can find the first formulation of the idea of the performative, and the hunch that it may in fact be the inner truth of speech and not just one species of it, in Austin's early essay, 'Other Minds', 103: 'To suppose that "I know" is a descriptive phrase, is only one example of the *descriptive fallacy*, so common in philosophy. Even if some language is now purely descriptive, language was not in origin so, and much of it is still not so. Utterance of obvious ritual phrases, in the appropriate circumstances, is not *describing* the action we are doing, but *doing* it ("I do"): in other cases it functions, like tone and expression, or again like punctuation and mood, as an intimation that we are employing language in some special way ("I warn", "I ask", "I define").'

The trajectory of the turn in England was striking, but it was the product of more than clever minds. For while the war affected Britain profoundly—and philosophers like Austin and Ryle directly—it left the basic social and political structure of the United Kingdom intact. For sure, it was a different, more social democratic country after the war, with a new kind of working-class presence in politics and culture and perhaps even a new class, but there was continuity in its political institutions and the philosophers who had led the linguistic charge before the war could continue their campaign after it.

Continental Europe was obviously a different matter. There was physical devastation and mass killing, of course, and a dramatic reshaping of the political landscape. New political and social institutions had to be built and several nations were either invented or dramatically reconfigured. Could language still provide a model of social cohesion and democratic deliberation? In this case, while one set of linguistic turns—the one described in this book—came to an end, another linguistic turn arose in its place. The linguistic turns of early twentieth-century continental Europe mutated, were transformed. The change can be described in five significant journeys.

1. Ernst Cassirer, who had witnessed the return of myth in a form more virulent than he could have ever expected, made his escape during the war. After a two-year sojourn in what had seemed like relatively safe Sweden, Cassirer realized he needed to put an ocean between himself and the Nazi advance. On 2 May 1941 he and his family boarded the freighter *Remmaren* bound for New York City. He was not the only person obsessed with symbols on the ship: Roman Jakobson, who had also been dodging the Nazis through Northern Europe, was on the same liner. Of course, they met and talked.[27] As a result, when Jakobson helped found yet another linguistic circle—the Linguistic Circle of New York—he arranged for his new friend Cassirer to deliver a lecture to the Circle in early 1945, which was then published in the second issue of the Circle's journal, *Word*. 'Structuralism in Modern Linguistics' gave a name to 'a general tendency of thought that, in these last decades, has become more and more prominent in almost all fields of scientific research'.[28]

2. Jakobson himself had begun to teach at an institution founded in New York in 1941–2, the École libre des Hautes Études de New York. There he met the young anthropologist Claude Lévi-Strauss, and the two began to attend one another's classes.[29] For Lévi-Strauss this meant attending classes on 'Six leçons sur le son et le sens' and 'sur la doctrine linguistique de Ferdinand de Saussure'.[30]

In Jakobson's linguistics, Lévi-Strauss thought he had found a scientific approach to the material of the human sciences, scientific because it dealt with structures

---

[27] See Thomas A. Sebeok, *Semiotics in the United States* (Bloomington: Indiana University Press, 1991), 37–8; Bert Jangfeldt, 'Roman Jakobson in Sweden 1940-41', *Cahiers de l'ILSL* 9 (1997): 141–9.

[28] Ernst A. Cassirer, 'Structuralism in Modern Linguistics', *Word* 1.2 (1945), 120. Thomas Sebeok, who attended, claims the lecture took place in the autumn of 1944: see his *Global Semiotics* (Bloomington: Indiana University Press, 2001), 139.

[29] The circumstances are briefly described in Claude Lévi-Strauss and Didier Eribon, *Conversations with Claude Lévi-Strauss*, trans. Paula Wissing (Chicago: University of Chicago Press, 1991), 40–3.

[30] John E. Joseph, 'The Genesis of Jakobson's "Six Lectures on Sound and Meaning"', *Historiographia Linguistica* 16.3 (1989): 415–20.

that worked below the level of consciousness and without its interference. Now 'language' could serve as the model for a much broader turn, which issued in a 'structuralist' version of anthropology. In this case the homology between language and society that had been so central to Saussure was utterly apt, for the object of Lévi-Strauss's analysis would not be texts (although myths would get their turn soon) but societies, which turned out, if you dug deep enough, to be structured like a language system. For Lévi-Strauss the lack of reflexivity in Saussure's system was not a weakness, but an advantage.

3. Roland Barthes was in Romania for much of the war; afterwards he found a teaching post in Alexandria. When he went there in 1949, he was already a literary critic and a confirmed champion of avant-garde writing. In Alexandria he would meet the Lithuanian A. J. Greimas; they became friends. Barthes showed Greimas the manuscript of what would eventually become *Michelet*. "'It's very good", Greimas commented, "but you could use Saussure".'[31] Thus the literary critic became a semiotician and one of structuralism's leading figures. More importantly, Saussure acquired a new and different kind of relevance. Until the spread of structuralism as a general method, Saussure was merely an important source for theoretical linguistics. But as structuralism began its imperial adventure, his works had to be consulted by an ever-widening circle. The *Cours de linguistique générale* was reprinted ten times between 1916 and 1963; in the twenty-two years following it went through another twenty-three reprints and sold more than 150,000 copies; rather a lot for a work in linguistic theory.[32] Of course, the point was that from the 1960s onwards the *Cours* was no longer a work of linguistic theory—it was the *ürtext* of structuralism, the place to which one turned for pithily expressed insights on the nature of the sign, the importance of differences, and the inseparability of language and thought. Saussure's linguistics had been exported; the idea of language had an unrivalled sphere of influence.[33]

4 and 5. Tzvetan Todorov travelled from Bulgaria to Paris in 1963, where he would establish himself as a literary critic and, just as importantly, introduce the Russian Formalists to Paris, in the shape of an edited collection of Formalist pieces translated into French in 1965.[34] Finally, another Bulgarian, Julia Kristeva, would leave Sofia for Paris, where Todorov would introduce her to Barthes's seminar. Like Todorov, she was, courtesy of the Soviet sphere of influence, able in Russian. Todorov had brought the Formalists; in 1965–6, she brought Bakhtin, whose works on Dostoevsky and Rabelais (republished in Russian in 1963 and 1965)

---

[31] Louis-Jean Calvet, *Roland Barthes: A Biography*, trans. Sarah Wykes (Cambridge: Polity Press, 1994), 94.

[32] This information comes from Gadet, *Saussure and Contemporary Culture*, 11.

[33] On the exportation of structuralist linguistics see Thomas G. Pavel, *The Feud of Language: A History of Structuralist Thought* (Oxford: Basil Blackwell, 1989); John E. Joseph, 'The Exportation of Structuralist Ideas from Linguistics to Other Fields: An Overview', in Sylvain Auroux, E. F. K. Koerner, Hans-Joseph Niederehe, and Kees Versteegh (eds.), *History of the Language Sciences: An International Handbook on the Study of Language from the Beginnings to the Present* (Berlin: Walter de Gruyter, 2000), 1880–908.

[34] Tzvetan Todorov (ed.), *Théorie de la littérature, textes des formalistes russes* (Paris: Le Seuil, 1965).

she was familiar with.[35] The set was complete: Paris had avant-garde literary criticism to go with its scientific linguistics. In fact, it seemed that most roads went to Paris. The linguistic turns of the early twentieth century were spread around; the turn that dominated the latter half of the century—structuralism and its progeny—was very much a French affair. France had had Sorel and linguists who expanded on Saussure's insights (such as Antoine Meillet and Benveniste), but phenomenology seemed to block 'language' otherwise (as Dummett pointed out, it provided an alternative route out of psychologism and subjectivism).[36] After the war, however, language appeared to provide a new model of society.

In its way, structuralism proved to be the grandest and most extravagant linguistic turn of them all, in part because it was also the most self-conscious. The linguistic philosophers in England and Austria knew they were focusing intently on language, but the structuralists in France knew they were focusing on a model of language. But something else added to the extravagance. When he ascended to a chair at the Collège de France in 1977, Barthes reminisced: 'It seemed to me (around 1954) that a science of signs might stimulate social criticism, and Sartre, Brecht, and Saussure could concur in this project.'[37] Earlier turns had looked to language as a sphere that might hold the key to social order in a politically precarious Europe; Barthes, in a way that was entirely typical, looked to language for a key to disturbing the social order. The France in which structuralism flourished was the relatively successful France of the Fourth and Fifth Republics—the question was how to shake the nation from its social democratic slumber.

In this respect, one of Barthes's earliest forays, the pieces collected as *Mythologies*, is entirely characteristic. Barthes's confessed target was the bourgeois consumerism of the 1950s: the objects of his critique were ads for soda powder, popular journalism, and French obsessions like steak, wine, and Catholicism. When the occasional pieces were put together in a published book, he added a lengthy theoretical addendum, 'Myth Today'. It was a sustained attempt to make language do an enormous amount of political work.

Myth, he insisted, was '*a type of speech*', 'a mode of signification'.[38] Myth was not defined by its objects or topics, 'but by the way in which it utters this message'.[39] In short, myth was something language could do and could do with anything; it was a strictly formal operation. To illustrate its workings, Barthes described the cover of an issue of *Paris-Match*, which portrayed a black soldier saluting, 'with his eyes uplifted, probably fixed on a fold of the tricolour'.[40] This not so subtle appeal to French imperialism nevertheless relied on a complex operation, according to Barthes. The soldier himself was a constituted sign (we could see, from the lines and colours of the picture, that this was a soldier saluting), but this sign then became a signifier in turn of something else, the idea (meaning) that even the victims of colonialism are loyal subjects of France. For Barthes, myth was a second-order

---

[35] Calvet, *Barthes*, 155–6.   [36] See Dummett, *Origins of Analytical Philosophy*, 22–7.
[37] Roland Barthes, 'Lecture in Inauguration of the Chair of Literary Semiology, Collège de France, January 7, 1977', translated by Richard Howard, *October* 8 (1979): 11.
[38] Roland Barthes, 'Myth Today', in *Mythologies*, trans. Annette Lavers (London: Vintage, 1993), 109.
[39] Barthes, 'Myth Today', 109.   [40] Barthes, 'Myth Today', 116.

system, built on the ordinary operations of signs: its trick was to efface the second join, so that the passage from lines and colours to French imperialism acquired the sheer immediacy of myth.

Immediacy, or, if you like, naturalness: this was the essential quality of myth. It set language up as the vehicle of 'naturalization', as if the danger of thinking language was a nomenclature—which so concerned Saussure—was an issue of everyday experience, part of the ordinary phenomenology of signs. What's notable about the argument is how it aligns certain formal features of language with the interests and world-view of bourgeois France: its perceived smugness and self-satisfaction, its false universality. France, Barthes will say, 'is steeped in this anonymous ideology'.[41] Indeed, reading the analysis it is easy to understand the anonymity, because the operation of myth looks a lot like the normal operating procedures of signs themselves. Second-order systems, signifiers being layered with new levels of meaning and connotation are part of the ordinary complexity of language, not a distortion of or deviation from it.

Saussure's linguistics thereby became a theory of ideology, while social cohesion and order became ideological per se. The flip side of this was a distinctly avant-garde notion of left-wing signification. If language so easily gives itself to myth, then one must disturb and wrench, prevent its normal operation, to fight the battle against ideology. Barthes will try, in 'Myth Today' to describe a kind of naturally left-wing speech (spoken, in the text, by a woodcutter), but that speech will be defined as an action that avoids the sign completely. Far more typical is the kind of signification Barthes will suggest at the end of one of the more interesting mythological analyses, where he suggests an 'ethic of signs'. Signs, Barthes says, must be either 'openly intellectual' (Brecht is the obvious inspiration) or 'deeply rooted'.[42] Ordinary language is the unhappy middle. From Saussure Barthes inherits belief in the cohesiveness and conservatism of *langue*, the language system. For Saussure, this had been one of its virtues; for Barthes—gay, left-wing, avant-garde—it is a defect, and its disruption is essential to political and social progress. It's a model he will share and pass on to a generation of structuralist and post-structuralist critics.

SOME FINAL REFLECTIONS

It should come as no surprise that in the final analysis the writers we've looked at did not provide a better model of social order and cohesion, did not imagine a public sphere that mixed political passion with cool deliberation, and did not figure a workable scenario for just political arrangements. These were problems no one solved and they were problems that would never be solved by sheer intellectual effort alone. But the writers involved in the linguistic turns had faced an additional difficulty, peculiar to their project. For, as I've argued throughout this book, language served as a metonym for the larger social and political whole and this unsurprisingly led writers to invest too much in it: to overestimate what 'language

---

[41] Barthes, 'Myth Today', 140.   [42] Barthes, 'The Romans in Films', in *Mythologies*, 28.

as such' might accomplish and to exaggerate the degree to which actually existing language was defective or disappointing.

Thus, Saussure made language as such too conservative in its nature; he endowed it with an inertia that resisted all directed linguistic change and when such change happened, he decried it as artificial. Benjamin, Bakhtin, Cassirer, and Shklovskii on the other hand, probably gave language as such too much political credit. Benjamin's distinction between language as such and human language burdened the former with utopian powers and aspirations: the pure language was the vehicle of an ideal community, transparent to itself and spontaneously just. That every element of calculation, of science, and of institutionalization found itself delegated to actually existing human language was a sign that politics would have no positive project in his work. That the divine language was just but destructive, that dialectical images were insightful but explosive, was just the logical result of the initial and enduring division.

In Bakhtin the distinction between novelistic dialogism and a variety of antitheses—official culture, monologism, the poetic, epic—had similar consequences: the deck was permanently stacked in the novel's favour, but the winnings were reduced. Bakhtin had embedded the open ethico-political situation of modernity—the need for ethical and political self-invention and creativity—in a distinctive literary style: its modest appearance belied the substantial and dramatic social energy he claimed was behind it. The style was historical, novelistic and modern, and at the same time the mere expression of a basic condition of language as such. But, as we discovered, the satirical, ironizing element of this style, which seemed necessary for its 'inconclusive spontaneity', left it with no purchase on the social world of roles, positions, and institutions, each of which became no more than a temporary mask. Democracy became no more than permanent forward movement, triggered by the inauthenticity of everything symbolic.

Cassirer had tried to be more nuanced; the multiple volumes of the *Philosophy of Symbolic Forms* were his statement of faith in the plural nature of symbols. But myth, acknowledged and thoroughly researched, could not be successfully assimilated and, in the end, language found itself caught between the enchantments of myth and the achievements of science. In theory, of course, science would always win; in practice, this turned out not to be the case. For the constitutional politics that Cassirer's philosophy led him towards could not understand the need for passionate, magical public opinion, or the need to turn defeat into political capital.

Shklovskii was used to defeat: in fact, his resilience, personally and intellectually, in the face of it was one of his most remarkable qualities. But here, too, one could not avoid the impression that the practical, ordinary language of everyday life was somehow a disappointment to 'language' itself, the son or daughter who seems a little too willing to do the bare minimum. In Shklovskii's case the democracy of technique—which can come from anywhere, which is discovered by means of the same improvisatory ethic it puts in play—is complemented by the avant-gardism of its effects, the conviction that sensitivity to things will somehow lead to sensitivity in ethical and political matters.

What, then, of the great edifice of analytic philosophy, which invested so much for so long in language? We can deal with the tributary represented by Ogden and Richards first, which is almost a mirror image of the work we've just discussed. For their science of symbolism tells us that language is naturally analytical, and that its ability to combine and synthesize by means of naming, morphology, and syntax, has to be kept in check. Few of the writers we've discussed are as upfront about the social and political ramifications of their theory of language, but that does not prevent Ogden and Richards from their own overinvestment. Their conviction that an analytic language was a necessarily clearer one, and that a clearer language would inevitably lead to sharp, well thought out judgments not only sidelined everything rhetorical in language, but probably sidelined much of actual science as well.

Is it unfair to say that analytic philosophy was also overinvested in style? From the outset the analytic commitment to clarity is motivated by the sense that actual language is, in Ryle's famous expression, 'systematically misleading'. What followed was a continuous effort to frame a kind of language that would never mislead, to define linguistic forms and rules of syntax that would prevent, by their very exercise, the nonsense that seemed to haunt philosophy. But here, too, the effect, clarity, is conflated with a particular mode of expression, as if a particular way of writing and speaking ensured flawless communication. Through all this, however, there is a commitment to language as a particularly public institution, available for inspection and analysis. In a long and broad tradition such as this, there were bound to be significant variations, and Wittgenstein accounted for several of them. The early work, culminating in the *Tractatus*, will redefine clarity as an ironic sense of the world's limitations: it marked the return of the rhetorical or intersubjective element that was being excluded, in theory at any rate, from the analytical project. In the middle and later work, we see this intersubjective element continually press against Wittgenstein's numerous and inventive attempts to order language, to ensure that it always works. Wittgenstein's effort and agility in response is impressive, as he moves from rules, to a calculus, to forms of life; but he slips on music, because, in that historical moment, it doesn't work. Austin shrewdly sticks to language and he generates what looks like a style and method that, while essential to democracy, cannot be the whole story.

Each kind of metonymy and investment leads to a different set of problems. Saussure can explain consent in his social order, but must exclude discussion. The analytic tradition offers a route to a more rational, objective form of decision-making, but depends on expertise and training instead of public debate to produce reasonable conclusions. Benjamin can acknowledge, as few others, the weight of the past in language, and the degree to which historical consciousness is necessary in democracy; but he must exclude the institutional side of politics. Cassirer can explain that side well, but fails to understand public opinion and its mythic passions. Bakhtin finds ethics in language, but no social roles. Wittgenstein can draw in all of social life, except failure.

You might think that the imbrication of writing on language with social and political thought is fascinating (if you've got this far, you probably do), but that there's something wrong, something uncharitable about the approach I've taken. For the claim that these writers use language as a metonym for European social and political life assumes that we know where the boundary between language and that social life should be drawn. Wouldn't the case appear quite different if we drew the boundary somewhere else, so as to include a more generous portion of the social and political? More to the point: shouldn't we want writing on language to think of social and political matters as being internal to language, rather than as external circumstances? When Saussure tells us that when we deal with semiological phenomena '[t]he community and its laws are among their *internal*, rather than *external* elements' should we not think of this as insight rather than confusion? When Wittgenstein says that '[w]ithout language we couldn't influence people. Or console them. Or build houses and machines' shouldn't we congratulate him for a conception of language as more than a mere tool?

We should and I think that, in my own way, I have. The issue at stake is not whether or not language is coextensive with our social and political life, as it obviously is, or whether there are different ways to draw a boundary around language, as there obviously are. All the writers covered in this book have deepened our sense of what language is and how it operates, have provided some remarkable insights into its shape and work, precisely by thinking either hard and carefully or hard and adventurously about how language is social and what sort of social institution and activity it is. The issue is with language as such: that is, the assumption that one can isolate something called 'language' and assign it properties, a force, a tendency which can then be compared with actually existing language. If there is a move the linguistic turns share that makes their life difficult, it's that one. For there is no predetermined thing to isolate, no predetermined place to draw the boundary—Saussure, with whom we began this long trek, knew that straight off the bat. What you will call language and how you will define it will be a partly philosophical and partly empirical question, depending on what questions you're asking and how you hope to answer them. Those who took a linguistic turn had questions, but they thought they could answer them by turning to language for help: language as such, which could do much of the work that needed to be done, if only we recognized it.

The linguistic turns of the early twentieth century made words more than words, language more than just an instrument of communication. They focused our attention on language in ways that were unquestionably productive, but they also led us to both expect wonders from it and blame it for many of our misfortunes. We need to consider the language we use as neither wholly innocent of the world's wrongs nor as a well full of dark forces. If we expect too much of it, we are sure to be disappointed; if we fear its ordinary operation, we will never take advantage of its many talents.

Bibliography

Aarsleff, Hans. *From Locke to Saussure: Essays on the Study of Language and Intellectual History*. Minneapolis: University of Minnesota Press, 1982.
Adorno, Theodor W. 'Mahler'. In *Quasi una Fantasia*, 81–110. Translated by Rodney Livingstone. London: Verso, 1992.
Adorno, Theodor W. *Mahler: A Musical Physiognomy*. Translated by Edmund Jephcott. Chicago: University of Chicago Press, 1992.
Adorno, Theodor W. and Walter Benjamin. *The Complete Correspondence 1928–1940*. Translated by Nicholas Walker. Cambridge: Polity Press, 1999.
Akehurst, Thomas L. *The Cultural Politics of Analytic Philosophy*. London: Continuum, 2010.
Alpatov, Vladimir M. 'Filologiia i revoliutsiia'. *Novoe literaturnoe obozrenie* 53 (2002): 199–216. http://magazines.russ.ru/nlo/2002/53/alpat.html. Accessed 3 September 2012.
Alpatov, Vladimir M. *Voloshinov, Bakhtin i lingvistika*. Moscow: Iazyki slavianskikh kul'tur, 2005.
Alter, Robert. *The Five Books of Moses*. New York: W. W. Norton, 2004.
Altieri, Charles. 'What Theory Can Learn from New Directions in Contemporary American Poetry'. *New Literary History* 43.1 (2012): 65–87.
Altieri, Charles. *Reckoning with the Imagination: Wittgenstein and the Aesthetics of Literary Experience*. Ithaca, NY: Cornell University Press, 2015.
Altieri, Charles. 'Doubt and Display: A Foundation for a Wittgensteinian Approach to the Arts'. In Sebastian Sunday Grève and Jakub Mácha (eds.), *Wittgenstein and the Creativity of Language*, 177–97. London: Palgrave Macmillan, 2016.
Altieri, Charles and Sascha Bru. 'Trakl's Tone: Mood and the Distinctive Speech Act of the Demonstrative'. In Sascha Bru, Wolfgang Huemer, and Daniel Steuer (eds.), *Wittgenstein Reading*, 355–72. Berlin: Walter de Gruyter, 2013.
Amsterdamska, Olga. *Schools of Thought: The Development of Linguistics from Bopp to Saussure*. Dordrecht: D. Reidel, 1987.
Anderson, Benedict. *Imagined Communities: Reflections on the Origin and Spread of Nationalism*. Revised edn. London: Verso, 1991.
Anderson, Perry. 'Components of the National Culture'. In Alexander Cockburn and Robin Blackburn (eds.), *Student Power: Problems, Diagnosis, Action*, 214–84. Harmondsworth: Penguin, 1969.
Angenot, Mark. 'Structuralism as Syncretism: Institutional Distortions of Saussure'. In John Fekete (ed.), *The Structural Allegory*, 150–63. Manchester: Manchester University Press, 1984.
Antin, David. 'Wittgenstein among the Poets (Review of Marjorie Perloff, *Wittgenstein's Ladder*)'. *Modernism/Modernity* 5.1 (1998): 149–66.
Any, Carol. *Boris Eikhenbaum: Voices of a Russian Formalist*. Stanford, CA: Stanford University Press, 1994.
Apel, Karl-Otto. *Analytic Philosophy of Language and the Geisteswissenschaften*. Dordrecht: D. Reidel, 1967.
Arvatov, Boris. 'Iazyk poeticheskii i iazyk prakticheskii'. *Pechat' i revoliutsiia* 7 (1923): 58–67.

Arvatov, Boris. 'Rechetvorchestvo (po povodu "zaumnoi" poezii)'. *LEF* 2 (1923): 79–91.
Attridge, Derek. 'Language as History/History as Language: Saussure and the Romance of Etymology'. In Derek Attridge, Geoff Bennington, and Robert Young (eds.), *Post-Structuralism and the Question of History*, 183–211. Cambridge: Cambridge University Press, 1987.
Auerbach, Erich. *Mimesis: The Representation of Reality in Western Literature*. Translated by Willard R. Trask. Princeton, NJ: Princeton University Press, 2003.
Auroux, Sylvain. 'Deux hypothèses sur l'origine de la conception saussurienne de la valeur linguistique'. *Travaux de linguistique et de littérature* 23.1 (1985): 295–9.
Auroux, Sylvain. 'The Semiological Source of Semantics'. In Lia Formigari (ed.), *Historical Roots of Linguistic Theories*, 221–32. Amsterdam: John Benjamins, 1995.
Austin, J. L. Review of Gilbert Ryle, *The Concept of Mind*. *Times Literary Supplement*, 7 April 1950, 220.
Austin, J. L. *How to Do Things with Words*. Oxford: Clarendon Press, 1962.
Austin, J. L. *Philosophical Papers*. 2nd edn. Oxford: Clarendon Press, 1970.
Ayer, A. J. 'Atomic Propositions'. *Analysis* 1.1 (1933): 2–6.
Ayer, A. J. *Language, Truth, and Logic*. Harmondsworth: Penguin, 1971.
Ayer, A. J. *Russell and Moore: The Analytical Heritage*. London: Macmillan, 1971.
Ayer, A. J. et al. *The Revolution in Philosophy*. London: Macmillan, 1956.
Badiou, Alain. *Wittgenstein's Antiphilosophy*. Translated by Bruno Bosteels. London: Verso, 2011.
Baker, G. P. and P. M. S. Hacker. 'Dummett's Frege or through a Looking-Glass Darkly'. *Mind* 92 (1983): 239–46.
Baker, G. P. and P. M. S. Hacker. *Language, Sense and Nonsense: A Critical Investigation into Modern Theories of Language*. Oxford: Basil Blackwell, 1984.
Bakhtin, M. M. *Problemy tvorchestva Dostoevskogo*. Leningrad: Priboi, 1929.
Bakhtin, M. M. *Tvorchestvo Fransua Rable i narodnaia kul'tura srednevekov'ia i Renessansa*. Moscow: Khudozhestvennaia literatura, 1990.
Bakhtin, M. M. *Sobranie sochinenii. Tom 5: raboty 1940-x—nachalo 1960-x godov*. Moscow: Russkie slovari, 1996.
Bakhtin, M. M. *Sobranie sochinenii. Tom 2: Problemy tvorchestva Dostoevskogo, 1929; stat'i o L. Tol'stom, 1929; zapisi kursa lektsii po istorii russkoi literatury, 1922–1927*. Moscow: Russkie slovari, 2000.
Bakhtin, M. M. *Besedy c V. D. Duvakinym*. Moscow: Soglasie, 2002.
Bakhtin, M. M. *Sobranie sochinenii. Tom 6: Problemy poetiki Dostoevskogo, 1963; raboty 1960-x—1970-x gg*. Moscow: Russkie slovari, 2002.
Bakhtin, M. M. *Sobranie sochinenii. Tom 1: Filosofskaia estetika 1920-x godov*. Moscow: Russkie slovari, 2003.
Bakhtin, M. M. *Sobranie sochinenii. Tom 4 (1): Fransua Rable v istorii realizma (1940 g); materialy k knige o Rable (1930 gg–1950 gg); kommentarii i pripolozheniia*. Moscow: Iazyki slavianskikh kul'tur, 2008.
Bakhtin, M. M. *Sobranie sochinenii. Tom 3: teoriia romana (1930–1961 gg.)*. Moscow: Iazyki slavianskikh kul'tur, 2012.
Baldwin, Thomas. 'Moore's Rejection of Idealism'. In Richard Rorty, J. B. Schneewind, and Quentin Skinner (eds.), *Philosophy in History: Essays in the Historiography of Philosophy*, 357–74. Cambridge: Cambridge University Press, 1984.
Balibar, Etienne and Pierre Macherey. 'On Literature as an Ideological Form'. In Robert Young (ed.), *Untying the Text*, 79–99. London: Routledge & Kegan Paul, 1981.

Barankova, G. S. 'K istorii Moskovskogo Lingvisticheskogo Kruzhka: Materialy iz Rukopisnogo otdela Instituta russkogo iazyka'. In S. M. Gindin and N. N. Rozanova (eds.), *Iazyk, kul'tura, gumanitarnoe znanie: nauchnoe nasledie G. O. Vinokura i sovremennost'*, 359–82. Moscow: Nauchnyi mir, 1999.

Barooshian, Vahan D. *Russian Cubo-Futurism, 1900–1930*. The Hague: Mouton, 1974.

Barthes, Roland. 'Lecture in Inauguration of the Chair of Literary Semiology, Collège de France, January 7, 1977'. Translated by Richard Howard. *October* 8 (1979): 3–16.

Barthes, Roland. 'Saussure, the Sign, Democracy'. In *The Semiotic Challenge*, 151–6. Translated by Richard Howard. Oxford: Basil Blackwell, 1988.

Barthes, Roland. *Mythologies*. Translated by Annette Lavers. London: Vintage, 1993.

Baz, Avner. *When Words Are Called For: A Defense of Ordinary Language Philosophy*. Cambridge, MA: Harvard University Press, 2012.

Beaney, Michael. 'What is Analytic Philosophy?' and 'The Historiography of Analytic Philosophy, In Michael Beaney (ed.), *The Oxford Handbook of the History of Analytic Philosophy*, 3–39, 30–60. Oxford: Oxford University Press, 2013.

Benes, Kveta E. 'German Linguistic Nationhood, 1806–66: Philology, Cultural Translation, and Historical Identity in Preunification Germany'. PhD dissertation, University of Washington, 2001.

Benjamin, Walter. 'N [Re the Theory of Knowledge, Theory of Progress]'. Translated by Leigh Hafrey and Richard Sieburth. In Gary Smith (ed.), *Benjamin: Philosophy, Aesthetics, History*, 43–83. Chicago: University of Chicago Press, 1989.

Benjamin, Walter. *The Correspondence of Walter Benjamin, 1910–1940*. Edited by Gershom Scholem and Theodor W. Adorno. Translated by Manfred R. Jacobson and Evelyn M. Jacobson. Chicago: University of Chicago Press, 1994.

Benjamin, Walter. *Selected Writings: Volume 1, 1913–1926*. Translated by Edmund Jephcott and others. Cambridge, MA: Harvard University Press, 1996.

Benjamin, Walter. *The Arcades Project*. Translated by Howard Eiland and Kevin McLaughlin. Cambridge, MA: Harvard University Press, 1999.

Benjamin, Walter. *Selected Writings: Volume 2, 1927–1934*. Translated by Rodney Livingstone and others. Cambridge, MA: Harvard University Press, 1999.

Benjamin, Walter. *Selected Writings: Volume 3, 1935–1938*. Translated by Edmund Jephcott, Howard Eiland, and others. Cambridge, MA: Harvard University Press, 2002.

Benjamin, Walter. *Selected Writings: Volume 4, 1938–1940*. Translated by Edmund Jephcott and others. Cambridge, MA: Harvard University Press, 2003.

Benjamin, Walter. *Berlin Childhood around 1900*. Translated by Howard Eiland. Cambridge, MA: Harvard University Press, 2006.

Benjamin, Walter and Gershom Scholem. *The Correspondence of Walter Benjamin and Gershom Scholem, 1932–1940*. Edited by Gershom Scholem. Translated by Gary Smith and Andre Lefevere. Cambridge, MA: Harvard University Press, 1992.

Benveniste, Émile. *Problems of General Linguistics*. Translated by Mary Elizabeth Meek. Coral Gables, FL: University of Miami Press, 1971.

Berezin, Vladimir. *Viktor Shklovskii*. Moscow: Molodaia gvardiia, 2014.

Bergmann, Gustav. 'Two Types of Linguistic Philosophy'. *Review of Metaphysics* 5.3 (1952): 417–38.

Bergmann, Gustav. 'Strawson's Ontology'. *Journal of Philosophy* 57.19 (1960): 601–22.

Bergmann, Gustav. *The Metaphysics of Logical Positivism*. Madison, WI: University of Wisconsin Press, 1967.

Berlin, Adele and Marc Zvi Brettler (eds.). *The Jewish Study Bible (Tanakh Translation)*. Oxford: Oxford University Press, 2004.

Berlin, Isaiah. 'Austin and the Early Beginnings of Oxford Philosophy'. In Isaiah Berlin et al., *Essays on J. L. Austin*, 1–16. Oxford: Clarendon Press, 1973.

Berlina, Alexandra. '"Let Us Return *Ostranenie* to its Functional Role": On Some Lesser-Known Writings of Viktor Shklovsky'. *Common Knowledge* 24.1 (2017): 8–25.

Bernstein, J. M. *The Philosophy of the Novel: Lukács, Marxism and the Dialectics of Form*. Minneapolis: University of Minnesota Press, 1984.

Bernstein, R. J. 'I. One Step Forward, Two Steps Backward: Richard Rorty on Liberal Democracy and Philosophy'. *Political Theory* 15.4 (1987): 538–63.

Bernstein, Richard. 'Richard Rorty's Deep Humanism'. *New Literary History* 39.1 (2008): 1–16.

Biale, David. *Gershom Scholem: Kabbalah and Counter-History*. Cambridge, MA: Harvard University Press, 1979.

Biletzki, Anat and Anat Matar (eds.). *The Story of Analytic Philosophy: Plot and Heroes*. London: Routledge, 1998.

Bishop, Paul. 'The Politics of Myth: Cassirer, Bachofen, and Sorel'. In Paul Bishop and R. H. Stephenson (eds.), *The Persistence of Myth as Symbolic Form*, 219–42. Leeds: Maney Publishing, 2008.

Bloomfield, Leonard. *Language*. New York: Henry Holt and Company, 1933.

Blumenberg, Hans. *Work on Myth*. Translated by Robert M. Wallace. Cambridge, MA: MIT Press, 1985.

Boothman, Derek. 'Gramsci's Interest in Language: The Influence of Bartoli's *Dispense di glottologia* (1912–13) on the *Prison Notebooks*'. *Journal of Romance Studies* 12.3 (2012): 10–23.

Bourbon, Brett. 'Wittgenstein's Preface'. *Philosophy and Literature* 29.2 (2007): 428–43.

Bourdieu, Pierre. *Language and Symbolic Power*. Translated by Peter Raymond and Gino Adamson. Cambridge, MA: Harvard University Press, 1991.

Bouveresse, J. '"The Darkness of This Time": Wittgenstein and the Modern World'. In A. Philips Griffiths (ed.), *Wittgenstein: Centenary Essays*, 11–39. Cambridge: Cambridge University Press, 1991.

Boym, Svetlana. 'Poetics and Politics of Estrangement: Viktor Shklovsky and Hannah Arendt'. *Poetics Today* 26.4 (2005): 581–611.

Brandist, Craig. 'The Origins of Soviet Sociolinguistics'. *Journal of Sociolinguistics* 7.2 (2003): 213–31.

Brandist, Craig. 'Voloshinov's Dilemma: On the Philosophical Roots of the Dialogic Theory of the Utterance'. In Craig Brandist, David Shepherd, and Galin Tihanov (eds.), *The Bakhtin Circle: In the Master's Absence*, 97–124. Manchester: Manchester University Press, 2004.

Brandist, Craig. 'Marxism and the Philosophy of Language in Russia in the 1920s and 1930s'. *Historical Materialism* 13.1 (2005): 63–84.

Brandist, Craig. 'The Rise of Soviet Sociolinguistics from the Ashes of *Völkerpsychologie*'. *Journal of the History of the Behavioral Sciences* 42.3 (2006): 261–77.

Brandist, Craig. 'Sociological Linguistics in Leningrad: The Institute for the Comparative History of the Literatures and Languages of the West and East (Iljazv) 1921–1933'. *Russian Literature* 63 (2008): 171–200.

Brandist, Craig and Katya Chown (eds.). *Politics and the Theory of Language in the USSR, 1917–1938*. London: Anthem Press, 2011.

Bréal, Michel. *Semantics: Studies in the Science of Meaning* (1897). Translated by Mrs Henry Cust. New York: Dover, 1964.

Bréal, Michel. 'Language and Nationality'. In *The Beginnings of Semantics: Essays, lectures and reviews*, 199–220. Translated by George Wolf. London: Duckworth, 1991.

Brik, O. et al. *Poetika: sborniki po teorii poeticheskogo iazyka*. Petersburg: n.p., 1919.
Bru, Sascha. *Democracy, Law and the Modernist Avant-Gardes: Writing in the State of Exception*. Edinburgh: Edinburgh University Press, 2009.
Bruckstein, Almut Shulamit. 'Practicing "Intertextuality": Ernst Cassirer and Hermann Cohen on Myth and Monotheism'. In Jeffrey Andrew Barash (ed.), *The Symbolic Construction of Reality: The Legacy of Ernst Cassirer*, 174–88. Chicago: University of Chicago Press, 2008.
Brugmann, Karl. *Elements of the Comparative Grammar of the Indo-Germanic Languages, Vol. I: Introduction and Phonology*. Translated by Joseph Wright. London: Trübner & Co., 1888.
Bulatova, Asiya. '"I'm writing to you in this magazine": The Mechanics of Modernist Dissemination in Shklovsky's Open Letter to Jakobson'. *Comparative Critical Studies* 11.2–3 (2014): 185–202.
Burge, Tyler. 'Philosophy of Language and Mind: 1950–1990'. *Philosophical Review* 101.1 (1992): 3–51.
Burliuk, David, Aleksandr Kruchenykh, V. Mayakovsky, and Viktor Khlebnikov. 'Poshchechina obshchestvennomu vkusu' In D. Burliuk et al., *Poshchechina obshchestvennomu vkusu: v zashchitu svobodnago isskustva*. Moscow: G. L. Kuz′min, 1912. Getty Research Institute digital library. http://www.getty.edu/research/tools/guides_bibliographies/russian_avant_garde/index.html.
Burliuk, David et al. Untitled manifesto. In *Sadok sudei*, Vol. 2, 1–2. St Petersburg: Zhuravl′, 1913. Getty Research Institute digital library: http://www.getty.edu/research/tools/guides_bibliographies/russian_avant_garde/index.html.
Burrow, J. W. *The Crisis of Reason: European Thought, 1848–1914*. New Haven, CT: Yale University Press, 2000.
Busch, Kathrin. 'The Language of Things and the Magic of Language: On Walter Benjamin's Concept of Latent Potency'. *Transversal Texts* (2006). http://eipcp.net/transversal/0107/busch/en, accessed 18 June 2016.
Buse, Peter, Ken Hirschkop, Scott McCracken, and Bertrand Taithe. *Benjamin's Arcades: An unGuided tour*. Manchester: Manchester University Press, 2005.
Butler, Judith. *Gender Trouble*. London: Routledge, 1990.
Calvet, Louis-Jean. *Roland Barthes: A Biography*. Translated by Sarah Wykes. Cambridge: Polity Press, 1994.
Calvet, Louis-Jean. *Language Wars and Linguistic Politics*. Translated by Michel Petheram. Oxford: Oxford University Press, 1998.
Carlucci, Alessandro. *Gramsci and Languages: Unification, Diversity, Hegemony*. Chicago: Haymarket Books, 2013.
Cassirer, Ernst. 'Structuralism in Modern Linguistics'. *Word* 1.2 (1945): 99–120.
Cassirer, Ernst. *The Myth of the State*. New Haven, CT: Yale University Press, 1946.
Cassirer, Ernst. *Substance and Function*. Translated by William Curtis Swabey and Marie Collins Swabey. New York: Dover, 1953.
Cassirer, Ernst. *The Philosophy of Symbolic Forms, Volume 1: Language*. Translated by Ralph Manheim. New Haven, CT: Yale University Press, 1955.
Cassirer, Ernst. *The Philosophy of Symbolic Forms, Volume 2: Mythical Thought*. Translated by Ralph Manheim. New Haven, CT: Yale University Press, 1955.
Cassirer, Ernst. *The Philosophy of Symbolic Forms, Volume 3: The Phenomenology of Knowledge*. Translated by Ralph Manheim. New Haven, CT: Yale University Press, 1957.
Cassirer, Ernst. *The Philosophy of Symbolic Forms, Volume 4: The Metaphysics of Symbolic Forms*. Translated by John Michael Krois. New Haven, CT: Yale University Press, 1996.
Cassirer, Ernst. *The Individual and the Cosmos in Renaissance Philosophy*. Translated by Mario Domandi. New York: Dover Press, 2000.

Cassirer, Ernst. 'Seminar on Symbolism and Philosophy of Language, Vorlesung New Haven 1941/1942'. In *Nachgelassene Manuskripte und Texte*, Band 6, 191–343. Hamburg: Felix Meiner Verlag, 2005.

Cassirer, Ernst. 'Form and Technology' (1930). In Aud Sissel Hoel and Ingvild Folkvord (eds.), *Ernst Cassirer on Form and Technology: Contemporary Readings*, 15–53. Basingstoke: Palgrave Macmillan, 2012.

Cassirer, Ernst. *The Warburg Years (1919–1933)*. Translated by S. G. Lofts and Aldo Calcagno. New Haven, CT: Yale University Press, 2013.

Cassirer, Ernst. ['The Philosophy of Hermann Cohen and his Conception of Jewish Religion']. In Ernst Cassirer, *Nachgelassene Manuskripte und Texte*, Band 17, 141–57. Hamburg: Felix Meiner Verlag, 2014.

Cassirer, Ernst. 'The Idea of a Republican Constitution' (1928). Translated by Seth Berk. *Philosophical Forum* 49.1 (2018): 3–17.

Cavell, Stanley. *Must We Mean What We Say?* New York: Charles Scribner's Sons, 1969.

Cavell, Stanley. 'The Uncanniness of the Ordinary'. In *In Quest of the Ordinary: Lines of Skepticism and Romanticism*, 153–78. Chicago: University of Chicago Press, 1988.

Cavell, Stanley. 'What Did Derrida Want of Austin?' In *Philosophical Passages: Wittgenstein, Emerson, Austin, Derrida*, 42–65. Oxford: Basil Blackwell, 1995.

Cavell, Stanley. 'Declining Decline'. In *The Cavell Reader*, 321–52. Edited by Stephen Mulhall. Oxford: Basil Blackwell, 1996.

Cavell, Stanley. 'The Ordinary as the Uneventful'. In *The Cavell Reader*, 253–9. Edited by Stephen Mulhall. Oxford: Basil Blackwell, 1996.

Cavell, Stanley. 'Benjamin and Wittgenstein: Signals and Affinities'. *Critical Inquiry* 25.2 (1999): 235–46.

Cavell, Stanley. *The Claim of Reason: Wittgenstein, Skepticism, Morality, and Tragedy*. Oxford: Oxford University Press, 1999.

Cerbone, David. 'The Limits of Conservatism: Wittgenstein on "Our Life" and "Our Concepts"'. In Cressida J. Heyes (ed.), *The Grammar of Politics: Wittgenstein and Political Philosophy*, 43–62. Ithaca, NY: Cornell University Press, 2003.

Chambers, J. K., Sarah Cummins, and Jeff Tennant. 'Louis Gauchat – Patriarch of Variationist Linguistics'. *Historiographia Linguistica* 35.1/2 (2008): 213–74.

Chomsky, Noam. *Syntactic Structures*. The Hague: Mouton, 1957.

Chomsky, Noam. *The Logical Structure of Linguistic Theory*. Chicago: University of Chicago Press, 1985.

Chudakov, A. P. 'Dva pervykh desiatiletiia'. In Viktor Shklovskii, *Gamburgskii shchet: stat´i, vospominaniia, esse, 1914–1933*, 3–32. Moscow: Sovetskii pisatel´, 1990.

Chudakova, Marietta. 'Conversation with Viktor Borisovich Shklovsky, January 9, 1981'. *Poetics Today* 27.1 (2006): 237–44.

Clark, Katerina and Michael Holquist, *Mikhail Bakhtin*. Cambridge, MA: Harvard University Press, 1984.

Clark, T. J. 'Clement Greenberg's Theory of Art'. *Critical Inquiry* 9.1 (1982): 139–56.

Clark, T. J. *Farewell to an Idea: Episodes from a History of Modernism*. New Haven, CT: Yale University Press, 1999.

Cohen, Hermann. *Religion of Reason Out of the Sources of Judaism*, 2nd edn. Translated by Simon Kaplan. Atlanta: Scholars Press, 1995.

Collini, Stefan. 'On Highest Authority: The Literary Critic and Other Aviators in Early Twentieth-Century Britain'. In Dorothy Ross (ed.), *Modernist Impulses in the Human Sciences 1870–1930*, 152–70. Baltimore: Johns Hopkins University Press, 1994.

Compton, Susan P. *The World Backwards: Russian Futurist Books, 1912–16*. London: British Library, 1978.
Conant, James. 'Must We Show What We Cannot Say?'. In Richard Fleming and Michael Payne (eds.), *The Senses of Stanley Cavell*, 242–83. Lewisburg, PA: Bucknell University Press, 1989.
Conant, James. 'The Search for Logically Alien Thought: Descartes, Kant, Frege, and the *Tractatus*'. *Philosophical Topics* 20.1 (1991): 115–80.
Conant, James. 'Mild Mono-Wittgensteinianism'. In Alice Crary (ed.), *Wittgenstein and the Moral Life: Essays in Honor of Cora Diamond*, 29–142. Cambridge, MA: MIT Press, 2007.
Conant, James. 'A Prolegomenon to the Reading of Later Wittgenstein'. In Ludwig Nagel and Chantal Mouffe (eds.), *The Legacy of Wittgenstein: Pragmatism or Deconstruction*, 93–130. Frankfurt am Main: Peter Lang, 2010.
Conant, James. 'Wittgenstein's Methods'. In Oskari Kuusela and Marie McGinn (eds.), *The Oxford Handbook of Wittgenstein*, 620–45. Oxford: Oxford University Press, 2011.
Cook, Nicholas. *The Schenker Project: Culture, Race, and Music Theory in Fin-de-Siècle Vienna*. Oxford: Oxford University Press, 2007.
Courtine, Jean-Jacques. 'A Brave New Language: Orwell's Invention of *Newspeak* in *1984*'. *SubStance* 15.2 (1986): 69–74.
Crary, Alice. 'Wittgenstein's Philosophy in Relation to Political Thought'. In Alice Crary and Rupert Read (eds.), *The New Wittgenstein*, 118–45. London: Routledge, 2000.
Crary, Alice. 'The Happy Truth: J. L. Austin's *How to Do Things with Words*'. *Inquiry* 45.1 (2002): 59–80.
Croce, Benedetto. *Aesthetic as Science of Expression and General Linguistic*. Translated by Douglas Ainslie. London: Macmillan & Co., 1909.
Crossley, Nick and John Michael Roberts (eds.). *After Habermas: New Perspectives on the Public Sphere*. Malden, MA: Wiley-Blackwell, 2004.
Crowley, Tony. *Standard English and the Politics of Language*. 2nd edn. Basingstoke: Palgrave Macmillan, 2003.
Curthoys, Ned. *The Legacy of Liberal Judaism: Ernst Cassirer and Hannah Arendt's Hidden Conversation*. New York: Berghahn, 2013.
Darmesteter, Arsène. *The Life of Words as the Symbols of Ideas*. London: Kegan Paul, Trench & Co., 1886.
Davidson, Donald. 'Truth and Meaning'. *Synthese* 17.3 (1967): 304–23.
Davidson, Donald. 'On the Very Idea of a Conceptual Scheme'. *Proceedings and Addresses of the American Philosophical Association* 47 (1973): 5–20.
Davidson, Donald. 'Belief and the Basis of Meaning'. *Synthese* 27.3/4 (1974): 309–23.
Davidson, Donald. 'Communication and Convention'. *Synthese* 59.1 (1984): 3–17.
Davidson, Donald. 'A Nice Derangement of Epitaphs'. In Ernest Lepore (ed.), *Truth and Interpretation: Perspectives on the Philosophy of Donald Davidson*, 433–46. Oxford: Basil Blackwell, 1986.
de Man, Paul. 'The Resistance to Theory'. In *The Resistance to Theory*, 3–20. Minneapolis: University of Minnesota Press, 1986.
De Mauro, Tullio. 'Language from Nature to History: More on Gramsci the Linguist'. In Peter Ives and Rocco Lacorte (eds.), *Gramsci, Language, and Translation*, 51–62. Lanham, MD: Lexington Books, 2010.
Derrida, Jacques. 'Signature Event Context'. In *Margins of Philosophy*, 307–30. Translated by Alan Bass. Chicago: University of Chicago Press, 1982.

Desnitskaia, A. V. 'Frantsuzskie lingvisty i sovetskoe iazykoznanie 1920–1930-x godov'. *Izvestiia Akademii Nauk SSSR, Seriia literatury i iazyka* 50.5 (1991): 474–85.

Diamond, Cora. 'Having a Rough Story about What Moral Philosophy Is'. *New Literary History* 15.1 (1983): 155–69.

Diamond, Cora. 'Throwing Away the Ladder'. *Philosophy* 63 (1988): 5–27.

Diamond, Cora. 'Ethics, Imagination and the Method of Wittgenstein's *Tractatus*'. In Richard Heinrich and Helmuth Vetter (eds.), *Bilder der Philosophie: Reflexionen über das Bildliche und die Phantasie*, 55–90. Vienna: R. Oldenbourg, 1991.

Diamond, Cora. 'Wittgenstein, Ludwig [Josef Johann] (1889–1951)'. In Lawrence C. Becker and Charlotte B. Becker (eds.), *Encyclopedia of Ethics, Vol. II*, 1321. New York: Garland, 1992.

Diamond, Cora. 'Martha Nussbaum and the Need for Novels'. *Philosophical Investigations* 16.2 (1993): 128–53.

Diamond, Cora. ' "What Time Is It on the Sun?": An Interview with Cora Diamond'. *Harvard Review of Philosophy* 8 (2000): 69–81.

Diamond, Cora. 'The *Tractatus* and the Limits of Sense'. In Oskari Kuusela and Marie McGinn (eds.), *The Oxford Handbook of Wittgenstein*, 240–75. Oxford: Oxford University Press, 2011.

Doroszewski, W. 'Quelques remarques sur les rapports de la sociologie et de la linguistique: Durkheim et F. de Saussure'. *Journal de Psychologie normale et pathologique* 30 (1933): 82–91.

Dosse, François. *History of Structuralism: Vol. 1: The Rising Sign, 1945–1966*. Translated by Deborah Glassman. Minneapolis: University of Minnesota Press, 1997.

Duffy, Enda. 'Energy, Stress, and Modernist Style'. In Gregor Castle (ed.), *A History of the Modernist Novel*, 211–30. Cambridge: Cambridge University Press, 2015.

Dummett, Michael. *Frege: Philosophy of Language*. London: Duckworth, 1973.

Dummett, Michael. *The Interpretation of Frege's Philosophy*. London: Duckworth, 1981.

Dummett, Michael. *Origins of Analytical Philosophy*. London: Duckworth, 1993.

Düttman, Alexander García. *The Gift of Language: Memory and Promise in Adorno, Benjamin, Heidegger and Rosenzweig*. Translated by Arline Lyons. London: Athlone Press, 2000.

Easton, M. W. 'Analogy and Uniformity'. *American Journal of Philology* 5.2 (1884): 164–77.

Edelstein, Dan. 'The Modernization of Myth: From Balzac to Sorel'. *Yale French Studies* 111 (2007): 32–44.

Edelstein, Dan. 'The Birth of Ideology from the Spirit of Myth: Georges Sorel among the *Idéologues*'. In Joshua Landy and Michael Saler (eds.), *The Re-enchantment of the World: Secular Magic in a Rational Age*, 201–24. Stanford, CA: Stanford University Press, 2009.

Edmonds, David and John Eidinow. *Wittgenstein's Poker: The Story of a Ten-Minute Argument between Two Great Philosophers*. London: Faber and Faber, 2001.

Eiland, Howard and Michael W. Jennings. *Walter Benjamin: A Critical Life*. Cambridge, MA: Harvard University Press, 2014.

Eliot, T. S. 'The Idea of a Literary Review'. *The New Criterion* 4.1 (January 1926): 1–6.

Eliot, T. S. *Notes Toward the Definition of Culture*. London: Faber and Faber, 1948.

Eliot, T. S. '*Ulysses*, Order and Myth' (1923). In *Selected Prose of T. S. Eliot*, 175–8. London: Faber and Faber, 1975.

Engel, Pascal. Review of Michael Dummett, *Origins of Analytical Philosophy*. *Philosophical Quarterly* 45 (1995): 269–71.

Engelmann, Paul. *Letters from Ludwig Wittgenstein, With a Memoir*. Oxford: Basil Blackwell, 1967.

Engelmann, Mauro Luiz. 'Wittgenstein's "Most Fruitful Ideas" and Sraffa'. *Philosophical Investigations* 36.2 (2013): 155–78.
Engelmann, Mauro Luiz. *Wittgenstein's Philosophical Development: Phenomenology, Grammar, Method, and the Anthropological View*. Basingstoke: Palgrave Macmillan, 2013.
Erden, Yasemin J. 'Wittgenstein on Simile as the "Best Thing" in Philosophy'. *Philosophical Investigations* 35.2 (2012): 127–37.
Erlich, Viktor. *Russian Formalism: History—Doctrine*. 4th edn. The Hague: Mouton, 1980.
Etkind, Alexander. 'James and Konovalev: *The Varieties of Religious Experience* and Russian Theology between Revolutions'. In Joan Delaney Grossman and Ruth Rischin (eds.), *William James in Russian Culture*, 169–88. Lanham, MD: Lexington Books, 2003.
Falk, Julia S. 'Saussure and American Linguistics'. In Carol Sanders (ed.), *The Cambridge Companion to Saussure*, 107–23. Cambridge: Cambridge University Press, 2004.
Fann, K. T. *Symposium on J. L. Austin*. New York: Humanities Press, 1969.
Felman, Shoshana. *The Literary Speech Act: Don Juan with J. L. Austin, or a Seduction in Two Languages*. Translated by Catherine Porter. Ithaca, NY: Cornell University Press, 1983.
Feyerabend, Paul. *Against Method*. London: New Left Books, 1975.
Feyerabend, Paul. *Farewell to Reason*. London: Verso, 1987.
Fitzpatrick, Sheila. *The Commissariat of Enlightenment*. Cambridge: Cambridge University Press, 1970.
Fitzpatrick, Sheila (ed.). *Cultural Revolution in Russia, 1928–1931*. Bloomington: Indiana University Press, 1978.
Floyd, Juliet. 'Recent Themes in the History of Early Analytic Philosophy'. *Journal of the History of Philosophy* 47.2 (2009): 157–200.
Floyd, Juliet and Sanford Shieh (eds.). *Future Pasts: The Analytic Tradition in Twentieth-Century Philosophy*. New York: Oxford University Press, 2001.
Forguson, Lynd. 'Oxford and the "Epidemic" of Ordinary Language Philosophy'. *The Monist* 84.3 (2001): 325–45.
Foucault, Michel. *The Order of Things: An Archaeology of the Human Sciences*. London: Tavistock Publishers, 1974.
Francioni, Gianni. *L'Officina Gramsciana: Ipotesi sulla struttura dei 'Quaderni del carcere'*. Naples: Bibliopolis, 1984.
Franke, Damon. *Modernist Heresies: British Literary History, 1883–1924*. Columbus, OH: Ohio State University Press, 2008.
Frege, Gottlob. *The Basic Laws of Arithmetic*. Translated by Montgomery Furth. Berkeley, CA: University of California Press, 1964.
Frege, Gottlob. *Begriffsschrift: a formula language modeled upon that of arithmetic, for pure thought* (1879). Translated by Stefan Bauer-Mengelberg. In *Frege and Godel: Two Fundamental Texts in Mathematical Logic*. Edited by Jean van Heijenoort. Cambridge, MA: Harvard University Press, 1970.
Frege, Gottlob. 'On the Scientific Justification of a Conceptual Notation'. In *Conceptual Notation and Related Articles*, 83–9. Translated and edited by Terrell Ward Bynum. Oxford: Clarendon Press, 1972.
Frege, Gottlob. *Logical Investigations*. Translated by P. T. Geach and R. H. Stoothoff. Oxford: Basil Blackwell, 1977.
Frege, Gottlob. *Posthumous Writings*. Edited by Hans Hermes, Friedrich Kambartel, and Friedrich Kaulbach. Oxford: Basil Blackwell, 1979.
Frege, Gottlob. *Translations from the Philosophical Writings of Gottlob Frege*. Edited by Max Black and Peter Geach. 3rd edn. Oxford: Basil Blackwell, 1980.

Fried, Michael. 'Jeff Wall, Wittgenstein, and the Everyday'. *Critical Inquiry* 33 (2007): 495–526.
Friedman, Michael. *A Parting of the Ways: Carnap, Cassirer and Heidegger*. Chicago: Open Court, 2000.
Gadet, Françoise. *Saussure and Contemporary Culture*. Translated by Gregory Elliott. London: Hutchinson Radius, 1989.
Gadris, Stelios. 'Two Cases of Irony: Kant and Wittgenstein'. *Kant-Studien* 107.2 (2016): 343–68.
Garvía, Roberto. *Esperanto and its Rivals: The Struggle for an International Language*. Philadelphia: University of Pennsylvania Press, 2015.
Gasparov, Boris. 'The Ideological Principles of Prague School Phonology'. In Krystyna Pomorska et al. (eds.), *Language, Poetry and Poetics—the Generation of the 1890s: Jakobson, Trubetzkoy, Majakovskij*, 49–78. Berlin: Mouton de Gruyter, 1987.
Gasparov, Boris. 'Futurism and Phonology: Futurist Roots of Jakobson's Approach to Language'. In Françoise Gadet and Patrick Seriot (eds.), *Jakobson entre l'Est et l'Ouest 1915–1939*, Cahiers del'ILSL No. 9, 109–29. Lausanne: Presses Centrales de Lausanne, 1997.
Gasparov, Boris. *Beyond Pure Reason: Ferdinand de Saussure's Philosophy of Language and Its Early Romantic Antecedents*. New York: Columbia University Press, 2013.
Gawronsky, Dmitry. 'Ernst Cassirer: His Life and Work'. In Paul Arthur Schilpp (ed.), *The Philosophy of Ernst Cassirer*, 3–37. LaSalle, IL: Open Court Press, 1949.
Gellner, Ernest. *Words and Things*. London: Victor Gollancz, 1959.
Gellner, Ernest. *Language and Solitude: Wittgenstein, Malinowski and the Habsburg Dilemma*. Cambridge: Cambridge University Press, 1998.
Geuss, Raymond. 'Richard Rorty at Princeton: Personal Recollections'. *Arion* 15.3 (2008): 85–100.
Gindin, S. I. 'Druz'ia v zhizni – opponenty v nauke: Perepiska R. O. Jakobsona i G. O. Vinokura'. *Novoe literaturnoe obozrenie* 21 (1996): 59–111.
Ginneken, Jaap van. *Crowds, Psychology, and Politics, 1871–1899*. Cambridge: Cambridge University Press, 1992.
Glock, Hans-Johann. 'Cambridge, Jena or Vienna'. *Ratio* 5 (1992): 1–23.
Godel, Robert. *Les sources manuscrites du Cours de Linguistique Générale*. Geneva: Librarie Droz, 1969.
Goldfarb, Warren. 'Frege's Conception of Logic'. In Juliet Floyd and Sanford Shieh (eds.), *Future Pasts: The Analytic Tradition in Twentieth-Century Philosophy*, 25–41. New York: Oxford University Press, 2001.
Golec, Michael J. '"The Thinking Man's Filter": J. L. Austin's Ordinary Language Philosophy as Cultural Criticism'. *Cultural Critique* 72 (2009): 66–88.
Gordon, W. Terrence. *C. K. Ogden: A Bio-Bibliographical Study*. Metuchen, NJ: Scarecrow Press, 1990.
Gordon, W. Terrence. 'From "The Meaning of Meaning" to Basic English'. *Et cetera* (1991): 165–71.
Gorham, Michael S. 'Natsiia ili snikerizatsiia? Identity and Perversion in the Language Debates of Late- and Post-Soviet Russia'. *Russian Review* 59.4 (2000): 614–29.
Gornung, Boris. *Pokhod vremeni: stat'i i esse*. Moscow: RGGU, 2001.
Gramsci, Antonio. *Selections from Prison Notebooks*. Edited and translated by Quintin Hoare and Geoffrey Nowell-Smith. London: Lawrence & Wishart, 1971.
Gramsci, Antonio. *Letters from Prison*. Translated by Lynne Lawner. London: Jonathan Cape, 1975.

Gramsci, Antonio. *Selections from Political Writings (1910–1920)*. Translated by John Mathews. London: Lawrence & Wishart, 1977.
Gramsci, Antonio. *Selections from Cultural Writings*. Edited by David Forgacs and Geoffrey Nowell-Smith. Translated by William Boelhower. London: Lawrence & Wishart, 1985.
Gramsci, Antonio. *Prison Notebooks, Volumes I–III*. Edited and translated by Joseph A. Buttigieg. New York: Columbia University Press, 1992–2007.
Grasshoff, Gerd. 'Hertz's Philosophy of Nature in Wittgenstein's *Tractatus*'. In Davis Baird, R. I. G. Hughes, and Alfred Nordmann (eds.), *Heinrich Hertz: Classical Physicist, Modern Philosopher*, 243–68. Dordrecht: Kluwer Academic Publishers, 1998.
Greenberg, Udi E. 'Orthodox Violence: "Critique of Violence" and Walter Benjamin's Jewish Political Theology'. *History of European Ideas* 34 (2008): 324–33.
Griffin, Nicholas. 'Wittgenstein's Criticism of Russell's Theory of Judgment'. *Russell* 5 (1985): 132–45.
Grimm, Jacob Karl Ludwig. *On the Origin of Language* [1851]. Translated by Raymond A. Wiley. Leiden: Brill, 1984.
Gross, Neil. *Richard Rorty: The Making of an American Philosopher*. Chicago: University of Chicago Press, 2008.
Guter, Eran. '"A Surrogate for the Soul": Wittgenstein and Schoenberg'. In Enzo de Pellegrin (ed.), *Interactive Wittgenstein*, 109–52. Dordrecht: Springer, 2011.
Guter, Eran. 'Wittgenstein on Mahler'. In Danièle Moyal-Sharrock, Volker A. Munz, and Annalisa Coliva (eds.), *Mind, Language and Action: Contributions to the 36th International Wittgenstein Symposium*, 169–71. Austrian Ludwig Wittgenstein Society, 2013.
Guter, Eran. 'The Good, the Bad, and the Vacuous: Wittgenstein on Modern and Future Musics'. *Journal of Aesthetics and Art Criticism* 73.4 (2015): 425–39.
Habermas, Jürgen. 'What is Universal Pragmatics?' In *Communication and the Evolution of Society*, 21–5. Translated by Thomas McCarthy. London: Heinemann, 1979.
Habermas, Jürgen. *The Theory of Communicative Action, Volume I: Reason and the Rationalization of Society*. Translated by Thomas McCarthy. Boston: Beacon Press, 1981.
Habermas, Jürgen. 'Walter Benjamin: Consciousness-Raising or Rescuing Critique'. In *Philosophical-Political Profiles*, 129–64. Translated by Frederick G. Lawrence. Cambridge, MA: MIT Press, 1983.
Habermas, Jürgen. *On the Logic of the Social Sciences*. Translated by Shierry Weber Nicholsen and Jerry A. Stark. Cambridge, MA: MIT Press, 1988.
Habermas, Jürgen. *The Structural Transformation of the Public Sphere: An Inquiry into a Category of Bourgeois Society*. Translated by Thomas Burger and Frederick Lawrence. Cambridge, MA: MIT Press, 1989.
Habermas, Jürgen. 'Philosophy as Stand-In and Interpreter'. In *Moral Consciousness and Communicative Action*, 1–20. Translated by Christian Lenhardt and Shierry Weber Nicholsen. Cambridge, MA: MIT Press, 1990.
Habermas, Jürgen. *Between Facts and Norms*. Translated by William Rehg. Cambridge: Polity Press, 1997.
Habermas, Jürgen. 'The Liberating Power of Symbols: Ernst Cassirer's Humanistic Legacy and the Warburg Library'. In *The Liberating Power of Symbols: Philosophical Essays*, 1–29. Translated by Peter Dews. Cambridge: Polity Press, 2001.
Habermas, Jürgen. '"...And to define America, her athletic democracy": The Philosopher and the Language Shaper; In Memory of Richard Rorty'. *New Literary History* 39.1 (2008): 3–12.
Hacker, P. M. S. *Wittgenstein's Place in Twentieth-Century Analytic Philosophy*. Oxford: Basil Blackwell, 1996.

Hacker, P. M. S. 'The Rise of Twentieth Century Analytic Philosophy'. In Hans-Johann Glock (ed.), *The Rise of Analytic Philosophy*, 51–76. Oxford: Basil Blackwell, 1997.

Hacker, P. M. S. 'Was He Trying to Whistle It?' In Alice Crary and Rupert Read (eds.), *The New Wittgenstein*, 353–88. London: Routledge, 2000.

Hacker, P. M. S. 'Soames' History of Analytic Philosophy'. *Philosophical Quarterly* 56 (2006): 121–31.

Hacker, P. M. S. 'Analytic Philosophy: Beyond the Linguistic Turn and Back Again'. In Michael Beaney (ed.), *The Analytic Turn: Analysis in Early Analytic Philosophy*, 125–41. London: Routledge, 2007.

Hall Jr, Robert A. 'Bartoli's "Neolinguistics"'. *Language* 22.4 (1946): 273–83.

Hampshire, Stuart and Austin Duncan-Jones. 'Symposium: Are All Philosophical Questions Questions of Language?' *Proceedings of the Aristotelian Society, Supplementary Volume* 22 (1948): 31–78.

Hanfling, Oswald. '"I heard a plaintive melody": (*Philosophical Investigations*, p. 209)'. In A. Philips Griffiths (ed.), *Wittgenstein: Centenary Essays*, 117–33. Cambridge: Cambridge University Press, 1991.

Hanssen, Beatrice. 'Language and Mimesis in Walter Benjamin's Work'. In David S. Ferris (ed.), *The Cambridge Companion to Walter Benjamin*, 54–72. Cambridge: Cambridge University Press, 2004.

Harcourt, Edward. 'Frege on "I", "Now", "Today" and Some Other Linguistic Devices'. *Synthese* 121.3 (1999): 329–56.

Harcourt, Edward and Richard Marshall. 'Wittgenstein's Ethical Enterprise and Related Matters' (Interview with Edward Harcourt). *3:AM Magazine*, 19 November 2016. http://www.3ammagazine.com/3am/wittgensteins-ethical-enterprise-related-matters/, accessed 21 June 2017.

Harris, Roy. *Language, Saussure and Wittgenstein: How to Play Games with Words*. London: Routledge, 1990.

Harris, Roy. *The Language Connection: Philosophy and Linguistics*. Bristol: Thoemmes Press, 1996.

Harris, Roy. 'On Redefining Linguistics'. In Hayley G. Davis and Talbot J. Taylor (eds.), *Rethinking Linguistics*, 17–68. London: Routledge Curzon, 2003.

Hassler, Gerda. '"Analogy": The History of a Concept and a Term from the 17th to the 19th Century'. In Douglas A. Kibbee (ed.), *History of Linguistics 2005: Selected Papers from the ICHOLS X*, 156–68. Amsterdam: John Benjamins, 2007.

Heidegger, Martin. *An Introduction to Metaphysics*. Translated by Ralph Manheim. New Haven, CT: Yale University Press, 1959.

Heidegger, Martin. 'Review of Ernst Cassirer's Mythical Thought [1928]'. Translated by James G. Maraldo and John C. Hart. In *The Piety of Thinking*, 32–45. Bloomington: Indiana University Press, 1976.

Heidelberger, Michael. 'From Helmholtz's Philosophy of Science to Hertz's Picture-Theory'. In Davis Baird, R. I. G. Hughes, and Alfred Nordmann (eds.), *Heinrich Hertz: Classical Physicist, Modern Philosopher*, 9–24. Dordrecht: Kluwer Academic Publishers, 1998.

Heis, Jeremy. 'Arithmetic and Number in the Philosophy of Symbolic Forms'. In J. Tyler Friedman and Sebastian Luft (eds.), *The Philosophy of Ernst Cassirer: A Novel Assessment*, 123–9. Berlin: Walter de Gruyter, 2015.

Hertz, Heinrich. *The Principles of Mechanics Presented in a New Form*. Translated by D. E. Jones and J. T. Walley. London: Macmillan & Co., 1899.

Hertzberg, Lars. 'Trying to Keep Philosophy Honest'. In Alois Pichler and S. Säätela (eds.), *Wittgenstein: The Philosopher and His Works*, 82–97. Frankfurt am Main: ontos Verlag, 2006.

Hertzberg, Lars. 'Very General Facts of Nature'. In Oskari Kuusela and Marie McGinn (eds.), *The Oxford Handbook of Wittgenstein*, 351–72. Oxford: Oxford University Press, 2011.

Hintikka, Jaakko. 'Who Is About to Kill Analytical Philosophy?'. In Anat Biletzki and Anat Matar (eds.), *The Story of Analytic Philosophy: Plot and Heroes*, 252–69. London: Routledge, 1998.

Hirschkop, Ken. *Mikhail Bakhtin: An Aesthetic for Democracy*. Oxford: Oxford University Press, 1999.

Hobsbawm, Eric. *Age of Extremes: The Short Twentieth Century, 1914–1991*. London: Michael Joseph, 1994.

Hobsbawm, Eric. *The Age of Empire, 1875–1914*. London: Weidenfeld & Nicolson, 1995.

Hoel, Aud Sissel. 'Technics of Thinking'. In Aud Sissel Hoel and Ingvild Folkvord (eds.), *Ernst Cassirer on Form and Technology: Contemporary Readings*, 65–91. Basingstoke: Palgrave Macmillan, 2012.

Holenstein, Elmar. *Roman Jakobson's Approach to Language: Phenomenological Structuralism*. Bloomington: Indiana University Press, 1977.

Hölscher, Stefanie. 'Ernst Cassirer's *Die Begriffsform im mythischen Denken* and the Beginnings of his Friendship with Fritz Saxl and Aby Warburg'. In Paul Bishop and R. H. Stephenson (eds.), *The Persistence of Myth as Symbolic Form*, 71–83. Leeds: Maney Publishing, 2008.

Honneth, Axel. 'A Communicative Disclosure of the Past: On the Relation between Anthropology and Philosophy of History in Walter Benjamin'. *new formations* 20 (1993): 83–94.

Hughes, H. Stuart. *Consciousness and Society: The Reorientation of European Social Thought, 1890–1950*. London: MacGibbon & Kee, 1959.

Humboldt, Wilhelm von. *On Language: The Diversity of Human Language-Structure and its Influence on the Mental Development of Mankind*. Translated by Peter Heath. Cambridge: Cambridge University Press, 1988.

Husserl, Edmund. *Ideas: General Introduction to Pure Phenomenology*. Translated by W. R. Boyce Gibson. New York: Collier, 1962.

Hutton, Christopher. *Linguistics and the Third Reich: Mother-Tongue Fascism, Race and the Science of Language*. London: Routledge, 1999.

Hylton, Peter. 'The Nature of the Proposition and the Revolt against Idealism'. In Richard Rorty, J. B. Schneewind, and Quentin Skinner (eds.), *Philosophy in History: Essays in the Historiography of Philosophy*, 375–97. Cambridge: Cambridge University Press, 1984.

Hylton, Peter. 'The Significance of "On Denoting"'. In C. Wade Savage and C. Anthony Anderson (eds.), *Rereading Russell: Essays on Bertrand Russell's Metaphysics and Epistemology*, 88–107. Minnesota Studies in Philosophy of Science. Minneapolis: University of Minnesota Press, 1989.

Hylton, Peter. *Russell, Idealism and the Emergence of Analytical Philosophy*. Oxford: Clarendon Press, 1992.

Hylton, Peter. *Propositions, Functions, and Analysis*. Oxford: Clarendon Press, 2005.

Iakubinskii, L. 'O zvukakh stikhotvornogo iazyka'. In Osip Brik et al., *Poetika: sborniki po teorii poeticheskogo iazyka*, 37–49. Petrograd: n.p., 1919.

Iakubinskii, L. 'F. de Sossiur o nevozmozhnosti iazykovoi politiki'. In N. Ia. Marr (ed.), *Iazykovedenie i materializm*, 2. 91–104. Moscow: Gosudarstvennaia sotsialno-ekonomicheskaia izdatel', 1931.

Ikonen, Sirkku. 'Cassirer's Critique of Culture: Between the Scylla of *Lebensphilosophie* and the Charybdis of the Vienna Circle'. *Synthese* 179 (2011): 187–202.

Isaac, Joel. 'W. V. Quine and the Origins of Analytic Philosophy in the United States'. *Modern Intellectual History* 2.2 (2005): 205–34.
Ivanov, Viacheslav. *Selected Essays*. Translated by Robert Bird. Evanston, IL: Northwestern University Press, 2001.
Jacobson, Eric. *Metaphysics of the Profane: The Political Theology of Walter Benjamin and Gershom Scholem*. New York: Columbia University Press, 2003.
Jakobson, Roman. 'Vliv revoluce na ruský jazyk (Poznamky ke knize André Mazona, *Lexique de la guerre et de la révolution en Russie*)'. *Nové Atheneum* 2 (1920–1): 110–14, 200–12, 250–5, 310–18.
Jakobson, Roman. *Noveishaia russkaia poeziia: nabrosok pervyi*. Prague: Politika, 1921.
Jakobson, Roman. 'Closing Statement: Linguistics and Poetics'. In Thomas Sebeok (ed.), *Style in Language*. Cambridge, MA: MIT Press, 1960.
Jakobson, Roman. 'The Concept of the Sound Law and the Teleological Criterion' (1928). In *Selected Writings: Vol. I—Phonological Studies*, 1–2. The Hague: Mouton, 1962.
Jakobson, Roman. *Selected Writings: Vol. II—Word and Language*. The Hague: Mouton, 1971.
Jakobson, Roman. 'On Realism in Art'. In *Language in Literature*, 19–27. Cambridge, MA: The Belknap Press, 1987.
Jakobson, Roman. 'What is Poetry?' In *Language in Literature*, 368–78. Cambridge, MA: The Belknap Press, 1987.
Jakobson, Roman. *My Futurist Years*. Translated by Stephen Rudy. New York: Marsilio Publishers, 1992.
Jakobson, Roman. 'Moskovskii Lingvisticheskii Kruzhok'. *Philologica* 3.5/7 (1996): 361–80.
Jakobson, Roman and Petr Bogatyrev. *Slavianskaia filologiia v Rossii za gody voiny i revoliutsii*. Berlin: OPOIaZ, 1923.
Jakobson, Roman and Iurii Tynianov. 'Problemy izucheniia literatury i iazyka'. *Novyi LEF* 12 (1928, reprinted Mouton: The Hague, 1970).
Jameson, Fredric. *The Prison-House of Language: A Critical Account of Structuralism and Russian Formalism*. Princeton, NJ: Princeton University Press, 1972.
Janecek, Gerald. 'Kručenych and Chlebnikov Co-authoring a Manifesto'. *Russian Literature* 8 (1980): 483–98.
Janecek, Gerald. 'Baudouin de Courtenay versus Kručenych'. *Russian Literature* 10 (1981): 17–30.
Janecek, Gerald. *Zaum*. San Diego, CA: San Diego University Press, 1996.
Jangfeldt, Bert. 'Roman Jakobson in Sweden 1940–41'. *Cahiers de l'ILSL* 9 (1997): 141–9.
Janik, Alan and Stephen Toulmin. *Wittgenstein's Vienna*. New York: Simon & Schuster, 1973.
Jankowsky, Kurt R. *The Neogrammarians: A Re-Evaluation of Their Place in the Development of Linguistic Science*. The Hague: Mouton, 1972.
Jarvis, Simon. 'There Is No Science of Language' (Review of Jean-Jacques Lecercle, *A Marxist Philosophy of Language*). *Radical Philosophy* 146 (2007): 48–51.
Jennings, Michael W. 'The Will to Apokatastasis: Media, Experience and Eschatology in Benjamin's Late Theological Politics'. In Colby Dickinson and Stéphane Symons (eds.), *Walter Benjamin and Theology*, 93–109. New York: Fordham University Press, 2016.
Johns, Adrian. 'Coffeehouses and Print Shops'. In Katherine Park and Lorraine Daston (eds.), *The Cambridge History of Science, Vol. 3: Early Modern Science*, 320–40. Cambridge: Cambridge University Press, 2006.
Joseph, John E. 'The Genesis of Jakobson's "Six Lectures on Sound and Meaning"'. *Historiographia Linguistica* 16.3 (1989): 415–20.

Joseph, John E. 'The Exportation of Structuralist Ideas from Linguistics to Other Fields: An Overview'. In Sylvain Auroux, E. F. K. Koerner, Hans-Joseph Niederehe, and Kees Versteegh (eds.), *History of the Language Sciences: An International Handbook on the Study of Language from the Beginnings to the Present*, 1880–908. Berlin: Walter de Gruyter, 2000.

Joseph, John E. 'Language and "Psychological Race": Leopold de Saussure on French in Indochina'. *Language & Communication* 20 (2000): 29–53.

Joseph, John E. 'The Unconscious and the Social in Saussure'. *Historiographia Linguistica* 27.2/3 (2000): 307–34.

Joseph, John E. 'The Sources of the "Sapir-Whorf Hypothesis"'. In *From Whitney to Chomsky: Essays in the History of American Linguistics*, 71–105. Amsterdam: John Benjamins, 2002.

Joseph, John E. *Saussure*. Oxford: Oxford University Press, 2012.

Joseph, John E. 'Saussure's Value(s)', *Recherches sémiotique/Semiotic Inquiry* 34.1/3 (2014): 191–208.

Judson, Pieter M. *The Habsburg Empire: A New History*. Cambridge, MA: Harvard University Press, 2016.

Kagan, Iu. M. 'O starykh bumagakh iz semeinogo arkhiva (M. M. Bakhtin i M. I. Kagan)'. *Dialog Karnaval Khronotop* 1 (1992): 60–88.

Kalinin, Ilya. 'Viktor Shklovskii, ili Prevrashchenie poeticheskogo priema v literaturnyi fakt'. *Zvezda* 7 (2014). http://magazines.russ.ru/zvezda/2014/7, accessed 13 June 2018.

Kalinin, Ilya. 'Viktor Shklovsky *vs.* Roman Jakobson. Poetic Language or Poetic Function of Language'. *Enthymema* 19 (2017): 342–51.

Kant, Immanuel. *Prolegomena to Any Future Metaphysics*. Translated by James W. Ellington and Paul Carus. Indianapolis: Hackett Publishing Company, 1977.

Kartsevskii, S. I. *Iazyk, voina i revoliutsiia*. Berlin: Russkoe universal'noe izdatel'stvo, 1923.

Kenny, Anthony. 'From the Big Typescript to the *Philosophical Grammar*'. In *The Legacy of Wittgenstein*, 24–37. Oxford: Basil Blackwell, 1984.

Khlebnikov, Velimir. *Sobranie proizvedenii, tom 5*. Leningrad: Izdat. pisatelei v Leningrade, 1933.

Khlebnikov, Velimir. *Collected Works, Vol. 1*. Translated by Paul Schmidt. Cambridge, MA: Harvard University Press, 1987.

Khlebnikov, Velimir. *Collected Works, Vol. 3*. Translated by Paul Schmidt. Cambridge, MA: Harvard University Press, 1997.

Khlebnikov, Velimir. *Sobranie sochinenii, tom 1: literaturnaia avtobiografiia, stikhotvoreniia 1904–1916*. Moscow: IMLI RAN, 2000.

Khlebnikov, Velimir. *Sobranie sochinenii, tom 6, kniga 1: stat'i (nabroski), uchenye trudy, vozzvaniia, otkrytye pis'ma, vystupleniia, 1904–1922*. Moscow: IMLI RAN, 2005.

Khlebnikov, Velimir. *Sobranie sochinenii, tom 6, kniga 2: doski sud'by, mysli i zametki, pis'ma i drugie avtobiograficheskie materialy, 1897–1922*. Moscow: IMLI RAN, 2006.

Kienzler, Wolfgang. 'About the Dividing Line between Early and Late Wittgenstein'. In Gianluigi Oliveri (ed.), *From the Tractatus to the Tractatus and Other Essays*, 125–30. Frankfurt am Main: Peter Lang, 2001.

Kiparsky, Paul. 'From Paleogrammarians to Neogrammarians'. In Dell Hymes (ed.), *Studies in the History of Linguistics: Traditions and Paradigms*, 331–45. Bloomington: Indiana University Press, 1974.

Kittsteiner, H. D. 'Walter Benjamin's Historicism'. *New German Critique* 39 (1986): 179–215.

Klagge, James C. 'Wittgenstein and his Audience: Esotericist or Evangelist?' In Nuno Venturinha (ed.), *The Textual Genesis of Wittgenstein's Philosophical Investigations*, 52–64. London: Routledge, 2013.
Klippi, Carita. 'Vox populi, Vox Dei: The "People" as an Agent of Linguistic Norm'. *Language & Communication* 26 (2006): 356–68.
Koerner, E. F. K. *Ferdinand de Saussure: Origin and Development of His Linguistic Thought in Western Studies of Language*. Braunschweig: Vieweg, 1973.
Koerner, E. F. K. 'Jacob Grimm's Position in the Development of Linguistics as a Science'. In Elmer H. Antonsen, James W. Marchand, and Ladislav Zgusta (eds.), *The Grimm Brothers and the Germanic Past*, 7–23. Amsterdam: John Benjamins, 1990.
Koerner, E. F. K. 'The Authors of the Idea of Language as a "Système où tout se tient"'. In *Linguistic Historiography: Projects & Prospects*, 183–200. Amsterdam: John Benjamins, 1999.
Kremer, Michael. 'Ryle's "Intellectualist Legend" in Historical Context'. *Journal for the History of Analytical Philosophy* 5.5 (2017): 16–35.
Kripke, Saul. *Naming and Necessity*. Cambridge, MA: Harvard University Press, 1980.
Krois, John Michael. 'The Pathos Formulae of Mythic Thought'. In Paul Bishop and R. H. Stephenson (eds.), *The Persistence of Myth as Symbolic Form*, 1–17. Leeds: Maney Publishing, 2008.
Krois, John Michael. 'The Priority of "Symbolism" over Language in Cassirer's Philosophy'. *Synthese* 179 (2011): 9–20.
Kruchenykh, A. 'Novye puti slova'. In V. Khlebnikov, A Kruchenykh, and E. Guro, *Troe*, 22–37. St Petersburg: Zhuravl´, 1913. Getty Research Institute digital library: http://www.getty.edu/research/tools/guides_bibliographies/russian_avant_garde/index.html.
Kruchenykh, A. and Aliagrov. *Zaumnaia gniga*. Moscow: n. p., 1916.
Kruchenykh, A. and V. Khlebnikov. *Slovo kak takovoe.*. Moscow: n. p., 1913. Getty Research Institute digital library: http://www.getty.edu/research/tools/guides_bibliographies/russian_avant_garde/index.html
Krusanov, A. B. *Russkii avangard, 1907–1932, tom 2(1): Futuristicheskaia revoliutsiia, 1917–1921*. Moscow: Novoe literaturnoe obozrenie, 2003.
Kuusela, Oskari. 'From Metaphysics and Philosophical Theses to Grammar: Wittgenstein's Turn'. *Philosophical Investigations* 28.2 (2005): 95–133.
Kuusela, Oskari. 'The Development of Wittgenstein's Philosophy'. In Oskari Kuusela and Marie McGinn (eds.), *The Oxford Handbook of Wittgenstein*, 597–619. Oxford: Oxford University Press, 2011.
Labov, William. *Sociolinguistic Patterns*. Philadelphia: University of Pennsylvania Press, 1972.
Lähteenmaki, Mika. 'Vološinov and Cassirer: A Case of Plagiarism?' *Historiographia Linguistica* 29.1/2 (2002): 121–44.
Lähteenmaki, Mika. 'On the Interpretation of Baxtin's Linguistic Ideas: The Problem of the Texts from the 1950s–60s'. *Russian Linguistics* 27 (2003): 23–39.
Lähteenmaki, Mika. 'On Rules and Rule-Following: Obeying Rules Blindly'. *Language & Communication* 21 (2003): 45–61.
Lähteenmaki, Mika. 'The Role of "Sociology" in Lev Shcherba's Conception of Language'. *Slavica Helsingiensia* 35 (2008): 183–90.
Latour, Bruno. 'Gabriel Tarde and the End of the Social'. In Patrick Joyce (ed.), *The Social in Question: New Bearings*, 117–32. London: Routledge, 2002.
Laugier, Sandra. *Why We Need Ordinary Language Philosophy*. Chicago: University of Chicago Press, 2013.
Lawton, Anna and Herbert Eagle (eds.). *Russian Futurism Through Its Manifestoes, 1912–1928*. Ithaca, NY: Cornell University Press, 1988.

Lefort, Claude. *The Political Forms of Modern Society: Bureaucracy, Democracy, Totalitarianism.* Cambridge: Polity Press, 1986.

LeMahieu, Michael and Karen Zumhagen-Yekplé. *Wittgenstein and Modernism.* Chicago: University of Chicago Press, 2016.

Lepenies, Wolf. *Between Literature and Science: The Rise of Sociology.* Translated by R. J. Hollingdale. Cambridge: Cambridge University Press, 1988.

Lepschy, Giulio. *Mother Tongues and Other Reflections on the Italian Language.* Toronto: University of Toronto Press, 2002.

Levchenko, Jan. 'Towards the Formalist Dimension of War, or how Viktor Šklovskij used to be a Soldier'. *Studies in East European Thought* 66 (2014): 89–100.

Leventhal, Robert S. 'The Emergence of Philological Discourse in the German States, 1770–1810'. *Isis* 77.2 (1986): 243–60.

Levinas, Emmanuel. *The Theory of Intuition in Husserl's Phenomenology.* Translated by André Orianne. Evanston, IL: Northwestern University Press, 1973.

Levine, Emily J. *Dreamland of Humanists: Warburg, Cassirer, Panofsky, and the Hamburg School.* Chicago: University of Chicago Press, 2013.

Lévi-Strauss, Claude, *Structural Anthropology.* Translated by Claire Jacobson and Brooke Grundfest Schoepf. New York: Basic Books, 1963.

Lévi-Strauss, Claude and Didier Eribon. *Conversations with Claude Lévi-Strauss.* Translated by Paula Wissing. Chicago: University of Chicago Press, 1991.

Lipton, David R. *Ernst Cassirer: The Dilemma of a Liberal Intellectual in Germany, 1914–33.* Toronto: University of Toronto Press, 1978.

Livshits, Benedikt. *The One and a Half-Eyed Archer.* Translated by John Bowlt. Moscow: The State Russian Museum, n.d.

Lofts, Stephen G. *Ernst Cassirer: A 'Repetition' of Modernity.* Albany, NY: SUNY Press, 2000.

Lo Piparo, Franco. 'The Linguistic Roots of Gramsci's Non-Marxism'. In Peter Ives and Rocco Lacorte (eds.), *Gramsci, Language, and Translation,* 19–28. Lanham, MD: Lexington Books, 2010.

Love, Nigel. 'Science, Language and Linguistic Culture'. *Language & Communication* 29 (2009): 26–46.

Lovibond, Sabina. 'Wittgenstein, Tolstoy, and the "Apocalyptic View"'. *Philosophy of the Social Sciences* 46.6 (2016): 565–83.

Löwy, Michael. 'Capitalism as Religion: Walter Benjamin and Max Weber'. *Historical Materialism* 17 (2009): 60–73.

Lubenow, William C. *Liberal Intellectuals and Public Culture in Modern Britain, 1815–1914.* Woodbridge: Boydell Press, 2010.

Lukács, Georg. *The Theory of the Novel.* Translated by Anna Bostock. Cambridge, MA: MIT Press, 1973.

Lurie, Yuval. 'Wittgenstein as the Forlorn Caretaker of Language'. In Anat Biletzki and Anat Matar (eds.), *The Story of Analytic Philosophy: Plot and Heroes,* 209–25. London: Routledge, 1998.

Lynn-George, Michael. 'The Crossroads of Truth: Ferdinand de Saussure and the Dreyfus Affair'. *Modern Language Notes* 121 (2006): 961–88.

McElvenny, James. 'Meaning in the Age of Modernism: C. K. Ogden and his Contemporaries'. PhD dissertation, University of Sydney, 2013.

McGuinness, Brian. *Wittgenstein: A Life—Young Ludwig, 1889–1921.* Berkeley, CA: University of California Press, 1988.

McGuinness, Brian. 'Asceticism and Ornament'. In Brian McGuinness (ed.), *Approaches to Wittgenstein,* 17–26. London: Routledge, 2002.

McGuinness, Brian. '"It Will Be Terrible Afterwards, Whoever Wins"' In Brian McGuinness (ed.), *Approaches to Wittgenstein*, 43–52. London: Routledge, 2002.

McKenzie, D. 'Karl Pearson and the Professional Middle Class'. *Annals of Science* 36.2 (1979): 125–43.

Majer, Ulrich. 'Heinrich Hertz's Picture-Conception of Theories: Its Elaboration by Hilbert, Weyl and Ramsey'. In Davis Baird, R. I. G. Hughes, and Alfred Nordmann (eds.), *Heinrich Hertz: Classical Physicist, Modern Philosopher*, 225–42. Dordrecht: Kluwer Academic Publishers, 1998.

Malcolm, Norman. *Ludwig Wittgenstein: A Memoir*. London: Oxford University Press, 1958.

Mali, Joseph. 'The Reconciliation of Myth: Benjamin's Homage to Bachofen'. *Journal of the History of Ideas* 60.1 (1999): 165–87.

Mali, Joseph. 'The Myth of the State Revisited: Ernst Cassirer and Modern Political Theory'. In Jeffrey Andrew Barash (ed.), *The Symbolic Construction of Reality: The Legacy of Ernst Cassirer*, 135–62. Chicago: University of Chicago Press, 2008.

Malinowski, Bronislaw. 'The Concept of Meaning in Primitive Languages'. Supplement 1 in C. K. Ogden and I. A. Richards, *The Meaning of Meaning*, 296–336. London: Kegan Paul, Trench and Trübner, 1923.

Malinowski, Bronislaw. 'An Ethnographic Theory of Language and Some Practical Corollaries'. In *Coral Gardens and Their Magic, Vol. 2: The Language of Magic and Gardening*, 3–74. London: Allen & Unwin, 1935.

Marshall, David L. 'The Intrication of Political and Rhetorical Inquiry in Walter Benjamin'. *History of Political Thought* 34.4 (2013): 702–37.

Matejka, Ladislav. 'Chlebnikov and Jakobson's *Novejšaja Russkaja Poèzija*'. In Willem Weststeijn (ed.), *Velimir Chlebnikov (1885–1922): Myth and Reality*. Studies in Slavic Literature and Poetics, Vol. VIII, 529–42. Amsterdam: Rodopi, 1986.

Matejka, Ladislav. 'Sociological Concerns of the Moscow Linguistic Circle'. In Krystyna Pomorska et al. (eds.), *Language, Poetry and Poetics: The Generation of the 1890s: Jakobson, Trubetzkoy, Majakovskij*, 307–12. Berlin: Mouton de Gruyter, 1987.

May, Robert. 'Frege on Indexicals'. *Philosophical Review* 115.4 (2006): 487–516.

Mayakovsky, V. V. and O. M. Brik. 'Nasha slovesnaia rabota'. *LEF* 1 (1923): 40–1.

Mayer, Arno J. *The Persistence of the Old Regime: Europe to the Great War*. New York: Pantheon, 1981.

Mazower, Mark. *Dark Continent: Europe's Twentieth Century*. London: Allen Lane, 1998.

Merleau-Ponty, Maurice. *The Phenomenology of Perception*. Translated by Colin Smith. London: Routledge & Kegan Paul, 1962.

Michaels, Walter Benn. 'The Shape of the Signifier'. *Critical Inquiry* 27.2 (2001): 266–83.

Milkov, Nikolay. 'Wittgenstein's Method: The Third Phase of Its Development (1933–36)'. In António Marques and Nuno Venturinha (eds.), *Knowledge, Language and Mind: Wittgenstein's Thought in Progress*, 65–79. Berlin: Walter de Gruyter, 2012.

Mirowski, Philip. *More Heat Than Light: Economics as Social Physics, Physics as Nature's Economics*. Cambridge: Cambridge University Press, 1989.

Moi, Toril. *Revolution of the Ordinary: Literary Studies after Wittgenstein, Austin, and Cavell*. Chicago: University of Chicago Press, 2017.

Monk, Ray. *Ludwig Wittgenstein: The Duty of Genius*. London: Vintage, 1991.

Monk, Ray. *Bertrand Russell: The Spirit of Solitude*. London: Jonathan Cape, 1996.

Monk, Ray. 'Was Russell an Analytic Philosopher?'. In Hans-Johann Glock (ed.), *The Rise of Analytic Philosophy*, 35–50. Oxford: Basil Blackwell, 1997.

Moore, G. E. 'The Nature of Judgement'. *Mind* (1899): 176–93.

Moore, G. E. 'The Justification of Analysis'. *Analysis* 1.2 (1934): 28–30.
Moore, G. E. 'Propositions'. In *Some Main Problems of Philosophy*, 1–20. London: Allen & Unwin, 1953.
Moore, G. E. 'Wittgenstein's Lectures in 1930–33'. In James Klagge and Alfred Nordmann (eds.), *Philosophical Occasions, 1912–1951*, 45–114. Indianapolis: Hackett Publishing, 1993.
Moretti, Franco. *The Way of the World: The Bildungsroman in European Culture*. London: Verso, 1987.
Moretti, Franco. *Modern Epic: The World System from Goethe to García Márquez*. Translated by Quintin Hoare. London: Verso, 1996.
Moretti, Franco. *Atlas of the European Novel, 1800–1900*. London: Verso, 1999.
Moretti, Franco. 'The Slaughterhouse of Literature'. *Modern Language Notes* 61.1 (2000): 207–27.
Morpurgo Davies, Anna. *History of Linguistics, Volume IV: Nineteenth-Century Linguistics*. London: Longman, 1998.
Morris, Michael and Julian Dodd. 'Mysticism and Nonsense in the *Tractatus*'. *European Journal of Philosophy* 17.2 (2009): 247–76.
Moses, Stéphane. 'Émile Benveniste and the Linguistics of Dialogue'. *Revue de Métaphysique et de Morale* 4 (2001): 509–25.
Moyal-Sharrock, D. 'Cora Diamond and the Ethical Imagination'. *The British Journal of Aesthetics* 52.3 (2012): 223–40.
Moynahan, Gregory B. *Ernst Cassirer and the Critical Science of Germany, 1899–1919*. London: Anthem Press, 2013.
Mulhall, Stephen. *Inheritance and Originality: Wittgenstein, Heidegger, Kierkegaard*. Oxford: Clarendon Press, 2001.
Mulhall, Stephen. 'Realism, Modernism and the Realistic Spirit: Diamond's Inheritance of Wittgenstein, Early and Late'. *Nordic Wittgenstein Review* 1 (2012): 7–33.
Mulhern, Francis. *Culture/Metaculture*. London: Routledge, 2000.
Negt, Oskar and Alexander Kluge. *Public Sphere and Experience: Toward an Analysis of the Bourgeois and Proletarian Public Sphere*. Translated by Peter Labanyi, Jamie Owen Daniel, and Assenka Oksoloff. Minneapolis: University of Minnesota Press, 1993.
Nerlich, Brigitte and David D. Clarke. *Language, Action, and Context: The Early History of Pragmatics in Europe and America, 1780–1930*. Amsterdam: John Benjamins, 1996.
Newman, Jane O. 'Enchantment in Times of War: Aby Warburg, Walter Benjamin, and the Secularization Thesis'. *Representations* 105 (2009): 133–67.
Nicholls, Peter. *Modernisms: A Literary Guide*. London: Macmillan, 1995.
Nietzsche, Friedrich. *The Birth of Tragedy and Other Writings*. Translated by Ronald Speirs. Cambridge: Cambridge University Press, 1999.
Nikolaev, N. I. '"Dostoevskii i antichnost'" kak tema Pumpianskogo i Bakhtina (1922–1963)'. *Voprosy literatury* 3 (1996): 115–27.
Nordmann, Alfred. ' "Everything Could Be Different": *The Principles of Mechanics* and the Limits of Physics'. In Davis Baird, R. I. G. Hughes, and Alfred Nordmann (eds.), *Heinrich Hertz: Classical Physicist, Modern Philosopher*, 155–72. Dordrecht: Kluwer Academic Publishers, 1998.
Norton, Bernard J. 'Karl Pearson and Statistics: The Social Origins of Scientific Innovation'. *Social Studies of Science* 8.1 (1978): 3–34.
Nyíri, J. C. 'Wittgenstein's Later Work in Relation to Conservatism'. In Anthony Kenny and Brian McGuinness (eds.), *Wittgenstein and His Times*, 44–69. Chicago: University of Chicago Press, 1982.

Odesskii, M. P. 'Vokrug polemiki G. O. Vinokura i A. M. Selishcheva: nauchnyi i sotsiial'nyi aspekty'. In S. I. Gindin and N. N. Rozanova (eds.), *Iazyk, kul'tura, gumanitarnoe znanie: nauchnoe nasledie G. O. Vinokura i sovremennost*, 382–9. Moscow: Nauchnyi mir, 1999.

[Ogden, C. K.]. 'Another Jungle Story'. *The Cambridge Magazine* 9.14 (1920): 193–4.

[Ogden, C. K.]. 'The Linguistic Conscience'. *The Cambridge Magazine* Double Number (Summer 1920): 31.

[Ogden, C. K.]. 'What is What?'. *The Cambridge Magazine* Double Number (Summer 1920): 40.

[Ogden, C. K.]. 'Thoughts, Words and Things'. *The Cambridge Magazine* Decennial Number (1912–1921): 29–31.

[Ogden, C. K.]. 'The Power of Words'. *The Cambridge Magazine* Early Spring Double Number (1923): 5–50.

Ogden, C. K. 'Preface'. In James Joyce, *Tales Told of Shem and Shaun: Three Fragments from Work in Progress*, i–xv. Paris: The Black Sun Press, 1929.

Ogden, C. K. *Debabelization*. London: Kegan Paul, Trench, Trübner & Co., 1931.

Ogden, C. K. *Basic English: A General Introduction with Rules and Grammar*, 3rd edn. London: Kegan Paul, Trench, Trübner & Co., 1932.

Ogden, C. K. 'Word Magic'. *Psyche* 18 (1938–52): 9–126.

Ogden, C. K. 'Basic English and Grammatical Reform' (1937). In W. Terrence Gordon (ed.), *C. K. Ogden and Linguistics, Vol. II: From Bentham to Basic English*, 188–215. London: Routledge Thoemmes Press, 1994.

Ogden, C. K. 'The Progress of Significs' (1911). In W. Terrence Gordon (ed.), *C. K. Ogden and Linguistics, Vol. I: From Significs to Orthology*, 1–47. London: Routledge Thoemmes Press, 1994.

Ogden, C. K. and I. A. Richards. 'Symbolism'. *The Cambridge Magazine*. Double Number (Summer 1920): 32–40.

Ogden, C. K. and I. A. Richards. 'On Talking'. *The Cambridge Magazine* Decennial Number (1912–1921): 57–65.

Ogden, C. K. and I. A. Richards. 'The Art of Conversation'. *The Cambridge Magazine* 10.2 (January–March 1921): 94–100.

Ogden, C. K. and I. A. Richards. *The Meaning of Meaning: A Study of The Influence of Language Upon Thought and the Science of Symbolism*. London: Kegan Paul, Trench, Trübner & Co., 1923.

Ogien, Albert. 'Obligation and Impersonality: Wittgenstein and the Nature of the Social'. *Philosophy of the Social Sciences* 46.6 (2016): 604–23.

Olender, Maurice. *The Languages of Paradise: Race, Religion and Philology in the Nineteenth Century*. Cambridge, MA: Harvard University Press, 1992.

Orwell, George. *Nineteen Eighty-Four*. Harmondsworth: Penguin, 1954.

Orwell, George. 'Letter to C. K. Ogden, 16 December 1942'. In *The Complete Works of George Orwell, Vol. 14: Keeping Our Little Corner Clean, 1941–1942*, 239. London: Secker & Warburg, 1998.

Orwell, George. 'As I Please', *Tribune*, 18 August 1944. In *The Complete Works of George Orwell, Vol. 16: I Have Tried to Tell the Truth, 1943–1944*, 336–8. London: Secker & Warburg, 1998.

Orwell, George. 'Politics and the English Language' (1946). In *The Complete Works of George Orwell, Vol. 17: I Belong to the Left, 1945*, 421–38. London: Secker & Warburg, 1998.

Orwell, George. 'Why I Write' (1946). In *The Complete Works of George Orwell, Vol. 18: Smothered Under Journalism*, 316–21. London: Secker & Warburg, 1998.

Osthoff, Hermann and Karl Brugmann. 'Preface' to *Morphological Investigations in the Sphere of the Indo-European Languages* I (Leipzig, 1878). Translated in Winfred P. Lehmann (ed.), *A Reader in Nineteenth-Century Historical Indo-European Linguistics*, 197–209. Bloomington: Indiana University Press, 1967.

Paul, Hermann. *Principles of the History of the Language*. Translated by H. A. Strong. London: Swan Sonnenschein, Lowrey & Co., 1888.

Pavel, Thomas G. *The Feud of Language: A History of Structuralist Thought*. Oxford: Basil Blackwell, 1989.

Pearson, Karl. *The Grammar of Science*. London: Walter Scott, 1892.

Pearson, Karl. *National Life from the Standpoint of Science*. London: Cambridge University Press, n.d. [1901?].

Pearson, Karl and Margaret Moul. 'The Problem of Alien Immigration into Great Britain, Illustrated by an Examination of Russian and Polish Jewish Children, Part 1'. *Annals of Eugenics* 1.1 (1925): 5–54.

Perloff, Marjorie. *The Futurist Moment: Avant-Garde, Avant Guerre, and the Language of Rupture* Chicago: University of Chicago Press, 1986.

Perloff, Marjorie. *Wittgenstein's Ladder: Poetic Language and the Strangeness of the Ordinary*. Chicago: University of Chicago Press, 1996.

Pertzov, Natalia. *Slovar' neologizmov Velimira Khlebnikova*. Vienna: Wiener Slawistischer Almanach, 1995.

Petrilli, Susan. *Signifying and Understanding: Reading the Works of Victoria Welby and the Signific Movement*. Berlin: De Gruyter Mouton, 2009.

Pichler, Alois. 'Wittgenstein's Later Manuscripts: Some Remarks on Style and Writing'. In Paul Henry and Arild Utaker (eds.), *Wittgenstein and Contemporary Theories of Language*, 219–51. Wittgenstein Archive Bergen Working Papers No. 5 (1992).

Pichler, Alois. 'The Interpretation of the *Philosophical Investigations*: Style, Therapy, *Nachlass*'. In Guy Kahane, Edward Kanterian, and Oskari Kuusela (eds.), *Wittgenstein and his Interpreters: Essays in Memory of Gordon Baker*, 123–44. Oxford: Basil Blackwell, 2007.

Pichler, Alois. 'Wittgenstein and Us "Typical Western Scientists"'. In Sebastian Sunday Grève and Jakub Mácha (eds.), *Wittgenstein and the Creativity of Language*, 55–75. London: Palgrave Macmillan, 2016.

Pitcher, George. 'Austin: A Personal Memoir'. In Isaiah Berlin et al. *Essays on J. L. Austin*, 17–30. Oxford: Clarendon Press, 1973.

Pitken, Hannah Fenichel. *Wittgenstein and Justice*. Berkeley, CA: University of California Press, 1972.

Poole, Brian. 'Bakhtin and Cassirer: The Philosophical Origins of Bakhtin's Carnival Messianism'. *South Atlantic Quarterly* 97.3/4 (1998): 537–78.

Porter, Theodore M. 'The Death of the Object: *Fin-de-Siècle* Philosophy of Physics'. In Dorothy Ross (ed.), *Modernist Impulses in the Human Sciences, 1870–1930*, 128–51. Baltimore: Johns Hopkins University Press, 1994.

Porter, Theodore M. *Trust in Numbers: The Pursuit of Objectivity in Science and Public Life*. Princeton, NJ: Princeton University Press, 1995.

Porter, Theodore M. 'Statistical Utopianism in an Age of Aristocratic Efficiency'. *Osiris*, 2nd series 17 (2002): 210–27.

Porter, Theodore M. *Karl Pearson: The Scientific Life in a Statistical Age*. Princeton, NJ: Princeton University Press, 2004.

Pospelov, N. S. 'O lingvisticheskom nasledstve S. Kartsevskogo'. *Voprosy iazykoznaniia* 6.4 (1957): 46–56.

Pratt, Mary Louise. *Towards a Speech Act Theory of Literary Discourse*. Bloomington: Indiana University Press, 1977.
Preston, Aaron. *Analytic Philosophy: The History of an Illusion*. London: Continuum, 2007.
Putnam, Hilary. 'The Analytic and the Synthetic'. In Herbert Feigl and Grover Maxwell (eds.), *Scientific Explanation, Space and Time*, Minnesota Studies in the Philosophy of Science 3, 358–97. Minneapolis: University of Minnesota Press, 1962.
Putnam, Hilary. 'The "Innateness Hypothesis" and Explanatory Models in Linguistics'. *Synthese* 17 (1967): 12–22.
Putnam, Hilary. 'A Half Century of Philosophy, Viewed from Within'. *Daedalus* 126.1 (1997): 175–208.
Putnam, Hilary. *The Threefold Cord: Mind, Body, and World*. New York: Columbia University Press, 1999.
Quine, W. V. O. 'Mr. Strawson on Logical Theory' (Review of P. F. Strawson, *Introduction to Logical Theory*). *Mind* 62 (1953): 433–51.
Quine, W. V. O. *Word and Object*. Cambridge, MA: MIT Press, 1960.
Quine, W. V. O. *From a Logical Point of View*. 2nd edn. Cambridge, MA: Harvard University Press, 1980.
Radunović, Dušan. 'Debates on Form in Russian Studies of Language and Art (1915–1929): Theoretical and Institutional Dynamics'. PhD dissertation, University of Sheffield, 2008.
Ram, Harsha. 'The Futurist Eurasianism of Roman Jakobson and Velimir Khlebnikov'. In Mark Bassin, Sergey Glebov, and Marlene Laruelle (eds.), *Between Europe and Asia: The Origins, Theories and Legacies of Russian Eurasianism*, 137–49. Pittsburgh: University of Pittsburgh Press, 2015.
Ramsey, Frank Plumpton. 'Philosophy'. In *The Foundations of Mathematics and other Logical Essays*, 263–9. London: Kegan Paul, Trench, Trübner & Co., 1931.
Rancière, Jacques. *Hatred of Democracy*. Translated by Steve Corcoran. London: Verso, 2009.
Rée, Jonathan. 'English Philosophy in the Fifties'. *Radical Philosophy* 65 (1993): 3–21.
Reznik, Vladislava. 'From Saussure to Sociolinguistics: The Evolution of Soviet Sociology of Language in the 1920s and 1930s'. PhD dissertation, University of Exeter, 2004.
Richards, I. A. 'What Happens When We Think'. *The Cambridge Magazine* Decennial Issue (1912–1921): 32–41.
Richards, I. A. 'Co-Author of the "Meaning of Meaning": Some Recollections of C. K. Ogden'. In P. Sargent Florence and J. R. L. Anderson (eds.), *C. K. Ogden: A Collective Memoir*, 96–109. London: Elek Pemberton, 1977.
Ricketts, Thomas. 'Truth and Propositional Unity in Early Russell'. In Juliet Floyd and Sanford Shieh (eds.), *Future Pasts: The Analytic Tradition in Twentieth-Century Philosophy*, 101–21. New York: Oxford University Press, 2001.
Ringer, Fritz K. *The Decline of the German Mandarins: The German Academic Community, 1890–1933*. Cambridge, MA: Harvard University Press, 1969.
Rogers, Ben. *A. J. Ayer*. New York: Grove Press, 1999.
Rorty, Richard. 'Realism, Categories, and the "Linguistic Turn"'. *International Philosophical Quarterly* 2 (1962): 307–22.
Rorty, Richard. 'Mind-Body Identity, Privacy and Categories'. *The Review of Metaphysics* 19.1 (1965): 24–54.
Rorty, Richard (ed.). *The Linguistic Turn: Recent Essays in Philosophical Method*. Chicago: University of Chicago Press, 1967.
Rorty, Richard. 'The World Well Lost'. *Journal of Philosophy* 69.19 (1972): 649–55.
Rorty, Richard. 'Introduction: Pragmatism and Philosophy'. In *The Consequences of Pragmatism (Essays 1972–1980)*. Minneapolis: University of Minnesota Press, 1982.

Rorty, Richard. 'II. Thugs and Theorists: A Reply to Bernstein'. *Political Theory* 15.4 (1987): 564–80.
Rorty, Richard. 'Ten Years After'. In Richard Rorty (ed.), *The Linguistic Turn*, 2nd edn., 361–70. Chicago: University of Chicago Press, 1992.
Rorty, Richard. 'Twenty-Five Years After'. In Richard Rorty (ed.), *The Linguistic Turn*, 2nd edn., 371–4. Chicago: University of Chicago Press, 1992.
Rorty, Richard. 'Wittgenstein and the Linguistic Turn'. In *Philosophy as Cultural Politics: Philosophical Papers, Volume 4*, 160–75. Cambridge: Cambridge University Press, 2007.
Rosanvallon, Pierre. *Democracy Past and Future*. New York: Columbia University Press, 2006.
Rosanvallon, Pierre. 'Democratic Universalism as a Historical Problem'. Books & Ideas.net. http://www.booksandideas.net/Democratic-Universalism-as-a.html, accessed 8 April 2008.
Rosiello, Luigi. 'Linguistics and Marxism in the Thought of Antonio Gramsci'. In Peter Ives and Rocco Lacorte (eds.), *Gramsci, Language, and Translation*, 29–49. Lanham, MD: Lexington Books, 2010.
Ross, Alison. 'The Distinction between Mythic and Divine Violence: Walter Benjamin's "Critique of Violence" from the Perspective of "Goethe's *Elective Affinities*"'. *New German Critique* 41.1 (2014): 93–120.
Ross, J. J. 'Analytic Philosophy as a Matter of Style'. In Anat Biletzki and Anat Matar (eds.), *The Story of Analytic Philosophy: Plot and Heroes*, 56–70. London: Routledge, 1998.
Russell, Bertrand. *The Principles of Mathematics. Vol. 1*. Cambridge: Cambridge University Press, 1903.
Russell, Bertrand. 'On Denoting'. *Mind* 14 (1905): 479–93.
Russell, Bertrand. 'On Scientific Method in Philosophy' (1914). In *Mysticism and Logic and Other Essays*, 97–124. London: Longmans, Green and Co., 1918.
Russell, Bertrand. 'Philosophy in the Twentieth Century'. *The Dial* 77 (October 1924): 271–90.
Russell, Bertrand. *Sceptical Essays*. London: Allen & Unwin, 1928.
Russell, Bertrand. *The History of Western Philosophy and its Connection with Political and Social Circumstances from the Earliest Times to the Present Day*. London: George Allen & Unwin, 1946.
Russell, Bertrand. 'Logical Atomism' (1924). In *Logic and Knowledge: Essays, 1901–1950*. London: Allen & Unwin, 1956.
Rüting, Torsten. 'History and Significance of Jacob von Uexküll and of his Institute in Hamburg'. *Sign Systems Studies* 32.1/2 (2004): 35–71.
Rutkoff, Peter M. and William B. Scott. *New School: A History of the New School for Social Research*. New York: The Free Press, 1986.
Ryan, Alan. 'Russell: The Last Great Radical?'. *Philosophy of the Social Sciences* 26.2 (1996): 247–66.
Ryle, Gilbert. 'Are There Propositions?'. *Proceedings of the Aristotelian Society*, New Series 30 (1929–30): 91–126.
Ryle, Gilbert. 'Systematically Misleading Expressions'. *Proceedings of the Aristotelian Society*, New Series 32 (1931–2): 139–70.
Ryle, Gilbert. '"About"'. *Analysis* 1.1 (1933): 10–12.
Ryle, Gilbert. 'Knowing How and Knowing That: The Presidential Address'. *Proceedings of the Aristotelian Society*, New Series 46 (1945–6): 1–16.
Ryle, Gilbert. *The Concept of Mind*. London: Hutchinson, 1949.
Ryle, Gilbert. 'Ordinary Language'. *Philosophical Review* 62.2 (1953): 167–86.
Salzer, Felix. *Structural Hearing: Tonal Coherence in Music*. New York: Dover, 1962.

Santner, Eric L. *On the Psychotheology of Everyday Life*. Chicago: University of Chicago Press, 2001.

Saussure, Ferdinand de. *Course in General Linguistics*. Translated by Wade Baskin. London: Fontana, 1974.

Saussure, Ferdinand de. *Course in General Linguistics*. Translated by Roy Harris. London: Duckworth, 1983.

Saussure, Ferdinand de. *Cours de Linguistique Générale*. Edited by Tullio de Mauro. Paris: Payot, 1985.

Saussure, Ferdinand de. *Saussure's Third Course of Lectures on General Linguistics (1910–1911)*. Edited by Eisuke Komatsu. Translated by Roy Harris. Oxford: Pergamon Press, 1993.

Saussure, Ferdinand de. *Saussure's First Course of Lectures on General Linguistics (1907)*. Edited by Eisuke Komatsu. Translated by George Wolf. Oxford: Pergamon Press, 1996.

Saussure, Ferdinand de. *Saussure's Second Course of Lectures on General Linguistics (1908–1909)*. Edited by Eisuke Komatsu. Translated by George Wolf. Oxford: Pergamon Press, 1997.

Saussure, Ferdinand de. *Writings in General Linguistics*. Translated by Carol Sanders, Matthew Pires, and Peter Figueroa. Oxford: Oxford University Press, 2006.

Saussure, Louis de and Peter Schulz. 'Subjectivity out of Irony'. *Semiotica* 173.1/4 (2009): 397–416.

Savickey, Beth. 'Wittgenstein's Use of Examples'. In Oskari Kuusela and Marie McGinn (eds.), *The Oxford Handbook of Wittgenstein*, 667–96. Oxford: Oxford University Press, 2011.

Savickey, Beth. 'Wittgenstein and Hacker: *Übersichtliche Darstellung*'. *Nordic Wittgenstein Review* 3.2 (2014): 99–123.

Saxl, F. 'Ernst Cassirer'. In Paul Arthur Schilpp (ed.), *The Philosophy of Ernst Cassirer*, 47–51. LaSalle, IL: Open Court Press, 1949.

Scheler, Max. *The Nature of Sympathy*. Translated by Peter Heath. London: Routledge & Kegan Paul, 1954.

Schenker, Heinrich. *Five Graphic Music Analyses*. New York: Dover, 1969.

Schiller, F. C. S. et al. 'The Meaning of "Meaning": A Symposium'. *Mind* 29 (1920): 385–414.

Schlaps, Christiane. 'The "Genius of Language": Transformations of a Concept in the History of Linguistics'. *Historiographia Linguistica* 31.2/3 (2004): 367–88.

Schmitt, Carl. 'Preface to the Second Edition (1926): On the Contradiction between Parliamentarism and Democracy'. In *The Crisis of Parliamentary Democracy*. Translated by Ellen Kennedy. Cambridge, MA: MIT Press, 1988.

Scholem, Gershom. *Walter Benjamin: The Story of a Friendship*. London: Faber and Faber, 1982.

Scholem, Gershom. *Lamentations of Youth: The Diaries of Gershom Scholem, 1913–1919*. Translated by Anthony David Skinner. Cambridge, MA: Harvard University Press, 2007.

Schor, Esther. 'L. L. Zamenhof and the Shadow People'. *Language Problems & Language Planning* 34.2 (2010): 183–92.

Schorske, Carl E. 'The New Rigorism in the Human Sciences, 1940–1960'. *Daedalus* 126.1 (1997): 289–309.

Schuchardt, Hugo. 'On Sound Laws: Against the Neogrammarians [1885]'. Translated by Theo Vennemen and Terence H. Wilbur. In Theo Vennemen and Terence H. Wilbur (eds.), *Schuchardt, the Neogrammarians, and the Transformational Theory of Phonological Change*, 39–72. Frankfurt: Athenäum Verlag, 1972.

Searle, John. *Speech Acts*. Cambridge: Cambridge University Press, 1969.

Sebeok, Thomas A. *Semiotics in the United States*. Bloomington: Indiana University Press, 1991.

Sebeok, Thomas A. *Global Semiotics*. Bloomington: Indiana University Press, 2001.
Seifrid, Thomas. *The Word Made Self: Russian Writings on Language, 1860–1930*. Ithaca, NY: Cornell University Press, 2005.
Seigel, Jerrold. 'The Human Subject as Language-Effect'. *History of European Ideas* 18.4 (1994): 481–95.
Sériot, Patrick. 'The Impact of Czech and Russian Biology on the Linguistic Thought of the Prague Linguistic Circle'. In *Travaux du Cercle linguistique de Prague* 3, 15–24. Amsterdam: John Benjamins, 1999.
Shapere, Dudley. 'Philosophy and the Analysis of Language'. In Richard Rorty (ed.), *The Linguistic Turn: Recent Essays in Philosophical Method*, 271–83. Chicago: University of Chicago Press, 1967.
Shepherd, David (ed.). *The Contexts of Bakhtin: Philosophy, Authorship, Aesthetics*. Amsterdam: Harwood, 1998.
Shiach, Morag. ' "To Purify the Dialect of the Tribe": Modernism and Language Reform'. *Modernism/Modernity* 14.1 (2007): 21–34.
Shklovskii, Viktor. *Voskreshenie slova*. St Petersburg: Z. Sokolinskago, 1914.
Shklovskii, Viktor. 'Isskustvo kak priem'. In Osip Brik et al., *Poetika: sborniki po teorii poeticheskogo iazyka*, 101–14. Petrograd: n.p., 1919.
Shklovskii, Viktor. 'O poezii i zaumnom iazyke'. In Osip Brik et al., *Poetika: sborniki po teorii poeticheskogo iazyka*, 13–26. Petrograd: n.p., 1919.
Shklovskii, Viktor. 'Sviaz' priemov siuzhetoslozheniia c obshchimi priemami stilia'. In Osip Brik et al., *Poetika: sborniki po teorii poeticheskogo iazyka*, 115–50. Petrograd: n.p., 1919.
Shklovskii, Viktor. *Razvertyvanie siuzheta*. Petrograd: OPOIaZ, 1921.
Shklovskii, Viktor. *Rozanov*. Petrograd: OPOIaZ, 1921; reprinted Letchworth: Prideaux Press, 1974.
Shklovskii, Viktor. 'Pis'mo k Romanu Iakobsonu'. *Veshch/Objet/Gegenstand* 1–2. Berlin: Skify, 1922; reprinted Baden: Verlag Lars Müller, 1994: 5.
Shklovskii, Viktor. *Khod konia*. Moscow/Berlin: Gelikon, 1923; reprinted Orange, CT: Antiquary, 1986.
Shklovskii, Viktor. *Sentimental'noe puteshestvie: vospominaniia, 1917–1922*. Moscow: Gelikon, 1923.
Shklovskii, Viktor. *Zoo, ili Pis'ma ne o liubvi*. Berlin: Helikon, 1923.
Shklovskii, Viktor. *Tret'ia fabrika*. Moscow: Krug, 1926.
Shklovskii, Viktor. *Third Factory*. Translated by Richard Sheldon. Ann Arbor: Ardis, 1977.
Shklovskii, Viktor. *Gamburgskii schet: stat'i—vospominaniia—esse (1914–1933)*. Moscow: Sovetskii pisatel', 1990.
Shor, R. *Iazyk i obshchestvo*. 2nd edn. Moscow: Rabotnik prosveshcheniia, 1926.
Shor, R. 'Krizis sovremennoi lingvistiki'. *Iaficheskii sbornik* 5 (1927): 32–71.
Silverstein, Michael. 'From the Meaning of Meaning to the Empires of the Mind: Ogden's Orthological English'. *Pragmatics* 5.2 (1995): 185–95.
Simmel, Georg. 'The Metropolis and Mental Life' (1903). In *On Individuality and Social Forms*, 324–39. Chicago: University of Chicago Press, 1971.
Skidelsky, Edward. *Ernst Cassirer: The Last Philosopher of Culture*. Princeton, NJ: Princeton University Press, 2008.
Skinner, Quentin. 'Meaning and Understanding in the History of Ideas ' In James Tully (ed.), *Meaning and Context: Quentin Skinner and His Critics*, 29–67. Princeton, NJ: Princeton University Press, 1988.
Skorupski, John. 'Dummett's Frege'. *Philosophical Quarterly* 34.136 (1984): 402–14.

Skorupski, John. 'Language, Expressibility and the Mystical'. In Anat Matar (ed.), *Understanding Wittgenstein, Understanding Modernism*, 13–35. London: Bloomsbury Academic, 2017.

Sliusareva, N. A. and V. G. Kuznetsov. 'Iz istorii sovetskogo iazykoznaniia: rukopisnye materialy S. N. Bernshteina o F. de Sossiura'. *Izvestiia Akademii Nauk, Seriia literatury i iazyka* 35.5 (1976): 440–50.

Sluga, Hans. *Gottlob Frege*. London: Routledge & Kegan Paul, 1980.

Sluga, Hans. 'What Has History to Do with Me? Wittgenstein and Analytic Philosophy'. *Inquiry* 41 (1998): 99–121.

Smith, Barry. 'Law and Eschatology in Wittgenstein's Early Thought'. *Inquiry* 21 (1978): 425–41.

Smith, Barry. 'On the Origins of Analytical Philosophy' (review of Michael Dummett, *Origins of Analytical Philosophy*). *Grazer philosophische Studien* 35 (1989): 153–73.

Smith, Michael. *Language and Power in the Creation of the USSR, 1917–1953*. Berlin: Mouton de Gruyter, 1998.

Somavilla, Ilsa. 'Wittgenstein's Coded Remarks in the Context of His Philosophizing'. In Nuno Venturinha (ed.), *Wittgenstein After His Nachlass*, 30–50. Basingstoke: Palgrave Macmillan, 2010.

Somers, Matthias. 'Modernism and Rhetoric: Literary Culture and Public Speech, 1900–1940'. PhD dissertation, Katholieke Universiteit Leuven, 2015.

Sontag, Susan. 'Against Interpretation'. In *Against Interpretation and Other Essays*, 13–23. New York: Dell, 1969.

Sorel, Georges. *Introduction à l'économie moderne*. 2nd edn. Paris: G. Jacques, 1922.

Sorel, Georges. 'On the Barbarism of Revolution'. In Richard Vernon, *Commitment and Change: Georges Sorel and the Idea of Revolution*, 111–20. Toronto: University of Toronto Press, 1978.

Sorel, Georges. *Reflections on Violence*. Translated by T. E. Hulme and Jeremy Jennings. Cambridge: Cambridge University Press, 1999.

Spiegel, Gabrielle M. 'Orations of the Dead/Silences of the Living: The Sociology of the Linguistic Turn'. In *The Past as Text: The Theory and Practice of Medieval Historiography*, 19–43. Baltimore: Johns Hopkins University Press, 1997.

Stanley, John L. 'Sorel's Study of Vico: The Uses of the Poetic Imagination'. *The European Legacy* 3.5 (1998): 17–34.

Starobinski, Jean. *Words upon Words: The Anagrams of Ferdinand de Saussure*. Translated by Olivia Emmet. New Haven, CT: Yale University Press, 1979.

Stebbing, L. Susan. 'Language and Misleading Questions'. *Journal of Unified Science (Erkenntnis)* 8.1/3 (1939): 1–6.

Stedman Jones, Gareth. 'The Determinist Fix: Some Obstacles to the Further Development of the Linguistic Approach to History in the 1990s'. *History Workshop Journal* 42 (1996): 19–35.

Steiner, Peter. *Russian Formalism: A Metapoetics*. Ithaca, NY: Cornell University Press, 1984.

Sterenberg, Matthew. 'Tradition and Revolution in the Rhetoric of Analytic Philosophy'. *Philosophy and Literature* 34.1 (2010): 161–72.

Stern, David G. 'The Significance of Jewishness for Wittgenstein's Philosophy'. *Inquiry* 43 (2000): 383–402.

Stern, David G. 'The Methods of the *Tractatus*: Beyond Positivism or Metaphysics?'. In Paolo Parrini, Wesley C. Salmon, and Merrilee H. Salmon (eds.), *Logical Empiricism: Historical and Contemporary Perspectives*, 125–56. Pittsburgh: University of Pittsburgh Press, 2003.

Stern, David G. *Wittgenstein's Philosophical Investigations: An Introduction*. Cambridge: Cambridge University Press, 2004.
Stern, David G. 'How Many Wittgensteins?'. In Alois Pichler and S. Säätela (eds.), *Wittgenstein: The Philosopher and His Works*, 205–29. Frankfurt am Main: ontos Verlag, 2006.
Stjernfelt, Frederik. 'Simple Animals and Complex Biology: Von Uexküll's Two-Fold Influence on Cassirer's Philosophy'. *Synthese* 179 (2011): 169–86.
Strawson, P. F. 'On Referring'. *Mind* 59 (1950): 320–44.
[Strawson, P. F.]. 'The Post-Linguistic Thaw'. *Times Literary Supplement*, 9 September 1960, lx.
Stroll, Avrum. *Twentieth-Century Analytic Philosophy*. New York: Columbia University Press, 2001.
Szabados, Béla. 'Wittgenstein the Musical: Notes toward an Appreciation'. *Canadian Aesthetics Journal* 10 (2004). http://www.uqtr.uquebec.ca/AE/Vol_10/wittgenstein/szabados.htm, accessed 11 April 2017.
Szabados, Béla. 'Wittgenstein Listens to Mahler: How to Do Philosophy and Compose Music in the Breakdown of Tradition?'. *Dialogue* 46 (2007): 91–113.
Tarde, Gabriel. *The Laws of Imitation*. Translated by Elsie Clews Parsons. New York: Henry Holt, 1903.
Tarde, Gabriel. 'Opinion and Conversation' (1898). In *On Communication and Social Influence*, 297–318. Chicago: University of Chicago Press, 1969.
Tarde, Gabriel. 'The Public and the Crowd' (1901). In *On Communication and Social Influence*, 277–94. Chicago: University of Chicago Press, 1969.
Taylor, Talbot J. 'Language Constructing Language: The Implications of Reflexivity for Linguistic Theories'. In Hayley G. Davis and Talbot J. Taylor (eds.), *Rethinking Linguistics*, 95–119. London: Routledge Curzon, 2003.
Thompson, E. P. 'The Moral Economy of the English Crowd in the Eighteenth Century'. *Past and Present* 50 (1971): 76–136.
Tihanov, Galin. 'Why Did Modern Literary Theory Originate in Central and Eastern Europe? (And Why Is It Now Dead?)'. *Common Knowledge* 10 (2004): 61–81.
Tihanov, Galin. 'Politics of Estrangement: The Case of the Early Shklovsky'. *Poetics Today* 26.4 (2005): 665–96.
Timpanaro, Sebastiano. 'Structuralism and Its Successors'. In *On Materialism*, 135–219. Translated by Lawrence Garner. London: New Left Books, 1975.
Toddes, E. A. and M. O. Chudakova. 'Pervyi russkii perevod "Kursa Obshchei Lingvistiki" F. de Sossiura i deiatel'nost' Moskovskogo Lingvisticheskogo Kruzhka'. *Fedorovskie chteniia* 1 (1978): 229–49.
Todorov, Tzvetan (ed.). *Théorie de la littérature: textes des formalistes russes*. Paris: Le Seuil, 1965.
Toews, J. E. 'Intellectual History after the Linguistic Turn'. *American Historical Review* 92.4 (1987): 879–907.
Toman, Jindřich (ed.). *Letters and Other Materials from the Moscow and Prague Linguistic Circles, 1912–1945*. Ann Arbor: Michigan Slavic Publications, 1994.
Tseitlin, R. M. *Grigorii Osipovich Vinokur*. Moscow: Izdatel' Moskovskogo universiteta, 1965.
Tully, James. 'The Pen Is a Mighty Sword: Quentin Skinner's Analysis of Politics'. In James Tully (ed.), *Meaning and Context: Quentin Skinner and His Critics*, 7–25. Princeton, NJ: Princeton University Press, 1988.
Tully, James. 'Wittgenstein and Political Philosophy: Understanding Practices of Critical Reflection'. In Cressida J. Heyes (ed.), *The Grammar of Politics: Wittgenstein and Political Philosophy*, 17–42. Ithaca, NY: Cornell University Press, 2003.
Turner, James. *Philology: The Forgotten Origins of the Modern Humanities*. Princeton, NJ: Princeton University Press, 2014.

Tynianov, Iurii. 'Dostoevskii i Gogol: K teorii parodii' (1921). In *Arkhaisty i novatory*, 412–55. Leningrad: Priboi, 1929; reprinted Ann Arbor: Ardis, 1985.
Urmson, J. O. 'Austin's Philosophy'. In K. T. Fann (ed.), *Symposium on J. L. Austin*, 22–32. New York: Humanities Press, 1969.
Varro. *De Lingua Latina X*. Studies in the History of the Language Sciences 85. Translated by Daniel J. Taylor. Amsterdam: John Benjamins, 1996.
Venturinha, Nuno. 'Sraffa's Notes on Wittgenstein's "Blue Book"'. *Nordic Wittgenstein Review* 1 (2012): 181–92.
Vernon, James. 'Who's Afraid of the Linguistic Turn?: The Politics of Social History and Its Discontents'. *Social History* 19.1 (1994): 81–97.
Vinokur, G. O. 'Futuristy – stroiteli iazyka'. *LEF* 1 (1923): 204–13.
Vinokur, G. O. 'Kul'tura iazyka (zadachi sovremennogo iazykoznaniia)'. *Pechat' i revoliutsiia* 5 (1923): 100–11.
Vinokur, G. O. 'Novaia literatura po poetike' (Review). *LEF* 1 (1923): 239–43.
Vinokur, G. O. 'O revoliutsionnoi fraseologii (Odin iz voprosov iazykovoi politiki)'. *LEF* 2 (1923): 104–18.
Vinokur, G. O. 'Poetika, lingvistika, sotsiologiia. (Metodologicheskaia spravka)'. *LEF* 3 (1923): 104–13.
Vinokur, G. O. 'Khlebnikov'. *Russkii sovremennik* 4 (1924): 222–6.
Vinokur, G. O. *Kul'tura iazyka: ocherki lingvisticheskoi tekhnologii*. Moscow: Rabotnik prosveshcheniia, 1925.
Vinokur, G. O. 'Poeziia i nauka'. In G. Vinokur and F. Vermel' (eds.), *Chet i nechet: almanakh poezii i kritiki*, 21–31. Moscow: n.p., 1925.
[Vinokur, G. O.] 'Preface'. In G. Vinokur and F. Vermel' (eds.), *Chet i nechet: almanakh poezii i kritiki*, 5. Moscow: n.p., 1925.
Vinokur, G. O. Review of A. M. Selishchev, *Iazyk revoliutsionnoi epokhi*. *Pechat' i revoliutsiia* 2 (1928): 181–3.
Vinokur, G. O. *Kul'tura iazyka*. 2nd edn. Moscow: Federatsiia, 1929.
Vinokur, G. O. 'Neskol'ko slov pamiati Iu. N. Tynianova' [1943–4]. In V. A. Kaverin (ed.), *Vospominaniia o Iu. Tynianova*, 65–8. Moscow: Sovetskii pisatel', 1983.
Vinokur, G. O. '<Slovarnaia Avtobiograficheskaia Zametka. Konets 1925–1926 gg.>'. In S. I. Gindin and N. N. Rozanova (eds.) *Iazyk, kul'tura, gumanitarnoe znanie: nauchnoe nasledie G. O. Vinokura i sovremennost'*, 454–7. Moscow: Nauchnyi mir, 1999.
Vinokur, G. O. *Vvedenie v izuchenie filologicheskikh nauk*. Moscow: Labirint, 2000.
Voloshinov, V. N. *Marksizm i filosofiia iazyka*. 2nd edn. Leningrad, 1930; reprinted The Hague: Mouton, 1972.
von Wright, G. H. *Wittgenstein*. Oxford: Basil Blackwell, 1982.
Warnock, G. J. *English Philosophy since 1900*. Oxford: Oxford University Press, 1969.
Warnock, G. J. 'John Langshaw Austin, a Biographical Sketch'. In K. T. Fann (ed.), *Symposium on J. L. Austin*, 3–21. New York: Humanities Press, 1969.
Warnock, G. J. 'Saturday Mornings'. In Isaiah Berlin et al., *Essays on J. L. Austin*, 31–45. Oxford: Clarendon Press, 1973.
Weber, Max. *The Vocation Lectures*. Translated by Rodney Livingstone. Indianapolis: Hackett Publishing, 2004.
Welby, V. 'Sense, Meaning, and Interpretation'. *Mind* New Series 5.17 (1896): 24–37.
Welby, Victoria. *Significs and Language: The Articulate Form of our Expressive and Interpretative Resources*. London: Macmillan and Co., 1911.
Weststeijn, W. G. *Velimir Chlebnikov and the Development of Poetical Language in Russian Symbolism and Futurism*. Amsterdam: Rodopi, 1983.

Wheeler, Benjamin Ide. *Analogy and the Scope of Its Application in Language*. Ithaca, NY: John Wilson and Sons, 1887.
Wheeler, Wendy. 'Postscript on Biosemiotics: Reading Beyond Words – and Ecocriticism'. *new formations* 64 (2008): 137–54.
Wijdeveld, Paul. *Ludwig Wittgenstein, Architect*. Amsterdam: The Pepin Press, 1993.
Willett, John. *The New Sobriety, 1917–1933: Art and Politics in the Weimar Period*. London: Thames and Hudson, 1978.
Williams, Bernard and Alan Montefiore (eds.). *British Analytical Philosophy*. London: Routledge & Kegan Paul, 1966.
Williams, Raymond. *Culture and Society, 1780–1950*. London: Chatto & Windus, 1958.
Williams, Raymond. *Keywords: A Vocabulary of Culture and Society*. London: Fontana, 1976.
Williams, Raymond. *Marxism and Literature*. Oxford: Oxford University Press, 1977.
Williamson, Timothy. 'Past the Linguistic Turn?'. In Brian Leiter (ed.), *The Future for Philosophy*, 106–28. Oxford: Clarendon Press, 2004.
Wilson, Deirdre and Dan Sperber. 'On Verbal Irony'. *Lingua* 87 (1992): 53–76.
Wilson, Leigh. 'Bringing Language Back to Life: Language Reform, Literary Experiment, and Magic'. Unpublished paper, 2009.
Wittgenstein, Ludwig. *Philosophical Investigations*. 3rd edn. Translated by G. E. M. Anscombe. Oxford: Basil Blackwell, 1967.
Wittgenstein, Ludwig. *The Blue and Brown Books*. 2nd edn. Oxford: Basil Blackwell, 1969.
Wittgenstein, Ludwig. *On Certainty*. Translated by G. E. M. Anscombe and Denis Paul. Oxford: Basil Blackwell, 1969.
Wittgenstein, Ludwig. *Philosophical Remarks*. Translated by Raymond Hargreaves and Roger White. Oxford: Basil Blackwell, 1975.
Wittgenstein, Ludwig. *Wittgenstein and the Vienna Circle: Conversations Recorded by Friedrich Waismann*. Translated by Joachim Schulte and Brian McGuinness. Oxford: Basil Blackwell, 1979.
Wittgenstein, Ludwig. *Philosophical Grammar*. Translated by Anthony Kenny. Oxford: Basil Blackwell, 1980.
Wittgenstein, Ludwig. *Wittgenstein's Lectures: Cambridge, 1930–1932, from the Notes of John King and Desmond Lee*. Edited by Desmond Lee. Oxford: Basil Blackwell, 1980.
Wittgenstein, Ludwig. *Tractatus Logico-Philosophicus*. Translated by C. K. Ogden. Oxford: Basil Blackwell, 1981.
Wittgenstein, Ludwig. *Notebooks 1914–1916*. 2nd edn. Translated by G. E. M. Anscombe. Chicago: University of Chicago Press, 1984.
Wittgenstein, Ludwig. *Philosophical Occasions, 1912–1951*. Edited by James Klagge and Alfred Nordmann. Indianapolis: Hackett Publishing, 1993.
Wittgenstein, Ludwig. *Cambridge Letters: Correspondence with Russell, Keynes, Moore, Ramsey and Sraffa*. Edited by Brian McGuinness and G. H. von Wright. Oxford: Basil Blackwell, 1995.
Wittgenstein, Ludwig. *Culture and Value*. Revised edn. Translated by Peter Winch. Oxford: Basil Blackwell, 1998.
Wittgenstein, Ludwig. *Ludwig Wittgenstein: Public and Private Occasions*. Edited by James C. Klagge and Alfred Nordmann. Lanham, MD: Rowman & Littlefield, 2003.
Wittgenstein, Ludwig. *The Big Typescript: TS 213*. Edited and translated by C. Grant Luckhardt and Maximilian A. E. Aue. Oxford: Basil Blackwell, 2005.
Wittgenstein, Ludwig. *Wittgenstein in Cambridge: Letters and Documents 1911–1951*. Edited by Brian McGuinness. Oxford: Blackwell, 2008.

Wittgenstein, Ludwig. *Philosophical Investigations*. Revised 4th edn. Edited by P. M. S. Hacker and Joachim Schulte. Translated by G. E. M. Anscombe, P. M. S. Hacker, and Joachim Schulte. Oxford: Wiley-Blackwell, 2009.

Wittgenstein, Ludwig. *Lecture on Ethics*. Edited by Edoardo Zamuner, Ermelinda Valentina Di Lascio, and D. K. Levy. Oxford: Wiley Blackwell, 2014.

Wohlfarth, Irving. 'Walter Benjamin's Image of Interpretation'. *New German Critique* 17 (2008): 70–98.

Wolf, George. 'C. K. Ogden'. In Roy Harris (ed.), *Linguistic Thought in England, 1914–1945*, 85–105. London: Duckworth, 1988.

Wolf, George. 'A Glance at the History of Linguistics: Saussure and Historical-Comparativism'. In Sheila Embleton, John E. Joseph, and Hans-Joseph Niederehe (eds.), *The Emergence of the Modern Language Sciences: Vol. 1: Historiographical Perspectives*, 129–37. Amsterdam: John Benjamins, 1999.

Wollen, Peter. *Raiding the Icebox: Reflections on Twentieth-Century Culture*. London: Verso: 1993.

Yaguello, Marina. *Lunatic Lovers of Language: Imaginary Languages and Their Inventors*. Translated by Catherine Slater. London: Athlone Press, 1991.

Young, Robert J. C. 'Race and Language in the Two Saussures'. In Peter Osborne and Stella Sanford (eds.), *Philosophies of Race and Ethnicity*, 63–78. London: Continuum, 2002.

Zager, David. 'On Orientation, or Constraining False Analogy'. *Linguistics* 19.11/12 (1981): 1107–31.

Žižek, Slavoj. *The Sublime Object of Ideology*. London: Verso, 1989.

Žižek, Slavoj. *For They Know Not What They Do: Enjoyment as a Political Factor*. London: Verso, 1991.

Žižek, Slavoj. *Looking Awry: An Introduction to Jacques Lacan through Popular Culture*. Cambridge, MA: MIT Press, 1992.

ARCHIVAL MATERIALS

C. K. Ogden fonds, RC 0060. McMaster University Library, Hamilton, Ontario.

Index

Aarsleff, Hans 142n.55
abbreviations, Soviet 115–16, 124
Adorno, Theodor 55, 235, 262, 270
Akehurst, Thomas 155
Alpatov, Vladimir 107n.9, 112n.30
Altieri, Charles 207
Amsterdamska, Olga 14, 37–8, 142n.55
analogy 22, 29–52, 91–9, 154–5, 193
   in Futurist poetry 118, 209–13
Analysis 86, 89–90
analytic philosophy
   linguistic turn within 1–2, 22–3, 53–104, 154, 247–53, 271–7, 282
   and nationalism 155–6
anarchism 235–6
Anderson, Benedict 42–3
Anderson, Perry 269
Apel, Karl-Otto 87, 91n.180, 169n.36
Aragon, Louis, *Paris Peasant* 228
arbitrariness, in signs 40, 112–16
art
   and estrangement 216–17
   and perspicuous representation 254–7
   relation of, to myth 198, 205
Ascoli, Graziadio Isaia 241, 244
assertion 54–5, 66–7
astrology 213–14, 230–2
Auerbach, Eric, *Mimesis* 181
Austin, J. L. 25, 88, 90, 101n.225, 264–70, 277, 282
   How to Do Things with Words 276
   'Ifs and Cans' 267, 268, 269
   and linguistic turn 1–2, 4–5, 275–6
   'Other Minds' 265, 269, 276n.26
   'A Plea for Excuses' 265–6, 269
   'Three Ways of Spilling Ink' 265–6, 269–70
   'Truth' 269
   'Unfair to Facts' 269
avant-gardism 84, 215, 227, 280, 281
   see also Futurism, Russian; Surrealism
awakening, as enlightenment 224, 228–9, 237
Ayer, A. J. 88, 89–90, 268n.110
   The Revolution in Philosophy 271

Baden-Powell, Robert, *Aid to Scouting* 71
Badiou, Alain 62, 74
Bakhtin, M. M. 24, 93, 156, 199, 278–9, 282
   on analogy 97
   'Discourse in the Novel' 137–41, 178–80, 182
   on heteroglossia 43, 130–1, 137–9
   linguistic turn in 3, 103, 131–4, 138

   as modernist 144–5
   on myth and word magic 24, 177–85, 247
   on novelistic style 130–41, 152–3, 178–9, 182, 281
   Problems of Dostoevsky's Art 132–7, 178
Bally, Charles 29, 50, 107n.8, 111, 123n.77, 128, 133
Balzac, Honoré de 238
Barthes, Roland 46, 50–1, 278–80
   Mythologies 25, 279–80
Bartoli, Matteo 240, 241–2, 244
Basic English 160, 172–6
Baudelaire, Charles 78, 146, 148, 234, 238
Baudouin de Courtenay, Jan 106, 118n.50, 214
Beauzée, Nicolas, *Encyclopédie méthodique* 33
Bebel, August 169–70
Beethoven, Ludwig von 261
Begriffsschrift (concept-script) 53–4, 88, 273
Belmore, Herbert 225
Benjamin, Walter 3, 25, 101, 281, 282
   on analogy 96–7
   on creativity in language 23–4, 147–53, 185, 224–6
   on crisis 7, 202
   on divine language 24, 149–50, 224–7
   on intoxication 146–7, 150–2, 156
   on language as such 130–1, 146–50, 225–6
   method of 93, 186
   and myth 103, 162, 224–36, 247
   on naming 182, 224–5
   and Sorel 237, 239
   on urban crowds 146
Benjamin, Walter, Works
   'Antitheses Concerning Word and Name' 149–50, 231
   Arcades Project 96–7, 141–3, 152, 227–9, 234
   Berlin Childhood 229–30
   'On the Concept of History' 234
   'Doctrine of the Similar' 229–31
   'On Language as Such and Human Language' 4, 96, 141, 147–8, 149–50, 224–6
   'On the Mimetic Faculty' 231
   'The Task of the Translator' 96, 148–9
   'Theological-Political Fragment' 235
   'The Work of Art in the Age of its Technological Reproducibility' 235
Benveniste, Émile 65–7, 98, 148–9, 154, 233, 252, 279
Berezin, Vladimir 221n.164
Bergmann, Gustav 2, 4, 271
Berlin, Isaiah 268n.110

Bernshtein, S. I. 107–8
Bernstein, J. M. 80n.135
Blanqui, Louis-Auguste 153, 234–6
Bloomfield, Leonard 38
Bocharov, S. G. 133n.16
Boothman, Derek 240
Bopp, Franz 10, 33–4
Bottomley, Horatio 167–8
Bourdieu, Pierre 10, 43, 102
Brahms, Johannes 255, 261
Bréal, Michel 10, 15–16, 33, 102, 148, 168
  and the Dreyfus affair 48–9
  and Gramsci 245
Breton, André 228
Brik, Osip 118, 214–15
Bru, Sascha 205
Bruckstein, Almut Shulamit 200
Brugmann, Karl 15
  Comparative Grammar of the Indo-Germanic Languages 15, 37
  Morphological Investigations 14, 33n.13, 34n.17, 37
Buber, Martin 20, 224
Bühler, Karl 133
Bukharin Nikolai, *The Theory of Historical Materialism* 244–5
Burge, Tyler 66
Burke, Kenneth 26, 66n.62
Butler, Judith, *Gender Trouble* viii, 276n.25

Caille, Louis 46
calculus, as model 92, 188–9, 252–4, 259–60
Cambridge Magazine 164
Carlucci, Alessandro 240
Cassirer, Ernst 11, 21, 138, 263, 277, 282
  Einstein's Theory of Relativity 190–1
  'Form and Technology' 201, 204
  'The Idea of a Constitutional Republic' 201–3
  'Language and Myth' 194, 196–7, 200
  linguistic turn in 2, 6, 190–1
  on myth 24, 162, 185, 187–205, 207–8, 212n.119, 213, 220, 226, 227, 229, 230, 243, 247–8, 249, 281
  Philosophy of Symbolic Forms 133–4, 190–200, 203, 275, 281
  Substance and Function 187–9, 199
  on theoretical science 100–1, 187–9, 206, 232
Cavell, Stanley 251, 257–8, 266
charisma 160, 222–3
Chomsky, Noam 35
  Syntactic Structures 94
cities, and linguistic change 146–53
clarity 55–6, 58–9, 269–70
  in analytic philosophy 22–3, 84–90, 154, 282

and intersubjectivity 65–72, 154
  in political discourse 175–6, 185
  Wittgenstein's conception of 55–6, 64–5, 71–2, 78–9, 84–5, 250–1
Clark, T. J. 215
Clarke, David 165
cliché 78, 175–6
Cohen, Hermann 189, 200, 227
  Religion of Reason Out of the Sources of Judaism 226
collaboration, in philosophy 264–5, 268–70
collective will
  and analogy 33–4, 44–50
  in Gramsci 242–6
  language as expression of 16
  and leadership 270
  and myth 247
  and urban life 146
  see also nationalism; people(s); political will
comparative philology 10–16, 31–2, 33, 141–3, 147, 149
Conan Doyle, Arthur 38
Conant, James 72–5, 81
consciousness
  and analogy 44–5
  collective 47
consent and agreement 21–2
  as basis of *langue* 32, 45–9, 102–3, 105–6, 145–6, 153
  in language as such 103, 154–6
  and linguistic productivity 141
  in philosophy 267–8
conservatism of language 6, 110–11, 281
constitutions
  in interwar Europe 7–8
  as symbolic forms 201–3
conventions, *see* consent and agreement
conversational idiom
  in analytic philosophy 89–90
  and public opinion 171–2
  in Wittgenstein 97–8, 268
Cook, Nicholas 260n.72
creativity, linguistic 39, 44–6. *See also under* Benjamin, Walter; Shklovskii, Viktor
crisis, personal and social 6–7, 135–41, 202–3
Croce, Benedetto 133, 233–4, 242
crowds 20–1
  and linguistic change 146–7, 151–3
  and grammar 46
  and reason 54–5
Cubism 207
Cusa, Nicholas de 200

Dameth, Henri 145n.62
Darmesteter, Arsène 10
Davidson, Donald 101n.227, 233n.223
de la Mare, Walter 76

deliberation
  collective, and linguistic change 15–16, 22, 33–4, 44–52, 110–31, 144–9, 153–6
  excluded from linguistic convention 103, 105
  liberal, as opposed to myth 161
  opposed to literature 76–7
  and the state 13
demagoguery, fear of 169–71
de Man, Paul 3–4, 220
De Mauro, Tullio 240
democracy 6–10, 20–1, 25–6
  and culture 76–7
  within language 45, 47, 50, 102–3, 185
  and leadership 269–70
  and liberalism 135n.26
  and linguistic change 105–6, 141, 213–14
  role of myth in 160–1, 170
  and social order 42–3
  and technique 220–2
  see also collective will; politics; public sphere
Derrida, Jacques 276n.25
descriptivism 69–72
dialectology 43, 128–9
dialogism 136–8
Diamond, Cora 72–7, 78, 81–3, 85n.154
Dickens, Charles 76
discourse, instances of
  and language structure 65–6, 232–3
  and Wittgenstein's style 97–8, 252–4
distinctive features 212–13
diversity, of existing languages 130–53
Doroszewksi, Witold 46
dramatization, as philosophical method 97–9, 252–3, 263–4, 266–7
Dreyfus Affair 9, 48–9, 170
Drumont, Édouard, *La libre parole* 48–9, 243
Duffy, Enda 220n.160
Dummett, Michael 53
  Origins of Analytical Philosophy 273–4, 279
Durkheim, Émile 46–7

Edelstein, Dan 238
Edenic language 100, 225. *See also* perfect language; pure language; religion
Eikhenbaum, Boris 137, 221
Eiland, Howard 226
Eliot, T. S. 237, 247, 270
El Lissitsky 204
Engelmann, Mauro Luiz 92, 259
Engelmann, Paul 77, 254
Esperanto 172–3
estrangement 220–1
ethics
  in Bakhtin 132–7
  and science, in Cassirer 199–200
  in Wittgenstein 74–8
Eurasianism 208
Europe
  and constitutionalism 201–3
  and democracy 6–10
  postwar, and structuralism 277–80
Evans, Gareth 273

facts, world as totality of 62–4, 79–80
Feuerbach, Ludwig 197
Feyerabend, Paul 51
Ficker, Ludwig von 74, 78
Flaubert, Gustave 78–9
Floyd, Juliet 86, 273
force 4–6, 21, 188n.10
  and myth 160–1, 165, 175–7, 185, 187, 224–7
  public opinion as 170–1
Formalism, Russian 3–4, 24, 79n.132, 117–18, 214–24, 278–9
  and Bakhtin 131
  and Vinokur 120–2
  and word magic 160, 214
forms of life 257–8, 259–60, 264
France, linguistic turns in 278–80
Frazer, J. G., *The Golden Bough* 248–9
Frege, Gottlob
  and intersubjectivity 66–7
  and linguistic turn 1–2, 22, 273
  and logical analysis 53–7, 84, 154, 169, 188
  and myth 24, 168–71, 184
  and nonsense 88
  'On Sense and Reference' 168–70
Freud, Sigmund 20
Fried, Michael 254–5
functional conception of language 119–23, 128–31
functions, concepts as 187–9
Futurism, Italian 209, 217
Futurism, Russian 24, 106–7, 117–19, 121–3, 205–15
  and Jakobson 217
  and Shklovskii 160, 205–6, 220–1

Galileo Galilei 188
Gasparov, Boris 212–13
Gauchat, Louis 128n.3
Gawronsky, Dmitri 190
Geistesgegenwart (alertness) 146–7, 149–50, 223, 232
Gellner, Ernest, *Words and Things* 268–9
General Strike, myth of 238–9
Genette, Gerard 219
genius of a language 13, 102–3, 144, 210–11
gesture, language as 253–4, 259–60
Galliéron, Jules 128n.3
glossolalia 215–16
Godel, Robert 29, 49
gods, names of 196
Goethe, J. W. von 202, 204–5
Gordon, W. Terrence 164n.13, 173
Gornung, B. V. 108n.12, 115n.40, 117n.49

grammar
　and analogy 34–5, 95–6
　ironizing of 263
　and linguistic mythology 250–1
　and linguistic revolution 112–13
　and logic 57–8, 60–2, 93–5, 193
　and word-creation 115–16, 118–19, 123–4, 210–11
Gramsci, Antonio 1, 2–3, 21, 24–5, 236, 240–7, 259, 262
　on Sorel 237, 242
Greimas, A. J. 278
Grimm, Jacob 10–13, 31
Grimm Brothers 76, 149
Grimm-Rask Law 11–13, 31
Guter, Eran 255, 260

Habermas, Jürgen 59, 76, 229n.206, 268n.111
　on Cassirer 134n.18, 192
　on public sphere 22, 68, 71, 86n.158, 135n.26, 154
　on success of language 101n.225
Hacker, P. M. S. 251–2, 274
Hampshire, Stuart 56–7, 88, 268n.110
Harcourt, Edward 84–5
Harris, Roy 101n.227
Harrison, Jane 159
Hassler, Gerda 32–3
Havet, Louis 48–9
Hawthorne, Nathaniel 76
Hegel, G. W. F. 41
hegemony 240n.16
Heidegger, Martin 5, 20, 275
Henry, Victor 10
Heretics Society, Cambridge 159, 162–3
Hertz, Heinrich 63, 69–70, 72
　Principles of Mechanics 188
Hobsbawm, Eric 7–8
Hoel, Aud Sissel 201
Holbo, John 78
Honneth, Axel 150–1, 234
Humboldt, Wilhelm von 12–13, 95–6, 114–15, 191, 193
Husserl, Edmund 79n.132, 199
Hutton, Christopher 156n.104
Hylton, Peter 57–8

Iakubinskii, L. 23, 125–7, 138, 146, 214–16
ideology, theory of 280
image, concept of 229, 236–9
imitation 46–9, 77–8, 145–6, 175–7
improvisation, *see* dramatization
inner form 114–15, 121, 191, 201–2, 210–11
institution
　language as 21–4, 99–101, 144–5, 235
　language as hostile to 281
　see also collective will; order, social and political
intellectuals, and working of language 103, 116

intersubjectivity
　in analytic philosophy 23, 154, 282
　and logic 53–6, 65–72
　myth as form of 198–9
　in Wittgenstein 83–4, 252–4, 257
irony
　in Mahler 261–2
　in Wittgenstein 78–85, 154, 282

Jacobinism 243–4
Jakobson, Roman 56n.12, 79, 205, 217–20, 223n.172, 277–8
　and avant-gardism 117n.49, 217
　Contemporary Russian Poetry 217–18
　and functional conception of language 128–9
　and Khlebnikov 212–13, 217–18
　on linguistic revolution 112, 117
　in Moscow Linguistic Circle 115n.40
　on Saussure 21, 108–9, 214, 219, 277–8
　and Vinokur 122
James, Henry 76
James, William 216
Jameson, Fredric 146
Jarvis, Simon 98, 99
Jennings, Michael W. 226, 235n.231
Joseph, John E. 30, 40, 45, 47, 48–9, 50, 103–4, 111n.23
Joyce, James 78–9
Judaism 155, 200, 235n.231
judgment 54, 59–60, 66–7
Jung, Carl 151
Jünger, Ernst 151
justice 186–7, 202–3, 226–7, 234–5, 281

Kant, Immanuel 91, 202
Kartsevskii, S. I. 23, 107–8, 123–5, 210
　Language, War and Revolution 112–17
Kenigsberg, M. M. 110, 115n.40
Khlebnikov, Velimir 185, 205–7, 247
　and Jakobson 217–18
　and nationalism 208–10
　word-creation in 209–14
Kienzler, Wolfgang 92
Kittsteiner, H. D. 142n.51
Klages, Ludwig 203
Klippi, Carita 10, 102
Koerner, E. F. K. 46–7
Konovalev, Dmitri 216
Kraus, Karl 20, 79
Kripke, Saul 63
Kristeva, Julia 278–9
Krois, John Michael 191–2
Kruchenykh, Aleksandr 106, 210
　'Dyr bul shchyl' 119, 208
Kuusela, Oskari 92, 95n.199, 260

Labov, William 242n.25
Lacan, Jacques 105

Lacis, Asja 227
Laclau, Ernesto viii
Landauer, Gustav 20
Langer, Suzanne 275
language
    atomization of 14–15, 17–18, 37–41
    and ethical expression 73–7
    as ideological 280
    as internally divided 4, 6, 19–20
    as mimesis 229–34
    and the people 10–16, 21–2
    and poetic function 217–20. *See also* poetic language
    productivity of 137–53
    as something that 'works' 43, 51–2, 98–103, 126–7, 154–5, 184–5. *See also under* Wittgenstein
    as symbolic form 191–4, 196
language as such 19–21
    and analogy 22, 33–4, 95–9
    in analytic philosophy 54–60, 154–5
    as democratic 141
    and ethics 74–5
    heterogeneity of 98–9, 122
    and nationalism 43, 155–6
    and nonsense 88–9, 91
    overestimation of 280–3
    propensity to myth in 24–5, 161–2, 184, 238
    as residue of divine 225–6
    and social order 41, 103, 153–6, 186–7, 235, 280–1
    as unreflective 49–50, 116
    as urban 152
    see also word as such
language games 101–2
langue (language system) 17–19, 35–6,
    and analogy 30, 39–40, 44–52, 95–6
    and collective change 44–6, 109–13, 145–6
    patchwork nature of 102–3, 105, 144, 210–11
    relation of, to discourse 62, 65–6
    as tradition 109–11, 122–3
law 226–7
Lazarus, Moritz 37
Leavis, F. R. 76, 269
LEF 118
Lefort, Claude 140–1
Lepschy, Giulio 241
Levinas, Emmanuel 199
Lévi-Strauss, Claude 50–1, 277–8
Lewis, Wyndham 78–9
liberalism 42, 135
linguistic communism 10, 43
linguistic conscience 163
linguistic philosophy 1–2, 3, 22–3, 25.
    See also analytic philosophy
linguistic politics 119–22
linguistics
    and language in general 2–3, 16–19, 51–2

and politics, in Gramsci 240–2, 245
    see also comparative philology; Saussure, Ferdinand de
linguistic turn
    and clarity in philosophy 87–8
    as historical phenomenon 1–6, 19–20, 271–7, 280–3
    and myth 160–2
    postwar 277–80
literary language 50, 128–9
literature, as ethical expression 75–81
Livshits, Benedikt 209
Lobachevsky, N. I. 211
Lofts, Stephen 198
logical analysis
    of belief sentences 169, 252
    evolution of 57–68
    and grammar 93–4
    and natural language 53–4, 154
logical syntax 64–5, 67, 93
Loos, Adolf 84–5
Lo Piparo, Franco 240, 242
Lukács, Georg
    History and Class Consciousness 228
    Theory of the Novel 79–81, 83–5
Lyotard, Jean-François, *The Postmodern Condition* vii

McGuinness, Brian 84n.151, 255
Mach, Ernst 194
Machiavelli, Niccolò, *The Prince* 242
magic, word and language 160–2
    in Benjamin 147–50, 224–34
    critique of, by Ogden and Richards 2, 6, 159–60, 162–8
    see also myth
Mahler, Gustav 255, 261–3
Maimonides, Moses 200
Malcolm, Norman 87
Malinowski, Bronislaw 165
Mann, Thomas 204
Manzoni, Alessandro 241, 244
Marinetti, Filippo 209
markets, as metaphor 5–6, 145–6
Marr, Nikolai Ia. 126
Marshall, David L. 232n.221
Marty, Anton 114, 133
Marx, Karl 8, 41, 142, 185
Marxism 228, 244–5
Mauthner, Fritz 20
Mayakovsky, Vladimir 106, 108, 117, 118
Mayer, Arno 42
Mazower, Mark, *Dark Continent* 7–9, 155
mediation, *see* technology and technique, and *under* public opinion
Meillet, Antoine 17, 47, 279
    Linguistique générale et linguistique historique 108

metaculture 186
metaphysics, as myth 249, 265
metonymy, as relation of language to
  society 6, 19–21, 52, 155, 184–5, 280–3
Milkov, Nikolay 92
mimetic faculty 96, 149–50, 229–34
misleadingness, of language 88–98
modernism 76–85, 144–5, 207, 227.
  See also avant-gardism
modernity 138–41, 144–53, 281
  and myth 162, 178–9, 226–7, 238
  and public opinion 170–2
Monk, Ray 84n.151, 104, 273
monologism 178–9
Montefiore, Alan, *British Analytical Philosophy* 271
Moore, G. E. 94, 265, 273
  'The Justification of Analysis' 86–7
Moretti, Franco 38–9, 146
Morpurgo Davies, Anna, *Nineteenth-century Linguistics* 11–12, 36–8, 142n.55
Moscow Linguistic Circle 107–11, 115nn.40, 42, 117, 217
motivation of signs 113–16
Mouffe, Chantal viii
Moyal-Sharrock Danièle 76
Moynahan, Gregory B. 189, 199
Mozart, W. A. 256
Mulhall, Stephen 75n.109
Mulhern, Francis 176, 186
Müller, Max 187
music 78, 255–63
Mussolini, Benito 2–3, 237
myth 24–5, 281
  and collectivity 151, 161, 242–7
  critiques of 162–83, 249, 279–80
  and linguistic turns 160–2
  and names 63, 159–60, 162–3
  proponents of 184–246
  and science 247–9

names and naming
  in analytic philosophy 62–3, 266n.98
  and divine word 100–1, 225–6
  and mimesis 231
  as source of word magic 159–60, 162–6, 182–3, 195–6
  Soviet abbreviations as 115–16, 124–5
narcotic historicism 23–4, 141–2, 146–7, 224
nationalism 42–3, 102–3, 151, 155–6
  and comparative philology 10–16, 143–4, 149, 185–6
  and Russian Futurism 208–10
national languages 241, 243–6
nations
  and democracy 8–9
  and public opinion 172
Neogrammarians 14–16, 33–9, 43, 96
neolinguistics 240–1
neologisms 115–16, 118–19, 123–4, 209–13

NEP 125
Nestroy, Johannes 79
Neue Sachlichkeit 84n.150
Newspeak 174–7
New Wittgensteinians 72–7, 81–3, 92
Nicholls, Peter 78
Nikolaev, N. I. 133n.16
nonsense
  as philosophical topic 72–7, 88–9, 91–8, 154–5
  and transrational poetry 215–16, 218
Nussbaum, Martha 76

Offenbach, Jacques, *Orfée aux enfers* 171n.41
Ogden, C. K. 2, 6, 20–1, 24, 161, 282
  The Meaning of Meaning 165–8, 187
  on myth and word magic 159–60, 162–8, 170, 172–6, 182–6, 190, 195, 207, 247
  'The Progress of Significs' 159–60, 175
OPOIaZ 107, 119, 214–15, 217
order, social and political
  and atomized society 14
  and democracy 9–10
  and linguistic order 19–22, 41–52, 145–6, 152–6, 185–7
  and myth 161
  and structuralism 279–80
ordinary language, as philosophical topic 25, 93–5, 265–6, 269–70
organicism 36–7
Orwell, George 6, 24, 184–6, 247
  Nineteen Eighty-Four 124, 174–7, 179, 181
  'Politics and the English Language' 175–7
Osthoff, Hermann 15
  Morphological Investigations 14, 33n.13, 34n.17, 37

Paris 23–4, 146–7, 150–3
Paris, Gaston 48–9
parliamentarianism, rejection of 8, 237
Pasternak, Boris 108
Paul, Hermann 14–15, 17, 36–43
  Principles of the History of Language 34–5, 37
Pearson, Karl 69–71, 77, 83n.146, 154
  The Grammar of Science 70–1
Peirce, C. S. 163, 192
people(s)
  and democracy 8–10
  and languages 11–13, 153
  will of the 169–72, 203–4
  see also collective will; nationalism
Perelman, Chaim 25–6
perfect language 100–1. See also pure language
perspicuous representation 251–8, 260, 263–4
Peterson, M. N. 109
Petrilli, Susan 163nn.7, 12
phenomenology 279. See also Husserl, Edmund
Pichler, Alois 98

picture theory of meaning 61–4
Pitcher, George 265
pleasure 25, 264–5, 269
  in perspicuous representation 251–2, 257–8, 263–4
poetic language/function 119, 214–20
political will, and mediation 200–4.
  See also collective will; public sphere
politics
  Bakhtin's conception of 141, 185
  and Frege 169–70
  and the market 5–6
  and myth 24, 226–7, 237–40, 242–6
  and religion 234–5
  and scientific method 70–2
  'unleashing' of 9, 16–17, 21–2, 41–2
  and Wittgenstein 71–2, 262–3
  and word magic 166–8
Polivanov, Evgenii 214–15
popular etymology 49
popular speech, status of 10, 14
Porter, Theodore, *Trust in Numbers* 68–9
Potebnia, Aleksandr 114–15
Pott, August Friedrich 31n.8
Pound, Ezra 78–9
pragmatism 274–5
press 170–1, 243, 245
profane illumination 150–2
professionals, and objectivity 67–72, 154, 168
propositions, analysis of 54–65, 255–7
Proust, Marcel 229
public opinion 48–9, 68–9, 169–72
  and mediation 202–4, 243–6
public sphere 8
  and democracy 42, 76–7
  and philosophical style 82, 90
  and professional expertise 23, 68, 70–2, 85–6, 154, 269–70
  word magic in 167–8, 185
  See also collective will; deliberation; political will
pure language 148–50, 152, 281. See also Edenic language; language as such
purism 129
Pushkin, Aleksandr 218
Putnam, Hilary 87, 99–100, 274n.15

Quine, W. V. O. 87
  Word and Object 5–6

race 8–9, 43, 155–6
Ram, Harsha 208
Ramsey, Frank 259
Rancière, Jacques 41n.44
Ranke, Leopold 142
Rask, Rasmus 10, 11, 12
Ravel, Maurice 255

reason
  and analogical change 32–3, 47–8
  and democracy 42
  and language 54–5, 67–8
  and language system 36, 128
  see also deliberation; public sphere
religion 150–1, 195–8, 200, 216, 224, 227, 235
republican model 145–6
revolution, linguistic 23, 106–7, 110–16
Rhees, Rush 251
rhetoric 23, 25–6, 55, 176, 184–5.
  See also deliberation
Richards, I. A. 2, 6, 20–1, 24, 164–8, 172, 182–3, 207, 282
  The Meaning of Meaning 165–8
Ricketts, Thomas 59
Riefenstahl, Leni, *The Triumph of the Will* 203–4
Rilke, Rainer Maria 78
Romm, A. I. 109–15 *passim*
Rorty Richard 73–4, 98–9
  The Consequences of Pragmatism 73–4
  The Linguistic Turn 271–5
Rosanvallon, Pierre 5, 9, 22, 41, 145, 235
Rosiello, Luigi 240
Ross, Alison 226–7
Ross, J. J. 86, 90
Russell, Bertrand
  'On Denoting' 57–8, 66
  History of Western Philosophy 85–6
  and linguistic turn 1–2, 22, 273
  and logical analysis 55–65, 84, 88, 154, 188
  and Ogden 165n.18
  and science 67–8, 71–2, 85–6, 154
Russian Revolution 105–6, 111–16
Ryle, Gilbert 59, 277
  The Concept of Mind 90, 275–6
  The Revolution in Philosophy 271
  'Systematically Misleading Expressions' 89
  on value of clarification 87, 89–90, 282

sacredness 195–6, 220–1. See also religion
Salzer, Felix 255
Santner, Eric 176–7
satire 139–40
Saussure, Ferdinand de 29–52, 93, 168, 232
  on analogy 22, 29–49, 95–6, 193, 210
  and Benveniste 65
  Cours de linguistique générale 29–30, 49–51, 107–12, 278
  and the Dreyfus affair 48–9, 155
  'On the Dual Essence of Language' 36, 51
  and Jakobson 21, 109, 214, 219, 277–8
  on 'language in general' 2, 16–19, 23, 51–2, 93, 98, 283
  and language that works 100–4, 155

Saussure, Ferdinand de (*cont.*)
   on mutability of language 88–9, 110–11
   and myth 24, 183, 187, 196
   on productivity of language 23–4, 130–1,
      141–7, 149, 151–3, 155–6
   on relative arbitrariness 112–13
   on social nature of language vii, 6, 54–5, 67,
      102–3, 105–7, 120, 153,
      185, 281–3
   Soviet reception of 106–27, 219, 240
   and structuralism 25, 50–1, 278, 280
Saussure, Léopold de 43, 48–9
Savickey, Beth 252, 264
Saxl, Fritz 190
Scheler, Max 199
Schenker, Heinrich 255–6, 260–1
Schlaps, Christiane 13
Schlegel, Friedrich 10–11
   *On the Language and Wisdom of the
      Indians* 11
Schleicher, August 33–4, 36–7
Schmitt, Carl 8–9
Scholem, Gershom 224, 227, 230, 231
   Major Trends in Jewish Mysticism 235n.231
Schuchardt, Hugo 43, 128n.3
science
   Cassirer and 187–9, 192, 194, 199
   culture of 67–72, 85–6, 154, 168,
      268–9, 274
   ironized 82–4
   linguistics, as model of 277–8
   relation of, to philosophy 63–5, 71–2, 85–7,
      247–9, 258, 268–9, 272, 274–5
Searle, John 276n.25
Sebeok, Thomas 277n.28
Sechehaye, Albert 29, 50, 111
seeing, as method 79, 94–9
semantic function of language 65–6, 148–9
seriousness, official and unofficial 180–2
Shklovskii, Viktor 2, 6, 24, 160, 214–24
   'Art as Technique' 216–17
   on improvisation 221–3, 232, 281
   and Jakobson 217, 221, 223n.172
   and magic of words 2, 4, 160, 162, 184,
      185, 205–6, 214–24, 229
   on narrative 218–19
   'On Poetry and Transrational
      Language' 215–16
   and politics 6, 20–1, 222, 247
   'The Resurrection of the Word' 2, 205
   style of 186–7, 218–19, 223n.172
Shor, Rozaliia 109
Shpet, Gustav 108, 111, 114–15, 121
similarity, *see* analogy; mimetic faculty
Simmel, Georg 150
Skidelsky, Edward 190–1, 198
Sorel, Georges 162, 185–6, 235–40, 247, 279
   on image 229, 236–8
   influence of, on Gramsci 24–5, 237, 242

parliament, hostility to 6, 8, 238, 247
Reflections on Violence 237
style of 186–7, 249
sound change 11–13, 31, 35–6
Soviet Union, linguistics in 106–27
speaking mass (*masse parlante*) 52, 102–3, 120,
   123–5, 144–6
Spengler, Oswald 204, 260
Spitzer, Leo 138
Sraffa, Piero 92, 259, 262–3, 263n.83
standardized vernaculars 13n.41
statistics 68–9
Stedman Jones, Gareth viii
Steinthal, Heymann 37, 114–15
Stern, David G. 92, 259–60
Stjernfelt, Frederick 203
Strawson, Peter 276
structuralism vii–viii, 25, 50–1, 217, 277–80
style 89–90, 92–3, 186–7, 218–19
stylistics 120–3, 128–41, 181
subjectivity 139–41, 150–2
suffrage 7–8, 10, 167, 238–9
Surrealism 149–51, 227–9
symbolic form 190–202
symbolism, science of 164–8
synchronic point of view 29–30, 35–41, 49,
   51, 143
   Soviet reaction to 108–11
Szabados, Béla 261n.76, 263

Tarde, Gabriel
   and imitation 46–9
   The Laws of Imitation 47–8
   'Opinion and Conversation' 48
   on public opinion 170–2, 204, 243, 245
technology and technique
   and intersubjectivity 235
   in literature 205, 216–23, 281
   in politics 200–5
Thompson, E. P. 41
Tiedemann, Rolf 235
Tihanov, Galin 217n.142
Timpanaro, Sebastiano 232n.220
Todorov, Tzvetan 278–9
Toman, Jindřich 107n.8
Trakl, George 78
translation
   logical analysis as 22–3, 57–9, 154
   theory of, in Benjamin 24, 148–9, 152
transrational language 106–7, 118–19, 205–16
Trubetskoi, N. S. 106
Tynianov, Iurii 109, 137
types, theory of 60–1
typology, language 11, 12–13, 194

übersichtliche Darstellung, *see* perspicuous
   representation
Uexküll, Jacob von 203
uncanny, language as 254–8, 263

uniformitarianism 33n.13
universal languages 172–3, 213
Usener, Hermann, *Names of the Gods* 196

Varro, *De lingua latina* 32
Vico, Giambattista 238
Vienna Circle 20, 86, 87, 88
Vinokur, G. O. 115n.40, 117–25, 128–31, 210–11
  on Saussure 23, 107–8
  The Culture of Language 121–5, 129
Voloshinov, V. N. 99n.222, 137
  Marxism and the Philosophy of Language 133–4
Vossler, Karl 233–4

Wall, Jeff 254
Walras, Léon 145n.62
Walter, Bruno 255
war, and estrangement 221–2
Warburg, Aby 190
Warnock, G. J. 265, 268, 269–70
Watson, John 165n.18
Weber, Max 79–80, 222–3, 239
Welby, Victoria 159–60, 163
Wertheimer, Joseph 30
Williams, Bernard, *British Analytical Philosophy* 271
Williams, Raymond 76–7, 269
Williamson, Timothy 84n.149, 274
Wittgenstein, Ludwig 4–5, 6, 21, 155, 185, 282, 283
  changing conceptions of language 250–65, 266
  on clarity 71–2, 84–8, 250–1, 267, 282
  development of work 91–2
  and expression of ethics 72–7, 91, 249–50
  as ironist 77–85
  and language that works 98–104, 155, 250–1, 253–4, 258, 262–4
  and linguistic turn 1–2, 4, 22–3, 73
  and logical analysis 60–8, 154–5
  on method in philosophy 90–8, 249–54, 260, 264–9
  and myth 25, 248–50
  and politics 71–2, 262–3
  and science 63, 72, 82–3, 248–9, 258
Wittgenstein, Ludwig, Works
  'Big Typescript' 92, 95, 100, 186, 249, 252, 253–4, 258, 259, 260
  Blue Book 98, 253
  On Certainty 259–60
  'Lecture on Ethics' 75, 91, 257
  Nachlass 92–3, 98
  Philosophical Grammar 253, 259–60
  Philosophical Investigations 56, 79, 92, 250–4, 256, 259, 263–4, 274
  Philosophical Remarks 93, 248, 251–2, 253
  Tractatus Logico-Philosophicus 2, 55–6, 61–7, 72–84, 90, 91–2, 93, 95, 98, 248, 249, 252, 259–60, 263, 274, 282
Wittgenstein, Paul 255
Wolf, George 33–4, 165n.18
word as such 106–7, 206–14
Wordsworth, William 76
Wundt, Wilhelm 215

Zamenhof, L. L. 172–3
Zhirmunskii, Viktor 129n.3, 138
Žižek, Slavoj 125, 152, 170

Cannot measure concepts, but you can measure linguistic expressions. p. 274.